The PRODUCTION of REALITY

FOURTH EDITION

TITLES OF RELATED INTEREST FROM PINE FORGE PRESS

Sociology: Exploring The Architecture of Everyday Life, Fifth Edition, by David M. Newman

Sociology: Exploring The Architecture of Everyday Life, Readings, Fifth Edition, edited by David M. Newman and Jodi O'Brien

Social Problems, by Anna Leon-Guerrero

McDonaldization of Society, Revised New Century Editon, by George Ritzer

Second Thoughts: Seeing Conventional Wisdom Through the Sociological Eye, Third Edition, by Janet M. Ruane and Karen A. Cerulo

Sociological Theory in the Classical Era: Text and Readings, by Laura D. Edles and Scott A. Appelrouth

Illuminating Social Life 3/e, by Peter Kivisto

Key Ideas in Sociology, Second Edition, by Peter Kivisto

Cultures and Societies in a Changing World, Second Edition, by Wendy Griswold

The Social Theory of W. E. B. Du Bois, edited by Phil Zuckerman

Explorations in Classical Sociological Theory, by Ken Allan

The Globalization of Nothing, by George Ritzer

Enchanting a Disenchanted World, Second Edition, by George Ritzer

McDonaldization: The Reader, edited by George Ritzer

Development and Social Change, Third Edition, by Philip McMichael

Investigating the Social World, Fourth Edition, by Russell K. Schutt

Race, Ethnicity, Gender, and Class: The Sociology of Group Conflict and Change, Third Edition, by Joseph F. Healey

Diversity and Society: Race, Ethnicity, and Gender, by Joseph F. Healey

Race, Ethnicity, and Gender: Selected Readings, edited by Joseph F. Healey and Eileen O'Brien

The PRODUCTION *of* REALITY

FOURTH EDITION

Essays and Readings on Social Interaction

Jodi O'Brien
Seattle University

PINE FORGE PRESS
An Imprint of Sage Publications, Inc.
Thousand Oaks • London • New Delhi

Cover: *Gossiping Together,* by Salma Arastu. Used by permission.

For information:

Pine Forge Press
An imprint of Sage Publications, Inc.
2455 Teller Road
Thousand Oaks, California 91320
E-mail: order@sagepub.com

Sage Publications Ltd.
1 Oliver's Yard
55 City Road
London EC1Y 1SP
United Kingdom

Sage Publications India Pvt. Ltd.
B-42, Panchsheel Enclave
Post Box 4109
New Delhi 110 017 India

Printed in the United States of America

Library of Congress Cataloging-in-Publication Data

The production of reality: Essays and readings on social interaction /
edited by Jodi O'Brien.—4th ed.
　　　p. cm.
Rev. ed. of: The production of reality / Jodi O'Brien. c2001.
Includes bibliographical references and index.
ISBN 1-4129-1519-8 (pbk.)
　1. Social psychology. I. O'Brien, Jodi. II. O'Brien, Jodi. Production of reality.
HM1033.O27 2006
302—dc22

　　　　　　　　　　　2005009387
This book is printed on acid-free paper.

06　07　9　8　7　6　5　4　3　2

Acquiring Editor:	Jerry Westby
Editorial Assistant:	Laura Shigemitsu
Production Editor:	Diana E. Axelsen
Typesetter:	C&M Digitals (P) Ltd.
Indexer:	Jeanne Busemeyer
Cover Designer:	Michelle Lee Kenny

BRIEF CONTENTS

DETAILED CONTENTS

PART II
HUMANS AS SYMBOL-USING CREATURES

PART III
PRODUCING SOCIAL ORDER THROUGH INTERACTION

PART VI

AMBIGUITY, COMPLEXITY, AND
CONFLICT IN SOCIAL INTERACTION   425

PREFACE

In my class syllabus for a course in social psychology, I make this statement:

> The main goal of this course is that you understand how we become social creatures and how, through our everyday interactions with one another, we make and remake ourselves and our social worlds. One important implication of the ideas covered in this course is that if we understand how it is that we participate in the construction of our own realities, then we can take a more active and purposeful approach toward making this the sort of world in which we want to live.

During the production of this book, I was reminded of a scene in *Annie Hall,* wherein Woody Allen (as a young man) reports that he is depressed because he has read that the universe is expanding. As the universe expands, it changes shape. Consequently, what we think we know about it changes as well—whatever we think we know today may change tomorrow. Believing that this will eventually mean "the end of everything," young Woody refuses to do his homework: "What's the point?" he sighs.

Indeed, why bother to learn anything if, in fact, everything that we learn now will be invalid later on?

WHY BOTHER?

The Production of Reality was initially compiled in order to provide students with a social psychology text that was useful and relevant to their everyday lives. One thing that you will probably learn in your sojourn through higher education, if you haven't already, is that there are many voices, many points of view, and many ways of learning and knowing. Diversity and complexity are hallmarks of life in the new millennium. Our social universe is continually expanding, and as it expands, so too does our stockpile of knowledge. Even more profound is the fact that the more we learn about our social universe, the more it changes shape. How do we make sense of this shifting and complexity? This is one of the most significant questions of the day. Several relatively new fields (for example, cultural studies) have emerged in the past few decades with the aim of studying this particular question. Scholars within established disciplines—such as anthropology, communications, English, history, philosophy, and even geography—have also taken up this question. The commonality across disciplines of the themes of global expansion, diversity, and complexity is a sign of the importance of this inquiry. It is an exciting time to be a part of this intellectual dialogue.

Sociologists and social psychologists have toiled for more than a century to unearth patterns of human social behavior. As sociologists, we know a great deal about patterns—how to look for them, how to read them, and how to interpret the consequences. In particular, sociologists have a lot to contribute regarding "structured relations of power." *Structured* is the operative word in this phrase. Sociologists and social psychologists know a great deal about "structure" and the ways in which "structure" matters in everyday life. Anyone who wants to make sense of her or his own life needs an understanding of the underlying patterns and material conditions that make up the particular cultural milieu in which she or he lives. Racism, for example, is a persistent problem in U.S. society. The tools for understanding and potentially eradicating racism can be forged through an understanding of *why* and *how* people, even self-professed nonracists, are stuck in a social groove that produces patterns of racism. These "grooves" or "ruts" are what sociologists mean when we talk about "social patterns" and "social structures."

New Emphases for the Fourth Edition

In the first edition of *The Production of Reality,* the intent was to ground social psychology in the experiences of students. The second edition was expanded to include an emphasis on the social self as a product of interaction, conflict, and contradiction. The third edition underscored contemporary questions regarding how people make sense of themselves and others in a social universe that is continually expanding and shifting. This fourth edition takes its shape from the enduring question "How do we account for the theoretical possibility that our worlds are in constant flux and simultaneously identify and analyze what appear to be stable social patterns and structures?" The book provides a theoretical framework for making sense of the apparent contradiction between stability and change. A central theoretical framework for this exploration is *Symbolic Interactionism.*

Symbolic Interactionism offers a theory of self and society whereby people create their own stability through interactions with one another. People participate in these stabilizing processes as a way of establishing social anchors—anchors of meaning—in constantly changing seas. The experiences of "authenticity," "meaning," "value," and "self-worth" are embedded in social relations. Who you are and your ideas of what you think you can do and who you think you can be are shaped by the social relations in which you participate. The "structure" of these social relations, including the meaning that they hold for you, is shaped in turn by your participation. We therefore believe that you will be better equipped to grapple with the timely questions of "What is real?" and "What is good?" by studying the social-psychological structure of social relations. In response to the contemporary zeitgeist, we emphasize how people make sense of an expanding, diverse, complex, contradictory world in which there are multiple perspectives about what is true and good—and real.

This *multivocal* perspective is a focus in this edition. The book is intended as one contribution to the current dialogue of complexity and diversity. Complexity is a hallmark of a *relevant* social science. I am hopeful that readers of this text will gain an understanding of this complex, expanding terrain so that they can navigate their own life courses more clearly.

THE LOGIC OF THE BOOK

This book is organized as a combination of *essays* and *readings*. The essays introduce relevant themes and concepts. They constitute the theoretical logic of the book. The readings have been selected to illustrate and elaborate various aspects of social interaction that are described in the essays. The readings span several decades and represent many different voices and points of view. Some of the readings are considered sociological classics—material that every well-educated student should be familiar with. Some of the language and examples used by the authors of these older pieces may seem outdated and even offensive. We encourage you to read these selections as a form of social history as well as social theory. In other words, ask yourself what it was that was different about the times in which these authors wrote. Can you be critical and still comprehend why the ideas might have been groundbreaking at the time they were written? The contemporary readings include research studies, narrative essays, and some fiction. It is likely that different readings will resonate for different readers. As you read these diverse selections, consider why it is that certain types of writing and particular themes seem more or less appealing to you. What does your own response as a reader indicate about your social biography?

MANY QUESTIONS, YOUR OWN ANSWERS

The general intent is to immerse you in the puzzles and issues of contemporary social psychology and to provide a framework from which you can begin to construct your own understanding of the social world. Toward this end, many questions are posed, and you are invited to reflect on them in light of the concepts and theories presented in the book. As you will discover in reading this text, there are no absolute or final answers to the most important human questions. This is because we are constantly creating new ways of understanding ourselves and our social worlds. Through our ability to think and communicate, we are expanding our social universe. The material in this text is intended to provide you with a framework for understanding this creative social-psychological process (as well as for avoiding some of the pitfalls that appear when we fail to recognize our own involvement in the process). We suggest that you approach this material as a set of building blocks that you can assemble and reassemble to construct a framework for making sense of your own life.

If you (unlike Woody) are willing to do your homework, I am confident that your own universe of knowledge will expand in useful and profound ways.

ACKNOWLEDGMENTS

The creation of any product is always a collective enterprise. There are many who have helped to shape this book. My editor, Jerry Westby, has been an engaging coconspirator in the effort to push the boundaries of the traditional textbook. I appreciate his confidence in my vision. Editorial assistant Laura Shigemitsu has been tremendously helpful in dealing with the myriad details and headaches that accompany book production. I am especially appreciative of the editorial assistance provided by Rachel Hile Bassett and Diana Axelsen.

My commitment to bridging the gap between teaching and scholarship was fostered by role models such as Hubert (Tad) Blalock, Howard Becker, Karen Cook, and Judy Howard. Over the course of my career, my commitment has been continuously renewed through interactions with colleagues who struggle valiantly in the quest to provide relevant and useful knowledge for students. I am repeatedly impressed with the dedication of these teacher-scholars. We are tremendously grateful for the honest and constructive comments from the reviewers of this book. For the first edition, these reviewers were the following:

Dick Adams
University of California, Los Angeles

Peter Callero
Western Oregon State College

Jeff Chin
LeMoyne College

Andy Deseran
Louisiana State University

Jennifer Friedman
University of South Florida

John Kinch
San Francisco State University

Ken Plummer
University of Essex

Reviewers for the second edition were the following:

Timothy Anderson
Bentley College

Jeff Breese
St. Mary's College

Ellen Cohn
University of Pittsburgh

Robert E. Emerick
San Diego State University

Rebecca Erickson
University of Akron

Heather Fitz Gibbon
College of Wooster

Tom Gerschick
Illinois State University

Chris Hunter
Grinnell College

Tracy Luff
Viterbo College

Charles Marske
St. Louis University

Bruce Mork
University of Minnesota

Judith Richlin-Klonsky
University of Southern California

Marty Shockey
St. Ambrose University

Ronald Schultz
Queens College

Barbara Smalley
University of North Carolina

Douglas Smith
Pennsylvania State University

Barbara Trepagnier
*University of California,
Santa Barbara*

Sherry Walker
Middle Tennessee State University

James Zaffiro
University of Minnesota

Several persons have provided extensive and constructive comments and reviews of the third edition. Our thanks to the following:

Linda Belgrave
University of Miami

Amy Best
San Jose State University

Laura Fingerson
University of Wisconsin, Milwaukee

Tom Gershick
Illinois State University

Norman Goodman
SUNY at Stony Brook

Anne Marie Kinnell
University of Southern Mississippi

Gretchen Peterson
California State University, Los Angeles

Angus Vail
Williamette University

Tony Vigorito
Ohio University

Andy Weigert
University of Notre Dame

Much of my thinking as it developed in this book is the result of conversations with my students. I thank them for sharing their intellectual passion. I am fortunate to have several friends and colleagues who are always responsive to my requests for feedback or my need for inspiring company. They include Michele Berger, Peter Burke, Kate Bornstein, Mark Cohan, Wendy Chapkis, Jennifer Eichstedt, Melissa Embser-Herbert, Sarah Fenstermaker, Lori Homer, Kevin Krycka, Chuck Lawrence, Tom Linneman, Kari Lerum, Nancy Naples, Peter Nardi, Ken Plummer, Rich Serpe, Mary Romero, Cecilia Ridgeway, Leila Rupp, Beth Schneider, Arlene Stein, Eve Shapiro, Marty Shockey, Pepper Schwartz, Judy Taylor, Verta Taylor, France

Winddance Twine, and Angus Vail. Carol Lombardi, who copyedited the third edition, gets credit for the Woody Allen reference. I owe many drinks to Scott Harris, who provided me with several new ideas and references for this edition. Thanks especially to my good buddy Val Jenness for always reminding me that laughter really is the best medicine. The original idea and content for this book resulted from a collaboration with Peter Kollock. The book would not have existed without him. Thanks, Pete, for an inspired and always inspiring collaboration. May your new gardens bring similarly wonderful fruits. As always, thanks to Ron Obvious just for being there. Finally, thank you, Cristina, for insisting on balance.

Jodi O'Brien

ABOUT THE COVER ARTIST

Salma Arastu was born in Ajmer, Rajasthan, India. She graduated with an MFA in painting from Maharaja Sayajirao University in Baroda, India, and for the last thirty years has been exhibiting her paintings in India, Iran, Kuwait, and the United States.

Hindu by birth and Muslim by marriage, her work expounds on the unity of an all-encompassing God, common in all religions. She seeks out the Universal in her art.

Artist's Statement

"I am creating a body of work of through continuous, lyrical line, to express joy in the universal spirit that unites our humanity. I have a deep intention to bring world harmony through art. The human form, of people moving together, merging together, conversing or dancing together, influences me and I am inspired by the differences. The people are faceless, as I do not want to give them any name. They do not belong to any religion or ethnicity, any color or creed. It is a flow of humanity and it is moving, melodious and harmonious."

PART I

INTRODUCTION

A father said to his double-seeing son, "Son, you see two instead of one."

"How can that be?" the boy replied. "If that were true, I would see four moons up there in place of two."

—Idries Shah (1972), *Caravan of Dreams*

I have come to see that knowledge contains its own morality, that it begins not in neutrality but in a place of passion within the human soul. Depending on the nature of that passion, our knowledge will follow certain courses and head toward certain ends.

—Parker Palmer (1993), *To Know as We Are Known*

WHAT IS REAL?

Jodi O'Brien

In rural villages, religious festivals are an important part of the local culture. A documentary film crew was around to record one of these events in another country. The film shows brightly colored decorations, music, dancing, and a variety of delicious and special foods made for the festival. The special treats are clearly a highlight for everyone, especially the children, who crowd around the stands. In the middle of one crowd of children waiting for a treat is a very large stone bowl. A large stone pillar rises out of the center of the bowl. The pillar seems alive. It is completely covered by shiny black beetles crawling around and over each other. The person in charge takes a tortilla, spreads some sauce on the inside, grabs a handful of live beetles, and fills the burrito with them, quickly folding the tortilla so that the beetles cannot escape. Playfully pushing the beetles back into the tortilla between bites, a gleeful child eats the burrito with relish. Would you be willing to try a beetle burrito? Is a strip of burnt cow muscle (also known as a steak) inherently any more or less desirable than a beetle burrito? If you had grown up in that village, would you be eating and enjoying beetle burritos? What does your answer have to say about the social and cultural origins of what seems like an almost biological trait—our tastes in food?

In his book *The Te of Piglet* (1992), Benjamin Hoff recounts the following narratives, based on the writings of Chinese Taoist philosophers:

> A man noticed that his axe was missing. Then he saw the neighbor's son pass by. The boy looked like a thief, walked like a thief, behaved like a thief. Later that day, the man found his axe where he had left it the day before. The next time he saw the neighbor's son, the boy looked, walked, and behaved like an honest, ordinary boy.
>
> A man dug a well by the side of the road. For years afterward, grateful travelers talked of the Wonderful Well. But one night, a man fell into it and drowned. After that, people avoided the Dreadful Well. Later it was discovered that the victim was a drunken thief who had left the road to avoid being captured by the night patrol—only to fall into the Justice-Dispensing Well. (p. 172)

What sort of reality do these Chinese tales illustrate? Does the essence of the neighbor boy or the nature of the well change? Or do people's perceptions change? Consider occasions when your perceptions of someone or something may have been influenced by your own momentary experiences. Is it possible that reality depends on how you look at something? How much does your point of view depend on your own interests?

Consider further: A group of workers from a local factory gathers every night after work to share drinks and conversation. They express dissatisfaction with the conditions of their job and the atrocities committed by the shop manager. One young man recalls a recent incident in which an employee lost her arm to unsafe machinery. "I'm terrified every second of every working hour that the same will happen to me," he admits. A woman complains of sexual harassment from the shop manager and threatens to "give him a piece of my foot in a place that he won't soon forget next time he lays his dirty hands on me." Several of the workers discuss plans for a walkout, and in a final burst of enthusiasm, they agree that at noon on the following day, they will step away from their machines and cease to work as a show of protest. The next day, life resumes at the factory. The young man endures his fear in terrified silence and even manages a friendly nod to fellow employees. The woman smiles sweetly when the boss pats her backside and tells her she looks marvelous in blue. At noon a few employees, remembering last night's talk of strike and rebellion, look sheepishly around the plant floor and are relieved to note that no one else has ceased to work. The status quo prevails.

Think about the difference in the late-night and workday activities of these people. What is the source of the disparity between the behaviors in each setting? Are these people being any more or less truthful in either situation? What forces compel people to change their circumstances? What forces constrain resistance in the face of injustice? When are people likely to think their actions or resistance might be successful?

One more story. Imagine a small child with a high fever. The child has been bedridden for a few days. At one point, the fever is so severe that she becomes delirious, seeing monsters in her bedroom. She begins to cry and call out. When her father enters the room, the child is sobbing, saying that monsters are everywhere. Her father comforts her. "There aren't any monsters, dear, it's just a bad dream," he says.

"But I'm not *asleep*," complains the child. "And I can *see* them!"

The father tries again: "I know you can see them, but they aren't real."

"Then why can I see them?"

"Because you're sick," the father explains. "You have germs."

"What are germs? Where are they?" the little girl asks.

"Well, you can't see germs, but they're real," the father answers with great confidence. Is this a reasonable argument? Should we be surprised if the child does not believe it? Have you ever seen a germ? Could you identify one? Do you believe they exist? Most of us do, yet for most of us this belief is probably based on what others have told us rather than on direct evidence.

These scenarios have in common a focus on the intersection between social forms of expression and individual perceptions, tastes, and behaviors. In each case, a taken-for-granted body of cultural knowledge influences individual action. Children in some villages consume beetles with gusto, whereas others might look on in horror. Yet we all feel that our personal tastes are reasonable.

A person's reactions to the world depend on how he or she defines the situation. The definition of the situation can differ from moment to moment, depending on what the person is inclined to see. People also may appear perfectly reasonable in one situation and then appear the opposite in another situation. Indeed, a great deal of human behavior appears unreasonable and illogical if viewed out of context.

Cultural beliefs and practices include rules about what is "real" and what is "not real." These rules are often taken for granted, and we may follow them without being aware of them. They are not necessarily based on logic or sensory perception. The study of culture and behavior involves figuring out these rules and making them explicit. This book is about how human beings learn and conform to the rules of reality in various situations. These rules enable us to organize and to make sense of our experiences and to share our understanding with others.

When people interact with one another, they do so according to these cultural rules. The result of this interaction is a set of meaningful patterns that we think of as society. It is important to note that these rules are constructed by human beings and that they are meaningful only within a specific social context. In other words, behavior is contextually meaningful. Taken out of context, many behaviors appear contradictory, silly, or even immoral.

How do people know what to expect and what to do in different contexts, especially in situations that may appear contradictory? How do we learn the rules of reality? The ability to distinguish between contexts and to behave in accordance with social expectations is a defining feature of humanness. It is also the main subject of this book.

WHAT IS HUMANNESS?

I used to be a *Star Trek* fan. Through the years, I've been particularly fascinated by the observation that the portrayal of certain characters parallels the major currents of thought in social psychology over the past three decades. Consider the contrast between the rational Vulcan Mr. Spock of the first *Star Trek* series and the android Data, who is featured in *Star Trek: The Next Generation*. Consistent with the dominant cognitive perspective of the 1970s, Spock epitomized the being who operated according to the dictates of pure reason. Unencumbered by emotions (those messy "hot flashes") and cognitive biases, Spock was able to assess his environment and formulate hypotheses with a detachment and accuracy that resembled a computer. The show often made contrasts between Spock and Doctor McCoy, who, although a man of science, was frequently amiss in his judgment because of his human biases and social attachments. Other characters would occasionally shake their heads over Spock's lack of emotion. However, in the end, it was always Spock's unerring rationality that saved the day. The message seemed clear: Emotion and human quirks, endearing and meaningful as they might seem, get in the way of the human project, which in this case was to explore and chart (and master?) the universe.

Star Trek: The Next Generation was just as fixated as its predecessor on the ideal of a reasoned, universal harmony orchestrated by sentient beings. But its claims for the virtue and virility of rationality were more modest. In the new show, Spock was replaced with a potentially more perfect form of rational life, an android named Data. Data was capable of calculation and theory construction that far surpassed the abilities of even the most rational Vulcan. In a fascinating twist, however, *Star Trek: The Next Generation* deemphasized Data's rational capabilities in order to insert a theme of humanness as nonrational. Data is a featured character not because of his amazing cognitive abilities, but because of the limitations his technological nature places on his endeavors to be human.

Data is an amazing piece of machinery. He is stronger than any humanoid, has a life span of unguessed potential, and can assimilate and process any amount of information. He is even programmed to simulate perfectly many of the masters of universal culture. For example, he can play the violin like Isaac Stern, paint like Picasso, and act like Sir Laurence Olivier. Yet despite this technical mastery, he is not human.

The character of Data the android raises the question: What is the nature of humanness? If humanness is not rational, cognitive decision making, as it was characterized by social psychology in the 1970s, what *is* the distinctive mark of our species? Spock represented the quest to become more rational, like a computer. Data, who *is* a computer, symbolizes the search for something beyond perfect cognitive activity—an integration of thought, body, and feeling. It's the ideal that has shifted, not the definition of humanness: Spock considered humans to be disorganized and silly. Data thinks they're wonderful. As a scientific culture, we have long admired the computer for its rational, objective, calculating approach to information. A great deal of our industrial technology, cognitive science, and popular mythology focus on how humans can be more like computers, how we can be more objective and rational. For many years, social psychology has separated what are known as "cold" topics (rationality, cognition, and decision making) from "hot" topics (attraction and emotion). In past decades, any young scholar who wished to make a mark in the field was admonished to pursue study of the "cold" topics. In recent years, social psychologists have begun to look more closely at those aspects of humanness that are not epitomized by computer technology and to ask what purpose these nonrational human characteristics have in our personal and cultural experiences. The understanding of human behavior has been enriched by studies that focus more holistically on the body, emotions, and cognition.

Among the features that endear Data to other members of the crew are his earnest attempts to be human and his continual failure to hit the mark. In one episode, Data works fervently to understand humor, but the concept is beyond his otherwise "perfect" abilities. In another episode, he explores the question of love and affection and finds that, although he can intellectually comprehend this state of being and is capable of the act of physical sex, he is unable to experience love. To enhance his understanding of humanness, Data attempts to do human things, such as developing hobbies and social attachments. One by one, Data explores various human institutions. His factual knowledge of these institutions would overwhelm even the most advanced student of human culture. But despite this knowledge, the android is incapable of experiencing life as a human being.

This is a different message from that of earlier social psychology. That is, perfect factual knowledge and cognitive ability do not make a human. Humanness is a situated, interactional process. This process is anchored in personal experience and embodied in emotions.

Little by little, Data appears to advance in his comprehension of the human experience— not through his impressive information-processing abilities, but through interactions with human beings. Through exposure to various human experiences—such as love, humor, grief, and betrayal—Data begins to respond to some situations in a particularly humanlike fashion. To the extent that Data is able to experience humanness, it is through his interactions with humans and their endeavors to teach him what otherwise abstract concepts such as friendship and sorrow mean. Through this learning process, Data is being *socialized* into the human community.

Two points are worth noting here. First, Data's various experiences suggest that humanness involves not only a general comprehension of myriad facts and the ability to calculate probable hypotheses, but also an empathic understanding of highly nuanced, situated meaning. Sociologist Thomas Scheff (1990) tells a story about a computer that is directed to translate the sentence "The spirit is willing but the flesh is weak" into Russian. The computer has the necessary glossary and grammar to make this translation, but it translates the phrase as "The vodka is good but the meat is rotten." The computer provides a literal translation, but the translation does not convey the intended meaning of the phrase. The computer is unable to translate the essence of the phrase, because it does not have the comprehension of metaphor that humans do. Meaning is situated.

Second, Data begins to comprehend human metaphorical meaning not through his private cognitive calculations but through interactions with his companions. He notes their reactions to his utterances and behaviors and then queries them regarding the reasons for their responses—which are often not what Data would have predicted based on rational calculation alone. In this way, he assembles a litany of human metaphors and expected behaviors that, although not always rational, more closely approximates actual human experience. Thus, to the extent that Data does achieve humanness, it occurs as the result of social interactions with humans. These interactions provide Data's schooling in the nuanced richness of human life. He learns that the meanings of objects and ideas, despite what his computer archives tell him, are relative to the context. Humans create and re-create meaning in interaction with one another. Reality is not just a codified series of facts and possibilities; it is something produced and reproduced through ongoing human activity.

Star Trek Voyager, a more recent show in the ongoing saga, depicts several changes that reflect cultural shifts. One noteworthy change is that the captain of *Voyager* is a woman. Another is the replacement of a Data-like character (an android) with a holographic physician. This new character plays a role similar to Data, in that he is nonhuman in body and has perfected cognitive capabilities but struggles in his attempts to interact *meaningfully* with other members of the crew. What we find interesting is that the doctor's advanced programming (he has many abilities that far surpass those of Data) reflects his creators' increasingly complex understanding of human nature. Frequent references to his programming make the audience aware that the doctor has been created with the ability to comprehend nuance and to respond to human ambiguity. There is no presupposition of rationality. At the same time, his ability to become increasingly "human" (i.e., to engage in meaningful behavior) is a consequence of his *interactions* with the crew. He has perfect encyclopedic knowledge of human history, but the crew members are the ones who teach him how to use this knowledge in meaningful ways. Sometimes I wonder if the writers of the series took social psychology courses with ideas similar to the material presented in this book.

Recent developments in the fields of biotechnology and genetic engineering, as well as computer-mediated communications, have led to renewed conversations about the nature of humanness. Current debates about stem cell research, genetic social engineering, and the "realness" of online relationships indicate that our definitions of humanness are always a matter of debate. The rules for deciding what, or in this case "who," is real shift and change in response to contemporary social, cultural, and technological developments. The material in this book will provide you with a template for understanding the cultural rules and ideals that underlie many of these debates.

HUMANNESS IS ACHIEVED THROUGH SYMBOLIC INTERACTION

The production of meaningful realities through human interaction is the focus of this book. Human culture is achieved through interactions among individuals who share highly complex, richly nuanced definitions of themselves and the situations in which they participate. We *learn* to be human, and our learning depends on and is achieved through interactions with other humans. The basis for meaningful human behavior is in our capacity for language—not just definitions and grammar, but metaphor.

As illustrated by Data, perfect rationality does not make one human. In some cases, literal, rational calculation may even be a hindrance to meaningful human interaction. Nevertheless, cognitive capabilities are a necessary foundation for the development of humanness and the achievement of culture. To extend the computer analogy, neurological cognitive functions constitute the "hardware" of human existence. But it is the meaningful use of symbols—the "software"—that makes this existence what it is.

This book focuses on everyday interactions and explores the ways in which these interactions constitute the basis of human existence. The aim is to demonstrate how humans learn to participate in culture and ultimately to produce and reproduce themselves and their various cultures. We will explore a number of questions: What cognitive and emotive capacities are necessary for people to be able to engage in meaningful social interaction? How is social behavior affected by a disruption of these processes? How do interactional dynamics shape our behavior and our sense of who we are and what we can do? How do these processes contribute to the production of culture? How is it possible that, through our own behavior, we may be perpetuating cultural systems to which we may think ourselves opposed (e.g., racism)? The general aim is to explore the social foundations of mind, self, and culture. The framework for this exploration is a theoretical perspective known as *symbolic interactionism*. This perspective is described in detail in the next essay, "Symbolic Interactionism: A Perspective for Understanding Self and Social Interaction" (pp. 44–62, this volume). For now, we invite you to ponder further the question, What is real? Ideally, by now you realize that the answer depends to some extent on the rules that your culture gives you for determining real/unreal. This includes rules for what is true/false, fact/fiction, and right/wrong and rules for what counts as "real" knowledge versus superstition or opinion.

Cultural Rules

Consider two additional examples. You may recall that in 1995, former football player and actor O. J. Simpson was accused of murdering his ex-wife and Ron Goldman, a male companion. After several months of nationally televised trials in criminal court, a jury found him not guilty. Immediately following this verdict, Goldman's family filed a civil suit against Simpson accusing him of wrongful death and demanding several million dollars in damages. This time, a civil court found Simpson guilty and awarded Goldman's family the money. What's the truth here? Is Simpson guilty or not guilty? According to the criminal court (wherein the rules are that one must be found "guilty beyond a reasonable doubt" in order to be convicted of a crime), the case was not adequately made, and therefore Simpson is not guilty and is a free man. According to the civil court, an injustice occurred, damages were incurred, and someone should be responsible for those damages. This court determined that it was reasonable to hold Simpson accountable for the damages. The outcome of the two trials is that he is a free man (not guilty) who must pay damages (guilty). One noteworthy feature of this example is that the supposedly contradictory verdicts don't seem to bother people too much. We understand that the different courts are engaged in different activities with different rules of proof. For some observers, money was the common denominator that made sense of this contradiction: Simpson had enough money to buy a good defense in the criminal trial and was perceived in the civil trial as having enough money that he should give some to the Goldman family. However you choose to interpret this case, it's clear that even in such high-profile and supposedly rigorous undertakings as legal deliberations, there are contradictory rules about what is real, true, and right. Strange as it may seem to an outsider, within a commonly understood context, these contradictory rules make sense.

A second illustration: In many states, when a man beats or kills a male-to-female transgendered person, it is acceptable for the man to enter a plea of "arousal under false pretenses." The logic of this defense plea is that a man may approach someone whom he presumes to be a woman but whom he later discovers to have the sex characteristics of a physiological male. The shock of this discovery may lead him to react violently toward the person, administering a severe beating or even committing murder. What sort of rules for what is real and what is right are operating in the logic of this defense plea? Is the man heeding the cues of attraction (body/experience) or his cultural training regarding gender and sexuality? The logic of the defense rests on the "fact" that the man is indeed aroused by the other person. Apparently, he is attracted enough to initiate contact and to pursue amorous relations—at least according to the logic of the defense plea. But when the physiological features don't match the packaging, the man flies into a rage, and in many cases that come before judges, this rage is considered reasonable—a basis that justifies the attack.

This example raises questions about what constitutes "real" gender, "real" feelings of attraction and arousal, and "real" attempts to deceive. It also raises questions about the unspoken rules for who really has rights. In this culture, if someone sells you a product and it doesn't turn out to be what you expected, you have the right to sue but not to beat up or kill the seller. How are the rules different in the case of this defense plea? What do you make of the information that many judges find this a perfectly acceptable defense plea and usually find the defendant not guilty? The point with this example is that many people take for granted that this is a reasonable defense plea. Even if the death of another strikes them as unfortunate, their presumption about why the transgendered person was attacked ("He/She was asking for it") makes sense to them.

So, What's Real?

What is reality anyway? Nothin' but a collective hunch.

—Trudy the bag lady

According to the symbolic interactionist perspective, "truth" and "reality" are determined by the context in which they are practiced. Does this mean that anything goes? Far from it. Reality may differ across social groups, but within each group, a taken-for-granted system of knowledge establishes boundaries about what is real, true, and right. A central line of inquiry in symbolic interactionism is uncovering what these boundaries consist of and how members of a community produce and reproduce their systems of knowledge through their interactions. For instance, symbolic interactionists have noted that people living in modern, Western cultures act as if their reality is based on a "natural" truth (things are the way they are because nature intended them to be that way). Other cultures might have a faith-based reality (things are the way they are because a transcendent god intends them to be that way). These realities include complex, culturally specific rules for how one can know things. Thus, people in one society may believe in the existence of germs that cause illness. They may invest considerable resources to develop the technology necessary to "see" and "control" these germs. In another culture, people may invest similar resources to perfect ceremonies and rituals to "see" and "communicate with" the spirits that control health and well-being.

Cultural rules about what is real are often contradictory as well. It is fascinating to observe human behavior and culture to see the ways in which seemingly contradictory systems of reality exist side by side. For instance, in the United States, systems of rationality and Christianity often coexist, despite some apparent contradictions. Even so, contradictory belief systems have rules for navigating the contradictions. For example, it is considered normal for the president of the United States to make statements such as "one nation under God" in his speeches. But if he were to say that he was leading the country based on "visions" he received from God, people might question his abilities. Similarly, citing your religious beliefs as a basis for not dating someone is considered reasonable, but these same beliefs are unacceptable as a reason for not paying taxes. Knowing which cultural rules apply in specific contexts is considered "common sense" or "what everybody knows."

In place of the question "What is real?" try asking, "What are some of the beliefs and practices that make up commonsense realities? What are the implications and consequences of these realities? How do different realities depict the world and the place of humans in it?" These questions remind us to scrutinize our own rules of interaction and their implications for self and society. We must make the "taken for granted" explicit. One of the major strengths of the symbolic interactionist perspective is that it encourages us to see our own roles as authors in the human story and, ideally, to take responsibility for the scripts we produce and the parts we play.

ORGANIZATION OF THE BOOK

One general aim of this book is to establish a foundation for understanding symbolic activity based on human thought processes (social cognition) and then to use this foundation to address questions about social order and change. By way of summary, the basic components of this foundation are symbols, the social self, interaction, and social patterns. The materials in this book are organized to present a picture of society as the product of human interactions based on the use of shared social symbols that are incorporated into human conduct through cognitive-emotive processes. Because humans derive cognitive schemas from cultural patterns, these processes reflect a preexisting social structure. Through our interactions with one another we learn, enact, reproduce, and potentially change this structure.

Part I introduces some of these basic components and explores the general idea of socially constructed realities.

In Part II, the focus is on the ways our thoughts and feelings reflect cultural learning and values as well as distinct, private personal experiences. For symbolic interactionists, the key to this puzzle is the *symbol,* an abstract representation of something that may or may not exist in a tangible form. For example, *table* is the symbolic representation of a class of objects constructed from hard substances and designed to serve certain purposes. *Guilt* symbolizes a feeling that you are probably familiar with, but it has no actual, physical referent. Complex combinations of symbols used for communication are known as language. Through language, humans are able to identify meaningful symbols; understand cultural expectations; and incorporate these expectations into conscious, reflexive behavior. Language is the encyclopedia of human culture. It is also through language that humans generate, conserve, and alter social structure.

In Part III, the subject is interaction. Humans develop a social self and learn and re-create their culture through interaction. Social relationships, such as love or power, are given meaning and come to life when they are acted out by members of a social group. These patterns are discernible in the encounters of everyday life, such as conversations. Basic interaction requires people to project an image of what part they wish to play, what part they want others to play, and how they intend to define the situation. For an interaction to proceed smoothly, the actors must agree on a definition of the situation and perform it together. Even arguments, as we will discuss, hold to a particular definition of the situation ("this is a fight") and follow specific rules of interaction. In addition to defining situations, people negotiate how they will define themselves and others.

The *social self* is the focus of Part IV. Students of the material are especially interested in the relationship between the persona or identity that we present in our interactions with others, and our inner feelings about who and what we are. What is the source of these inner ideas of "self"? What ideas and information do we use to make self-assessments and to guide our own behavior? To what extent are our ideas about who we think we are (or can be) shaped by others in our social environment? These are the questions that will be addressed in Part IV.

The social construction of reality is the focus of Part V. In this section, we explore the implications of the points raised in Parts II, III, and IV for the production and reproduction of social realities. That is, realities are social constructs that exist through shared expectations about how the world is organized. These realities are quite fragile, because they depend on the participation of people who are socialized to comprehend and perform patterns and rituals that follow highly structured (but often unrecognized) rules of interaction. Ironically, these implicit rules can be made explicit by violating them and forcing interaction to a confused halt. We present several such "violations" in Part V as a way of demonstrating how to "see" the rules of interaction. An important question in this section is why certain patterns of reality endure so well, given that they are based on such fragile dynamics.

In Part VI, we consider how people grapple with multiple perspectives and contradictions. People have the ability to occupy multiple positions and are able to take on a variety of roles and behaviors. However, many of these positions are contradictory and thus present dilemmas for individuals and groups who seek to establish meaningful patterns of existence. We do not attempt to resolve these contradictions. Rather, we draw your attention to the point that social life is dynamic and complex. Our understanding of who we are and of what is meaningful is forged by wrestling with everyday contradictions.

REFERENCES AND SUGGESTIONS FOR FURTHER READING

Hoff, B. (1992). *The Te of Piglet.* New York: Penguin.
Palmer, P. (1993). *To know as we are known.* San Francisco: Harper.
Scheff, T. (1990). *Discourse, emotion, and social structure.* Chicago: University of Chicago Press.
Shah, I. (1972). *Caravan of dreams.* Baltimore: Penguin.

————————————))))(————————————

REALITY AS A COLLECTIVE HUNCH

Most of us know that different cultures have distinct values and beliefs. Everyday life also consists of patterns of thinking, organizing time, and making sense of things in ways that differ across cultures and between groups of people. The readings in this section illustrate some of the differences in how people perceive everyday reality.

"Islands of Meaning" is written by a sociologist, Eviatar Zerubavel. In this essay, he gives many examples to illustrate the ways we carve up our lives with respect to divisions such as time and geography. We tend to think of these divisions as natural, but Zerubavel demonstrates that these divisions are actually social creations that are so entrenched that we come to think of them as natural.

"The Search for Signs of Intelligent Life in the Universe" is a selection from a popular Broadway play written by Jane Wagner and performed by Lily Tomlin. In this excerpt, the character Trudy-the-bag-lady ponders the meaning of life and the arbitrariness of cultural rules for what is real.

Questions for Discussion and Review

1. As you read the articles in this section, think of examples of cultural rules that you take for granted and assume to be fixed in nature.

2. What does it mean to say that cultural rules are "arbitrary"?

3. Consider your relationship to time. Do you think people's rhythms have been altered by the invention of digital clocks that carve time into units of seconds, versus clocks that signal only quarter hours? What about people who organize time in terms of the sun only?

4. Spend a day thinking of yourself as an anthropologist from Mars (remember Mork from Ork?). What do you see when you look at your world from the perspective of an outsider?

REALITY AS A COLLECTIVE HUNCH

1

Islands of Meaning

Eviatar Zerubavel

(1991)

In the beginning . . . the earth was unformed and void . . . and God divided the light from the darkness. And God called the light Day, and the darkness He called Night.[1]

The very first act of the Creation was one of dividing. It was through being separated from one another that entities began to emerge. The first day was thus spent on dividing the light from the darkness while the next two were dedicated to separating the waters under the heaven from those above it as well as from the dry land.[2] Indeed, according to Genesis, the first three days of the Creation were devoted exclusively to making distinctions.

Like most cosmogonies, the biblical story of the Creation is an allegorical account of the process through which we normally create order out of chaos. These theories of the origin of the universe almost invariably describe the formation of essences (the heavens, the earth, life) out of a boundless, undifferentiated void.[3] Distinctions, they all tell us, are at the basis of any orderliness.

Separating entities from their surroundings is what allows us to perceive them in the first place. In order to discern any "thing," we must distinguish that which we attend from that which we ignore. Such an inevitable link between differentiation and perception is most apparent in color-blindness tests or camouflage, whereby entities that are not clearly differentiated from their surroundings are practically invisible.[4] It is the fact that it is differentiated from other entities that provides an entity with a distinctive meaning[5] as well as with a distinctive identity that sets it apart from everything else.

The way we cut up the world clearly affects the way we organize our everyday life. The way we divide our surroundings, for example, determines what we notice and what we ignore, what we eat and what we avoid eating. By the same token, the way we classify people determines whom we trust and whom we fear, whom we marry and whom we consider sexually off limits. The way we partition time and space likewise determines when we work and when we rest, where we live and where we never set foot.

Indeed, our entire social order is a product of the ways in which we separate kin from nonkin, moral from immoral, serious from merely playful, and what is ours from what is not. Every class system presupposes a fundamental distinction between personal features that are relevant for placing one in a particular social stratum (for example, occupation, color of skin, amount of formal education) and those that are not (for example, sexual attractiveness, height, intelligence), and any society that wishes to implement a welfare or retirement policy must first distinguish the well-to-do from the needy and those who are fully competent to work from those who are "too old." By the same token, membership in particular social categories qualifies us for, or disqualifies us from, various benefits, exemptions, and jobs.[6] It is the need to distinguish "us" from "them" that likewise generates laws against intermarriage, and the wish to separate mentally the "masculine" from the "feminine" that leads to the genderization of professions and sports.

It is boundaries that help us separate one entity from another: "To classify things is to arrange them in groups . . . separated by clearly determined lines of demarcation. . . . At the bottom of our conception of class there is the idea of a circumscription with fixed and definite outlines."[7] Indeed, the word *define* derives from the Latin word for *boundary*, which is *finis*. To define something is to mark its boundaries,[8] to surround it with a mental fence that separates it from everything else. As evidenced by our failure to notice objects that are not clearly differentiated from their surroundings, it is their boundaries that allow us to perceive "things" at all. These lines play a critical role in the construction of social reality, since only with them do meaningful social entities (families, social classes, nations) emerge out of the flux of human existence. Examining how we draw them is therefore critical to any effort to understand our social order. It also offers us a rare glimpse into the not-so-orderly world that underlies our social world, the proverbial chaos that preceded the Creation.

Boundaries are normally taken for granted[9] and, as such, usually manage to escape our attention. After all, "Nothing evades our attention so persistently as that which is taken for granted. . . . Obvious facts tend to remain invisible."[10] In order to make them more "visible," we must suspend our usual concern with what they separate and focus instead on the process by which we cut up the world and create meaningful entities. In short, we must examine how we actually separate entities from one another, whether it be humans from animals, work from hobby, official from unofficial, or vulgar from refined.

The way we cut up the world in our mind manifests itself in how we construct age, gender, and ethnicity as well as in how we arrange food in supermarkets and books and movies in bookstores and video stores. It is manifested as well in how we divide our homes into separate rooms, and in our sexual taboos. Conventional metaphors such as *closed*, *detached*, and *clear-cut* similarly reveal how we experience reality as made up of insular entities, while our need to keep such discrete islands of meaning neatly separate from one another is evident from our gut response to ambiguous creatures.

The way we draw lines varies considerably from one society to another as well as across historical periods within the same society. Moreover, their precise location, not to mention their very existence, is often disputed and contested within any given society. Nonetheless, like the child who believes the equator is a real line[11] or the racist who perceives an actual divide separating blacks from whites, we very often experience boundaries as if they were part of nature....

Things assume a distinctive identity only through being differentiated from other things, and their meaning is always a function of the particular mental compartment in which we place them. Examining how we draw lines will therefore reveal how we give meaning to our environment as well as to ourselves. By throwing light on the way in which we distinguish entities from one another and thereby give them an identity, we can explore the very foundations of our social world, which we normally take for granted.

At a time when political and moral distinctions are constantly blurred—when the international order we have regarded for nearly half a century as a given is virtually collapsing and our definitions of work, art, and gender are in flux—the very notion of a social order is being questioned. At such a point it is therefore critical for us to understand the actual process by which we establish boundaries and make distinctions. How we draw these fine lines will certainly determine the kind of social order we shall have.

* * * * *

The first man who, having enclosed a piece of ground, bethought himself of saying "This is mine," and found people simple enough to believe him, was the real founder of civil society.[12]

We transform the natural world into a social one by carving out of it mental chunks we then treat as if they were discrete, totally detached from their surroundings. The way we mark off islands of property is but one example of the general process by which we create meaningful social entities....

Chunks of Space

The perception of supposedly insular chunks of space is probably the most fundamental manifestation of how we divide reality into islands of meaning. Examining how we partition space, therefore, is an ideal way to start exploring how we partition our social world.

The way we carve out of ecological continuums such as continents and urban settlements supposedly insular countries and neighborhoods is a classic case in point.[13] Despite the fact that Egypt and Libya or Chinatown and Little Italy are actually contiguous, we nevertheless treat them as if they were discrete. Such discontinuous perception of space is nicely captured by the map shown here, which almost literally lifts Montana out of its actual context. Not only does it represent that state as a discrete three-dimensional chunk jutting out of a flat backdrop, it also portrays both the Missouri River and the Rocky Mountains as if they indeed broke off at its borders.

Spatial partitions clearly divide more than just space. The lines that mark off supposedly insular chunks of space often represent the invisible lines that separate purely mental entities such as nations or ethnic groups from one another, and crossing them serves to articulate passage through such mental partitions. That is why we attribute such great symbolic significance to acts such as trespassing[14] or crossing a picket line and regard the crossing of the Red Sea by the ancient Israelites coming out of Egypt as an act of liberation. That is also why the Berlin Wall could represent the mental separation of democracy from communism and why opening the border between Austria and Hungary in 1989 could serve as a symbolic display of the spirit of glasnost.

Often abstract and highly elusive, mental distinctions need to be concretized. Wearing different sets of clothes, for example, helps substantiate the mental distinction between business and casual or ordinary and festive, just as color coding helps us mentally separate different types of information we put in our notebooks, calendars, or files. Choosing among different variants of a language (such as the one used for speeches and the one used for intimate conversations) likewise helps express the mental contrast between the formal and the informal.[15] In a similar manner, we often use differentiation in space to reinforce mental differentiation. Partitioning our home into separate rooms, for example, helps us compartmentalize our daily activity into separate clusters of functions (eating, resting, playing, cleaning) as well as mentally separate culture (study) from nature (bathroom)[16] or the formal (living room) from the informal (family room). Along similar lines, separate aisles in music stores help reinforce the mental separation of classical and popular music, just as separate floors of department stores help us keep the worlds of men and women separate in our mind. In a similar manner, we express discontinuities among supposedly separate bodies of information by relegating them to separate drawers, newspaper sections, and library floors; and keep different categories of food separate in our mind by assigning them to separate pages of restaurant menus, chapters of cookbooks, aisles of supermarkets, and sections of the refrigerator. Similar forms of zoning help give substance to the mental contrasts between even more abstract entities such as the sacred and the profane,[17] the

permitted and the forbidden,[18] the dangerous and the safe, and the good and the evil.[19]

The mental role of spatial partitions is also evident from the way neighborhood boundaries graphically outline rather elusive social class differences.[20] Even more revealing is the way separate bathrooms in the army help articulate status differences between officers and soldiers. The conspicuous absence of doors from rooms we define as public likewise highlights the role of spatial partitions in keeping the private and public spheres separate.[21] "A lock on the door," notes Virginia Woolf in her aptly titled study of privacy and selfhood, *A Room of One's Own*, "means the power to think for oneself."[22] It is the realization that the definition of our selfhood is at stake that makes us so sensitive to the symbolism of having the license to close the door to our room or office.

BLOCKS OF TIME

The way we divide time is evocative of the manner in which we partition space. Just as we cut supposedly discrete chunks like countries and school districts off from ecological continuums, we also carve seemingly insular segments such as "the Renaissance" or "adolescence" out of historical continuums. Such discontinuous experience of time is quite evident from the way we isolate from the flow of occurrences supposedly freestanding events such as meetings, classes, and shows, some of which we further subdivide into smaller though still discrete particles—meals into courses, baseball games into innings.[23] It is also manifested in our ability to create stories with beginnings and ends as well as in the way we break down novels, sonatas, and plays into chapters, movements, and acts.

In a similar manner, we isolate in our mind supposedly discrete blocks of time such as centuries, decades, years, months, weeks, and days, thus perceiving actual breaks between "last week" and "this week"[24] or "the fifties" and "the sixties."

That is why many of us may not carry over sick days from one year to the next and why officials try to use up their entire budget before the end of the fiscal year. A similar discontinuity between successive tax years also leads some couples to plan the births of their offspring for December, even to the point of inducing those that would naturally have occurred in January.

Central to such discontinuous perception of time is our experience of beginnings, endings, and "turning points." Most revealing in this regard is the sense of conclusion we experience as a performance, picnic, or season is coming to an end,[25] the radical change we expect at the turn of a century or a millennium or even between two contiguous decades, and the experience of a "fresh" start (or "turning over a new leaf") often associated with the beginning of a "new" year. Even in services that operate around the clock, night staff are often expected to allow the day ("first") shift a fresh start with a "clean desk."[26] A pregnant friend of mine who came back to the same clinic that had handled her previous pregnancy within the same year was asked to provide her entire medical history all over again, as she would now be considered a "new" case.

Temporal differentiation helps substantiate elusive mental distinctions. Like their spatial counterparts, temporal boundaries often represent mental partitions and thus serve to divide more than just time. For example, when we create special "holy days," we clearly use time to concretize the mental contrast between the sacred and the profane.[27] In a similar manner, we use it to give substance to the equally elusive contrast between the private and the public domains, using, for example, the boundary of the workday to represent the mental partition between being "on" and "off" duty.[28] Groups likewise use the way they periodize their own history to highlight certain ideological distinctions, as evident, for example, in the Zionist use of "the Exile"[29] or the American use of "the Great Depression" or "Vietnam" as discrete

historical eras. The boundaries of the Sabbath, the workday, and "the Vietnam era" clearly represent major mental discontinuities. Like neighborhoods, drawers, and wings of museums, what they define are clearly more than mere chunks of time.

FRAMES

Temporal differentiation often entails an experience of discontinuity among different sorts of reality as well. Transitions from televised news to commercials or from live coverage to replay, for example, obviously involve more than just breaks in time. Along similar lines, warmup and "real" jumps in long-jump competitions are clearly anchored not only within two distinct blocks of time but also within two separate realms of experience, as are comments made before meetings begin and those included in the official minutes.[30]

Spatial differentiation often entails similar experiential discontinuity. The knight on the chessboard and the glass of water on the table are obviously situated not only within two distinct chunks of space but also within two separate "realities." That is also true of what occurs on and off the stage or inside and outside the picture frame.

Crossing the fine lines separating such experiential realms from one another involves a considerable mental switch from one "style" or mode of experiencing to another, as each realm has a distinctive "accent of reality."[31] At the sound of the bell that signals the end of a boxing match, as brutal punches are instantly transformed into friendly hugs, our entire sense of what is real is dramatically altered. That also happens, of course, when actors enter the stage and are immediately transformed into fictional characters. Picture frames similarly remind viewers that they cannot smell the flowers or eat the apples they see in pictures,[32] as pictorial space is "a structure altogether different from the real space we experience. Within actual space an object can be touched, whereas in a painting it can only be looked at; each portion of real space is experienced as part of an infinite expanse, but the space of a picture is experienced as a self-enclosed world. . . . [The work of art] builds a sovereign realm."[33]

It is precisely that quality that makes frames the ideal prototype of all boundaries delineating the various realms of our experience,[34] those mental lines that separate ordinary reality from the "worlds" of art, dream, play, and symbolism as well as off-the-record from official statements, parenthetical from ordinary remarks,[35] the metaphoric from the literal, satire from sheer slander, commentary from pure coverage, parody from plagiarism, and maneuvers from actual war. Framing is the act of surrounding situations, acts, or objects with mental brackets[36] that basically transform their meaning by defining them as a game, a joke, a symbol, or a fantasy. Play, for example, is actually "a name for contexts in which the constituent acts have a different sort of relevance . . . from that which they would have had in non-play. . . . The essence of play lies in a partial denial of the meanings that the actions would have had in other situations."[37]

A frame is characterized not by its contents but rather by the distinctive way in which it transforms the contents' meaning. The way framing helps de-eroticize what we normally consider sexual is quite suggestive of the remarkable transformational capacity of frames. The party frame, for example, allows even perfect strangers to hold one another while moving together in a pronounced rhythmic fashion (though only while the music is playing).[38] In a similar manner, in the context of art, respectability is granted to otherwise obscene literary passages and poetic metaphors as well as to nude modeling and photography,[39] just as the play frame helps de-eroticize games such as "house" and "doctor." Ordinary sexual meanings are likewise antisepticized by science, which allows genital display in anatomy books, and medicine, which de-eroticizes mouth-to-mouth resuscitation and gynecological examinations.[40]

In cutting chunks of experience off from their surroundings, frames obviously define not only different but also separate realms of experience. In delineating a space which the viewer cannot enter, picture frames, for example, "[cut] the artist's statement off from the room in which it is hung,"[41] thus visually articulating an experiential cleavage between ordinary reality and the artistic realm.[42] Supposedly bounded, experiential realms do not spill over into one another,[43] and the "reality" of any object is therefore always confined to the boundaries of the particular frame within which it is situated. That is why it is so difficult to prolong a dream after waking up or to sustain an erotic experience when someone knocks on the door, as well as why we normally do not hold others responsible for any harm they may have caused us in our fantasies. Along similar lines, terrified as we are by Captain Hook, Darth Vader, or the Wicked Witch of the West when we read about them or watch them on the screen, we nonetheless know that they can never step out of the fictional frames in which they belong and therefore cannot really hurt us.

Picture frames also make us disregard the wall surrounding the picture.[44] Like them, all frames basically define parts of our perceptual environment as irrelevant, thus separating that which we attend in a focused manner from all the out-of-frame experience[45] that we leave "in the background" and ignore. Thus, for example, when we play checkers, the material of which the pieces are made is considered totally irrelevant to the game and, therefore, out of frame. In fact, when a piece is missing, we often replace it with a coin, totally disregarding the latter's ordinary monetary value. Likewise, within an erotic context, we normally perceive others as attractive or not, ignoring ordinary distinctions based on social class, status, or ethnic origin.[46]

Moreover, frames make us ignore entire acts or objects despite their obvious physical presence in the situation. At concerts, for example, we usually disregard such acts as replacing a mouthpiece or wiping spittle off one's horn, which are clearly not part of the framed performance in which they are visually embedded. We likewise ignore "background" activity such as nail biting or doodling at meetings and routinely skip page numbers and translators' notes when reading books.[47] And just as we exclude from the game frame such accidents as unintentionally knocking a piece off the chessboard (in sharp contrast to removing deliberately a captured piece), we also instruct jurors to ignore "unacceptable" evidence presented to them.

The experiential discontinuity between what is situated "inside" and "outside" frames also applies to human objects, as mere presence at a social situation may not always guarantee inclusion in the frame surrounding it.[48] In social gatherings, full-fledged participants are often surrounded by a mental partition[49] that keeps mere bystanders practically "out of focus." (Such discontinuity becomes apparent when we poke fun at those who laugh at jokes that were not addressed to them or when cardplayers scold kibitzers who offer unsolicited advice: "Who asked you, anyway?")[50] Cabdrivers, waiters, stenographers, and children are often assigned such out-of-frame status. So are technicians installing equipment at rock concerts, attendants who clean after the animals at circuses, food vendors at sports events, and photographers at weddings, all of whom are clearly situated outside the entertainment frame that surrounds everyone else. Despite their obvious physical presence at these situations, they are considered "non-persons"[51] and thus relegated to the out-of-frame "background." That is also why we sometimes fail to notice the very presence of those we assume do not understand the language we speak or the topic we discuss.[52]

CHUNKS OF IDENTITY

The manner in which we isolate supposedly discrete "figures" from their surrounding "ground" is also manifested in the way we come to experience ourselves.[53] It involves a form of mental differentiation that entails a fundamental distinction between us and the rest of the world. It is known as our sense of identity.

The most obvious form of identity is the experience of an insular self that is clearly cut off from one's surrounding environment,[54] a self with "clear and sharp lines of demarcation" that we experience as autonomous and "marked off distinctly from everything else."[55] Such self presupposes the experience of some "ego boundary"[56] that marks the "edge" of our personhood,[57] the point where we end and the rest of the world begins. Such boundary is at the heart of the fundamental experiential separation of what is "inside" the self from what lies "outside" it.[58]

The experience of a self presupposes some "psychological division from the rest of the world."[59] It is a product of a long process that begins when, as infants, we psychologically disengage ("hatch") from our initial "symbiotic" relationship with our most immediate other, usually our mother.[60] As a result of such process of individuation, we withdraw from a somewhat fluid reality into one where the self as well as other individuals with sharp and firm contours seem to emerge as discrete entities that are clearly separate from their environment.[61]

The self is but one particular focus of identity. There are many other answers to the existential question of where we end and the rest of the world begins, and they all involve supposedly bounded clusters of individuals (a family, a profession, a political party, a nation) who experience themselves collectively—and are usually perceived by others—as insular entities[62] clearly separate from everyone else. In short, we experience ourselves not only as "I" but also collectively as "we," that is, as liberals, baseball fans, Muslims, women, humans. It is such perceptions of social clusters as discrete entities that lead us to regard a marriage between a Christian and a Jew or an Armenian and a Pole as "mixed."

The experience of such discrete entities presupposes a perception of some boundaries surrounding them.[63] Even a couple going steady experiences some clear partition separating them from others around them.[64] Such fine mental lines help us perceive a fundamental discontinuity between insiders and outsiders, those included in a social cluster and those who are left outside its confines. Only in relation to those lines do sentiments such as fidelity, loyalty, or patriotism, for example, evolve, and only in relation to them do we learn whom we can trust and of whom we should beware, who is available to us as a sexual partner and whom we must avoid. These are the boundaries that basically define the mental entities we come to experience as "us" and "them." They constitute the basis of our sense of identity and determine much of the scope of our social relations.

MENTAL FIELDS

Early in life space is the only mode available for organizing a self.[65] Indeed, our individuation begins with the development of locomotor functions such as crawling, which allow us to literally withdraw from others.[66] Later we establish some nonspatial sense of selfhood,[67] actualizing our separateness by acts such as saying no[68] and experiences such as ownership of toys, yet the basic way in which we experience the self and its relations with others remains spatial nonetheless. We thus associate selfhood with a psychological "distance" from others[69] and experience privacy (including its non-spatial aspects, such as secrecy) as having some "space" for ourselves or as a "territory" of inaccessibility surrounding us.[70] We experience others as being "close" to or "distant" from us and portray our willingness or unwillingness to make contact with them using topological images such as "opening up" (or "reaching out") and being "closed" (or "removed").[71] We also use the image of

"penetration" to depict the essence of the process of becoming intimate.[72]

Similar spatial imagery captures our experience of groups as bounded, "closed"[73] entities that one almost literally "enters" and "exists."[74] We thus "*incorporate*" members into, "expel" them from, and assign them "central" or "marginal" places in groups. We also use images such as "*extra*marital" (or "*out of* wedlock"), "mobility,"[75] and "knows his place"; perceive actual social "distance"[76] between blacks and whites or senior and junior executives; and mentally locate "distant" relatives in terms of the number of "steps" they are "removed" from us.[77] Such mental geography has no physical basis but we experience it as if it did.

We likewise use spatial images to depict supposedly discrete chunks of professional jurisdiction (boundary, turf, territory, arena)[78] as well as knowledge. We thus perceive academic disciplines as surrounded by mental "walls"[79] and works as lying on the "fringes" of sociology or outside our "area" of expertise, and regard those whose interest does not transcend the confines of their "field" as "limited" or "narrow minded." Similar spatial imagery seems to underlie our perception of the *extra*curricular, *extra*judicial, and *eso*teric as well as of insular "domains" such as work, religion, or art.

Somewhat similar is our experience of the fine mental lines that separate acceptable from unacceptable behavior—the assertive from the rude, the funny from the crude. We basically "confine [ourselves] to a particular radius of activity and . . . regard any conduct which drifts outside that radius as somehow inappropriate or immoral. . . . Human behavior can vary over an enormous range, but each community draws a symbolic set of parentheses around a certain segment of that range and limits its own activities within that narrower zone."[80] Our quasi-spatial experience of such "normative outlines" of society[81] is quite evident from our use of verbs such as "*trans*gress" or "*ex*ceed" (which literally mean to step or go beyond), prefixes such as "over-" (as in "*over*ambitious"), "out-" (as in "*out*law"), or "extra-" (as in "*extra*vagant"), and metaphors such as "line of decency"[82] or "limits of authority."

In a somewhat similar manner, we also "enter" conversations, go "out of" business, portray breakthroughs as the crossing of a Rubicon[83] or a forbidden frontier,[84] and can appreciate a cartoon depicting someone reaching a line demarcated by the sign "Boundary of Self Respect."[85] Similar spatial imagery also underlies such concepts as "*extra*ordinary," "*out*standing," or "*ex*otic."

Spatial metaphors pervade much of our thinking.[86] In a wide variety of contexts, we use them to depict purely mental relations among entities. In fact, we basically experience reality as a "space"[87] made up of discrete mental fields delineated by mental "fences"[88] that define[89] and separate them from one another. Given the significance of proximity in perceptual grouping (the closer things are to one another, the more we tend to perceive them as a single entity[90]), we use closeness as a metaphor for conceptual similarity,[91] essentially seeing difference in terms of mental distance.[92] We thus consider similar mental items as belonging "together"[93] and different ones as being "worlds apart," and we may even try to locate an item "exactly halfway" between two others.[94]

A foremost prerequisite for differentiating any entity from its surrounding environment are exceptionally strong intra-entity relations.[95] A mental field is basically a cluster of items that are more similar to one another than to any other item. Generating such fields, therefore, usually involves some lumping. As we group items in our mind (that is, categorize the world), we let their similarity outweigh any differences among them. As a result we perceive mental fields as relatively homogeneous lumps and regard their constituent items as functionally interchangeable variants ("allo-" variants) of a single unit of meaning.[96] Even when we notice differences among them, we dismiss them as totally irrelevant[97]—"making no difference"—and consequently ignore them.

Thus, despite the obvious differences among them, we regard the prefixes of the adjectives "*in*accurate," "*im*proper," "*dis*honest," and "*un*usual" as functionally equivalent variants of a single morpheme.[98] We regard them as basically "the same" because no confusion of meaning is likely to occur if one of them is substituted for another (that is, if we say "disaccurate" or "unproper"). Nor do we normally attribute much significance to the difference between right-eye and left-eye winks, which we perceive as functionally interchangeable variants of a single gesture,[99] or between a kiss and an affectionate look, which we often substitute for each other as tokens of intimacy.[100] Along similar lines, we usually ignore the obvious difference between 490- and 540-millimicron-long light waves, regarding both as variants of the color "green,"[101] and casually substitute pretzels for potato chips as party snacks. And though clearly aware of the difference between thirty-one- and twenty-eight-day blocks of time, we nonetheless regard both as structurally equivalent variants of the unit "month"[102] and expect identical monthly paychecks for January and February. Along similar lines, we usually perceive conventional historical periods as relatively homogeneous stretches, often lumping together events that occurred centuries apart from one another yet within the same "period" (as in "the Middle Ages").[103]

In a similar manner, we establish social clusters in our mind by regarding all cluster members as similar and ignoring all differences among them, as when we lump together all those whose income falls below a certain "poverty line" as an undifferentiated lot—"the poor." We generally tend to downplay differences within our own group as well as among others,[104] as evident from the extremely broad categories ("Orientals") in which we lump those who came to America[105] or from various catchall categories for outsiders, such as the ancient Greek "barbarian," the Armenian *odar*,[106] the Gypsy *gadjo*, or the Jewish *goy*.

Ignoring intracluster differences and regarding all cluster members as basically "the same" often results in stereotypes, as when racists claim that all blacks are lazy or that all Orientals look alike. Nonetheless, without some lumping, it would be impossible ever to experience any collectivity, or mental entity for that matter. The ability to ignore the uniqueness of items and regard them as typical members of categories is a prerequisite for classifying any group of phenomena. Such ability to "typify"[107] our experience is therefore one of the cornerstones of social reality.

RITUAL TRANSITIONS

Most of the fine lines that separate mental entities from one another are drawn only in our own head and, therefore, totally invisible. And yet, by playing up the act of "crossing" them, we can make mental discontinuities more "tangible." Many rituals, indeed, are designed specifically to substantiate the mental segmentation of reality into discrete chunks. In articulating our "passage" through the mental partitions separating these chunks from one another, such rituals, originally identified by Arnold Van Gennep as "rites of passage,"[108] certainly enhance our experience of discontinuity.

The various rites we perform when we cross the equator, tropic of Cancer, or arctic circle[109] are perfect cases in point. In dramatizing our passage through these imaginary lines that exist only on maps, they certainly make them more "tangible" (somewhat like the road sign Welcome to Massachusetts). In a similar manner, we also dramatize the mental discontinuity between the public and private domains by knocking on the door before entering a room as well as by altering our appearance, as in the following caricature of a stereotypical return home, "from 'a hard day at the office': a banal scene in which the social passage is signified by the man successively removing his hat ... taking off his jacket, stripping away his tie (exaggerated gesture), opening his shirt collar. . . . A whole set of statements about the contrast between [home] and the 'larger world' is going on."[110] Along similar lines, soldiers coming home even for a few hours often change into civilian clothes just to actualize their "exit" from the military world. Lowering their voices on entering church similarly helps congregants substantiate the mental separation of the sacred from the profane, whereas the ritual apology ("I beg your pardon") we offer on entering each other's "personal space" likewise promotes our experience of an insular self.

In a similar manner, weddings substantiate the boundaries of the family, whose crossing transforms people into spouses and in-laws. They also signal, of course, the crossing of the mental partition that separates marriage from singlehood, just like puberty rites[111] (or modern equivalents such as obtaining a driver's license or going for the first time to an R-rated film), which dramatize the transition from childhood to adulthood. (The fact that we rarely celebrate divorces and usually articulate second weddings considerably less than first ones suggests that entering marriage entails a much greater break in identity than exiting or reentering it.) In dramatizing the moments of entering and exiting it, birth and death rituals[112] likewise substantiate the experience of life as a discrete block of time (as well as the mental contrast between life and nonlife). The need to substantiate the way we segment time into discrete blocks also accounts for the holidays we create to commemorate critical transition points between historical epochs[113] as well as for the rituals we design to articulate significant changes in our relative access to one another—greetings, first kisses, farewell parties, bedtime stories.[114] Changes of lighting or background music likewise signal transitions among successive segments of theatrical performances, films,[115] rock concerts, and circus shows, whereas ritual switches from sitting to standing help to "punctuate" religious services[116] and demarcate featured solos in jazz.

The ritual of raising the curtain before the beginning of a show[117] and the almost obligatory "once upon a time" or "and they lived happily ever after"[118] that signal crossings of the line separating fairy tales from "real" life similarly serve to substantiate the boundaries of frames.[119] So do the ritual glove touch or kickoff that prefaces sports events, the suspension of meter that signals the dissolution of the poetic frame,[120] and the caption "The End" that used to announce the conclusion of films. (Within films, conventional cues such as soft focus, overexposure, change from color to black and white, and suspension of background music often signal transitions from characters' here and now into their memories, fantasies, or dreams.) Along similar lines, organ preludes are often used to announce a religious frame,[121] "soft" music (and candlelight) a romantic frame, and dance music (and hors d'oeuvres) a party.

By switching from one language to another or even from standard to colloquial speech, we often articulate transitions from formality to informality or from just talking to quoting.[122] In a similar manner, speakers often clear their throats to announce the conclusion of their informal introductory remarks (just as chairpersons use gavels to announce the formal parts of meetings), change their tone to signal diversions from the general thrust of their talk to "parenthetical" remarks, and sit down to announce the beginning of the more informal question-and-answer part.[123] Children likewise use a change of voice to "enter" the make-believe frame[124] and the ritual call "Time" to exit from a game in order to tie a loose shoelace or get a drink.

Along similar lines, by punishing deviants who transgress its moral boundaries, society not only forces us to see that such lines do indeed exist but also demarcates their precise "location." Like weddings, funerals, and bedtime stories, punishment is a ritual that dramatizes the act of crossing some mental partition. In substantiating the mental segmentation of human behavior into acceptable and unacceptable, it serves to "locate and publicize"[125] moral edges:

> The deviant is a person whose activities have moved outside the margins of the group, and when the community calls him to account for that vagrancy it is making a statement about the nature and placement of its boundaries. . . . Members of a community inform one another about the placement of their boundaries by participating in the confrontations which occur when persons who venture out to the edges of the group are met by policing agents. . . . Whether these confrontations take the form of criminal trials, excommunication hearings, courts-martial, or even psychiatric case conferences, they [demonstrate] where the line is drawn. . . . Morality and immorality meet at the public scaffold, and it is during this meeting that the line between them is drawn. . . . Each time the community moves to censure some act of deviation, then, and convenes a formal ceremony to deal with the responsible offender, it . . . restates where the boundaries of the group are located.[126]

Moral boundaries remain a meaningful point of reference, of course, only as long as society indeed curbs all attempts to transgress them.[127] When society fails to punish deviants who venture beyond the limit of what it defines as acceptable, members will wonder whether such a line really exists.

Only the need to announce crossings of frame boundaries prompts us to indent quotations like the one above on a page of text[128] and only the need to substantiate an insular self compels us to say grace before we ingest parts of the environment into our body through the act of eating. Substantiating the insularity of conventional chunks of space, time, and identity is likewise the only reason for the rites we perform around doorsills,[129] the birthday cards[130] and New Year midnight kisses with which we "punctuate" life as well as history, and the various initiation rites (such as baptism, adoption, and naturalization) by which we dramatize the incorporation of new members into religious communities, families, or nations. Such rituals of "passage" are all products of some basic need to substantiate in our acts the mental discontinuities we perceive in our mind. As such, they play a major role in our ability to think analytically.

Notes

1. Genesis 1:1–5.
2. Ibid., 6–10.
3. See, for example, Paul Seligman, *The Apeiron of Anaximander* (London: Athlone Press, 1962).
4. Gyorgy Kepes, *Language of Vision* (Chicago: Paul Theobald, 1951 [1944]), p. 45; Wolfgang Köhler, *Gestalt Psychology* (New York: New American Library, 1947), pp. 84, 93.
5. See also Ferdinand de Saussure, *Course in General Linguistics* (New York: Philosophical Library, 1959 [1915]), pp. 116–22; Michel Foucault, *The Order of Things* (New York: Vintage, 1973 [1966]), p. 144.
6. Paul Starr, "Social Categories and Claims in the Liberal State," in Mary Douglas, ed., *How Classification Works* (Edinburgh: Edinburgh University Press, forthcoming).
7. Emile Durkheim and Marcel Mauss, *Primitive Classification* (Chicago: University of Chicago Press, 1963 [1903]), p. 4. See also Karl W. Deutsch, "Autonomy and Boundaries according to Communications Theory," in Roy R. Grinker, ed., *Toward a Unified Theory of Human Behavior* (New York: Basic Books, 1956), pp. 278–79; Anatol Rapoport, "Statistical Boundaries," in *Toward a Unified Theory of Human Behavior*, p. 308. In Hebrew, the words for *classifying* (*sivug*) and *boundary* (*syag*) indeed derive from the same root.
8. Kenneth Burke, *A Grammar of Motives* (Berkeley: University of California Press, 1969 [1945]), p. 24. See also Gottlob Frege, "Logic in Mathematics," in *Post-humous Writings* (Chicago: University of Chicago Press, 1979 [1914]), pp. 155, 179, 195, 229, 241; Joan Weiner, "The Philosopher Behind the Last Logicist," in Crispin Wright, ed., *Frege—Tradition and Influence* (Oxford: Basil Blackwell, 1984), p. 72n.

9. Don Handelman, "The Ritual Clown: Attributes and Affinities." *Anthropos* 76 (1981):340.
10. Gustav Ichheiser, *Appearances and Realities* (San Francisco: Jossey-Bass, 1970), p. 8.
11. See also Henning Henningsen, *Crossing the Equator* (Copenhagen: Munksgaard, 1961), pp. 99–101.
12. Jean Jacques Rousseau, "A Discourse on the Origin of Inequality," in *The Social Contract and Discourses* (New York: E. P. Dutton, 1950 [1754]), p. 234.
13. See also Robert C. Tryon, *Identification of Social Areas by Cluster Analysis* (Berkeley: University of California Press, 1955), p. 71.
14. Barry Schwartz, "The Social Psychology of Privacy," *American Journal of Sociology* 78 (1968):747.
15. Charles A. Ferguson, "Diglossia," *Word* 15 (1959):325–40.
16. Stanley J. Tambiah, "Animals Are Good to Think and Good to Prohibit," *Ethnology* 8 (1969): 423–59; Pierre Bourdieu, "The Berber House," in Mary Douglas, ed., *Rules and Meanings* (Harmondsworth, England: Penguin, 1973 [1971]), pp. 98–110.
17. Robert Hertz, "The Pre-eminence of the Right Hand: A Study in Religious Polarity," in Rodney Needham, ed., *Right and Left* (Chicago: University of Chicago Press, 1973 [1909]); Barry Schwartz, *Vertical Classification* (Chicago: University of Chicago Press, 1981).
18. Kurt Lewin, *Principles of Topological Psychology* (New York: McGraw-Hill, 1936), p. 44.
19. Helms, *Ulysses' Sail*, pp. 22–31.
20. Gerald D. Suttles, *The Social Order of the Slum* (Chicago: University of Chicago Press, 1968), pp. 13–38, 225; Albert Hunter, *Symbolic Communities* (Chicago: University of Chicago Press, 1982 [1974]), pp. 84, 88.
21. See also Schwartz, "The Social Psychology of Privacy," pp. 747–49.
22. Virginia Woolf, *A Room of One's Own* (San Diego: Harcourt Brace Jovanovich, 1957 [1929]), p. 110. See also pp. 4, 109; Christopher Alexander et al., *A Pattern Language* (New York: Oxford University Press, 1977), pp. 669–71.
23. On such segmentation of everyday life, see Kenneth L. Pike, *Language in Relation to a Unified Theory of the Structure of Human Behavior* (The Hague: Mouton, 1967 [1954]), pp. 73–82; Roger G. Barker and Herbert F. Wright, *Midwest and Its Children* (Hamden,

Conn.: Archon, 1971 [1955]), pp. 225–73; Roger G. Barker, ed., *The Stream of Behavior* (New York: Appleton-Century-Crofts, 1963).

24. Zerubavel, *The Seven-Day Circle*, pp. 121–29. See also pp. 102–6 and Zerubavel, *Patterns of Time in Hospital Life*, pp. 98–101. That is why nurses can take four-day blocks off only if no more than two of these days are within "the same" week (*Patterns of Time in Hospital Life*, p. 21; *The Seven-Day Circle*, pp. 128–29).

25. See also Barbara H. Smith, *Poetic Closure* (Chicago: University of Chicago Press, 1968), pp. 2–4.

26. Zerubavel, *Patterns of Time in Hospital Life*, pp. 31–32.

27. Zerubavel, *Hidden Rhythms*, pp. 101–37; Zerubavel, *The Seven-Day Circle*, pp. 118–20.

28. Zerubavel, *Hidden Rhythms*, pp. 138–66.

29. Yael Zerubavel, "The Last Stand: On the Transformation of Symbols in Modern Israeli Culture," (Ph.D. diss., University of Pennsylvania, 1980), pp. 301–21; Yael Zerubavel, "Collective Memory and Historical Metaphors: Masada and the Holocaust as National Israeli Symbols" (paper presented at the meetings of the Association for Jewish Studies, Boston, December 1987).

30. See also Roy Turner, "Some Formal Properties of Therapy Talk," in David Sudnow, ed., *Studies in Social Interaction* (New York: Free Press, 1972), pp. 367–96.

31. Alfred Schutz, "On Multiple Realities," in *Collected Papers* (The Hague: Martinus Nijhoff, 1973 [1945]), vol. 1, pp. 230–31. See also William James, *The Principles of Psychology* (Cambridge: Harvard University Press, 1983 [1890]), pp. 920–23.

32. See also Gregory Bateson, "A Theory of Play and Fantasy," in *Steps to an Ecology of Mind* (New York: Ballantine, 1972 [1955]), pp. 187–88; Marion Milner, *The Suppressed Madness of Sane Men* (London: Tavistock, 1987), pp. 80–81, 225–26.

33. Georg Simmel, "The Handle," in Kurt H. Wolff, ed., *Georg Simmel, 1858–1918* (Columbus: Ohio State University Press, 1959 [1911]), p. 267.

34. Bateson, "A Theory of Play and Fantasy," pp. 184–92; Erving Goffman, *Frame Analysis* (New York: Harper Colophon, 1974).

35. See also Goffman, ibid., pp. 496–559; Erving Goffman, *Forms of Talk* (Philadelphia: University of Pennsylvania Press, 1981), pp. 144–57, 173–86, 226–327.

36. Schutz, "On Multiple Realities," p. 233; Goffman, *Forms of Talk*, pp. 251–69.

37. Gregory Bateson, *Mind and Nature* (New York: E. P. Dutton, 1979), p. 125.

38. See also Georg Simmel, "Sociability: An Example of Pure, or Formal Sociology," in Kurt H. Wolff, ed., *The Sociology of Georg Simmel* (New York: Free Press, 1950 [1917]), pp. 47–53.

39. Goffman, *Frame Analysis*, pp. 77–78; Murray S. Davis, *Smut* (Chicago: University of Chicago Press, 1983), pp. 216–19.

40. Joan P. Emerson, "Behavior in Private Places: Sustaining Definitions of Reality in Gynecological Examinations," in Hans P. Dreitzel, ed., *Recent Sociology No. 2* (London: Macmillan, 1970), pp. 74–97; Davis, *Smut*, pp. 219–24.

41. Goffman, *Frame Analysis*, p. 412.

42. Rudolf Arnheim, *Art and Visual Perception* (Berkeley: University of California Press, 1967 [1954]), p. 231; Edward T. Cone, *Musical Form and Musical Performance* (New York: W. W. Norton, 1968), p. 15; Meyer Schapiro, "On Some Problems in the Semiotics of Visual Art: Field and Vehicle in Image-Signs," *Semiotica* 1 (1969):224; Boris Uspensky, *A Poetics of Composition* (Berkeley: University of California Press, 1973), p. 143; Rudolf Arnheim, *The Power of the Center* (Berkeley: University of California Press, 1982), pp. 50–52, 63.

43. Schutz, "On Multiple Realities," pp. 230–33.

44. Bateson, "A Theory of Play and Fantasy," p. 187.

45. Goffman, *Frame Analysis*, pp. 201–46.

46. Davis, *Smut*, pp. 29–30.

47. Michel Butor, "The Book as Object," in *Inventory* (New York: Simon & Schuster, 1968), pp. 50–51; Goffman, *Frame Analysis*, pp. 227–30. See also Erving Goffman, *Behavior in Public Places* (New York: Free Press, 1963), pp. 43, 50–53; Goffman, *Frame Analysis*, p. 220.

48. Goffman, *Frame Analysis*, pp. 224–25; Goffman, *Forms of Talk*, pp. 131–40.

49. See, for example, Erving Goffman, *Encounters* (Indianapolis: Bobbs-Merrill, 1961), pp. 65–66; Harland G. Bloland, "Opportunities, Traps, and Sanctuaries: A Frame Analysis of Learned Societies," *Urban Life* 11 (1982):87ff.

50. See also Goffman, *Encounters*, pp. 63–64.

51. Erving Goffman, *The Presentation of Self in Everyday Life* (Garden City, N.Y.: Anchor, 1959), pp. 151–53; Goffman, *Behavior in Public Places*, p. 84; Goffman, *Frame Analysis*, p. 207.

52. Our assumption, however, may be false. Traveling in Europe and speaking together in Hebrew, my wife and I were once surprised on a bus by the woman sitting in front of us, who turned and asked us in Hebrew something about the weather. It was a subtle hint designed to remind us that "nonpersons" may interact with us in a far more "focused" way than we realize.

53. Heinz Werner, *Comparative Psychology of Mental Development* (New York: International Universities Press, 1957 [1940]), pp. 452–53; Witkin et al., *Psychological Differentiation*, p. 5; Herman A. Witkin, "Psychological Differentiation and Forms of Pathology," *Journal of Abnormal Psychology* 70 (1965):319.

54. Victor Tausk, "On the Origin of the 'Influencing Machine' in Schizophrenia," in Robert Fliess, ed., *The Psychoanalytic Reader* (New York: International Universities Press, 1948 [1919]), vol. 1, p. 68; Witkin et al., *Psychological Differentiation*, p. 14; Witkin, "Psychological Differentiation and Forms of Pathology," pp. 320–21.

55. Sigmund Freud, *Civilization and Its Discontents* (New York: W. W. Norton, 1962 [1930]), p. 13.

56. Tausk, "On the Origin of the 'Influencing Machine.'"

57. Paul Federn, "The Ego as Subject and Object in Narcissism," in *Ego Psychology and the Psychoses* (London: Imago Publishing Co., 1953 [1928]), p. 285.

58. Paul Federn, "Ego Psychological Aspect of Schizophrenia," in *Ego Psychology and the Psychoses*, p. 225. See also Tausk, "On the Origin of the 'Influencing Machine,'" p. 69; Jean Piaget, *The Construction of Reality in the Child* (New York: Basic Books, 1954), p. 281; Ernst Prelinger, "Extension and Structure of the Self," *Journal of Psychology* 47 (1959):13–23; Witkin et al., *Psychological Differentiation*, p. 134.

59. Nancy Chodorow, *The Reproduction of Mothering* (Berkeley: University of California Press, 1978), p. 68. See also Otto Fenichel, *The Psychoanalytic Theory of Neurosis* (New York: W. W. Norton, 1945), pp. 35–36.

60. Margaret S. Mahler and Kitty La Perriere, "Mother-Child Interaction during Separation-Individuation," in Margaret S. Mahler, *Separation-Individuation* (New York: Jason Aronson, 1979 [1965]), p. 36; Margaret S. Mahler, "On the First Three Subphases of the Separation-Individuation Process," in *Separation-Individuation*, pp. 121–22; Margaret S. Mahler et al., *The Psychological Birth of the Human Infant* (New York: Basic Books, 1975), pp. 52–54, 63.

61. Arthur Koestler, *The Act of Creation* (New York: Macmillan, 1964), p. 292.

62. Donald T. Campbell, "Common Fate, Similarity, and Other Indices of the Status of Aggregates of Persons as Social Entities," *Behavioral Science* 3 (1958):17–18. See also Reuben Hill, *Families Under Stress* (Westport, Conn.: Greenwood, 1971 [1949]), pp. 3–5; Fredrik Barth, *Ethnic Groups and Boundaries* (Boston: Little, Brown, 1969), p. 9.

63. See, for example, Kurt Koffka, *Principles of Gestalt Psychology* (New York: Harbinger, 1935), p. 665; Hill, *Families Under Stress*, pp. 3–5; Kai T. Erikson, *Wayward Puritans* (New York: John Wiley, 1966), pp. 11, 13, 196; Richard Handler, *Nationalism and the Politics of Culture in Quebec* (Madison: University of Wisconsin Press, 1988).

64. Mark Krain, "A Definition of Dyadic Boundaries and an Empirical Study of Boundary Establishment in Courtship," *International Journal of Sociology of the Family* 7 (1977): 120. See also Erving Goffman, *Relations in Public* (New York: Harper Colophon, 1972), pp. 19–23.

65. Sigmund Freud, *The Ego and the Id* (New York: W. W. Norton, 1962 [1923]), p. 16; Stanley R. Palombo and Hilde Bruch, "Falling Apart: The Verbalization of Ego Failure," *Psychiatry* 27 (1964):250, 252, 256.

66. Mahler and La Perriere, "Mother-Child Interaction," p. 36; Margaret S. Mahler, "On Human Symbiosis and the Vicissitudes of Individuation," in *Separation-Individuation*, pp. 85–86; Mahler, "On the First Three Subphases," pp. 124–25; Mahler et al., *The Psychological Birth of the Human Infant*, p. 72; Louise J. Kaplan, *Oneness and Separateness* (New York: Touchstone, 1978), pp. 191–98.

67. See, for example, James, *Principles of Psychology*, pp. 280–83.

68. Kaplan, *Oneness and Separateness*, p. 200.

69. Werner, *Comparative Psychology of Mental Development*, p. 452.

70. Georg Simmel, "The Secret and the Secret Society," in Kurt H. Wolff, ed., *The Sociology of Georg Simmel* (New York: Free Press, 1950 [1908]), pp. 321–22; Goffman, *Relations in Public*, pp. 38–39; Eviatar Zerubavel, "Personal Information and Social Life," *Symbolic Interaction* 5 (1982):102–5.

71. See also Lewin, *Principles of Topological Psychology;* Maria A. Rickers-Ovsiankina, "Social Accessibility in Three Age Groups," *Psychological Reports* 2 (1956):283–94; Maria A. Rickers-Ovsiankina and Arnold A. Kusmin, "Individual Differences in Social Accessibility," *Psychological Reports* 4 (1958):391–406; Prelinger, "Extension and Structure of the Self."

72. Irwin Altman and Dalmas A. Taylor, *Social Penetration* (New York: Holt, Rinehart and Winston, 1973).

73. Max Weber, *Economy and Society* (Berkeley: University of California Press, 1978 [1925]), pp. 43–46; Campbell, "Common Fate," p. 22.

74. Arnold Van Gennep, *The Rites of Passage* (Chicago: University of Chicago Press, 1960 [1908]), pp. 103, 113.

75. Pitirim A. Sorokin, *Social and Cultural Mobility* (New York: Free Press, 1964 [1927]), p. 133. See also pp. 1–10; Pierre Bourdieu, "The Social Space and the Genesis of Groups," *Theory and Society* 14 (1985):723–44.

76. Georg Simmel, "The Stranger," in Kurt H. Wolff, ed., *The Sociology of Georg Simmel* (New York: Free Press, 1950 [1908]), pp. 402–8; Robert E. Park, "The Concept of Social Distance," *Journal of Applied Sociology* 8 (1924):339–44.

77. See, for example, Ward H. Goodenough, "Yankee Kinship Terminology: A Problem in Componential Analysis," in Stephen A. Tyler, ed., *Cognitive Anthropology* (New York: Holt, Rinehart and Winston, 1969 [1965]), pp. 269–71; David M. Schneider, *American Kinship* (Chicago: University of Chicago Press, 1980), pp. 23, 73.

78. Eliot Freidson, *Doctoring Together* (Chicago: University of Chicago Press, 1980 [1975]), pp. 69–85; Carol L. Kronus, "The Evolution of Occupational Power: An Historical Study of Task Boundaries between Physicians and Pharmacists," *Sociology of Work and Occupations* 3 (1976):3–37; Andrew Abbott, *The System of Professions* (Chicago: University of Chicago Press, 1988).

79. Margaret Mead, "Crossing Boundaries in Social Science Communications," *Social Science Information* 8 (1969):7.

80. Erikson, *Wayward Puritans*, p. 10.

81. Ibid., p. 12.

82. "Next: R-Rated Record Albums?" *Newsweek*, August 26, 1985, p. 69.

83. "Botha Goes Slow," *Newsweek*, August 26, 1985, p. 27.

84. Elihu Katz and Daniel Dayan, "Contests, Conquests, Coronations: On Media Events and Their Heroes," in Carl F. Graumann and Serge Moscovici, eds., *Changing Conceptions of Leadership* (New York: Springer-Verlag, 1986), p. 139.

85. *Newsday*, January 30, 1986, Part 2, p. 19.

86. Mark Johnson, *The Body in the Mind* (Chicago: University of Chicago Press, 1987).

87. Fred Attneave, "Dimensions of Similarity." *American Journal of Psychology* 63 (1950):516–56; Charles E. Osgood et al., *The Measurement of Meaning* (Urbana: University of Illinois Press, 1957), pp. 86, 89–97; Foucault, *The Order of Things*, pp. xviii–xix, xxii; Richard Beals et al., "Foundations of Multidimensional Scaling," *Psychological Review* 75 (1968):132; Samuel Fillenbaum and Amnon Rapoport, *Structures in the Subjective Lexicon* (New York: Academic Press, 1971), p. 4; J. Douglas Carroll and Myron Wish, "Multidimensional Perceptual Models and Measurement Methods," in Edward C. Carterette and Morton P. Friedman, eds., *Handbook of Perception, vol. 2: Psychophysical Judgment and Measurement* (New York: Academic Press, 1974), pp. 425–26; Eugene Hunn, "Toward a Perceptual Model of Folk Biological Classification," *American Ethnologist* 3 (1976): 515; Robert Darnton, *The Great Cat Massacre and Other Episodes in French Cultural History* (New York: Vintage, 1985), p. 192; Frederick L. Bates and Walter G. Peacock, "Conceptualizing Social Structure: The Misuse of Classification in Structural Modeling," *American Sociological Review* 54 (1989):569n.

88. Anthony F. Wallace and John Atkins, "The Meaning of Kinship Terms," *American Anthropologist* 62 (1960):67.

89. The Hebrew words for *fence (gader)* and *definition (hagdara)* indeed derive from the same root.

90. Max Wertheimer, "Untersuchungen zur Lehre von der Gestalt," *Psycholo. Forsch.* 4 (1923):301–50.

91. See also Werner, *Comparative Psychology of Mental Development*, pp. 222–25.

92. See, for example, Attneave, "Dimensions of Similarity"; Osgood et al., *The Measurement of Meaning*, pp. 89–97; Warren S. Torgerson, *Theory and Methods of Scaling* (New York: John Wiley, 1958), pp. 250, 260ff; Werner S. Landecker, "Class Boundaries," *American Sociological Review* 25 (1960):873; Roger N. Shepard, "The Analysis of Proximities: Multidimensional Scaling with an Unknown Distance Function," *Psychometrika* 27 (1962): 126; R. E. Bonner, "On Some Clustering Techniques," *IBM Journal of Research and Development* 8 (1964):22–32; Warren S. Torgerson, "Multidimensional Scaling of Similarity," *Psychometrika* 30 (1965): 379–93; Peter M. Blau and Otis D. Duncan, *The American Occupational Structure* (New York: John Wiley, 1967), pp. 67–75, 152–61; Beals et al., "Foundations of Multidimensional Scaling," p. 127; Jack B. Arnold. "A Multidimensional Scaling Study of Semantic Distance," *Journal of Experimental Psychology* 90 (1971):349–72; Fillenbaum and Rapoport, *Structures in the Subjective Lexicon*; Abraham A. Moles, *Théorie des Objets* (Paris: Éditions Universitaires, 1972), pp. 59–61, 74; Stephen K. Reed, "Pattern Recognition and Categorization," *Cognitive Psychology* 3 (1972): 382–407; Peter H. A. Sneath and Robert R. Sokal, *Numerical Taxonomy* (San Francisco: W. H. Freeman, 1973), p. 119; Carroll and Wish, "Multidimensional Perceptual Models," p. 393; Robert R. Sokal, "Classification: Purposes, Principles, Progress, Prospects," *Science* 185 (1974): 1119; Victor Turner, "Metaphors of Anti-Structure in Religious Culture," in *Dramas, Fields, and Metaphors* (Ithaca: Cornell University Press, 1975 [1974]), p. 294; Alfonso Caramazza et al., "Subjective Structures and Operations in Semantic Memory," *Journal of Verbal Learning and Verbal Behavior* 15 (1976): 103–17; Hunn, "Toward a Perceptual Model," p. 515; Carol L. Krumhansl, "Concerning the Applicability of Geometric Models to Similarity Data: The Interrelationship between Similarity and Spatial Density," *Psychological Review* 85 (1978): 445–63; Edward E. Smith and Douglas L.

Medin, *Categories and Concepts* (Cambridge: Harvard University Press, 1981), p. 105.

93. See, for example, Kurt Goldstein and Martin Scheerer, "Abstract and Concrete Behavior: An Experimental Study with Special Tests." *Psychological Monographs* 53 (1941), #2, pp. 59–60, 75–82, 103–7, 128.

94. Foucault, *The Order of Things*, p. 136.

95. Köhler, *Gestalt Psychology*, p. 93; Federn, "Ego Psychological Aspect of Schizophrenia," p. 222; Talcott Parsons, *The Social System* (New York: Free Press, 1964 [1951]), p. 482; Campbell, "Common Fate," pp. 18–20; Bonner, "On Some Clustering Techniques," p. 22; Smith, *Poetic Closure*, pp. 23–24; Robert R. Sokal, "Clustering and Classification: Background and Current Directions," in J. Van Ryzin, ed., *Classification and Clustering* (New York: Academic Press, 1977), p. 7; Smith and Medin, *Categories and Concepts*, pp. 110–11.

96. See also Jerome S. Bruner et al., *A Study of Thinking* (New York: John Wiley, 1956), pp. 2–4; Stephen C. Johnson, "Hierarchical Clustering Systems," *Psychometrika* 32 (1967): 242; Yehudi A. Cohen, "Social Boundary Systems," *Current Anthropology* 10 (1969): 109–11.

97. Foucault, *The Order of Things*, p. 140.

98. On "allomorphs," see Pike, *Language in Relation to a Unified Theory*, pp. 164, 176–77, 206; Dwight Bolinger, *Aspects of Language* (New York: Harcourt, Brace & World, 1968), pp. 58–63. On their functional phonological analogues, "allophones," see Roman Jakobson, *Six Lectures on Sound and Meaning* (Cambridge: MIT Press, 1978 [1942]), pp. 28–33; Pike, *Language in Relation to a Unified Theory*, pp. 44–46, 325–28; Mario Pei, *Glossary of Linguistic Terminology* (New York: Columbia University Press, 1966), p. 10; Bolinger, *Aspects of Language*, pp. 43–44.

99. See Ray L. Birdwhistell, *Kinesics and Context* (Philadelphia: University of Pennsylvania Press, 1970), pp. 166, 193–95, 229.

100. Murray S. Davis, *Intimate Relations* (New York: Free Press, 1973), pp. 76–77.

101. Umberto Eco, *A Theory of Semiotics* (Bloomington: Indiana University Press, 1976), p. 77.

102. See also Zerubavel, *Patterns of Time in Hospital Life*, p. 4.

103. See also Y. Zerubavel, "The Last Stand," p. 309.

104. Henri Tajfel, *Human Groups and Social Categories* (Cambridge, England: Cambridge University Press, 1981), pp. 115–16, 121, 133, 243.

105. See also Richard Williams, *Hierarchical Structures and Social Value* (Cambridge, England: Cambridge University Press, 1990).

106. Howard F. Stein, *Developmental Time, Cultural Space.* Norman: Oklahoma Press, 1987), p. 6.

107. Berger and Luckmann, *The Social Construction of Reality*, pp. 30–34, 54–58; Schutz and Luckmann, *The Structures of the Life-World*, pp. 73–79, 238–41.

108. Van Gennep, *The Rites of Passage.*

109. Henningsen, *Crossing the Equator.*

110. Marshall Sahlins, *Culture and Practical Reason* (Chicago: University of Chicago Press, 1976), pp. 181–82n.

111. Van Gennep, *The Rites of Passage*, pp. 65–88.

112. Ibid., pp. 50–64, 146–65; Robert Hertz, "A Contribution to the Study of the Collective Representation of Death," in *Death and the Right Hand* (Aberdeen, Scotland: Cohen and West, 1960 [1907]), pp. 80–86; Michael C. Kearl, *Endings* (New York: Oxford University Press, 1989), p. 95.

113. Y. Zerubavel, "Collective Memory and Historical Metaphors."

114. Goffman, *Relations in Public*, pp. 73–94; Davis, *Intimate Relations*, pp. 56ff; Stuart Albert and William Jones, "The Temporal Transition from Being Together to Being Alone: The Significance and Structure of Children's Bedtime Stories," in Bernard S. Gorman and Alden E. Wessman, eds., *The Personal Experience of Time* (New York: Plenum, 1977), p. 131. See also Emanuel A. Schegloff and Harvey Sacks, "Opening up Closings," *Semiotica* 8 (1973):289–327; Stuart Albert and Suzanne Kessler, "Processes for Ending Social Encounters: The Conceptual Archaeology of a Temporal Place," *Journal for the Theory of Social Behavior* 6 (1976):147–70; Goffman, *Forms of Talk*, p. 130.

115. See also John Carey, "Temporal and Spatial Transitions in American Fiction Films," *Studies in the Anthropology of Visual Communication* 1 (1974):45.

116. Pike, *Language in Relation to a Unified Theory*, p. 76.

117. On ways of invoking or suspending the theatrical frame before the introduction of the curtain, see William Beare, *The Roman Stage* (London: Methuen, 1964), p. 179; Elizabeth Burns, *Theatricality* (New York: Harper Torchbooks, 1973), p. 41.

118. Michel Butor, "On Fairy Tales," in *Inventory* (New York: Simon & Schuster, 1968 [1960]), p. 213.

119. For a general discussion of "metamessages," see Gregory Bateson et al., "Toward a Theory of Schizophrenia," in *Steps to an Ecology of Mind* (New York: Ballantine, 1972 [1956]), p. 222; Bateson, "A Theory of Play and Fantasy."

120. Smith, *Poetic Closure*, pp. 24–25. See also pp. 50–95, 98–150, 158–66, 172–86.

121. Cone, *Musical Form and Musical Performance*, p. 13.

122. Jan-Peter Blom and John J. Gumperz, "Social Meaning in Linguistic Structure: Code-Switching in Norway," in John J. Gumperz and Dell Hymes, eds., *Directions in Sociolinguistics* (New York: Holt, Rinehart and Winston, 1972), pp. 425–26; John J. Gumperz, *Discourse Strategies* (Cambridge, England: Cambridge University Press, 1982), p. 76.

123. Goffman, *Forms of Talk*, p. 176.

124. Holly Giffin, "The Coordination of Meaning in the Creation of a Shared Make-Believe Reality," in Inge Bretherton, ed., *Symbolic Play* (Orlando, Fla.: Academic Press, 1984), p. 86.

125. Erikson, *Wayward Puritans*, p. 11.

126. Ibid., pp. 11–13.

127. Ibid., p. 13.

128. Butor, "The Book as Object," pp. 54–55.

129. H. Clay Trumbull, *The Threshold Covenant* (New York: Charles Scribner's Sons, 1906), pp. 3–12, 25–28, 66–68.

130. Vered Vinitzky-Seroussi, "Classification of Special Days and Specific People" (paper presented at the annual meeting of the Midwest Modern Language Association, Kansas City, November 1990). See also Esther Lavie, "Age as an Indicator for Reference in the Construction of Social Contexts" (Ph.D. diss., Tel-Aviv University, 1987), pp. 242–81.

2

The Search for Signs of Intelligent Life in the Universe

Jane Wagner

(1986)

Here we are, standing on the corner of
"Walk, Don't Walk."
You look away from me, tryin' not to catch
my eye,
  but you didn't turn fast enough, *did* you?

You don't like my *ras*py voice, do you?
I got this *ras*py voice
'cause I have to yell all the time
'cause nobody around here ever
LISTENS to me.

You don't like that I scratch so much: yes, and
excuse me,
  I scratch so much
  'cause my neurons are
  on *fire*.

And I admit my smile is not at its Pepsodent best
'cause I think my
caps must've somehow got
osteo*porosis*.

And if my eyes seem to be twirling around like
fruit flies—
  the better to see you with, my dears!
  Look at me,
  you mammalian-brained LUNKHEADS!

I'm not just talking to myself. I'm talking to
you, too.
  And to you

and you
and you
and you and you and you!

I know what you're thinkin'; you're thinkin' I'm
crazy.
  You think I give a hoot? You people
  look at my shopping bags,
  call me crazy 'cause I save this junk. What
should we call the
  ones who
  buy it?

It's my belief we all, at one time or another,
secretly ask ourselves the question,
"Am *I* crazy?"
In my case, the answer came back: A resounding
YES!

You're thinkin': How does a person know if
they're crazy
  or not? Well, sometimes you don't know.
Sometimes you
  can go through life suspecting you *are*
  but never really knowing for sure. Sometimes
you know for sure
  'cause you got so many people tellin' you you're
crazy
  that it's your word against everyone else's.

Another sign is when you see life so clear
sometimes
  you black out.

This is your typical visionary variety
who has flashes of insight
but can't get anyone to listen to 'em
'cause their insights make 'em sound so *crazy!*

In my case,
the symptoms are subtle
but unmistakable to the trained eye. For instance,
here I am,
standing at the corner of "Walk, Don't Walk,"
waiting for these aliens from outer space to
show up.
I call that crazy, don't you? If I were sane,
I should be waiting for the light like everybody
else.

They're late
as usual.

You'd think,
as much as they know about time travel,
they could be on time *once* in a while.

I could kick myself.
I told 'em I'd meet 'em on the corner of "Walk,
Don't Walk"
'round lunchtime.
Do they even know what "lunch" means?
I doubt it.

And " 'round." Why did I say " 'round"? Why
wasn't I more
specific? This is so typical of what I do.

Now they're probably stuck somewhere in time,
wondering
what I meant by
" 'round lunchtime." And when they get here,
they'll be
dying to know what "lunchtime" means. And
when they
find out it means going to Howard Johnson's for
fried

clams, I wonder, will they be just a bit letdown?
I dread having to explain
tartar sauce.

This problem of time just points out
how far apart we really are.
See, our ideas about time and space are different
from theirs. When we think of time, we tend to
think of
clock radios, coffee breaks, afternoon naps,
leisure time,
halftime activities, parole time, doing time,
Minute Rice, instant
tea, mid-life crises, that time of the month,
cocktail hour.
And if I should suddenly
mention *space*—aha! I bet most of you thought
of your
closets. But when they think of time and space,
they really think
of
Time and Space.

They asked me once my thoughts on infinity
and I told 'em
with all I had to think about, infinity was not on
my list
of things to think about. It could be time on an
ego trip,
for all I know. After all, when you're pressed for
time,
infinity may as well
not be there.
They said, to them, infinity is
time-released time.
Frankly, infinity doesn't affect
me personally one way or the other.

You think too long about infinity, you could go
stark raving mad.
But I don't ever want to sound negative about
going crazy.
I don't want to overromanticize it either, but
frankly,

goin' crazy was the *best* thing ever happened to me.

I don't say it's for everybody;
some people couldn't cope.

But for me it came at a time when nothing else seemed to be
working. I got the kind of madness Socrates talked about,
"A divine release of the soul from the yoke of
custom and convention." I refuse to be intimidated by
reality anymore.
After all, what is reality anyway? Nothin' but a
collective hunch. My space chums think reality was once a
primitive method of
crowd control that got out of hand.
In my view, it's absurdity dressed up
in a three-piece business suit.

I made some studies, and
reality is the leading cause of stress amongst those in
touch with it. I can take it in small doses, but as a lifestyle
I found it too confining.
It was just too needful;
it expected me to be there for it *all* the time, and with all
I have to do—
I had to let something go.

Now, since I put reality on a back burner, my days are
jam-packed and fun-filled. Like some days, I go hang out
around Seventh Avenue; I love to do this old joke:
I wait for some music-loving tourist from one of the hotels
on Central Park to go up and ask someone.
"How do I get to Carnegie Hall?"

Then I run up and yell,
"Practice!"
The expression on people's faces is priceless. I never
could've done stuff like that when I was in my
right mind.
I'd be worried people would think I was *crazy*.
When I think of the fun I missed,
I try not to be bitter.

See, the human mind is kind of like . . .
a piñata. When it breaks open,
there's a lot of surprises inside. Once you get the piñata
perspective, you see that losing your mind
can be a peak experience.

I was not always a bag lady, you know.
I used to be a designer and creative consultant. For big
companies!
Who do you think thought up the color scheme for Howard Johnson's?
At the time, nobody was using
orange and aqua
in the same room together.
With fried clams.

Laugh tracks:
I gave TV sitcoms the idea for canned laughter.
I got the idea, one day I heard voices
and no one was there.

Who do you think had the idea to package panty hose
in a plastic goose egg?

One thing I personally don't like about panty hose:
When you roll 'em down to the ankles the way I like 'em, you
can't walk too good. People seem amused, so what's a little

loss of dignity? You got to admit:
It's a look!

The only idea I'm proud of—

my umbrella hat. Protects against sunstroke, rain and
muggers. For *some* reason, muggers steer clear of people
wearing umbrella hats.

So it should come as no shock . . . I am now creative consultant to
these aliens from outer space. They're a kinda cosmic
fact-finding committee. Amongst other projects, they've been
searching all over for Signs of Intelligent Life.

It's a lot trickier than it sounds.

We're collecting all kinds of data
about life here on Earth. We're determined to figure out,
once and for all, just what the hell it all means.
I write the data on these Post-its and then we study it.
Don't worry, before I took the consulting job, I gave 'em my whole
psychohistory.

I told 'em what drove *me* crazy was my *last* creative consultant
job, with the Ritz Cracker mogul, Mr. Nabisco. It was
my job to come up with snack inspirations to increase sales.
I got this idea to give Cracker Consciousness to the entire
planet.

I said, "Mr. Nabisco, sir! You could be the first to sell the
concept of munching to the Third World. We got an untapped

market here! These countries got millions and millions of
people don't even know where their next *meal* is *coming* from.
So the idea of eatin' *between* meals is somethin' just never
occurred to 'em!"

I heard myself sayin' *this!*
Must've been when I went off the deep end.
I woke up in the nuthouse. They were hookin' me up.
One thing they don't tell you about shock treatments, for
months afterwards you got
flyaway hair. And it used to *be* my best feature.

See, those shock treatments gave me new electrical circuitry
(frankly, I think one of the doctors' hands must've been wet).
I started having these time-space continuum shifts, I guess
you'd call it. Suddenly, it was like my central nervous system
had a patio addition out back.
Not only do I have a linkup to extraterrestrial
channels. I also got a hookup with humanity as a whole.
Animals and plants, too. I used to talk to plants all the time;
then, one day, they started talking back. They said,
"Trudy,
shut up!"

I got like this . . .

built-in Betamax in my head. Records anything.
It's like somebody's using my brain to dial-switch
through humanity. I pick up signals that seem to transmit
snatches of people's lives.

My umbrella hat works as a satellite dish. I hear this
  sizzling sound like white noise. Then I know it's
  trance time.
  That's how I met my space chums. I was in one of my trances,
  watching a scene from someone's life, and I suddenly sense
    others were there
    watching with me.

  Uh-oh.
  I see this skinny
  punk kid.
  Got hair the color of
  Froot Loops and she's wearin' a T-shirt says "Leave Me Alone."
    There's a terrible family squabble going on.
    If they're listening to each other,
    they're all gonna get their feelings hurt.

  I see glitches—
  Now I see this dark-haired actress
    on a Broadway stage. I know her. I see her all the time outside
    the Plymouth Theater, Forty-fifth Street . . .

  Dial-switch me outta this!
  I got enough worries of my own.
  These trances are entertaining but distracting, especially since
    someone *else* has the remote control, and if the pause button
    should somehow get punched, I could have a neurotransmitter
    mental meltdown. Causes "lapses of the synapses." I forget
    things. Never underestimate the power of the human mind to
    forget. The other day, I forgot where I put my house keys—
    looked everywhere, then I remembered
  I don't have a house. I forget more important things, too.

Like the meaning of life.
I forget that.
It'll come to me, though.
Let's just hope when it does,
I'll be in . . .

My space chums say they're learning so much about us
  since they've begun to time-share my trances.
  They said to me, "Trudy, the human mind is so-o-o strange."
  I told 'em, "That's nothin' compared to the human genitals."
  Next to my trances they love goin' through my shopping bags.
  Once they found this old box of Cream of Wheat. I told 'em, "A
  box of cereal." But they saw it as a picture of infinity. You know
  how on the front is a picture of that guy holding up a box of
    Cream of Wheat
    and on *that* box is a picture of that guy holding up a box of
    Cream of Wheat
    and on *that* box is a picture of that guy holding up a box of
    Cream of Wheat
    and on *that* box is a picture of that guy holding up a box of
    Cream of Wheat . . .

We think so different.

They find it hard to grasp some things that come easy to us,
  because they simply don't have our frame of reference.
  I show 'em this can of Campbell's tomato soup.
  I say,
  "This is soup."
  Then I show 'em a picture of Andy Warhol's painting

of a can of Campbell's tomato soup.
I say,
"This is art."

"This is soup."

"And this is art."

Then I shuffle the two behind my back.

Now what is this?

No,
this is soup
and *this is art*! . . .

Hey, what's this?

"Dear Trudy, thanks for making our stay here so jam-packed and
fun-filled. Sorry to abort our mission—it is not over,
just temporarily scrapped.

We have orders to go to a higher bio-vibrational plane.

Just wanted you to know, the neurochemical imprints of our
cardiocortical experiences here on earth will remain with us
always, but what we take with us into space that we cherish the
most is the 'goose bump' experience."

Did I tell you what happened at the play? We were at the back
of the theater, standing there in the dark,

all of a sudden I feel one of 'em tug my sleeve,
whispers, "Trudy, look." I said, "Yeah, goose bumps. You
definitely
got goose bumps. You really like the play that much?" They said
it wasn't the play
gave 'em goose bumps,
it was the audience.

I forgot to tell 'em to watch the play; they'd been watching
the *audience*!

Yeah, to see a group of strangers sitting together in the dark,
laughing and crying about the same things . . . that just knocked
'em out.
They said, "Trudy,
the play was soup . . .
the audience . . .
art."

So they're taking goose bumps
home with 'em.
Goose bumps!
Quite a souvenir.

I like to think of them out there
in the dark, watching us.
Sometimes we'll do something and they'll laugh.
Sometimes we'll do something and they'll cry.
And maybe one day we'll do something so magnificent,
everyone in the universe will get
goose bumps.

——————————— \\\\ ———————————

RESEARCHING SOCIAL LIFE

Social researchers who work from the perspective of symbolic interactionism face the challenge of trying to understand what people themselves think they are doing. It is not enough simply to observe a behavior. Symbolic interactionists are interested in people's *interpretations* of the situation and their own behavior.

"Truth, Objectivity, and Agreement" is a fun essay written by social methodologist Earl Babbie. Babbie wants his readers to understand that everyone, even scientists, is always interpreting information based on preexisting ideas. This subjectivity is a fact of human experience. Scientists and other systematic researchers deal with their own subjectivity by creating rules for observation and explicit theoretical starting points. One implication is that there is no "objective" truth. Truth is arrived at through "intersubjective" agreement about what is being observed and how to observe it.

"Constructivist, Interpretivist Approaches to Human Inquiry" is written by a symbolic interactionist, Thomas Schwandt. He discusses some of the philosophical and method-ological dilemmas that symbolic interactionists face in their research. He also describes some of the methods that have been developed in response to these methodological challenges.

Questions for Discussion and Review

1. What does *Verstehen* mean? What is its relevance to social research?

2. Think of some examples of "intersubjective" agreement. Why do we believe the intersubjective truths proposed by some groups and not others?

3. Do you think you have to be similar to members of a culture to understand them (e.g., do you have to be a priest to understand a culture of priests)? Or is it possible to devise methods that would enable you to "put yourself in another's shoes" or "look over their shoulder" to gain insight into their worldviews and experiences?

4. What methods do you currently use in your own life when you're trying to understand someone else?

RESEARCHING SOCIAL LIFE

3

Truth, Objectivity, and Agreement

Earl Babbie

(1986)

Science is often portrayed as a search for the truth about reality. That sounds good, but what is *truth*? What is *reality*? Look those words up in a good dictionary, such as the *Oxford English Dictionary*, and you'll find definitions like "the quality of being true" and "the quality of being real." Beyond these basic tautologies are some additional definitions (from the *OED*):

Truth:

- Conformity with fact; agreement with reality
- Agreement with a standard or rule; accuracy, correctness
- Genuineness, reality, actual existence
- That which is in accordance with fact
- That which is true, real, or actual; reality

Reality:

- The quality of . . . having an actual existence
- Correspondence to fact; truth
- Real existence

Definitions of the words *true* and *real* are similar:

True:

- Consistent with fact; agreeing with reality; representing the thing as it is
- Agreeing with a standard, pattern, or rule; exact, accurate, precise, correct, right

- Consistent with, exactly agreeing with
- Conformable to reality; natural
- In accordance with reality

Real:

- Having an objective existence; actually existing as a thing
- Actually present or existing as a state or quality of things; having a foundation in fact; actually occurring or happening
- Consisting of actual things

These definitions point to the inherent circularity of language, which is inevitable as long as we use words to define words. In this case, things are true if they're real and real if they're true. The relationship between truth and reality can also be seen in the preponderance of words dealing with agreement: *conformity, accordance, correspondence, consistent with, representing.*

Here's a useful way of seeing the relationship between truth and reality: It is possible to make statements about reality; those that agree with (conform to, are consistent with, represent) reality are true. None of this tells us what truth or reality is, however. It only tells us about their relationship to one another.

Other words in the definitions we've seen may clarify the meanings of truth and reality—words such as *actual, existence,* and *fact.*

Actuality:

- The state of being actual or real; reality, existing objective fact

Actual:

- Existing in act or fact; really acted or acting; carried out; real

Factual:

- Pertaining to or concerned with facts; of the nature of fact, actual, real

Fact:

- Something that has really occurred or is actually the case
- Truth attested by direct observation or authentic testimony; reality

Existence:

- Actuality; reality
- Being; the fact or state of existing

Exist:

- To have place in the domain of reality, have objective being

By now, the incestuous circularity of language is getting a little annoying. Consider this abbreviated search for truth:

Truth is "That which is real; **reality.**"

Reality is "Having an actual **existence.**"

Existence is "**Actuality;** reality."

Actuality is "Existing objective **fact.**"

Fact is "**Truth** attested by direct observation."

In addition to the circularity of these relatively few words defining each other, let's take a cue from the definitions of *exist* and *existence* and add the term *being.*

Being:

- Existence
- That which exists or is conceived as existing

Be:

- To have or take place in the world of fact; to exist, occur, happen
- To have place in the objective universe or realm of fact, to exist
- To come into existence
- To be the case or the fact

For the most part, these new words simply add to the circularity of definitions that is becoming very familiar in this exercise. . . .

From time to time throughout these definitions, and now in the definition of *be*, the quality of objectivity has appeared as part of the background of a definition. In these cases, *real* does not just have existence, it has "objective existence"; *actuality* is not just a matter of fact but of "objective fact." Now, to *be* is to have a place in the "objective universe." Implicit in these uses is the contrast between objectivity and subjectivity.

Subjectivity:

- The quality or condition of viewing things exclusively through the medium of one's own mind or individuality
- The character of existing in the mind only

Subjective:

- Relating to the thinking subject, proceeding from or taking place within the subject; having its source in the mind

In stark contrast, *objective* is defined this way:

Objective:

- That which is external to the mind

The truth about *truth* eventually comes down to the recognition that we know most of the world through our minds. Moreover, we recognize that our individual minds are not altogether reliable. We have colloquial phrases such as "a figment of your imagination," and we realize that people often "see what they want to see." Simply put, the subjective realm refers to the possibly inaccurate perceptions and thoughts we have through the medium of our minds, yours and mine, whereas the objective realm refers to that which lies outside and is independent of our minds. We often term that objective realm *reality*, and term *true* a statement that accurately describes reality.

A couple of snags lie hidden in this construction of objectivity. First, neither you nor I, perceiving reality through our subjective minds, can know whether we perceive it accurately or not. The following scene should make the matter painfully clear.

Imagine that you are sitting in a room that has a small window with a view into another room. A light located in the other room can be turned on or off. Reality in this illustration is simply whether the light is on or off in the other room. Truth is a function of your ability to say accurately whether the light is on or off.

At first impression, nothing could be simpler. I turn the light on in the other room, and you say, "The light is on." I turn it off, and you say, "The light is off." This would be a model of objectivity.

The defect in this model is that your mind and its subjectivity have not been taken into account. But imagine that the small window before you has two shutters. The first shutter has a picture of the other room with the light on, and the second has a picture of the room with the light off. Sometimes the first shutter will close your view of the other room, sometimes the second shutter will, and sometimes there won't be any shutter—but you'll never know.

Now when I ask you whether the light is on in the other room, you will answer based on what you see, but what you see may be the open window or it may be one of the shutters. If you see one of the shutters, the scene you see may correspond with the real condition of the room or it may not.

Relating this illustration to real life, however, you would not be conscious of the possibility that you were looking at a shutter; instead, you would think that what you perceived was reality. You would feel sure that you knew the truth about whether the light was on or off because you saw it with your own eyes. And even if you became aware of the existence of the shutters, you couldn't be sure of reality because you still wouldn't know if what you were seeing was the other room or one of the shutters.

The point of this illustration is that you have no way out. In the normal course of life, you cannot be sure that what you see is really there. But there's a bigger problem than this. Given the subjectivity of your mind, you can't be sure there is *anything* out there at all. In the two-room illustration, maybe there is no window and no other room—only two shutters. Maybe it's all in your mind. How could you ever know?

The answer to both of these dilemmas is the same. If you can't be sure that what your mind tells you is true, you can at least gain some confidence in that regard if you find that my mind has told me the same thing. You say the light is on, and I say the light is on: case closed. Now you may feel doubly sure you know the light is on, not to mention that there's a window, a room, and a light.

Ultimately, our only proof of objectivity is intersubjectivity, and some dictionaries even define *objectivity* that way. When different subjects—with their individual, error-prone subjectivities—report the same thing, we conclude that what they report is objective, existing, actual, factual, real, and true.

Thus, the basis of truth is agreement. Basically, things are true if we agree they are. When Copernicus first said that the earth revolved around the sun, few people agreed; today, most people agree. We say that this view is not only true today but was true when Copernicus first expressed it, and was even true before Copernicus. But we say all that *today* when virtually everyone agrees with the view. Moreover, if all the world's astronomers were to announce a new discovery showing the sun revolved around the earth, we'd soon be saying that

Copernicus was wrong and that the sun had always revolved around the earth, even before Copernicus.

When you think about the past history of agreements that were eventually overturned, you won't find much basis for confidence in what you and I now agree to be so. . . . [M]ost of what we "know" today will be thrown out as inaccurate tomorrow.

Where does science figure in all this? What about social science? Don't they offer an exception to this? Aren't they a dependable channel to the truth?

Ultimately, science—social or otherwise—also operates on the basis of agreement: in this case, agreement among fellow scientists. But there are some differences. Scientists recognize that knowledge is continually changing. They know that what they know today may be replaced tomorrow. In fact, the goal of science is to keep changing the truth.

Scientists are aware of the power of subjective biases and are explicitly committed to avoiding them in their research. Social researchers have an advantage in this respect, since bias itself is a subject matter for social science. On the other hand, social researchers have a disadvantage in that their subject matter—religion and politics, for example—is more likely to provoke personal biases than is the subject matter of the natural sciences.

For scientists, observation is a conscious and deliberate activity, whereas it is generally casual and semiconscious for most people in normal life. Thus, you might mistakenly recall that your best friend wore a blue dress yesterday, when it was really green. If you had been recording dress colors as part of a research project, however, you wouldn't have made that mistake.

Moreover, scientists have developed procedures and equipment to aid them in making observations. This also avoids some of the mistakes we make in casual observations. For example, scientists are explicit about the basis for their agreements. Rules of proof are contained within the system of logic prevailing at the time.

More important, perhaps, in the context of this essay, scientists are explicit about the intersubjective nature of truth. Peer review is an established

principle: Scientists review each other's work to guard against errors of method or reasoning. Scientific journals perform what is called a gatekeeper function in this regard. Articles submitted for publication are typically circulated among independent reviewers—other scientists knowledgeable in the area covered by the article. Unless the reviewers agree that the article represents a sound and worthwhile contribution to the field, it will not be published.

Scientists are by no means above error, however. Being human, they are susceptible to all the human foibles that afflict nonscientists. Though the scientific enterprise commits them to keeping an open mind with regard to truth, individual scientists can grow attached to particular views. . . .

To understand the nature of science, it is essential to recognize that scientific knowledge at any given time is what scientists agree it is. Because scientific proof is fundamentally based on agreement among scientists, scientific knowledge keeps changing over time. It is probably unavoidable that we see this evolution of scientific knowledge over time as a process through which we get closer and closer to the truth. This view cannot be verified, however. All we can know for sure is that what we know keeps changing.

We can't even bank on views that haven't changed for a long time. Bear in mind, for example, that the idea that the earth was stationary and the sun moved was accepted much longer than our current view has been. Years ago, when I was living in a house on the slopes of a volcano in Hawaii, I took comfort in knowing that the volcano hadn't erupted for 25,000 years and hence probably wouldn't ever erupt again. Then I learned that its previous period of dormancy had been longer than that.

In the case of scientific knowledge, changes are generally occurring faster, not slower, than in the past. . . . [W]hat we learn about social life is often changed by just having the knowledge we've gained. On the whole, then, we'd do better simply to settle for the thrill of discovery than to worry about whether what we've discovered is the ultimate truth or simply a new and currently useful way of viewing things.

RESEARCHING SOCIAL LIFE

4

Constructivist, Interpretivist Approaches to Human Inquiry

Thomas A. Schwandt

(1994)

Constructivist, constructivism, interpretivist, and *interpretivism* are terms that routinely appear in the lexicon of social science methodologists and philosophers. Yet, their particular meanings are shaped by the intent of their users. As general descriptors for a loosely coupled family of methodological and philosophical persuasions, these terms are best regarded as sensitizing concepts (Blumer, 1954). They steer the interested reader in the general direction of where instances of a particular kind of inquiry can be found. However, they "merely suggest directions along which to look" rather than "provide descriptions of what to see" (p. 7).

Proponents of these persuasions share the goal of understanding the complex world of lived experience from the point of view of those who live it. This goal is variously spoken of as an abiding concern for the life world, for the emic point of view, for understanding meaning, for grasping the actor's definition of a situation, for *Verstehen*. The world of lived reality and situation-specific meanings that constitute the general object of investigation is thought to be constructed by social actors. That is, particular actors, in particular places, at particular times, fashion meaning out of events and phenomena through prolonged, complex processes of social interaction involving history, language, and action.

The constructivist or interpretivist believes that to understand this world of meaning one must interpret it. The inquirer must elucidate the process of meaning construction and clarify what and how meanings are embodied in the language and actions of social actors. To prepare an interpretation is itself to construct a reading of these meanings; it is to offer the inquirer's construction of the constructions of the actors one studies. . . .

Furthermore, what is unusual about these approaches cannot be explained through an examination of their methods. They are principally concerned with matters of knowing and being, not method per se. As Harry Wolcott (1988, 1992) and Frederick Erickson (1986) have noted, not only are methods the most unremarkable aspect of interpretive work, but a focus on methods (techniques for gathering and analyzing data) often masks a full understanding of the relationship between method and inquiry purpose. The aim of attending carefully to the details, complexity, and situated meanings of the everyday life world can be achieved through a variety of methods. Although we may feel professionally compelled to use a special language for these procedures (e.g., participant observation, informant interviewing, archival research), at base, all

AUTHOR'S NOTE: Thanks to Colleen Larson, John K. Smith, Harry Wolcott, Norman Denzin, and Yvonna Lincoln for their comments on an earlier draft of this chapter.

interpretive inquirers watch, listen, ask, record, and examine. How those activities might best be defined and employed depends on the inquirer's purpose for doing the inquiry. Purpose, in turn, is shaped by epistemological and methodological commitments....

INTERPRETIVIST THINKING

Painted in broad strokes, the canvas of interpretivism is layered with ideas stemming from the German intellectual tradition of hermeneutics and the *Verstehen* tradition in sociology, the phenomenology of Alfred Schutz, and critiques of scientism and positivism in the social sciences influenced by the writings of ordinary language philosophers critical of logical empiricism (e.g., Peter Winch, A. R. Louch, Isaiah Berlin).[1] Historically, at least, interpretivists argued for the uniqueness of human inquiry. They crafted various refutations of the naturalistic interpretation of the social sciences (roughly the view that the aims and methods of the social sciences are identical to those of the natural sciences). They held that the mental sciences (*Geisteswissenschaften*) or cultural sciences (*Kulturwissenschaften*) were different in kind than the natural sciences (*Naturwissenschaften*): The goal of the latter is scientific explanation (*Erklären*), whereas the goal of the former is the grasping or understanding (*Verstehen*) of the "meaning" of social phenomena.[2]

Owing in part to unresolved tensions between their rationalist and romanticist roots, interpretivists wrestle with maintaining the opposition of subjectivity and objectivity, engagement and objectification (Denzin, 1992; Hammersley, 1989). They celebrate the permanence and priority of the real world of first-person, subjective experience. Yet, in true Cartesian fashion, they seek to disengage from that experience and objectify it.[3] They struggle with drawing a line between the object of investigation and the investigator. The paradox of

how to develop an objective interpretive science of subjective human experience thus arises....

SYMBOLIC INTERACTIONISM

One interpretive science in search of portraying and understanding the process of meaning making is the social psychological theory of symbolic interactionism. This approach to the study of human action is difficult to summarize briefly because of the many theoretical and methodological variants of the position (for summaries, see Denzin, 1992; Hammersley, 1989; Meltzer, Petras, & Reynolds, 1975; Plummer, 1991). I offer a characterization of the Blumer-Mead model of symbolic interactionism, followed by an outline of a postmodern version of the approach, namely, Norman Denzin's interpretive interactionism.

Drawing on the work of G. H. Mead, Herbert Blumer (1969, p. 2) claims that symbolic interactionism rests on three premises: First, human beings act toward the physical objects and other beings in their environment on the basis of the meanings that these things have for them. Second, these meanings derive from the social interaction (communication, broadly understood) between and among individuals. Communication is symbolic because we communicate via languages and other symbols; further, in communicating we create or produce significant symbols. Third, these meanings are established and modified through an interpretive process: "The actor selects, checks, suspends, regroups, and transforms the meanings in light of the situation in which he is placed and the direction of his action. . . . meanings are used and revised as instruments for the guidance and formation of action" (p. 5).

The Blumer-Mead version of symbolic interactionism regards human beings as purposive agents. They engage in "minded," self-reflexive behavior (Blumer, 1969, p. 81); they confront a world that they must interpret in order to act rather than a set of environmental stimuli to which they are forced to respond. Despite disavowing a substantive or philosophical behaviorism, symbolic interactionism does endorse a kind of methodological behaviorism (Denzin, 1971, p. 173). In other words, the symbolic interactionist holds that a necessary (although not sufficient) condition for the study of social interaction is careful attention to the overt behaviors and behavior settings of actors and their interaction (i.e., "behavior specimens"; see Denzin, 1989c, pp. 79ff.). Thus symbolic interactionists evince a profound respect for the empirical world. Whether they overestimate the obduracy of that world or imagine that it can be directly apprehended is a matter of some dispute (Blumer, 1980; Denzin, 1989c; Hammersley, 1989).

Blumer (1969) objects to methodologies in which "participants in . . . a societal organization are logically merely media for the play and expression of the forces or mechanisms of the system itself; [in which] one turns to such forces or mechanisms to account for what takes place" (pp. 57–58). On the contrary, symbolic interactionism requires that the inquirer actively enter the worlds of people being studied in order to "see the situation as it is seen by the actor, observing what the actor takes into account, observing how he interprets what is taken into account" (p. 56). The process of actors' interpretation is rendered intelligible not merely through the description of word and deed, but by taking that rich description as a point of departure for formulating an interpretation of what actors are up to.

As Denzin (1971) explains, symbolic interactionists begin with a "sensitizing image of the interaction process" (p. 168) built around such concepts as self, language, social setting, social object, and joint act. The inquirer then "moves from sensitizing concepts to the immediate world of social experience and permits that world to shape and modify his conceptual framework [and, in this way, the inquirer] moves continually

between the realm of the more general social theory and the worlds of native people" (p. 168). Symbolic interactionists seek explanations of that world, although, they view explanatory theories as interpretive, grounded, and hovering low over the data (Denzin, 1989c).

Pragmatism informs the philosophical anthropology, epistemology, and social philosophy of the Blumer-Mead version of symbolic interactionism. Like Dewey, Mead and Blumer criticize associationist theories of cognition that reduce action to environmentally determined conduct. They view human beings as acting (not responding) organisms who construct social action (Blumer, 1969). Consequently, such epistemological terms as *truth* and *meaning* are not expressions of relationships of correspondence to reality, but refer to the consequences of a purposeful action. Mead's political pragmatism also shaped the symbolic interactionist persuasion. Denzin (1992), for one, claims that Mead's political philosophy was more culturally conservative and less critical than Dewey's and often issued in a "conservative cultural romanticism which turned the modern self and its interactional experiences into a moral hero" (p. 6).

INTERPRETIVE INTERACTIONISM

Denzin finds several faults with the Blumer-Mead version of symbolic interactionism: a naive empirical realism, a romantic conception of the "other," and a conservative social philosophy. He thinks it important that Blumer's respect for the empirical world—his call for "close and reasonably full familiarity with area[s] of life under study" (Blumer, 1969, p. 37)—remain at the heart of symbolic interactionism. However, he is keen on developing a postmodern politics of "interpretive interactionism" (Denzin, 1989a, 1989b) that does not offer inscription in the place of description; present a romantic realist picture of human actors;

or obscure, decontextualize, or overtheorize the presentation of the voices, emotions, and actions—that is, the lived experience—of respondents.

To become more self-consciously "interpretive," symbolic interactionism must, in Denzin's view, shed its pretensions to ethnographic realism and adopt insights from poststructural philosophy, principally work in cultural and feminist studies. The former facilitates connecting the study of meaning making in social interaction to the communication process and the communication industry "that produce and shape the meanings that circulate in everyday life" (Denzin, 1992, p. 96). Cultural studies directs the interpretive interactionist toward a critical appraisal of "how interacting individuals connect their lived experiences to the cultural representations of those experiences" (p. 74). From feminist studies, the interactionist learns that the language and activity of both inquirer and respondent must be read in gendered, existential, biographical, and classed ways. As a result, a "phenomenologically, existentially driven view of humans and society positions self, emotionality, power, ideology, violence, and sexuality at the center of the interactionist's interpretive problems [and] [t]hese are the topics that an interactionist cultural studies aims to address" (p. 161).

Finally, in Denzin's (1992) reformulation, interpretive interactionism must explicitly engage in cultural criticism. He argues that this can be accomplished through the development of an "oppositional cultural aesthetic" (p. 151) crafted through a rereading of the pragmatic tradition and an appropriation of insights from critical theory. In true deconstructionist fashion, this approach (a) "aims to always subvert the meaning of a text, to show how its dominant and negotiated meanings can be opposed"; (b) "expose[s] the ideological and political meanings that circulate within the text, particularly those which hide or displace racial, class, ethnic and gender biases"; and (c) "analyze[s] how texts address the problems of presence, lived experience, the real and its representations, and the issues of subjects, authors, and their intentionalities" (p. 151). . . .

REFERENCE

Blumer, H. (1954). What is wrong with social theory? *American Sociological Review, 19,* 3–10.

Blumer, H. (1969). *Symbolic interactionism: Perspective and method.* Englewood Cliffs, NJ: Prentice Hall.

Blumer, H. (1980). Mead and Blumer: The convergent methodological perspectives of social behaviorism and symbolic interactionism. *American Sociological Review, 45,* 409–419.

Denzin, N. K. (1971). The logic of naturalistic inquiry. *Social Forces. 50,* 166–182.

Denzin, N. K. (1989a). *Interpretive biography.* Newbury Park, CA: Sage.

Denzin, N. K. (1989b). *Interpretive interactionism.* Newbury Park, CA: Sage.

Denzin, N. K. (1989c). *The research act: A theoretical introduction to sociological methods* (3rd ed.). Englewood Cliffs, NJ: Prentice Hall.

Denzin, N. K. (1992). *Symbolic interactionism and cutural studies.* Cambridge, UK: Basil Blackwell.

Erickson, F. (1986). Qualitative methods. In M. C. Wittrock (Ed.), *Handbook of research on teaching* (3rd ed., pp. 119–161). New York: Macmillan.

Hammersley, M. (1989). *The dilemma of qualitative method: Herbert Blumer and the Chicago tradition.* London, Routledge.

Meltzer, B. N., Petras, J. W., & Reynolds, L. T. (1975). *Symbolic interactionism: Genesis, varieties and criticism.* London: Routledge & Kegan Paul.

Plummer, K. (Rd.). (1991). *Symbolic interactionism: Vols. 1 and 2. Classic and contemporary issues.* Hauts, England: Edward Elgar.

Wolcott, H.F. (1988). Ethnographic research in education. In R. M. Jaeger (Ed.), *Complementary methods for research in education* (pp. 187–249). Washington, DC: American Educational Research Association.

Wolcott, H.F. (1992). Posturing in qualitative inquiry. In M. D. LeCompte, W. L. Millroy, & J. Preissle (Eds.), *The handbook of qualitative research in education* (pp. 3–52). New York: Academic Press.

SYMBOLIC INTERACTIONISM

A Perspective for Understanding Self and Social Interaction

Jodi O'Brien

Social psychology is the study of the relationship between the individual and the rules and patterns that constitute society. Most sociologists and psychologists agree that human behavior is shaped to some extent by physiological, biological, and neurological processes that are beyond the scope of social psychology. However, social psychologists emphasize that the majority of the activities people engage in and encounter in others on a day-to-day basis constitute *social* behavior—behavior that is both influenced by and expressed through social interaction. Some of the questions that social psychologists ask are: How does a person become "socialized"? What are the implications of human socialization for the transmission of culture? How does human action contribute to the production and reproduction of cultural and social institutions?

There is no single answer to these questions. Rather, the answers depend on which group of social psychologists is responding and the context in which their knowledge was developed. Social psychology consists of different theoretical perspectives, each focused on a different version of "reality" regarding human activity and social institutions. This book is written according to a perspective known as *symbolic interactionism*. Although the many approaches to the study of human social behavior have their own strengths and limitations, we find symbolic interactionism to be the most useful perspective for our purposes. In Parts II through V, we will sketch the basic tenets of symbolic interactionism and demonstrate why we think it is a useful approach to the study of the ongoing relationship between the individual and society.

As a point of comparison (and to provide some context for symbolic interactionism as it is developed in this book), this essay will explore some basic themes and perspectives in social psychology. Our lists are not complete, and people with other purposes might offer other themes and perspectives. Nevertheless, our organization of the material represents the intellectual background from which many social-psychological theories have developed.

Our discussion is organized around three major themes in the social sciences. If you understand these themes, you will have enough information to place most social-psychological perspectives that you may encounter within the historical context from which they were developed. The three major themes addressed are (1) assumptions about human nature and society, (2) how we "know" things (epistemology), and (3) the relationship between the individual and society.

As you read about the themes, pay attention to the contrasts between symbolic inter-actionism and the other perspectives. It is helpful to imagine that each perspective is similar to a different pair of glasses. Ask yourself, "What do I see through this particular lens?" and "What *don't* I see?" Each perspective contains an untold story as well as the story that it explicitly represents.

THEME 1: ASSUMPTIONS ABOUT HUMAN NATURE AND SOCIETY

All theoretical perspectives are based on assumptions—unquestioned beliefs used as a foundation on which to construct a theory. Every theory must have a starting point, a point at which some central ideas are fixed for the purpose of pursuing the implications of the ideas. Proponents of various perspectives do not necessarily believe that these assumptions are true. They realize that such assumptions allow them to construct and solve puzzles. In order to comprehend and evaluate a social theory, we need to know the assumptions on which the theory is based.

In addition, no program of study can pursue every possible line of thought. Therefore, different perspectives scrutinize specific aspects of the social story. Each theory allows us to observe details that might otherwise go unnoticed. Microbiologists, for instance, focus primarily on the cellular structure of the physical body in order to construct theories about how organisms behave; psychologists focus on the internal thoughts and impulses of indi-viduals; sociologists emphasize groups of individuals. Each type of research gives primary emphasis to different units of analysis: cells, individuals, groups.

Researchers sometimes become so focused on their own unit of analysis that they forget it is part of a larger picture. Thus, you will note (even in this book) statements such as "The most interesting aspects of behavior are social." It would be just as easy to say that the most interesting aspects of behavior are biological—although, of course, we personally don't think so. The noteworthy point is that different perspectives give primacy to different aspects of behavior. To effectively evaluate a perspective, we need to be able to mentally locate the primary focus within its larger context—such as the cell within the organ of the body from which it was taken or individual psychology within a social context.

The debate about human nature and its relationship to society centers around two questions: What can be assumed about the human creature in order to build theories of behavior and society? Which aspects of behavior should be the primary focus in the study of the relationship between the individual and society? Social psychologists have addressed these questions from a variety of perspectives. Here we discuss three—utilitarianism, behaviorism, and the cognitive/interpretive perspective—before sketching the basic premises of symbolic interactionism.

Utilitarianism

Several philosophers in the seventeenth, eighteenth, and nineteenth centuries (such as Thomas Hobbes, Jeremy Bentham, John Stuart Mill, and Adam Smith) were interested in new forms of government that would provide peace and order for as many people as possible. These thinkers lived in times characterized by the upheaval and rapid changes forged by the industrial revolution. They were also reacting to social structures in which the many were ruled by a privileged few.

In theorizing about alternative forms of government, these philosophers began with the assumption, based on the writings of Aristotle, that humans have a rational nature. They postulated that the human creature is intelligent and self-interested and is thus motivated to achieve its desires in a pragmatic way. Conflict arises because, in the attempt to satisfy their own desires and pursue scarce resources, people often exploit and injure others.

Hobbes suggested that, because they are reasonable and know what is in their own best interest, people cooperate with laws that provide order for all. In other words, humans are not dumb brutes who need to be ruled by an intelligent few (as Niccolò Machiavelli, among others, had argued), but reasonable beings who govern themselves because they desire order. Without laws and order, each person has to be constantly alert to the possibility of attack. Such alertness and defense require a lot of energy and personal resources. Therefore, rational individuals would be willing to give up some degree of freedom, such as the right to harm others, in order to have a government to protect them.

A corresponding assumption of utilitarianism is that a person will pursue the course of action that is most likely to produce the greatest returns for the least cost. Behavior is therefore the result of cost/benefit analysis in the pursuit of desired ends.

From the utilitarian perspective, society consists of two or more individuals exchanging resources that have some value to each. How available a resource is and who holds the resource determine the structure of society. For example, if you own a small forest in an area where there is little wood, others may very well want to exchange something they own for some of your wood. One neighbor may offer you sheep in return for firewood. Another might offer wine in exchange for lumber. If you already have enough sheep of your own, you will probably opt to exchange your wood for wine. When you convert the trees from your forest into lumber, others may approach you to purchase lumber as well. If these exchanges are profitable, you might become a major producer of lumber over time. But to continue exchanging lumber for wine if another neighbor offered you a better deal for your wood would not be rational. The key point is that these exchange relationships are rational; they're based on the law of supply and demand and on rules of trade that promote free exchange.

Utilitarianism is a pillar of modern Western thought. For example, the discipline of economics is based on the utilitarian assumption that humans are rational beings who calculate risks, costs, and benefits and make decisions accordingly. A major branch of political science is also founded on this tradition. Social psychologists whose research is based on the utilitarian perspective address such questions as how social order is possible among people with competing interests and how people establish power over others to get what they want. This tradition is known as *rational choice theory* in sociology and as *exchange theory* in social psychology.

All these versions of utilitarianism assume that people behave rationally to maximize the attainment of their desires at minimal cost. What their desires are often remains untold, although frequently these desires are assumed to include some form of material rewards and power. The key point is that these theories assume that individual action is rational. In these versions of utilitarianism, it is also assumed that social institutions emerge from rational exchange relationships. In other words, institutions exist and operate as they do because they meet the needs of rational human beings.

The utilitarian tradition does not attempt to explain how humans become rational calculators; it simply assumes that they are. One theoretical implication of utilitarianism is that those individuals who fail to act rationally will not be successful competitors in the exchange market. Because they are not successful, they will not exist as observable cases for a researcher to study. Therefore, theoretically speaking, the perspective needn't be concerned with non-rational actors, because such actors, if they did exist, would eventually be weeded out of society. Another implication is that society is very fluid and changes constantly with the redistribution of tangible resources. One noteworthy contribution of utilitarian theory is the idea that we can figure out what people value by looking at what sorts of choices they make. This notion, which economists refer to as "revealed utility," holds that we can know what a person *really* values only when the person has to make a choice. When making a choice, people deliberate, and this process of deliberation reveals their preferences and values. Thus, there are no real values independent of choice-making actions.

The following theoretical perspectives derive from utilitarianism but specifically address questions of individual psychology. Behaviorism, which is closely related to utilitarianism, makes even fewer assumptions about human nature than its theoretical predecessor. The cognitive/interpretive perspective and symbolic interactionism, on the other hand, offer more complex theories of the individual and make different initial assumptions about human nature.

Behaviorism

Behaviorism is a school of thought generally associated with B. F. Skinner, who assumed behavior to be hedonistic. In other words, humans and other animals seek pleasure and avoid punishment. This logic is similar to utilitarianism, except that it incorporates no assumptions about rational behavior. Organisms, including humans, simply become conditioned by particular stimuli and learn to behave in a manner that produces positive results and avoids negative ones.

Humans are socialized through a process that teaches them that certain actions are accompanied by punishments and certain actions are followed by rewards, or positive reinforcement. For example, if a child is repeatedly spanked for throwing food, the child will learn to associate the conduct with punishment and will avoid this behavior. When the child is rewarded for a behavior, such as successful toilet training, the child will repeat the behavior and thus become socialized to engage in acceptable behavior. In short, a person's behavior is predicted by the person's reinforcement history.

This relationship between the environment and behavior is often referred to as the stimulus-response relationship. A stimulus is anything in a person's environment that provokes an action (response). The environment includes internal physiology as well as external forces. Stimuli usually exist in a tangible form, such as food or money, although some researchers also recognize less tangible stimuli, such as approval or affection.

According to behaviorism, human action can be, and often is, irrational or "neurotic." Neurotic behavior is the result of conditioned responses to stimuli that may not actually be associated with the outcome but that the actor associates with the desired outcome because of prior conditioning. For example, an animal that has been trained (conditioned) by electric shock not to venture beyond specific boundaries will continue to stay within these boundaries, even when the electric shock is removed. Humans often engage in superstitious behaviors (such as wearing a lucky sweater for exams) in the neurotic belief that certain actions and outcomes are correlated. That is, if a person *perceives* a connection between a particular action and outcome, he or she will persist in the behavior in hopes of producing (or avoiding) the anticipated response.

Behaviorism and its derivative, *social learning theory,* constitute one building block in most of the predominant social psychology theories. The theories differ, however, with regard to whether a particular stimulus will produce the same response in all subjects. Some behaviorists think that all people desire certain "universal" or "objective" resources and that all avoid certain punishments. Something is said to be "objective" if its effect is independent of the subject's comprehension of it; it is "universal" if it produces the same response in all subjects. The pain of fire, for example, can be considered objective and universal: Pain appears to occur in all who come into contact with a flame, regardless of the person's opinion or thoughts about fire.

On the other hand, money, which many assume to be a universal motivator, may have little or no effect on subjects who do not consider it to be important. In other words, the effect of money as a potential stimulus to action depends on a person's *subjective* interpretation of the stimulus. Let's say that a researcher places a subject in a situation where she is predicted to cheat an acquaintance in order to get money. If the subject wants to be seen as a good person more than she wants the money, she may respond in a manner that contradicts the researcher's predictions. Behavior based on subjective perceptions can be predicted only if the researcher knows what the person values. Determining individual values and desires is difficult to do.

Nonetheless, all variants of social psychology depend in some way on the assumption that behavior is based on the desire to gain rewards and avoid punishments. However, just what these rewards and punishments are and how the researcher should figure them out is a complex puzzle.

Behaviorism does not offer much of a picture of society. It assumes preexisting socialized beings who socialize the next generations through conditioned stimulus-response patterns. (How the first humans became socialized and why they valued certain things are questions that are addressed by evolutionary anthropologists and biologists, among others.) The primary emphasis in behaviorism is on the individual's reinforcement history—in other words, the patterns of learning achieved through the application of particular rewards and punishments. Why, for example, humans in each culture prefer to wear particular types of clothing and why some costumes convey different impressions and are accorded more prestige than others is not a story that can be told from the behaviorist perspective. The story that can be told is how people learn that they must wear clothes if they wish to avoid punishment, such as being spanked or jailed, and that certain clothes bring rewards, such as popularity and dates.

This perspective offers the possibility that one might construct an "ideal" society and train people to behave in a manner that supports its ideals. In *Walden Two* (Skinner, 1976), which was very influential during the 1970s, Skinner illustrates the construction of a utopian society based on "behavioral engineering." His premise is that with the right "reinforcement schedule" (that is, behavioral engineering), people can be taught to engage in socially desirable activities and to avoid socially undesirable actions.

Freud and the Unconscious

Although we do not offer a full review here, the theories of Freud are a useful point of comparison. In contrast to the behaviorists, Sigmund Freud and his followers argue that behavior is largely the result of *unconscious* desires and impulses that arise in the human psyche. From this perspective, Skinner's utopian society is doomed to failure, because people can never be perfectly socialized. Unconscious desires and impulses, such as sexuality and aggression, counteract the effects of even the most careful behavioral conditioning. Thus, the Freudian perspective sees humans as nonrational and unlikely to act on a reasonable calculation of costs and benefits—quite the opposite of the utilitarian view. Freudians believe that most behavior is an attempt to arrive at some tolerable compromise between the impulses that surge through our unconscious and the desire to live within the boundaries established by our social community.

Freud was one of the first researchers to direct his attention to the human unconscious. In so doing, he unlocked a black box previously ignored by most students of human social behavior. Behaviorists discount the distinction between the conscious and the unconscious. They prefer to focus on the link between an observable stimulus and an observable response. In conversation with a Freudian, a behaviorist might say that unconscious impulses are simply a form of stimulus—in this case, an internal rather than an external stimulus. The important feature for the behaviorist is what happens to a person when he or she acts on impulse. Is the behavior punished and thereby eventually extinguished, or is it rewarded and therefore repeated?

Freud might not have disagreed with this analysis, but he wanted to document what human impulses and drives consist of and how the contradictions inherent in these forces are reconciled through human development. That is, his agenda was to demonstrate that civilization is the product of our attempt to temper and harness our unruly impulses. Social institutions exist to bring some modicum of order where there would otherwise be only the chaos of beasts raping and murdering one another. At the same time, although we may become socialized, we may never be fully reconciled to the "rules" of society.

The Cognitive/Interpretive Perspective

Another perspective that offers a more complex view of human beings than that assumed by the utilitarians or the behaviorists is the cognitive/interpretive approach. In addition to examining the human psyche, it examines human thought processes, or *cognition*.

Many researchers who agree with the basic proposition of behaviorism—that behavior is the result of learning which actions produce punishments and which ones produce rewards—also conclude that most forms of stimuli are subjective rather than objective. In other words, the way a person responds to a stimulus depends on how the person *interprets* the stimulus. For example, a person who is hugged will respond differently if the hug is interpreted as an aggressive clinch than if it is thought to be a show of affection. Same stimulus, different subjective interpretations, different responses.

Cognitive social psychologists believe that *interpretation*—in other words, thought—intervenes between the stimulus and response. The thought processes include paying attention to certain information, storing it, and later recalling it. That is, according to most variants of this perspective, behavior is the result of an individual's selective interpretation of the stimulus. For example, it's not likely that you would drool in anticipation if offered a burrito filled with live beetles. But some people, as discussed in the essay "What Is Real?" (pp. 2–11, this volume), consider a tortilla filled with beetles a delicacy and would respond with enthusiasm. Again, same stimulus, different subjective interpretations, different responses. (We say a great deal more about the process of interpretation in the essay that accompanies Part II.)

Another element of the cognitive/interpretive perspective concerns the question of whether humans are capable of rational thought. In a major research program conducted over the past three decades, two cognitive social psychologists, Daniel Kahnemann and Amos Tversky, have explored this question (Tversky, Kahnemann, & Slovic, 1982). One assumption of rationality is that if you prefer A to B and B to C, then you should prefer A to C. Tversky and colleagues decided to test this assumption, known as *transitivity*. In one experiment, people were asked to select panty hose from a variety of styles and colors. The experiments demonstrated that people who preferred panty hose A to panty hose B and panty hose B to panty hose C did not necessarily prefer A to C. In fact, after having selected A in the choice between A and B and B in the choice between B and C, many participants selected C when given a choice between A and C. In other words, someone who claims to prefer nylon to wool and wool to cotton will presumably prefer nylon to cotton as well. But Tversky and colleagues demonstrated that this is not necessarily the case. Many people who preferred nylon to wool and wool to cotton selected cotton in the choice between cotton and nylon.

In another study, a group of researchers observed that even the ability to perform complex mathematical calculations depends on context (Lave, 1988). Women who performed poorly on written math exams were tested on the same skills while grocery shopping. These women performed very rational calculations while shopping for the best bargains. Conversely, men who performed well on written math tests but whose wives generally did the shopping did not fare well in locating bargains at the grocery store. The same cognitive skill operated differently in different contexts.

Another assumption of rationality that has not held up to experimental scrutiny is decision making based on the laws of probability. Consider this test: A researcher holds 100 cards that contain short biographical statements taken from thirty engineers and seventy lawyers. The following card is selected at random and read: "Bob is in his middle 40s. He enjoys mathematical puzzles, dislikes social gatherings, and likes to build model trains." Is Bob a lawyer or an engineer? Most people guess that he is an engineer. Yet, based on probability, the most rational guess is that he is a lawyer. The tendency to guess Bob's profession based on types of behavior or activities associated with certain professions is a form of stereotyping, which is very different from applying the laws of rational probability.

Social cognition is the manner in which people impose preexisting categories of thought—schemas—on the stimuli in their environment and use these categories to select what to pay attention to, how to interpret the information, and whether to store it in and recall it from memory. In one study of schemas, subjects were shown a film of a woman and a man having a celebration dinner. Half the subjects were told that the woman was a librarian; the others were told that she was a waitress. When asked later to recall details from the film, the subjects recalled information consistent with role schemas, for example, that the librarian wore glasses and mentioned a trip to Europe or that the waitress liked to bowl and drink beer. The subjects not only recalled information consistent with their preestablished stereotypes, but actually made up information that affirmed these schemas as well. For example, subjects reported that the waitress ate a hamburger. Those believing her to be a librarian reported that she ate roast beef. But in the film, she ate neither (Cohen, 1981).

The implication is not that people lie or make things up but rather that perception is influenced by social categories and is a constructive as well as an interpretive process. This perspective also implies that society "exists" in the structure of a person's thoughts.

But if social institutions are individually relative, then how do human groups come to have the shared perceptions and interpretations necessary for communication and the transmission of culture? The cognitive/interpretive perspective theorizes that our social group is the source of our shared schemas. The untold story is how the ideas of "society" get into human minds and influence individual perceptions to begin with. We have placed the term *society* in quotes here to underscore another point regarding the cognitive conception of society—the idea that society is somehow "out there," independent of human actors but able to shape and direct human thought. In addition, because of its emphasis on human thought processes, the cognitive/interpretive perspective has not focused much on actual human behavior. It assumes that thoughts somehow predict behavior. However, without a more developed idea of the relationship between thought and behavior, this perspective cannot easily explain how human actions lead to social patterns.

Symbolic Interactionism

The foregoing theoretical traditions each have a different view of human nature and focus on different aspects of the relationship between the individual and society. The utilitarian tradition depicts human beings as rational calculators, and thus the primary lines of inquiry are the implications of the exchange of goods between rational actors and the effect of these economic exchanges on the structure of society. Behaviorists view the human being as the sum of a history of rewards and punishment. Each person learns to pursue certain lines of action and to avoid others. Social behavior within any particular group is the result of this conditioned learning. Theoretically it should be possible, according to this perspective, to "engineer" different types of social behavior that would result in alternative types of societies. Utilitarians and behaviorists emphasize observable actions and are interested in the effects of these actions on the social environment. In contrast, Freudians and cognitive/interpretivists focus on internal processes. Freudians are interested in how unconscious impulses are dealt with in the process of socializing the human into a healthy adult. Cognitive/interpretivists focus on human thought. For them, a central line of inquiry is how people make sense of the stimuli they encounter, that is, how they perceive and deal with the environment in an organized fashion.

This book presents social psychology from the perspective of *symbolic interactionism*. This perspective depicts the production of society as an ongoing process of negotiation among social actors. Like the cognitive/interpretive perspective, symbolic interactionism suggests that the potential for society exists in the minds of people who share common expectations about reality. Society is enacted in momentary, situational encounters among humans. In other words, there is no society independent of the human mind and human expressions of culture. The implication, in a strict theoretical sense, is that humans exist as embryonic potential and that anything the mind can conceive is possible. However, symbolic interactionists point out that humans limit these possibilities by creating and maintaining social boundaries that make life orderly and predictable.

Two main points are worth underlining. One is that stable patterns of interaction among human beings can be observed. These patterns, which include relationships of power, affection, exchange, and so forth, give meaning to social existence—they constitute social structure. The second point is that, enduring as these patterns may seem, they are fragile in that they require constant coordination by and shared understanding from the people involved to maintain them. The tacit compliance of each of the participants is what makes social patterns endure.

Pragmatism

Symbolic interactionism shares with utilitarianism the assumption that humans are motivated to make practical use of the things they encounter in their environment (including other people). According to the symbolic interactionist, people may not be necessarily *rational*, but they are *pragmatic*. Humans attempt to mold the environment to their own ends. Symbolic interactionists assume that the ends a person desires and the means he or she employs to achieve these ends are based on socially constructed meanings. Anthropologists—who also study human groups—have long debated whether human interactions should be viewed primarily as an exchange of utilities or as an exchange of socially meaningful symbols. The difference between symbolic interactionists and utilitarians is that the latter focus on the exchange of tangible resources that have some intrinsic utility, whereas the former focus on the exchange of symbolically meaningful items and actions. From the utilitarian perspective, the value of an item used in exchange is in its potential use—for example, as food or currency. Symbolic interactionists would view an item used in exchange in terms of the symbolic gesture it communicates, such as a show of respect, friendship, or solidarity. They consider exchange to be one line of action that occurs within the more general ceremony constituting social life. From the symbolic interactionist perspective, the exchange of utilities would not be possible without the underlying "trust" that exists among those who share the same social expectations.

Deliberation

Unlike utilitarians, symbolic interactionists make no assumptions about rationality, except insofar as rationality constitutes one set of cultural rules (in modern culture, we are *expected* to be rational). Another significant feature that symbolic interactionism shares with utilitarian theory is the assumption that deliberations—pragmatic choices—*reveal* something about what people value and how they make sense of their circumstances. For instance, if you are deliberating between reading this text and going to a movie with friends, ask yourself whether your decision to read the text is based on your desire to enhance your knowledge (one type of motivation) or your desire to get a good grade on an exam (an altogether different motivation). You may in fact be influenced by both forms of motivation. The point is that you can probably learn more about yourself by focusing on the sorts of deliberations you make than you can by simply responding to a question such as "Do you value education?" When you deliberate and make pragmatic decisions, you are doing so in accordance with your own understanding and valuation of a particular context.

This deliberative process also shares common assumptions with behaviorism. When you deliberate, you are considering possible rewards and punishments and weighing the pros and cons. This is actually a cognitive-emotive process, but it reflects your particular "reinforcement history." What do you perceive to be rewarding or punishing? What has occurred to you in the past, and what systems of belief do you hold that lead you to these particular assessments?

Symbolic interactionism is similar to behaviorism in emphasizing that human action is motivated by a desire to seek rewards and avoid punishments. However, symbolic interactionists study the *interactional context;* that is, they study how participants in an interaction negotiate the meaning of the situation to get one another to respond in a desirable way. The emphasis on meaning negotiated through interaction is a more social focus than the individual stimulus-response patterns studied by behaviorists.

Symbolic interactionists acknowledge (in concert with Freudians) that humans are bundles of drives and impulses. Both theories emphasize the manner in which humans learn to observe, comment on, and direct their own impulses. Deliberation can be seen as an internal conversation in which the person considers whether and how to bring his or her behavior into line with the expectations of others (a specific reference group).

The symbolic interactionist portrays humans as creatures who are reasonable and pragmatic in the pursuit of rewards and the avoidance of punishment. People learn which behaviors produce which outcomes by observing their own actions and other's reactions. The point to underscore is that symbolic interactionism focuses on subjective interpretations of events that occur in an *interactional* context. The assumption is that, whether we are dealing with someone face to face or having an internal dialogue with an imagined other, most human activity involves evaluating how to respond to others in specific contexts. *In this regard, symbolic interaction is the most social of the social psychologies.*

The important questions of study from this perspective are what meaning people give to a social context and how they negotiate and enact this meaning through interaction with others. For this reason, symbolic interactionists talk of "performing reality." Society consists of an ongoing, negotiated performance of socially meaningful interactions.

Two points are noteworthy regarding symbolic interactionism in contrast to other social-psychological perspectives and the major themes of debate:

1. Symbolic interactionism gives primacy to the social situation over individual psychology. In other words, behavior is assumed to be organized primarily in response to social factors.

2. The focus of study is on observable behavior, but the cause of this behavior is assumed to be nonobservable processes of individual interpretation. In other words, behavior is based on subjective interpretation of the social environment instead of being a direct response to objective stimuli.

THEME 2: EPISTEMOLOGY

It is the theory that determines what we can observe.

—Albert Einstein

How do we "know" things? How do we discover "truth"? Can the methods of science uncover the "real" truth? Sociologist Earl Babbie (1986) suggests that "truth" is a matter of agreement based on shared rules of what is real (see Reading 3). This holds for scientific claims of truth as well as for superstitious beliefs. For a long time, scientists believed in a universal "truth" and sought the underlying natural patterns that would reveal this truth. The metaphor that guided their inquiries was that of a watch or clock: They saw the universe as a grand watch ticking merrily away. The scientist's job was to take it apart piece by piece in order to figure out how this amazing machine worked. It's probably no historical accident that this perspective developed alongside the rise of industrial mechanization in the eighteenth and nineteenth centuries.

In the twentieth century, however, physicists, including Werner Heisenberg and Albert Einstein, began to question the possibility of a universal, objective "truth." They observed that different experiments designed to address the same question yielded different results depending on how the question was asked. For example, when light was hypothesized to be composed of waves, the experiments produced a pattern that suggested it was waves. But when light was hypothesized to be made up of particles, the tests revealed a pattern of particles. Was it possible that light was both wave and particle, both energy and matter, at the same time? Heisenberg concluded that the experimental process itself interacts with reality, that there is no completely objective stance from which to view truth (Biggs & Peat, 1984). That is, scientists shape the outcome to some extent by their interaction with the phenomenon. Even scientific interpretations are based on preexisting perspectives, or what are usually called theories. This led Einstein to make his often quoted remark, "It is the theory that determines what we can observe."

These observations set the stage for the contemporary debate between those who practice science with the goal of discovering and verifying truth (sometimes referred to as "positivism") and those who argue that truth is relative—in the case of science, relative to the theories themselves ("constructivism"). That is, theories do not reflect "natural" reality. They are a social construction. The philosophy underlying positivism is that natural laws govern the universe and that these laws can be known. The philosophy underlying what came to be known as constructivism is that any order we perceive in nature is the product of our own perspectives for organizing the "facts," or theories. In other words, our theories do not simply verify or refute reality; they actually interact with the observed phenomenon to construct a truth that reflects the original perspective.

The Symbolic Interactionist View

Symbolic interactionism is a constructivist perspective. According to this perspective, knowledge, including scientific knowledge, is *subjective*. It is the product of the context within which it was constructed. Humans do not experience the world in its natural state. We do not gather and observe "facts" that interpret themselves; rather, the selection and interpretation of data are based on classification schemes constructed by the observer. No matter how logical and insightful these schemes are, they influence how we make sense of the data and how we arrive at conclusions about "truth."

The case of Copernicus, who was able to convince some of his fellow astronomers in the 1500s that the earth revolved around the sun rather than the other way around, is an example of the relationship between scientific discovery and sociohistorical context. During the time of Copernicus, most people believed that the sun and all other planets known to exist in the heavens circled the earth. This belief was based on mathematical calculations made by Ptolemy in the second century AD.

Several of Copernicus's contemporaries suspected, based on years of charting the movement of the planets, that the earth might actually revolve around the sun. However, the language of the day (the dominant system of thought characterizing the historical epoch) incorporated Ptolemy's scheme of mathematics because it supported the Catholic theology that the earth was the center of the universe and humans the center of all things. Most mathematical calculations, the predominant method for charting the movement of celestial bodies, were based on this theory and in turn supported it.

Copernicus was successful in launching a scientific revolution not because he gathered new empirical evidence that demonstrated conclusively the earth's movement around the sun, but because he developed a mathematical statement that suggested this to be the case. He used the perspective of the time, with a slightly new twist, to advance an alternative theory. The lesson is that existing systems of thought can be used either to affirm or to alter a particular version of scientific truth. The accuracy of a scientific proposition is assessed by the prevailing standards of the time. These standards are also shaped by perspectives. Copernicus was able to reach his colleagues by using the shared language of their knowledge to cast new light on an old question. He met with resistance from the church, however, because his "findings" did not coincide with another, very powerful perspective of the day. A century later, even with the evidence of his telescope to back him up, Galileo was still made to recant similar assertions that the earth revolved around the sun when the church found them to be "incorrect" according to its standards.

A more recent example from paleontology shows how existing classification schemes shape scientific discoveries. In the book *It's a Wonderful Life* (1989), evolutionary biologist, paleontologist, and natural history essayist Stephen Jay Gould tells the story of the Burgess Shale. This limestone quarry, which was formed more than 530 million years ago, supported more life forms than can be found in the oceans today. The Burgess Shale was discovered by modern paleontologists in 1909. According to Gould, its discovery could have changed our entire understanding of biological evolution. However, the first discoverers classified every fossil according to a preexisting taxonomy, which consisted of only two categories: worms and arthropods. This scheme supported the two dominant perspectives in the study of human evolution: the hierarchical "ladder of progress" theory (that humans are the ultimate goal/result of evolution) and the "inverted cone" theory (which holds that creatures evolve with increasing diversity and complexity). Gould points out that the first taxonomists were unable to "see" the richness of the Burgess Shale because they were "trapped by history. . . . The familiar iconographies of evolution are all directed toward reinforcing a comfortable view of human inevitability and superiority. The comfortably familiar becomes a prison of thought" (p. 1).

An alternative classification scheme might have enabled paleontologists to see evidence for a different set of theories. For example, a more recent theory, which acknowledges the rich diversity of the species fossilized in the Burgess Shale, does not assume the superiority of human evolution. Instead, its model is based on the image of an "incredibly prolific bush," in which branches occupied by particular species either break off, branch out, or continue. From this theoretical vantage point, human evolution is an awesome improbability, not an inevitable truth.

So the Burgess Shale fossils were first classified according to theories that assumed the superior nature of the human species, a theme prevalent in the early part of the twentieth century. More recently, the fossils have been reclassified, this time according to theories that question assumptions of human superiority. Which perspective is correct? Symbolic interactionists would say that both are "correct" according to the criteria for scientific research holding sway when the classification schemes were developed. The two classifications of the Burgess Shale are consistent with the perspectives of their respective dates of publication.

This story illustrates that "evidence" is inevitably classified and interpreted. The theories that shape the process of classification and interpretation determine the picture of reality that emerges, because these systems of thought provide a lens through which to collect, organize, and interpret the information. The implication, then, is that scientific knowledge is not a direct representation of the natural world but is based on systems of thought that are culturally and historically bound. Thus, theoretical perspectives generally reflect the prevalent paradigms of thought that characterize a particular culture at a particular time in its history.

Symbolic Interactionist Methodology

The following points summarize the symbolic interactionist position regarding the debate over the pursuit of scientific truth:

- Scientific communities create and affirm systems of thought known as *theoretical paradigms.* These paradigms shape what we can know and how we can know it.
- Theoretical paradigms are socially constructed and reflect the historical context in which they are developed.

- Symbolic interactionism uses *interpretive* methodologies. The researcher attempts to take the perspective of the subject and to interpret the context in which the behavior takes place. In other words, the researcher tries to "look over the shoulder" of the subject or group of interest. Some of the methods used to gather information about human relations include fieldwork, interviews, and participant observation. The aim is to understand how humans see and enact their own beliefs and ideals and to trace the implications of these beliefs and actions.

THEME 3: THE RELATIONSHIP BETWEEN THE INDIVIDUAL AND SOCIETY

One of the most interesting things you will learn in the study of social psychology is that people simultaneously shape and are shaped by the societies in which they live. Who are you really? Are you a product of your social group, or are you the result of some independent genetic, psychological, or perhaps even spiritual factors? How did you get to be you? Would you be different if your significant associations were with another family and other friends than those you now have? What if you had been raised in another culture? How much are you aware of the influence of others in shaping who you are and what you think you can do and be?

In 1954, social psychologists Kuhn and McPartland published what they called the "twenty statements test." They asked people to give twenty responses to the question "Who am I?" Most people can do so quickly, without thinking too hard about the question. What Kuhn and McPartland noted was that the answers people gave tended to fall into two categories: social roles (e.g., mother, son, sister, boyfriend, student, politician) or personality expressions (e.g., happy, friendly, helpful, trustworthy, generous). What's interesting about this list is that the ways in which people see themselves involve reference to others. You can't be a father without a child to be a father to. Nor can you be "friendly" without someone to be friendly toward or someone who has let you know that he or she considers you to be friendly. How do you develop your distinctive sense of self? Where does your individuality come from?

The study of social psychology will help you avoid two common errors people tend to make when they try to figure out themselves and others. One is the error of "individualism." The other is the error of falsely separating "nature" and "nurture."

Individualism

We see ourselves in terms of our relationships to other people (social roles), and we evaluate ourselves in terms of cultural expectations. Even when we are resisting, we are resisting specific cultural values. One cherished social role in modern Western society is the image of strong individuals who do not allow "society" to influence their actions and beliefs. Consider for a moment how you may have learned about this image. Ironically, "individualism" is a culturally learned value. If you think about it, you will recall many sources of learning about the desirability of being distinctly individual, the "leader of the pack," the "lone hero." When was the last time you saw a movie that featured a group or community as the "star"? If you grew up in Western society, chances are you learned that the individual is the most important social unit in most situations. This ideal is usually associated with the belief that you achieved your uniqueness independently of any social influences.

There is evidence that average people act in accordance with this belief. Social psychologists demonstrated some years ago that people are inclined to attribute observed behaviors to individual agency rather than to social or environmental factors. For example, if someone performs poorly on an exam, the cause is likely to be seen as lack of intelligence or lack of studying—that is, as individual ability or choice. The likelihood that poor performance might be due to the exam's cultural bias (a social factor), which might make it difficult for some people to interpret the questions, is often not considered to be a valid explanation. Similarly, if one person is observed hitting another, we are likely to assume that the person is angry or hostile, has a short temper, and lacks self-control. We will probably assume that the behavior is connected to certain "personality traits." The possibility that the person was induced to act aggressively through the dynamics of the situation often doesn't enter into our assessment. This tendency to assume individual responsibility over social forces is known as the *fundamental attribution error*. People are more likely to attribute behaviors to individual personality and character traits than to social context.

In recent years, some researchers have suggested that the fundamental attribution error is a U.S. phenomenon (e.g., Hewstone, 1983). People in other cultures do not tend to make such individualistic judgments when trying to explain things. This tendency underscores the U.S. cultural attitude that single, individual actions are the primary forces shaping the world. Several observers and critics have also noted that the myth of individualism pervades the U.S. study of social behavior and organizations. The criticism is that individual psychology and development, not environmental factors (particularly social context), are presumed to explain social behavior. European social psychologists criticize their counterparts in the United States for this imbalance between individual psychology and social context.

From the perspective of symbolic interaction, you will learn that the relationship between individual personality and social values is a *dynamic and ongoing process*. You learn possible ways of seeing yourself and evaluating your own behavior from your family and other significant cultural sources, but as your sense of self develops, you also make choices about the ways in which you wish to respond to these possibilities. In this way, you are both uniquely you and a product of your cultural environment. Similarly, your own choices and actions will contribute to the maintenance of cultural values and patterns, or, depending on some of the choices you make, your actions may disrupt cultural patterns. When you consider the effects of such actions at the collective level, you will begin to see how many individuals supposedly acting on their own impulses and desires can collectively actually reinforce or change society. Recognizing that you are shaped by cultural forces does not take away from your individuality. In fact, students of social psychology often find that they have a better sense of themselves once they learn to identify the cultural influences that are shaping how they think and feel. "Individualism," the belief that you are not influenced by cultural factors, is one of the cultural myths that a thoughtful social psychologist learns to recognize as incorrect and even misleading in the quest for understanding human behavior.

Nature Versus Nurture

You may have participated in conversations in which people argue about whether certain behaviors are primarily determined by your genetic makeup or your cultural environment. As an undergraduate student, I studied biology with considerable enthusiasm. One of the first things we learned in our biology courses was the dictum *nature doesn't determine, nature hints.* The theories that we studied as budding biologists instructed us to think of the human organism in relation to its material and environmental surroundings. For instance, an infant born with a genetic propensity for great height may not actually grow to above average, or even normal, height if fed a very poor diet. The human genome project is an attempt to chart the DNA territory of humans. This has been a vast undertaking. Throughout the project, many of the most highly regarded scientists involved have continually reminded the rest of us that just because we can now map genetic combinations, it does not necessarily mean that we understand how the genes actually operate in shaping the complexity of human life. Again, they remind us of the dictum: Nature only hints. Genetic researchers can now identify a gene for Parkinson's disease quite easily. However, the likelihood that the disease will manifest actively in persons who carry the gene is less than 50%. What other factors influence the likelihood that someone carrying the gene may actually develop the disease? Geneticists have been among the most consistent in saying that the rest of the story involves a complex interaction of environmental factors, which may include diet, health patterns, stress, and other cultural-material influences.

Thoughtful, well-trained biological and genetic scientists tend to agree that human behavior is a *complex combination* of nature and nurture. Unfortunately, in recent decades many social psychologists seem to have lost sight of this understanding. Nature and nurture are not opposing positions in a debate that can be settled rhetorically. They are two sides of the same coin. A full understanding of the richness of human life involves knowledge of both the physical and cultural aspects of behavior. For that matter, we should probably consider spiritual knowledge as well. As you develop your understanding of social psychology, keep in mind that it's one aspect of a much larger puzzle. See if you can formulate questions that take into account the connections between nature and nurture, rather than falsely separate them. One example that I like to share with students in my classes is the example of chromosomal structures and reproductive structures in birds. Culturally, we tend to think of the bird that does the egg laying as "female" and the bird that does the fertilizing as "male." This fits with the gender categorization system we have for humans. Consider this, however: The chromosomal structure of the egg-laying bird is usually XY, or what in many humans is the structure linked to males. Correspondingly, the fertilizing bird does not have a Y chromosome. Does that mean the egg layer is male? How do we decide? Thus far, scientists have identified at least five distinct chromosomal structures in humans alone (you probably thought there were only two, to correspond with the two genders). What is nature "hinting" at here? Nature doesn't speak for itself. Whatever conclusions we draw are cultural conclusions. What should be of interest to the social psychologist willing to explore this complexity is that the two-gender cultural system does not reflect the much wider array of sex-typification combinations that exist in nature. This might lead a social psychologist to conclude that cultural processes of gender *socialization* are significant factors in developing and sustaining the two-gender system that we consider not only normal, but natural.

In addition to learning to think of nature and nurture as related, rather than oppositional, aspects of human development, symbolic interactionism will enable you to learn that social patterns, like natural ones, are extremely powerful in shaping human feeling, behavior, and thought. Many people assume, incorrectly, that social influences are not very strong and are therefore easy to change. For instance, in recent years it has become fashionable to think of behavioral patterns such as alcohol abuse as physiological diseases. Drinking behaviors are *both* physiological and cultural. However, it is assumed that by calling the behavior a physical disease, we take some of the blame off the individual. In other words, if the behavior is attributed primarily to nature, then it is easy to explain why it is so difficult to change the behavior culturally. The problem with this line of reasoning, in addition to the false separation of nature and society, is that it deemphasizes the extent to which deeply entrenched cultural patterns *do* contribute to chronic drinking. Just because a behavior is entrenched in cultural patterns does not lead to the conclusion that it is a behavior that can be easily changed. Think about the previous example about gender. To say that gender is, in large part, socially constructed does not mean it is easy to disassemble. If you were asked to live your life as another gender and couldn't do so, we wouldn't say it was because you hadn't tried hard enough. Rather, we would recognize that cultural patterns, like natural ones, are not easily altered. This is perhaps one of the most misunderstood aspects of cultural life: that it is easy to change.

The study of social psychology through the perspective of symbolic interaction will enable you to understand both the significance and the entrenchment of the cultural patterns that shape our lives and our choices. Symbolic interactionism focuses on the ways in which we learn, enact, and ultimately reinforce cultural patterns, including myths such as "individualism" and "naturalism."

Reading Notes for Understanding Symbolic Interactionism

The following "reading notes" are drawn from the experiences of teachers and students who have used this material. Readers sometimes fall into the traps of "psychologism" and "reification."

Psychologism

Social psychologists who study human cognition note that each of us has a tendency to interpret information in terms of its specific relevance to our own experiences. This information-processing bias is termed *psychologism* (or the self-consensus bias). Psychologism, when coupled with the ideal of individualism, makes it difficult for students to comprehend theories that pertain to the social group. The tendency is to interpret and evaluate the information offered by these theories in terms of individual psychology and experience. Readers tend to ask, "Does the theoretical perspective match my personal situation?"

Many people view theories that emphasize group knowledge and socialization as antithetical to their own individuality. But this separation of individual and group is based on a false dichotomy. As we discuss throughout this book, there is no possibility of the concept of the "individual" (including individual rights, feelings, and so forth) without the social group.

Remember that you do not have to deny personal experience in order to explore the implications of group knowledge. The question to ask yourself is "How might collective meanings and social interactions shape how I see the world and how I act?" What humans do in interaction with others may or may not be harmonious with their private thoughts. However, and this is the point to emphasize, whether or not people accept or believe in their own public actions, these actions are observable by others and come to be real in their consequences.

Reification

Reification means to treat an abstract concept as if it were real, independent of human activity. For example, people tend to think of "IQ" as a real thing that exists inside our brains and shapes our intelligence. In fact, IQ is simply a score derived from a battery of tests that are not meaningful beyond their direct application. In spite of this, parents and educators often act "as if" IQ is real and make decisions accordingly. Similarly, people sometimes treat sociological concepts—for example, norms—as if they were physical structures that exist somewhere in a state of nature and "do" things to humans. When a concept is reified, or given a life of its own, we tend to forget the extent to which our own beliefs and actions contribute to the construction and perpetuation of the processes described by the concept. Thus students are inclined to write papers in which they make claims such as "Society causes people to be poor."

It's more than a little bit ironic that we tend to think of ourselves as *individuals* who are entirely free of social influence and, at the same time, see many social forces and their consequences for other people as if the forces had a life of their own. This way of thinking reflects a kind of social illiteracy. We fail to see just how firmly entrenched certain social "rules" are and how they shape our personal lives, and at the same time fail to see how our own behavior reflects and contributes to the perpetuation of these social forces. The false separation of the individual and society deters us from a comprehensive and complex understanding of the ways in which we are both products of and producers of society.

Symbolic interactionism offers a way to reconcile the false separation of the individual and society. The perspective teaches us that social reality is the product of coordinated activity among real individuals. The puzzle is how abstract concepts are communicated, shared, and reproduced and how they take on patterns of stability that make them appear "real." The enduring, stable character of social interaction is what we come to know, in a reified way, as "society."

CONCLUSION

Symbolic interactionism is conducted at the intersection of individuals and society. From this perspective, it is not possible to make sense of one without incorporating the other. The challenge for symbolic interactionism has been to represent society in a way that avoids reification—in other words, to model social patterns and relationships as the products of ongoing individual activity. At the same time, symbolic interactionism must account for the observation that existing social patterns do influence and constrain individual actions. The ultimate aim of symbolic interactionism, as presented in this book, is to place the individual and society on the same level and to analyze the reciprocal relationships between individual action and social patterns and institutions. Social life is conceived as a dynamic web of reciprocal influences among members of a social group. This web is made up of the interactions of individuals. Individuals spin and respin the web. At the same time, they are influenced by the existing patterns of previously spun strands.

Symbolic interactionism is unique in the study of both psychology and sociology in that it is the only perspective that assumes an active, expressive model of the human actor and treats individual and social phenomena at the same level of analysis. In gaining an understanding of this perspective, think in terms of process and feedback. This viewpoint is admittedly more complicated than representing social life in terms of simple dichotomies and cause-and-effect reasoning. However, in reality individual existence and social patterns are mutually constitutive—the relationship between the individual and society is reciprocal. Symbolic interactionism offers a rich story about human behavior and its social consequences. We think you will find this story to be instructive and relevant to your personal life and the social world in which you are a participant.

References

Babbie, E. (1986). *Observing ourselves: Essays in social research.* Belmont, CA: Wadsworth.

Biggs, J., & Peat, D. (1984). *Looking glass universe: The emerging science of wholeness.* New York: Simon & Schuster.

Cohen, C. (1981). Person categories and social perception: Testing some boundaries of the processing effects of prior knowledge. *Journal of Personality and Social Psychology, 40,* 441–452.

Gould, S. J. (1989). *It's a wonderful life: The Burgess Shale and the nature of history.* New York: Norton.

Hewstone, M. (Ed.). (1983). *Attribution theory: Social and functional extensions.* Oxford, UK: Basil Blackwell.

Kuhn, M., & McPartland, T. (1954). An empirical investigation of self-attitude. *American Sociological Review, 19,* 68–76.

Lave, J. (1988). *Cognition in practice: Mind, mathematics, and culture in everyday life.* New York: Cambridge University Press.

Skinner, B. F. (1976). *Walden two.* New York: Macmillan.

Tversky, A., Kahnemann, D., & Slovic, P. (Eds.). (1982). *Judgment under uncertainty: Heuristics and biases.* New York: Cambridge University Press.

PART II

HUMANS AS SYMBOL-USING CREATURES

Human beings act toward things on the basis of the meanings that the things have for them.

—Herbert Blumer (1969), *Symbolic Interactionism*

The limits of my language mean the limits of my world.

—Ludwig Wittgenstein (in Lee, 1980)

SHARED MEANING AS THE BASIS OF HUMANNESS

Jodi O'Brien

Imagine that you have just been kicked in the knee. How do you respond? Your immediate physical response is probably an upward jerk of the leg. Perhaps a rush of air and a surprised gasp escape your lips. In a behaviorist's terms, the blow to the knee is considered the stimulus, and your direct, physical response is your jerking leg and cry of pain. This physical response to the stimulus of being kicked is the same for most humans.

In addition to this physiological response, you are likely to have reactions that are not as predictable. How do you respond to the person who kicked you? You may kick the person in return. You may apologize for being in the way. You may flee. Your response to the person who kicked you depends on how you *interpret* the incident. Do you perceive it to be an act of aggression, an accident, a playful joke? Your interpretation of the incident is in turn based on the situation and the cues you pick up from the person who kicked you. If you are in a crowded space and the kicker smiles apologetically, you are likely to interpret the act as an accident and to respond accordingly. If you have been reading quietly in an empty room and the kicker glares at you menacingly, you are more likely to interpret the kick as an act of aggression than as an accident.

Symbolic interactionists are interested in the process of assigning meaning to actions and in the responses that follow. The meaning that you assign to being kicked determines how you will respond to the kicker and, in turn, how the kicker will respond to you. That is, how you *perceive* the incident will determine how you *feel* about it and your subsequent course of action. This perception will also be the basis for how you store the event in your memory and recall it later.

A jerk of the knee and a cry of pain may be predictable, universal, physical responses. However, there is nothing inherent in the interpretation that can be placed on the event. To symbolic interactionists, the most interesting aspects of human behavior are those that take place when we assign meaning to our own actions or interpret the actions of others. Although it is possible to chart direct stimulus-response patterns in human behavior, symbolic interactionists maintain that these patterns are of limited interest in understanding human behavior and institutions. Most noteworthy behavior involves a process of *interpretation* between stimulus and response. Thus, the interesting question for the student of human behavior is not what the objective stimulus is (for example, the blow to the knee) but what *meaning* the receiver of the kick assigns to the stimulus (that is, how the blow is perceived). It is the process of assigning meaning that determines how people feel and act.

Symbolic interactionists claim that symbolic activity mediates between stimulus and response. This essay explores the implications of being symbol-using creatures who interpret the world. We will also discuss human thought as a process of symbolic gestures achieved through the acquisition of language. From this perspective, social behavior is a manifestation of shared patterns of symbolic meaning.

"Physical reality seems to recede in proportion as man's symbolic activity advances."

The philosopher Ernst Cassirer makes this assertion in his essay on humans as symbol-using creatures (see Reading 6). For Cassirer, symbol-using creatures do not exist in a direct state of nature. To exist in a state of nature is to be nonconscious, nonreflective, and nonsymbolic. In such a state, the organism is propelled directly by the forces of nature, which include internal physiology and the external environment. In contrast, the symbolic creature is able to comprehend, comment on, and organize behavior in accordance with abstract representations that are removed from the state of nature. This does not necessarily imply that humans are "superior" to animals, nor does it suggest that we do not have an animal form (biologically and physiologically). The point is that most noteworthy human activity is symbolic (abstracted from a direct state of nature). Thus, the symbolic interactionist focuses on human behavior and culture *primarily* as expressions of meaningful symbol systems.

A comparison with elephants illustrates this point. When elephants meet, one places its trunk in the mouth of the other. Body temperature and fluids in the mouth indicate whether each elephant is in a state of arousal or aggression or is passive. This encounter triggers the appropriate response—copulating, fighting, fleeing, or traveling together. The elephants, as far as we can tell, do not think about this encounter; they do not interpret the event and assign meaning to it. They simply engage in a series of stimulus-response behaviors with each other in a direct state of nature.

The difference between humans and elephants is that humans do not respond directly to the physical environment. Rather, humans impose symbolic interpretations on experiences and draw conclusions based on these interpretations. It is true that we are attuned to odors and other physiological manifestations of our fellow humans and that we may experience these directly rather than through a process of interpretation. But most of our responses to others are determined by our *interpretation* of various cues. These cues include physiological features; gestures; and accessories and adornments, such as clothing and other symbolically meaningful items.

Those of you who have driven across a border into another country know that it is the duty of border guards to ascertain whether you are bringing merchandise into (or out of) the country in violation of international or national laws. These guards cannot read your mind. Nor can they experience directly whether you are telling the truth when you claim not to be carrying illicit goods. The guards must infer your intentions based on symbolic cues, such as the type of car you are driving, your gender, and the style of your clothes and hair. In other words, the guards guess at your integrity based on their symbolic interpretation of you and the situation. Similarly, the police officer who stops a motorist cannot experience directly whether the accosted driver will be hostile or compliant. The officer must make an inference based on available symbolic cues.

Consider the process of cue interpretation you engage in when you are trying to figure out if the person across the room is flirting with you. In such a situation, you have no direct knowledge of the person's actual mood or intentions. Is this someone who is a potential date? If you approach, will the person be hostile or receptive? Before making a move, the individual trying to assess the situation is likely to consider many cues and will probably discuss the cues with a group of friends before deciding to act. All of this is interpretive behavior.

Sociologists are interested in the signs people use to make inferences and the reliability of these signs for predicting the intentions of others. This predictability is not a function of directly reading the "natural" world. Rather, it is the product of the symbolic codes through which we assign meaning to objects. Human behavior is not determined directly from our encounters with the physical world. Our bodies are physical entities that exist in the physical world, but our experience of our own bodies, of other people, and of things in our environment is anchored in the internal conversation that constitutes our conscious thought.

Symbolic Meaning: It's the Name, Not the Thing

Herbert Blumer is credited with first use of the term *symbolic interactionism* to define the approach to the study of human behavior and society that we have been discussing (Fine, 1990). Blumer, who was a sociologist at the University of California, Berkeley, suggested three basic premises:

1. Humans act toward a thing on the basis of the meaning they assign to the thing.

2. Meanings are socially derived, which is to say that meaning is not inherent in a state of nature. There is no absolute meaning. Meaning is negotiated through interaction with others.

3. The perception and interpretation of social symbols are modified by the individual's own thought processes (Blumer, 1969, p. 2).

Naming (Assigning Meaning)

When we make sense of a person, space, or occasion, we attach meaning to it. This process is known as *naming*. Naming has three elements: a label, a cognitive-emotive evaluation, and a recommended course of action. The conceptual names we have for persons, spaces, and things include each of these three components. Consider a round, hollow tube made of glass with a single closed end. We can label it a glass. But *glass* is a fairly abstract term, and we might each be imagining a different type of glass. Let's say that we further narrow the meaning of the label by imposing additional classifications—for example, the glass has a stem attached. This description suggests a wineglass, which we may evaluate subjectively as, perhaps, an elegant sort of glass or a decadent sort of glass. Regardless of the specific glass that each of us has in mind, we are in agreement as to its general purpose. That is, we know the recommended course of action toward the object that we have labeled a glass: It is a container from which we can drink.

Philosophers, linguists, and cognitive social psychologists agree that to name something is to know it. This process of object identification is central to human perception and appraisal. Humans name things and then respond according to the implications carried by the name. They do not respond to the essence of the thing itself. Thus, we say that human behavior involves not just a response to a stimulus but a process—naming—that mediates between stimulus and response.

Try the following exercise. Work up some saliva in your mouth. How does it feel? Now spit it into a glass. How does it look? Now drink it up. Most of you will probably respond to this last request with some hesitation. Yet we have simply asked you to reabsorb a substance that, in fact, you swallow continually all through the day. Why did you hesitate? Probably because you have an aversion to spit. This aversion is not a direct response to the natural essence of the substance. It is an aversion to the *name,* not the thing. Your reaction is based on a symbolic process whereby you have conceptualized bodily fluids that have left the body as repulsive. The name *spit* implies an evaluative response ("Yuck!") and a course of action (avoidance). You do not respond to the nature of the fluid. Instead, you assign meaning to the fluid and respond to that meaning. Cassirer reminds us of the words of Epictetus: "What disturbs [people] are not things, but their opinions and fancies about things."

Symbols and Signifying

Emotional and behavioral responses to environmental stimuli are shaped by this naming process. Thus, behavior differs not in response to a particular stimulus but in response to the meaning human actors assign to the stimulus. In Jane Wagner's "The Search for Signs of Intelligent Life in the Universe" (Reading 2), Trudy, a bag lady giving lessons about earth life to some space chums, attempts to explain the difference between a can of Campbell's soup and Andy Warhol's painting of a can of Campbell's soup. One is soup, the other is art. Warhol's rendering of the can of soup is not merely a stand-in image for the soup itself; rather, as "art" it constitutes a class of meaning unto itself. In contemplating the painting, a person doesn't consider whether the actual soup tastes good; instead, the person evaluates the "worth" of the painting based on what he or she knows about art. "Soup" and "art" are both abstract ideas, although each term conjures a different meaning. These different meanings imply different lines of action or responses toward the object. Similarly, the conversation we are now having, in which we are removed from one another's immediate presence, would not be possible if we did not share the abstract ideas of "book," "reading," and a similar symbolic system called "written English."

What are these symbols that we use to assign meaning to our experiences? Symbols are abstract representations. Brand names are a form of symbolic representation that even young children are familiar with. Many parents are familiar with the exasperation of trying to locate, not to mention pay for, a pair of shoes that a teenager insists he or she *must* have. It's often the case that the materials and construction of the desired brand differ little from those of other brands, but the brand itself stands for something—in this case, being hip or cool—and in a social world, this makes all the difference.

Consider another example: A rectangular piece of cloth with red and white horizontal stripes and a blue square filled with white stars in the upper left-hand corner has significance beyond this physical description—it is a symbol, an abstract representation, of the United States of America.

A flag is a symbol not only of the nation "for which it stands" but also of the social convention of dividing the world into mutually exclusive geopolitical units known as "nations." The U.S. flag not only stands for what is considered uniquely American but also symbolizes a *distinction* from other nations. To be American is also to *not be* Russian, for example. Thus, a symbol defines both what something is and what it is not. The essence of the item you hold in your hands at this moment is tree pulp flattened and pressed into connected sheets with splotches of ink all over them. Most likely you do not think of the item this way, but rather as a book with abstract symbols in the form of written language for you to absorb. It is also likely that you do not consider the book as a source of toilet paper, although its natural essence has properties similar to those of the materials in toilet paper.

The study of semiotics and sociolinguistics is the study of the cultural systems of meaning that are conveyed through various symbolic representation. Roland Barthes (1964/1967), for example, has studied food symbolism. All societies have cultural systems that *signify* what foods can be eaten and what foods should be excluded; how certain foods are supposed to be grouped (for example, breakfast, lunch, dinner, or appetizers, main courses, desserts); and the various rituals of use ("table manners," "picnics," "feasts"). Trudy's space chums have difficulty comprehending the distinction between "soup" and "art" because they do not share the symbolic understanding whereby an apparently similar material image is *assigned* to entirely different domains of meaning (food/art). In both examples, the symbolic system *signifies* how things are supposed to be grouped (classified) and how we are supposed to feel about them. Thus:

Naming = assigning symbolic meaning to things/persons/events

Symbolic meaning = a sign system that conveys messages about how to feel about and respond to the thing/person/event

Harlem Renaissance artist and writer Langston Hughes wrote a story called "That Powerful Drop" to illustrate the significance of symbolic meaning within specific cultural contexts (see Reading 5). In the story, Hughes's characters ponder the significance of "Negro blood." Physiologically, there is no difference between white and black blood. However, in the context of this story—the 1950s Southern states—identifying certain people as having "Negro blood" conveys the symbolic message that black blood is less desirable and more problematic than white blood. Technically speaking, the characters in the story cannot see one another's blood, nor can most of us most of the time. It's not the blood per se, but the idea of what the blood stands for, in this case, skin hues and phenotypical characteristics such as nose and other facial features that are presumed to signify one's standing as a human being in relation to other human beings. This racial marker is mutually understood by people who share a cultural system of meaning premised on racial differentiation and prejudice. In a culture in which differentiation is based more on class position than on race, the phenotypical characteristics associated with "blood" might be overlooked, but people's accents—do they sound educated or not?—might be highly notable and symbolic.

Symbols, Experience, and Culture

Because symbols are abstractions, we can use them to transcend the concrete environment and to have experiences that are not rooted in time and space. Abstraction also allows us to remember, fantasize, plan, and have vicarious experiences. When we imagine something, we formulate an image, a symbolic representation, of something that is not present in the immediate state of nature. Remembering is a similar activity. When we fantasize and make plans, we are manipulating symbolic images. Vicarious experience allows us to learn by observing the actions of others; we need not experience everything ourselves to comprehend what someone else is experiencing. This is a key element in individual survival and in the transmission of culture.

Symbolic interactionists claim that without symbol systems, human experience and culture would not be possible. To comprehend the significance of the human ability to engage in symbolic abstraction, consider how much time you spend in the presence of your intimate friends versus how much time you spend thinking, remembering, fantasizing, and planning about them. Ask yourself if it would be possible for you to experience "love" for someone if you could not imagine (represent conceptually) the person when he or she was not actually physically present.

A great deal of human symbolic activity involves learning to sort and group people into social roles (for example, stranger, teacher, judge, soldier, priest, and so on). Culturally specific expectations are associated with different social roles. For example, we think, feel, and behave very differently with "friends" than we do with "grandparents."

In a case study titled "Yes, Father-Sister" (see Reading 7), neurologist Oliver Sacks describes a woman who has lost the ability to recognize and name people according to recognized social groups. She has a neurological dissolution associated with language processing that has left her without "any 'center' to the mind." She is no longer able to comprehend or express symbolic *meaning*. All social roles are the same for her and can be interchanged at will. Thus, someone in her presence can be "Father," "Sister," or "Doctor" at any given moment. Imagine how disconcerting it would be if one of your parents named you indiscriminately "child," "parent," "lover," "salesclerk." People who are unable to engage in appropriate symbolic activity are islands isolated from meaningful relationships. They are unable to access and express the cultural "script" that others share and find significant.

THE SOURCE OF SYMBOLIC SYSTEMS OF MEANING: LANGUAGE

The primary way by which humans exchange symbolic meaning is through language. Language is a system of symbols that allows humans to communicate and share abstract meaning. Language gives humans the capacity to become social creatures—which is to say, the capacity to comprehend and to participate in culture.

The basic unit of language is the word. Words are symbols that denote the meaning of something. Words can be conveyed through writing, speech, and sign. The power of words to represent the range of human activity can be seen in the following exercise: Try listing words for as many emotions as you can think of. Then read your list to someone else. Chances are that the person will comprehend the states of being that each word suggests. Now, select an emotion word that is well understood among those who share your language and attempt to communicate this emotion to someone through direct physical contact without the use of words. General emotions such as anger, lust, and fright may possibly be communicated by touch. However, it is likely that the list of emotion words that you generated conveys a much wider range of emotion and greater emotional subtlety than you can communicate effectively without resorting to words. Does this exercise show that there are more emotions than there are ways of expressing them? No. It implies that there are as many emotions as there are words for describing them.

Words give meaning to our experiences. In many instances, a physiological state of arousal is meaningless and may even go unnoticed until the experience has been named. Consider, for example, a young man who, while traveling by plane, experiences a shaky stomach and sweaty palms. He is unable to ascertain whether he is experiencing airsickness or attraction to the woman sitting next to him. Both experiences entail the same physiological responses, but different courses of action are deemed appropriate, depending on whether one labels the experience "nausea" or "love."

Meaning consists not only of isolated words or names but of the additional ideas and experiences associated with particular words. An instructive exercise is to note words that have parallel definitions but carry very different connotations. *Spinster* and *bachelor* are one example. Both are defined simply as the male and female state of being unmarried. But *spinster* raises much less attractive images in the minds of most people than does the term *bachelor*. Language comprehension involves much more than just knowing words. Meaningful communication is based on shared understanding of a *cluster of meanings* associated with particular words. Recall the discussion of "naming"—words are the basis of naming and provide not only identification of objects, but instructions for how to feel and respond to objects and situations that we encounter.

Language and Social Behavior

Language, thought, and social behavior are closely related. We interact with each other by observing ourselves and steering our behavior according to our interpretations of the expectations of others. This process is internal; we *talk* with ourselves about how to name situations, how to name our role in the situation, and how to assign meaning to others in the situation. We determine recipes for action based on the meaning we assign to the situation and experience feelings about the situation depending on how we have defined it. Without language, we would be unable to assign meaning to our own actions or to bring our actions into line with the expectations of our culture. We would be unsocialized.

Language and Socialization

The social philosopher George Herbert Mead lectured and wrote in the 1930s (see Reading 22). He theorized that language acquisition is an interactional process. The meanings that the child learns to assign to things in the environment, including the self, derive from interactions with significant others. The child does not simply learn to name a spherical object "ball." She learns that a certain activity associated with the ball, such as hurling it across space, meets with particular responses from those around her. She also learns that these responses are either positive or negative and come in the form of reactions toward herself. Thus, she learns that she is the source of the activity that generates the response. She also learns that in certain situations, for example, in an enclosed space, people react more negatively when she hurls the ball than they do when she is on the green stuff called "grass."

The child also learns to distinguish between the responses of differently named persons in her environment. "Dad" may praise her "athletic ability" when she hurls the ball. "Mom" may attempt to "settle her down." In this way, the child learns to form complex associations among persons, things, and situations. Most important, the child learns what stance to adopt in a given setting in relationship to specifically named others and objects. This process of learning "names" and the associated rewards and punishments is the foundation of human socialization.

Much research has been done on the relationship between language acquisition and human development. Researchers are particularly interested in the few documented cases of "feral children"—children raised in isolation from adult human interaction.

In the 1940s, sociologist Kingsley Davis described the case of a young girl who was subjected to extreme isolation during crucial developmental years (see Reading 8). In presenting her case, Davis pursued the hypothesis that social intercourse is necessary for the development of language and intellectual activity. Without exposure to language, children do not achieve the ability to engage in normal human activities.

Further information about the relationship between language and social behavior comes from studies of people who have experienced damage to the language centers of the brain. The neurological disorders that result from such damage are referred to as "aphasia." These disorders usually impair a person's ability to engage in normal social interactions. Recall the woman described by Oliver Sacks who could no longer recognize social roles and therefore responded to everyone as if they were anything that popped into her mind.

Other researchers have documented similar consequences of aphasia (see, for example, Lindesmith, Strauss, & Denzin, 1991). In one tragic case, a well-known symphony conductor contracts a virus that impairs his neurological language center. As a result of this impairment, his conceptual memories are wiped out to the extent that he no longer recognizes his own wife. When she hugs him, his sense of smell and touch serve as triggers that remind him, briefly, who she is. Thus reminded, he sobs and clings to her and asks where she has been for so long. Minutes later, when she returns to his room from taking a break, the entire scene is played over again. Without the capacity for language, specifically the ability to formulate a concept of "wife" and retain all his memories of her as wife in his mind, the man simply doesn't know who she is.

Together, these curious and often tragic cases suggest to neurologists, linguists, and social psychologists that the relationships among the brain, language, and social behavior is highly complex and also crucial for what we consider "normal" human behavior.

Language and Thought

As powerful as a single word may be in assigning meaning, the full power of language is in the relationships among words, or the *structure* of language. Words are juxtaposed in such a way as to convey one meaning rather than another. For example, the words *cat, dog,* and *chases* each suggest a particular meaning. The first two are nouns that denote certain types of four-legged mammals, and the third is a verb that names a particular action. Presumably we have a shared understanding of the general class of meaning to which these words refer. Now, consider the alignment of the words "dog chases cat" and "cat chases dog." Does each combination suggest the same events? Try writing other possible combinations of these three words. How many of these combinations make sense to you?

The structure of language, called *syntax,* comprises the rules of grammar. Syntax allows humans to combine words to create strings or clusters of meaning more complex than the meaning suggested by isolated words. The syntax of a language also permits us to convey entirely different meanings by recombining symbols, as in the example of *cat, dog,* and *chases.* Another interesting feature of syntax is that humans appear to learn and use the rules of language without necessarily being aware of what these rules are. For example, although most people can give an example of a "yes-or-no" question (for instance, "Is your car red?"), very few could state the formal rules for constructing such a sentence. Nevertheless, people recognize when the rules have been violated. (We will return to this simple but profound point in Part IV in discussing the similarities between language syntax and "social grammar." As with rules of grammar, people are implicitly aware of the rules of interaction and recognize when these rules have been violated, but they cannot state explicitly what these rules are.) Thus, the power of language derives from human ability to employ rules to convey meaning without necessarily being aware of the rules. Humans are continually able to represent new meanings, and these novel combinations will be understood by others, provided that the combinations follow accepted syntactical structure.

Linguists refer to the ability to formulate novel but mutually understood statements as the *generative* property of language. Humans generate their own ideas and codes of meaning; in other words, language and meaning are not predetermined by nature. The extent of this generative ability is profound—it allows small children to formulate novel sentences (rather than just repeating preprogrammed speech) and nuclear physicists to develop abstract and complex theories.

Nonetheless, not all combinations of words are equally meaningful or likely to be generated. What is intriguing is that people can ascertain the difference between "gibberish" and mutually comprehensible strings of words.

The meaning of what is generated is determined by the underlying structure of the language, or the particular "patterns of discourse." Different languages entail distinct patterns of meaning. These language patterns profoundly influence culture. In short, different languages provide different ways to make sense of ourselves, others, and our circumstances.

During the past few decades, social scientists have debated whether language shapes thought or thought comes before language. Mead (see Reading 22) theorized that, in the process of learning language, the mind develops and becomes structured in a manner that reflects the individual's culture. Anthropologists, too, have pursued the claim that distinct languages cause people of different cultures to view and think about the world differently. For instance, many anthropologists demonstrate ways in which different cultures divide up "time" and "space" as expressed in their various languages. Some cultures express time in a nonlinear way as compared with Western linear conceptions, for example. Think about what your relationship to time might be if you could refer only to the concepts of "now" and "not now" and had no notion of "past" or "future."

Language: Innate or Socially Produced?

Scholars agree that language is a bedrock of human behavior and social life. There is disagreement, however, about whether language is socially learned (nurture) or physiologically innate (nature). Linguists such as Noam Chomsky consider language an innate human ability. Chomsky (1972) has made a convincing case that the "deep structure" of language is more complex than anyone could "learn" through social contact alone. He argues instead that one feature of the human brain is an inborn "computational modality." That is, humans are "hardwired" to comprehend and generate abstract representations and to piece together complex strings of words that require them to compute various possible lines of meaning and association. This activity is so complex and so unavailable to general consciousness that, according to Chomsky and his supporters, it would be impossible for children to perform the incredible mental gymnastics required to communicate if the brain were not hardwired for language.

One of Chomsky's students, Stephen Pinker, author of the popular book *The Language Instinct* (1994), offers a simple but noteworthy illustration of the computational modality using these three statements:

Ralph is an elephant.

Elephants live in Africa.

Elephants have tusks.

Pinker continues thus:

> Our inference-making device [innate computational processor] . . . would deduce "Ralph lives in Africa" and "Ralph has tusks." This sounds fine but isn't. Intelligent you, the reader, knows that the Africa Ralph lives in is the same Africa that all the other elephants live in, but that Ralph's tusks are his own. (Pinker, 1994, p. 79)

Pinker's point is that people make this distinction on the basis of common sense, but there is nothing in the words themselves that conveys this common sense; thus, the meaning is not logically explicit. The fact that people can make the distinction without hesitation is, for Pinker, a demonstration that people "know" things independently of the words used to express them. Thus, the way people think about and structure understanding precedes the language they use to express this understanding. Language itself contains so many ambiguities and oversimplifications that humans must have a larger picture in mind before speaking; otherwise, we would be unable to fill in the blanks and sort through the ambiguities with such unconscious ease.

Rather than debate the nature/nurture aspects of language, there is a more useful and accurate (albeit more complex) way to think about human behavior. Chomsky is probably correct, in part—the ability for abstraction and linguistic computation is innate. It is a fundamental property of humanness. But what is the *source* of the conceptual abstractions that the mental processors are acting on? This puzzle is the untold story in contemporary linguistics.

Let's return to Ralph the elephant. If humans were preprogrammed with information, infants would be born knowing all there is to know about elephants, Africa, and tusks. Clearly, this is a silly speculation. Let's assume, then, that we comprehend the distinction between the sharing of one Africa by many elephants and the possession of tusks by single elephants because we have learned a distinction between being physically located in a space and possessing physical traits. Our ability to generalize these experiential observations and to incorporate them in language is the computational element that Chomsky refers to.

Language, Thought, and Social Interaction

Our capacity for the abstraction and computation necessary to process language may be innate, but the actual content is *learned* through social contact. What Chomsky and colleagues can't tell us, as observers trying to make sense of human behavior, is the *significance* of Ralph in particular and of elephants, tusks, and Africa in general. This significance—people's attitudes, feelings, and behavior toward such strings of words—is determined by the context in which the words appear and the attributes people have learned to associate with these contexts. This is a social process. That is, the human capacity for the abstraction and computation necessary to process language may be innate, but the actual content is learned through social contact. Adults use language to teach children not necessarily how to think about, say, elephants, tusks, or Africa, but what to think about these things—and subsequently, how to respond. People don't need to be taught how to respond physiologically, as, for example, *what* to do physically when kicked in the knee. But the range of possible *social* responses to being kicked that occurs to a person, and her or his understanding of their appropriateness and consequences, are the result of having been taught, through language, what she or he should think about the incident. The name that we each ascribe to an experience acts as a sort of shorthand that shapes our subsequent thoughts about how to respond to the situation. In this way, language, experience, and thought continually interact—they are mutually determining.

A helpful analogy is the relationship between computer hardware and software: Here, the human brain is the hardware and language the software. Humans are born with brain hardware that enables us to engage in complex, computational, abstract, representational thought, but the content—*what* we process—is input by others who provide us with meaningful ideas through the activity of language. In the same way that a fully functional computer cannot operate without being switched on and fed some software, there is considerable evidence that children who are not exposed to language fail to develop normal conceptual abilities.

Oliver Sacks (1989) explores this issue in his book about the congenitally deaf, *Seeing Voices* (see Reading 9). On the basis of several case studies, Sacks asserts that those born without hearing are endowed with the same intellectual capacity as those who can hear. But in an oral-based culture, the congenitally deaf, in the absence of aural stimulation, fail to develop conceptual thought. The cognitive hardware of the congenitally deaf child may be in perfect working order, but the hearing impairment (deficient perceptual hardware) gets in the way of the necessary start-up. The child's language ability never really gets turned on. For this reason, many deaf children are mistakenly assumed to be developmentally disabled. However, when a congenitally deaf infant is exposed to sign language, the child not only proceeds along a normal course of cognitive development but actually begins to communicate in sign earlier than hearing infants learn to talk. Some specialists suggest that the ability for communication is switched on before the infant's vocal cords are physically ready for speech. Signing infants don't have to wait for their vocal cords to develop.

Studies of "feral children"—children raised in isolation, who are often assumed to be developmentally disabled—suggest similar conclusions. The capacity for abstract thought may be innate, but in order to develop this capacity, the child must be exposed to language-based social interaction. When the child lacks such access, then he or she is effectively denied access to the "switch" (language-based interaction) and the "software" (a specific language) through which conceptual thought develops. The implication is that humans require social stimulation and exposure to abstract symbol systems—language—in order to embark upon the conceptual thought processes that characterize our species.

Thus, human experience is given meaning and is organized through language, and the ability to form complex strings of words and to communicate verbally is innate. But the source of the meaning assigned to the words is social.

Experience and Conceptualization

In the late 1600s, the philosophers Gottfried Leibnitz and John Locke are said to have exchanged letters in which they debated the following question: Imagine a man who is born blind. How will he learn the difference between the concepts "triangle," "square," and "circle"? Like all children, he can be given blocks to play with. The "platonic solids" consist of blocks that are triangular, cubed, and round. The blind man could learn to tell the difference through his sense of touch. He could *feel* each one and be told the name, and then, whenever someone mentioned the name (for example, "triangle"), he would have an *idea* of what the triangle was. Now here is the question: What would happen if the man were suddenly able to see, and the three different blocks were set in front of him? Would he be able to *see* the difference and name them accordingly, or would he still have to *feel* each one? According to Locke, the man would not necessarily be able to *see* the different shapes. His *conceptual* understanding of the shapes would be based in his *experience* of touch. Leibnitz disagreed. He believed that the man would be able to conjecture what each was based on the concept that he held in his mind (a concept that was rooted in the experience of touch, not sight).

One of the questions that interests sociolinguists is the relationship among experience, perception, and conceptualization. In the title case from his well-known book *The Man Who Mistook His Wife for a Hat*, Oliver Sacks (1987) describes a man who has retained his ability for abstraction but has lost the "commonsensical" meaning tracks used in ordinary, day-to-day conversation. While trying to figure out what is wrong with the man, Sacks holds up a glove and asks him what he sees. The man studies it for a bit and then declares that it appears to be "some sort of container with five out-pouchings." Technically, this is an accurate description of the item. But is it meaningful? Sacks notes that "seeing" is a matter of conceptualization, not just sensory perception. We use our conceptual knowledge to make sense of what our senses are seeing. *Meaningful* concepts resonate with experience. A "glove" is really not the same thing as "a continuous surface unfolded on itself with five out-pouchings." The implication is that we learn conceptual meaning *in context*. Socially meaningful concepts reflect specific experiences, experiences that are visceral and imbued with feeling. Thus, when studying how children learn to assign meaning to concrete things in their environment, we have to take into account both the social content and the context of experience.

The Russian linguist and social psychologist Lev Vygotsky wrote extensively on the relationship between language and thought during the 1920s, but his writings have been available in English only since 1960 (for example, Vygotsky, 1961). Writing independently of the North American debate regarding linguistic determinism, Vygotsky, like his fellow Eastern European social scientists, was inclined to see a mutual relationship between individual neurological-cognitive processes and social learning.

According to Vygotsky (1961), children make sense of their environment by grouping things (persons and objects) that seem, through their own experiences, to be connected. The result is "complex thinking," or grouping seemingly related things into "complexes." Concepts generated from the complexes stand in as abstract representations of meaningful relationships between concrete things and experiences. For instance, a child's experiential complex for the family dog might consist of "Ruffy, big, furry, tail, bite." Conceptual thinking replaces the complex when the child learns the general name for the complex—"dog." Initially, the child may attempt to interchange the specific name, "Ruffy," with the general name, "dog." She may also experience fear whenever she hears of a "dog," because her complex or cluster includes the experience "bite."

Comprehending a parent's explanation that "the dog will bite you only if you pull its tail" is an illustration of the child's ability to generalize based on abstract thinking. It is also an illustration of the child's ability to learn vicariously through language. The child needn't experiment with pulling the tail of every dog that she encounters to gain an understanding of the conceptual relationship between tail pulling and biting. Rather, she uses the words to formulate a more general idea and to encode both the specific experience and her general interpretation of it in her memory. Thus, she begins to develop a lexicon of experientially based but socially influenced "names" complete with evaluative and action codes ("Dogs can bite, so beware").

Vygotsky bridges individual and social-cognitive linguistics through his idea of "pseudo-concepts," generalizations that are like concepts but that are actually complexes:

In the experimental setting, the child produces a pseudo-concept every time he surrounds a sample with objects that could just as well have been assembled on the basis of an abstract concept. For instance, when the sample is a yellow triangle and the child picks out all the triangles in the experimental material, he could have been guided by the general idea or concept of a triangle. Experimental analysis shows, however, that in reality the child is guided by concrete, visible likeness and has formed only an associative complex limited to a certain kind of perceptual bond. Although the results are identical, the process by which they are reached is not at all the same as in conceptual thinking.

Pseudo-concepts predominate over all other complexes in the child's thinking for the simple reason that in real life complexes corresponding to word meanings are not spontaneously developed by the child: The lines along which a complex develops are predetermined by the meaning a given word already has in the language of adults. . . . This language, with its stable, permanent meanings, points the way that a child's generalizations will take. The adult cannot pass on to the child his mode of thinking. He merely supplies the ready-made meaning of a word, around which the child forms a complex. . . . The pseudo-concept serves as the connecting link between thinking in complexes and thinking in concepts. Verbal intercourse with adults becomes a powerful factor in the intellectual development of the child. (Vygotsky, 1961, pp. 67–69)

The point that we derive from Vygotsky is that, in normal cognitive development, children operate at the nexus of practical experience and preestablished concepts. Even as they are forming experience-based groupings of things in their environment, children are learning to use ready-made words that are based on conceptualizations that are already socially established. Thus, both the child's own experiences and social influence, through preexisting language, play a role in the development of language and cognition. The resulting conceptual knowledge is a combination of experience and social learning. Concrete experiences enable the child to *comprehend* in an embodied, fully feeling way, but without preexisting language, the child would not be able to transcend the immediate experience and "make sense" of it in a more general way.

LANGUAGE, THOUGHT, AND CULTURE

We can discuss language and cognitive structure from one additional angle. Chomsky and others, in their zeal to make the point that humans have an innate capacity for representational computation, have rejected the notion that the particular language of a culture determines the way in which members of the culture classify persons, objects, and events. Many social scientists disagree and argue instead that language categories do in fact structure the way in which individuals perceive, organize, evaluate, feel about, and respond to their experiences and environments.

Language, as we have already noted, has evaluative and emotive components that make up concepts. Concepts, as Vygotsky details, do not necessarily emerge through direct experience but, rather, are handed down to us through social intercourse with other members of our culture. These concepts shape the way we focus on, categorize, evaluate, respond to, and remember people, objects, and events; in other words, language *does* structure how we think.

Consider the following string of words: *Race is not biologically significant; it is only skin deep.* When considered from a chromosomal perspective, this statement may indeed be correct. But is it representative of social reality as you know it? The chromosomes of humans with brown and pink skin may be identical, but the words *black* and *white* carry an entire history of meaning in this country and shape, to a large extent, the way in which Americans are inclined to see, evaluate, and remember others. In short, "race" in the United States is socially significant.

In learning the customs and belief systems of their culture, people learn to classify humans in a variety of ways. They learn that humans can be big, small, short, tall, fat, brown, black, yellow, white, and so forth, and each of these "names" includes emotive-evaluative components and behavioral cues.

Let us stress the point one more time—left to themselves, free of preexisting cultural influence, children would develop "complexes" that reflect their particular experience with their environment. The meaning that they would attach to words (that is, the abstract concepts and names that emerge from complexes) would thus accurately portray the world as they experienced it. Note that this path of learning leads to a process of stereotyping—if the child is bitten by a big fluffy animal that she later comes to name "dog," she may, through experience, later presume that all such creatures are scary. In other words, her conceptual notion would stand in for "real" experience and would shape her response to such creatures. However, as generations of social scientists have demonstrated, children do not learn in a vacuum. More likely, they begin forming complex associations between named objects, people, and spaces by asking, "What's that?" The concepts given to them by others contain preconceived associations that reflect shared cultural evaluations. For example, a child who has no direct experience with lions can still learn to identify a picture of one—and, most important, the child will absorb whatever emotive-evaluative-behavioral cues are expressed by the adults explaining what a lion is. Thus, a child can become "scared" by the *thought* of a lion without ever encountering one, because he or she has been taught that lions are "scary."

This process of "naming" has serious implications for the structure of society. For instance, without ever having encountered a Mexican American before, an Anglo American middle-class employer can find himself wondering whether a young "Mexican-looking" job candidate from Texas is likely to be "illegal." The sources of such a stereotype are subtle and many. The employer may not even be aware that he is evaluating the candidate on the basis of a preconceived stereotypical framework. His response is based on a cultural representation that may have no connection to his direct experience or the abilities of the prospective employee.

By studying the way in which names are associated with other emotive-evaluative words, we can learn a great deal about the way in which culture, through language, shapes the thoughts of individuals. The power of language is not simply in words but in the manner in which words can be combined to create clusters of meaning. These associations, which we often take as "common sense," reflect social divisions, not natural ones.

Categorization

The process of naming is an act of *categorization.* To categorize is to impose conceptual categories of meaning on things. Categories group things in a way that makes them related and gives them order. Cognitively, this is a very efficient operation, akin to a mental filing system (consider the "system" you use to organize your notes and materials for different classes so that you don't have to file through one big heap every time you need something). But categorization also presents problems. In her book *Mindfulness*, Harvard psychologist Ellen Langer (1989) tells the story of a man who is approached in his home by eager scavenger hunters looking for a 9.5- × 3-foot piece of wood. They offer to pay him $10,000 if he can find such a piece of wood for them. The man searches his home unsuccessfully. Who has such large pieces of wood lying around, he wonders? The next day, he realizes belatedly that the average door meets these measurements. In the moment, it never occurred to him that a "door" is often also a "piece of wood." Different categories.

Langer refers to this as "mindlessness." Mindlessness occurs when we rely on a few symbolic cues to fill in all the blanks. This "shortcut" perception is efficient to the extent that it allows humans to process massive quantities of information quickly and efficiently. The dangers, however, include the omission of other relevant features of the object or person in question and the perpetuation of stereotypes. Langer gives examples of elderly people or persons with physical disabilities who are often assumed to be mentally deficient as well because, stereotypically, it is common to associate physical slowness or inability with mental slowness.

Stereotypes and Default Assumptions

All languages suggest categorical relationships based on notable symbols. In the absence of specific information, people use these general word-based categories to impose meaning on other people, things, and events and to form judgments that they then rely on to guide their behavior. A border guard, in the absence of any other information, may see a male with a shaved head and five earrings in one ear and infer, based on categorical associations among clusters of symbols, that the person is a punker trying to smuggle drugs into the country. We all have a tendency to make these types of inferences. What is your general image of the border guard? Where did you get this information? Your ability to envision a border guard, even if you have personally never encountered one, is a process of stereotyping. You conjure up the image based on a classification scheme. Chances are that the border guard you imagine is based on a stereotype. This stereotype is most likely male, wearing some type of uniform, and carrying a gun.

Douglas Hofstadter is another scholar who writes about stereotypical thinking. He discusses what he calls *default assumptions*. Default assumptions are preconceived notions about the likely state of affairs—what we assume to be true in the absence of specific information. Given no other information, when I mention my "secretary," you are likely to assume the secretary is female, because female and secretary are associated stereotypically. In the absence of specific details, people rely on the stereotype as a *default assumption* for filling in the blanks. Default assumptions have a tendency, in Hofstadter's words, to "permeate our mental representations and channel our thoughts" (Hofstadter, 1986, p. 137). For instance, given the words *cat, dog,* and *chases,* you are likely to think first of a dog chasing a cat.

This line of thought reflects a default assumption that, all else being equal, the dog is more likely to chase the cat than the other way around. Default assumptions are based on prior experience and knowledge of circumstances. They are useful in that people cannot always afford the time it would take to consider every theoretical possibility that confronts them.

Nonetheless, it is possible that default assumptions are wrong. An interesting question is how we might know if we are wrong. Another is whether we change our default assumptions if the facts of the situation prove us wrong. If, for example, the shaved motorist does not have drugs in the car, will the border guard revise her categorical expectations regarding the relationship between male, shaved head, earrings, and drug use? Or will she reaffirm these general expectations with an account to herself of why this particular incident was not as expected? She may decide that the person does, in fact, have drugs in the car; she was simply unable to find them. Thus, the general category shaved head = punker = drugs is confirmed. Furthermore, the category may now be associated with deviousness as well.

Default assumptions are only one type of language-based categorization. Hofstadter is particularly interested in race-based and sex-based categorization and default assumptions. For instance, if you hear that your school basketball team is playing tonight, do you assume it's the men's team? Most people would assume so unless a "qualifier" were added to provide specific information. In this case the qualifier would be "the *women's* basketball team is playing tonight." Hofstadter means to show us that language is a powerful reflection of cultural associations and stereotypes. These associations are revealed in the way we use language. The phrase "my *black* doctor" reflects the cultural assumption that, all else being equal, the speaker knows that her audience does not expect the physician to be black. She adds a qualifier to offset the expected default assumption. Similarly, consider the practice of hyphenation in racial and ethnic labeling. Anglo Americans rarely refer to themselves as such. Rather, the default assumption, in the absence of a qualifier such as Japanese American, is that an American is Anglo and white. The qualifier is considered unnecessary, because it is assumed to be the default. One of the problems with default assumptions such as these is that, in addition to being taken for granted, the categorical associations tend to include notions such as "normal" and sometimes even "culturally desirable."

Hofstadter offers another exercise for finding culture embedded in language. He refers to these as "language asymmetries" (p. 103, Question 2). Consider the following terms: *Mr., Mrs.,* and *Miss.* Presumably each is the polite form of address for someone you don't know well. Why are there two terms for women and only one for men? "Well," you might respond, "it's because the Miss/Mrs. lets you know if a woman is married or not." Correct. But why is there no corresponding distinction for men? The asymmetry suggests that a woman's marital status is significant information, whereas a man's marital status is not. Indeed, it is probably the case that in modern Western culture, marital status is one of *the* most important bits of information about a woman. This is reflected in the prominence of language that provides this information.

CONCLUSION

By way of conclusion, consider the following statements. These are real headlines that linguist Stephen Pinker collected from various newspapers:

Child's Stool Great for Use in Garden

Stud Tires Out

Stiff Opposition Expected to Casketless Funeral Plan

Drunk Gets Nine Months in Violin Case

Iraqi Head Seeks Arms

Queen Mary Having Bottom Scraped

Columnist Gets Urologist in Trouble With His Peers (Pinker, 1994, p. 79)

It's both mundane and amazing that we understand the double meanings and the underlying humor. The computational ability required to recognize these double entendres is innate and universal, but the content of each—or rather, its double content—and, more significantly, the fact that people find the phrases funny, is a consequence of social learning.

The complicated mental process that enables "generative grammar" is a universal human feature. But the lexicon of meanings available to individuals—the concepts through which they make sense of their experiences, encode these in memory, and feel about and act on them—derives from cultural learning. That is, we are interested in what is said, not said, and how it is said—what names do and don't exist and the evaluative-emotive components of those names. Different languages represent reality differently; particular languages highlight certain features of life and leave others in the haze of "preconceived" thought. Names/words/concepts reveal certain lines of action and possibilities to individual humans. In this way, although it may be theoretically possible for all humans to generate infinite and similar grammars and lexicons of meanings, it is not probable that members of a given culture will do so. And that which is unnamed is unknown. The idea has been summarized by the mathematician and philosopher Bertrand Russell: "Language serves not only to express thought but to make possible thoughts which could not exist without it."

The assertion that humans process all experience through socially constructed symbol systems has been a source of both caution and enthusiasm. This tension is expressed in the following quotation from a brooding poet in *Hyperion,* a science fiction novel (Simmons, 1990):

Words are the supreme objects. They are minded things. As pure and transcendent as any idea that ever cast a shadow into Plato's dark cave of our perceptions. But they are also pitfalls of deceit and misperception. Words bend our thinking to infinite paths of self-delusion, and the fact that we spend most of our mental lives in brain mansions built of words means that we lack the objectivity necessary to see the terrible distortion of reality which language brings. . . . [Yet] here is the essence of [humankind's] creative genius: not the edifices of civilization nor the bang-flash weapons which can end it, but the *words* which fertilize new concepts. . . . You see, in the beginning was the Word. And the Word was made flesh in the weave of the human universe. Words are the only bullets in truth's bandolier. (pp. 190–191)

It is important to emphasize that the process of associating meaning with objects, persons, and events is an ongoing negotiation. In making sense of your world, you negotiate abstract meanings with others (interpersonal negotiation), and you negotiate with yourself to maintain a "fit" between your existing conceptual frameworks and concrete experience (intrapersonal negotiation). This negotiation is done through language: Even as you experience "unnamed" thoughts, emotions, and acts, you make sense of them by "fitting" them into the language categories available to you. For instance, if your culture has a category for "lover" that includes the default assumption that the pairing consists of one each of the two sexes, and you are paired with someone of the same sex, then you may find yourself without a "name" for this person when conversing with others who want to know about your attachments. Your experience may lead you to search for "alternative names" that stretch the category of "husband/wife" to include those who have same-sex partners. In this way, you are generating new concepts reflective of individual experience, but the fact that you have to search for a name for what you do is structured by the existing cultural classifications.

"Meaning" is not simply "out there"; it is something that is created and re-created through everyday interactions. The process reflects the complex interplay between individual experience and social structure. Individuals are constantly working to "fit" their individual thoughts and experiences into a form that can be expressed and shared with others. As you read the articles in this section, ask yourself: How do significant categories of language carve up my world? How do various concepts shape who I think I can be and what I think I can do? What are some of my default assumptions as a result of having absorbed the concepts of my culture? Am I aware that my language reflects a cultural value system?

REFERENCES AND SUGGESTIONS FOR FURTHER READING

Barthes, R. (1967). *Elements of semiology.* New York: Hill & Wang. (Original work published 1964)

Blumer, H. (1969). *Symbolic interactionism.* Englewood Cliffs, NJ: Prentice Hall.

Brown, R. (1986). *Social psychology* (2nd ed.). New York: Free Press.

Charon, J. (1989). *Symbolic interactionism* (3rd ed.). Englewood Cliffs, NJ: Prentice Hall.

Chomsky, N. (1972). *Language and the mind.* New York: Harcourt Brace Jovanovich.

Fine, G. (1990). Symbolic interactionism in the post-Blumerian age. In G. Ritzer (Ed.), *Frontiers of social theory* (pp. 117–157). New York: Columbia University Press.

Hofstadter, D. (1986). Changes in default words and images. In *Metamagical themas: Questing for the essence of mind and pattern* (pp. 136–158). New York: Bantam Books.

Langer, E. (1989). *Mindfulness.* Reading, MA: Addison-Wesley.

Lee, D. (Ed.). (1980). *Wittgenstein's lectures, Cambridge 1930–1932.* Chicago: University of Chicago Press.

Lindesmith, A. R., Strauss, A. L., & Denzin, N. K. (Eds.). (1991). *Social psychology* (7th ed.). Englewood Cliffs, NJ: Prentice Hall.

Mead, G. H. (1934). *Mind, self and society.* Chicago: University of Chicago Press.

Pinker, S. (1994). *The language instinct: How the mind creates language.* New York: Harper Perennial.

Sacks, O. (1987). *The man who mistook his wife for a hat.* New York: Harper & Row.

Sacks, O. (1989). *Seeing voices.* Berkeley: University of California Press.

Sapir, E. (1921). *Language.* New York: Harcourt, Brace and World.

Simmons, D. (1990). *Hyperion.* New York: Bantam.

Vygotsky, L. S. (1961). *Thought and language* (E. Hanfmann & G. Vahar, Trans.). Cambridge: MIT Press.

—————————— ⦚ ——————————

NAMING

The readings in this section are illustrations of a basic component of symbolic interactionism: People respond to things, people, and situations in terms of the *meaning* they assign to the object, person, or event. We do not just respond to stimuli in our environment. We *interpret* the stimuli. Interpretation is an act of assigning meaning. The act of assigning a meaning or definition is known as *naming*.

"That Powerful Drop" is a brief excerpt from a story by Langston Hughes. Hughes was an artist and writer during the period in the 1920s known as the Harlem Renaissance. In this short story, the characters are pondering the significance of a "single drop of Negro blood." The story illustrates that it is the cultural meaning that matters, not the physical properties.

"A Clue to the Nature of Man" is written by a philosopher, Ernst Cassirer. Cassirer's classic essay describes humans as living in a symbolic world, a world of culturally created ideas, and not in a state of nature. He reminds us that it is our opinions and fancies of things that disturb (or delight) us, not the nature of the thing itself.

"Yes, Father-Sister" is a reading taken from the case files of the well-known neurologist Oliver Sacks. In this case, Sacks presents a woman who has lost the ability to "name" the people she encounters. She no longer recognizes the symbolic cues that enable her to place people into meaningful social categories.

Questions for Discussion and Review

1. Explain to someone who is not in your class the difference between responding to symbolic cues and responding directly to stimuli.

2. Practice slowing down your thinking in situations and see if you can catch yourself "interpreting" the situation.

3. When you encounter a stranger, what do you notice first in deciding what to think about the person?

4. Think of something that disturbs or frightens you. See if you can trace your feelings to your original experiences of "naming." Is your fear or disgust based on direct experience, or is it based on an idea that you learned from someone else?

NAMING

5

That Powerful Drop

Langston Hughes

(1953)

Leaning on the lamp post in front of the barber shop, Simple was holding up a copy of the *Chicago Defender* and reading about how a man who looks white had just been declared officially colored by an Alabama court.

"It's powerful," he said.

"What?"

"That one drop of Negro blood—because just *one* drop of black blood makes a man colored. *One* drop—you are a Negro! Now, why is that? Why is Negro blood so much more powerful than any other kind of blood in the world? If a man has Irish blood in him, people will say, 'He's *part* Irish.' If he has a little Jewish blood, they'll say, 'He's *half Jewish*.' But if he has just a small bit of colored blood in him, BAM!— '*He's a Negro!*' Not, '*He's part* Negro.' No, be it ever so little, if that blood is black, '*He's a Negro!*' Now, this is what I do not understand—why our *one* drop is so powerful. Take paint—white will not make black *white*. But black will make white *black*. One drop of black in white paint—and the white ain't white no more! Black is powerful. You can have ninety-nine drops of white blood in your veins down South—but if that other *one* drop is black, shame on you! Even if you look white, you're black. That drop is really powerful. Explain it to me. You're colleged."

"It has no basis in science," I said, "so there's no logical explanation.". . .

NAMING

6

A Clue to the Nature of Man: The Symbol

Ernst Cassirer

(1944)

In the human world we find a new characteristic which appears to be the distinctive mark of human life. The functional circle of man is not only quantitatively enlarged; it has also undergone a qualitative change. Man has, as it were, discovered a new method of adapting himself to his environment. Between the receptor system and the effector system, which are to be found in all animal species, we find in man a third link which we may describe as the *symbolic system*. This new acquisition transforms the whole of human life. As compared with the other animals man lives not merely in a broader reality; he lives, so to speak, in a new *dimension* of reality. There is an unmistakable difference between organic reactions and human responses. In the first case a direct and immediate answer is given to an outward stimulus; in the second case the answer is delayed. It is interrupted and retarded by a slow and complicated process of thought. At first sight such a delay may appear to be a very questionable gain. Many philosophers have warned man against this pretended progress. "L'homme qui médite," says Rousseau, "est un animal dépravé": It is not an improvement but a deterioration of human nature to exceed the boundaries of organic life.

Yet there is no remedy against this reversal of the natural order. Man cannot escape from his own achievement. He cannot but adopt the conditions of his own life. No longer in a merely physical universe, man lives in a symbolic universe. Language, myth, art, and religion are parts of this universe. They are the varied threads which weave the symbolic net, the tangled web of human experience. All human progress in thought and experience refines upon and strengthens this net. No longer can man confront reality immediately; he cannot see it, as it were, face to face. Physical reality seems to recede in proportion as man's symbolic activity advances. Instead of dealing with the things themselves man is in a sense constantly conversing with himself. He has so enveloped himself in linguistic forms, in artistic images, in mythical symbols or religious rites that he cannot see or know anything except by the interposition of this artificial medium. His situation is the same in the theoretical as in the practical sphere. Even here man does not live in a world of hard facts, or according to his immediate needs and desires. He lives rather in the midst of imaginary emotions, in hopes and fears, in illusions and disillusions, in his fantasies and dreams. "What disturbs and alarms man," said Epictetus, "are not the things, but his opinions and fancies about the things."

From the point of view at which we have just arrived we may correct and enlarge the classical definition of man. In spite of all the efforts of modern irrationalism this definition of man as an *animal rationale* has not lost its force. Rationality is indeed an inherent feature of all human activities. Mythology itself is not simply a crude mass of superstitions or gross delusions. It is not merely chaotic, for it possesses a systematic or conceptual form.[1] But, on the other hand, it would be impossible to characterize the structure of myth as rational. Language has often been identified with reason, or with the very source of reason. But it is easy to see that this definition fails to cover the whole field. It is a *pars pro toto;* it offers us a part for the whole. For side by side with conceptual language there is an emotional language; side by side with logical or scientific language there is a language of poetic imagination. Primarily language does not express thoughts or ideas, but feelings and affections. And even a religion "within the limits of pure reason" as conceived and worked out by Kant is no more than a mere abstraction. It conveys only the ideal shape, only the shadow, of what a genuine and concrete religious life is. The great thinkers who have defined man as an *animal rationale* were not empiricists, nor did they ever intend to give an empirical account of human nature. By this definition they were expressing rather a fundamental moral imperative. Reason is a very inadequate term with which to comprehend the forms of man's cultural life in all their richness and variety. But all these forms are symbolic forms. Hence, instead of defining man as an *animal rationale,* we should define him as an *animal symbolicum*. By so doing we can designate his specific difference, and we can understand the new way open to man—the way to civilization.

NOTE

1. See E. Cassirer (1922), *Die Begriffsform im mythischen Denken*. Leipzig: B. G. Teubner.

NAMING

7

Yes, Father-Sister

Oliver Sacks

(1970)

Mrs. B., a former research chemist, had presented with a rapid personality change, becoming "funny" (facetious, given to wisecracks and puns), impulsive—and "superficial." ("You feel she doesn't care about you," one of her friends said. "She no longer seems to care about anything at all.") At first it was thought that she might be hypomanic, but she turned out to have a cerebral tumor. At craniotomy there was found, not a meningioma as had been hoped, but a huge carcinoma involving the orbitofrontal aspects of both frontal lobes.

When I saw her, she seemed high-spirited, volatile—"a riot" (the nurses called her)—full of quips and cracks, often clever and funny.

"Yes, Father," she said to me on one occasion.

"Yes, Sister," on another.

"Yes, Doctor," on a third.

She seemed to use the terms interchangeably.

"What *am* I?" I asked, stung, after a while.

"I see your face, your beard," she said, "I think of an Archimandrite Priest. I see your white uniform—I think of the Sisters. I see your stethoscope—I think of a doctor."

"You don't look at *all* of me?"

"No, I don't look at all of you."

"You realize the difference between a father, a sister, a doctor?"

"I *know* the difference, but it means nothing to me. Father, sister, doctor—what's the big deal?"

Thereafter, teasingly, she would say: "Yes, father-sister. Yes, sister-doctor," and other combinations.

Testing left-right discrimination was oddly difficult, because she said left or right indifferently (though there was not, in reaction, any confusion of the two, as when there is a lateralizing defect of perception or attention). When I drew her attention to this, she said: "Left/right. Right/left. Why the fuss? What's the difference?"

"*Is* there a difference?" I asked.

"Of course," she said, with a chemist's precision. "You could call them *enantio-morphs* of each other. But they mean nothing to *me*. They're no different for *me*. Hands . . . Doctors . . . Sisters . . . ," she added, seeing my puzzlement. "Don't you understand? They mean nothing—nothing to me. *Nothing means anything* . . . at least to me."

"And . . . this meaning nothing . . . ," I hesitated, afraid to go on, "This meaninglessness . . . does *this* bother you? Does *this* mean anything to you?"

"Nothing at all," she said promptly, with a bright smile, in the tone of one who makes a joke, wins an argument, wins at poker.

Was this denial? Was this a brave show? Was this the "cover" of some unbearable emotion? Her face bore no deeper expression whatever. Her world had been voided of feeling and meaning. Nothing any longer felt "real" (or "unreal"). Everything was now "equivalent" or "equal"—the whole world reduced to a facetious insignificance.

I found this somewhat shocking—her friends and family did too—but she herself, though not without insight, was uncaring, indifferent, even with a sort of funny-dreadful nonchalance or levity.

Mrs. B., though acute and intelligent, was somehow not present—"de-souled"—as a person. I was reminded of William Thompson (and also of Dr. P.). This is the effect of the "equalization" described by Luria. . . .

Postscript

The sort of facetious indifference and "equalization" shown by this patient is not uncommon—German neurologists call it *Witzelsucht* ("joking disease"), and it was recognized as a fundamental form of nervous "dissolution" by Hughlings Jackson a century ago. It is not uncommon, whereas insight is—and the latter, perhaps mercifully, is lost as the "dissolution" progresses. I see many cases a year with similar phenomenology but the most varied etiologies. Occasionally I am not sure, at first, if the patient is just "being funny," clowning around, or schizophrenic. Thus, almost at random, I find the following in my notes on a patient with cerebral multiple sclerosis, whom I saw (but whose case I could not follow up) in 1981:

She speaks very quickly, impulsively, and (it seems) indifferently . . . so that the important and the trivial, the true and the false, the serious and the joking, are poured out in a rapid, unselective, half-confabulatory stream. . . . She may contradict herself completely within a few seconds . . . will say she loves music, she doesn't, she has a broken hip, she hasn't . . .

I concluded my observation on a note of uncertainty:

How much is cryptannesia-confabulation, how much frontal-lobe indifference-equalization, how much some strange schizophrenic disintegration and shattering-flattening?

Of all forms of "schizophrenia" the "silly-happy," the so-called "hebephrenic," most resembles the organic amnestic and frontal lobe syndromes. They are the most malignant, and the least imaginable—and no one returns from such states to tell us what they were like.

In all these states—"funny" and often ingenious as they appear—the world is taken apart, undermined, reduced to anarchy and chaos. There ceases to be any "center" to the mind, though its formal intellectual powers may be perfectly preserved. The end point of such states is an unfathomable "silliness," an abyss of superficiality, in which all is ungrounded and afloat and comes apart. Luria once spoke of the mind as reduced, in such states, to "mere Brownian movement." I share the sort of horror he clearly felt about them (though this incites, rather than impedes, their accurate description). They make me think, first, of Borges' "Funes," and his remark, "My memory, Sir, is like a garbage-heap," and finally, of the *Dunciad*, the vision of a world reduced to Pure Silliness—Silliness as being the End of the World:

Thy hand, great Anarch, lets the curtain fall;
And Universal Darkness buries All.

LANGUAGE AND SOCIALIZATION

Language is an organized symbol system that enables us to think, imagine, learn vicariously, plan, direct our own behavior, and communicate with others. It is the basis of social life. Without language, individuals would not be able to learn or understand cultural expectations and would not be able to participate in social life. The study of the relationships among the brain, the mind, language, and culture is a fascinating area of research. The readings in this section illustrate some of the basic ideas that researchers agree on regarding language and social development.

"Final Note on a Case of Extreme Isolation" is a research note written by sociologist Kingsley Davis in 1947. Davis and his contemporaries were interested in the cases of children who had been raised in isolation from normal human interaction. When found, such children are considered more animal than human. They lack many of the basic signs of socialization that even severely developmentally delayed children raised in normal environments possess. Davis reviews the case of Anna and raises the question of whether it is possible for a child who is not exposed to human culture, especially language, by a certain age to ever become fully socialized.

"Seeing Voices" is another excerpt from the files of neurologist Oliver Sacks. In this article, Sacks explores the implications of being born deaf into a hearing world. Congenitally deaf children were historically mistaken as developmentally delayed. Sacks points out that there is nothing wrong with these children mentally. They simply haven't had their mental "switch" flipped on, because they have not been exposed to language. Deaf children who are exposed to sign language develop as normally as any other child. Sacks takes this as evidence that we are hardwired for language ability but require social contact to switch on the process and input the content.

Questions for Discussion and Review

1. Consider how often you imagine or think about someone you love. If you had no language or ability for abstract thought, could you remember that person when they weren't in your presence?

2. Think of an example of something that you've learned vicariously. How much of what you know is based on others telling you things?

3. The forms we use for expressing language influence us as much as the content of the language. Consider how your life might be different if you lived in a culture that had no written language. How would such a culture pass on learning and knowledge? Do you think people in such a culture would have stronger or weaker abilities to memorize?

8

Final Note on a Case of Extreme Isolation

Kingsley Davis

(1947)

Early in 1940 there appeared . . . an account of a girl called Anna.[1] She had been deprived of normal contact and had received a minimum of human care for almost the whole of her first six years of life. At this time observations were not complete and the report had a tentative character. Now, however, the girl is dead, and with more information available,[2] it is possible to give a fuller and more definitive description of the case from a sociological point of view.

Anna's death, caused by hemorrhagic jaundice, occurred on August 6, 1942. Having been born on March 1 or 6,[3] 1932, she was approximately ten and a half years of age when she died. The previous report covered her development up to the age of almost eight years; the present one recapitulates the earlier period on the basis of new evidence and then covers the last two and a half years of her life.

EARLY HISTORY

The first few days and weeks of Anna's life were complicated by frequent changes of domicile. It will be recalled that she was an illegitimate child, the second such child born to her mother, and that her grandfather, a widowed farmer in whose house her mother lived, strongly disapproved of this new evidence of the mother's indiscretion. This fact led to the baby's being shifted about.

Two weeks after being born in a nurse's private home, Anna was brought to the family farm, but the grandfather's antagonism was so great that she was shortly taken to the house of one of her mother's friends. At this time a local minister became interested in her and took her to his house with an idea of possible adoption. He decided against adoption, however, when he discovered that she had vaginitis. The infant was then taken to a children's home in the nearest large city. This agency found that at the age of only three weeks she was already in a miserable condition, being "terribly galled and otherwise in very bad shape." It did not regard her as a likely subject for adoption but took her in for a while anyway, hoping to benefit her. After Anna had spent nearly eight weeks in this place, the agency notified her mother to come to get her. The mother responded by sending a man and his wife to the children's home with a view to their adopting Anna, but they made such a poor impression on the agency that permission was refused. Later the mother came herself and took the child out of the home and then gave her to this couple. It was in the home of this pair that a social worker found the girl a short time thereafter. The social worker went to the mother's home and pleaded with Anna's grandfather to allow the mother to bring the child home. In spite of threats, he refused. The child, by then more than four months old, was next taken to another children's home in a near-by town. A medical examination at this time revealed that she had impetigo, vaginitis, umbilical hernia, and a skin rash.

Anna remained in this second children's home for nearly three weeks, at the end of which time she was transferred to a private foster-home. Since, however, the grandfather would not, and the mother could not, pay for the child's care, she was finally taken back as a last resort to the grandfather's house (at the age of five and a half months). There she remained, kept on the second floor in an attic-like room because her mother hesitated to incur the grandfather's wrath by bringing her downstairs.

The mother, a sturdy woman weighing about 180 pounds, did a man's work on the farm. She engaged in heavy work such as milking cows and tending hogs and had little time for her children. Sometimes she went out at night, in which case Anna was left entirely without attention. Ordinarily, it seems, Anna received only enough care to keep her barely alive. She appears to have been seldom moved from one position to another. Her clothing and bedding were filthy. She apparently had no instruction, no friendly attention.

It is little wonder that, when finally found and removed from the room in the grandfather's house at the age of nearly six years, the child could not talk, walk, or do anything that showed intelligence. She was in an extremely emaciated and undernourished condition, with skeletonlike legs and a bloated abdomen. She had been fed on virtually nothing except cow's milk during the years under her mother's care.

Anna's condition when found, and her subsequent improvement, have been described in the previous report. It now remains to say what happened to her after that.

LATER HISTORY

In 1939, nearly two years after being discovered, Anna had progressed, as previously reported, to the point where she could walk, understand simple commands, feed herself, achieve some neatness, remember people, etc. But she still did not speak, and, though she was much more like a normal infant of something over one year of age in mentality, she was far from normal for her age.

On August 30, 1939, she was taken to a private home for retarded children, leaving the county home where she had been for more than a year and a half. In her new setting she made some further progress, but not a great deal. In a report of an examination made November 6 of the same year, the head of the institution pictured the child as follows:

> Anna walks about aimlessly, makes periodic rhythmic motions of her hands, and, at intervals, makes guttural and sucking noises. She regards her hands as if she had seen them for the first time. It was impossible to hold her attention for more than a few seconds at a time—not because of distraction due to external stimuli but because of her inability to concentrate. She ignored the task in hand to gaze vacantly about the room. Speech is entirely lacking. Numerous unsuccessful attempts have been made with her in the hope of developing initial sounds. I do not believe that this failure is due to negativism or deafness but that she is not sufficiently developed to accept speech at this time. . . . The prognosis is not favorable. . . .

More than five months later, on April 25, 1940, a clinical psychologist, the late Professor Francis N. Maxfield, examined Anna and reported the following: large for her age; hearing "entirely normal"; vision apparently normal; able to climb stairs; speech in the "babbling stage" and "promise for developing intelligible speech later seems to be good." He said further that "on the Merrill-Palmer scale she made a mental score of 19 months. On the Vineland social maturity scale she made a score of 23 months."[4]

Professor Maxfield very sensibly pointed out that prognosis is difficult in such cases of isolation. "It is very difficult to take scores on tests standardized under average conditions of environment and experience," he wrote, "and interpret them in a case where environment and experience have been so unusual." With this warning he gave it as his opinion at that time that Anna would eventually "attain an adult mental level of six or seven years."[5]

The school for retarded children, on July 1, 1941, reported that Anna had reached 46 inches in height and weighed 60 pounds. She could bounce and catch a ball and was said to conform to group socialization, though as a follower rather than a leader. Toilet habits were firmly established. Food habits were normal, except that she still used a spoon as her sole implement. She could dress herself except for fastening her clothes. Most remarkable of all, she had finally begun to develop speech. She was characterized as being at about the two-year level in this regard. She could call attendants by name and bring in one when she was asked to. She had a few complete sentences to express her wants. The report concluded that there was nothing peculiar about her, except that she was feeble-minded—"probably congenital in type."[6]

A final report from the school made on June 22, 1942, and evidently the last report before the girl's death, pictured only a slight advance over that given above. It said that Anna could follow directions, string beads, identify a few colors, build with blocks, and differentiate between attractive and unattractive pictures. She had a good sense of rhythm and loved a doll. She talked mainly in phrases but would repeat words and try to carry on a conversation. She was clean about clothing. She habitually washed her hands and brushed her teeth. She would try to help other children. She walked well and could run fairly well, though clumsily. Although easily excited, she had a pleasant disposition.

INTERPRETATION

Such was Anna's condition just before her death. It may seem as if she had not made much progress, but one must remember the condition in which she had been found. One must recall that she had no glimmering of speech, absolutely no ability to walk, no sense of gesture, not the least capacity to feed herself even when the food was put in front of her, and no comprehension of cleanliness. She was so apathetic that it was hard to tell whether or not she could hear. And all this at the age of nearly six years. Compared with this condition, her capacities at the time of her death seem striking indeed, though they do not amount to much more than a two-and-a-half-year mental level. One conclusion therefore seems safe, namely, that her isolation prevented a considerable amount of mental development that was undoubtedly part of her capacity. Just what her original capacity was, of course, is hard to say; but her development after her period of confinement (including the ability to walk and run, to play, dress, fit into a social situation, and, above all, to speak) shows that she had at least this capacity—capacity that never could have been realized in her original condition of isolation.

A further question is this: What would she have been like if she had received a normal upbringing from the moment of birth? A definitive answer would have been impossible in any case, but even an approximate answer is made difficult by her early death. If one assumes, as was tentatively surmised in the previous report, that it is "almost impossible for any child to learn to speak, think, and act like a normal person after a long period of early isolation," it seems likely that Anna might have had a normal or near-normal capacity, genetically speaking. On the other hand, it was pointed out that Anna represented "a marginal case, [because] she was discovered before she had reached six years of age," an age "young enough to allow for some plasticity."[7] While admitting, then, that Anna's isolation may have been the major cause (and was certainly a minor cause) of her lack of rapid mental progress during the four and a half years following her rescue from neglect, it is necessary to entertain the hypothesis that she was congenitally deficient.

In connection with this hypothesis, one suggestive though by no means conclusive circumstance needs consideration, namely, the mentality of Anna's forebears. Information on this subject is easier to obtain, as one might guess, on the mother's than on the father's side. Anna's maternal grandmother, for example, is said to have been college educated and wished to have her children receive a good education, but her husband, Anna's stern grandfather, apparently a shrewd, hard-driving, calculating farmowner, was so penurious that her ambitions in this direction were thwarted. Under the circumstances her daughter (Anna's mother) managed, despite having to do hard work on the farm, to complete the eighth grade in a country school. Even so, however, the daughter was evidently not very smart. "A schoolmate of [Anna's mother] stated that she was retarded in school work; was very gullible at this age; and that her morals even at this time were discussed by other students." Two tests administered to her on March 4, 1938, when she was thirty-two years of age, showed that she was mentally deficient. On the Stanford Revision of the Binet-Simon Scale her performance was equivalent to that of a child of eight years, giving her an I.Q. of 50 and indicating mental deficiency of "middle-grade moron type."[8]

As to the identity of Anna's father, the most persistent theory holds that he was an old man about seventy-four years of age at the time of the girl's birth. If he was the one, there is no indication of mental or other biological deficiency, whatever one may think of his morals. However, someone else may actually have been the father.

To sum up: Anna's heredity is the kind that *might* have given rise to innate mental deficiency, though not necessarily.

COMPARISON WITH ANOTHER CASE

Perhaps more to the point than speculations about Anna's ancestry would be a case for comparison.

If a child could be discovered who had been isolated about the same length of time as Anna but had achieved a much quicker recovery and a greater mental development, it would be a stronger indication that Anna was deficient to start with.

Such a case does exist. It is the case of a girl found at about the same time as Anna and under strikingly similar circumstances. A full description of the details of this case has not been published, but in addition to newspaper reports, an excellent preliminary account by a speech specialist, Dr. Marie K. Mason, who played an important role in the handling of the child, has appeared.[9] Also the late Dr. Francis N. Maxfield, clinical psychologist at Ohio State University, as was Dr. Mason, has written an as yet unpublished but penetrating analysis of the case.[10] Some of his observations have been included in Professor Zingg's book on feral man.[11] The following discussion is drawn mainly from these enlightening materials. The writer, through the kindness of Professors Mason and Maxfield, did have a chance to observe the girl in April, 1940, and to discuss the features of her case with them.

Born apparently one month later than Anna, the girl in question, who has been given the pseudonym Isabelle, was discovered in November, 1938, nine months after the discovery of Anna. At the time she was found she was approximately six and a half years of age. Like Anna, she was an illegitimate child and had been kept in seclusion for that reason. Her mother was a deaf-mute, having become so at the age of two, and it appears that she and Isabelle had spent most of their time together in a dark room shut off from the rest of the mother's family. As a result Isabelle had no chance to develop speech; when she communicated with her mother, it was by means of gestures. Lack of sunshine and inadequacy of diet had caused Isabelle to become rachitic. Her legs in particular were affected; they were so bowed that as she stood erect the soles of her shoes came nearly flat together, and she got about with a skittering gait.[12]

Her behavior toward strangers, especially men, was almost that of a wild animal, manifesting much fear and hostility. In lieu of speech she made only a strange croaking sound. In many ways she acted like an infant. "She was apparently utterly unaware of relationships of any kind. When presented with a ball for the first time, she held it in the palm of her hand, then reached out and stroked my face with it. Such behavior is comparable to that of a child of six months."[13] At first it was even hard to tell whether or not she could hear, so unused were her senses. Many of her actions resembled those of deaf children.

It is small wonder that, once it was established that she could hear, specialists working with her believed her to be feeble-minded. Even on nonverbal tests her performance was so low as to promise little for the future. Her first score on the Stanford-Binet was 19 months, practically at the zero point of the scale. On the Vineland social maturity scale her first score was 39, representing an age level of two and a half years.[14] "The general impression was that she was wholly uneducable and that any attempt to teach her to speak, after so long a period of silence, would meet with failure."[15]

In spite of this interpretation, the individuals in charge of Isabelle launched a systematic and skillful program of training. It seemed hopeless at first. The approach had to be through pantomime and dramatization, suitable to an infant. It required one week of intensive effort before she even made her first attempt at vocalization. Gradually, she began to respond, however, and, after the first hurdles had at last been overcome, a curious thing happened. She went through the usual stages of learning characteristic of the years from one to six not only in proper succession but far more rapidly than normal. In a little over two months after her first vocalization she was putting sentences together. Nine months after that she could identify words and sentences on the printed page, could write well, could add to ten, and could retell a story after hearing it. Seven months beyond this point she

had a vocabulary of 1,500–2,000 words and was asking complicated questions. Starting from an educational level of between one and three years (depending on what aspect one considers), she had reached a normal level by the time she was eight and a half years old. In short, she covered in two years the stages of learning that ordinarily require six.[16] Or, to put it another way, her I.Q. trebled in a year and a half.[17] The speed with which she reached the normal level of mental development seems analogous to the recovery of body weight in a growing child after an illness, the recovery being achieved by an extra fast rate of growth for a period after the illness until normal weight for the given age is again attained.

When the writer saw Isabelle a year and a half after her discovery, she gave him the impression of being a very bright, cheerful, energetic little girl. She spoke well, walked and ran without trouble, and sang with gusto and accuracy. Today she is over fourteen years old and has passed the sixth grade in a public school. Her teachers say that she participates in all school activities as normally as other children. Though older than her classmates, she has fortunately not physically matured too far beyond their level.[18]

Clearly the history of Isabelle's development is different from that of Anna's. In both cases there was an exceedingly low, or rather blank, intellectual level to begin with. In both cases it seemed that the girl might be congenitally feeble-minded. In both a considerably higher level was reached later on. But the Ohio girl achieved a normal mentality within two years, whereas Anna was still marked inadequate at the end of four and a half years. This difference in achievement may suggest that Anna had less initial capacity. But an alternative hypothesis is possible.

One should remember that Anna never received the prolonged and expert attention that Isabelle received. The result of such attention, in the case of the Ohio girl, was to give her speech at an early stage, and her subsequent rapid development seems to have been a consequence of that. "Until Isabelle's speech and language development, she had all the characteristics of a feeble-minded child." Had Anna, who, from the standpoint of psychometric tests and early history, closely resembled this girl at the start, been given a mastery of speech at an earlier point by intensive training, her subsequent development might have been much more rapid.[19]

The hypothesis that Anna began with a sharply inferior mental capacity is therefore not established. Even if she were deficient to start with, we have no way of knowing how much so. Under ordinary conditions she might have been a dull normal or, like her mother, a moron. Even after the blight of her isolation, if she had lived to maturity, she might have finally reached virtually the full level of her capacity, whatever it may have been. That her isolation did have a profound effect upon her mentality, there can be no doubt. This is proved by the substantial degree of change during the four and a half years following her rescue.

Consideration of Isabelle's case serves to show, as Anna's case does not clearly show, that isolation up to the age of six, with failure to acquire any form of speech and hence failure to grasp nearly the whole world of cultural meaning, does not preclude the subsequent acquisition of these. Indeed, there seems to be a process of accelerated recovery in which the child goes through the mental stages at a more rapid rate than would be the case in normal development. Just what would be the maximum age at which a person could remain isolated and still retain the capacity for full cultural acquisition is hard to say. Almost certainly it would not be as high as age fifteen; it might possibly be as low as age ten. Undoubtedly various individuals would differ considerably as to the exact age.

Anna's is not an ideal case for showing the effects of extreme isolation, partly because she was possibly deficient to begin with, partly because she did not receive the best training available, and partly because she did not live long enough. Nevertheless, her case is instructive when

placed in the record with numerous other cases of extreme isolation. This and the previous article about her are meant to place her in the record. It is to be hoped that other cases will be described in the scientific literature as they are discovered (as unfortunately they will be), for only in these rare cases of extreme isolation is it possible "to observe *concretely separated* two factors in the development of human personality which are always otherwise only analytically separated, the biogenic and the sociogenic factors."[20]

NOTES

1. K. Davis (1940, January), "Extreme social isolation of a child," *American Journal of Sociology, 45*, 554–565.

2. Sincere appreciation is due to the officials in the Department of Welfare, Commonwealth of Pennsylvania, for their kind co-operation in making available the records concerning Anna and discussing the case frankly with the writer. Helen C. Hubbell, Florentine Hackbusch, and Eleanor Meckelnburg were particularly helpful, as was Fanny L. Matchette. Without their aid neither of the reports on Anna could have been written.

3. The records are not clear as to which day.

4. Letter to one of the state officials in charge of the case.

5. Ibid.

6. Progress report of the school.

7. Davis (1940), p. 564.

8. The facts set forth here as to Anna's ancestry are taken chiefly from a report of mental tests administered to Anna's mother by psychologists at a state hospital where she was taken for this purpose after the discovery of Anna's seclusion. This excellent report was not available to the writer when the previous paper on Anna was published.

9. M. K. Mason (1942), "Learning to speak after six and one-half years of silence," *Journal of Speech Disorders, 7*, 295–304.

10. F. N. Maxfield (no date), "What happens when the social environment of a child approaches zero." Unpublished manuscript. The writer is greatly indebted

to Mrs. Maxfield and to Professor Horace B. English, a colleague of Professor Maxfield, for the privilege of seeing this manuscript and other materials collected on isolated and feral individuals.

11. J. A. L. Singh & R. M. Zingg (1941), *Wolf-children and feral man*. New York: Harper & Bros., pp. 248–251.

12. Maxfield (no date).

13. Mason (1942), p. 299.

14. Maxfield (no date).

15. Mason (1942), p. 299.

16. Mason (1942), pp. 300–304.

17. Maxfield (no date).

18. Based on a personal letter from Dr. Mason to the writer, May 13, 1946.

19. This point is suggested in a personal letter from Dr. Mason to the writer, October 22, 1946.

20. Singh & Zingg (1941), pp. xxi–xxii, in a foreword by the writer.

LANGUAGE AND SOCIALIZATION

9

Seeing Voices

Oliver Sacks

(1989)

Why *is the uneducated deaf person isolated in nature and unable to communicate with other men? Why is he reduced to this state of imbecility? Does his biological constitution differ from ours? Does he not have everything he needs for having sensations, acquiring ideas, and combining them to do everything that we do? Does he not get sensory impressions from objects as we do? Are these not, as with us, the occasion of the mind's sensations and its acquired ideas?* Why *then does the deaf person remain stupid while we become intelligent?*

To ask this question—never really or clearly asked before—is to grasp its answer, to see that the answer lies in the use of symbols. It is, Sicard continues, because the deaf person has "no symbols for fixing and combining ideas . . . that there is a total communication-gap between him and other people.". . .

I first became interested in the deaf—their history, their predicament, their language, their culture—several years ago when I was sent Harlan Lane's books to review. In particular, I was haunted by descriptions of isolated deaf people who had failed to acquire any language whatever:

their evident intellectual disabilities and, equally seriously, the mishaps in emotional and social development to which they might fall prey in the absence of any authentic language or communication. What is necessary, I wondered, for us to become complete human beings? Is our humanity, so-called, partly dependent on language? What happens to us if we fail to acquire any language? Does language develop spontaneously and naturally, or does it require contact with other human beings? . . .

Language must be introduced and acquired as early as possible or its development may be permanently retarded and impaired, with all the problems in "propositionizing" which Hughlings-Jackson discussed. This can be done, with the profoundly deaf, only by Sign. Therefore deafness must be diagnosed as early as possible. Deaf children must first be exposed to fluent signers, whether these be their parents, or teachers, or whoever. Once signing is learned—and it may be fluent by three years of age—then all else may follow: a free intercourse of minds, a free flow of information, the acquisition of reading and writing, and perhaps that of speech. There is no evidence that signing inhibits the acquisition of speech. Indeed the reverse is probably so.

Have the deaf always and everywhere been seen as "handicapped" or "inferior"? Have they always suffered, must they always suffer, segregation and isolation? Can one imagine their situation otherwise? If only there were a world where being deaf did not matter, and in which all deaf people could enjoy complete fulfillment and integration! A world in which they would not even be perceived as "handicapped" or "deaf." . . .

Such worlds do exist, and have existed in the past, and such a world is portrayed in Nora Ellen Groce's beautiful and fascinating *Everyone Here Spoke Sign Language: Hereditary Deafness on Martha's Vineyard.* Through a mutation, a recessive gene brought out by inbreeding, a form of hereditary deafness existed for 250 years on Martha's Vineyard, Massachusetts, following the arrival of the first deaf settlers in the 1690s. By the mid-nineteenth century, scarcely an up-Island family was unaffected, and in some villages (Chilmark, West Tisbury), the incidence of deafness had risen to one in four. In response to this, the entire community learned Sign, and there was free and complete intercourse between the hearing and the deaf. Indeed the deaf were scarcely seen as "deaf," and certainly not seen as being at all "handicapped."

In the astonishing interviews recorded by Groce, the island's older residents would talk at length, vividly and affectionately, about their former relatives, neighbors, and friends, usually without even mentioning that they were deaf. And it would only be if this question was specifically asked that there would be a pause and then, "Now you come to mention it, yes, Ebenezer *was* deaf and dumb." But Ebenezer's deaf-and-dumbness had never set him apart, had scarcely even been noticed as such: he had been seen, he was remembered, simply as "Ebenezer"—friend, neighbor, dory fisherman—not as some special, handicapped, set-apart, deaf-mute. The deaf on Martha's Vineyard loved, married, earned their livings, worked, thought, wrote, as everyone else did—they were not set apart in any way, unless it was that they were, on the whole, better educated than their neighbors, for virtually all of the deaf on Martha's Vineyard were sent to be educated at the Hartford Asylum—and were often looked at as the most sagacious in the community.

Intriguingly, even after the last deaf Islander had died in 1952, the hearing tended to preserve Sign among themselves, not merely for special occasions (telling dirty jokes, talking in church, communicating between boats, etc.) but generally. They would slip into it, involuntarily, sometimes in the middle of a sentence, because Sign is "natural" to all who learn it (as a primary language), and has an intrinsic beauty and excellence sometimes superior to speech.

I was so moved by Groce's book that the moment I finished it I jumped in the car, with only a toothbrush, a tape recorder, and a camera—I had to see this enchanted island for myself. I saw how some of the oldest inhabitants still preserved Sign, delighted in it, among themselves. My first sight of this, indeed, was quite unforgettable. I drove up to the old general store in West Tisbury on a Sunday morning and saw half a dozen old people gossiping together on the porch. They could have been any old folks, old neighbors, talking together—until suddenly, very startlingly, they all dropped into Sign. They signed for a minute, laughed, then dropped back into speech. At this moment I knew I had come to the right place. And, speaking to one of the very oldest there, I found one other thing, of very great interest. This old lady, in her nineties, but sharp as a pin, would sometimes fall into a peaceful reverie. As she did so, she might have seemed to be knitting, her hands in constant complex motion. But her daughter, also a signer, told me she was not knitting but thinking to herself, thinking in Sign. And even in sleep, I was further informed, the old lady might sketch fragmentary signs on the counterpane— she was dreaming in Sign. Such phenomena cannot be accounted as merely social. It is evident that if a person has learned Sign as a primary language, his brain/mind will retain this, and use it, for the rest of that person's life, even though hearing and speech be freely available and unimpaired. Sign, I was now convinced, was a fundamental language of the brain. . . .

Two years ago, at the Braefield School for the Deaf, I met Joseph, a boy of eleven who had just entered school for the first time—an eleven-year-old with no language whatever. He had been born deaf, but this had not been realized until he was in his fourth year. His failure to talk, or understand speech, at the normal age was put down to "retardation," then to "autism," and these diagnoses had clung to him. When his deafness finally became apparent he was seen as "deaf and dumb," dumb not only literally, but metaphorically, and there was never any real attempt to teach him language.

Joseph longed to communicate, but could not. Neither speaking nor writing nor signing was available to him, only gesture and pantomime, and a marked ability to draw. What has happened to him, I kept asking myself? What is going on inside, how has he come to such a pass? He looked alive and animated, but profoundly baffled: his eyes were attracted to speaking mouths and signing hands—they darted to our mouths and hands, inquisitively, uncomprehendingly, and, it seemed to me, yearningly. He perceived that something was "going on" between us, but he could not comprehend what is was—he had, as yet, almost no idea of symbolic communication, of what it was to have a symbolic currency, to exchange meaning.

Previously deprived of opportunity—for he had never been exposed to Sign—and undermined in motive and affect (above all, the joy that play and language should give), Joseph was now just beginning to pick up a little Sign, beginning to have some communication with others. This, manifestly, gave him great joy; he wanted to stay at school all day, all night, all weekend, all the time. His distress at leaving school was painful to see, for going home meant, for him, return to the silence, return to a hopeless communicational vacuum, where he could have no converse, no commerce, with his parents, neighbors, friends; it meant being overlooked, becoming a nonperson, again.

This was very poignant, extraordinary— without any exact parallel in my experience. I was partly reminded of a two-year-old infant trembling on the verge of language—but Joseph was eleven, was like an eleven-year-old in most other ways. I was partly reminded in a way of a nonverbal animal, but no animal ever gave the feeling of yearning for language as Joseph did. Hughlings-Jackson, it came to me, once compared aphasics to dogs—but dogs seem complete and contented in their languagelessness, whereas the aphasic has a tormenting sense of loss. And Joseph, too: he clearly had an anguished sense of something missing, a sense of his own crippledness and deficit. He made me think of wild children, feral children, though clearly he was not "wild" but a creature of our civilization and habits—but one who was nonetheless radically cut-off.

Joseph was unable, for example, to communicate how he had spent the weekend—one could not really ask him, even in Sign: he could not even grasp the *idea* of a question, much less formulate an answer. It was not only language that was missing: there was not, it was evident, a clear sense of the past, of "a day ago" as distinct from "a year ago." There was a strange lack of historical sense, the feeling of a life that lacked autobiographical and historical dimension, the feeling of a life that only existed in the moment, in the present.

His visual intelligence—his ability to solve visual puzzles and problems—was good, in radical contrast to his profound difficulties with verbally based problems. He could draw and liked drawing: he did good diagrams of the room, he enjoyed drawing people; he "got" cartoons, he "got" visual concepts. It was this that above all gave me the feeling of intelligence, but an intelligence largely confined to the visual. He "picked up" tic-tac-toe and was soon very good at it; I had the sense that he might readily learn checkers or chess.

Joseph saw, distinguished, categorized, used; he had no problems with *perceptual* categorization or generalization, but he could not, it seemed, go much beyond this, hold abstract ideas in mind, reflect, play, plan. He seemed completely literal—unable to juggle images or hypotheses or possibilities, unable to enter an imaginative or figurative realm. And yet, one still felt, he was of normal intelligence, despite these manifest limitations of intellectual functioning. It was not that he lacked a mind, but that he was not *using his mind fully*.

It is clear that thought and language have quite separate (biological) origins, that the world is examined and mapped and responded to long before the advent of language, that there is a huge range of thinking—in animals, or infants—long before the emergence of language. . . . A human being is not mindless or mentally deficient without language, but he is severely restricted in the range of his thoughts, confined, in effect, to an immediate, small world.

For Joseph, the beginnings of a communication, a language, had now started, and he was tremendously excited at this. The school had found that it was not just formal instruction that he needed, but playing with language, language games, as with a toddler learning language for the first time. In this, it was hoped, he might begin to acquire language and conceptual thinking, to acquire it in the *act* of intellectual play. . . .

The very word "infant" means nonspeaking, and there is much to suggest that the acquisition of language marks an absolute and qualitative development in human nature. Though a well-developed, active, bright eleven-year-old, Joseph was in this sense still an infant—denied the power, the world, that language opens up. In Joseph Church's words:

> Language opens up new orientations and new possibilities for learning and for action, dominating and transforming preverbal experiences. . . . Language is not just one function among many . . . but an all-pervasive characteristic of the individual such that he becomes a *verbal organism* (all of whose experiences and actions and conceptions are now altered in accordance with a verbalized or symbolic experience).
>
> Language transforms experience. . . . Through language . . . one can induct the child into a purely symbolic realm of past and future, of remote places, of ideal relationships, of hypothetical events, of imaginative literature, of imaginary entities ranging from werewolves to pi-mesons. . . .
>
> At the same time the learning of language transforms the individual in such a way that he is enabled to do new things for himself, or to do old things in new ways. Language permits us to deal with things at a distance, to act on them without physically handling them. First, we can act on other people, or on objects through people. . . . Second, we can manipulate symbols in ways impossible with the things they stand for, and so arrive at novel and even creative versions of reality. . . . We can verbally rearrange situations which in themselves would resist rearrangement . . . we can isolate features which in fact cannot be isolated . . . we can juxtapose objects and events far separated in time and space . . . we can, if we will, turn the universe symbolically inside out.

We can do this, but Joseph could not. Joseph could not reach that symbolic plane which is the normal human birthright from earliest childhood on. He seemed, like an animal, or an infant, to be stuck in the present, to be confined to literal and immediate perception, though made aware of this by a consciousness that no infant could have. . . .

None of us can remember how we "acquired" language; St. Augustine's description is a beautiful myth. Nor are we, as parents, called on to "teach" our children language; they acquire it, or seem to, in the most automatic way, through virtue of being children, our children, and the communicative exchanges between us.

It is customary to distinguish grammar, verbal meanings, and communicative intent—the syntax, the semantics, the pragmatics of language—but as Bruner and others remind us, these always go together in the learning and use of language; and therefore, it is not language but language *use* we must study. The *first* language use, the first communication, is usually between mother and child, and language is acquired, arises, *between* the two.

One is born with one's senses; these are "natural." One can develop motor skills, naturally, by oneself. But one cannot acquire language by oneself: *this* skill comes in a unique category. It is impossible to acquire language without some essential innate ability, but this ability is only activated by another person who already possesses linguistic power and competence. It is only through transaction (or, as Vygotsky would say, "negotiation") with another that the language is achieved. (Wittgenstein writes in general terms of the "language games" we must all learn to play, and Brown speaks of "the original word game" played by mother and child.)

The mother—or father, or teacher, or indeed anyone who talks with the child—leads the infant step by step to higher levels of language; she leads him into language, and into the world picture it embodies (*her* world-picture, because it is her language; and beyond this, the world-picture of the culture she belongs to). The mother must always be a step ahead, in what Vygotsky calls the "zone of proximal development"; the infant cannot move into, or conceive of, the next stage ahead except

through its being occupied and communicated to him by his mother. . . .

Charlotte, a little girl of six, is also, like Joseph, congenitally deaf. But Charlotte is tremendously animated, playful, full of curiosity, turned vividly to the world. She is almost indistinguishable from a hearing six-year-old—totally different from poor, cut-off Joseph. What made the difference? As soon as Charlotte's parents realized she was deaf—when she was a few months old—they decided to learn a signed language, knowing that she would not be able to pick up spoken language easily. They did this, as did several of their relatives and friends. As Charlotte's mother, Sarah Elizabeth, wrote when Charlotte was four:

> Our daughter Charlotte was diagnosed profoundly deaf at ten months old. During these past three years we have experienced a range of emotions: disbelief, panic and anxiety, rage, depression and grief, and finally acceptance and appreciation. As our initial panic wore off it became clear that we needed to use sign language with our daughter while she was young.
>
> We started a sign language class at our home studying Signed Exact English, SEE, an exact replication of spoken English in signs, which we felt would help us in passing on our English language, literature, and culture to our child. As hearing parents we were overwhelmed by the task of learning a new language ourselves and having to teach it to Charlotte simultaneously, so the familiarity of English syntax made sign language seem accessible to us. . . . We desperately wanted to believe that Charlotte was similar to us.
>
> After a year we decided to move away from the rigidity of SEE to pidgin Signed English, a mixture of American Sign Language vocabulary, which is more visually descriptive, and English syntax, which is familiar . . . [but] the elaborate linear structures of spoken English don't translate into interesting sign language, so we had to reorient the way we thought to produce visual sentences. We were introduced to the most lively and exciting aspects of signing: idioms, humor, mime, whole-concept signs, and facial

expression.... Now we are moving to American Sign Language, studying it with a deaf woman, a native signer who can communicate in signs without hesitation and can codify the language for us hearing people. We are excited and stimulated by the process of learning an ingenious and sensible language which has such beauty and imagination. It is a delight to realize that Charlotte's signing reflects visual thought patterns. We are startled into thinking differently about physical objects, and their placement and motion, because of Charlotte's expressions.

I found this narrative powerful and fascinating, indicating how Charlotte's parents first wanted to believe their daughter essentially similar to themselves, despite the fact that she uses her eyes, not her ears; how they first used SEE, which has no real structure of its own, but is a mere transliteration of an auditory language, and how they only gradually came to appreciate the fundamental visuality of their child, her use of "visual thought patterns," and how this both needed and generated a visual language. Rather than imposing their auditory world on their child, as so many parents of the deaf do, they encouraged her to advance into her own (visual) world, which they were then able to share with her. By the age of four, indeed, Charlotte had advanced so far into visual thinking and language that she was able to provide new ways of thinking—revelations—to her parents.

Early in 1987, Charlotte and her family moved from California to Albany, New York, and her mother wrote again to me:

Charlotte is now a six-year-old first-grader. We, of course, feel she is a remarkable person because, although profoundly deaf, she is interested, thoughtful, competent within her (mainly) hearing world. She seems comfortable in both ASL and English, communicates enthusiastically with deaf adults and children and reads and writes at a third-grade level. Her hearing brother, Nathaniel, is fluent and easy in Sign; our family conducts many conversations and much business in sign language.... I

feel our experience bears out the idea that early exposure to visually coherent language develops complex conceptual thought processes. Charlotte knows how to think and how to reason. She uses effectively the linguistic tools she has been given to build complicated ideas.

When I went to visit Charlotte and her family, the first thing that struck me was that they *were* a family—full of fun, full of liveliness, full of questions, all together. There was none of the isolation one so often sees with the deaf—and none of the "primitive" language ("What's this? What's that? Do this! Do that!"), the condescension, of which Schlesinger speaks. Charlotte herself was full of questions, full of curiosity, full of life—a delightful, imaginative, and playful child, vividly turned to the world and to others. She was disappointed that I did not sign, but instantly commandeered her parents as interpreters and questioned me closely about the wonders of New York.

About thirty miles from Albany is a forest and river, and here I later drove with Charlotte, her parents, and her brother. Charlotte loves the natural world as much as the human world, but loves it in an intelligent way. She had an eye for different habitats, for the way things live together; she perceived cooperation and competition, the dynamics of existence. She was fascinated by the ferns that grew by the river, saw that they were very different from the flowers, understood the distinction between spores and seeds. She would exclaim excitedly in Sign over all the shapes and colors, but then attend and pause to ask, "How?", and "Why?", and "What if?" Clearly, it was not isolated facts that she wanted, but connections, understanding, a world with sense and meaning. Nothing showed me more clearly the passage from a perceptual to a conceptual world, a passage impossible without complex dialogue—a dialogue that first occurs with the parents, but is then internalized as "talking to oneself," as thought.

Dialogue launches language, the mind, but once it is launched we develop a new power, "inner speech," and it is this that is indispensable for our further development, our thinking. "Inner speech," says Vygotsky, "is speech almost without words . . . it is not the interior aspect of external speech, it is a function in itself. . . . While in external speech thought is embodied in words, in inner speech words die as they bring forth thought. Inner speech is to a large extent thinking in pure meanings." We start with dialogue, with language that is external and social, but then to think, to become ourselves, we have to move to a monologue, to inner speech. Inner speech is essentially solitary, and it is profoundly mysterious, as unknown to science, Vygotsky writes, as "the other side of the moon." "We are our language," it is often said; but our real language, our real identity, lies in inner speech, in that ceaseless stream and generation of meaning that constitutes the individual mind. It is through inner speech that the child develops his own concepts and meanings; it is through inner speech that he achieves his own identity; it is through inner speech, finally, that he constructs his own world. And the inner speech (or inner Sign) of the deaf may be very distinctive. . . .

There was no linguistic attention, no scientific attention, given to Sign until the late 1950s when William Stokoe, a young medievalist and linguist, found his way to Gallaudet College. Stokoe thought he had come to teach Chaucer to the deaf; but he very soon perceived that he had been thrown, by good fortune or chance, into one of the world's most extraordinary linguistic environments. Sign language, at this time, was not seen as a proper language, but as a sort of pantomime or gestural code, or perhaps a sort of broken English on the hands. It was Stokoe's genius to see, and prove, that it was nothing of the sort; that it satisfied every linguistic criterion of a genuine language, in its lexicon and syntax, its capacity to generate an infinite number of propositions. In 1960 Stokoe published *Sign Language Structure*, and in 1965 (with his deaf colleagues Dorothy Casterline and Carl Croneberg) *A Dictionary of American Sign Language*. Stokoe was convinced that signs were *not* pictures, but complex abstract symbols with a complex inner structure. He was the first, then, to look for a structure, to analyze signs, to dissect them, to search for constituent parts. Very early he proposed that each sign had at least three independent parts—location, handshape, and movement (analogous to the phonemes of speech)—and that each part had a limited number of combinations. In *Sign Language Structure* he delineated nineteen different handshapes, twelve locations, twenty-four types of movements, and invented a notation for these—American Sign Language had never been *written* before. His *Dictionary* was equally original, for the signs were arranged not thematically (e.g. signs for food, signs for animals, etc.) but systematically, according to their parts, and organization, and principles of the language. It showed the lexical structure of the language—the linguistic interrelatedness of a basic three thousand sign "words."

It required a quiet and immense self-confidence, even obstinacy to pursue these studies, for almost everyone, hearing and deaf alike, at first regarded Stokoe's notions as absurd or heretical; his books, when they came out, as worthless or nonsensical. This is often the way with works of genius. But within a very few years, because of Stokoe's works, the entire climate of opinion had been changed, and a revolution—a double revolution—was under way: a scientific revolution, paying attention to sign language, and its cognitive and neural substrates, as no one had ever thought to do before; and a cultural and political revolution.

The *Dictionary of American Sign Language* listed three thousand root signs—which might seem to be an extremely limited vocabulary (compared, for instance, with the 600,000 words or so in the *Oxford English Dictionary*). And yet, manifestly, Sign is highly expressive; [it] can express essentially anything that a spoken language can. . . .

To be deaf, to be born deaf, places one in an extraordinary situation; it exposes one to a range of linguistic possibilities, and hence to a range of intellectual and cultural possibilities, which the rest of us, as native speakers in a world of speech, can scarcely even begin to imagine. We are neither deprived nor challenged, linguistically, as the deaf are: we are never in danger of languagelessness, or severe linguistic incompetence; but nor do we discover, or create, a startlingly new language.

The unspeakable experiment of King Psammetichos—who had two children raised by shepherds who never spoke to them, in order to see what (if any) language they would speak naturally—is repeated, potentially, with all children born deaf. A small number—perhaps ten percent of these—are born of deaf parents, exposed to Sign from the start, and become native signers. The rest must live in an aural-oral world, neither biologically, nor linguistically, nor emotionally well-equipped to deal with them. Deafness as such is not the affliction; affliction enters with the breakdown of communication and language. If communication cannot be achieved, if the child is not exposed to good language and dialogue, we see all the mishaps Schlesinger describes—mishaps at once linguistic, intellectual, emotional, and cultural. These mishaps are imposed, to a larger or smaller degree, upon the majority of those born deaf: "most deaf children," as Schein remarks, "grow up like strangers in their own households."

LANGUAGE AND CULTURE

When we learn language, we also acquire a kind of social encyclopedia that provides us with an entire system of cultural knowledge. The way we talk about things shapes our experiences. Language shapes our focus—what we pay attention to and what we ignore; it shapes our values and our perceptions. Language can be dissected and examined to reveal underlying cultural beliefs and value systems.

"Metaphors We Live By" is written by two psycholinguists, George Lakoff and Mark Johnson. They provide several illustrations of the ways in which metaphors shape our thinking and behavior. For example, the metaphor of "time as money" leads us to organize our behavior in terms of "not wasting time," "saving time," and so forth. We even "spend" time with others.

"Pills and Power Tools" is a feminist analysis of the metaphors used in everyday conversation, in medicine, and by pharmaceutical companies to describe male sexuality. Susan Bordo points out that men are treated like "tools" or "hydraulic systems." She discusses some of the implications of these metaphors for men and the expectations they have of themselves.

"Racism in the English Language" is a dissection of language asymmetries and metaphors that convey a cultural value system. Readers are usually surprised at the many examples Robert Moore writes about. Many of these illustrations are aspects of language people rarely think about. Taken together, however, the cultural message indicates deeply entrenched meanings and values.

Questions for Discussion and Review

1. Make a list of some of the metaphors discussed by Lakoff and Johnson. Try inserting new words that convey a different meaning. For example, consider the expression, "I'd like to *share* some time with you" rather than "*spend* some time with you."

2. Make a list of "language asymmetries" (see Part II, p. 80, and Reading 12 for definitions) and consider what underlying cultural values these asymmetries indicate.

3. Consider the use of the masculine *he* or *man* to refer to all people. Some people say that this "generic use" is perfectly acceptable because the terms "imply" women as well as men. Others argue that the term not only leaves out half the population but also perpetuates an image of women as "auxiliary" and men as "central." Discuss this.

4. Discuss the cultural practice of women taking men's names when they marry. What cultural values does this practice convey?

5. Keep track of all the "medicalized" terms you hear for a few days (for example, *erectile dysfunction, hyperkinesis*). Try substituting more common terms and see if you think about the "problem" differently. For example, *clinically depressed* versus *tired and really burnt out.* Do these problems seem more real or authentic with the use of some terms rather than others?

LANGUAGE AND CULTURE

10

Metaphors We Live By

George Lakoff and Mark Johnson

(1980)

The concepts that govern our thought are not just matters of the intellect. They also govern our everyday functioning, down to the most mundane details. Our concepts structure what we perceive, how we get around in the world, and how we relate to other people. Our conceptual system thus plays a central role in defining our everyday realities. If we are right in suggesting that our conceptual system is largely metaphorical, then the way we think, what we experience, and what we do every day is very much a matter of metaphor.

But our conceptual system is not something we are normally aware of. In most of the little things we do every day, we simply think and act more or less automatically along certain lines. Just what these lines are is by no means obvious. One way to find out is by looking at language. Since communication is based on the same conceptual system that we use in thinking and acting, language is an important source of evidence for what that system is like.

Primarily on the basis of linguistic evidence, we have found that most of our ordinary conceptual system is metaphorical in nature. And we have found a way to begin to identify in detail just what the metaphors are that structure how we perceive, how we think, and what we do.

To give some idea of what it could mean for a concept to be metaphorical and for such a concept to structure an everyday activity, let us start with the concept ARGUMENT and the conceptual metaphor ARGUMENT IS WAR. This metaphor is reflected in our everyday language by a wide variety of expressions:

ARGUMENT IS WAR

Your claims are *indefensible*.

He *attacked every weak point* in my argument.

His criticisms were *right on target*.

I *demolished* his argument.

I've never *won* an argument with him.

You disagree? Okay, *shoot*!

If you use that *strategy*, he'll *wipe you out*.

He *shot down* all of my arguments.

It is important to see that we don't just *talk* about arguments in terms of war. We can actually win or lose arguments. We see the person we are arguing with as an opponent. We attack his positions and we defend our own. We gain and lose ground. We plan and use strategies. If we find a position indefensible, we can abandon it and take a new line of attack. Many of the things we *do* in arguing are partially structured by the concept of war. Though there is no physical battle, there is a verbal battle, and the structure of an argument—attack, defense, counterattack, etc.—reflects this.

It is in this sense that the ARGUMENT IS WAR metaphor is one that we live by in this culture; it structures the actions we perform in arguing.

Try to imagine a culture where arguments are not viewed in terms of war, where no one wins or loses, where there is no sense of attacking or defending, gaining or losing ground. Imagine a culture where an argument is viewed as a dance, the participants are seen as performers, and the goal is to perform in a balanced and aesthetically pleasing way. In such a culture, people would view arguments differently, experience them differently, carry them out differently, and talk about them differently. But *we* would probably not view them as arguing at all: They would simply be doing something different. It would seem strange even to call what they were doing "arguing." Perhaps the most neutral way of describing this difference between their culture and ours would be to say that we have a discourse form structured in terms of battle and they have one structured in terms of dance.

This is an example of what it means for a metaphorical concept, namely, ARGUMENT IS WAR, to structure (at least in part) what we do and how we understand what we are doing when we argue. *The essence of metaphor is understanding and experiencing one kind of thing in terms of another.* It is not that arguments are a subspecies of war. Arguments and wars are different kinds of things—verbal discourse and armed conflict—and the actions performed are different kinds of actions. But ARGUMENT is partially structured, understood, performed, and talked about in terms of WAR. The concept is metaphorically structured, the activity is metaphorically structured, and, consequently, the language is metaphorically structured.

Moreover, this is the *ordinary* way of having an argument and talking about one. The normal way for us to talk about attacking a position is to use the words "attack a position." Our conventional ways of talking about arguments presuppose a metaphor we are hardly ever conscious of. The metaphor is not merely in the words we use—it is in our very concept of an argument. The language of argument is not poetic, fanciful, or rhetorical; it is literal. We talk about arguments that way because we conceive of them that way—and we act according to the way we conceive of things. . . .

In each of the examples that follow we give a metaphor and a list of ordinary expressions that are special cases of the metaphor. The English expressions are of two sorts: simple literal expressions and idioms that fit the metaphor and are part of the normal everyday way of talking about the subject.

THEORIES (AND ARGUMENTS) ARE BUILDINGS

Is that the *foundation* for your theory? The theory needs more *support.* The argument is *shaky.* We need some more facts or the argument will *fall apart.* We need to *construct* a *strong* argument for that. I haven't figured out yet what the *form* of the argument will be. Here are some more facts to *shore up* the theory. We need to *buttress* the theory with *solid* arguments. The theory will *stand* or *fall* on the *strength* of that argument. The argument *collapsed.* They *exploded* his latest theory. We will show that theory to be without *foundation.* So far we have put together only the *framework* of the theory.

IDEAS ARE FOOD

What he said *left a bad taste in my mouth.* All this paper has in it are *raw facts, half-baked ideas, and warmed-over theories.* There are too many facts here for me to *digest* them all. I just can't *swallow* that claim. That argument *smells fishy.* Let me *stew* over that for a while. Now there's a theory you can really *sink your teeth into.* We need to let that idea *percolate* for a while. That's *food for thought.* He's a *voracious* reader. We don't need to *spoon-feed* our students. He *devoured* the book. Let's let that idea *simmer on the back burner* for a while. This is the *meaty* part of the paper. Let that idea *jell* for a while. That idea has been *fermenting* for years.

With respect to life and death IDEAS ARE ORGANISMS, either PEOPLE or PLANTS.

IDEAS ARE PEOPLE

The theory of relativity *gave birth to* an enormous number of ideas in physics. He is the *father* of modern biology. Whose *brainchild* was that? Look at what his ideas have *spawned.* Those ideas *died off* in the Middle Ages. His ideas will *live on* forever. Cognitive psychology is still in its *infancy.* That's an idea that ought to be *resurrected.* Where'd you *dig up* that idea? He *breathed new life into* that idea.

IDEAS ARE PLANTS

His ideas have finally come to *fruition.* That idea *died on the vine.* That's a *budding* theory. It will take years for that idea to *come to full flower.* He views chemistry as a mere *offshoot* of physics. Mathematics has many *branches.* The *seeds* of his great ideas were *planted* in his youth. She has a *fertile* imagination. Here's an idea that I'd like to *plant* in your mind. He has a *barren* mind.

IDEAS ARE PRODUCTS

We're really *turning (churning, cranking, grinding) out* new ideas. We've *generated* a lot of ideas this week. He *produces* new ideas at an astounding rate. His *intellectual productivity* has decreased in recent years. We need to *take the rough edges off* that idea, *hone it down, smooth it out.* It's a rough idea; it needs to be *refined.*

IDEAS ARE COMMODITIES

It's important how you *package* your ideas. He won't *buy* that. That idea just won't *sell.* There is always a *market* for good ideas. That's a *worthless* idea. He's been a source of *valuable* ideas. I wouldn't *give a plugged nickel for* that idea. Your ideas don't have a chance in the *intellectual marketplace.*

IDEAS ARE RESOURCES

He *ran out of* ideas. Don't *waste* your thoughts on small projects. Let's *pool* our ideas. He's a *resourceful* man. We've *used up* all our ideas. That's a *useless* idea. That idea will *go a long way.*

IDEAS ARE MONEY

Let me put in my *two cents' worth*. He's *rich* in ideas. That book is a *treasure trove* of ideas. He has a *wealth* of ideas.

IDEAS ARE CUTTING INSTRUMENTS

That's an *incisive* idea. That *cuts right to the heart of* the matter. That was a *cutting* remark. He's *sharp*. He has a *razor* wit. He has a *keen* mind. She *cut* his argument *to ribbons*.

IDEAS ARE FASHIONS

That idea went *out of style* years ago. I hear sociobiology *is in* these days. Marxism is currently *fashionable* in western Europe. That idea is *old hat*! That's an *outdated* idea. What are the new *trends* in English criticism? *Old-fashioned* notions have no place in today's society. He keeps *up-to-date* by reading the New York Review of Books. Berkeley is a center of *avant-garde* thought. Semiotics has become quite *chic*. The idea of revolution is no longer *in vogue* in the United States. The transformational grammar *craze* hit the United States in the mid-sixties and has just made it to Europe.

UNDERSTANDING IS SEEING; IDEAS ARE LIGHT-SOURCES; DISCOURSE IS A LIGHT-MEDIUM

I *see* what you're saying. It *looks* different from my *point of view*. What is your *outlook* on that? I *view* it differently. Now I've got the *whole picture*. Let me *point something out* to you. That's an *insightful* idea. That was a *brilliant* remark. The argument is *clear*. It was a *murky* discussion. Could you *elucidate* your remarks? It's a *transparent* argument. The discussion was *opaque*.

LOVE IS A PHYSICAL FORCE (ELECTROMAGNETIC, GRAVITATIONAL, ETC.)

I could feel the *electricity* between us. There were *sparks*. I was *magnetically drawn* to her. They are uncontrollably *attracted* to each other. They *gravitated* to each other immediately. His whole life *revolves* around her. The *atmosphere* around them is always *charged*. There is incredible *energy* in their relationship. They lost their *momentum*.

LOVE IS A PATIENT

This is a *sick* relationship. They have a *strong, healthy* marriage. The marriage is *dead*—it can't be *revived*. Their marriage is *on the mend*. We're getting *back on our feet*. Their relationship is *in really good shape*. They've got a *listless* marriage. Their marriage is *on its last legs*. It's a *tired* affair.

LOVE IS MADNESS

I'm *crazy* about her. She *drives me out of my mind*. He constantly *raves* about her. He's gone *mad* over her. I'm just *wild* about Harry. I'm *insane* about her.

LOVE IS MAGIC

She *cast her spell* over me. The *magic* is gone. I was *spellbound*. She had me *hypnotized*. He has me *in a trance*. I was *entranced* by him. I'm *charmed* by her. She is *bewitching*.

LOVE IS WAR

He is known for his many rapid *conquests*. She *fought for* him, but his mistress *won out*. He *fled from* her *advances*. She *pursued* him *relentlessly*. He is slowly *gaining ground* with her. He *won* her hand in marriage. He *overpowered* her. She is *besieged* by suitors. He has to *fend* them *off*. He *enlisted the aid* of her friends. He *made an ally* of her mother. Theirs is a *misalliance* if I've ever seen one.

WEALTH IS A HIDDEN OBJECT

He's *seeking* his fortune. He's flaunting his *new-found* wealth. He's a *fortune-hunter*. She's a *gold-digger*. He *lost* his fortune. He's *searching for* wealth.

SIGNIFICANT IS BIG

He's a *big* man in the garment industry. He's a *giant* among writers. That's the *biggest* idea to hit advertising in years. He's *head and shoulders above* everyone in the industry. It was only a *small* crime. That was only a *little* white lie. I was astounded at the *enormity* of the crime. That was one of the *greatest* moments in World Series history. His accomplishments *tower over* those of *lesser* men.

SEEING IS TOUCHING; EYES ARE LIMBS

I can't *take* my eyes *off* her. He sits with his eyes *glued to* the TV. Her eyes *picked out* every detail of the pattern. Their eyes *met*. She never *moves* her eyes *from* his face. She *ran* her eyes *over* everything in the room. He wants everything *within reach of* his eyes.

THE EYES ARE CONTAINERS FOR THE EMOTIONS

I could see the fear *in* his eyes. His eyes were *filled* with anger. There was passion *in* her eyes. His eyes *displayed* his compassion. She couldn't *get* the fear *out* of her eyes. Love *showed in* his eyes. Her eyes *welled* with emotion.

EMOTIONAL EFFECT IS PHYSICAL CONTACT

His mother's death *hit* him *hard*. That idea *bowled me over*. She's a *knockout*. I was *struck* by his sincerity. That really *made an impression* on me. He *made his mark on* the world. I was *touched* by his remark. That *blew me away*.

PHYSICAL AND EMOTIONAL STATES ARE ENTITIES WITHIN A PERSON

He has a pain *in* his shoulder. Don't *give* me the flu. My cold has *gone from my head to my chest*. His pains *went away*. His depression *returned*. Hot tea and honey will *get rid of* your cough. He could barely *contain* his joy. The smile *left* his face. *Wipe* that sneer *off* your face, private! His fears *keep coming back*. I've got to *shake off* this depression—it keeps *hanging on*. If you've got a cold, drinking lots of tea will *flush it out* of your system. There isn't a *trace* of cowardice *in* him. He hasn't got *an honest bone in his body*.

VITALITY IS A SUBSTANCE

She's *brimming* with vim and vigor. She's *overflowing* with vitality. He's *devoid* of energy. I don't *have* any energy *left* at the end of the day. I'm *drained*. That *took a lot out of* me.

LIFE IS A CONTAINER

I've had a *full* life. Life is *empty* for him. There's *not much left* for him *in* life. Her life is *crammed* with activities. *Get the most out of* life. His life *contained* a great deal of sorrow. Live your life *to the fullest*.

LIFE IS A GAMBLING GAME

I'll *take my chances*. The *odds are against me*. I've got an *ace up my sleeve*. He's *holding all the aces*. It's a *toss-up*. If you play your cards right, you can do it. He *won big*. He's a real *loser*. Where is he when the *chips are down*? That's my *ace in the hole*. He's *bluffing*. The president is *playing it close to his vest*. Let's *up the ante*. Maybe we need to *sweeten the pot*. I think we should *stand pat*. That's *the luck of the draw*. Those are *high stakes*.

In this last group of examples we have a collection of what are called "speech formulas," or "fixed-form expressions," or "phrasal lexical items." These function in many ways like single words, and the language has thousands of them. In the examples given, a set of such phrasal lexical items is coherently structured by a single metaphorical concept. Although each of them is an instance of the LIFE IS A GAMBLING GAME metaphor, they are typically used to speak of life, not of gambling situations. They are normal ways of talking about life situations, just as using the word "construct" is a normal way of talking about theories. It is in this sense that we include them in what we have called literal expressions structured by metaphorical concepts. If you say "The odds are against us" or "We'll have to take our chances," you would not be viewed as speaking metaphorically but as using the normal everyday language appropriate to the situation. Nevertheless, your way of talking about, conceiving, and even experiencing your situation would be metaphorically structured. . . .

The most fundamental values in a culture will be coherent with the metaphorical structure of the most fundamental concepts in the culture. As an example, let us consider some cultural values in our society that are coherent with our UP-DOWN spatialization metaphors and whose opposites would not be.

"More is better" is coherent with MORE IS UP and GOOD IS UP.

"Less is better" is not coherent with them.

"Bigger is better" is coherent with MORE IS UP and GOOD IS UP.

"Smaller is better" is not coherent with them.

"The future will be better" is coherent with THE FUTURE IS UP and GOOD IS UP. "The future will be worse" is not.

"There will be more in the future" is coherent with MORE IS UP and THE FUTURE IS UP.

"Your status should be higher in the future" is coherent with HIGH STATUS IS UP and THE FUTURE IS UP.

These are values deeply embedded in our culture. "The future will be better" is a statement of the concept of progress. "There will be more in the future" has as special cases the accumulation of goods and wage inflation. "Your status should be higher in the future" is a statement of careerism. These are coherent with our present spatialization metaphors; their opposites would not be. So it seems that our values are not independent but must form a coherent system with the metaphorical concepts we live by. . . .

NEW MEANING

The metaphors we have discussed so far are *conventional* metaphors, that is, metaphors that structure the ordinary conceptual system of our culture, which is reflected in our everyday language. We would now like to turn to metaphors that are outside our conventional conceptual system, metaphors that are imaginative and creative. Such metaphors are capable of giving us a new understanding of our experience. Thus, they can give new meaning to our pasts, to our daily activity, and to what we know and believe.

To see how this is possible, let us consider the new metaphor LOVE IS A COLLABORATIVE WORK OF ART. This is a metaphor that we personally find particularly forceful, insightful, and appropriate, given our experiences as members of our generation and our culture. The reason is that it makes our experiences of love coherent—it makes sense of them. We would like to suggest that new metaphors make sense of our experience in the same way conventional metaphors do: They provide coherent structure, highlighting some things and hiding others.

Like conventional metaphors, new metaphors have entailments, which may include other metaphors and literal statements as well. For example, the entailments of LOVE IS A COLLABORATIVE WORK OF ART arise from our beliefs about, and experiences of, what it means for something to be a collaborative work of art. Our personal views of work and art give rise to at least the following entailments for this metaphor:

Love is work.

Love is active.

Love requires cooperation.

Love requires dedication.

Love requires compromise.

Love requires a discipline.

Love involves shared responsibility.

Love requires patience.

Love requires shared values and goals.

Love demands sacrifice.

Love regularly brings frustration.

Love requires instinctive communication.

Love is an aesthetic experience.

Love is primarily valued for its own sake.

Love involves creativity.

Love requires a shared aesthetic.

Love cannot be achieved by formula.

Love is unique in each instance.

Love is an expression of who you are.

Love creates a reality.

Love reflects how you see the world.

Love requires the greatest honesty.

Love may be transient or permanent.

Love needs funding.

Love yields a shared aesthetic satisfaction from your joint efforts.

Some of these entailments are metaphorical (e.g., "Love is an aesthetic experience"); others are not (e.g., "Love involves shared responsibility"). Each of these entailments may itself have further entailments. The result is a large and coherent network of entailments, which may, on the whole, either fit or not fit our experiences of love. When the network does fit, the experiences form a coherent whole as instances of the metaphor. What we experience with such a metaphor is a kind of reverberation down through the network of entailments that awakens and connects our memories of our past love experiences and serves as a possible guide for future ones.

Let's be more specific about what we mean by "reverberations" in the metaphor LOVE IS A COLLABORATIVE WORK OF ART.

First, the metaphor highlights certain features while suppressing others. For example, the active side of love is brought into the foreground through the notion of WORK both in COLLABORATIVE WORK and in WORK OF ART. This requires the masking of certain aspects of love that are viewed passively. In fact, the emotional aspects of love are almost never viewed as being under the lovers' active control in our conventional conceptual system. Even in the LOVE IS A

JOURNEY metaphor, the relationship is viewed as a vehicle that is not in the couple's active control, since it can be *off the tracks,* or *on the rocks,* or *not going anywhere.* In the LOVE IS MADNESS metaphor ("I'm crazy about her," "She's driving me wild"), there is the ultimate lack of control. In the LOVE IS HEALTH metaphor, where the relationship is a patient ("It's a healthy relationship," "It's a sick relationship," "Their relationship is reviving"), the passivity of health in this culture is transferred to love. Thus, in focusing on various aspects of activity (e.g., WORK, CREATION, PURSUING GOALS, BUILDING, HELPING, etc.), the metaphor provides an organization of important love experiences that our conventional conceptual system does not make available.

Second, the metaphor does not merely entail other concepts, like WORK or PURSUING SHARED GOALS, but it entails very specific *aspects* of these concepts. It is not just any work, like working on an automobile assembly line, for instance. It is work that requires that special balance of control and letting-go that is appropriate to artistic creation, since the goal that is pursued is not just any kind of goal but a joint aesthetic goal. And though the metaphor may suppress the out-of-control aspects of the LOVE IS MADNESS metaphor, it highlights another aspect, namely, the sense of almost demonic possession that lies behind our culture's connection between artistic genius and madness.

Third, because the metaphor highlights important love experiences and makes them coherent while it masks other love experiences, the metaphor gives love a new meaning. If those things entailed by the metaphor are for us the most important aspects of our love experiences, then the metaphor can acquire the status of a truth; for many people, love *is* a collaborative work of art. And because it is, the metaphor can have a feedback effect, guiding our future actions in accordance with the metaphor.

Fourth, metaphors can thus be appropriate because they sanction actions, justify inferences, and help us set goals. For example, certain actions, inferences, and goals are dictated by the LOVE IS A

COLLABORATIVE WORK OF ART metaphor but not by the LOVE IS MADNESS metaphor. If love is madness, I do not concentrate on what I have to do to maintain it. But if it is work, then it requires activity, and if it is a work of art, it requires a very special *kind* of activity, and if it is collaborative, then it is even further restricted and specified.

Fifth, the meaning a metaphor will have for me will be partly culturally determined and partly tied to my past experiences. The cultural differences can be enormous because each of the concepts in the metaphor under discussion—ART, WORK, COLLAB-ORATION, and LOVE—can vary widely from culture to culture. Thus, LOVE IS A COLLABORATIVE WORK OF ART would mean very different things to a nineteenth-century European Romantic and an Eskimo living in Greenland at the same time. There will also be differences within a culture based on how individuals differ in their views of work and art. LOVE IS A COLLABORATIVE WORK OF ART will mean something very different to two fourteen-year-olds on their first date than to a mature artist couple.

As an example of how the meaning of a metaphor may vary radically within a culture, let us consider some entailments of the metaphor for someone with a view of art very different from our own. Someone who values a work of art not for itself but only as an object for display and someone who thinks that art creates only an illusion, not reality, could see the following as entailments of the metaphor:

Love is an object to be placed on display.

Love exists to be judged and admired by others.

Love creates an illusion.

Love requires hiding the truth.

Because such a person's view of art is different, the metaphor will have a different meaning for him. If his experience of love is pretty much like ours, then the metaphor simply will not fit. In fact, it will be grossly inappropriate. Hence, the same metaphor that gives new meaning to our experiences will not give new meaning to his.

Another example of how a metaphor can create new meaning for us came about by accident. An Iranian student, shortly after his arrival in Berkeley, took a seminar on metaphor from one of us. Among the wondrous things that he found in Berkeley was an expression that he heard over and over and understood as a beautifully sane metaphor. The expression was "the solution of my problems"—which he took to be a large volume of liquid, bubbling and smoking, containing all of your problems, either dissolved or in the form of precipitates, with catalysts constantly dissolving some problems (for the time being) and precipitating out others. He was terribly disillusioned to find that the residents of Berkeley had no such chemical metaphor in mind. And well he might be, for the chemical metaphor is both beautiful and insightful. It gives us a view of problems as things that never disappear utterly and that cannot be solved once and for all. All of your problems are always present, only they may be dissolved and in solution, or they may be in solid form. The best you can hope for is to find a catalyst that will make one problem dissolve without making another one precipitate out. And since you do not have complete control over what goes into the solution, you are constantly finding old and new problems precipitating out and present problems dissolving, partly because of your efforts and partly despite anything you do.

The CHEMICAL metaphor gives us a new view of human problems. It is appropriate to the experience of finding that problems which we once thought were "solved" turn up again and again. The CHEMICAL metaphor says that problems are not the kind of things that can be made to disappear forever. To treat them as things that can be "solved" once and for all is pointless. To live by the CHEMICAL metaphor would be to accept it as a fact that no problem ever disappears forever. Rather than direct your energies toward solving your problems once and for all, you would direct your energies toward finding out what catalysts will dissolve your most pressing problems for the longest time without precipitating out worse ones. The reappearance of a problem is viewed as a natural occurrence rather than a failure on your part to find "the right way to solve it."

To live by the CHEMICAL metaphor would mean that your problems have a different kind of reality for you. A temporary solution would be an accomplishment rather than a failure. Problems would be part of the natural order of things rather than disorders to be "cured." The way you would understand your everyday life and the way you would act in it would be different if you lived by the CHEMICAL metaphor.

We see this as a clear case of the power of metaphor to create a reality rather than simply to give us a way of conceptualizing a preexisting reality. This should not be surprising. As we saw in the case of the ARGUMENT IS WAR metaphor, there are natural kinds of *activity* (e.g., arguing) that are metaphorical in nature. What the CHEMICAL metaphor reveals is that our current way of dealing with problems is another kind of metaphorical activity. At present most of us deal with problems according to what we might call the PUZZLE metaphor, in which problems are PUZZLES for which, typically, there is a correct solution—and, once solved, they are solved forever. The PROBLEMS ARE PUZZLES metaphor characterizes our present reality. A shift to the CHEMICAL metaphor would characterize a new reality.

But it is by no means an easy matter to change the metaphors we live by. It is one thing to be aware of the possibilities inherent in the CHEMICAL metaphor, but it is a very different and far more difficult thing to live by it. Each of us has, consciously or unconsciously, identified hundreds of problems, and we are constantly at work on solutions for many of them—via the PUZZLE metaphor. So much of our unconscious everyday activity is structured in terms of the PUZZLE metaphor that we could not possibly make a quick or easy change to

the CHEMICAL metaphor on the basis of a conscious decision.

Many of our activities (arguing, solving problems, budgeting time, etc.) are metaphorical in nature. The metaphorical concepts that characterize those activities structure our present reality. New metaphors have the power to create a new reality. This can begin to happen when we start to comprehend our experience in terms of a metaphor, and it becomes a deeper reality when we begin to act in terms of it. If a new metaphor enters the conceptual system that we base our actions on, it will alter that conceptual system and the perceptions and actions that the system gives rise to. Much of cultural change arises from the introduction of new metaphorical concepts and the loss of old ones. For example, the Westernization of cultures throughout the world is partly a matter of introducing the TIME IS MONEY metaphor into those cultures.

The idea that metaphors can create realities goes against most traditional views of metaphor. The reason is that metaphor has traditionally been viewed as a matter of mere language rather than primarily as a means of structuring our conceptual system and the kinds of everyday activities we perform. It is reasonable enough to assume that words alone don't change reality. But changes in our conceptual system do change what is real for us and affect how we perceive the world and act upon those perceptions.

The idea that metaphor is just a matter of language and can at best only describe reality stems from the view that what is real is wholly external to, and independent of, how human beings conceptualize the world—as if the study of reality were just the study of the physical world. Such a view of reality—so-called objective reality— leaves out human aspects of reality, in particular the real perceptions, conceptualizations, motivations, and actions that constitute most of what we experience. But the human aspects of reality are most of what matters to us, and these vary from culture to culture, since different cultures have different conceptual systems. Cultures also exist within physical environments, some of them radically different—jungles, deserts, islands, tundra, mountains, cities, etc. In each case there is a physical environment that we interact with, more or less successfully. The conceptual systems of various cultures partly depend on the physical environments they have developed in.

Each culture must provide a more or less successful way of dealing with its environment, both adapting to it and changing it. Moreover, each culture must define a social reality within which people have roles that make sense to them and in terms of which they can function socially. Not surprisingly, the social reality defined by a culture affects its conception of physical reality. What is real for an individual as a member of a culture is a product both of his social reality and of the way in which that shapes his experience of the physical world. Since much of our social reality is understood in metaphorical terms, and since our conception of the physical world is partly metaphorical, metaphor plays a very significant role in determining what is real for us. . . .

Metaphor, Truth, and Action

In the preceding section we suggested the following:

> Metaphors have entailments through which they highlight and make coherent certain aspects of our experience.

> A given metaphor may be the only way to highlight and coherently organize exactly those aspects of our experience.

> Metaphors may create realities for us, especially social realities. A metaphor may thus be a guide for future action. Such actions will, of course, fit the metaphor. This will, in turn, reinforce the power of the metaphor to make experience coherent. In this sense metaphors can be self-fulfilling prophecies.

For example, faced with the energy crisis, President Carter declared "the moral equivalent of war." The WAR metaphor generated a network of entailments. There was an "enemy," a "threat to national security," which required "setting targets," "reorganizing priorities," "establishing a new chain of command," "plotting new strategy," "gathering intelligence," "marshaling forces," "imposing sanctions," "calling for sacrifices," and on and on. The WAR metaphor highlighted certain realities and hid others. The metaphor was not merely a way of viewing reality; it constituted a license for policy change and political and economic action. The very acceptance of the metaphor provided grounds for certain inferences: there was an external, foreign, hostile enemy (pictured by cartoonists in Arab headdress); energy needed to be given top priorities; the populace would have to make sacrifices; if we didn't meet the threat, we would not survive. It is important to realize that this was not the only metaphor available.

Carter's WAR metaphor took for granted our current concept of what ENERGY is, and focused on how to get enough of it. On the other hand, Amory Lovins (1977) observed that there are two fundamentally different ways, or PATHS, to supply our energy needs. He characterized these metaphorically as HARD and SOFT. The HARD ENERGY PATH uses energy supplies that are inflexible, nonrenewable, needing military defense and geopolitical control, irreversibly destructive of the environment, and requiring high capital investment, high technology, and highly skilled workers. They include fossil fuels (gas and oil), nuclear power plants, and coal gasification. The SOFT ENERGY PATH uses energy supplies that are flexible, renewable, not needing military defense or geopolitical control, not destructive of the environment, and requiring only low capital investment, low technology, and unskilled labor. They include solar, wind, and hydroelectric power, biomass alcohol, fluidized beds for burning coal or other combustible materials, and a great many other possibilities currently available. Lovins' SOFT

ENERGY PATH metaphor highlights the technical, economic, and sociopolitical *structure* of the energy system, which leads him to the conclusion that the "hard" energy paths—coal, oil, and nuclear power—lead to political conflict, economic hardship, and harm to the environment. But Jimmy Carter is more powerful than Amory Lovins. As Charlotte Linde (in conversation) has observed, whether in national politics or in everyday interaction, people in power get to impose their metaphors.

New metaphors, like conventional metaphors, can have the power to define reality. They do this through a coherent network of entailments that highlight some features of reality and hide others. The acceptance of the metaphor, which forces us to focus *only* on those aspects of our experience that it highlights, leads us to view the entailments of the metaphor as being *true.* Such "truths" may be true, of course, only relative to the reality defined by the metaphor. Suppose Carter announces that his administration has won a major energy battle. Is this claim true or false? Even to address oneself to the question requires accepting at least the central parts of the metaphor. If you do not accept the existence of an external enemy, if you think there is no external threat, if you recognize no field of battle, no targets, no clearly defined competing forces, then the issue of objective truth or falsity cannot arise. But if you see reality as defined by the metaphor, that is, if you do see the energy crisis as a war, then you can answer the question relative to whether the metaphorical entailments fit reality. If Carter, by means of strategically employed political and economic sanctions, forced the OPEC nations to cut the price of oil in half, then you would say that he would indeed have won a major battle. If, on the other hand, his strategies had produced only a temporary price freeze, you couldn't be so sure and might be skeptical.

Though questions of truth do arise for new metaphors, the more important questions are those of appropriate action. In most cases, what is at issue is not the truth or falsity of a metaphor but the perceptions and inferences that follow from it and the actions that are sanctioned by it. In all aspects of life, not just in politics or in love, we define our reality in terms of metaphors and then proceed to act on the basis of the metaphors. We draw inferences, set goals, make commitments, and execute plans, all on the basis of how we in part structure our experience, consciously and unconsciously, by means of metaphor. . . .

Metaphors, as we have seen, are conceptual in nature. They are among our principal vehicles for understanding. And they play a central role in the construction of social and political reality. Yet they are typically viewed within philosophy as matters of "mere language," and philosophical discussions of metaphor have not centered on their conceptual nature, their contribution to understanding, or their function in cultural reality. Instead, philosophers have tended to look at metaphors as out-of-the-ordinary imaginative or poetic linguistic expressions, and their discussions have centered on whether these linguistic expressions can be *true.* . . .

We do not believe that there is such a thing as *objective* (absolute and unconditional) *truth,* though it has been a long-standing theme in Western culture that there is. We do believe that there are *truths* but think that the idea of truth need not be tied to the objectivist view. We believe that the idea that there is absolute objective truth is not only mistaken but socially and politically dangerous. As we have seen, truth is always relative to a conceptual system that is defined in large part by metaphor. Most of our metaphors have evolved in our culture over a long period, but many are imposed upon us by people in power—political leaders, religious leaders, business leaders, advertisers, the media, etc. In a culture where the myth of objectivism is very much alive and truth is always absolute truth, the people who get to impose their metaphors on the culture get to define what we consider to be true—absolutely and objectively true. . . .

An Experientialist Synthesis

What we are offering in the experientalist account of understanding and truth is an alternative which denies that subjectivity and objectivity are our only choices. . . . The reason we have focused so much on metaphor is that it unites reason and imagination. Reason, at the very least, involves categorization, entailment, and inference. Imagination, in one of its many aspects, involves seeing one kind of thing in terms of another kind of thing—what we have called metaphorical thought. Metaphor is thus *imaginative rationality.* Since the categories of our everyday thought are largely metaphorical and our everyday reasoning involves metaphorical entailments and inferences, ordinary rationality is therefore imaginative by its very nature. Given our understanding of poetic metaphor in terms of metaphorical entailments and inferences, we can see that the products of the poetic imagination are, for the same reason, partially rational in nature.

Metaphor is one of our most important tools for trying to comprehend partially what cannot be comprehended totally: our feelings, aesthetic experiences, moral practices, and spiritual awareness. These endeavors of the imagination are not devoid of rationality; since they use metaphor, they employ an imaginative rationality.

An experientialist approach also allows us to bridge the gap between the objectivist and subjectivist myths about impartiality and the possibility of being fair and objective. . . . [T]ruth is relative to understanding, which means that there is no absolute standpoint from which to obtain absolute objective truths about the world. This does not mean that there are no truths; it means only that truth is relative to our conceptual system, which is grounded in, and constantly tested by, our experiences and those of other members of our culture in our daily interactions with other people and with our physical and cultural environments. . . .

Reference

Lovins, A. (1977). *Soft energy paths.* Cambridge: Ballinger.

11

Pills and Power Tools

Susan Bordo

(1998)

Viagra. When it went on sale in April of 1998, it broke all records for "fastest takeoff of a new drug" that the Rite Aid drugstore chain had ever seen. It was all over the media. Users were jubilant, claiming effects that lasted through the night, youth restored, better-"quality" erections.

Some even viewed Viagra as a potential cure for social ills. Bob Guccione, publisher of *Penthouse*, hails the drug as "freeing the American male libido" from the emasculating clutches of feminism. This diagnosis doesn't sit very comfortably with current medical wisdom, which has declared impotence to be a physiological problem. I, like Guccione, am skeptical of that declaration—but would suggest a deeper meditation on what's put the squeeze on male libido.

Think, to begin with, of the term: *Impotence.* It rings with disgrace, humiliation—and it's not feminists who invented it. Writer Philip Lopate, in an essay on the body, says that merely to say the word out loud makes him nervous.

Unlike other disorders, impotence implicates the whole man, not merely the body-part. *He is impotent.* Would we ever say about a person with a headache, "*He is a headache*"? Yet this is just what we do with impotence, as Warren Farrell notes. "We make no attempt to separate impotence from the total personality," writes Farrell. "Then, we

expect the personality to perform like a machine." "Potency" means power. So I guess it's correct to say that the machine we expect men to perform like is a power tool.

Think of our slang-terms, so many which encase the penis, like a cyborg, in various sorts of metal or steel armor. Big rig. Blow torch. Bolt. Cockpit. Crank. Crowbar. Destroyer. Dipstick. Drill. Engine. Hammer. Hand tool. Hardware. Hose. Power tool. Rod. Torpedo. Rocket. Spear. Such slang—common among teen-age boys—is violent in what it suggests the machine penis can do to another, "softer" body. But the terms are also metaphorical protection against the failure of potency. A human organ of flesh and blood is subject to anxiety, ambivalence, uncertainty. A torpedo or rocket, on the other hand, would never let one down.

Contemporary urologists have taken the metaphor of man the machine even further. Erectile functioning is "all hydraulics," says Irwin Goldstein of the Boston University Medical Center, scorning a previous generation of researchers who stressed psychological issues. Goldstein was quoted in a November 1997 *Newsweek* cover story called "The New Science of IMPOTENCE," announcing the dawn of the age of Viagra. At the time, the trade name meant little to the casual reader. What caught my eye were the contradictory messages. On the one hand, that ugly shame-inducing word *IMPOTENCE* was emblazoned throughout the piece. On the other hand, we were told in equally bold letters that science was "REBUILDING THE MALE MACHINE." If it's all a matter of fluid dynamics, I thought, why keep the term *impotent*, whose definitions (according to *Webster's Unabridged*) are: "want of power," "weakness," "lack of effectiveness, helplessness" and (only lastly) "lack of ability to engage in sexual intercourse"? In keeping the term *impotence*, I figured, the drug companies would get to have it both ways: reduce a complex human condition to a matter of chemistry, while keeping the old shame-machine working, helping to assure the flow of men to their doors.

It's remarkable, really, when you think about it, that *impotence* remained a common nomenclature among medical researchers (instead of the more forgiving, if medicalized, *erectile dysfunction*) for so long. *Frigidity*—with its suggestion that the woman is "cold," like some barren tundra—went by the board a long while ago. But *impotence*, no less loaded with ugly gender implications, remained the term of choice—not only for journalists but also for doctors—throughout all of the early reportage on Viagra. "THE POTENCY PILL," *Time* magazine called it, in its May 4th, 1998, issue three weeks after Viagra went on sale. At the same time, inside the magazine, fancy charts with colored arrows, zigzags, triangles, circles, and boxes show us "How Viagra Works," a cartoonlike hot dog the only suggestion that a penis is involved in any of this.

The drug companies eventually realized that *impotence* was as politically incorrect as *frigidity*. They also, apparently, began to worry about the reputation that Viagra was getting as a magic bullet that could produce rampant erections out of thin air. Pfizer's current ad for Viagra announces "A pill that helps men with erectile dysfunction respond again." *Respond*. The word attempts to create

a counter-image not only to the early magic-bullet hype, but also to the curious absence of partners in men's descriptions of the effects of the drug. *It's* "Stronger." *It's* "Harder." "Longer-lasting." "Better quality." *It's* "Firmer." "The characters in the drama of Viagra were three: a man, his blessed power pill, and his restored power tool.

The way Viagra is supposed to work—as the Pfizer ad goes on to say—is by helping you "achieve erections the natural way—in response to sexual stimulation." *Natural. Response.* It illustrates its themes with a middle-aged man in a suit dipping his gray-haired partner, smiling ecstatically. *Partners. Happy partners.* A playful, joyous, moment. "Let the dance begin," announces Pfizer at the very bottom of the ad, as though it were orchestrating a timeless, ritual coupling. The way men *had* been talking about the effects of Viagra, that dance was entirely between them and their members.

It wasn't playful rumba though. More like a march performed to the finale of the "1812 Overture," accompanied with cannon-blasts. "This little pill is like a package of dynamite," says one user. "Turned into a monster" (says another, with pleasure). "You just keep going all night. The performance is unbelievable," said one. I'm not making fun of these responses; I find them depressing. The men's explosive pride, to me, is indicative of how small and snail-like these men had felt before, and of the extravagant relief now felt at becoming a "real man," imagined in these comments as some kind of monster Energizer Bunny (pardon me, *Rabbit*.).

Something else is revealed, too, by the absence of partners in these descriptions of the effects of Viagra. The first "sex life" of most men in our culture—and a powerful relationship that often continues throughout their lives—involves a male, his member, and a magazine (or some other set of images seemingly designed with male libido in mind). Given the fast-trigger nature of adolescent sexuality, it doesn't take much; indeed, it sometimes seems to the teenage boy as though everything female has been put on the face of the earth just to get men hot. Philip Roth's descriptions of Alex Portnoy masturbating at the sight of his sister's bra, capable of getting a hard-on even at the sound of the *word* "panties," are hilarious—and true to life. Despite myths to the contrary, it's sometimes not so different for adolescent girls, either. But when we grow up, those "hard-on" moments (if, to make a point, I may use that metaphor in a unisexual way) aren't transformed into launch-off preparations for a sexual "performance."

It's often been noted that women's sexual readiness can be subtle to read. We are not required to cross a dramatic dividing line in order to engage in intercourse. And we aren't expected—as men are expected, as men seem to expect of themselves— to retain that hair-trigger sexuality of adolescence. Quite the opposite, in fact; the mythology about women is that we're "slow-cookers" when it comes to sex. Men, in contrast, get hit with a double whammy: they feel that they have to perform and they expect themselves to do so at the mere sight of a fancy brassiere! It's one reason, I think, why so many men "trade up" for younger wives as they get older; they're looking for that quick sexual fix of adolescence. It's their paradigm of sexual response, their criterion (ironically, since it represents the behavior of a fifteen-year-old) of manliness.

It comes as no surprise then, to learn that as sexual "performers," many men seem to expect no tactile help from the audience except— hopefully—applause at the end. Gail Sheehy . . . reports that Leonore Tiefer's interviews with hundreds of cops, firemen, sanitation workers, and blue-collar workers at Montefiore Medical Center in the Bronx revealed that most of these men expect, even in their fifties, to be able to get an erection just from paging through *Playboy*. Sheehy goes on: "When the sexologist suggests that at this age a man often needs physical stimulation they balk: 'C'mon, Doc, it's not *masculine* for a woman

to have to get it up for me.' Their wives often echo that rigid code: 'He should get it up.'"

Some dance, huh?

Most studies of Viagra's "effectiveness" leave partners out of the picture, too. When you put them in, you get a somewhat different picture of the "success" of the drug. In England, they used something called a "RigiScan" to measure the penis's "resistance" against a cloth-covered ring while Viagra-treated men watched porn movies. In the United States, the 69 percent "success rate" that Pfizer submitted to the F.D.A. was based on questionnaires filled out by patients. "Real soft data, no pun intended, "William Steers, Chief of Urology at the University of Virginia was quoted as saying in the July 6, 1998, *New Yorker*. He went on to note that Pfizer's study included no spousal questionnaires. Steers, cheers to him, *did* ask spouses. It turns out that when you ask women about sex with their "Viagra-enhanced" husbands, their estimation of the success of the drug is always lower than men—is about 48 percent for the women, no matter what measure of "success" you use.

Steers does not provide detail as to what those different measures were. Perhaps "monsters" were not what partners were looking for in bed. Perhaps they didn't appreciate the next-day chafing that usually accompanies "going all night." . . . Perhaps partners didn't want *just* a proud member, but the kind of romantic attention that goes along with the proud member in romance novels. . . .

Since the initial wave of enthusiasm about Viagra, therapists have begun to worry that Viagra is providing couples with a way to sidestep dealing not only with relationship problems that may have *contributed* to their sexual difficulties ("just because there is a physiological problem doesn't mean there is no psychological cause," reminds Eileen Palace, director of the Center for Sexual Health at Tulane) but also patterns of alienation, resentment, and anger that may develop *because* of those difficulties. A number of studies have found that when men begin to have erectile difficulties, a common response is to turn away from *all* romantic and affectionate gestures—kissing, caressing, hugging—so as not to (as one said) "stir things up." Many don't offer manual or oral stimulation in place of intercourse, because that would be to admit to themselves that they can't "perform" the "way a man should." They're often uncomfortable talking about the situation with their wives (and even their doctors, who report that most of the men who are asking for prescriptions for Viagra never mentioned their dysfunction before.) "I would tend to kind of brush the problem under the rug," says one man. "It isn't an easy topic to deal with. It goes to the heart of your masculinity."

Into the middle of all this distance, confusion, anxiety, and strain walks Viagra, and with it the news that the problem is only a malfunctioning hydraulic system—which, like any broken machinery, can be fixed. And "let the dance begin!" Many couples, unsurprisingly, don't know the steps, stumble, and step all over each other's toes.

Let me make it clear that I have no desire to withhold Viagra from the many men who have been deprived of the ability to get an erection by accidents, diabetes, cancer, and other misfortunes to which the flesh—or psyche—is heir. I would, however, like CNN and *Time* to spend a fraction of the time they devote to describing "how Viagra cures" to thinking about that gentleman's astute comment—"It goes to the heart of your masculinity"—and perhaps devoting a few features to exploring the functioning of *that* body part as well. . . .

Some of what we now call "impotence" may indeed be physiological in origin. Some may be grounded in deep fears and anxieties. But whatever the cause of a man's sexual problems, the "heart of masculinity" isn't a mechanical pump, and in imagining the penis as such, Viagran science actually administers more of the poison it claims to counteract. Dysfunction is no longer defined as "inability to get an erection" but inability to get an erection that is adequate for "satisfactory

sexual performance." *Performance*. Not pleasure. Not feeling. *Performance*. Eighty-five-year-old men are having Viagra heart attacks trying to keep those power tools running.

Sometimes, perhaps, a man's "impotence" may simply be his penis instructing him that his *feelings* are not in synch with the job he's supposed to do—or with the very fact that it's a "job." So, I like Philip Lopate's epistemological metaphor for the penis much better than the machine images. Over the years, he has come to appreciate, he writes, that his penis has its "own specialized form of intelligence." The penis knows that it is not a torpedo, no matter what a culture expects of it or what drugs are relayed to its blood vessels. If we accepted that, the notion that a man requires understanding and "tolerance" when he doesn't "perform" would go by the wayside. ("It's O.K. It happens" still assumes that there is something to be excused.) So, too, would the idea that there ought to be one model for understanding nonarousal. Sometimes, the penis's "specialized intelligence" should be listened to rather than cured.

Viagra, unfortunately, seems to be encouraging rather than deconstructing the expectation that men perform like power tools with only one switch—on or off. Until this expectation is replaced by a conception of manhood that permits men *and* their penises a full range of human feeling, we won't yet have the kind of "cure" we really need.

References

Broder, David. (1998). "Side Effect of Viagra May Be End of a Great Stupidity," *Lexington Herald Leader*, July 27.

Cameron, Deborah. (1992). "Naming of Parts Gender, Culture, and Terms for the Penis Among American College Students," *American Speech* Vol. 67, No. 4 pp. 367–382.

Cowley, Geoffrey. (1998). "Is Sex a Necessity," *Newsweek*, May 11, pp. 62–63.

Farrell, Warren. (1986). *Why Men Are the Way They Are* New York: Berkley Books.

Goldstein, Irwin. (1997). "The New Science of IMPO-TENCE," *Newsweek*, November.

Handy, Bruce. (1998). "The Viagra Craze," *Time*, May 4, pp. 50–57.

Hendren, John. (1998). "Pfizer Presses Insurers on Viagra," *Washington Post*, July 7, p. E3.

Hitchens, Christopher. (1998). "Viagra Falls," *The Nation*, May 25, p. 8.

Leland, John. (1997). "A Pill for Impotence?" *Newsweek*, November 17, pp. 62–68.

Lopate, Phillip. (1993). "Portrait of My Body," *Michigan Quarterly Review*, Volume XXXII, Number 4, Fall, pp. 656–665.

Martin, Douglas. (1998). "Thanks a Bunch, Viagra," *New York Times*, May 3.

Risher, Michael T. (1998). "Controlling Viagra-Mania," *New York Times*, July 20, p. A19.

Safire, William. (1998). "Is There a Right to Sex?" *New York Times*, July 13, p. A21.

Sharpe, Rochelle. (1998). "FDA Received Data on Adverse Effects from Using Viagra," *Wall Street Journal*, June 29, p. B5.

Steinhauer, Jennifer. (1998). "Viagra's Other Side Effect: Upsets in Many a Marriage," *New York Times*, June 23, pp. B9, B11.

Tiefer, Leonore. (1994). "The Medicalization of Impotence," *Gender and Society*, Vol. 8, No. 3, September, pp. 363–377.

Time, May 4, 1998.

LANGUAGE AND CULTURE

12

Racism in the English Language

Robert B. Moore

(1976)

LANGUAGE AND CULTURE

An integral part of any culture is its language. Language not only develops in conjunction with a society's historical, economic and political evolution; it also reflects that society's attitudes and thinking. Language not only *expresses* ideas and concepts but actually *shapes* thought.[1] If one accepts that our dominant white culture is racist, then one would expect our language—an indispensable transmitter of culture—to be racist as well. Whites, as the dominant group, are not subjected to the same abusive characterization by

our language that people of color receive. Aspects of racism in the English language that will be discussed in this essay include terminology, symbolism, politics, ethnocentrism, and context.

Before beginning our analysis of racism in language we would like to quote part of a TV film review which shows the connection between language and culture.[2]

Depending on one's culture, one interacts with time in a very distinct fashion. One example which gives some cross-cultural insights into the concept of time is language. In Spanish, a watch is said to "walk." In English, the watch "runs." In German, the watch "functions." And in French, the watch "marches." In the Indian culture of the Southwest, people do not refer to time in this way. The value of the watch is displaced with the value of "what time it's getting to be." Viewing these five cultural perspectives of time, one can see some definite emphasis and values that each culture places on time. For example, a cultural perspective may provide a clue to why the negative stereotype of the slow and lazy Mexican who lives in the "Land of Mañana" exists in the Anglo value system, where time "flies," the watch "runs" and "time is money."

A SHORT PLAY ON "BLACK" AND "WHITE" WORDS

Some may blackly (angrily) accuse me of trying to blacken (defame) the English language, to give it a black eye (a mark of shame) by writing such black words (hostile). They may denigrate (to cast aspersions; to darken) me by accusing me of being blackhearted (malevolent), of having a black outlook (pessimistic, dismal) on life, of being a blackguard (scoundrel)—which would certainly be a black mark (detrimental fact) against me. Some may black-brow (scowl at) me and hope that a black cat crosses in front of me because of this black deed. I may become a black sheep (one who causes shame or embarrassment because of deviation from the accepted standards), who will be blackballed (ostracized) by being placed on a blacklist (list of undesirables) in an attempt to blackmail (to force or coerce into a particular action) me to retract my words. But attempts to blackjack (to compel by threat) me will have a Chinaman's chance of success, for I am not a yellow-bellied Indian-giver of words, who will whitewash (cover up or gloss over vices or crimes) a black lie (harmful, inexcusable). I challenge the purity and innocence (white) of the English language. I don't see things in black and white (entirely bad or entirely good) terms, for I am a white man (marked by upright firmness) if there ever was one. However, it would be a black day when I would not "call a spade a spade," even though some will suggest a white man calling the English language racist is like the pot calling the kettle black. While many may be niggardly (grudging, scanty) in their support, others will be honest and decent—and to them I say, that's very white of you (honest, decent).

The preceding is of course a white lie (not intended to cause harm), meant only to illustrate some examples of racist terminology in the English language.

OBVIOUS BIGOTRY

Perhaps the most obvious aspect of racism in language would be terms like "nigger," "spook," "chink," "spic," etc. While these may be facing increasing social disdain, they certainly are not dead. Large numbers of white Americans continue to utilize these terms. "Chink," "gook," and "slant-eyes" were in common usage among U.S. troops in Vietnam. An NBC nightly news broadcast, in February 1972, reported that the basketball team in Pekin, Illinois, was called the "Pekin Chinks" and noted that even though this had been protested by Chinese Americans, the term continued to be used because it was easy, and meant no harm. Spiro Agnew's widely reported "fat Jap" remark and the "little Jap" comment of lawyer John Wilson during the Watergate hearings, are surface indicators of a deep-rooted Archie Bunkerism.

Many white people continue to refer to Black people as "colored," as for instance in a July 30, 1975 *Boston Globe* article on a racist attack by whites on a group of Black people using a public beach in Boston. One white person was quoted as follows:

We've always welcomed good colored people in South Boston but we will not tolerate radical blacks or Communists. . . . Good colored people are welcome in South Boston, black militants are not.

Many white people may still be unaware of the disdain many African Americans have for the term "colored," but it often appears that whether used intentionally or unintentionally, "colored" people are "good" and "know their place," while "Black" people are perceived as "uppity" and "threatening" to many whites. Similarly, the term "boy" to refer to African American men is now acknowledged to be a demeaning term, though still in common use. Other terms such as "the pot calling the kettle black" and "calling a spade a spade" have negative racial connotations but are still frequently used, as for example when President Ford was quoted in February 1976 saying that even though Daniel Moynihan had left the U.N., the U.S. would continue "calling a spade a spade."

COLOR SYMBOLISM

The symbolism of white as positive and black as negative is pervasive in our culture, with the black/white words used in the beginning of this essay only one of many aspects. "Good guys" wear white hats and ride white horses, "bad guys" wear black hats and ride black horses. Angels are white, and devils are black. The definition of *black* includes "without any moral light or goodness, evil, wicked, indicating disgrace, sinful," while that of *white* includes "morally pure, spotless, innocent, free from evil intent."

A children's TV cartoon program, *Captain Scarlet,* is about an organization called Spectrum, whose purpose is to save the world from an evil extraterrestrial force called the Mysterons. Everyone in Spectrum has a color name—Captain Scarlet, Captain Blue, etc. The one Spectrum agent who has been mysteriously taken over by the Mysterons and works to advance their evil aims is Captain Black. The person who heads Spectrum, the good organization out to defend the world, is Colonel White.

Three of the dictionary definitions of white are "fairness of complexion, purity, innocence." These definitions affect the standards of beauty in our culture, in which whiteness represents the norm. "Blondes have more fun" and "Wouldn't you really rather be a blonde" are sexist in their attitudes toward women generally, but are racist white standards when applied to third world women. A 1971 *Mademoiselle* advertisement pictured a curly-headed, ivory-skinned woman over the caption, "When you go blonde go all the way," and asked: "Isn't this how, in the back of your mind, you always wanted to look? All wide-eyed and silky blonde down to there, and innocent?" Whatever the advertising people meant by this particular woman's innocence, one must remember that "innocent" is one of the definitions of the word white. This standard of beauty when preached to all women is racist. The statement "Isn't this how, in the back of your mind, you always wanted to look?" either ignores third world women or assumes they long to be white.

Time magazine in its coverage of the Wimbledon tennis competition between the black Australian Evonne Goolagong and the white American Chris Evert described Ms. Goolagong as "the dusky daughter of an Australian sheepshearer," while Ms. Evert was "a fair young girl from the middle-class groves of Florida." *Dusky* is a synonym of "black" and is defined as "having dark skin; of a dark color; gloomy; dark; swarthy." Its antonyms are "fair" and "blonde." *Fair* is defined in part as "free from blemish, imperfection, or anything that impairs the appearance, quality, or character; pleasing in appearance, attractive; clean; pretty; comely." By defining Evonne Goolagong as "dusky," *Time* technically defined her as the opposite of "pleasing in appearance; attractive; clean; pretty; comely."

The studies of Kenneth B. Clark, Mary Ellen Goodman, Judith Porter and others indicate that this persuasive "rightness of whiteness" in U.S. culture affects children before the age of four, providing white youngsters with a false sense of superiority and encouraging self-hatred among third world youngsters.

ETHNOCENTRISM OR FROM A WHITE PERSPECTIVE

Some words and phrases that are commonly used represent particular perspectives and frames of reference, and these often distort the understanding of the reader or listener. David R. Burgest[3] has written about the effect of using the terms "slave" or "master." He argues that the psychological impact of the statement referring to "the master raped his slave" is different from the impact of the same statement substituting the words: "the white captor raped an African woman held in captivity."

> Implicit in the English usage of the "master-slave" concept is ownership of the "slave" by the "master," therefore, the "master" is merely abusing his property (slave). In reality, the captives (slave) were African individuals with human worth, right and dignity and the term "slave" denounces that human quality thereby making the mass rape of African women by white captors more acceptable in the minds of people and setting a mental frame of reference for legitimizing the atrocities perpetuated against African people.

The term "slave" connotes a less than human quality and turns the captive person into a thing. For example, two McGraw-Hill Far Eastern Publishers textbooks (1970) stated, "At first it was the slaves who worked the cane and they got only food for it. Now men work cane and get money." Next time you write about slavery or read about it, try transposing all "slaves" into "African people held in captivity," "Black people forced to work for no pay" or "African people stolen from their families and societies." While it is more cumbersome, such phrasing conveys a different meaning. . . .

POLITICS AND TERMINOLOGY

"Culturally deprived," "economically disadvantaged" and "underdeveloped" are other terms which mislead and distort our awareness of reality.

The application of the term "culturally deprived" and third world children in this society reflects a value judgment. It assumes that the dominant whites are cultured and all others without culture. In fact, third world children generally are bicultural, and many are bilingual, having grown up in their own culture as well as absorbing the dominant culture. In many ways, they are equipped with skills and experiences which white youth have been deprived of, since most white youth develop in a monocultural, monolingual environment. Burgest[5] suggests that the term "culturally deprived" be replaced by "culturally dispossessed," and that the term "economically disadvantaged" be replaced by "economically exploited." Both these terms present a perspective and implication that provide an entirely different frame of reference as to the reality of the third world experience in U.S. society.

Similarly, many nations of the third world are described as "underdeveloped." These less wealthy nations are generally those that suffered under colonialism and neo-colonialism. The "developed" nations are those that exploited their resources and wealth. Therefore, rather than referring to these countries as "underdeveloped," a more appropriate and meaningful designation might be "over exploited." Again, transpose this term next time you read about "underdeveloped nations" and note the different meaning that results.

Terms such as "culturally deprived," "economically disadvantaged" and "underdeveloped" place the responsibility for their own conditions on those being so described. This is known as "Blaming the Victim."[6] It places responsibility for poverty on the victims of poverty. It removes the blame from those in power who benefit from, and continue to permit, poverty.

Still another example involves the use of "non-white," "minority" or "third world." While people of color are a minority in the U.S., they are part of the vast majority of the world's population, in which white people are a distinct minority. Thus, by utilizing the term minority to describe people of color in the U.S., we can lose sight of the global majority/minority reality—a fact of some importance in the increasing and interconnected struggles of people of color inside and outside the U.S.

To describe people of color as "non-white" is to use whiteness as the standard and norm against which to measure all others. Use of the term "third world" to describe all people of color overcomes the inherent bias of "minority" and "non-white." Moreover, it connects the struggles of third world people in the U.S. with the freedom struggles around the globe.

The term "third world" gained increasing usage after the 1955 Bandung Conference of "non-aligned" nations, which represented a third force outside of the two world superpowers. The "first world" represents the United States, Western Europe and their sphere of influence. The "second world" represents the Soviet Union and its sphere. The "third world" represents, for the most part, nations that were, or are, controlled by the "first world" or West. For the most part, these are nations of Africa, Asia and Latin America.

"LOADED" WORDS AND NATIVE AMERICANS

Many words lead to a demeaning characterization of groups of people. For instance, Columbus, it is said, "discovered" America. The word *discover* is defined as "to gain sight or knowledge of something previously unseen or unknown; to discover may be to find some existent thing that was previously unknown." Thus, a continent inhabited by millions of human beings cannot be "discovered." For history books to continue this usage represents a Eurocentric (white European) perspective on world history and ignores the existence of, and the perspective of, Native Americans. "Discovery," as used in the Euro-American context, implies the right to take what one finds, ignoring the rights of those who already inhabit or own the "discovered" thing.

Eurocentrism is also apparent in the usage of "victory" and "massacre" to describe the battles between Native Americans and whites. *Victory* is defined in the dictionary as "a success or triumph over an enemy in battle or war; the decisive defeat of an opponent." *Conquest* denotes the "taking over of control by the victor, and the obedience of the conquered." *Massacre* is defined as "the unnecessary, indiscriminate killing of a number of human beings, as in barbarous warfare or persecution, or for revenge or plunder." *Defend* is described as "to ward off attack from; guard against assault or injury; to strive to keep safe by resisting attack."

Eurocentrism turns these definitions around to serve the purpose of distorting history and justifying Euro-American conquest of the Native American homelands. Euro-Americans are not described in history books as invading Native American lands, but rather as defending *their* homes against "Indian" attacks. Since European communities were constantly encroaching on land already occupied, then a more honest interpretation would state that it was the Native Americans who were "warding off," "guarding" and "defending" their homelands.

Native American victories are invariably defined as "massacres," while the indiscriminate killing, extermination and plunder of Native American nations by Euro-Americans is defined as "victory." Distortion of history by the choice of "loaded" words used to describe historical events is a common racist practice. Rather than portraying Native Americans as human beings in highly defined and complex societies, cultures and civilizations, history books use such adjectives as "savages," "beasts," "primitive," and "backward." Native people are referred to as "squaw," "brave," or "papoose" instead of "woman," "man," or "baby."

Another term that has questionable connotations is *tribe*. The Oxford English Dictionary defines this noun as "a race of people; now applied especially to a primary aggregate of people in a primitive or barbarous condition, under a headman or chief." Morton Fried,[7] discussing "The Myth of Tribe," states that the word "did not become a general term of reference to American Indian society until the nineteenth century. Previously, the words commonly used for Indian populations were 'nation' and 'people.'" Since "tribe" has assumed a connotation of primitiveness or backwardness, it is suggested that the use of "nation" or "people" replace the term whenever possible in referring to Native American peoples.

The term *tribe* invokes even more negative implications when used in reference to American peoples. As Evelyn Jones Rich[8] has noted, the term is "almost always used to refer to third world people and it implies a stage of development which is, in short, a put-down."

"Loaded" Words and Africans

Conflicts among diverse peoples within African nations are often referred to as "tribal warfare," while conflicts among the diverse peoples within European countries are never described in such terms. If the rivalries between the Ibo and the Hausa and Yoruba in Nigeria are described as "tribal," why not the rivalries between Serbs and Slavs in Yugoslavia, or Scots and English in Great Britain, Protestants and Catholics in Ireland, or the Basques and the Southern Spaniards in Spain? Conflicts among African peoples in a particular nation have religious, cultural, economic and/or political roots. If we can analyze the roots of conflicts among European peoples in terms other than "tribal warfare," certainly we can do the same with African peoples, including correct reference to the ethnic groups or nations involved. For example, the terms "Kaffirs," "Hottentot" or "Bushmen" are names imposed by white Europeans. The correct names are always those by which a people refer to themselves. (In these instances Xhosa, Khoi-Khoin and San are correct.[9])

The generalized application of "tribal" in reference to Africans—as well as the failure to acknowledge the religious, cultural and social diversity of African peoples—is a decidedly racist dynamic. It is part of the process whereby Euro-Americans justify, or avoid confronting, their oppression of third world peoples. Africa has been particularly insulted by this dynamic, as witness the pervasive "darkest Africa" image. This image, widespread in Western culture, evokes an Africa covered by jungles and inhabited by "uncivilized," "cannibalistic," "pagan," "savage" peoples. This "darkest Africa" image avoids the geographical reality. Less than 20 percent of the African continent is wooded savanna, for example. The image also ignores the history of African cultures and civilizations. Ample evidence suggests this distortion of reality was developed as a convenient rationale for the European and American slave trade. The Western powers, rather than exploiting, were civilizing and christianizing "uncivilized" and "pagan savages" (so the rationalization went). This dynamic also served to justify Western colonialism. From Tarzan movies to racist children's books like *Doctor Dolittle* and *Charlie and the Chocolate Factory*, the image of "savage" Africa and the myth of "the white man's burden" has been perpetuated in Western culture.

A 1972 *Time* magazine editorial lamenting the demise of *Life* magazine, stated that the "lavishness" of *Life*'s enterprises included "organizing safaris into darkest Africa." The same year, the *New York Times'* C. L. Sulzberger wrote that "Africa has a history as dark as the skins of many of its people." Terms such as "darkest Africa," "primitive," "tribe" ("tribal") or "jungle," in reference to Africa, perpetuate myths and are especially inexcusable in such large circulation publications.

Ethnocentrism is similarly reflected in the term "pagan" to describe traditional religions. A February 1973 *Time* magazine article on Uganda stated, "Moslems account for only 500,000 of Uganda's 10 million people. Of the remainder,

5,000,000 are Christians and the rest pagan." *Pagan* is defined as "Heathen, a follower of a polytheistic religion; one that has little or no religion and that is marked by a frank delight in and uninhibited seeking after sensual pleasures and material goods." *Heathen* is defined as "Unenlightened; an unconverted member of a people or nation that does not acknowledge the God of the Bible. A person whose culture or enlightenment is of an inferior grade, especially an irreligious person." Now, the people of Uganda, like almost all Africans, have serious religious beliefs and practices. As used by Westerners, "pagan" connotes something wild, primitive and inferior—another term to watch out for.

The variety of traditional structures that African people live in are their "houses," not "huts." A *hut* is "an often small and temporary dwelling of simple construction." And to describe Africans as "natives" (noun) is derogatory terminology—as in, "the natives are restless." The dictionary definition of *native* includes: "one of a people inhabiting a territorial area at the time of its discovery or becoming familiar to a foreigner; one belonging to a people having a less complex civilization." Therefore, use of "native," like use of "pagan" often implies a value judgement of white superiority.

QUALIFYING ADJECTIVES

Words that would normally have positive connotations can have entirely different meanings when used in a racial context. For example, C. L. Sulzberger, the columnist of the *New York Times,* wrote in January 1975, about conservations he had with two people in Namibia. One was the white South African administrator of the country and the other a member of SWAPO, the Namibian liberation movement. The first is described as "Dirk Mudge, who as senior elected member of the administration is a kind of acting Prime Minister. . . ." But the second person is introduced

as "Daniel Tijongarero, an intelligent Herero tribesman who is a member of SWAPO. . . ." What need was there for Sulzberger to state that Daniel Tijongarero is "intelligent"? Why not also state that Dirk Mudge was "intelligent"—or do we assume he wasn't?

A similar example from a 1968 *New York Times* article reporting on an address by Lyndon Johnson stated, "The President spoke to the well-dressed Negro officials and their wives." In what similar circumstances can one imagine a reporter finding it necessary to note that an audience of white government officials was "well-dressed?"

Still another word often used in a racist context is "qualified." In the 1960s white Americans often questioned whether Black people were "qualified" to hold public office, a question that was never raised (until too late) about white officials like Wallace, Maddox, Nixon, Agnew, Mitchell, et al. The question of qualifications has been raised even more frequently in recent years as white people question whether Black people are "qualified" to be hired for positions in industry and educational institutions. "We're looking for a qualified Black" has been heard again and again as institutions are confronted with affirmative action goals. Why stipulate that Blacks must be "qualified," when for others it is taken for granted that applicants must be "qualified"?

SPEAKING ENGLISH

Finally, the depiction in movies and children's books of third world people speaking English is often itself racist. Children's books about Puerto Ricans or Chicanos often connect poverty with a failure to speak English or to speak it well, thus blaming the victim and ignoring the racism which affects third world people regardless of their proficiency in English. Asian characters speak a stilted English ("Honorable so and so" or "Confucius say") or have a speech impediment ("rots or ruck," "very solly," "flied lice"). Native American characters speak another variation of stilted English ("Boy not hide. Indian take boy."), repeat certain Hollywood-Indian phrases ("Heap big" and "Many moons") or simply grunt out "Ugh" or "How." The repeated use of these language characterizations functions to make third world people seem less intelligent and less capable than the English-speaking white characters.

WRAP-UP

A *Saturday Review* editorial[10] on "The Environment of Language" stated that language

> . . . has as much to do with the philosophical and political conditioning of a society as geography or climate. . . . people in Western cultures do not real-ize the extent to which their racial attitudes have been conditioned since early childhood by the power of words to ennoble or condemn, augment or detract, glorify or demean. Negative language infects the subconscious of most Western people from the time they first learn to speak. Prejudice is not merely imparted or superimposed. It is metabolized in the bloodstream of society. What is needed is not so much a change in language as an awareness of the power of words to condition attitudes. If we can at least recognize the underpinnings of prejudice, we may be in a position to deal with the effects.

To recognize the racism in language is an impor-tant first step. Consciousness of the -influence of language on our perceptions can help to negate much of that influence. But it is not enough to simply become aware of the affects of racism in conditioning attitudes. While we may not be able to change the language, we can definitely change our usage of the language. We can avoid using words that degrade people. We can make a conscious effort to use terminology that reflects a progressive perspective, as opposed to a distorting perspective. It is important for educators to provide students with opportunities to explore racism in language and to increase their awareness of it, as well as learning terminology that is positive and does not perpetuate negative human values.

NOTES

1. Simon Podair, "How Bigotry Builds Through Language," *Negro Digest,* March 1967.

2. Jose Armas, "Antonio and the Mayor: A Cultural Review of the Film," *The Journal of Ethnic Studies,* Fall, 1975.

3. David R. Burgest, "The Racist Use of the English Language," *Black Scholar,* Sept. 1973.

4. Thomas Greenfield, "Race and Passive Voice at Monticello," *Crisis,* April 1975.

5. David R. Burgest, "Racism in Everyday Speech and Social Work Jargon," *Social Work,* July 1973.

6. William Ryan, *Blaming the Victim,* Pantheon Books, 1971.

7. Morton Fried, "The Myth of Tribe," *National History,* April 1975.

8. Evelyn Jones Rich, "Mind Your Language," *Africa Report,* Sept./Oct. 1974.

9. Steve Wolf, "Catalogers in Revolt Against LC's Racist, Sexist Headings," *Bulletin of Interracial Books for Children,* Vol. 6, Nos. 3&4, 1975.

10. "The Environment of Language," *Saturday Review,* April 8, 1967.

Further Readings

Roger Bastide, "Color, Racism and Christianity," *Daedalus,* Spring 1967.

Kenneth J. Gergen, "The Significance of Skin Color in Human Relations," *Daedalus,* Spring 1967.

Lloyd Yabura, "Towards a Language of Humanism," *Rhythm,* Summer 1971.

UNESCO, "Recommendations Concerning Terminology in Education on Race Questions," June 1968.

PART III

PRODUCING SOCIAL ORDER THROUGH INTERACTION

All the world's a stage.

And all the men and women merely players:

They have their exits and their entrances;

And one man in his time plays many parts.

—William Shakespeare, *As You Like It*

We are told on good authority, Callicles, that heaven and earth and their respective inhabitants are held together by the bonds of society and love and order and discipline and righteousness, and that is why the universe is an ordered whole or cosmos and not a state of disorder and license.

—Plato, *Gorgias*

MEANING IS NEGOTIATED THROUGH INTERACTION

Jodi O'Brien

In the early 1950s, during what has come to be known as the "beatnik era," Howard Becker, a young graduate student, spent his evenings playing jazz piano in Chicago-area nightclubs. Becker noticed that many patrons tried the drug marijuana, but only a few continued to use it. As a budding sociologist, Becker wondered why some people merely "experimented" and others became routine users. He was familiar with the "personality" and "physical" theories of his day, which suggested that those who continued to smoke marijuana were likely to have the sort of personality or physical makeup that inclined them to use drugs. But Becker wasn't satisfied with these theories. They didn't mesh with his observations.

Becker noted that those who continued to use marijuana described it as a "pleasurable" experience; they could rattle off lists of effects that they associated with marijuana, and when they introduced the drug to their friends, they tended to pass on this information. He concluded that those who continued smoking marijuana had "learned" to define the experience and the effects as enjoyable. He wrote a paper titled "Becoming a Marihuana User," in which he suggested that people learn to "name" experiences and physical responses (see Reading 13). This "naming" process shapes a person's reactions to the event—in this case, the smoking of a drug and the corresponding physical reaction. He emphasized that people learn these "names," or responses, through interaction with others. Regardless of how people might feel privately, they get cues from others about how they are expected to feel and behave. They adjust their perceptions and behavior in response. This profoundly "social" explanation for individual behavior—even in response to something as physically based as drug ingestion—helped alter the course of sociology and gained young Becker a reputation as a formidable social scientist.

Humans become social creatures through their ability to formulate language-based systems of meaning. We live in a symbolic universe rather than a direct state of nature. Humans organize their existence into a meaningful reality through symbols, and language is the primary form of symbol. One implication of this thesis is that social order exists in the human mind, in the form of meaningful conceptual associations that organize each person's experiences and perceptions. This essay explores how this internal, cognitive system is learned, manifested, and reproduced among groups of people. For a cognitive system to be "social," it must be enacted or made real—"realized." Realization of a symbolic order is achieved through ongoing interactions in which we each express ourselves to others.

Naming: An Interactional Process

To engage in meaningful expression, people must translate the thoughts and images in their minds into a form—names—that will be understood by others. The transcription of thought into language is social interaction. If others can be relied upon to use similar names and make similar associations among objects, persons, and events, then the naming process becomes stable. It becomes something that we can take for granted as social "order." The process of naming includes several elements: Ideas and intentions must be *projected* to others. Meaning must be *negotiated.* The ability to successfully project and negotiate intentions is, in part, a function of the *resources* that one has, in the form of interpersonal skills and material goods. The world does not speak for itself. To interact at all, we must learn to *associate* socially significant meanings with objects, persons, and events. Finally, people learn these meanings or names through *interaction.*

In thinking about Becker's question—What does it take to become a marijuana user?—consider the possible range of responses from someone who ingests marijuana but doesn't know what it is. As a child, I once accidentally inhaled Clorox bleach. The physical sensation was similar to the one marijuana might produce when it is first inhaled: choking, followed by a burning sensation. When I inhaled the bleach, I thought I was going to die. I was so convinced of my imminent demise that I wrote a note for my parents to find when they came across my body and didn't know how to explain my death.

Becker asks a pertinent question when considering the relationship between physical stimuli and human response: Why would someone voluntarily seek out and continue to do something that, if evaluated simply as an undefined physical experience, is not likely to be considered immediately pleasant? Technically, when you first smoke marijuana, you are just as likely to feel like you have inhaled bleach as you are to feel like you have inhaled something that might be a source of pleasure. Becker illustrates the process of interaction and learning that helps us to identify an experience with a particular meaning. One of the key points of his article is that getting high is something that must be *learned in interaction* with other, more experienced users. Becker points out, for example, that it is very common for novices not to feel high the first time they smoke marijuana and for an experienced user to smoke a placebo that smells like marijuana and report feeling high. In other words, smoking marijuana is not a simple physiological response to a psychoactive drug but a socially constructed experience that must be identified or named before people are able to recognize the intended effect. The fact that Becker's article is more than fifty years old is also important for the contemporary reader. It allows us to study a culture in its infancy, before the general public knew much about marijuana and its effects.

Becker's article demonstrates that people do not respond directly to stimuli within a state of nature but to the meaning assigned to the situation. Further, we learn responses, even some physiological ones, from others. Consider some more examples. How do you know when you are sick? In the course of your daily activities, you may notice aspects of your body or behavior that feel "off." As you attend to these often uncomfortable feelings, you attempt to make sense of them. In doing so, you rely not only on your observations of the specific symptoms—scratchy throat, upset stomach, aches and pains—but on input from others. One sociologist, Bernice Pescosolido, researches the process of deliberation people use to determine whether they should go to the doctor when something feels "off." Her research suggests that people rely on networks of friends and acquaintances to help them name the situation. People confer with an average of at least seven others before they decide to visit the doctor's office. Other people help us interpret the situation by drawing our attention to specific symptoms ("Do you have a fever? If you don't have a fever, you don't have the flu.") or reminding us of associations we may not have considered ("You've been partying every night the past two weeks, of course you feel run down"). Pescosolido's study reminds us that we must recognize and name even basic physiological experiences before we can act on them.

There is some very interesting research done by endocrinologists that shows that men experience regular hormonal fluctuations. Similar to the experiences of menstruating women, these fluctuations may be associated with mood change and related physiological effects such as a decrease or increase in appetite, sexual desire, and so forth. Although the fluctuations may have a pattern and be a source of mood shifts among men, it is unlikely that most men recognize the effects of these shifts. Culturally, men simply don't have a "script" for talking about, let alone recognizing, hormonal fluctuations in their bodies. In fact, the prevailing cultural attitude is that most men have stable hormones and only women experience hormonal cycles. One conclusion that can be drawn from this research is that a significant physical process may be occurring, but without a name for it, it's not likely to be recognized or understood. Conversely, most women have considerable experience talking with others about bodily symptoms that they learn to associate with a menstrual cycle. Whether or not these symptoms are actually associated with the hormonal shifts that are presumed to be their source, most women talk with one another *as if* this were the case.

Even if you don't know what your body is doing, you know your heart, right? Sociological research is also filled with studies of ways in which young people learn through their interactions with others about love and romance. What are some of the "symptoms" of love? Ask some of your friends to generate a list of symptoms associated with "falling" in love. It's likely this list will include terms such as "distracted," "nervous," "anxious," "giddy," and similar words that convey a sense of being "out of control." Does this sound like fun to you? In the absence of a culturally learned context, an anthropologist from Mars might conclude that the human experience of attraction is similar to the experience of taking a dreaded exam.

These examples illustrate that the ways we make sense of our experiences, even things as basic as bodily functions, are based on interactions with others. In these interactions, we learn how to define our experiences, we learn whether something is supposed to be pleasurable or painful, and we learn the attitudes and postures that are associated with the experience.

WHAT'S GOING ON? PROJECTING A DEFINITION OF THE SITUATION

Once you've accumulated a stockpile of cultural knowledge, the kind of information that enables you to name and make sense of your experiences in a culturally meaningful way, you're on your way to successful interaction. But you still need to let others know what your expectations of the situation are. Sociologists call this "framing."

In his novel *Tom Sawyer,* Mark Twain (1875/1946) tells an entertaining story. Tom has been given the thankless task of whitewashing a long fence on a weekend afternoon. One of his friends comes by and begins to taunt him:

"Hello, old chap, you got to work, hey?"

Tom wheeled suddenly and said: "Why, it's you, Ben! I warn't noticing."

"Say—I'm going in a-swimming, I am. Don't you wish you could? But of course you'd druther work—wouldn't you? Course you would!"

Tom contemplated the boy a bit, and said: "What do you call work?"

"Why, ain't *that* work?"

Tom resumed his whitewashing, and answered carelessly: "Well, maybe it is, and maybe it ain't. All I know, is, it suits Tom Sawyer."

"Oh come, now, you don't mean to let on that you *like* it?" The brush continued to move.

"Like it? Well, I don't see why I oughtn't to like it. Does a boy get a chance to whitewash a fence every day?"

That put the thing in a new light. Ben stopped nibbling his apple. Tom swept his brush daintily back and forth—stepped back to note the effect—added a touch here and there—criticized the effect again—Ben watching every move and getting more and more interested, more and more absorbed. Presently he said: "Say, Tom, let me whitewash a little." (pp. 18–19)

Soon, boy after boy comes by and begs to exchange food, a toy, or some other treasure for an opportunity to whitewash the fence.

In this story, Tom is an entrepreneur of meaning. Using great skill, he has managed to *reframe* a presumably unpleasant activity into a rare and desirable opportunity. He has successfully defined the situation in a way that allows him to accomplish his goal (to avoid spending the day whitewashing the fence) and to benefit from it.

If an interaction is to proceed successfully, the participants must establish their identities and agree on the sort of situation they find themselves in. Although it is usually not apparent to the casual observer, there is considerable work that goes into defining a situation and maintaining a particular definition. This process of letting others know your situational identity and your corresponding definition of the situation is called an *interaction routine.*

Some people attempt to define a situation in a novel way, as Tom Sawyer did. However, most of us don't project novel definitions of a situation in most circumstances. Rather, we tend to rely on known "scripts" or "plot lines." When we "name" something, we categorize the situation and then follow the culturally expected line of response. One sociological perspective uses the imagery and language of the theater to explain the process of interaction among symbolic actors who are attempting to establish and maintain a shared definition of what's going on. According to this perspective, we "frame" the situation (for example, wedding, funeral, trip to the grocery store, classroom, and so forth) and then use the stockpile of cultural information at our disposal to inform us about what to expect and which roles befit ourselves and others in the particular situation.

Life as Theater

"Life as theater" uses the metaphor of *performance* to explain interaction routines. Like any metaphor, it is not a complete description of social reality, but in many ways, our interactions with others do seem to resemble a theatrical performance.

The theater metaphor can be seen in the origins of the word *person,* which comes from the Latin *persona,* meaning a mask worn by actors. We behave differently (play different roles) in front of different people (audiences). We pick out clothing (a costume) that is consistent with the image we wish to project. We enlist the help of friends, caterers, and decorators (fellow actors and stage crew) to help us successfully "stage" a dinner for a friend, a birthday party for a relative, or a rush party for a sorority or fraternity. And if we need to adjust our clothing or wish to say something unflattering about one of our guests, we are careful to do so out of sight from others (backstage).

The presentation of ourselves to others is known as *dramaturgy,* and the use of the theatrical metaphor for analyzing human interaction is known as the *dramaturgical perspective.* The most noted writer on this perspective is Erving Goffman, who in 1959 published *The Presentation of Self in Everyday Life.* In this classic book, Goffman analyzes everyday "performances." He details the care people take in preparing and presenting their performances—that is, the manner in which people *manage* the impressions others form of them.

Why do people spend so much time and energy thinking about what they should say and how they should look? Some would say that we should simply "be ourselves" and that only those who are deceitful need to worry about managing their image. They would concede that con artists and the insincere have to be concerned about these issues, but what about good, decent people? In fact, however, even saints are concerned with the presentation of self. To tell us to simply "be" ourselves implies that who we are is easily, quickly, and accurately perceived by those with whom we interact. But if we have just met someone or will be interacting with someone for only a short length of time (for example, in a job interview), we certainly can't count on the person to see us as we see ourselves. Dramaturgy can be an issue even when we interact with people who have known us for some time. Who we are may not be obvious to others—most of us do not wear our personal characteristics and convictions tattooed onto our foreheads.

Private Minds, Public Identities

A simple but profound truth about human interaction is that minds are private. Our thoughts, desires, beliefs, and character cannot be directly perceived and evaluated by others. We are not a race of mind readers, and so we must depend on signs and gestures to comprehend one another. Recall the example of the border guard from the essay in Part II. The guard sizes people up and treats them according to their appearance. Therefore, it is in people's best interest to appear in a way that gets them treated as they wish. In this case, they want to appear "law-abiding."

The fact that minds are private doesn't mean that people are obligated to accurately display their thoughts and desires to others, but it does mean that even the most honest people must be concerned about how they come across to others. In Goffman's (1959) words:

> Whether an honest performer wishes to convey the truth or whether a dishonest performer wishes to convey a falsehood, both must take care to enliven their performances with appropriate expressions, exclude from their performances expressions that might discredit the impression being fostered, and take care lest the audience impute unintended meanings. (p. 66)

It is crucial to remember that *impression management* is something everyone does in all everyday activities. To one degree or another, we all manage others' impressions of us in interactions. We have to "perform" or "project" our intentions and desires, because people can't read our minds.

Because minds are private, people typically behave so as to highlight important facts about themselves that might otherwise go unnoticed. Goffman calls this activity *dramatic realization.* For example, when you are in a job interview, you might describe in great detail a position of responsibility you held in the past. Or if you are in traffic court, you might point out the absence of any past traffic violations to the judge. But although this feature may be true about you, you probably wouldn't bring it up as a way to impress a potential date. Instead, you might focus on highlighting your favorite bands or activities. Dramatic realization is an attempt to make traits and characteristics that might otherwise go unnoticed "real" and noticeable. If these traits are not noticed, they don't exist as "real" aspects of the performance. It is up to the individual to bring them into play.

Goffman also makes the point that we often try to present ourselves in a favorable light, a process he calls *idealization.* We might simply accent those aspects about ourselves that are positive (for example, mentioning that you are on the varsity team but not mentioning that you have just lost your job), or we might engage in outright deception (saying you are on the varsity team when you are not).

People also have a general tendency to convey the impression that the role they are currently engaged in is their most important role. For example, when an individual walks into a store to buy an expensive suit, she will be interacting with a "salesperson." The salesperson may also be a spouse, parent, community volunteer, jogger, gardener, and so forth, but if that salesperson is good at the job, he will take part in the interaction as if serving customers is the only (or at least the most important) role in his life at that moment.

Before an interaction can proceed successfully, two actors must agree about the sort of situation they are in and the role each is to play. Is it a friendly chat between acquaintances, a seduction between lovers, or a coaching session between subordinate and supervisor? This process is referred to as *identity negotiation.*

People in an interaction each project an identity, and their responses to each other indicate whether they accept the projected identity. For example, if you ask your boss how old she is and she doesn't acknowledge the question, she has chosen not to grant you the identity of "familiar acquaintance." When two people agree on the identities they are both going to play in an interaction, they have arrived at what Goffman refers to as a *working consensus.*

Public agreement on identities does not necessarily reflect the actor's *private* beliefs. People often have pleasant chats with coworkers they dislike. There are many possible reasons for doing this—to be polite, to prevent an awkward scene, to ensure good relations in the workplace, or perhaps to stay in the good graces of a person who controls resources that might be needed sometime. Whatever the private reality might be, it is the public, socially agreed upon definition of the situation that will guide the interaction.

Once a public agreement has been reached (whether implicitly or explicitly), it carries the weight of a contract. The working consensus has a moral character to it. Each actor *feels as if* he or she has the right to be treated in a particular way by other actors. The actors also *feel as if* they have an obligation to behave in ways that are consistent with the presented identity. For example, in an interaction between a teacher and a student, the person who is in the role of the teacher expects certain behavior from the person who is the student; these behaviors include being treated respectfully, being treated as a status superior, being treated as an expert in the subject, and so on. At the same time, the person who has claimed the identity of teacher has numerous obligations or duties, such as competently carrying out the teacher's role, being respectful of students, knowing a great deal about the subject, and being able to convey that knowledge to students. The rights and duties associated with an identity that has been publicly accepted must be respected if the small social order of the interaction is to continue. If a math teacher is unable to solve a problem in front of the class or if a student treats the teacher as a younger sibling, the interaction grinds to an uncomfortable halt.

In sum, interaction has two key elements—publicly defining (and presenting) a personal identity and defining what sort of situation the individual is in with others. There are many possible answers to the questions "Who am I?" "Who are you?" "What's going on?" For successful interaction to occur, these definitions must be projected and negotiated by the participants. The participants jockey to claim identities and to define the situation in ways that will help them accomplish their personal goals. Once identities are established, they must be actively maintained.

This process leads people to reproduce taken-for-granted cultural patterns. Because minds are private, we all must dramatize (in other words, signal) the identities we wish to claim and our definition of the situation. To be effective in interactions, we select symbolic representations that we know to be reliable signals of our intentions. This selection of culturally typical or expected symbols is a process of *idealization.* You may not like business suits, for instance, but you will put one on for a job interview because you believe it to be the appropriate costume for presenting the identity of an eager and professional potential employee. When you present yourself with the appropriate costume, props, and mannerisms, you effectively reproduce a set of cultural expectations or *ideals*—one of them being "Businesspeople wear suits." In other words, you will be presenting a symbolic *ideal type,* and through your self-presentation, you will be affirming the ideal type. The implications of idealization for perpetuating social norms are significant. Some of the consequences of "dramatizing the ideal" are discussed in Parts III and IV of this book.

Who Are We and What Are We Doing Here?

> When an individual enters the presence of others, they commonly seek to acquire information about him [*sic*] or to bring into play information already possessed. They will be interested in his general socio-economic status, his conception of self, his attitude toward them, his competence, his trustworthiness, etc. (Goffman, 1959, p. 1)

When they come together, people must actively strive to present a definition of the role they wish to play in the interactional moment and the definition of the situation as they see it. Failure to do so may lead to misunderstandings, embarrassment, and the breakdown of the interaction. In a study of gym trainers and their clients, Linda Van Leuven (2001) describes the different definitions that client and trainer may bring to the interaction. Clients sometimes define the situation as a personal friendship or even a romantic encounter. Accordingly, they may enter the situation prepared to act out the identity of "engaging flirt." Trainers, who are aware of this propensity in some clients, develop strategies designed to let the client know immediately what they can expect of the situation—a "workout" and not an occasion to "visit" or to "flirt." For instance, a trainer may grill a potential client about her or his commitment in advance. During the sessions, the trainer might carefully avoid eye contact so as to discourage conversation. These interactional strategies help to establish a frame around the situation and to signal to participants what the boundaries and expectations are.

Goffman notes that there are many skills required to bring off a reasonable interactional performance. Because interaction requires the ongoing cooperation of participants, it is vulnerable and can break down. A situation might be defined in an inappropriate way. Or the identities the participants claim might somehow be discredited (as when a math teacher cannot solve a problem in front of the class). In that case, the result is embarrassment.

From a dramaturgical perspective, embarrassment can be defined as a breakdown in a projected identity. It is striking to note how uncomfortable we are made by embarrassment and how hard we work to avoid it. Indeed, embarrassment makes us so uncomfortable that we usually cooperate to prevent or smooth over other people's embarrassing actions, even if they are strangers. We might look away when someone stumbles clumsily, pretend not to hear the fight the couple is having at a nearby table, or readily and eagerly accept other people's explanations for their unacceptable behavior. Engaging in cooperative support of each other's identities to avoid or repair embarrassment is called *tact*. The presence and prevalence of tact is an extraordinary thing. Humans apparently have a very deep commitment to support each other's identities, even the identities of strangers.

True, there are times when someone might react to an embarrassing moment without tact (or even have engineered the moment, if it involves a rival), but these instances stand out because they are exceptions. Practical jokes that make someone look foolish (that is, those that discredit someone's "face") would not be funny if they were not a deviation from the usual norm of tact.

The mutual obligation to avoid "scenes" and to be who we claim to be means that whenever a situation or identity is threatened, someone must repair the interaction. When the audience helps in the repair work, they are being tactful—but, of course, the person whose identity is threatened can also work to repair the interaction. Following behavior that threatens an identity, people usually can offer explanations or give an *account* of the actions.

Offering accounts after an inappropriate act does not guarantee that others will accept ("honor") the account. Not every explanation is acceptable. "I had car trouble" might be a reasonable excuse for failing to get to class on time, but not "Voices told me to come late today." And some explanations are acceptable in some situations but not in others. Burning the stew because "I was distracted by a phone call" is acceptable, but the same excuse would certainly not be honored as an explanation for why someone failed to show up for her wedding. What is judged to be an acceptable account varies from situation to situation. It can also vary tremendously from one culture to another.

Goffman emphasizes just how fragile and potentially disruptable interaction routines really are. His intent is not so much to present people as cynical and calculating as to draw our attention to the tricky interpersonal gymnastics required of social actors. What is remarkable—and Goffman's respectful awe is apparent in his voluminous writings—is that people somehow do manage to project mutually understood definitions of self and situation, despite all the things that could go wrong.

It's important to note that people *learn* acceptable definitions of identity and situation. Some of these learning processes are very explicit. For instance, business schools frequently hold "mock cocktail parties" in order to teach students how to network with clients. Informal social networking is an important factor in successful business encounters. For this reason, business schools provide students with an opportunity to "try on" and practice performing social networking identities. Students learn tips such as "don't have both hands full with drink and food, because you won't be able to shake someone else's hand" and "you have to appear eager but not like you're a 'social climber.'"

Whether one intends to project an identity of competent instructor, capable business-woman, earnest priest, or intimidating thug, we all have to engage in impression management; we have to signal to others our definition of the situation and our intended position.

Negotiating a Working Consensus

The generative quality of social structure is observable in face-to-face encounters. Individuals bring different ideas, goals, and expectations to social encounters. As they strive to achieve a working definition of what is going on, they transcribe their private definitions, as well as their immediate feelings, into a form that they think others will understand and accept. In other words, people manage, despite many differences, to engage in meaningful, sustainable discourses. We all do this through continual negotiation.

The theatrical form most indicative of the generative, negotiated quality of interaction is improvisation. "Theater sports" is a form of entertainment in which the audience calls out a "frame" or "setting"—usually one involving some sort of controversy or misunderstanding—and the actors then improvise their roles within the parameters of the setting. The actors and audience share a general understanding of what the scene or setting consists of, but how it is played out is largely determined by each actor's performance repertoire (that is, each actor's familiarity with how people might react in this situation) and how the other performers respond. If you have participated in theater sports, you know that the fun is in seeing how diverse actors play off one another when they don't know what the others are likely to do.

Everyday interaction is an ongoing series of such moments. The ability to negotiate working understandings of different situations is the genius of human sociability. The fact that everyday encounters feel more or less like comfortable routines—rather than a madcap scramble of miscues, misunderstandings, and maladies—is a testament to the existence of shared social scripts.

The negotiation process becomes apparent in situations that are less familiar and routine. On those occasions, people are likely to be more aware of the potential gap between the private and projected definitions of various participants. These situations are often "precarious."

In a study of interaction between patients and staff in gynecological exams, Joan Emerson illustrates the impression management that must take place when participants have strongly competing definitions of the situation (see Reading 19). The patient is likely to feel that the examination is a violation of her body and her dignity, whereas the medical staff wants to establish an air of professional detachment. The doctors and nurses performing this medical procedure must take care to ensure that the situation continues to be defined as a medical examination, because the exam includes many sensitive behaviors that could threaten this definition. Although most interactions are not as precarious as this situation, any interaction can end up being redefined in a negative light ("I thought you were being helpful. Now I just think you're being patronizing and manipulative!"). Thus, the concerns and dramaturgical activity that are brought out so clearly in the gynecological examination are relevant to many more ordinary settings.

Even so-called deviant settings require impression management and negotiation of a working consensus. In an article on strip clubs (see Reading 20), Kari Lerum describes how employees in an erotic dance club work to maintain specific definitions of the situation. In contrast with gynecological exams, in which the intent is to desexualize the situation, this study reveals that there are also interaction rules for erotic situations. Employees must actively strive to create an impression that the atmosphere in the club is distinctly erotic. At the same time, dancers also wish to convey the impression that their performances are strictly work. Lerum points out the additional difficulties that arise because this work is not considered as legitimate as other forms of wage earning. All of this makes for some complicated impression management.

Performing Interaction Rituals

Goffman (1959) opens *The Presentation of Self in Everyday Life* with the following lines from the philosopher George Santayana:

Masks are arrested expressions and admirable echoes of feelings, at once faithful, discreet, and superlative. Living things in contact with the air acquire a cuticle, and it is not urged against cuticles that they are not hearts; yet some philosophers seem to be angry with images for not being things, and with words for not being feelings. Words and images are like shells, no less integral parts of nature than are the substances they cover, but better addressed to the eye and more open to observation. (p. vi)

Through this quotation, Goffman anticipates readers' reactions to his theory that we "perform" ourselves, our ideals, and our beliefs rather than somehow simply exuding them naturally. Some people are inclined to associate "performance" with fakery or trickery. They assume that, behind the stage, there is something "more real."

Goffman and sociologists of his persuasion do not disavow the existence of a physiology, a psyche, and perhaps even a soul that may be independent of social forces, but their theoretical and analytical focus is on *social* relations. "Reality" is in the expression of social meaning achieved through interaction. We are, first and foremost, *expressive* creatures. To express ourselves, we must transform individual urges, amorphous images, and fuzzy ideas into communicable form. We do so through interactional speech and gesture. Thus, "reality" consists of shared forms of expression that, as we have noted, take on patterns. Goffman calls these patterns "interaction rituals."

Producing a shared reality requires give and take, concession, and acknowledgment of others. Interaction rituals are enactments of ceremony that reinforce cultural symbols and expectations. The rituals range from simple greeting exchanges (in which people acknowledge the presence of other people) to elaborate ceremonies (such as weddings and funerals). And these interaction rituals have a conservative aspect: Through ritual presentations of the "ideal," people conserve or maintain the status quo.

For Goffman (1959), everyday ceremonies, or rituals, give meaning to our collective existence:

> To the degree that a performance highlights the common official values of the society in which it occurs, we may look upon it as a ceremony—as an expressive rejuvenation and reaffirmation of the moral values of the community. . . . To stay in one's room away from the place where the party is being given . . . is to stay away from where reality is being performed. The world, in truth, is a wedding. (pp. 35–36)

CONCLUSION

Interaction is a fluid, intricately coordinated dance that requires actors to participate in meaningful symbolic routines. These interaction routines serve to define who people are, relative to one another, and what the situation is. The implication is that social life is a production or performance staged by the participants. Even the self is a social construction arrived at through processes of meaningful interaction with others.

By way of conclusion, ponder the paradox of the social self. Many Western individuals are uncomfortable with the notion that the self is a social construction. We are all more or less aware that we engage in impression management, but many of us like to think that our "true self" is unchanging and is the product of forces independent of society. Thus, many of us rebel against the "chains of society," thinking that if only we could break loose from these chains, we would be "free" (Charon, 1989).

Herein lies the paradox: To gain control over our own behavior, we must each develop a self that is capable of observing, reflecting on, and directing that behavior. Without such a self, we are merely passive organisms propelled by the forces of nature. In the process of developing this self, we determine what position to take on our own behavior by observing and experiencing the reactions of others to our behavior. The implication is that all the behavior we reflect on holds meaning for us only because it has been derived from some form of social interaction. The ability to consider whether we are "free" agents or "controlled" by society is therefore possible only through our ability to engage in internal dialogue regarding the self as an object—which, ironically, is a product of socialization. Free agency is a moot point for the unsocialized being. Such a being cannot reflect on or guide its own behavior and therefore cannot make active choices.

Resolution of this paradox may lie in the recognition that we are all, in Goffman's phrase, "sweet conspirators" in social patterns and interaction rituals. It is more useful to ask ourselves what purpose these patterns and rituals serve, and with what consequences, than to shrug them off as someone else's chains. To ignore our socialization is, according to Goffman, to leave the stage where reality is being performed. The pertinent question for the enlightened social actor is "Just what sort of a performance am I a part of?" Hence the focus on the questions "What is the definition of the situation?" and "What role(s) am I playing?"

References and Suggestions for Further Reading

Charon, J. (1989). *Symbolic interactionism* (3rd ed.). Englewood Cliffs, NJ: Prentice Hall.

Goffman, E. (1959). *The presentation of self in everyday life.* Garden City, NY: Doubleday.

Kuhn, M. H., & McPartland, T. S. (1954). An empirical investigation of self-attitudes. *American Sociological Review, 19,* 68–76.

Turner, R. (1976). The real self: From institution to impulse. *American Journal of Sociology, 81,* 989–1016.

Twain, M. (1946). *The adventures of Tom Sawyer.* New York: Grosset & Dunlap. (Original work published 1875)

Van Leuven, L. (2001). What does this service include? In J. O'Brien & P. Kollock (Eds.), *The production of reality* (3rd ed., pp. 254–264). Thousand Oaks, CA: Pine Forge Press.

———————— ﷽ ————————

NAMING AS AN INTERACTIONAL PROCESS

We learn meaning from others. People learn from one another what to think, feel, and expect from their experiences. Even when we experience the physical symptoms of illness, we talk with others about these symptoms in order to figure out what is really going on.

"Becoming a Marihuana User" is a classic sociological article written by Howard Becker in 1953. Becker observed that people who use marijuana for pleasure have to *learn* how to smoke the drug, identify its effects, and consider the effects to be pleasant. If they don't learn these things, they don't continue smoking. It's an acquired taste—acquired through interaction with others who tell you what to do and feel. This article was a milestone in demonstrating that even physiological experiences have to be interpreted.

"The Development of Feeling Norms Underlying Romantic Love" addresses the question "How do you know if you're in love?" Based on interviews with adolescent girls, Robin Simon describes the social process young people go through—especially talking to one another—that enables them to understand and respond to social expectations about love and romance.

Questions for Discussion and Review

1. Think about a new job or new experience you've had, and recall in detail the process you went through to learn the "routine." Who explained it to you? What mistakes did you make in first learning?

2. Recall an occasion when you were confused about something. Whom did you talk with, and what can you remember about how they defined the situation for you?

3. When did you first become aware of "sex" (not your own sexuality, just the idea of sex)? Can you remember a particular event or set of events that made you realize this was culturally significant? What emotions or feelings do you associate with that experience? Were people helpful in their explanations, or did they seem embarrassed and abstract? Have subsequent experiences altered your first impressions, or do you still have the same initial feeling imprint?

NAMING AS AN INTERACTIONAL PROCESS

13

Becoming a Marihuana User

Howard S. Becker

(1953)

The use of marihuana is and has been the focus of a good deal of attention on the part of both scientists and laymen. One of the major problems students of the practice have addressed themselves to has been the identification of those individual psychological traits which differentiate marihuana users from nonusers and which are assumed to account for the use of the drug. That approach, common in the study of behavior categorized as deviant, is based on the premise that the presence of a given kind of behavior in an individual can best be explained as the result of some trait which predisposes or motivates him to engage in the behavior.[1]

This study is likewise concerned with accounting for the presence or absence of marihuana use

AUTHOR'S NOTE: This paper was read at the meetings of the Midwest Sociological Society in Omaha, Nebraska, April 25, 1953. The research on which this paper is based was done while I was a member of the staff of the Chicago Narcotics Survey, a study done by the Chicago Area Project, Inc., under a grant from the National Institute of Mental Health. My thanks to Solomon Kobrin, Harold Finestone, Henry McKay, and Anselm Strauss, who read and discussed with me earlier versions of this paper.

in an individual's behavior. It starts, however, from a different premise: that the presence of a given kind of behavior is the result of a sequence of social experiences during which the person acquires a conception of the meaning of the behavior, and perceptions and judgments of objects and situations, all of which make the activity possible and desirable. Thus, the motivation or disposition to engage in the activity is built up in the course of learning to engage in it and does not antedate this learning process. For such a view it is not necessary to identify those "traits" which "cause" the behavior. Instead, the problem becomes one of describing the set of changes in the person's conception of the activity and of the experience it provides for him.[2]

This paper seeks to describe the sequence of changes in attitude and experience which lead to *the use of marihuana for pleasure*. Marihuana does not produce addiction, as do alcohol and the opiate drugs; there is no withdrawal sickness and no ineradicable craving for the drug.[3] The most frequent pattern of use might be termed "recreational." The drug is used occasionally for the pleasure the user finds in it, a relatively casual kind of behavior in comparison with that connected with the use of addicting drugs. The term "use for pleasure" is meant to emphasize the noncompulsive and casual character of the behavior. It is also meant to eliminate from consideration here those few cases in which marihuana is used for its prestige value only, as a symbol that one is a certain kind of person, with no pleasure at all being derived from its use.

The analysis presented here is conceived of as demonstrating the greater explanatory usefulness of the kind of theory outlined above as opposed to the predispositional theories now current. This may be seen in two ways: (1) predispositional theories cannot account for that group of users (whose existence is admitted)[4] who do not exhibit the trait or traits considered to cause the behavior and (2) such theories cannot account for the great variability over time of a given individual's behavior with reference to the drug. The same person will at one stage be unable to use the drug for pleasure, at a later stage be able and willing to do so, and still later, again be unable to use it in this way. These changes, difficult to explain from a predispositional or motivational theory, are readily understandable in terms of changes in the individual's conception of the drug as is the existence of "normal" users.

The study attempted to arrive at a general statement of the sequence of changes in individual attitude and experience which have always occurred when the individual has become willing and able to use marihuana for pleasure and which have not occurred or not been permanently maintained when this is not the case. This generalization is stated in universal terms in order that negative cases may be discovered and used to revise the explanatory hypothesis.[5]

Fifty interviews with marihuana users from a variety of social backgrounds and present positions in society constitute the data from which the generalization was constructed and against which it was tested.[6] The interviews focused on the history of the person's experience with the drug, seeking major changes in his attitude toward it and in his actual use of it, and the reasons for these changes. The final generalization is a statement of that sequence of changes in attitude which occurred in every case known to me in which the person came to use marihuana for pleasure. Until a negative case is found, it may be considered as an explanation of all cases of marihuana use for pleasure. In addition, changes from use to nonuse are shown to be related to similar changes in conception, and in each case it is possible to explain variations in the individual's behavior in these terms.

This paper covers only a portion of the natural history of an individual's use of marihuana,[7] starting with the person having arrived at the point of willingness to try marihuana. He knows that others use it to "get high," but he does not know what this means in concrete terms. He is curious about the experience, ignorant of what it may turn out to be, and afraid that it may be more than he has bargained for. The steps outlined below, if he undergoes them all and maintains the attitudes developed in them, leave him willing and able to use the drug for pleasure when the opportunity presents itself.

I

The novice does not ordinarily get high the first time he smokes marihuana, and several attempts are usually necessary to induce this state. One explanation of this may be that the drug is not smoked "properly," that is, in a way that ensures sufficient dosage to produce real symptoms of intoxication. Most users agree that it cannot be smoked like tobacco if one is to get high:

> Take in a lot of air, you know, and . . . I don't know how to describe it, you don't smoke it like a cigarette, you draw in a lot of air and get it deep down in your system and then keep it there. Keep it there as long as you can.

Without the use of some such technique[8] the drug will produce no effects, and the user will be unable to get high:

> The trouble with people like that [who are not able to get high] is that they're just not smoking it right, that's all there is to it. Either they're not holding it down long enough, or they're getting too much air and not enough smoke, or the other way around or something like that. A lot of people just don't smoke it right, so naturally nothing's gonna happen.

If nothing happens, it is manifestly impossible for the user to develop a conception of the drug as an object which can be used for pleasure, and use will therefore not continue. The first step in the sequence of events that must occur if the person is to become a user is that he must learn to use the proper smoking technique in order that his use of the drug will produce some effects in terms of which his conception of it can change.

Such a change is, as might be expected, a result of the individual's participation in groups in which marihuana is used. In them the individual learns the proper way to smoke the drug. This may occur through direct teaching:

> I was smoking like I did an ordinary cigarette. He said, "No, don't do it like that." He said, "Suck it, you know, draw in and hold it in your lungs till you . . . for a period of time."
>
> I said, "Is there any limit of time to hold it?"
>
> He said, "No, just till you feel that you want to let it out, let it out." So I did that three or four times.

Many new users are ashamed to admit ignorance and, pretending to know already, must learn through the more indirect means of observation and imitation:

> I came on like I had turned on [smoked marihuana] many times before, you know. I didn't want to seem like a punk to this cat. See, like I didn't know the first thing about it—how to smoke it, or what was going to happen, or what. I just watched him like a hawk—I didn't take my eyes off him for a second, because I wanted to do everything just as he did it. I watched how he held it, how he smoked it, and everything. Then when he gave it to me I just came on cool, as though I knew exactly what the score was. I held it like he did and took a poke just the way he did.

No person continued marihuana use for pleasure without learning a technique that supplied sufficient dosage for the effects of the drug to appear. Only when this was learned was it possible for a conception of the drug as an object which could be used for pleasure to emerge. Without such a conception marihuana use was considered meaningless and did not continue.

II

Even after he learns the proper smoking technique, the new user may not get high and thus not form a conception of the drug as something which can be used for pleasure. A remark made by a user suggested the reason for this difficulty in getting high and pointed to the next necessary step on the road to being a user:

> I was told during an interview, "As a matter of fact, I've seen a guy who was high out of his mind and didn't know it."
>
> I expressed disbelief: "How can that be, man?"
>
> The interviewee said, "Well, it's pretty strange, I'll grant you that, but I've seen it. This guy got on with me, claiming that he'd never got high, one of those guys, and he got completely stoned. And he kept insisting that he wasn't high. So I had to prove to him that he was."

What does this mean? It suggests that being high consists of two elements: the presence of symptoms caused by marihuana use and the recognition of these symptoms and their connection by the user with his use of the drug. It is not enough, that is, that the effects be present; they alone do not automatically provide the experience of being high. The user must be able to point them out to himself and consciously connect them with his having smoked marihuana before he can have this experience. Otherwise, regardless of the actual effects produced, he considers that the drug has had no effect on him: "I figured it either had no effect on me or other people were exaggerating its effect on them, you know. I thought it was probably psychological, see." Such persons believe that the whole thing is an illusion and that the wish to be high leads the user to deceive himself into believing that something is happening when, in fact, nothing is. They do not continue marihuana use, feeling that "it does nothing" for them.

Typically, however, the novice has faith (developed from his observation of users who do get high) that the drug actually will produce some new experience and continues to experiment with it until it does. His failure to get high worries him, and he is likely to ask more experienced users or provoke comments from them about it. In such conversations he is made aware of specific details of his experience which he may not have noticed or may have noticed but failed to identify as symptoms of being high:

> I didn't get high the first time . . . I don't think I held it in long enough. I probably let it out, you know, you're a little afraid. The second time I wasn't sure, and he [smoking companion] told me, like I asked him for some of the symptoms or something, how would I know, you know. . . . So he told me to sit on a stool. I sat on—I think I sat on a bar stool—and he said, "Let your feet hang," and then when I got down my feet were real cold, you know.
>
> And I started feeling it, you know. That was the first time. And then about a week after that, sometime pretty close to it, I really got on. That was the first time I got on a big laughing kick, you know. Then I really knew I was on.

One symptom of being high is an intense hunger. In the next case the novice becomes aware of this and gets high for the first time:

> They were just laughing the hell out of me because like I was eating so much. I just scoffed [ate] so much food, and they were just laughing at me, you know. Sometimes I'd be looking at them, you know, wondering why they're laughing, you know, not knowing what I was doing. [Well, did they tell you why they were laughing eventually?] Yeah, yeah, I come back, "Hey, man, what's happening?" Like, you know, like I'd ask, "What's happening?" and all of a sudden I feel weird, you know. "Man, you're on you know. You're on pot [high on marihuana]." I said, "No, am I?" Like I don't know what's happening.

The learning may occur in more indirect ways:

I heard little remarks that were made by other people. Somebody said, "My legs are rubbery," and I can't remember all the remarks that were made because I was very attentively listening for all these cues for what I was supposed to feel like.

The novice, then, eager to have this feeling, picks up from other users some concrete referents of the term "high" and applies these notions to his own experience. The new concepts make it possible for him to locate these symptoms among his own sensations and to point out to himself a "something different" in his experience that he connects with drug use. It is only when he can do this that he is high. In the next case, the contrast between two successive experiences of a user makes clear the crucial importance of the awareness of the symptoms in being high and re-emphasizes the important role of interaction with other users in acquiring the concepts that make this awareness possible:

[Did you get high the first time you turned on?] Yeah, sure. Although, come to think of it, I guess I really didn't. I mean, like that first time it was more or less of a mild drunk. I was happy, I guess, you know what I mean. But I didn't really know I was high, you know what I mean. It was only after the second time I got high that I realized I was high the first time. Then I knew that something different was happening.

[How did you know that?] How did I know? If what happened to me that night would of happened to you, you would've known, believe me. We played the first tune for almost two hours—one tune! Imagine, man! We got on the stand and played this one tune, we started at nine o'clock. When we got finished I looked at my watch, it's a quarter to eleven. Almost two hours on one tune. And it didn't seem like anything. I mean, you know, it does that to you. It's like you have much more time or something. Anyway, when I saw that, man, it was too much. I knew I must really be high or something if anything

like that could happen. See, and then they explained to me that that's what it did to you, you had a different sense of time and everything. So I realized that that's what it was. I knew then. Like the first time, I probably felt that way, you know, but I didn't know what's happening.

It is only when the novice becomes able to get high in this sense that he will continue to use marihuana for pleasure. In every case in which use continued, the user had acquired the necessary concepts with which to express to himself the fact that he was experiencing new sensations caused by the drug. That is, for use to continue, it is necessary not only to use the drug so as to produce effects but also to learn to perceive these effects when they occur. In this way marihuana acquires meaning for the user as an object which can be used for pleasure.

With increasing experience the user develops a greater appreciation of the drug's effects; he continues to learn to get high. He examines succeeding experiences closely, looking for new effects, making sure the old ones are still there. Out of this there grows a stable set of categories for experiencing the drug's effects whose presence enables the user to get high with ease.

The ability to perceive the drug's effects must be maintained if use is to continue; if it is lost, marihuana use ceases. Two kinds of evidence support this statement. First, people who become heavy users of alcohol, barbiturates, or opiates do not continue to smoke marihuana, largely because they lose the ability to distinguish between its effects and those of the other drugs.[9] They no longer know whether the marihuana gets them high. Second, in those few cases in which an individual uses marihuana in such quantities that he is always high, he is apt to get this same feeling that the drug has no effect on him, since the essential element of a noticeable difference between feeling high and feeling normal is missing. In such a situation, use is likely to be given up completely, but temporarily, in order that the user may once again be able to perceive the difference.

III

One more step is necessary if the user who has now learned to get high is to continue use. He must learn to enjoy the effects he has just learned to experience. Marihuana—produced sensations are not automatically or necessarily pleasurable. The taste for such experience is a socially acquired one, not different in kind from acquired tastes for oysters or dry martinis. The user feels dizzy, thirsty; his scalp tingles; he misjudges time and distances; and so on. Are these things pleasurable? He isn't sure. If he is to continue marihuana use, he must decide that they are. Otherwise, getting high, while a real enough experience, will be an unpleasant one he would rather avoid.

The effects of the drug, when first perceived, may be physically unpleasant or at least ambiguous:

It started taking effect, and I didn't know what was happening, you know, what it was, and I was very sick. I walked around the room, walking around the room trying to get off, you know; it just scared me at first, you know. I wasn't used to that kind of feeling.

In addition, the novice's naive interpretation of what is happening to him may further confuse and frighten him, particularly if he decides, as many do, that he is going insane:

I felt I was insane, you know. Everything people done to me just wigged me. I couldn't hold a conversation, and my mind would be wandering, and I was always thinking, oh, I don't know, weird things, like hearing music different. . . . I get the feeling that I can't talk to anyone. I'll goof completely.

Given these typically frightening and unpleasant first experiences, the beginner will not continue use unless he learns to redefine the sensations as pleasurable:

It was offered to me, and I tried it. I'll tell you one thing. I never did enjoy it at all. I mean it was just nothing that I could enjoy. [Well, did you get high when you turned on?] Oh, yeah, I got definite feelings from it. But I didn't enjoy them. I mean I got plenty of reactions, but they were mostly reactions of fear. [You were frightened?] Yes, I didn't enjoy it. I couldn't seem to relax with it, you know. If you can't relax with a thing, you can't enjoy it, I don't think.

In other cases the first experiences were also definitely unpleasant, but the person did become a marihuana user. This occurred, however, only after a later experience enabled him to redefine the sensations as pleasurable:

[This man's first experience was extremely unpleasant, involving distortion of spatial relationships and sounds, violent thirst, and panic produced by these symptoms.] After the first time I didn't turn on for about, I'd say, ten months to a year. . . . It wasn't a moral thing; it was because I'd gotten so frightened, bein' so high. An' I didn't want to go through that again, I mean, my reaction was, "Well, if this is what they call bein' high, I don't dig [like] it." . . . So I didn't turn on for a year almost, accounta that. . . .

Well, my friends started, an' consequently I started again. But I didn't have any more, I didn't have that same initial reaction, after I started turning on again.

[In interaction with his friends he became able to find pleasure in the effects of the drug and eventually became a regular user.]

In no case will use continue without such a redefinition of the effects as enjoyable.

This redefinition occurs, typically, in interaction with more experienced users who, in a number of ways, teach the novice to find pleasure in this experience which is at first so frightening.[10] They may reassure him as to the temporary character of the unpleasant sensations and minimize their seriousness, at the same time calling attention to the more enjoyable aspects. An experienced user describes how he handles newcomers to marihuana use:

> Well, they get pretty high sometimes. The average person isn't ready for that, and it is a little frightening to them sometimes. I mean, they've been high on lush [alcohol], and they get higher that way than they've ever been before, and they don't know what's happening to them. Because they think they're going to keep going up, up, up till they lose their minds or begin doing weird things or something. You have to like reassure them, explain to them that they're not really flipping or anything, that they're gonna be all right. You have to just talk them out of being afraid. Keep talking to them, reassuring, telling them it's all right. And come on with your own story, you know: "The same thing happened to me. You'll get to like that after awhile." Keep coming on like that; pretty soon you talk them out of being scared. And besides they see you doing it and nothing horrible is happening to you, so that gives them more confidence.

The more experienced user may also teach the novice to regulate the amount he smokes more carefully, so as to avoid any severely uncomfortable symptoms while retaining the pleasant ones. Finally, he teaches the new user that he can "get to like it after awhile." He teaches him to regard those ambiguous experiences formerly defined as unpleasant as enjoyable. The older user in the following incident is a person whose tastes have shifted in this way, and his remarks have the effect of helping others to make a similar redefinition:

> A new user had her first experience of the effects of marihuana and became frightened and hysterical. She "felt like she was half in and half out of the room" and experienced a number of alarming physical symptoms. One of the more experienced users present said, "She's dragged because she's high like

that. I'd give anything to get that high myself. I haven't been that high in years."

In short, what was once frightening and distasteful becomes, after a taste for it is built up, pleasant, desired, and sought after. Enjoyment is introduced by the favorable definition of the experience that one acquires from others. Without this, use will not continue, for marihuana will not be for the user an object he can use for pleasure.

In addition to being a necessary step in becoming a user, this represents an important condition for continued use. It is quite common for experienced users suddenly to have an unpleasant or frightening experience, which they cannot define as pleasurable, either because they have used a larger amount of marihuana than usual or because it turns out to be a higher-quality marihuana than they expected. The user has sensations which go beyond any conception he has of what being high is and is in much the same situation as the novice, uncomfortable and frightened. He may blame it on an overdose and simply be more careful in the future. But he may make this the occasion for a rethinking of his attitude toward the drug and decide that it no longer can give him pleasure. When this occurs and is not followed by a redefinition of the drug as capable of producing pleasure, use will cease.

The likelihood of such a redefinition occurring depends on the degree of the individual's participation with other users. Where this participation is intensive, the individual is quickly talked out of his feeling against marihuana use. In the next case, on the other hand, the experience was very disturbing, and the aftermath of the incident cut the person's participation with other users to almost zero. Use stopped for three years and began again only when a combination of circumstances, important among which was a resumption of ties with users, made possible a redefinition of the nature of the drug:

IV

It was too much, like I only made about four pokes, and I couldn't even get it out of my mouth, I was so high, and I got real flipped. In the basement, you know, I just couldn't stay in there anymore. My heart was pounding real hard, you know, and I was going out of my mind; I thought I was losing my mind completely. So I cut out of this basement, and this other guy, he's out of his mind, told me, "Don't, don't leave me, man. Stay here." And I couldn't.

I walked outside, and it was five below zero, and I thought I was dying, and I had my coat open; I was sweating. I was perspiring. My whole insides were all . . . , and I walked about two blocks away, and I fainted behind a bush. I don't know how long I laid there. I woke up, and I was feeling the worst, I can't describe it at all, so I made it to a bowling alley, man, and I was trying to act normal, I was trying to shoot pool, you know, trying to act real normal, and I couldn't lay and I couldn't stand up and I couldn't sit down, and I went up and laid down where some guys that spot pins lay down, and that didn't help me, and I went down to a doctor's office. I was going to go in there and tell the doctor to put me out of my misery . . . because my heart was pounding so hard, you know. . . . So then all weekend I started flipping, seeing things there and going through hell, you know, all kinds of abnormal things. . . . I just quit for a long time then.

[He went to a doctor who defined the symptoms for him as those of a nervous breakdown caused by "nerves" and "worries." Although he was no longer using marihuana, he had some recurrences of the symptoms which led him to suspect that "it was all his nerves."] So I just stopped worrying, you know; so it was about thirty-six months later I started making it again. I'd just take a few pokes, you know. [He first resumed use in the company of the same user-friend with whom he had been involved in the original incident.]

A person, then, cannot begin to use marihuana for pleasure, or continue its use for pleasure, unless he learns to define its effects as enjoyable, unless it becomes and remains an object which he conceived of as capable of producing pleasure.

In summary, an individual will be able to use marihuana for pleasure only when he goes through a process of learning to conceive of it as an object which can be used in this way. No one becomes a user without (1) learning to smoke the drug in a way which will produce real effects; (2) learning to recognize the effects and connect them with drug use (learning, in other words, to get high); and (3) learning to enjoy the sensations he perceives. In the course of this process he develops a disposition or motivation to use marihuana which was not and could not have been present when he began use, for it involves and depends on conceptions of the drug which could only grow out of the kind of actual experience detailed above. On completion of this process he is willing and able to use marihuana for pleasure.

He has learned, in short, to answer "Yes" to the question: "Is it fun?" The direction his further use of the drug takes depends on his being able to continue to answer "Yes" to this question and, in addition, on his being able to answer "Yes" to other questions which arise as he becomes aware of the implications of the fact that the society as a whole disapproves of the practice: "Is it expedient?" "Is it moral?" Once he has acquired the ability to get enjoyment out of the drug, use will continue to be possible for him. Considerations of morality and expediency, occasioned by the reactions of society, may interfere and inhibit use, but use continues to be a possibility in terms of his conception of the drug. The act becomes impossible only when the ability to enjoy the experience of being high is lost, through a change in the user's conception of the drug occasioned by certain kinds of experience with it.

In comparing this theory with those which ascribe marihuana use to motives or predispositions rooted deep in individual behavior, the evidence makes it clear that marihuana use for pleasure can occur only when the process described above is undergone and cannot occur without it. This is apparently so without reference to the nature of the individual's personal makeup, or psychic problems. Such theories assume that people have stable modes of response which predetermine the way they will act in relation to any particular situation or object and that, when they come in contact with the given object or situation, they act in the way in which their makeup predisposes them.

This analysis of the genesis of marihuana use shows that the individuals who come in contact with a given object may respond to it at first in a great variety of ways. If a stable form of new behavior toward the object is to emerge, a transformation of meanings must occur, in which the person develops a new conception of the nature of the object.[11] This happens in a series of communicative acts in which others point out new aspects of his experience to him, present him with new interpretations of events, and help him achieve a new conceptual organization of his world, without which the new behavior is not possible. Persons who do not achieve the proper kind of conceptualization are unable to engage in the given behavior and turn off in the direction of some other relationship to the object or activity.

This suggests that behavior of any kind might fruitfully be studied developmentally, in terms of changes in meanings and concepts, their organization and reorganization, and the way they channel behavior, making some acts possible while excluding others.

Notes

1. See, as examples of this approach, the following: E. Marcovitz & H. J. Meyers (1944, December), "The marihuana addict in the army," *War Medicine, 6,* 382–391; H. S. Gaskill (1945, September), "Marihuana, an intoxicant," *American Journal of Psychiatry, 102,* 202–204; S. Charen & L. Perelman (1946, March), "Personality studies of marihuana addicts," *American Journal of Psychiatry, 102,* 674–682.

2. This approach stems from George Herbert Mead's (1934) discussion of objects in *Mind, self, and society,* Chicago: University of Chicago Press, pp. 277–280.

3. Cf. R. Adams (1942, November), "Marihuana," *Bulletin of the New York Academy of Medicine, 18,* 705–730.

4. Cf. L. Kolb (1938, July), "Marihuana," *Federal Probation, 2,* 22–25; and W. Bromberg (1939, July 1), "Marihuana: A psychiatric study," *Journal of the American Medical Association, 113,* 11.

5. The method used is that described in A. R. Lindesmith (1947), *Opiate addiction,* Bloomington, IN: Principia, chap. i. I would like also to acknowledge the important role Lindesmith's work played in shaping my thinking about the genesis of marihuana use.

6. Most of the interviews were done by the author. I am grateful to Solomon Kobrin and Harold Finestone for allowing me to make use of interviews done by them.

7. I hope to discuss elsewhere other stages in this natural history.

8. A pharmacologist notes that this ritual is in fact an extremely efficient way of getting the drug into the blood stream. R. P. Walton (1938), *Marihuana: America's new drug problem,* Philadelphia: J. B. Lippincott, p. 48.

9. "Smokers have repeatedly stated that the consumption of whiskey while smoking negates the potency of the drug. They find it very difficult to get 'high' while drinking whiskey and because of that smokers will not drink while using the 'weed.'" Cf. New York City Mayor's Committee on Marihuana (1944), *The marihuana problem in the city of New York,* Lancaster, PA: Jacques Cattel, p. 13.

10. Charen & Perelman (1946), p. 679.

11. Cf. A. Strauss (1952, June), "The development and transformation of monetary meanings in the child," *American Sociological Review, 17,* 275–286.

14

The Development of Feeling Norms Underlying Romantic Love Among Adolescent Females

Robin W. Simon

Donna Eder

Cathy Evans

(1992)

In American society, love is an important emotion (Cancian 1985, 1987; Cancian and Gordon 1988; Hochschild 1983a; Swidler 1980). Like other feelings, romantic love is a *social* sentiment, for which a cultural label and a set of ideological beliefs exist (Gordon 1981). Embodied in ideological beliefs about love are "feeling norms" which guide individuals' romantic feelings and behaviors.* (Hochschild 1979, 1983a). Feeling norms that underlie romantic love not only influence whether we should or should not love (Hochschild 1983a), but also help us identify the appropriate object of romantic feelings. Yet in spite of the importance attached to love in American culture, we know little about the content of the feeling norms that govern romantic love and the ways in which cultural knowledge about love is acquired socially. . . .

In this paper we discuss the content of feeling and expression norms underlying romantic love as they emerge in adolescent girls' peer culture. We also discuss the various ways in which feeling norms are communicated to group members. Although adolescent girls may obtain normative information about romantic feelings in other social relationships and in other social contexts—as well as through media such as romance novels, music, television, and films—the focus of this paper is limited to affective socialization processes among peers in school contexts because we do not have data on those other socialization agents. Peer groups, however, are an important source of emotional socialization because of the primacy of these groups to youths. In interaction with peers, young people draw on norms and beliefs that are available in the broader culture and make them meaningful by applying them to their everyday concerns and activities (Corsaro and Rizzo 1988; Mead 1934). By focusing on peer group socialization, we show that while adolescent girls are acquiring cultural knowledge about love, they also are creating and continuously negotiating feeling norms which pertain to the emergent concerns of their peer culture.

---

*Feeling norms are social norms that prescribe the appropriate intensity, duration, and target of emotions in social situations and relationships (Gordon 1981; Hochschild 1979).

DATA AND METHODS

We collected the data for this paper as part of an ethnographic study of adolescent socialization and peer interaction in a middle school. The school that was selected for the study was located in a medium-sized midwestern community. The school enrolls sixth-, seventh-, and eighth-grade students from a range of socioeconomic backgrounds, including youths from upper middle-class and lower working-class families. Most of the students were white, but a small number of black youths were enrolled at the school. The school was large, with approximately 250 students in each grade.

Data on peer interaction and relations were collected over a three-year period and involved a variety of methods, including participant observation, audio and audiovisual recording, and in-depth group interviews. Three female researchers observed a total of 10 female peer groups during lunch periods twice a week, over periods ranging from five to nine months. Three of these groups were studied for two years. . . .

At the beginning of the study, we told the students that we were interested in their lunchroom activities and conversations. Because we spent time with each group and avoided assuming any authority over the students, a high degree of rapport was established. Several weeks into the study, many students felt free to swear in front of us and often assured other students that we were "okay."

After observing groups for a minimum of three months, we made and transcribed audio and/or video recordings of conversations with eight of the groups. In addition, we conducted in-depth interviews on romance with the girls in two groups that had a strong interest in this topic. Field notes and transcriptions of naturally occurring conversations among these girls show that their views about romance were similar to those of girls in other groups that also had romantic interests. We coded each type of data for content relevant to the topic of romance. We conducted computer searches on the codes in order to identify all references to romance and feeling norms.

Data from interviews, recorded conversations, and field notes are employed in this paper. It is important to combine these various types of data to study thoroughly the development of feeling norms underlying romance. Data from in-depth interviews reveal the girls' current beliefs and norms about romantic love but fail to show how their knowledge is acquired through daily activities. For that purpose we turned to an examination of field notes and transcripts of naturally occurring conversations. These types of data are essential for identifying not only the content of feeling norms that underlie romantic love, but also the processes through which these norms are developed and conveyed in day-to-day interaction. Also, by examining daily speech activities we can examine how emotion norms and beliefs are reflected in actual discourse. Without this level of analysis, it is easy to assume greater conformity to emotion norms than actually exists. Finally, our analysis of field notes helps us identify certain feeling norms which are so taken for granted that they are no longer regarded as constraints.

Although data from all of the groups were analyzed for this paper, some groups of girls were more interested in romance and had more contact with boys than others. Among the girls who had romantic interests, relationships with boys varied considerably. In fact, at this school, the term "going together" was used widely by both girls and boys to refer to a variety of romantic relationships, ranging from those which lasted several months to those which lasted one or two days. In some cases, the girl and the boy spent their lunch period together; in others, the couple had minimal contact at school.* In most cases, the relationships

---

*Often the best friend of the girl and of the boy arranged these relationships by contracting the interested parties over the telephone, so that the couple might not have had much direct contact either before or after they started "going together."

were brief (less than two weeks) and were limited to some social contact at school, which sometimes included expressions of affection such as hand holding and kissing. . . .

FEELING NORMS UNDERLYING ROMANTIC LOVE IN ADOLESCENT FEMALE PEER CULTURE

We begin with the observation that romantic love was a frequent topic of conversation among the female students. By the seventh grade, most of the girls at the school had become concerned with romance and had begun to form relationships with boys. While the girls were obtaining normative information about romantic love, the feelings and behavior that group members considered appropriate were still in the process of negotiation. Some feeling norms were generally accepted; others were not shared by all group members. An examination of the girls' talk about romantic love revealed that they used a variety of discourse strategies to communicate normative information and clarify feeling norms.

Norm 1: Romantic relationships should be important, but not everything in life. Previous research shows that white adolescent females tend to embrace traditional feminine concerns of romance, marriage, and domesticity and to reject both academic and athletic values (Eder 1985; Griffin 1985; Kessler et al. 1985; Lever 1978; McRobbie 1978). Although romance was salient to most of the girls in this study, group members

had mixed attitudes about the importance of relationships with boys in relation to their other interests and activities. Some girls thought "they could not live without boys"; others believed that "learning about themselves and their school-work" was primary (interview, eighth-grade group, March 30, 1983). Concerns about the relative importance of romantic love required the development of a feeling norm among adolescent females.

One such norm that had begun to emerge in some peer groups was that romantic relationships should be important, but not everything in life. Many seventh-and eighth-grade girls agreed that relationships with boys were important. Group members, however, also were becoming critical of friends who were perceived as "boy-crazy," a term used by adolescents to describe girls who made boys their primary interest and activity. As the following two examples illustrate, this norm still was being negotiated when the girls were in the eighth grade.

In the first example, one group of girls debates the relative importance of romantic relationships. This exchange was part of an in-depth group interview about romance novels, which many eighth-grade girls liked to read. Ellen, Hanna, Natalie, Peg, and Tricia* had been discussing why they liked reading romance novels when the researcher asked them how important romantic love was to them. Ellen began by expressing her view that boys are the most important thing in her life, a view that runs counter to the emerging feeling norm.

---

*All names are pseudonyms. The following notations are used in the examples from transcripts:

( )   refers to an uncertain or unclear utterance or speaker;

(( )) refers to nonverbal behavior;

//   refers to the point at which the next speaker begins talking during someone else's turn;

/1/   first interruption; /2/ second interruption;

\#   refers to a brief pause.

1. Ellen:	Boys [are] the most important thing in my life. That's what I
2.	marked it on my value chart today.
3. Hanna:	Yes. I know.
4. Researcher:	Why? Why are boys the most important / / thing?
5. Hanna:	Boys, um (pleasure)
6. Ellen:	You can't live without 'em!
7. Natalie:	You can't live / / with 'em and you can't live without 'em!
8. Peg:	You can't live with 'em.
9. Ellen:	You can too.
10. Tricia:	That's / / a matter of opinion.
11. Ellen:	There is no way—there is no way a girl could live her
12.	whole life without a boy.
13. Tricia:	I can.
14. Ellen:	You can live your whole life without a boy?
15. Tricia:	Yeah. / / I'm not goin' to, though.
16. Peg:	Uh uh!
17. Ellen:	(be isolated) you never kissed one or nothin'.
18. Natalie:	Lesbies can.
19. Researcher:	That's true.
20. Tricia:	You wouldn't know, Natalie. ((laughing)) (interview, eighth grade, March 30).

In this example it is clear that group members had conflicting views about the relative importance of romance, and expressed their opinions openly. Yet even though the girls engaged in a normative debate, they expressed conflict in a playful, nonserious way. Rather than responding defensively to Ellen's question in Line 14, Tricia said teasingly that even though she could live without boys, she was not going to do so. In Line 18, Natalie's substitution of the word "lesbies" for lesbians contributes to the playfulness of this exchange.

Whereas normative debates often were carried out in a playful and joking manner, conflict exchanges over normative issues were sometimes quite serious. This was especially true when lighter disputes were unsuccessful at producing normative consensus, as in the next example. The following exchange was part of the same group interview. At this point Ellen not only had stated repeatedly that boys were her central interest, but also had been flirting with some boys at a nearby table.

1.	Researcher:	What about you, Tricia? How do you feel / / about it all?
2.	Peg:	Ellen, / / I'm only teasin', gosh! ((singsong voice))
3.	Tricia:	I feel the same way that Peg does. Especially now when
4.		we're just about to go into high school, our grades are more
5.		important than / / boys.
6.	Natalie:	See, we may be friends / / with them, but we're not sluts.
7.	Researcher:	Um hum, ((To Tricia))
8.	Hanna:	Will you repeat that, please? ((angry voice))
9.	Tricia:	No, /1/ you /2/ don't qualify.
10.	Natalie:	/1/ I know, but we're not sluts.
11.	Ellen:	/2/ ( ) fuck you (you guys))! ((Ellen stomps off, angry
12.		and upset)) (interview, eighth grade, March 30).

In both examples, the girls' openly expressed their conflicting views about the relative importance of romance and clarified this feeling norm to group members. In the second example, however, the conflict escalated and became more serious and more heated. Tricia and Peg became annoyed when the emerging norm was violated repeatedly, and engaged in confrontations when their friends' attitudes and behaviors did not match their expectations. In Lines 6 and 10, for example, Natalie accuses violators of this norm of being "sluts." Responses to norm violations are important ways in which group members develop and communicate knowledge about interpersonal and interactional norms (Eder and Sanford 1986; Mehan 1979). Although conflict was not resolved in either of these exchanges, the girls learned through these debates what their friends viewed as appropriate and inappropriate feeling and behavior with respect to this norm. Romantic love was a salient emotion for most of these girls, but several were concerned with setting some limits on its importance.

The Object of Romantic Feelings

According to Gordon (1981, p. 567), "sentiments," such as romantic love, are feelings that are "organized around a relationship to a social object, usually another person." While the girls were developing a norm about the relative importance of romance, they also were acquiring cultural knowledge about the object of romance. In fact, by the eighth grade, three norms concerning the object of romantic feelings had emerged.

Norm 2: One should have romantic feelings only for someone of the opposite sex. The most basic feeling norm concerning the object of romance was that one should have romantic feelings only for someone of the opposite sex. By the time they had become actively interested in romance, a norm of heterosexuality had developed in these groups of girls. In contrast to the previously discussed feeling norm, there was considerable consensus for this norm. In view of the general negative view of homosexuality at the school and the label attached to alleged norm violators, it is not surprising that this norm was widely accepted. We found that the girls used a variety of discourse strategies to clarify and reinforce the norm of heterosexuality to friends. The way in which this norm was communicated depended upon whether alleged norm violators were nongroup or group members.

One way in which the norm of heterosexuality was communicated was through gossip about nongroup members' deviant affect and behavior. Girls who did not express romantic interest in boys or who had gender-atypical interests often were the targets of gossip. For example, Sandy and Paula were discussing Sandy's sister in the sixth grade, who did not share their romantic interest in boys and who was interested in sports and in becoming a mechanic.

> Sandy said her sister is extremely different from her and has absolutely no interest in boys—she considers boys pests. Sandy referred to her sister as a tomboy. She said that since her sister is a tomboy, if she liked boys then she would be queer, but on the other hand, if she liked girls then she would really be queer. Then Paula added jokingly that if she didn't like anyone at all she would still be queer. I [researcher] said, "It sounds like she doesn't have a chance" (field notes, seventh grade, May 24).

This example shows that Sandy and Paula were reinforcing a feeling norm of which they had only limited understanding. Girls at this school were establishing violations of the norm of heterosexuality on the basis of gender-inappropriate behavior. Sandy's sister's outward disinterest in boys as well as her nontraditional interests and behaviors were considered by these group members to be deviant with regard to the norm of heterosexuality. Yet, by establishing violations of this norm on the basis of nonstereotypical gender-role behavior, the girls were reinforcing and reproducing existing gender norms that ultimately constrain their own behavior.

In general, it was not uncommon for girls and boys who were not actively pursuing romantic relationships or who routinely engaged in gender-inappropriate behavior to be labeled homosexual. In fact, children at the school who were perceived

to be deviant in other ways were the objects of these allegations as well (Evans and Eder 1989). Unpopular students who were viewed as unattractive and/or unintelligent also were singled out for group discussions in which they were accused indirectly of being homosexual.

> Annie said, "I'm gonna beat that girl up someday," referring to twins and a little chubby girl in a green sweater who were sitting at the middle of the table pretty far down. So we all turned to look at her and Marsha agreed that she was really disgusting, that "they're gay" (field notes, seventh grade, February 3).

Rather than relying on the display of romantic feelings toward someone of the same sex as an indication of affective deviance, Annie and Marsha accused these girls of being "gay" solely on the basis of physical appearance.

A second way in which the norm of heterosexuality was communicated was by teasing group members. Humor often was used when the girls confronted their friends about norm violations. Group members frequently teased one another about behaviors that could be interpreted as homosexual, such as close physical contact between friends. Although many girls still viewed close physical contact between friends as acceptable, others were beginning to redefine such expressions of affection as inappropriate.

> The little girl with glasses came over and actually sat on Andrea's lap. She's so tiny that she can do this easily, and Andrea laughed and said, "You're really not my type" (field notes, sixth grade, May 20).

Not only did the girls tease one another about overt expressions of affection, they also chided one another about their actual feelings. Statements concerning both positive and negative affect for females were a frequent source of group humor.

> . . . they were talking about why would somebody like this particular girl. Debby said, "I wouldn't like

her!" Melinda said, "Well, I should *hope* not" (field notes, eighth grade, April 20).

In addition to teasing one another about their feelings and behaviors, group members also chided each other about their best-friend relationships. In fact, adolescence is a period in which female friendships are faced with a dilemma. Even while intimate feelings between close friends usually deepen, girls routinely tease one another about the romantic implications of these relationships.

> Julie said something about how Bonnie and somebody were considered her best mates. Right away Mia said, "Ooooh . . ." as this sort of implied that they were gay. Hillary picked up on that and went "Ooooh!" (field notes, eighth grade, April 9).

The final way in which the norm of heterosexuality was communicated was through self-denial. Self-denials often were used to clarify the nature of intimate female friendships. Although many girls at the school continued to have strong positive feelings for their female friends, verbal and behavioral expressions of affection frequently were followed by a disclaimer. In light of the pressures for heterosexuality from peers and the seriousness of norm violations, it is not surprising that many girls at the school became quite concerned that their own feelings and behaviors towards their close friends might be perceived by others as homosexual.

> Sally was really talkative today, and it was interesting to see her being so talkative. She was going on and on about how somebody would sign her letters "love you queerly." She said, "I always sign my letters 'love you dearly, but not queerly.'" But then she was joking, saying, "I didn't know what that meant," until Mary explained it to her. Then they were joking about how innocent she was and didn't even know what "queer" meant (field notes, seventh grade, March 3).

Whereas self-denials often were humorous, denials of affective deviance with respect to the norm of heterosexuality sometimes were quite serious. The girls were especially self-conscious about expressions of affection that were overt and

therefore readily observable. They were concerned that nongroup members would misinterpret these visible signs of affection as romantic.

> Alice told me that she had taken a bunch of photographs recently. She said it was embarrassing because most of the pictures were taken when people happened to be hugging and kissing each other, and that she hoped she got hold of the pictures before her mother did when they got back from being developed. She said, for example, "Natalie and another girl were hugging each other in friendship" (which meant that she wanted me to know that that was differentiated from a romantic hug) (field notes, eighth grade, February 7).

Not only was Alice embarrassed by the hugging and kissing in the photographs, but she also was concerned that if her mother saw the pictures, she might interpret these actions as homosexual. By distinguishing between a "friendship" hug and a "romantic" hug, however, Alice clarified both to herself and to the researcher that this behavior was within the realm of acceptable conduct.

Overall the norm of heterosexuality was communicated among adolescent females through gossip, teasing, and self-denials. In these discussions, group members collectively explored what does and does not constitute homosexual feeling and behavior in order to develop an understanding of this feeling norm and of norm violations. Through these discussions, however, the girls not only expressed their own homophobic concerns but also supported and maintained the broader cultural norm of heterosexuality. Many girls at the school continued to value intimate relationships with females; nevertheless they upheld and reproduced what Rich (1980) called "the norm of compulsory heterosexuality."

Norm 3: One should not have romantic feelings for a boy who is already attached. Another feeling norm that had emerged in regard to the object of romance was that one should not have romantic feelings for a boy who is already attached. A corollary of this norm was that if one had such feelings, they should not be expressed. In most groups, the development of this norm was a direct response to changes in group members' romantic activities. The norm of exclusivity had only minimal relevance during an earlier phase, when the girls were first becoming interested in romance, but this norm had become highly salient by the time they began to form relationships with boys.

Early in the seventh grade, most of the girls talked about the boys they liked,* but often were shy about letting boys know their feelings. As long as romantic activities consisted of only talking about the objects of their affection, the norm of exclusivity had little significance. In fact, during this stage in the development of their romantic activities, it was not uncommon for many group members to like the same boy. Just as they might have other interests in common, sharing a romantic interest in a particular boy was considered to be acceptable, if not appropriate.

Interestingly enough, Marsha and Josephine talked about how they both liked this guy Jack. They pointed him out to me and I [researcher] said, "Oh, oh, you both like the same guy?" They said, "Oh yeah, it's okay. We can do that. We always like the same people, but we don't get mad at each other" (field notes, seventh grade, March 30).

In an interview with another group of seventh-grade girls, it became clear that the distinction between *liking* and *going with* the same boy is important. The former is permissible; the latter is not.

1.	Carrie:	They can like, like, like as much as they want, buy they
2.		don't / / (go)
3.	Marla:	They don't two-time!
4.	Researcher:	But what?
5.	Carrie:	They can like a person as much as they want.
6.	Researcher:	Can two friends *go* together / / with the same boy?
7.	(Alice):	Oh, they don't have any choice / / (they)
8.	Carrie:	No.
9.	Bonnie:	No (interview, seventh grade, May 24).

Throughout this year, many girls began to pursue boys openly and to make their feelings more public, often through a friend who served as an intermediary. Once a group member had acted openly on her feelings and formed a relationship with a boy, it was no longer acceptable for other girls either to have or to express romantic feelings for him. At this point in the development of their romantic activities, the norm of exclusivity had become highly salient, and violations began to be perceived as a serious threat. Most of the girls became concerned about violations; they were resentful and jealous of those who did not abide by the norm of exclusivity.

Gossip was one way in which the girls clarified and reinforced this norm. In the following example from a seventh-grade interview, Natalie is accusing Rhoda, an attractive group member, of flirting with her and Tricia's boyfriends.

---

*Although Zick Rubin's (1970, 1973) research shows that "liking" and "loving" are distinct emotional states, the girls in this study used these emotion words interchangeably, especially when referring to their romantic feelings for boys.

1.	Natalie:	Rhoda, every time I get a boyfriend or Tricia gets a boyfriend
2.		# or or we like somebody, she starts # y'know messing around
3.		with him and everything and # y'know—and everything, she
4.		shows her ass off and so, they start *likin'* her, right? And she
5.		did that, she was trying to do that to Sammy Jones #
6.		Tricia's boyfriend # ya know, the one that broke up with her
7.		after four months (interview, seventh grade, May 24).

Although gossip episodes such as this do not inform norm violators about the deviant nature of their behavior, they communicate normative information to other group members (Eder and Enke 1988; Fine 1986; Goodwin 1980).

The girls considered it inappropriate to have or express romantic feelings not only for a boy who was involved with someone else, but also for a boy whom a group member was in the process of pursuing. Group members sometimes engaged in confrontations with alleged norm violators in order to communicate their inappropriate behavior and affect. In the next exchange, several members of a seventh-grade group directly accuse Carol of flirting with Ted, a boy Betty is pursuing but not currently going with. Although Carol argues initially that she has not done anything wrong, later she agrees to be an intermediary for Betty in order to resolve the dispute.

1.	Mary:	Ted came up to Carol and said she—that he loved her.
2.	Linda:	Who?
3.	Betty:	*Carol!*
4.	Carol:	What?
5.	Betty:	I don't like you no more.
6.	Carol:	What'd I do?
7.	Linda:	Taking Betty's boyfriend.
8.	Carol:	I didn't either! ((pounds table as she half laughs))
9.	Mary:	It wasn't Carol's *fault*, though.
10.	Betty:	*Yes it was!* She *flirts!*
11.	Carol:	I was just walking there / / ( ).
12.	Betty:	You *flirt*. You *flirt*. Yes, you / /
13.	Carol:	I didn't even do nothing. ((laughter))

(Continued)

(Continued)

14.	Betty:	You *flirt*, Carol! You're mean! I don't like you no more.
15.	Carol:	You won't (mind me) after I get done talking # *if* you still
16.		want me to.
17.	Betty:	Huh?
18.	Carol:	If you—do you want me to still talk to him? / / ((Betty
19.		nods)) Alright, shut up. God.
20.	Nancy:	Hell, she called me up, she goes, "Nancy, call Ted and talk to
21.		him."
22.	Betty:	(I sank you) ((silly voice)) (taped conversation, seventh grade, May 5).

This example is interesting because it shows that these girls expect their friends to know not only with whom they are going, but also their *intentions* to become romantically involved with certain boys. Acceptable contact with these boys is limited to behavior that will promote their friends' romantic interests (e.g., serving as intermediaries), and excludes any friendly behavior that might encourage romantic feelings to develop. As shown in the previous example, such behavior makes a girl subject to the negative label "flirt."* It is also noteworthy that group members use confrontations such as this to sanction inappropriate behavior and affect. Because violations of the norm of exclusivity have serious consequences for group members, including the possibility of being in competition with friends over boys, it is not surprising that confrontations sometimes are used to clarify and reinforce this norm.

Although most group members increasingly saw the need for the norm of exclusivity to protect themselves from unpleasant feelings of jealousy, some girls were reluctant to give up the freedom to have or express romantic feelings whenever they desired. Because norm violations were viewed as serious, girls who continued to defy this norm occasionally engaged in playful modes of interaction whereby they could express their "deviant" feelings while acknowledging the norm of exclusivity.

For example, several seventh-grade girls were teasing Mary about "liking" Wally and dragged her over to the ball diamond, where Wally was playing softball. The teasing consisted of trying to get Mary to talk with him and telling Wally that Mary wanted to "go in the stairwell" with him. Mary refused to talk to Wally. This reaction led to some joking exchanges among the other group members, several of whom also had romantic feelings for Wally.

---

*The label "flirt" has a double meaning among adolescent females. Whereas the term sometimes is used to describe girls who express romantic feelings toward a group member's boyfriend, it is also used to describe girls who express romantic feelings for more than one boy. In the previous example, the girls used it in the former sense. Like the labels "gay" and "slut," the girls also use the label "flirt" to refer to an emotional social type. Emotional social types are persons who routinely violate emotion norms and who serve as examples in correcting young people's feeling and/or expression. See Gordon (1989) for a discussion of the functions of the emotional social type in childhood emotional socialization.

1.	Carol:	I'll take him if you don't.
2.	Elaine:	Whoo! You hear that one, Wally?
3.	Carol:	Well, I don't care.
4.	Elaine:	Wally, Wally, Wally, Wally. She says she'll take
5.		ya if Mary don't want ya. ((Unrelated talk for
6.		five turns.))
7.	Elaine:	She said she'd take ya if Mary don't want ya.
8.	Mary:	What'd you tell him Elaine? Elaine / / ( )
9.	Linda:	Hey you! If Mary don't want ya and Carol don't
10.		want ya, I'll take ya!
11.	Carol:	Uh uh, I will. I'll take him if Mary don't and
12.		then if I don't, you do (taped conversation, seventh grade, April 7).

Here the girls use playful teasing to inform Wally of their romantic feelings, while acknowledging at the same time that they will wait to act on these feelings until Mary no longer "wants" him. The joking nature of this exchange provides these girls with more freedom to express their feelings for Wally and thus to violate the norm of exclusivity.*

This finding suggests that feeling and expression norms do not determine adolescent girls' affect and behavior, but serve as an important cultural resource which is incorporated into their action. Through expressing their knowledge of this norm, in fact, these girls succeed in expressing their feelings for a boy who is being pursued by a friend. At the same time, their ability to transform cultural knowledge into a playful frame gives them an opportunity to violate the norm without negative sanctions.

In brief, when group members began to pursue boys and form romantic relationships, the girls developed the norm of exclusivity to deal with their new concerns. They communicated this norm through gossip and confrontations as well as in more playful modes of discourse. Yet even

though norm violations were viewed negatively by most of the girls, several group members did not feel compelled to abide by this norm. Instead they responded with "resistance" by continuing to hold and express romantic feelings for boys who were already "taken." In some cases their resistance was communicated through playful teasing, which allowed them to express their normatively inappropriate feelings while simultaneously showing their awareness of the norm of exclusivity.

Norm 4: One should have romantic feelings for only one boy at a time. The third feeling norm pertaining to the object of romance was that one should have romantic feelings for only one boy at a time. A corollary was that if one had romantic feelings for more than one boy, these feelings should not be expressed. In some groups, the development of the norm of monogamy reflected the girls' awareness of the societal norm of monogamy. In other groups, however, this norm was developed to deal with the problems created by having multiple boyfriends.

For example, when we asked one group of seventh-grade girls about the possibility of going

---

*Although an alternative interpretation of this exchange is that the girls actually are supporting Mary's romantic interest rather than violating the norm of exclusivity, ethnographic data on these girls show that several of them in fact had romantic feelings for Wally. Because Mary was somewhat overweight, the girls did not take her interest in him seriously.

with more than one person at a time, the reason they gave for avoiding this behavior was the likelihood of creating jealousy among boyfriends. Because jealousy and other forms of conflict among males were expressed frequently in physical fights, the consequences of creating jealousy were considered to be quite serious.

> I asked if you could only go with one person at a time and she said, "It depends on who you're talking about." She said that you should only go with one at a time but that some girls went with more than one. I asked why they shouldn't do that, and she said because "then you get a couple of jealous boyfriends on your hands" and they might end up getting into a fight, and that it was best to avoid that (field notes, seventh grade, April 27).

Some girls continued to have multiple boyfriends, but were careful to become involved only with boys who were separated geographically. As long as a boy was unaware of his girlfriend's other romantic involvements, jealousy and its negative consequences could be avoided. For some of these girls, in fact, having multiple boyfriends was a source of status—something they bragged about to their female friends.

> Effie and Laura had a long conversation. Laura told Effie that she was going with two guys, one from Royalton and another from California. She said that they were both going to be coming down this summer and she didn't know what to do. She presented this as a dilemma, but she was laughing about it. She really wanted to show that she was popular with boys (field notes, eighth grade, April 6).

Although some groups developed the norm of monogamy to deal with the practical problems associated with having multiple boyfriends, in other groups the development of this norm reflected group members' knowledge of the cultural norm of monogamy. When we asked one group of seventh-grade girls whether two people could go with the same boy, their response turned to the inappropriateness of having multiple romantic partners.

1.	Researcher:	How come two people can't go with the same boy at the same
2.		time? It seems like you could logi—
3.	Ellen:	Because you're only supposed to—when you go with a person
4.		like if you
5.	Natalie:	It's like a bigamist.
6.	Ellen:	Oh . . .
7.	Natalie:	You know, when you
8.	Ellen:	Like a what?
9.	Natalie:	A bigamist. Like when you go with somebody. Like it's, it's
10.	Ellen:	Two-timing.
11.	Natalie:	When you go with each other the same—when you go with each
12.		other it's kinda like gettin' married or somethin', you
13.		know, and like if you're goin' with two people at the same
14.		time it's like a bigamist.
15.	Ellen:	Like Natalie did!
16.	Natalie:	Yeah, I did that once.
17.	Ellen:	Yeah, with Steve and Robert.
18.	Natalie:	I did it twice. ((Natalie and Ellen burst out laughing)) (interview, seventh grade, May 24).

This example illustrates that the girls are drawing on their knowledge of the societal norm of monogamy (which pertains to marriage) in order to develop a feeling norm regarding multiple partners which is relevant to their own romantic relationships. The exchange also shows that even though these girls agreed that it was inappropriate to have romantic feelings for more than one boy at a time, violations of this norm were not perceived as serious.

By the time these girls were in eighth grade, however, having romantic feelings for more than one boy was no longer viewed as acceptable. Moreover, they used different strategies to clarify this norm and to sanction deviant affect and behavior. In the following exchange, Ellen and Hanna are telling the other girls about what happened at church the night before. Because Ellen is already going with Craig, she is first accused and later reprimanded for going to church solely to meet other boys.

1.	Ellen:	We were sittin' there startin' at guys at church last night,
2.		me and Hanna were, and—
3.	Hanna:	And she saw one that looked just like Craig.
4.	Natalie:	But # / / I was—
5.	Ellen:	I wasn't starin' at him.
6.	Hanna:	That was groaty.
7.	(Natalie:)	You're going with Craig.
8.	Ellen:	I know. I stared at Steve. ((laughs))
9.	Hanna:	I know, but he looks like him in the face,
10.	Natalie:	But, um, he just—
11.	Peg:	You / / go to church for a different reason than that, Ellen!
12.	Natalie:	I / / get stuck on one guy.
13.	Peg:	Then you shouldn't of been there (interview, eighth grade, March 30).

Although Peg and Natalie considered this violation to be serious, Ellen continued to view it as humorous, laughing as she acknowledged that she "stared" at another boy. Given Ellen's reluctance to consider the seriousness of her violation, Peg and Natalie used more confrontive strategies to inform her about the inappropriateness of her affect and behavior with respect to this norm.

As girls begin to take this norm seriously, they need to become more aware of their romantic feelings. They may even begin to modify their emotions on certain occasions, changing romantic attractions to nonromantic feelings in order to avoid norm violations. Sometimes the girls explicitly discussed their feelings toward boys, thus showing their close monitoring of these feelings. Awareness of romantic feelings was especially important during times of transition from one boyfriend to another. Because "going together" arrangements typically lasted less than two weeks, these transitions were frequent.

Gwen and Ellen went "cruising" with some boys over the weekend. The boy Gwen was with asked her to go with him but he broke up with her the next morning because another boy that Gwen went with last week threatened to beat him up. So then the other boy asked her back with him Monday morning and she's going with him again now. She said that "one thing I can say for certain is that I love (the boy she's going with), but I can also say for certain that I really like (the boy she went with on Saturday)" (field notes, eighth grade, March 30).

Through Gwen's claim that she "loves" the boy she is currently going with and "likes" the boy she went with on Saturday, her feelings appear to conform with the norm of monogamy. Although it is not clear whether her current feelings are the result of emotion (or expression) work, it is clear that she pays close attention to her feelings and can discuss them with "certainty."

Other girls expressed more confusion about their emotions. In some cases, their confusion stemmed from the discrepancy between their *actual* feelings and the feelings they thought they *ought* to have. Even though they knew that they *should* have romantic feelings for only one boy at a time, girls sometimes found themselves feeling multiple attractions.

I heard Karla being teased when a specific boy walked by. Her friends were saying that she had a crush on him and once they yelled it at the boy. Karla acted rather embarrassed and angry about this. When they yelled at the boy, they asked Karla if it was true that she liked him. Karla said that she did like him "for a friend." They said that they had seen her walking with him in the halls. After a long pause Karla asked Laura rather indignantly, "How could I like him when I'm already going with somebody?" Effie said, "Two-timing." Karla was embarrassed and seemed rather mild in her denial (field notes, eighth grade, April 21).

Karla's feelings are creating some discomfort for her because they do not conform readily to this feeling norm. She claims that she likes the other boy only "for a friend," but she expresses embarrassment as well as anger toward her friends, who perceive it to be a stronger attraction. Although we do not know whether Karla subsequently modified her feelings and/or expressions toward this boy, emotion work might be necessary in situations such as this, if girls are to abide by the norm of monogamy.

Norm 5: One should always be in love. The final feeling norm emerged was that one should always be in love. This norm differed from those discussed previously in that it was not devised to deal with group concerns, but was developed largely to deal with the concerns of individuals. Whereas violations of most feeling norms had consequences for other group members and peers (e.g., the norms of heterosexuality, exclusivity, and monogamy), violations of this final norm had consequences only for individual girls. Because such violations did not affect others, this norm was held even less widely than those discussed previously. For many girls at the school, however, this emotion norm was a basic part of their knowledge and understanding of romantic love.

For some girls, the onset of their first romantic attraction was the beginning of a continuous state of being in love, often with frequent changes in the object of their feelings. In fact, simply having romantic feelings may have been more important than the actual boys to whom these feelings were directed. For example, a researcher noticed that a girl had "I love" written on her hand and asked her about it. Although this girl's romantic feelings had no particular target, she explained that she was ready to add the name of a boy as soon as a suitable target was found.

The importance of always being in love became particularly evident when relationships with boys ended. For instance, when girls realized that a boy they had been going with now liked someone else, they often redirected their romantic feelings toward someone new.

> She said that she was just going to go up and ask him if he had any intention of going with her again, and if he didn't, she was just "going to have to find someone else." I don't think she has the concept in her mind that she could possibly not be involved with anyone (field notes, eighth grade, March 23).

The salience of this norm was related to the duration of adolescent romantic relationships. Although it might seem that "long-term" relationships would be preferred because girls would not continually have to seek out new boyfriends, some girls reported that being in a long-term relationship was a disadvantage because it took them out of circulation.

> Apparently Alice's boyfriend broke up with her today and she was unhappy. She saw him walk by the media center and called to him several times, but he ignored her purposely. She said that the worst of it was that she had gone with him several months, and during that time had progressively cut herself off from contact with other boys so that she didn't even have any male friends left (field notes, eighth grade, March 4).

Within four days Alice had a new boyfriend, but her comments show that replacing her old boyfriend was an important concern.

During the early stage in the development of their romantic activities, when the girls were beginning to have romantic feelings but did not act on them, all group members could adhere easily to this norm. Once they started to form romantic relationships, however, only the girls who were popular with boys could continually attract new boyfriends. In fact, the status associated with being popular with boys contributed to the salience of this norm among the girls at this school. At the same time, group members also had a hand in reinforcing this feeling norm.

> When Nancy came up she asked "Who do you like now, Carol?," a question which Nancy often asks Carol. Carol said, "Pete." Nancy said, "Oh yeah." Shortly after that Linda said, "Guess who Pete likes?" Betty said, "Carol." Nancy said, "God, you guys get everything you want" (field notes, seventh grade, April 14).

Even though less popular girls could not attract new boyfriends so easily, nevertheless they were able to abide by this norm. One strategy commonly used by these as well as by the more popular girls was to "recycle" the boys with whom they had had a previous relationship.

1.	Ellen:	And then she went with George and then she went to likin' Tom
2.		again.
3.	Natalie:	Yeah. ((pause)) But sometimes it kinda switches on and off, like
4.		s—like you'll like one boy and then you'll get tired of 'im and
5.		you go with somebody else and then you'll like him again. Like
6.		with Bryan and Dale. I used to do that a lot (interview, seventh grade, May 24).

Natalie's comments suggest that her and her friends' feelings for former boyfriends sometimes are recreated for the purpose of conforming to this norm. Natalie's comments also imply that conformity is likely to result in emotion work on the part of these girls, who sometimes evoke romantic feelings for boys they were previously "tired of."

The advantages of conforming to this norm include appearing to be popular with boys as well as providing ongoing evidence of a heterosexual orientation; both are important concerns to girls at this age. At the same time, however, conformity carries several possible costs. One such cost is that emotion work may be necessary in order to always be in love. Although we can only speculate at this point, adolescent girls sometimes may create romantic feelings for boys to whom they are not attracted so they can conform to this norm. Hochschild (1983b) argued that when insincere feelings are created routinely, people lose touch with their actual feelings. Insofar as girls have insincere feelings, it is possible that eventually they will have difficulty in distinguishing between their "real" romantic feelings and their less authentic feelings, which they created in order to satisfy the requirements of this norm.

A second potential cost stems from the dilemma faced by adolescent females as a result of their adherence to this norm. On the one hand, girls consider being continuously in love as socially desirable because it is a way to reaffirm their popularity with boys and thus to increase their own status in relation to other females. On the other hand, group members who both attract too much attention from males and appear to be indiscriminate in their choice of romantic partners are often criticized by their friends for being "sluts," and ultimately are viewed in a negative manner.

DISCUSSION

In this paper we argue that adolescence is a period during which females acquire cultural knowledge about romantic love, including the social norms that guide romantic feelings. In addition to obtaining normative information about romance, we found that the girls in this study had developed several feeling and expression norms to deal with their own concerns about romantic love. By the seventh and eighth grade, norms concerning the relative importance of romantic relationships as well as the appropriate object of romantic feelings had emerged in these groups of friends. Whereas some of these norms were highly developed and generally accepted (e.g., the norms of heterosexuality, exclusivity, and monogamy), others were not held by all group members and still were being negotiated (e.g., the norm concerning the relative importance of romantic relationships).

We also found that adolescent girls used a variety of discourse strategies to communicate normative information and to reinforce emotion norms to friends. In general, group members informed one another about feeling and expression norms through light and playful language activities, as well as through serious and confrontive modes of discourse. Language that involved humor was one of the more common discourse strategies used by these girls. Through joking and teasing remarks, group members could point out their friends' norm violations in an indirect, nonthreatening manner. Moreover, teasing and joking were ways in which the girls could show their awareness of feeling norms while simultaneously expressing their own normatively inappropriate emotions.

The girls also commonly used gossip and confrontations to clarify and reinforce feeling norms. Although gossip did not directly inform norm violators of their inappropriate affect and behavior, it provided normative information to other group members. Finally, confrontations sometimes were used when indirect strategies were ineffective at producing normative consensus and when norm violations had negative consequences for group members. In these exchanges, girls expressed social disapproval of affective deviance through accusations, insults, and reprimands. Not surprisingly, such exchanges often involved considerable conflict and tension. Overall, through these various language activities and modes of discourse, the girls conveyed what they viewed as appropriate and inappropriate in regard to the group's feeling and expression norms.

Even though girls obtain normative information about romantic love from friends, they do not always abide by emotion norms. Rather, our analysis of discourse revealed that group members sometimes responded with "resistance" and intentionally defied their group's feeling and expression norms. Therefore, feeling and expression norms underlying romantic love constrain but do not determine adolescent females' affect and behavior. Further research is necessary to determine the degree to which girls resist other emotion norms, as well as to identify the full range of emotion management processes used by adolescent females.

Romance is highly salient, however, because having a boyfriend enhances girls' popularity with peers at an age when being popular is important for their self-image. In fact, two norms that emerged in these peer groups reveal the salience of romance to girls during this period: the norms concerning the relative importance of romantic relationships and the importance of being in love continually. It is possible that even after romantic relationships become tied less closely to peer group status, females continue to feel that they always should be in a romantic relationship with a male in order to validate their attractiveness and worth to self and to others.

Although it was not our purpose to examine the actual emotional experiences of adolescent girls, our findings support the view that emotions are in part socially constructed and that feeling and expression are subject to normative influences. By focusing on romantic socialization in adolescent peer groups, we have shown how, in everyday interaction with friends, females obtain normative information about romantic feelings as well as maintaining, reproducing, and recreating one aspect of their society's emotion culture. . . .

REFERENCES

Berger, Peter L., and Thomas Luckman. 1967. *The Social Construction of Reality: A Treatise in the Sociology of Knowledge.* New York: Anchor.

Cancian, Francesca M. 1985. "Gender Politics: Love and Power in the Private and Public Spheres." Pp. 253–264 in *Gender and the Life Course,* edited by Alice S. Rossi. New York: Aldine.

_____. 1987. *Love in America: Gender and Self Development.* Boston: Cambridge University Press.

Cancian, Francesca M., and Steven L. Gordon. 1988. "Changing Emotion Norms in Marriage: Love and Anger in U.S. Women's Magazines since 1900." *Gender and Society* 2(3):308–342.

Cantor, Muriel. 1987. "Popular Culture and the Portrayal of Women: Content and Control." Pp. 190–214 in *Analyzing Gender,* edited by Beth Hess and Myra Marx Ferree. New York: Sage.

Clark, Candice. 1987. "Sympathy Biography and Sympathy Margin." *American Journal of Sociology* 93:290–321.

Corsaro, William A., and Thomas A. Rizzo. 1988. "Discussione and Friendship: Socialization Processes in the Peer Culture of Italian Nursery School Children." *American Sociological Review* 53:879–894.

Eder, Donna. 1985. "The Cycle of Popularity: Interpersonal Relations Among Female Adolescents." *Sociology of Education* 58:154–165.

———. 1988. "Teasing Activities among Adolescent Females." Paper presented at conference "Gender Roles through the Life Span," Ball State University, Muncie, IN.

Eder, Donna, and Janet Enke. 1988. "Gossip as a Means of Strengthening Social Bonds." Paper presented at the annual meeting of the American Sociological Association, Atlanta.

Eder, Donna, and Stephanie Sanford. 1986. "The Development and Maintenance of Interactional Norms among Early Adolescents." *Sociological Studies of Child Development* 1:283–300.

Evans, Cathy, and Donna Eder. 1989. "'No Exit': Processes of Social Isolation in the Middle School." Paper preented at the annual meeting of the American Sociological Association, San Francisco.

Fine, Gary Alan. 1986. "The Social Organization of Adolescent Gossip: The Rhetoric of Moral Evaluation." Pp. 405–423 in *Children's Worlds and Children's Language,* edited by Jenny Cook-Gumperz, William Corsaro, and Jurgen Streeck. Berlin: Moulin.

Goodwin, Marjorie H. 1980. "He-Said-She-Said: Formal Cultural Procedures for the Construction of a Gossip Dispute Activity." *American Ethnologist* 7:674–695.

Gordon, Steven L. 1981. "The Sociology of Sentiments and Emotion." Pp. 562–592 in *Social Psychology: Sociological Perspectives,* edited by Morris Rosenberg and Ralph H. Turner. New York: Basic Books.

———. 1989. "The Socialization of Children's Emotions: Emotional Culture, Competence, and Exposure." Pp. 319–349 in *Children's Understanding of Emotion,* edited by Carolyn Saarni and Paul Harris. New York: Cambridge University Press.

Griffin, Christine. 1985. *Typical Girls?: Young Women from School to Job Market.* London: Routledge and Kegan Paul.

Harris, Paul, and Tjeert Olthof. 1982. "The Child's Concept of Emotion." Pp. 188–209 in *Social Cognition: Studies of the Development of Understanding,* edited by George Butterworth and Paul Light. Chicago: University of Chicago Press.

Hochschild, Arlie R. 1979. "Emotion Work, Feeling Rules, and Social Structure." *American Journal of Sociology* 85(3):551–575.

———. 1983a. "Attending to, Codifying and Managing Feelings: Sex Differences in Love." Pp. 250–262 in *Feminist Frontiers: Rethinking Sex, Gender, and Society,* edited by Laurel Richardson and Verta Taylor. New York: Addison-Wesley.

———. 1983b. *The Managed Heart: Commercialization of Human Feeling.* Berkeley: University of California Press.

Holland, Dorothy, and Margaret Eisenhart. 1990. *Educated in Romance: Women, Achievement, and College Culture,* Chicago: University of Chicago Press.

Kessler, S., D. Ashenden, R. Connell, and G. Dowsett. 1985. "Gender Relations in Secondary Schooling." *Sociology of Education* 58:34–47.

Lees, Sue. 1986. *Sexuality and Adolescent Girls.* London: Hutchinson.

Lever, Janet. 1978. "Sex Differences in the Complexity of Children's Play and Games." *American Sociological Review* 43:471–483.

Lofland, Lyn H. 1985. "The Social Shaping of Emotion: Grief in Historical Perspective." *Symbolic Interaction* 8:171–190.

McRobbie, Angela. 1978. "Working Class Girls and the Culture of Femininity." Pp. 96–108 in *Women Take Issue,* edited by The Women's Study Group, Centre for Contemporary Cultural Studies. London: Hutchinson.

Mead, George Herbert. 1934. *Mind, Self, and Society.* Chicago: University of Chicago Press.

Mehan, Hugh. 1979. *Learning Lessons: Social Organization in the Classroom.* Cambridge, MA: Harvard University Press.

Rich, Adrienne. 1980. "Compulsory Heterosexuality and Lesbian Existence." *Signs: Journal of Women in Culture and Society* 5:631–660.

Rosenberg, Florence, and Roberta Simmons. 1975. "Sex Differences in the Self-Concept in Adolescence." *Sex Roles* 1:147–159.

Rubin, Lillian B. 1977. *Worlds of Pain: Life in the Working-Class Family.* New York: Basic Books.

Rubin, Zick. 1970. "Measurement of Romantic Love." *Journal of Personality and Social Psychology* 16: 265–273.

———. 1973. *Liking and Loving: An Invitation to Social Psychology,* New York: Holt, Rinehart and Winston.

Saarni, Carolyn. 1979. "Children's Understanding of Display Rules for Expressive Behavior." *Developmental Psychology* 15(4):424–429.

Schofield, Janet. 1982. *Black and White in School.* New York: Praeger.

Stearns, Carol Z., and Peter N. Stearns. 1986. *Anger: The Struggle for Emotional Control in America's History.* Chicago: University of Chicago Press.

Swidler, Ann. 1980. "Love and Adulthood in American Culture." Pp. 120–147 in *Themes of Work and Love in Adulthood,* edited by Neil J. Smelser and Erik H. Erickson. Cambridge, MA: Harvard University Press.

Thoits, Peggy A. 1989. "The Sociology of Emotions." *Annual Review of Sociology* 15:317–342.

Waller, Willard. 1937. "The Rating and Dating Complex." *American Sociological Review* 2:727–734.

Wulff, Helena. 1988. *Twenty Girls: Growing Up, Ethnicity and Excitement in a South London Microculture.* Stockholm: University of Stockholm Press.

Youniss, James, and Jacqueline Smollar. 1985. *Parents and Peers in Social Development: A Sullivan-Piaget Perspective.* Chicago: University of Chicago Press.

PROJECTING THE DEFINITION OF THE SITUATION

Because we cannot read one another's minds, we have to signal our definition of the situation. This process includes signaling what kind of moment or event we think we're in (casual conversation at the store, an argument, a celebration, etc.) and what social role we are playing in the moment (flirtatious potential date, hassled shopper, betrayed spouse, etc.). Although most day-to-day behavior seems routine and automatic, we're actually working together all the time to signal to one another. The signaling may be as simple as "I see and acknowledge you as a comrade" or as complex as trying to get a raise from someone you disrespect. Much human social interaction can be analyzed in terms of the kinds of signaling of expectations that people are doing with one another.

"Acknowledgment Rituals" is based on a study done by sociologist Carl Edward Pate. Pate, who is a black man, was intrigued by the way in which black men acknowledge one another in public settings. His research explores some of the reasons for these greetings and investigates whether other groups engage in similar rituals of acknowledgment.

"Embarrassment and the Analysis of Role Requirements" is another classic sociological article written by Edward Gross in 1964. Gross notes that embarrassment is an emotion that indicates that we are aware of social expectations but are not always ideal performers. When we can't carry off the role requirements for the situation, we become embarrassed. Most people feel bad for those who mess up (we know what it feels like to be in their situation), so we try to be helpful in putting the expected situation back together. Gross's article was considered so intriguing that he was invited to talk about it on the *Tonight Show*. As a guest, he was asked to explain why people find shows such as *Candid Camera* so entertaining. What does embarrassment tell us about ourselves and our expectations? Why do we feel both amused and sorry when someone else is embarrassed?

Sociologist Arlie Hochschild is well known for her recent scholarship on working families and how they organize their time. The selection "The Managed Heart" is an excerpt from an earlier book based on a study of flight attendants and their interactions with the public. One of the services airlines try to provide in a highly competitive industry is a "friendly" experience. Flight attendants must present a friendly face despite the fact that the situation is often tense and passengers are frightened, rude, and sometimes drunk. What do flight attendants do to "signal" a friendly situation, and how does this "emotion work" affect them personally?

Questions for Discussion and Review

1. Think about some ways people signal to others through T-shirts, bumper stickers, and other symbolic displays. Would you wear a T-shirt that symbolized something you didn't like or agree with? Do you find yourself responding positively to strangers who are wearing some kind of symbol that you identify with?

2. Recall a situation in which you were embarrassed? Was the embarrassment due to playing the wrong role for the situation or due to misplaying the expected role for the situation?

3. Make a list of jobs that require "emotion work." When does emotional communication feel like work, and when does it feel like "authentic" self-expression?

4. Try an exercise in which you wear clothes that are not expected for the situation (for example, dress poorly to shop in a nice store, wear a suit on a casual date). Does the clothing seem to have any effect on people's perceptions of the situation and how they respond to you? What is the connection between a "dress code" and a definition of the situation?

PROJECTING THE DEFINITION OF THE SITUATION

15

Acknowledgment Rituals

The Greeting Phenomenon Between Strangers

Carl Edward Pate

(1998)

For years I've noticed and participated in a greeting phenomenon that occurs between African American males who do not know each other. The greeting can take several forms: a head nod only, a head nod accompanied by a verbal recognition, a verbal recognition only, or a nonverbal gesture. Why and how does this phenomenon happen? Does this greeting phenomenon occur out of an expression of a common experience (i.e., a shared definition of the situation which recognizes the oppression felt by people of color in general and African American males specifically)? Does

AUTHOR'S NOTE: This research could not have been completed without the support of the Minority Education Office, a part of the Graduate School Administrative Division at the University of Washington. I am also indebted to Judith A. Howard, Robert Crutchfield, Jodi O'Brien, and Howard Becker for providing guidance throughout this endeavor.

this greeting phenomenon happen because of a perceived in-group or a fictive kinship relationship? Would this phenomenon occur in situations where African American males are in the majority? Do acknowledgments occur in New York or Chicago as often as they do in Seattle or smaller communities or other mostly white communities? What is sociologically significant about Acknowledgment Rituals?

I will attempt to isolate and illuminate a micro level greeting phenomenon which occurs between *strangers*. Elijah Anderson's (1990) work on greetings between African American men provides the reference point for framing my inquiries. I attempt to extend his research across cultures and gender, examining greetings between and among African, Asian, White, Mexican, and Latino Americans, men, women, and gays, bisexuals, and lesbians. I attempt to tie this phenomenon to the importance of daily interaction as a means of group identification and as a means of defining self. I employ social psychological perspectives to establish that an acknowledgment ritual exists between strangers, to identify what situations facilitate these greetings, who participates in greetings between strangers, and what role they play or what importance they have in common everyday interaction. I use participant and non-participant observations, as well as interviewing strategies, both focus group and individual, to illuminate the complexities of this greeting phenomenon.

INTERACTIVE GREETINGS

Anderson (1990) addresses the issue of greetings in a chapter from his book *StreetWise,* titled "The Black Male in Public." In this chapter, he suggests that greetings serve the function of protection or as a way to determine whether someone is a "predator" or member of a "wolfpack." Anderson focused on the stigma black males face in public associated with their skin color, age, gender,

appearance, and self presentation. Anderson notes that these black men have to fight this stigma because most residents of Village-Northton ascribe to them (anonymous black males) the characteristics of criminality, incivility, toughness, and street smartness. Anderson also raises the issue of encounters between strangers in urban communities. He indicates that because "public encounters between strangers on the streets of urban America are by nature brief, the participants must draw conclusions about each other quickly, and they generally rely on a small number of cues. This process is universal, and it unavoidably involves some prejudging—prejudice—but its working out is especially prominent in the public spaces of the Village-Northton" (163). Some of the interactive dynamics Anderson describes refer to the etiquette of "strangers in the streets": for example, young black men making extended eye contact as a means of presenting self. According to Anderson, the response of the other person to this extended eye contact is to avert their eyes from the black males, and thus not provoke a potentially threatening response. The subtle averting of the eyes during interaction that Anderson refers to is but one example among many which I frame in terms of the interactive dynamics of greetings between strangers.

Anderson specifically addresses the issue of greetings between non-familiar African American males. Anderson not only establishes the existence of acknowledgment rituals between strangers, but also illuminates the intricate relationships between greetings and categorical characteristics (i.e., race), in terms of in-group/out-group dynamics. He suggests that greetings within the African American community are salient for the development of self as well as a community identity. His focus is mainly black men, but I suggest that greetings are also important for black women, other members of other racial/ethnic groups, and members of the gay community. Anderson's perspectives are captured in this passage:

Among blacks, the act of greeting is of great cultural importance . . . Blacks in the Village still spontaneously greet other blacks they are sure they do not [underline added] know. In fact Northton blacks, many of whom have southern roots, seem to be more forthcoming with such greetings to fellow blacks on the streets of the Village than they are on their home turf, reflecting a need to express color-caste solidarity. In contrast, middle-income blacks of the Village are more likely to greet their white counterparts, while remaining somewhat reserved in their overall behavior.

To many blacks, greetings carry an obligation to respond in kind. Not to return a greeting is uncommon, and the person is considered "strange." Blacks are more likely to speak to those they do not know, including whites, than whites are to speak to unfamiliar whites or to blacks in public places. (1990: 168–69)

Using Anderson's work as a starting point, I expand the scope of inquiry beyond African American males, adding a potentially illuminating comparative frame to understanding acknowledgment rituals. My intuitive sense is that other groups might participate in some form of acknowledgment ritual, since, like African Americans, commonalties exist between individuals and groups that may also encourage this greeting phenomenon. A comparative design allows me to address the following questions: Is the acknowledgment ritual an intra-group phenomenon (i.e., between women, or gay, bisexual and lesbians, or between individuals in the Asian community, or between Jewish people, or Anglo American males)? Or is it an inter-group phenomenon that occurs across races or cultural groups, across men and women, across age or generation and/or between homosexuals and heterosexuals? Do some groups participate in acknowledgment rituals more often than other groups? Are the reasons for participating in an acknowledgment ritual the same for all groups? Is the performance of solidarity the focal point of acknowledgment? Do acknowledgments that occur between oppressed individuals reflect their membership in subordinate groups in American society?

CONCEPTUAL FRAMEWORK

. . . Acknowledgment rituals represent a presentation of self, a statement of membership in a particular group, to another member of that group.

Howard (1994) suggests that social identities (as opposed to personal identities) are more important for dominated groups, not only in interactions with dominant group members, but also within their own self-concepts. Her point is that social power plays a salient role in the process of self and social categorization. This is consistent with my point that some groups use acknowledgment rituals as a show of intra-group solidarity in situations which may be potentially oppressive (i.e., college campuses for most minority groups such as gays, bisexuals, and lesbians or African Americans). This is also consistent with a finding noted below, that members of dominant groups, such as Anglo American males, do not participate in acknowledgment rituals as frequently.

In a section of his book, *Relations in Public,* titled "Supportive Interchanges," Goffman (1971) primarily focused on familiar individuals in terms of the social significance of greetings. He wrote:

Two individuals upon approaching orient frontally to each other. Their glances lock for a moment in communion, eyes glisten, smiling expressions of social recognition are conveyed, and a note of pleasure is briefly sustained. Hand-waving, hat-tipping, and other "appeasement gestures" may be performed. A verbal salutation is likely to be provided along with a term of address. When possible, embracing, hand-shaking, and other bodily contacting may occur. (74)

He referred to greetings among strangers as a guarantee for safe passage, and suggested that such greetings seldom occur. Even though Goffman wrote primarily about familiar individuals, I suggest that his implicit reference to the significance of social recognition and gestures fits for strangers.

In constructing definitions of the situation, Goffman (1959) suggested that individuals participate in performances in which each participant orchestrates gestures to present oneself in a specific manner.

> When an individual enters the presence of others, they commonly seek to acquire information about him or to bring into play information already possessed. They will be interested in his general conception of self, his attitude toward them, his competence, his trustworthiness, etc. Although some of this information seems to be sought almost as an end in itself, there are usually quite practical reasons for acquiring it. Information about the individual helps to define the situation, enabling others to know in advance what he will expect of them and what they may expect of him. Informed in these ways, the others will know how best to act in order to call forth a desired response from him. (1)

Goffman's point is that during interaction individuals look for clues as to who each other is, and how each person is bound to react to the other. My research indicates that acknowledgments are outcomes of the presentation of self and an aspect of impression management. People present themselves as a member of a group or show support for the other's presentation of self through the acknowledgment ritual.

Goffman (1971) refers to "tie-signs" as "evidence about relationships, that is, about ties between persons, whether involving objects, acts, expressions, and only excluding the literal aspects of explicit documentary statement" (194). That is, cues (such as gender, race, manner of dress, etc.,) may act as an anchoring mechanism for interacting individuals to quickly assess the other's in-group/out-group status, and thus facilitate greetings that express intra-group solidarity. Tie-signs, in conjunction with people's abilities to

schematically categorize and organize information, further explain how meaning-laden acknowledgments pass between one another on the street, at a bus stop or down a hallway.

METHODS

Research Sites

I used participant and non-participant observation, focus groups, and individual interviews, to assess the acknowledgment ritual phenomenon. The ubiquitous nature of greetings enabled me to conduct research almost anywhere; research sites varied according to my normal day-to-day travels and included interactions on buses and at bus stops; in restaurants and shopping malls; walking down streets, or on the University of Washington's and Humboldt State University's campuses; and while driving in cars. Observations were made and noted throughout the city of Seattle, as well as in adjacent cities and communities for a period of one year. Observations were also made elsewhere, including various locations in California (i.e., San Diego, San Francisco, and Oakland).

Observed Subjects

Subjects included anyone I encountered in the research sites. The varied locations enabled me to interact with both men and women, and individuals representative of multiple racial groups. I did not specifically select sites where I expected to see individuals from specific racial groups. However, I interacted with individuals from various racial groups, as a participant or non-participant observer, when the opportunity presented itself.

Participant and Non-Participant Observations

Participant and non-participant observations were conducted during the entire study period.

Initially, these methods were used to answer several questions: Does this greeting phenomenon occur? Who participates in it? What does it consist of? Participant and non-participant methods were also useful in the later stages of my study to facilitate ongoing, post interview observations.

Participant observations are defined in this study as observations collected while I actively participated in the acknowledgment ritual by being either the initiator of an acknowledgment or the recipient of an initiated acknowledgment. These interactions were noted on tape or in a notepad to be recorded at a later time on an acknowledgment ritual observation form. Non-participant observations were recorded while watching potential and actual interactions from the perspective of an unobtrusive observer.

To a limited degree, I used Goffman's (1974) notion of frame analysis to assist in "picking up" subtle differences between individuals' and groups' avoidance of or participation in this greeting phenomenon between non-familiar individuals. Paying attention to the smallest of details enabled me to distinguish and quickly categorize behaviors or actions.

As I note below, my observations seemed to support the hypothesis that individuals do participate in this greeting phenomenon. Several questions followed: What specific meanings are attached to this greeting phenomenon? Do these acknowledgments symbolize a common experience framed within a shared subordinate status or are they a response to a specific situation? What intra- or inter-group dynamics are occurring, if any? Focus group and individual interviews were conducted to analyze these questions.

Interviews and Interviewees

I conducted nineteen formal interviews, including 13 individual and six focus group interviews, and an unspecified amount of informal interviews. The majority of formal interviews were conducted on a West Coast university campus and primarily involved students. The interviewees ranged in age from early twenties to mid-forties, and included 45 females and 32 males (n = 77). The racial composition of the interviewees included African, White, Mexican, and Asian (including Filipino, Korean, Japanese, Chinese, and Vietnamese) Americans. Interviews were conducted to uncover and illuminate the process of acknowledgment rituals, to specify who was involved and to identify patterns in the interviewee's personal accounts of this greeting phenomenon. Informal interviewees included both students and non-students, males and females and had the same racial composition as the formal interviewees. Formal interviewees were contacted prior to the interview, met in a designated interview site and followed standard interview procedures. Informal interviewees were unscheduled but presented spontaneous opportunities to inquire about acknowledgment rituals and greetings. Informal interviews were not taped, because of their spur of the moment nature, however, any useful information was later recorded.

The largest focus group interview was with the Asian Student Commission, and included 25 participants. The remaining focus group interviews were conducted with ten members of the Black Student Union, six members of the Black Student Commission, five members of the Women's Commission, six members of the Women Engineers Association, and 12 members of the Gay, Bisexual, and Lesbian Commission. Focus group interviews were conducted prior to individual interviews as a means of generating multiple perspectives and conceptions that could then be further analyzed during individual interviews. Open ended questions were used to stimulate discussion. These interviews were conducted in a give-and-take conversational manner to minimize my influence on the information given and to not appear authoritarian or intimidating. Each focus group interview was taped and later transcribed.

The individual interview questions were all open ended. An initial set of questions was used to stimulate discussion, and additional questions were formulated to probe any comments that needed clarification or elaboration. The interviewees included both women and men, and people self-identifying as, Japanese, Mexican, white and black. Each interview was taped and later transcribed.

To facilitate understanding and theorizing about acknowledgement rituals, I conceived of three stages in the acknowledgment ritual: (1) The initial acknowledgment; (2) the actual acknowledgment or greeting; and (3) the post acknowledgment. During the *initial acknowledgment* there are three sub-stages. First, an assessment or definition of the situation, including an initial presentation of self; second, a cognitive assessment of who the other is and whether the acknowledgment is likely to occur; and third, a decision to acknowledge the other or not. The *actual acknowledgment* or greeting (when the decision to do so is made) involves five possible forms: (1) Nod only; (2) Nod and Verbal; (3) Verbal Only; (4) Non-Response; and (5) Other Non-Verbal (e.g., raising the eyebrows). The *post acknowledgment* is a period in which one takes the role of the other and attempts to ascribe meaning to the greeting, if warranted. This stage is also salient for continuing the presentation of self, in terms of showing the appropriate "face," as well as enabling the other to present "face" also, until each interactant is sure the greeting is complete. This final stage normally covers the period of time from the actual greeting until the interactants have passed by each other.

FINDINGS

The first question is whether acknowledgments between strangers occurred. My initial participant and non-participant observations indicated that strangers do participate in acknowledgment rituals, and that these greetings occurred intra-group, as well as inter-group. Interview transcripts indicated that, indeed, greetings between strangers occur and that there are shared understandings of the greetings as well as the symbolism of what a greeting means. In other words, individuals are collectively aware of the symbolism of a smile or a head nod as opposed to a quick glance or a verbal communication such as "hello."

The interviewees were very "Goffmanesque" in their descriptions, being able to relay minute detail describing (and at times demonstrating) subtle glances, intentional averting of the eyes to avoid eye contact or body language which made the other appear either open or closed to a greeting. For example, Interviewee C not only indicated, in relaying an experience, examples of what constituted a greeting but also illustrated the second step of the initial acknowledgment stage (described above). Interviewee C stated:

> if you see somebody, like I am walking, getting ready to acknowledge someone and I'm looking up and I'm getting ready to smile at them or nod at them or say good morning or something, and I see that they are not going to acknowledge me, then I'll ignore them. And sometimes you can tell that someone is determinedly looking away from you.

She is also clearly weighing whether to acknowledge the other by participating in a give-and-take interaction with the other where she is presenting self (looking up, getting ready to smile), but defines the situation, based on her perception of the other's body language, such that it is unlikely that a greeting will occur.

There was some disagreement as to precisely what form of non-verbal communication was "enough" to qualify as a greeting. The disagreement focused on whether eye contact alone constitutes a greeting or whether something beyond simple eye contact is necessary for an acknowledgment to have occurred. There also seemed to be a significant difference in the degree and form of eye contact which counted as an acknowledgment or greeting. Interviewee J felt that eye contact was not enough to qualify as an acknowledgment when she stated:

> If I make eye contact, I crack a smile, and that to me, I'm acknowledging that person. And so it's not enough that they make eye contact, but that they acknowledge that they've made eye contact with some emotional or physical manifestation.

However, Interviewee L indicates that eye contact is primary and does qualify as a greeting in and of itself, as well as in conjunction with other gestures. Interviewee L's reference to "meaningful contact" also fits well with my contention that some greetings are purposive and symbolic and are not only perfunctory acts:

> Well, I would have said at least eye contact. I mean I immediately want to qualify it by saying eye contact and then some facial expression that indicates that the person sees you, but I think, if a person is walking past and you just can tell they noticed that you were there and they're going to steer around you, that's not acknowledgment. But if there's some kind of meaningful contact.

Group Specific Findings

African Americans

The most striking finding was the difference in how often African American males participated in the acknowledgment ritual as compared to any other group. African American males acknowledge one another at a rate exceeding all other groups combined. I noted, in both participant and non-participant observations, hundreds of examples where, in multi-racial situations, African American males were the only ones to participate in acknowledgment rituals. There were literally hundreds of opportunities for individuals of all races and sexes to acknowledge one another; the only consistent acknowledgments were between African American males. (This is not to say that other groups do not participate in acknowledgment rituals; they do, as I comment on below.)

The interviews corroborated may claims that African American males participate repeatedly in this greeting phenomenon; all of the interviews (across sex, age, and race) perceived that African American males significantly acknowledge one another more often than any other group. One African American woman, during the Black Student Commission focus group interview, illustrated this fact with a humorous statement that initiated agreement and laughter from all of the participants:

> There's that damn nod, most of the guys go like this [she demonstrated an exaggerated head nod], when they're walking.

Anderson (1990) made reference to the 'amazement' White people express in terms of how often Black men greet one another. He also indicated that greetings hold "instrumental" meaning which is shared and understood collectively, including serving as a means of expressing one's tie to a particular "community" (i.e., black or gay community). Anderson wrote:

> When with a black person, a white person may be amazed that so many "unknown" black will speak. In this way, unacquainted blacks can give the appearance of a unified public community on the streets of the Village. Such greeting behavior is not simply an ingrained ritual; it may be viewed as instrumental, as a way for Northton blacks in the Village to come to terms with an environment they see as not always welcoming. (169)

Respondent 4 of the Black Student Union focus group, illustrated Anderson's point when she indicated the salience of greetings for establishing in-group cohesion and tie to one's community. She also implicitly suggests that an acknowledgement can serve as an antidote for the oppression felt by African American males, indicating an interesting nexus of race and gender. Respondent 4 said:

> I do believe that the black community is the lowest person on the pyramid. And us acknowledging one another is rising us up. I mean . . . the reason why I acknowledge men more than women is cos I believe that the black male has been brought down so low, that he needs to be pumped up. And I think a black sister needs to do that . . . And that's why I acknowledge people, cos I know I feel good when people acknowledge me, and I know they're doing it because I'm a black female.

She links self-esteem and social identity with her desire to give as well as receive acknowledgments, corresponding to one of Tajfel and Turner's (1986) main assumptions about social identity: "Individuals strive to maintain or enhance their self-esteem: they strive for a positive self-concept." (16) In doing so, Respondent 4 implicitly refers to the role that acknowledgment rituals play in "rising us up," which is a functional means of fighting against African American subordinate or oppressed status through a relatively simple symbolic gesture of unity. This particular function of acknowledgment rituals was a fairly common theme for some other minority groups as well, especially gay, bisexuals, and lesbians, Mexican and Chicano Americans and to some degree women in their mid-twenties and older. The question then is why are African Americans much more likely to participate in the acknowledgment ritual than other groups?

One explanation is that there is an unwritten law within the African American community that "brothers and sisters" should acknowledge one another. In other words, it is a group-specific norm, a shared understanding that to acknowledge one another is correct and to ignore someone within the community is non-normative (i.e., deviates from social expectations). Recently the cover of a *Newsweek* magazine read, "What Color is

Black?: Science, Politics and Racial Identity." The very first article dealing with the issue presented on the cover was written by a journalism student attending the University of Tennessee. Courtney's opening two sentences stressed exactly this point:

> As my friend Denise and I trudged across the University of Tennessee campus to our 9:05 a.m. class, we delivered countless head nods, "Heys" and "How ya' doin's" to other African Americans we passed along the way. We spoke to people we knew as well as people we didn't know because it's an unwritten rule that black people speak to one another when they pass. (*Newsweek*, February, 1995: 16)

Describing a black community in a Midwestern city, Stack (1974) discussed the concept of kinship and its importance to the Black social structure. She used the notion of "fictive kinship" to refer to those people who one can count on as family but are not genetically related. Stack (1974) stated, "The offering of kin terms to "those you count on" is a way people expand their personal networks." (58) Stack further suggested that "fictive kin relations are maintained by consensus between individuals" (59) and that "social relations are conducted within the idiom of kinship" (60). This notion of *fictive kinship* may be one explanation for why African American males, in particular, participate in the acknowledgment ritual, and why African American females feel compelled to prop up their "brothers" through greetings. I argue that fictive kinship is most salient in situations that are potentially oppressive, such as situations of extreme numerical disadvantage (i.e., most college campuses regarding racial groups).

A second explanation focuses on the stigma of being an African American male in American society today. My observation is that acknowledgments or greetings between African Americans serves the purpose of symbolically saying "society doesn't value you as an individual (or a people) but that by acknowledging you I am saying you count." This notion of giving respect is a plausible explanation why African Americans participate in the acknowledgment ritual to a much greater degree than other groups. This particular explanation is consistent with Howard's (1994) notion that dominated groups are more likely to rely on social identities, because I suggest that these identities are bolstered by the collective response to oppression. Finally, it is evident that race is not the only identifiable factor which explains the noted disproportionate participation in acknowledgment rituals; otherwise there would not be such a sharp distinction between African American men and women. Clearly, the unparalleled participation by African American males indicates that sex as well as race (i.e., the nexus of the two) helps to shape the interactive accomplishment framed within this greeting phenomenon.

Mexican Americans

The second most frequent rates of acknowledgment were among Mexican American or Latino males. Again, this held true both when I was a participant and an observer. Interview data indicate that many of the same issues prompted greetings between Mexicans or Chicanos who did not know each other. However, there was a notable difference in the meaning of an acknowledgment to Mexican Americans. According to Interviewee M, a Mexican male, acknowledgments by strangers serve as a means of acquiring "respect." He illustrated this frame of reference and also added issues of intergroup interactions and relations to the equation:

> It's just, sometimes I think the ones that acknowledge me, gives me a little bit more respect cos of who I am, just walking by the street. I know that other people sometimes, they give 'em dirty looks or just by their race or by the way they look, they dress or something. It really makes me feel good just walking down the street and someone saying "hi" to me, that I don't even know.

Interviewee M also stated a preference for acknowledging certain racial groups, besides his own, as well as corroborating my earlier point that African Americans are perceived to be the most active acknowledgment ritual participants:

> And it's mostly blacks and Filipinos and other Hispanics that acknowledge, I mean, and say "hi" with a head nod or just by saying, "How you doing?" or things like that. But, yeah, I mostly don't really interact with the Asians and the Chinese or Japanese or Whites, you know. It's mostly black people and then, uhm Filipinos.

African American Women

The next group among whom acknowledgments were most frequent were African American women. Their acknowledgment rates far exceeded those of other women, Asian males and White males. For African American women, race commonalty is a plausible explanation for their participation in acknowledgment rituals. Heterosexual attraction is also a feasible explanation for explaining the frequency of acknowledgment rituals among African American men and women. The frequency of interaction between African American women and men provides a salient illustration of the nexus of race and gender framed in an acknowledgment ritual context.

White, Mexican/Latina, and Asian Women

White, Mexican/Latina, and Asian women, in terms of participant observations, were as a group the next most likely to participate in acknowledgements. White women and Mexican, or Latino women were approximately equal in their receptiveness to initiated acknowledgments. Both far exceeded Asian women in this respect.

Asian and White Males

Asian males and White males were the least likely to participate in acknowledgment rituals. Asian males, however, were relatively more receptive to an initiated acknowledgment than were White males. Asian or Whites males often completely ignored my initiated greeting, both verbal and non-verbal, in situations where it was highly unlikely that they were unaware of me (i.e., stairwells, or empty hallways). In those situations, the usual reaction to my greeting was to look away or stare straight ahead without any noticeable physical change. Respondent 1 of the Asian Student Commission focus group interview corroborated this point when he said, in response to my question "what if you are walking down the hall and there is only one other person coming towards you, what do you do?": "I'm looking away." Interviewee H (a White male) said:

> I wouldn't necessarily greet people I don't know unless there's a particular situation . . . so, it's just like walking down the street, I tend not to really notice people too much."

I rarely observed either Asian or White males acknowledging someone of their own race or gender. And when Asian or White males initiated an acknowledgment, it was usually with someone outside of their racial group, and in a majority of the cases it was with a Black male. This is consistent with the general perception that Black males are the most receptive to acknowledgments and that they are the most active participants in acknowledgment rituals.

Asian Americans and Asians

Asians and Asian Americans may share a cultural aversion to participating in acknowledgment rituals, illustrated during my interview with the Asian Student Commission. Respondent 2, of the Asian Student Commission focus group interview, summed this up in cultural terms:

> In our culture, eye contact is considered rude.

Respondent 7, of the Asian Student Commission focus group interview, said:

> You just don't acknowledge people you don't know.

The aversion is manifest in three ways: first, a perceived lack of unity among different nationality groups; second, as tension between Asian Americans and Asians; and third, an apparent affinity to acknowledge out-group members. Addressing the first point, a participant in the Asian Student commission focus group interview came up to me after concluding the interview to emphasize that there was not as much unity within the Asian community as it appeared during the interview. A number of other Asian students stopped to contribute to our conversation; they expressed consensus that in fact Asian people would rather not acknowledge strangers, or if a greeting did occur it would most likely be with someone who is not Asian. The second point was illustrated well by Respondent 1, of the Asian Student Commission focus group interview, who stated:

> I tend to relate to people who grew up here than that's coming over here, or what we call as FOB, fresh off the boat.

Respondent 4, of the Asian Student Commission focus group interview, not only mentions the lack of intra-group acknowledgements but also indicates that African American people often do acknowledge others. He said:

> I walk like past an Asian person, they won't even look at me. I mean they'll just walk straight ahead. But if I'm like, when a black person or something walking past me, and they'll just like nod at me or something.

White Americans

It is obvious from the discussions above that White Americans as a group participate in the acknowledgment ritual less frequently than any other group. However, White women do participate considerably more often than White men. There is also the perception among other groups that White men in particular don't participate in any kind of acknowledgment ritual. The observations bear out this perception. Interestingly, when I asked the interviewees who tends to acknowledge whom and under what circumstances, White men were never mentioned without prompting. Interviewee A left no doubt about her perspective regarding White American participation in the acknowledgment ritual as well as implicitly naming the intersection of gender and race as a salient factor:

> I've never noticed White people acknowledging other White people in the way other Black people do it. Do you know what I'm saying, in the very outward . . . I mean White people walk by White people all of the time, but I, rarely do I see Black people not have some sort of eye contact and I think that is great. I mean I think it is a sense of comfort. At least I know when I'm a woman in the minority, do you know what I'm saying, it is a feeling of comfort and that's something I want to do.

Respondent 2, of the black student commission, suggested a theory for the lack of acknowledging among White people, while implicitly pointing to the influence of numerical inferiority on greeting behavior:

> And I think maybe it's because they don't have to, because of the fact that they see a ton of white people all day long. They don't feel that it's necessary to say "hi" to whoever that is over there, because they don't know that person. Maybe they don't feel that same kind of need.

Gay Males, Bisexuals, and Lesbians

For many observers, gay males and lesbians are not necessarily as easily identifiable as those of racial minority groups or women. I did observe on several occasions lesbian couples holding hands and have seen individuals pass by and acknowledge them. I was not able to determine visually whether the persons who greeted the couples were a part of the gay community, but the interview data indicate that there is a significant commonalty or

solidarity in the gay community which would suggest that the greeters were themselves gay.

For individuals in the gay community there appears to be a strong need to acknowledge another gay person to signal in-group support or, in this case, acknowledging the other's sexuality. Implicit in this discussion are issues of identity and self. Respondent 2, who self-identifies as a bisexual Mexican male, said:

> I think also straight people, they might acknowledge you, but they wouldn't necessarily acknowledge your sexuality. Where, in the queer community, an acknowledgment, even if I acknowledge a lesbian, I'm acknowledging her sexuality as well as her person.

This data also indicates the salience of the intersection of race, gender and sexuality during greetings.

Respondent 4, of the gay, bisexual, and lesbian student commission illustrated that greetings for him can simply be the courteous thing to do, but he did indicate that acknowledgments also are tied to in-group cohesion and identity:

> For me, it's mostly out of politeness sake. Like, I'll just like acknowledge someone . . . gay or straight, but if I do notice it or realize, oh, they are gay, then it's kind of letting them know I know and that they know, just kind of acknowledge who they are.

There is also the perception that gay men do far more cruising than lesbians. (Cruising refers to a gay person who is actively or purposefully trying to "hit on" or get a relationship going [sexually or otherwise] with another gay person.) This is an important distinction, because this subtle difference in greeting patterns between gay men and lesbians shows the importance of considering layered frames (i.e., the nexus of gender and sexuality) when investigating interactional accomplishments. Woman 3, of the Women's Commission focus group interview, (self-identified lesbian) referred to this perception:

Also that is different among men, between gay men and lesbians. Gay men do far, far more cruising than lesbians. I'm not saying that lesbians don't, but uhm, and that it is more blatant in a different way.

Gendered Patterns in Acknowledgments

Gender Differences

The difference in acknowledgments as a result of gender provided some of the most fascinating findings. For women, three themes consistently recurred in discussing when they engage in acknowledgment rituals: (1) a sense of common bond as women; (2) a sense of vulnerability, particularly in potentially dangerous situations; and (3) for very young women only, a sense of competition. Women, of course, also participate in acknowledgment rituals for other reasons, like those noted for men, including normative behavior (i.e., etiquette), mood, physical attraction, etc. The three themes noted above were the most frequently cited, however. I have already discussed above how acknowledgments can affirm a common bond (see commonalty and other sections). The issues of vulnerability and competition require more explanation.

Women and Situations of Vulnerability

When asked, "when do you acknowledge people and what characteristics of the other are important?," women responded consistently by referring to acknowledging women in situations of vulnerability. They said that women felt more secure in potentially dangerous situations when other women were around to provide support and help if necessary. This also indicates a sense of in-group cohesion and cooperation, as well as signaling trust, channeled through an acknowledgment ritual. Interviewee L said:

at bus stops, late at night, which tends to be the times that I would be out. And you're really kind of checking out your support, in a way. I mean you're standing there and you're thinking, I know I shouldn't be waiting for this bus late at night, I know

this is a risky thing to do. God knows when the bus is going to come, cos you can't ever tell in Philadelphia when the bus is going to come. And there's this other person standing there. And it's really common that someone will just sort of ask you for the time or say, "God, I can't believe how long it is between buses," or "I wish they had a shelter at this bus stop because it's raining" or whatever it is that they say . . . and you want to assess, if you get attacked, is this person going to support me, kind of. Yeah.

Woman 3 of the Women's Commission focus group interview, said:

I was in a drug store, a while back, and I bought a box of condoms. And I thought to myself I am not going to acknowledge anyone who just saw me buy these condoms, because it might be a guy who thinks I'm a slut. You know stuff like that. You know, where there is something about you that could create an impression of you that might be dangerous for the other person to have.

This aspect of acknowledgment rituals requires further examination, because the greeting phenomena played out among women speak of larger societal issues. For example, women deal with the increasing potential of being raped or becoming victims of other violent crimes. Women also have to contend with single or multiple minority statuses (i.e., being a white woman or a woman of color), in terms of power.

Women and the Issue of Competitiveness

The theme of competitiveness among women as being relevant to participation in acknowledgments was unexpected. This surfaced repeatedly throughout the interviews with women, regardless of race. Interestingly, there appears to be a transition from a focus in competitiveness with other women to a focus of commonality among women, that occurs approximately in women's mid-twenties. Interviewee K spoke of the connection between age and competition:

For women, I would say it's, well, it's difficult with women because with younger women, I'm finding I'm finally reaching this age, like mid-twenties, where women aren't so competitive with each other. So I can have friendly acknowledgments with women. But before then, like in my early twenties and teens, there was a lot of competition and I felt [it] in acknowledging women on the streets. Most women, like on campus, because they're primarily undergraduates, might check me over, see what I'm wearing. See if my outfit, you know, meets with their standards. And they they'll either smile, because they know that I've seen, caught them looking at me. Or they'll just like glance away. But recently I've noticed women, like around my age range, mid-twenties or thirty, will acknowledge me.

Heterosexual Dynamics

Other factors also come into play in cross-sex (and presumably heterosexual) acknowledgments. One theme is a fear of transmitting the wrong message to a member of the opposite sex during an acknowledgment (i.e., "I'm physically attracted to you"). This particular theme was expressed by both men and women, regardless of race, and dictated whether an acknowledgment occured. Interviewee F quite emphatically presented her choice of acknowledging women, because of the potential for an acknowledgment with a male to be seen as a "come on":

> I've worked in a lot of construction or male-dominated jobs, and any form of acknowledgment can be taken as a come-on, and more often than not, it is. So rather than put up with that horseshit I just don't.

Respondent 3, of the Black Student Union focus group interview, said:

> Some women will hold back saying "Hello" to men or acknowledging men cos they're like . . . he might get the wrong idea, he might follow me, that kind of thing, it's those kinds of things that go through your mind not just, why a person would say

"Hello" . . . I would rather acknowledge a woman knowing I feel comfortable saying "Hello, how you doing?" And she'd be like, "Hello, how you doing?" And there's not a sexuality issue. Rather than with a man, I know if I say, "Hey, how you doing?" I am going like, [going to] ask him out, you know.

In addition, attraction also influenced whether one acknowledged someone of the opposite sex, or of the same sex for members of the gay community. Interviewees mentioned others' physical features, the way the dress or any possibilities that make others seem attractive. The theme of attraction was mentioned by all groups and both sexes as a significant reason for deciding to acknowledge or not acknowledge someone.

Other Findings

Presenting Self and Community Solidarity

For some groups, acknowledgment rituals are conducted with the explicit intention of presenting self as a legitimate member of an in-group and as a means of expressing a sense of intra-group solidarity. Presenting self to the other and establishing a sense of "community" are two important interrelated aspects of the meaning expressed through acknowledgment rituals. The shared understanding obviously is something that requires cooperative group or cultural frames of reference. According to Mead (1934), cooperation and group life require knowing one's position in terms of a complex set of others. It is also through this process that identities are created and linked to particular communities. As Berger (1963) wrote, identities are "socially bestowed, socially maintained, and socially transformed." (98) In other words, defining self is undertaken via interaction with others, in this case, a greeting. Identity, then, is reaffirmed, and is changed through interaction. Respondent 2, of the Black Student Commission focus group, articulated in-group association in terms of commonality and cohesiveness, while also stressing identity:

The acknowledgment is the way of showing that there is cohesiveness, that I do care about what happens to my community. I do care about people who are like me. I do care about who I am.

Respondent 2 of the Gay, Bisexual, and Lesbian Commission also stressed the sense of community and identity, but for him the symbolism of the acknowledgment was important also in dealing with his feelings of oppression:

> even just kind of the need for support, like from within the community, because it, at least, for out gay, lesbian, bisexual people, it can be very exhausting. And so, it's nice to just kind of get that brief eye contact, it's kind of like, oh yeah, we're all here together.

Situational Commonality

I also observed commonality influencing acknowledgment rituals, both as a participant and nonparticipant observer. A sense of commonality expressed through greetings or acknowledgment rituals permeated all of my interviews. Thus greetings also happen because of very minute, seemingly inconsequential, factors. The diversity of common bonds does not diminish the salience of larger issues, such as oppression or vulnerability-driven acknowledgments, but is simply another aspect of greetings, that may influence who we are, how we perceive and present ourselves, and how we think we are perceived.

Respondent 2 of the Women Engineers Association focus group interview illustrated another example of commonality expressed between two people who overhear a funny comment made by a child and the resulting laugh and smile represented a greeting that might not otherwise have happened:

> I was downtown a long time ago, walking past one of these theaters, the X-rated whatever, triple X theaters, and there was a black gentleman walking the other way with a little girl in tow. And we probably

wouldn't have made eye contact, except the little girl looked up and I don't remember her exact words but she said something like, "Daddy, is that where they make something movies," and we caught each other's eyes and we both burst out laughing, because I overheard it . . . And so we smiled at each other and, you know, walked past. Otherwise, we probably wouldn't have even acknowledged each other.

Age

Age was also relevant to participation in acknowledgment rituals. Younger, teenage boys and girls hardly even greeted someone older. Except for a very few occasions, I was ignored by teenage boys and girls when I attempted to initiate an acknowledgment. However, on the rare occasion when I was acknowledged by a teenager, it normally was a solo African American male. In groups, the teenagers I observed did not interact with older people unless the situation necessitated an interaction (i.e., overly crowded bus). Interviewee F illustrated the salience of age as well as the process of defining the situation in terms of subtle cues during an interaction, which determine the outcome of that interaction:

> I think the first thing that I consciously do is, yeah, I say I'm walking down the street where there's long visibility. I see someone coming towards me. I try to, and this is actually a conscious process of looking at their body language and their face and are they looking at me or are they looking away, turning away, walking stiffly, whatever. If they look relaxed, if they're looking up, then I'm much, that's like a yes, I'll probably look at them. And whether or not I say "hi" depends on whether or not I get eye contact with them. I usually smile almost automatically. If they smile back warmly, then there's going to be a verbal greeting as well. Age probably has something to do with it . . . Very elderly people, I'm, I consciously say I'm going to acknowledge them regardless of what they say to me. And I tend not to acknowledge younger people, like elementary, middle school, or high school kids as often.

I also did not see older individuals, who by all appearances were strangers, acknowledge one another, regardless of race or sex. However, during informal interviews, several older interviewees have indicated that it is not uncommon for older people to acknowledge one another while walking (particularly in one's neighborhood). During my interviews most interviewees indicated an affinity for acknowledging older individuals out of respect, regardless of race or sex, but this was not apparent to any extensive degree during observations. This may indicate that "situation" really matters and perhaps my area of study did not include areas where older individuals are more likely to acknowledge one another.

DISCUSSION AND CONCLUSION

Acknowledgment rituals help define who one is in terms of community ties, social identity, and self-esteem; they may in fact be a symbolic statement in response to societal oppression. The development and maintenance of self and social identity were recurring themes given as reasons for participating in this greeting phenomenon. This was particularly evident for all groups except for White and Asian males. Why is this so? Are White males numerically so superior that they have no need for acknowledgment rituals as an explicit means of expressing social identity? Is personal identity their primary frame of reference? Do cultural factors block Asian male participation? Why do not some groups (for example elderly persons) participate in acknowledgment rituals on a regular basis? Or do they, perhaps, but in areas other than those where I conducted observations? Further investigation of acknowledgment rituals would illuminate whether other groups (e.g., the elderly, the obese) participate in this greeting phenomenon in ways similar to the groups discussed here. For instance, do physically challenged individuals or obese persons feel compelled to acknowledge

other people like themselves or would this draw too much unwanted attention to their stigmatized personal characteristics? . . .

Vulnerability, and the Intersection of Gender and Race: Issues to Reveal

Although the disproportionate participation of African Americans in this greeting phenomenon generates some of the most striking findings, there are other significant patterns. The theme of vulnerability as a catalyst for acknowledgments between women is particularly interesting. Greetings between female strangers that occurred out of a sense of vulnerability crossed all racial boundaries and seemed to be gender-specific. Marking "vulnerability" in gendered terms does not go far enough, however. I would surmise that a relationship between age and vulnerability exists. I speculate that Signaling *trust* is an important part of this aspect of acknowledgment rituals. How does a head nod or a smile signal trust to the other? Is this gender-specific? Is it even possible for a man to signal trust or for women to interpret greetings in this way in situations of vulnerability? Is perceived or potential physical attraction (between heterosexuals or homosexuals) such a salient factor that the signal of trust is often misinterpreted or at least conflated during an interaction where vulnerability would be a factor (i.e., a bus stop late at night)?

Other interesting issues related to women's participation in acknowledgment rituals require more research. For instance, non-African American women more often than not "avoided" acknowledgments by looking away or down as I approached and attempted to initiate a greeting. In comparison, African American women were significantly more likely to respond to, as well as initiate greetings, with me. Why are African American women more likely to participate in this greeting phenomenon compared to other women? There are other issues at play however. To what degree does physical attraction affect one's decision to acknowledge the other? What role do societal norms regarding physical attraction have to do with the amount of participation in acknowledgment rituals? Are taboos against interracial dating or attraction prevalent enough to prevent participation in an everyday behavior such as acknowledgement rituals? What role does an African American woman's multiple subordinate statuses (i.e., being female and a minority) play in how often they participate in acknowledgment rituals compared to other women or African American males who have one subordinate status (i.e., minority)? Because of their multiple subordinate statuses, I expected African American women to acknowledge one another more often than they did. What factors are involved in the decision-making processes for African American women in terms of when and with whom they choose to acknowledge? This indicates that this greeting phenomenon is not solely based on race, but that issues regarding the intersection of race and gender are also salient. This raises a general issue of whether women use public spaces differently than men. That is, are women less likely to be forward in public spaces even considering the subtle nature of acknowledgement rituals? . . .

Acknowledgment Rituals: A Final Word About Complexity and Interactional Achievement

Many other questions and issues regarding acknowledgment rituals deserve attention. Social cognition and symbolic interactionism as theoretical perspectives together provide a useful framework for understanding the intricacies and implications of this greeting phenomenon. Even something as taken-for-granted as an acknowledgment ritual can have profound social implications, and hence is sociologically important. The research shows that what appears to be a subtle, seemingly taken-for-granted behavior, is best characterized as a salient *interactional achievement* that is significantly intertwined in the development

and maintenance of identity and self. This research endorses the necessity of understanding the importance of *everyday* interactive behavior, and points to the necessity of "complicating" these issues. Understanding everyday interactive behavior necessitates viewing these phenomena within a frame of complexity built upon the nexus of factors such as race, gender, class, age, region, and sexual orientation.

References

Anderson, Elijah. 1990. *StreetWise: Race, Class, and Change in an Urban Community.* Chicago: The University of Chicago Press, 163–89.

Berger, Peter. 1963. *Invitation to Sociology.* New York, NY: Doubleday.

Charon, Joel M. 1989. *Symbolic Interactionism: An Introduction, An Interpretation, An Integration,* 3rd edn. New Jersey, NJ: Prentice Hall.

Cialdini, Robert, Richard J. Borden, Avril Thorne, Marcus Randall Walker, Stephen Freeman, and Lloyd Reynolds Sloan. 1976. "Basking in Reflected Glory: Three (Football) Field Studies." *Journal of Personality and Social Psychology* 34(3): 366–75.

Cialdini, Robert and Maralou E. De Nicholas. 1989. "Self-Presentation by Association." *Journal of Personality and Social Psychology* 57(4): 626–31.

Fiske, S. T. and Taylor, S. E. 1991. *Social Cognition.* 2nd edn. New York, NY: McGraw Hill.

Gates, Henry Louis, Jr. 1994. *Colored People: A memoir.* New York, NY: Vintage Books.

Goffman, Erving. 1959. *The Presentation of Self in Everyday Life.* New York, NY: Doubleday.

———. 1967. *Interaction Ritual: Essays on Face-to-Face Behavior.* New York: Pantheon Books.

———. 1971. *Relations in Public: Microstudies of the Public Order.* New York: Basic Books, Inc.

———. 1974. *Frame Analysis: An Essay on the Organization of Experience.* Cambridge, MA: Harvard University Press.

Howard, Judith A. 1995. "Social Cognition," in *Sociological Perspectives on Social Psychology,* Karen Cook, G. Fine, and J. House (eds) Needham Heights, MA: Allyn & Bacon, 90–117.

McCall, George J. and Simmons, J. L. 1996. *Identities and Interactions: An Examination of Human Associations in Everyday Life.* New York, NY: The Free Press.

Mead, George H. 1934. *Mind, Self and Society.* Chicago, IL: Chicago University Press.

Patterson, Orlando. 1982. *Slavery and Social Death: A Comparative Study.* Cambridge, MA: Harvard University Press.

Stack, Carol B. 1974. *All Our Kin: Strategies for Survival in a Black Community.* New York: Harper & Row publishers.

Tajfel, Henri and John C. Turner. 1986. "The Social Identity Theory of Intergroup Behavior," in *Psychology of Intergroup Relations,* 2nd edn. Stephen Worchel and William G. Austin. (eds) Chicago: Nelson-Hall Publishers, 7–24.

PROJECTING THE DEFINITION OF THE SITUATION

16

Embarrassment and the Analysis of Role Requirements

Edward Gross and Gregory P. Stone

(1964)

Embarrassment occurs whenever some central assumption in a transaction has been *unexpectedly* and unqualifiedly discredited for at least one participant. The result is that he is incapacitated for continued role performance.[1] Moreover, embarrassment is infectious. It may spread out, incapacitating others not previously incapacitated. It is destructive dis-ease. In the wreckage left by embarrassment lie the broken foundations of social transactions. By examining such ruins, the investigator can reconstruct the architecture they represent.

To explore this idea, recollections of embarrassment were expressly solicited from two groups of subjects: (1) approximately 800 students enrolled in introductory sociology courses; and (2) about 80 students enrolled in an evening extension class. Not solicited, but gratefully received, were many examples volunteered by colleagues and friends who had heard of our interest in the subject. Finally we drew upon many recollections of embarrassment we had experienced ourselves. Through these means at least one thousand specimens of embarrassment were secured.

We found that embarrassments frequently occurred in situations requiring continuous and coordinated role performance—speeches, ceremonies, processions, or working concerts. In such situations embarrassment is particularly noticeable because it is so devastating. Forgetting one's lines, forgetting the wedding ring, stumbling in a cafeteria line, or handing a colleague the wrong tool, when these things occur without qualification, bring the performance to an obviously premature and unexpected halt. At the same time, manifestations of the embarrassment—blushing, fumbling, stuttering, sweating[2]—coerce awareness of the social damage and the need for immediate repair. In some instances, the damage may be potentially so great that embarrassment cannot be allowed to spread among the role performer. The incapacity may be qualified, totally ignored, or pretended out of existence.[3] For example, a minister, noting the best man's frantic search for an absent wedding ring, whispers to him to ignore it, and all conspire to continue the drama with an imaginary ring. Such rescues are not always possible. Hence we suggest that every enduring social relation will provide means of preventing embarrassment, so that the entire transaction will not collapse when embarrassment occurs. A second general observation would take into account that some stages in the life cycle, for example, adolescence in our society, generate more frequent embarrassments than others. These are points to which we shall return.

To get at the content of embarrassment, we classified the instances in categories that remained as close to the specimens as possible. A total of seventy-four such categories were developed, some of which were forced choices between friends, public mistakes, exposure of false front, being caught in a cover story, misnaming, forgetting names, slips of the tongue, body exposure, invasions of others' back regions, uncontrollable laughter, drunkenness in the presence of sobriety (or vice versa), loss of visceral control, and the sudden recognition of wounds or other stigmata. Further inspection of these categories disclosed that most could be included in three general areas: (1) inappropriate identity; (2) loss of poise; (3) disturbance of the assumptions persons make about one another in social transactions.

Since embarrassment always incapacitates persons for role performance (to embarrass is, literally, to bar or stop), a close analysis of the conditions under which it occurs is especially fruitful in the revelation of the requirements *necessary* for role-playing, role-taking, role-making, and role performance in general. These role requirements are thus seen to include the establishment of identity, poise, and valid assumptions about one another among all the parties of a social transaction. We turn now to the analysis of those role requirements.

IDENTITY AND POISE

In every social transaction, selves must be established, defined, and accepted by the parties. Every person in the company of others is, in a sense, obligated to bring his best self forward to meet the selves of others also presumably best fitted to the occasion. When one is "not himself" in the presence of others who expect him to be just that, as in cases where his mood carries him away either by spontaneous seizure (uncontrollable laughter or tears) or by induced seizure (drunkenness), embarrassment ensues. Similarly, when one is "shown up" to other parties to the transaction by the exposure of unacceptable moral qualifications or inappropriate motives, embarrassment sets in all around. However, the concept, self, is a rather gross concept, and we wish to single out two phases that frequently provided focal points for embarrassment—identity and poise.[4]

Identity

Identity is the substantive dimension of the self.[5]

Almost all writers using the term imply that identity establishes what and where the person is in social terms. It is not a substitute word for "self." Instead, when one has identity, he is *situated*—that is, cast in the shape of a social object by the acknowledgement of his participation or membership in social relations. One's identity is established when others *place* him as a social object by assigning the same words of identity that he appropriates for himself or *announces*. It is in the coincidence of placements and announcements that identity becomes a meaning of the self.

Moreover, . . . identity stands at the base of role. When inappropriate identities are established or appropriate identities are lost, role performance is impossible.

If identity *locates* the person in social terms, it follows that locations or spaces emerge as symbols of identity, since social relations are spatially distributed. Moreover, as Goffman has remarked,[6] there must be a certain coherence between one's personal appearance and the setting in which he appears. Otherwise embarrassment may ensue with the resulting incapacitation for role performance. Sexual identity is pervasively established by personal appearance, and a frequent source of embarrassment among our subjects was the presence of one sex in a setting reserved for the other. Both men and women reported inadvertent invasions of spaces set aside for the other sex with consequent embarrassment and humiliation. The implication of such inadvertent invasions is, of course, that one literally does not know where one is, that one literally has no identity in the situation, or that the identity one is putting forward is so absurd as to render the proposed role performance totally irrelevant. Everyone is embarrassed, and such manifestations as, for example, cries and screams, heighten the dis-ease. In such situations, laughter cannot be enjoined to reduce the seriousness of the unexpected collapse of the encounter, and only flight can insure that one will not be buried in the wreckage.

To establish *what* he is in social terms, each person assembles a set of apparent[7] symbols which he carries about as he moves from transaction to transaction. Such symbols include the shaping of the hair, painting of the face, clothing, cards of identity, other contents of wallets and purses, and sundry additional marks and ornaments. The items in the set must cohere, and the set must be complete. Taken together, these apparent symbols have been called *identity documents*,[8] in that they enable others to validate announced identities. Embarrassment often resulted when our subjects made personal appearances with either invalid or incomplete identity documents. It was embarrassing for many, for example, to announce their identities as customers at restaurants or stores, perform the customer role and then, when the crucial validation of this identity

was requested—the payoff—to discover that the wallet had been left at home.

Because the social participation of men in American society is relatively more frequently caught up in the central structures, for example, the structure of work, than is the social participation of women who are relatively more immersed in interpersonal relations, the identities put forward by men are often *titles;* by women, often *names.* Except for very unusual titles,[9] such identities are shared, and their presentation has the consequence of bringing people together. Names, on the other hand, mark people off from one another. So it is that a frequent source of embarrassment for women in our society occurs when they appear together in precisely the same dress. Their identity documents are invalidated. The embarrassment may be minimized, however, if the space in which they make their personal appearance is large enough. In one instance, both women met the situation by spending an entire evening on different sides of the ballroom in which their embarrassing confrontation occurred, attempting to secure validation from social circles with minimal intersection, or, at least, where intersection was temporally attenuated. Men, on the other hand, will be embarrassed if their clothing does not resemble the dress of the other men present in public and official encounters. Except for "the old school tie" their neckties seem to serve as numbers on a uniform, marking each man off from every other. Out of uniform, their structural membership cannot be visibly established, and role performance is rendered extremely difficult, if not impossible.[10]

Not only are identities undocumented, they are also misplaced, as in misnaming or forgetting, or other incomplete placements. One relatively frequent source of embarrassment we categorized as "damaging someone's personal representation." This included cases of ethnically colored sneers in the presence of one who, in fact, belonged to the deprecated ethnic group but did not put that identity forward, or behind-the-back slurs about a woman who turned out to be the listener's wife. The victim of such misplacement, however inadvertent, will find it difficult to continue the transaction or to present the relevant identity to the perpetrators of the embarrassment in the future. The awkwardness is reflexive. Those who are responsible for the misplacement will experience the same difficulties and dis-ease.

Other sources of embarrassment anchored in identity suggest a basic characteristic of all human transactions, which, as Strauss puts it, are "carried on in thickly peopled and complexly imaged contexts."[11] One always brings to transactions more identities than are necessary for his role performance. As a consequence, two or more roles are usually performed at once by each participant.[12]

If we designate the relevant roles in transactions as *dominant roles*[13] then we may note that *adjunct roles*—a type of side involvement, as Goffman would have it,[14] or better, a type of side *activity*—are usually performed in parallel with dominant role performance. Specifically, a lecturer may smoke cigarettes or a pipe while carrying out the dominant performance, or one may carry on a heated conversation with a passenger while operating a motor vehicle. Moreover, symbols of *reserve identities* are often carried into social transactions. Ordinarily, they are concealed, as when a court judge wears his golfing clothes beneath his robes. Finally, symbols of abandoned or *relict identities* may persist in settings where they have no relevance for dominant role performances.[15] For example, photographs of the performer as an infant may be thrust into a transaction by a doting mother or wife, or one's newly constituted household may still contain the symbols of a previous marriage.

In these respects, the probability of avoiding embarrassment is a function of at least two factors: (1) the extent to which adjunct roles, reserve identities and relict identities are not incongruent with the dominant role performance;[16] and (2) the allocation of prime attention to the dominant role

performance so that less attention is directed toward adjunct role performance, reserve identities, and relict identities. Thus the professor risks embarrassment should the performance of his sex role appear to be the main activity in transactions with female students where the professorial role is dominant—for example, if the student pulls her skirt over her knees with clearly more force than necessary. The judge may not enter the courtroom in a golf cap, nor may the husband dwell on the symbols of a past marriage in the presence of a new wife while entertaining guests in his home. Similarly, should adjunct role performance prove inept, as when the smoking lecturer ignites the contents of a wastebasket or the argumentative driver fails to observe the car in front in time to avert a collision, attention is diverted from the dominant role performance. Even without the golf cap, should the judge's robe be caught so that his golfing attire is suddenly revealed in the courtroom, the transactions of the court will be disturbed. Fetishistic devotion to the symbols of relict identities by bereaved persons is embarrassing even to well-meaning visitors.

However, the matter of avoiding incongruence and allocating attention appropriately among the several identities a performer brings to a transaction verges very closely on matters of poise, as we shall see. Matters of poise converge on the necessity of controlling representations of the self, and identity-symbols are important self-representations.

Personal Poise

Presentation of the self in social transactions extends considerably beyond making the appropriate personal appearance. It includes the presentation of an entire situation. Components of situations, however, are often representations of self, and in this sense self and situation are two sides of the same coin. Personal poise refers to the performer's control over self and situation, and whatever disturbs that control, depriving the transaction, as we have said before, of any relevant future, is incapacitating and consequently embarrassing. . . .

First, *spaces* must be so arranged and maintained that they are role-enabling. This is sometimes difficult to control, since people appear in spaces that belong to others, over which they exercise no authority and for which they are not responsible. Students, invited to faculty parties where faculty members behave like faculty members, will "tighten up" to the extent that the students' role performance is seriously impeded. To avoid embarrassment, people will go to great lengths to insure their appearance in appropriate places, and to some to be deprived of access to a particular setting is to limit performance drastically. . . .

We have already touched upon problems presented by invasions of spaces, and little more need be said. Persons lose poise when they discover they are in places forbidden to them, for the proscription itself means they have no identity there and hence cannot act. They can do little except withdraw quickly. It is interesting that children are continually invading the territories of others—who can control the course of a sharply hit baseball?—and part of the process of socialization consists of indications of the importance of boundaries. . . .

Such considerations raise questions concerning both how boundaries are defined and how boundary violations may be prevented. Walls provide physical limits, but do not necessarily prevent communications from passing through.[17] Hence walls work best when there is also tacit agreement to ignore audible communication on the other side of the wall. Embarrassment frequently occurs when persons on one side of the wall learn that intimate matters have been communicated to persons on the other side. A common protective device is for the captive listeners to become very quiet so that their receipt of the communication will not be discovered by the unsuspecting intimates. When no physical boundaries are present, a group gathered in one section of a room may have developed a common mood which is bounded by a certain space that defines the limits of their engagement to one another. The entry of someone new may be followed by an embarrassed hush. It is not necessary that the group should have been talking about that person. Rather, since moods take time to build up, it will take time for the newcomer to "get with it" and it may not be worth the group's trouble to "fill him in." However unintentionally, he has destroyed a mood that took some effort to build up and he will suffer for it, if only by being stared at or by an obvious change of subject. In some cases, when the mood is partially sustained by alcohol, one can prepare the newcomer immediately for the mood by loud shouts that the group is "three drinks ahead" of him and by thrusting a drink into his hand without delay. So, too, a function of foyers, halls, anterooms, and other buffer zones or decompression chambers around settings is to prepare such newcomers and hence reduce the likelihood of their embarrassing both themselves and those inside. . . .

Next, every social transaction requires the manipulation of *equipment.* If props are ordinarily stationary during encounters, equipment is typically moved about, handled, or touched.[18] Equipment can range from *words* to *physical objects,* and a loss of control over such equipment is a frequent source of embarrassment. Here are included slips of the tongue, sudden dumbness when speech is called for, stalling cars in traffic, dropping bowling balls, spilling food, and tool failures. Equipment appearances that cast doubt on the adequacy of control are illustrated by the clanking motor, the match burning down to the fingers, tarnished silverware, or rusty work tools. Equipment sometimes extends beyond what is actually handled in the transaction to include the stage props. Indeed, items of equipment in disuse, reserve equipment, often become props—the Cadillac in the driveway or the silver service on the shelf—and there is a point at which the objects used or scheduled for use in a situation are both equipment and props. At one instant, the items of a table setting lie immobile as props; at the next, they are taken up and transformed into equipment. The close linkage of equipment and props may be responsible for the fact that *embarrassment* at times not only *infects* the participants in the transaction but the *objects* as well. For example, at a formal dinner, a speaker was discovered with his fly zipper undone. On being informed of this embarrassing oversight after he was reseated, he proceeded to make the requisite adjustment, unknowingly catching the table cloth in his trousers. When obliged to rise again at the close of the proceedings, he took the stage props with him and of course scattered the dinner tools about the setting in such a way that others were forced to doubt his control. His poise was lost in the situation. . . .

. . . [C]*lothing* must also be maintained, controlled, and coherently arranged. Its very appearance must communicate this. Torn clothing, frayed cuffs, stained neckties, and unpolished shoes are felt as embarrassing in situations where they are expected to be untorn, neat, clean, and polished. Clothing is of special importance since, as William James observed,[19] it is as much a part of the self as the body—a part of what he called the "material me." Moreover, since it is so close to the body, it conveys the impression of body maintenance, paradoxically, by concealing body-maintenance activities.[20] Hence, the double wrap—outer clothes and underclothes. Underclothes bear the marks of body maintenance and tonic state, and their unexpected exposure is a frequent source of embarrassment. The broken brassière strap sometimes produces a shift in appearance that few women (or men, for that matter) will fail to perceive as embarrassing.

. . . [T]he *body* must always be in a state of readiness to act, and its appearance must make this clear. Hence any evidence of unreadiness or clumsiness is embarrassing. Examples include loss of whole body control (stumbling, trembling, or fainting), loss of visceral control (flatulence, involuntary urination, or drooling), and the communication of other "signs of the animal." The actress who is photographed from her "bad side" loses poise, for it shakes the foundation on which her fame rests. So does the person who is embarrassed about pimples, warts, or missing limbs, as well as those embarrassed in his presence.

Ordinarily, persons will avoid recognizing such stigmata, turn their eyes away, and pretend them out of existence, but on occasion stigmata will obtrude upon the situation causing embarrassment all around. A case in point was a minor flirtation reported by one of our students. Seated in a library a short distance from a beautiful girl, the student began the requisite gestural invitation to a more intimate conversation. The girl turned, smiling, to acknowledge the bid, revealing an amputated left arm. Our student's gestural line was brought to a crashing halt. Embarrassed, he abandoned the role he was building even before the foundation was laid, pretending that his inviting gestures were directed toward some imaginary audience suggested by his reading. Such stigmata publicize body-maintenance activities, and, when they are established in social transactions, interfere with role performances. The pimples on the face of the job applicant cast doubt on his maturity, and, consequently, on his qualifications for any job requiring such maturity. . . .

MAINTENANCE OF CONFIDENCE

When identities have been validated and persons poised, interaction may begin. Its continuation, however, requires that a scaffolding be erected and that attention be given to preventing this scaffolding from collapsing. The scaffold develops as the relationship becomes stabilized. In time persons come to expect that the way they place the other is the way the other announces himself, and that poise will continue to be maintained. Persons now begin to count on these expectations and to have confidence in them. But at any time they may be violated. It was such violations of confidence that made up the greatest single source of embarrassment in our examples. Perhaps this is only an acknowledgment that the parties to every transaction must always maintain themselves *in role* to permit the requisite role-taking, or that identity-switching ought not be accomplished so abruptly that others are left floundering in the encounter as they grope for the new futures that the new identity implies.

This is all the more important in situations where roles are tightly linked together as in situations involving a division of labor. In one instance, a group of social scientists was presenting a progress report of research to a representative of the client subsidizing the research. The principal investigator's presentation was filled out by comments from the other researchers, his professional peers. Negatively critical comments were held to a bare minimum. Suddenly the principal investigator overstepped the bounds. He made a claim that they were well on the road to confirming a hypothesis which, if confirmed, would represent a major contribution. Actually, his colleagues (our informant was one of them) knew that they were very far indeed from confirming the hypothesis. They first sought to catch the leader's eye to look for a hidden message. Receiving none, they lowered their eyes to the table, bit their lips, and fell silent. In the presence of the client's representative, they felt they could not "call" their leader for that would be embarrassing, but they did seek him out immediately afterward for an explanation. The leader agreed that they were right, but said his claim was politic, that new data might well turn up, and that it was clearly too late to remedy the situation.

Careful examination of this case reveals a more basic reason for the researchers' hesitance to embarrass the leader before the client's representative.

If their leader were revealed to be the kind of person who goes beyond the data (or to be a plain liar), serious questions could have been raised about the kind of men who willingly work with such a person. Thus they found themselves coerced into unwilling collusion. It was not simply that their jobs depended on continued satisfaction of the client. Rather they were unwilling to say to themselves and to the client's representative that they were the kind of researchers who would be party to a fraud. To embarrass the leader, then, would have meant embarrassing themselves by casting serious question upon their identities as researchers. Indeed, it was their desire to cling to their identities that led, not long afterward (and after several other similar experiences), to the breakup of the research team.

Just as, in time, an identity may be discredited, so too may poise be upset. Should this occur, each must be able to assume that the other will render assistance if he gets into such control trouble, and each must be secure in the knowledge that the assumption is tenable. Persons will be alert for incipient signs of such trouble—irrelevant attitudes—and attempt to avert the consequences. Goffman has provided many examples in his discussion of dramaturgical loyalty, discipline, and circumspection in the presentation of the self, pointing out protective practices that are employed, such as clearing one's throat before interrupting a conversation, knocking on doors before entering an occupied room, or begging the other's pardon before an intrusion.[21]

The danger that one's confidence in the other's continued identity or his ability to maintain his poise may be destroyed leads to the generation of a set of *performance norms*. These are social protections against embarrassment.[22] If persons adhere to them, the probability of embarrassment is reduced. We discovered two major performance norms.

First, *standards of role performance almost always allow for flexibility and tolerance.* One is rarely, if ever, totally in role (an exception might be highly ritualized performances where to acknowledge breaches of expectation is devastatingly embarrassing).[23] To illustrate, we expect one another to give attention to what is going on in our transactions, but the attention we anticipate is always *optimal,* never total. To lock the other person completely in one's glance and refuse to let go is very embarrassing. A rigid attention is coerced eventuating in a loss of poise. . . . Similarly, never to give one's attention to the other is role-incapacitating. If one focuses his gaze not on the other's eyes, but on his forehead, let us say, the encounter is visibly disturbed.[24] Norms allowing for flexibility and tolerance permit the parties to social transactions ordinarily to assume that they will not be held to rigid standards of conduct and that temporary lapses will be overlooked. . . .

The second performance norm was that of *giving the other fellow the benefit of the doubt.* For the transaction to go on at all, one has at least to give the other fellow a *chance* to play the role he seeks to play. Clearly, if everyone went around watching for chances to embarrass others, so many would be incapacitated for role performance that society would collapse. Such considerate behavior is probably characteristic of all human society, because of the dependence of social relations on role performance. A part of socialization, therefore, must deal with the prevention of embarrassment by the teaching of tact. People must learn not only not to embarrass others, but to ignore the lapses that can be embarrassing whenever they occur. In addition, people must learn to *cope* with embarrassment. Consequently, embarrassment will occasionally be deliberately perpetrated to ready people for role incapacitation when it occurs.

Conclusion

In this paper, we have inquired into the conditions necessary for role performance. Embarrassment has been employed as a sensitive indicator of those conditions, for that which embarrasses incapacitates role performance. Our data have led us to describe the conditions for role performance in terms of identity, poise, and sustained confidence in one another. When these become disturbed and discredited, role performance cannot continue. Consequently, provisions for the avoidance or prevention of embarrassment, or quick recovery from embarrassment when it does occur, are of key importance to any society or social transaction, and devices to insure the avoidance and minimization of embarrassment will be part of every persisting social relationship. . . .

Notes

1. Not all incapacitated persons are always embarrassed or embarrassing, because others have come to expect their *incapacities* and are consequently prepared for them.

2. Erving Goffman, in "Embarrassment and Social Organization," *American Journal of Sociology,* LXII (November 1956), 264–71, describes these manifestations vividly.

3. A more general discussion of this phenomenon, under the rubric civil inattention, is provided in Erving Goffman, *Behavior in Public Places* (New York: Free Press of Glencoe, 1963), pp. 83–88 and *passim.*

4. Other dimensions of the self—value and mood—will be taken up in subsequent publications.

5. Gregory P. Stone, "Appearance and the Self," in Arnold Rose (ed.), *Human Behavior and Social Processes* (Boston: Houghton Mifflin, 1962), p. 93.

6. Erving Goffman, *The Presentation of Self in Everyday Life* (New York: Doubleday Anchor Books, 1959), p. 25.

7. We use the term "appearance" to designate that dimension of a social transaction given over to identifications of the participants. Apparent symbols are those symbols used to communicate such identifications. They are often nonverbal. Appearance seems, to us, a more useful term than Goffman's "front" (*ibid.*), which in everyday speech connotes misrepresentation.

8. Erving Goffman, *Stigma* (Englewood Cliffs, N.J.: Prentice-Hall, 1963), pp. 59–62. Goffman confines the concept to personal identity, but his own discussion extends it to include matters of social identity.

9. For example, the title, "honorary citizen of the United States," which was conferred on Winston Churchill, served the function of a name, since Churchill was the only living recipient of the title. Compare the titles, "professor," "manager," "punch-press operator," and the like.

10. The implication of the discussion is that structured activities are uniformed, while interpersonal activities emphasize individuation in dress. Erving Goffman suggests, in correspondence, that what may be reflected here is the company people keep in their transactions. The work of men in our society is ordinarily teamwork, and teams are uniformed, but housework performed by a wife is solitary work and does not require a uniformed appearance, though the "housedress" might be so regarded.

11. Anselm L. Strauss, *Mirrors and Masks* (Glencoe, Ill.: Free Press, 1959), p. 57.

12. This observation and the ensuing discussion constitute a contribution to and extension of present perspectives on role conflict. Most discussions conceive of such conflict as internalized contradictory obligations. They do not consider simultaneous multiple-role performances. An exception is Everett C. Hughes' discussion of the Negro physician innocently summoned to attend a prejudiced emergency case in "Dilemmas and Contradictions in Status," *American Journal of Sociology*, L (March 1945), pp. 353–59.

13. We have rewritten this discussion to relate to Goffman's classification which came to our attention after we had prepared an earlier version of this article. Goffman distinguishes between what people do in transactions and what the situation calls for. He recognizes that people do many things at once in their encounters and distinguishes those activities that command most of their attention and energies from those which are less demanding of energy and time. Here, the distinction is made between *main* and *side involvements*. On the other hand, situations often call for multiple activities. Those which are central to the situation, Goffman speaks of as *dominant involvements;*

others are called *subordinate involvements*. Dominant roles, therefore, are those that are central to the transactional situation—what the participants have come together to do (see Goffman, *Behavior in Public Places*, pp. 43–59).

14. Adjunct roles are one type of side involvement or activity. We focus on them because we are concerned here with identity difficulties. There are other side *activities* which are *not* necessarily adjunct *roles*, namely, sporadic nosepicking, scratching, coughing, sneezing, or stomach growling, which are relevant to matters of embarrassment, but not to the conceptualization of the problem in these terms. Of course, such activities, insofar as they are consistently proposed and anticipated, may become incorporated in the *personal role* (always an adjunct in official transactions), as in the case of Billy Gilbert, the fabulous sneezer.

15. This phenomenon provides the main theme and source of horror and mystery in Daphne du Maurier's now classic *Rebecca*.

16. Adjunct roles, reserve identities, and relict identities need not cohere with the dominant role; they simply must not clash so that the attention of participants in a transaction is not completely diverted from the dominant role performance.

17. See Erving Goffman, *Behavior in Public Places*, pp. 151–52.

18. Whether objects in a situation are meant to be moved, manipulated, or taken up provides an important differentiating dimension between equipment on the one hand and props (as well as clothing, to be discussed shortly) on the other. Equipment is meant to be moved, manipulated, or taken up *during* a social transaction whereas clothing and props are expected to remain unchanged during a social transaction but will be moved, manipulated, or taken up *between* social transactions. To change props, as in burning the portrait of an old girl friend (or to change clothes, as in taking off a necktie), signals a change in the situation. The special case of the strip-tease dancer is no exception, for her act transforms clothes into equipment. The reference above to the "stickiness" of props may now be seen as another way of describing the fact that they are not moved, manipulated, or taken up during transactions, but remain unchanged for the course of the transaction. Clothing is equally sticky but the object to which it

sticks differs. Clothing sticks to the body; props stick to the settings.

19. William James, *Psychology* (New York: Henry Holt & Co., 1892), pp. 177–78.

20. A complete exposition of the body-maintenance function of clothing is set forth in an advertisement for Jockey briefs, entitled: "A Frank Discussion: What Wives Should Know about Male Support," *Good Housekeeping,* May, 1963, p. 237.

21. Goffman, *The Presentation of Self in Everyday Life,* pp. 212–33.

22. Implicit in Georg Simmel, *The Sociology of Georg Simmel,* trans. Kurt H. Wolff (Glencoe, IL: Free Press, 1950), p. 308.

23. See the discussion of "role distance" in Erving Goffman, *Encounters* (Indianapolis, Ind.: Bobbs-Merrill Co., 1961), pp. 105–52.

24. Here we are speaking of what Edward T. Hall calls the "gaze line." He points out there are cultural variations in this phenomenon. See his "A System for the Notation of Proxemic Behavior," *American Anthropologist,* LXV (October 1963), 1012–14.

PROJECTING THE DEFINITION OF THE SITUATION

17

The Managed Heart

Commercialization of Human Feeling

Arlie Russell Hochschild

(1983)

BEHIND THE SUPPLY OF ACTING: SELECTION

. . . Even before an applicant for a flight attendant's job is interviewed, she is introduced to the rules of the game. Success will depend in part on whether she has a knack for perceiving the rules and taking them seriously. Applicants are urged to read a preinterview pamphlet before coming in. In the 1979–1980 *Airline Guide to Stewardess and Steward Careers,* there is a section called "The Interview." Under the subheading "Appearance," the manual suggests that facial expressions should be "sincere" and "unaffected." One should have a "modest but friendly smile" and be "generally alert, attentive, not overly aggressive, but not reticent either." Under "Mannerisms," subheading "Friendliness," it is suggested that a successful

candidate must be "outgoing but not effusive," "enthusiastic with calm and poise," and "vivacious but not effervescent." As the manual continues: "Maintaining eye contact with the interviewer demonstrates sincerity and confidence, but don't overdo it. Avoid cold or continuous staring." Training, it seems, begins even before recruitment.

Like company manuals, recruiters sometimes offer advice on how to appear. Usually they presume that an applicant is planning to put on a front; the question is which one. In offering tips for success, recruiters often talked in a matter-of-fact way about acting, as though assuming that it is permissible if not quite honorable to feign. As one recruiter put it, "I had to advise a lot of people who were looking for jobs, and not just at Pan

Am. . . . And I'd tell them the secret to getting a job is to imagine the kind of person the company wants to hire and then become that person during the interview. The hell with your theories of what you believe in, and what your integrity is, and all that other stuff. You can project all that when you've got the job." . . .

The trainees, it seemed to me, were also chosen for their ability to take stage directions about how to "project" an image. They were selected for being able to act well—that is, without showing the effort involved. They had to be able to appear at home on stage.

* * *

TRAINING

The training at Delta was arduous, to a degree that surprised the trainees and inspired their respect. Most days they sat at desks from 8:30 to 4:30 listening to lectures. They studied for daily exams in the evenings and went on practice flights on weekends. There were also morning speakers to be heard before classes began. One morning at 7:45 I was with 123 trainees in the Delta Stewardess Training Center to hear a talk from the Employee Representative, a flight attendant whose regular job was to communicate rank-and-file grievances to management and report back. Her role in the training process was different, however, and her talk concerned responsibilities to the company:

> Delta does not believe in meddling in the flight attendant's personal life. But it does want the flight attendant to uphold certain Delta standards of conduct. It asks of you first that you keep your finances in order. Don't let your checks bounce. Don't spend more than you have. Second, don't drink while in uniform or enter a bar. No drinking twenty-four hours before flight time. [If you break this rule] appropriate disciplinary action, up to and including dismissal, will be taken. While on line we don't want you to engage in personal pastimes such as knitting,

reading, or sleeping. Do not accept gifts. Smoking is allowed if it is done while you are seated.

The speaker paused and an expectant hush fell across the room. Then, as if in reply to it, she concluded, looking around, "That's all." There was a general ripple of relieved laughter from the trainees: so that was *all* the company was going to say about their private lives.

Of course, it was by no means all the company was going to say. The training would soon stake out a series of company claims on private territories of self. First, however, the training prepared the trainees to accept these claims. It established their vulnerability to being fired and their dependence on the company. Recruits were reminded day after day that eager competitors could easily replace them. I heard trainers refer to their "someone-else-can-fill-your-seat" talk. As one trainee put it, "They stress that there are 5,000 girls out there wanting *your* job. If you don't measure up, you're out."

Adding to the sense of dispensability was a sense of fragile placement vis-à-vis the outside world. Recruits were housed at the airport, and during the four-week training period they were not allowed to go home or to sleep anywhere but in the dormitory. At the same time they were asked to adjust to the fact that for them, home was an idea without an immediate referent. Where would the recruit be living during the next months and years? Houston? Dallas? New Orleans? Chicago? New York? As one pilot advised: "Don't put down roots. You may be moved and then moved again until your seniority is established. Make sure you get along with your roommates in your apartment."

Somewhat humbled and displaced, the worker was now prepared to identify with Delta. . . . Training seemed to foster the sense that it was safe to feel dependent on the company. Temporarily rootless, the worker was encouraged to believe that this company of 36,000 employees operated as a "family." The head of the training center, a gentle, wise, authoritative figure in her fifties, appeared each morning in the auditorium; she was "mommy," the real authority on day-to-day problems. Her company superior, a slightly younger man, seemed to be "daddy." Other supervisors were introduced as concerned extensions of these initial training parents. (The vast majority of trainees were between nineteen and twenty-two years old.) As one speaker told the recruits: "Your supervisor is your friend. You can go to her and talk about anything, and I mean *anything*." The trainees were divided up into small groups; one class of 123 students (which included three males and nine blacks) was divided into four subgroups, each yielding the more intimate ties of solidarity that were to be the prototype of later bonds at work.

* * *

The company claim to emotion work was mainly insinuated by example. As living illustrations of the right kind of spirit for the job, trainers maintained a steady level of enthusiasm despite the long hours and arduous schedule. On Halloween, some teachers drew laughs by parading through the classroom dressed as pregnant, greedy, and drunk passengers. All the trainers were well liked. Through their continuous cheer they kept up a high morale for those whose job it would soon be to do the same for passengers. It worked all the better for seeming to be genuine.

Trainees must learn literally hundreds of regulations, memorize the location of safety equipment on four different airplanes, and receive instruction on passenger handling. In all their courses, they were constantly reminded that their own job security and the company's profit rode on a smiling face. A seat in a plane, they were told, "is our most perishable product—we have to keep winning our passengers back." How you do it is as important as what you do. There were many direct appeals to smile: "Really work on your smiles." "Your smile is

your biggest asset—use it." In demonstrating how to deal with insistent smokers, with persons boarding the wrong plane, and with passengers who are sick or flirtatious or otherwise troublesome, a trainer held up a card that said "Relax and smile." By standing aside and laughing at the "relax and smile" training, trainers parried student resistance to it. They said, in effect, "It's incredible how much we have to smile, but there it is. We know that, but we're still doing it, and you should too."

HOME IN THE SKY

Beyond this, there were actual appeals to modify feeling states. The deepest appeal in the Delta training program was to the trainee's capacity to act as if the airplane cabin (where she works) were her home (where she doesn't work). Trainees were asked to think of a passenger *as if* he were a "personal guest in your living room." The workers' emotional memories of offering personal hospitality were called up and put to use. . . . As one recent graduate put it:

> You think how the new person resembles someone you know. *You see your sister's eyes in someone sitting at that seat.* That makes you want to put out for them. I like to think of the cabin as the living room of my own home. When someone drops in [at home], you may not know them, but you get something for them. You put that on a grand scale—thirty-six passengers per flight attendant—but *it's the same feeling.*

On the face of it, the analogy between home and airplane cabin unites different kinds of experiences and obscures what is different about them. It can unite the empathy of friend for friend with the empathy of worker for customer, because it assumes that empathy is the *same sort of feeling* in either case. Trainees wrote in their notebooks, "Adopt the passenger's point of view," and the understanding was that this could be done in the same way one adopts a friend's point of view. The analogy between home and cabin also joins the worker to her company; just as she naturally protects members of her own family, she will naturally defend the company. Impersonal relations are to be seen *as if* they were personal. Relations based on getting and giving money are to be seen *as if* they were relations free of money. The company brilliantly extends and uses its workers' basic human empathy, all the while maintaining that it is not interfering in their "personal" lives.

* * *

By the same token, the injunction to act "as if it were my home" obscured crucial differences between home and airplane cabin. Home is safe. Home does not crash. It is the flight attendant's task to convey a sense of relaxed, homey coziness while at the same time, at takeoff and landing, mentally rehearsing the emergency announcement, "Cigarettes out! Grab ankles! Heads down!" in the appropriate languages. Before takeoff, safety equipment is checked. At boarding, each attendant secretly picks out a passenger she can call on for help in an emergency evacuation. Yet in order to sustain the *if,* the flight attendant must shield guests from this unhomelike feature of the party. As one flight attendant mused:

> . . . If we were going down, if we were going to make a ditching in water, the chances of our surviving are slim, even though we [the flight attendants] know exactly what to do. *But I think I would probably—* and I think I can say this for most of my fellow flight attendants—*be able to keep them from being too worried about it.* I mean my voice might quiver a little during the announcements, but somehow I feel we could get them to believe . . . the best.

Her brave defense of the "safe homey atmosphere" of the plane might keep order, but at the price of concealing the facts from passengers who might feel it their right to know what was coming.

Many flight attendants spoke of enjoying "work with people" and adopted the living room analogy as an aid in being as friendly as they wanted to be. . . . Others spoke of being frustrated when the analogy broke down, sometimes as the result of passenger impassivity. One flight attendant described a category of unresponsive passengers who kill the analogy unwittingly. She called them "teenage execs." . . .

> Teenage execs are in their early to middle thirties. Up and coming people in large companies, computer people. They are very dehumanizing to flight attendants. You'll get to their row. You'll have a full cart of food. They will look up and then look down and keep on talking, so you have to interrupt them. They are demeaning . . . you could be R2-D2 [the robot in the film *Star Wars*]. They would like that better. . . .

It is when the going gets rough—when flights are crowded and planes are late, when babies bawl and smokers bicker noisily with nonsmokers, when the meals run out and the air conditioning fails—that maintaining the analogy to home, amid the Muzak and the drinks, becomes truly a monument to our human capacity to suppress feeling.

Under such conditions some passengers exercise the privilege of not suppressing their irritation; they become "irates." When that happens, back-up analogies are brought into service. In training, the recruit was told: "Basically, the passengers are just like children. They need attention. Sometimes first-time riders are real nervous. And some of the troublemakers really just want your attention." The passenger-as-child analogy was extended to cover sibling rivalry: "You can't play cards with just one passenger because the other passengers will get jealous." To think of unruly passengers as "just like children" is to widen tolerance of them. If their needs are like those of a child, those needs are supposed to come first. The worker's right to anger is correspondingly reduced;

as an adult he must work to inhibit and suppress anger at children.

Should the analogy to children fail to induce the necessary deep acting, surface-acting strategies for handling the "irate" can be brought into play. Attendants were urged to "work" the passenger's name, as in "Yes, Mr. Jones, it's true the flight is delayed." This reminds the passenger that he is not anonymous, that there is at least some pretension to a personal relation and that some emotion management is owed. Again, workers were told to use terms of empathy. As one flight attendant, a veteran of fifteen years with United, recalled from her training: "Whatever happens, you're supposed to say, I know just how you feel. Lost your luggage? I know just how you feel. Late for a connection? I know just how you feel. Didn't get that steak you were counting on? I know just how you feel." Flight attendants report that such expressions of empathy are useful in convincing passengers that they have misplaced the blame and misaimed their anger. . . .

* * *

RESPONSES TO THE CONTRADICTION

The slowdown is a venerable tactic in the wars between industrial labor and management. Those whose work is to offer "personalized service" may also stage a slowdown, but in a necessarily different way. Since their job is to act upon a commercial stage, under managerial directors, their protest may take the form of rebelling against the costumes, the script, and the general choreography. . . .

For a decade now, flight attendants have quietly lodged a counter-claim to control over their own bodily appearance. Some crews, for example, staged "shoe-ins." ("Five of us at American just walked on the job in Famolares [low-heeled shoes] and the supervisor didn't say anything. After that we kept wearing them.") Others, individually or in groups, came to work wearing an extra piece of jewelry, a beard a trifle shaggier, a new permanent, or lighter makeup. . . . Sometimes, as in the case of body-weight regulations, the issue was taken to court. . . .

Workers have also—in varying degrees—reclaimed control of their own smiles, and their facial expressions in general. According to Webster's Dictionary, "to smile" is "to have or take on a facial expression showing pleasure, amusement, affection, friendliness, irony, derision, etc., and characterized by an upward curving of the corners of the mouth and a sparkling of the eyes." But in the flight attendant's work, smiling is separated from its usual function, which is to express a personal feeling, and attached to another one—expressing a company feeling. The company exhorts them to smile more, and "more sincerely," at an increasing number of passengers. The workers respond to the speed-up with a slow-down: they smile less broadly, with a quick release and no sparkle in the eyes, thus dimming the company's message to the people. It is a war of smiles.

* * *

The smile war has its veterans and its lore. I was told repeatedly, and with great relish, the story of one smile-fighter's victory, which goes like this. A young businessman said to a flight attendant, "Why aren't you smiling?" She put her tray back on the food cart, looked him in the eye, and said, "I'll tell you what. You smile first, then I'll smile." The businessman smiled at her. "Good," she replied. "Now freeze, and hold that for fifteen hours." Then she walked away. In one stroke, the heroine not only asserted a personal right to her facial expressions but also reversed the roles in the company script by placing the mask on a member of the audience. She challenged the company's right to imply, in its advertising, that passengers have a right to her smile. This passenger, of course, got more: an expression of her genuine feeling.

The slowdown has met resistance from all quarters and not least from passengers who "misunderstand." Because nonstop smiling had become customary before the speed-up occurred, the absence of a smile is now cause for concern. Some passengers simply feel cheated and consider unsmiling workers facial "loafers." Other passengers interpret the absence of a smile to indicate anger. As one worker put it: "When I don't smile, passengers assume I'm angry. But I'm not angry when I don't smile. I'm just not smiling." . . .

What is distinctive in the airline industry slowdown is the manner of protest and its locus. If a stage company were to protest against the director, the costume designer, and the author of a play, the protest would almost certainly take the form of a strike—a total refusal to act. In the airline industry the play goes on, but the costumes are gradually altered, the script is shortened little by little, and the style of acting itself is changed—at the edge of the lips, in the cheek muscles, and in the mental activities that regulate what a smile means.

The general effect of the speed-up on workers is stress. As one base manager at Delta frankly explained: "The job is getting harder, there's no question about it. We see more sick forms. We see more cases of situational depression. We see more alcoholism and drugs, more trouble sleeping and relaxing." The San Francisco base manager for United Airlines commented:

> I'd say it's since 1978, when we got the Greyhound passengers, that we've had more problems with drug and alcohol abuse, more absenteeism, more complaints generally.
>
> It's mainly our junior flight attendants and those on reserve—who never know when they will be called up—who have the most problems. The senior flight attendants can arrange to work with a friend in first class and avoid the Friendship Express altogether.

There are many specific sources of stress—notably, long shifts, disturbance in bodily rhythms, exposure to ozone, and continual social contact with a fairly high element of predictability. But there is also a general source of stress, a thread woven through the whole work experience: the task of managing an estrangement between self and feeling and between self and display.

———————— \\\\ ————————

NEGOTIATING A WORKING CONSENSUS

When people encounter one another, whether they are strangers or close friends, they have to define their expectations. Social expectations are often taken for granted, and people play out the routines with enough ease that it seems "natural." Whether we are aware of it or not, we are constantly negotiating a definition of the situation. Hurt feelings, anger, and frustration are often results of differing expectations that cannot be reconciled. The readings in this section illustrate some of the interactional work that takes place in situations that are not automatic. Looking at these illustrations helps to highlight the extent to which interaction routines require ongoing work.

"Behavior in Private Places" is a well-known sociological study of gynecology exams. Joan Emerson highlights the potentially precarious situation between medical staff—who want to define this as a sterile medical procedure—and the patient—who may feel violated and embarrassed. In this situation, the patient's cooperation cannot be taken for granted. Thus, the staff uses several strategies designed to keep the patient in her appropriate role so that the exam can be completed in a "routine" manner.

Working from Emerson's article, another sociologist, Kari Lerum, explores the processes of defining the situation in a strip club in " 'Precarious Situations' in a Strip Club." In this particular case, the club owners want to convey a "high-class" impression. They use several strategies to balance the impression that the situation is *both* respectable and erotic.

"Encounters With the Hearing" is an excerpt from a book by a sociologist, Paul Higgins. Higgins, who is hearing but was raised by deaf parents and is therefore bilingual, spent several years studying the everyday experiences of people who are deaf. In this selection, he describes some of the mishaps that occur and problems that arise when hearing people encounter people who are deaf. Usually, the hearing don't know how to react, and the situation is often strained as a result.

Questions for Discussion and Review

1. Recall an occasion in which you mentally practiced an interaction before going into the situation. What impression were you hoping to convey? What resistance, if any, did you anticipate? Are you more likely to consciously practice a performance if the situation is new or if it's routine?

2. Use the concepts of interaction routines, idealization, definition of the situation, and negotiating a working consensus to explain why people become so upset when things go wrong at "special events" such as weddings.

3. Why are children and the socially incompetent not allowed at certain events?

4. Why do people often behave politely in encounters with someone they privately dislike?

5. Think about someone you know who is just a little bit "off" (for example, the aunt who talks too loudly about sex, the uncle who drinks too much, the classmate who never "gets it"). How is it that you and others "know" this person is "off"? What unspoken interaction rules do you hold in common that the "off" person seems not to get? How do you and others respond to this person? Do the responses preserve the definition of the situation (that is, do you "accommodate" the person), or do you respond in ways that give the person information that he or she is "off"?

NEGOTIATING A WORKING CONSENSUS

18

Behavior in Private Places

Sustaining Definitions of Reality in Gynecological Examinations

Joan P. Emerson

(1970)

INTRODUCTION

In *The Social Construction of Reality,* Berger and Luckmann discuss how people construct social order and yet construe the reality of everyday life to exist independently of themselves.[1] Berger and Luckmann's work succeeds in synthesizing some existing answers with new insights. Many sociologists have pointed to the importance of social consensus in what people believe; if everyone else seems to believe in something, a person tends to accept the common belief without question. Other sociologists have discussed the concept of legitimacy, an acknowledgment that what exists has the right to exist, and delineated various lines of argument which can be taken to justify a state of affairs. Berger and Luckmann emphasize three additional processes that provide persons with evidence that things have an objective existence apart from themselves. Perhaps most important is the experience that reality seems to be out there before we arrive on the scene. This notion is fostered by the nature of language, which contains an all-inclusive scheme of categories, is shared by a community, and must be learned laboriously by each new member. Further, definitions of reality are continuously validated by apparently trivial features of the social scene, such as details of the setting, persons' appearance and demeanor, and "inconsequential" talk. Finally, each part of a systematic world view serves as evidence for all the other parts, so that reality is solidified by a process of intervalidation of supposedly independent events.

Because Berger and Luckmann's contribution is theoretical, their units of analysis are abstract processes. But they take those processes to be grounded in social encounters. Thus, Berger and Luckmann's theory provides a framework for making sense of social interaction. In this paper observations of a concrete situation will be interpreted to show how reality is embodied in routines and reaffirmed in social interaction.

AUTHOR'S NOTE: Arlene K. Daniels has applied her talent for editing and organizing to several drafts of this paper. Robert M. Emerson, Roger Pritchard, and Thomas J. Scheff have also commented on the material. The investigation was supported in part by a predoctoral fellowship from the National Institute of Mental Health (Fellowship Number MPM-18,239) and by Behavioral Sciences Training Grant MH-8104 from the National Institute of Mental Health, as well as General Research Support Grant I-SOI-FR-05441 from the National Institutes of Health, U.S. Department of Health, Education, and Welfare, to the School of Public Health, University of California, Berkeley.

Situations differ in how much effort it takes to sustain the current definition of the situation. Some situations are relatively stable; others are precarious.[2] Stability depends on the likelihood of three types of disconforming events. Intrusions on the scene may threaten definitions of reality, as when people smell smoke in a theater or when a third person joins a couple and calls one member by a name the second member does not recognize. Participants may deliberately decline to validate the current reality, like Quakers who refused to take off their hats to the king. Sometimes participants are unable to produce the gestures which would validate the current reality. Perhaps a person is ignorant of the relevant vocabulary of gestures. Or a person, understanding how he should behave, may have limited social skills so that he cannot carry off the performance he would like to. For those who insist on "sincerity," a performance becomes especially taxing if they lack conviction about the trueness of the reality they are attempting to project.

A reality can hardly seem self-evident if a person is simultaneously aware of a counter-reality. Berger and Luckmann write as though definitions of reality were internally congruent. However, the ordinary reality may contain not only a dominant definition, but in addition counterthemes opposing or qualifying the dominant definition. Thus, several contradictory definitions must be sustained at the same time. Because each element tends to challenge the other elements, such composite definitions of reality are inherently precarious even if the probability of disconfirming events is low.

A situation where the definition of reality is relatively precarious has advantages for the analysis proposed here, for processes of sustaining reality should be more obvious where that reality is problematic. The situation chosen, the gynecological examination,[3] is precarious for both reasons discussed above. First, it is an excellent example of multiple contradictory definitions of reality, as described in the next section. Second, while intrusive and deliberate threats are not important, there is a substantial threat from participants' incapacity to perform.

Dramaturgical abilities are taxed in gynecological examinations because the less convincing reality internalized by secondary socialization is unusually discrepant with rival perspectives taken for granted in primary socialization.[4] Gynecological examinations share similar problems of reality-maintenance with any medical procedure, but the issues are more prominent because the site of the medical task is a woman's genitals. Because touching usually connotes personal intimacy, persons may have to work at accepting the physician's privileged access to the patient's genitals.[5] Participants are not entirely convinced that modesty is out of place. Since a woman's genitals are commonly accessible only in a sexual context, sexual connotations come readily to mind. Although most people realize that sexual responses are inappropriate, they may be unable to dismiss the sexual reaction privately and it may interfere with the conviction with which they undertake their impersonal performance. The structure of a gynecological examination highlights the very features which the participants are supposed to disattend. So the more attentive the participants are to the social situation, the more the unmentionable is forced on their attention.

The next section will characterize the complex composition of the definition of reality routinely sustained in gynecological examinations. Then some of the routine arrangements and interactional maneuvers which embody and express this definition will be described. A later section will discuss threats to the definition which arise in the course of the encounter. Measures that serve to neutralize the threats and reaffirm the definition will be analyzed. The concluding section will turn to the theoretical issues of precariousness, multiple contradictory definitions of reality, and implicit communication.

THE MEDICAL DEFINITION AND ITS COUNTERTHEMES

Sometimes people are in each other's presence in what they take to be a "gynecological examination." What happens in a gynecological examination is part of the common stock of knowledge. Most people know that a gynecological examination is when a doctor examines a woman's genitals in a medical setting. Women who have undergone this experience know that the examination takes place in a special examining room where the patient lies with her buttocks down to the edge of the table and her feet in stirrups, that usually a nurse is present as a chaperone, that the actual examining lasts only a few minutes, and so forth. Besides knowing what equipment to provide for the doctor, the nurse has in mind a typology of responses patients have to this situation, and a typology of doctors' styles of performance. The doctor has technical knowledge about the examining procedures, what observations may be taken to indicate ways of getting patients to relax, and so on.

Immersed in the medical world where the scene constitutes a routine, the staff assume the responsibility for a credible performance. The staff take part in gynecological examinations many times a day, while the patient is a fleeting visitor. More deeply convinced of the reality themselves, the staff are willing to convince skeptical patients. The physician guides the patient through the precarious scene in a contained manner: taking the initiative, controlling the encounter, keeping the patient in line, defining the situation by his reaction, and giving cues that "this is done" and "other people go through this all the time."

Not only must people continue to believe that "this is a gynecological examination," but also that "this is a gynecological examination going right." The major definition to be sustained for this purpose is "this is a medical situation" (not a party, sexual assault, psychological experiment, or anything else). If it is a medical situation, then it follows that "no one is embarrassed"[6] and "no one is thinking in sexual terms."[7] Anyone who indicates the contrary must be swayed by some nonmedical definition.

The medical definition calls for a matter-of-fact stance. One of the most striking observations about a gynecological examination is the marked implication underlying the staff's demeanor toward the patient: "Of course, you take this as matter-of-factly as we do." The staff implicitly contend: "In the medical world the pelvic area is like any other part of the body; its private and sexual connotations are left behind when you enter the hospital." The staff want it understood that their gazes take in only medically pertinent facts, so they are not concerned with an aesthetic inspection of a patient's body. Their nonchalant pose attempts to put a gynecological examination in the same light as an internal examination of the ear.

Another implication of the medical definition is that the patient is a technical object to the staff. It is as if the staff work on an assembly line for repairing bodies; similar body parts continually roll by and the staff have a particular job to do on them. The staff are concerned with the typical features of the body part and its pathology rather than with the unique features used to define a person's identity. The staff disattend the connection between a part of the body and some intangible self that is supposed to inhabit the body.

The scene is credible precisely because the staff act as if they have every right to do what they are doing. Any hint of doubt from the staff would compromise the medical definition. Since the patient's nonchalance merely serves to validate the staff's right, it may be dispensed with or without the same threat. Furthermore, the staff claim to be merely agents of the medical system, which is intent on providing good health care to patients. This medical system imposes procedures and standards which the staff are merely following in this particular instance. That is, what the staff do derives from external coercion—"We have to do it this way"—rather than from personal choices which they would be free to revise in order to accommodate the patient.

The medical definition grants the staff the right to carry out their task. If not for the medical definition the staff's routine activities could be defined as unconscionable assaults on the dignity of individuals. The topics of talk, particularly inquiries about bodily functioning, sexual experience, and death of relatives might be taken as offenses against propriety. As for exposure and manipulation of the patient's body, it would be a shocking and degrading invasion of privacy were the patient not defined as a technical object. The infliction of pain would be mere cruelty. The medical definition justifies the request that a presumably competent adult give up most of his autonomy to persons often subordinate in age, sex, and social class. The patient needs the medical definition to minimize the threat to his dignity; the staff need it in order to inveigle the patient into cooperating.

Yet definitions that appear to contradict the medical definition are routinely expressed in the course of gynecological examinations. Some gestures acknowledge the pelvic area as special; other gestures acknowledge the patient as a person. These counterdefinitions are as essential to the encounter as the medical definition. We have already discussed how an actor's lack of conviction may interfere with his performance. Implicit acknowledgments of the special meaning of the pelvic area help those players hampered by lack of conviction to perform adequately. If a player's sense of "how things really are" is implicitly acknowledged, he often finds it easier to adhere outwardly to a contrary definition.

A physician may gain a patient's cooperation by acknowledging her as a person. The physician wants the patient to acknowledge the medical definition, cooperate with the procedures of the examination, and acknowledge his professional competence. The physician is in a position to bargain with the patient in order to obtain this cooperation. He can offer her attention and acknowledgment as a person. At times he does so.

Although defining a person as a technical object is necessary in order for medical activities to proceed, it constitutes an indignity in itself. This indignity can be canceled or at least qualified by simultaneously acknowledging the patient as a person.

The medical world contains special activities and special perspectives. Yet the inhabitants of the medical world travel back and forth to the general community where modesty, death, and other medically relevant matters are regarded quite differently. It is not so easy to dismiss general community meanings for the time one finds oneself in a medical setting. The counterthemes that the pelvic area is special and that patients are persons provide an opportunity to show deference to general community meanings at the same time that one is disregarding them.

Sustaining the reality of a gynecological examination does not mean sustaining the medical definition, then. What is to be sustained is a shifting balance between medical definition and counterthemes.[8] Too much emphasis on the medical definition alone would undermine the reality, as would a flamboyant manifestation of the counterthemes apart from the medical definition. The next three sections will suggest how this balance is achieved.

Sustaining the Reality

The appropriate balance between medical definition and counterthemes has to be created anew at every moment. However, some routinized procedures and demeanor are available to participants in gynecological examinations. Persons recognize that if certain limits are exceeded, the situation would be irremediably shattered. Some arrangements have been found useful because they simultaneously express medical definition and countertheme. Routine ways of meeting the task requirements and also dealing with "normal trouble" are available. This section will describe how themes and counterthemes are embodied in routinized procedures and demeanor.

The pervasiveness of the medical definition is expressed by indicators that the scene is enacted under medical auspices.[9] The action is located in "medical space" (hospital or doctor's office). Features of the setting such as divisions of space, decor, and equipment are constant reminders that it is indeed "medical space." Even background details such as the loudspeaker calling, "Dr. Morris. Dr. Armand Morris" serve as evidence for medical reality (suppose the loudspeaker were to announce instead, "Five minutes until post time"). The staff wear medical uniforms, don medical gloves, use medical instruments. The exclusion of lay persons, particularly visitors of the patient who may be accustomed to the patient's nudity at home, helps to preclude confusion between the contact of medicine and the contact of intimacy.[10]

Some routine practices simultaneously acknowledge the medical definition and qualify it by making special provision for the pelvic area. For instance, rituals of respect express dignity for the patient. The patient's body is draped so as to expose only that part which is to receive the technical attention of the doctor. The presence of a nurse acting as "chaperone" cancels any residual suggestiveness of male and female alone in a room.[11]

Medical talk stands for and continually expresses allegiance to the medical definition. Yet certain features of medical talk acknowledge a nonmedical delicacy. Despite the fact that persons present on a gynecological ward must attend to many topics connected with the pelvic area and various bodily functions, these topics are generally not discussed. Strict conventions dictate what unmentionables are to be acknowledged

under what circumstances. However, persons are exceptionally free to refer to the genitals and related matters on the obstetrics-gynecology service. If technical matters in regard to the pelvic area come up, they are to be discussed nonchalantly.

The special language found in staff-patient contacts contributes to depersonalization and desexualization of the encounter. Scientific-sounding medical terms facilitate such communication. Substituting dictionary terms for everyday words adds formality. The definite article replaces the pronoun adjective in reference to body parts, so that for example, the doctor refers to "the vagina" and never "your vagina." Instructions to the patient in the course of the examination are couched in language which bypasses sexual imagery; the vulgar connotation of "spread your legs" is generally metamorphosed into the innocuous "let your knees fall apart."

While among themselves the staff generally use explicit technical terms, explicit terminology is often avoided in staff-patient contacts.[12] The reference to the pelvic area may be merely understood, as when a patient says: "I feel so uncomfortable there right now" or "They didn't go near to this area, so why did they have to shave it?" In speaking with patients the staff frequently uses euphemisms. A doctor asks: "When did you first notice difficulty down below?" and a nurse inquires: "Did you wash between your legs?" Persons characteristically refer to pelvic examinations euphemistically in staff-patient encounters. "The doctors want to take a peek at you," a nurse tells a patient. Or "Dr. Ryan wants to see you in the examining room."

In one pelvic examination there was a striking contrast between the language of staff and patient. The patient was graphic; she used action words connoting physical contact to refer to the examination procedure: feeling, poking, touching, and punching. Yet she never located this action in regard to her body, always omitting to state where the physical contact occurred. The staff used impersonal medical language and euphemisms: "I'm going to examine you"; "I'm just cleaning out some blood clots"; "He's just trying to fix you up a bit."

Sometimes the staff introduce explicit terminology to clarify a patient's remark. A patient tells the doctor, "It's bleeding now" and the doctor answers, "You? From the vagina?" Such a response indicates the appropriate vocabulary, the degree of freedom permitted in technically oriented conversation, and the proper detachment. Yet the common avoidance of explicit terminology in staff-patient contacts suggests that despite all the precautions to assure that the medical definition prevails, many patients remain somewhat embarrassed by the whole subject. To avoid provoking this embarrassment, euphemisms and understood references are used when possible.

Highly specific requirements for everybody's behavior during a gynecological examination curtail the leeway for the introduction of discordant notes. Routine technical procedures organize the event from beginning to end, indicating what action each person should take at each moment. Verbal exchanges are also constrained by the technical task, in that the doctor uses routine phrases of direction and reassurance to the patient. There is little margin for ad-libbing during a gynecological examination.

The specifications for demeanor are elaborate. Foremost is that both staff and patient should be nonchalant about what is happening. According to the staff, the exemplary patient should be "in play": showing she is attentive to the situation by her bodily tautness, facial expression, direction of glance, tone of voice, tempo of speech and bodily movements, timing and appropriateness of responses. The patient's voice should be controlled, mildly pleasant, self-confident, and impersonal. Her facial expression should be attentive and neutral, leaning toward the mildly pleasant and friendly side, as if she were talking to the doctor in his office, fully dressed and seated in a chair. The

patient is to have an attentive glance upward, at the ceiling or at other persons in the room, eyes open, not dreamy or "away," but ready at a second's notice to revert to the doctor's face for a specific verbal exchange. Except for such a verbal exchange, however, the patient is supposed to avoid looking into the doctor's eyes during the actual examination because direct eye contact between the two at this time is provocative. Her role calls for passivity and self-effacement. The patient should show willingness to relinquish control to the doctor. She should refrain from speaking at length and from making inquiries which would require the doctor to reply at length. So as not to point up her undignified position, she should not project her personality profusely. The self must be eclipsed in order to sustain the definition that the doctor is working on a technical object and not a person.

The physician's demeanor is highly stylized. He intersperses his examination with remarks to the patient in a soothing tone of voice: "Now relax as much as you can"; "I'll be as gentle as I can"; "Is that tender right there?" Most of the phrases with which he encourages the patient to relax are routine even though his delivery may suggest a unique relationship. He demonstrates that he is the detached professional and the patient demonstrates that it never enters her mind that he could be anything except detached. Since intimacy can be introduced into instrumental physical contact by a "loving" demeanor (lingering, caressing motions and contact beyond what the task requires), a doctor must take special pains to ensure that his demeanor remains a brisk, no-nonsense show of efficiency.[13]

Once I witnessed a gynecological examination of a forty-year-old woman who played the charming and scatterbrained Southern belle. The attending physician stood near the patient's head and carried on a flippant conversation with her while a resident and medical student actually performed the examination. The patient completely ignored the examination, except for brief answers to the examining doctor's inquiries. Under these somewhat trying circumstances she attempted to carry off a gay, attractive pose and the attending physician cooperated with her by making a series of bantering remarks.

Most physicians are not so lucky as to have a colleague conversing in cocktail-hour style with the patient while they are probing her vagina. Ordinarily the physician must play both parts at once, treating the patient as an object with his hands while simultaneously acknowledging her as a person with his voice. In this incident, where two physicians simultaneously deal with the patient in two distinct ways, the dual approach to the patient usually maintained by the examining physician becomes more obvious.[14]

The doctor needs to communicate with the patient as a person for technical reasons. Should he want to know when the patient feels pain in the course of examination or information about other medical matters, he must address her as a person. Also the doctor may want to instruct the patient on how to facilitate the examination. The most reiterated instruction refers to relaxation. Most patients are not sufficiently relaxed when the doctor is ready to begin. He then reverts to a primitive level of communication and treats the patient almost like a young child. He speaks in a soft, soothing voice, probably calling the patient by her first name, and it is not so much the words as his manner which is significant. This caressing voice is routinely used by hospital staff members to patients in critical situations, as when the patient is overtly frightened or disoriented. By using it here the doctor heightens his interpersonal relation with the patient, trying to reassure her as a person in order to get her to relax.

Moreover even during a gynecological examination, failing to acknowledge another as a person is an insult. It is insulting to be entirely instrumental about instrumental contacts. Some acknowledgment of the intimate connotations of touching must occur. Therefore, a measure of "loving"

demeanor is subtly injected. A doctor cannot employ the full gamut of loving insinuations that a lover might infuse into instrumental touching. So he indirectly implies a hint of intimacy which is intended to counter the insult and make the procedure acceptable to the woman. The doctor conveys this loving demeanor not by lingering or superfluous contact, but by radiating concern in his general manner, offering extra assistance, and occasionally by sacrificing the task requirements to "gentleness."

In short, the doctor must convey an optimal combination of impersonality and hints of intimacy that simultaneously avoid the insult of sexual familiarity and the insult of unacknowledged identity. The doctor must manage this even though the behavior emanating from each definition is contradictory. If the doctor can achieve this feat, it will contribute to keeping the patient in line. In the next section, we will see how the patient may threaten this precarious balance.

Precariousness in Gynecological Examinations

Threats to the reality of a gynecological examination may occur if the balance of opposing definitions is not maintained as described above. Reality in gynecological examinations is challenged mainly by patients. Occasionally a medical student, who might be considerably more of a novice than an experienced patient, seemed uncomfortable in the scene.[15] Experienced staff members were rarely observed to undermine the reality.

Certain threatening events which could occur in any staff-patient encounter bring an added dimension of precariousness to a gynecological examination because the medical aegis screens so much more audacity at that time. In general, staff expect patients to remain poised and in play like a friendly office receptionist; any show of emotion except in a controlled fashion is objectionable. Patients should not focus on identities of themselves or the staff outside those relevant to the medical exchange. Intractable patients may complain about the pain, discomfort, and indignities of submitting to medical treatment and care. Patients may go so far as to show they are reluctant to comply with the staff. Even if they are complying, they may indirectly challenge the expert status of the staff, as by "asking too many questions."

Failure to maintain a poised performance is a possible threat in any social situation. Subtle failures of tone are common, as when a performer seems to lack assurance. Performers may fumble for their lines: hesitate, begin a line again, or correct themselves. A show of embarrassment, such as blushing, has special relevance in gynecological examinations. On rare occasions when a person shows signs of sexual response, he or she really has something to blush about. A more subtle threat is an indication that the actor is putting an effort into the task of maintaining nonchalant demeanor; if it requires such an effort, perhaps it is not a "natural" response.

Such effort may be indicated, for example, in regard to the direction of glance. Most situations have a common visual focus of attention, but in a gynecological examination the logical focus, the patient's internal organs, is not accessible; and none of the alternatives, such as staring at the patient's face, locking glances with others, or looking out the window are feasible. The unavailability of an acceptable place to rest the eyes is more evident when the presence of several medical students creates a "crowd" atmosphere in the small cubicle. The lack of a visual focus of attention and the necessity to shift the eyes from object to object requires the participants to remain vaguely aware of their directions of glance. Normally the resting place of the eyes is a background matter automatically managed without conscious attention. Attentiveness to this background detail is a constant reminder of how awkward the situation is.

Certain lapses in patients' demeanor are so common as hardly to be threatening. When patients express pain it can be overlooked if the patient is giving other signs of trying to behave well, because it can be taken that the patient is temporarily overwhelmed by a physiological state. The demonstrated presence of pain recalls the illness framework and counters sexual connotations. Crying can be accredited to pain and dismissed in a similar way. Withdrawing attention from the scene, so that one is not ready with an immediate comeback when called upon, is also relatively innocuous because it is close to the required passive but in play demeanor.

Some threats derive from the patient's ignorance of how to strike an acceptable balance between medical and nonmedical definitions, despite her willingness to do so. In two areas in particular, patients stumble over the subtleties of what is expected: physical decorum (proprieties of sights, sounds, and smells of the body) and modesty. While the staff is largely concerned with behavioral decorum and not about lapses in physical decorum, patients are more concerned about the latter, whether due to their medical condition or the procedure. Patients sometimes even let behavioral decorum lapse in order to express their concern about unappealing conditions of their bodies, particularly discharges and odors. This concern is a vestige of a nonmedical definition of the situation, for an attractive body is relevant only in a personal situation and not in a medical one.

Some patients fail to know when to display their private parts unashamedly to others and when to conceal them like anyone else. A patient may make an "inappropriate" show of modesty, thus not granting the staff the right to view what medical personnel have the right to view and others do not. But if patients act as though they literally accept the medical definition this also constitutes a threat. If a patient insists on acting as if the exposure of her breasts, buttocks, and pelvic area are no different from exposure of her arm or leg, she is "immodest." The medical definition is supposed to be in force only as necessary to facilitate specific medical tasks. If a patient becomes nonchalant enough to allow herself to remain uncovered for much longer than is technically necessary she becomes a threat. This also holds for verbal remarks about personal matters. Patients who misinterpret the license by exceeding its limits unwittingly challenge the definition of reality.[16]

Neutralizing Threatening Events

Most gynecological examinations proceed smoothly and the definition of reality is sustained without conscious attention.[17] Sometimes subtle threats to the definition arise, and occasionally staff and patient struggle covertly over the definition throughout the encounters.[18] The staff take more preventive measures where they anticipate the most trouble: young, unmarried girls; persons known to be temporarily upset; and persons with reputations as uncooperative. In such cases the doctor may explain the technical details of the procedure more carefully and offer direct reassurance. Perhaps he will take extra time to establish personal rapport, as by medically related inquiries ("How are you feeling?" "Do you have as much pain today?"), personal inquiries ("Where do you live?"), addressing the patient by her first name, expressing direct sympathy, praising the patient for her behavior in this difficult situation, speaking in a caressing voice, and affectionate gestures. Doctors also attempt to reinforce rapport as a response to threatening events.

The foremost technique in neutralizing threatening events is to sustain a nonchalant demeanor even if the patient is blushing with embarrassment, blanching from fear, or moaning in pain. The patient's inappropriate gestures may be ignored as the staff convey, "We're waiting until you are ready to play along." Working to bring the scene off, the staff may claim that this is routine, or happens to patients in general; invoke the "for your own good" clause; counterclaim that something is less important than the patient indicates; assert that the unpleasant medical procedure is almost over; and contend that the staff do not like to cause pain or trouble to patients (as by saying, "I'm sorry" when they appear to be causing pain). The staff may verbally contradict a patient, give an evasive answer to a question, or try to distract the patient. By giving a technical explanation or rephrasing in the appropriate hospital language something the patient has referred to in a nonmedical way, the staff member reinstates the medical definition.

Redefinition is another tactic available to the staff. Signs of embarrassment and sexual arousal in patients may be redefined as "fear of pain." Sometimes sexual arousal will be labeled "ticklishness." After one examination the doctor thanked the patient, presumably for her cooperation, thus typifying the patient's behavior as cooperative and so omitting a series of uncooperative acts which he had previously acknowledged.

Humor may be used to discount the line the patient is taking. At the same time, humor provides a safety valve for all parties whereby the sexual connotations and general concern about gynecological examinations may be expressed by indirection. Without taking the responsibility that a serious form of the message would entail, the participants may communicate with each other about the events at hand. They may discount the derogatory implications of what would be an invasion of privacy in another setting by dismissing the procedure with a laugh. If a person can joke on a topic, he demonstrates to others that he possesses a laudatory degree of detachment.

For example, in one encounter a patient vehemently protests, "Oh, Dr. Raleigh, what are you doing?" Dr. Raleigh, exaggerating his southern accent, answers, "Nothin.' " His levity conveys: "However much you may dislike this, we have to go on with it for your own good. Since you know that perfectly well, your protest could not be calling for a serious answer." Dr. Raleigh also plays the seducer claiming innocence, thus obliquely referring to the sexual connotations of where his hand is at the moment. In another incident Dr. Ryan is attempting to remove some gauze which has been placed in the vagina to stop the bleeding. He flippantly announces that the remaining piece of gauze has disappeared inside the patient. After a thorough search Dr. Ryan holds up a piece of gauze on the instrument triumphantly: "Well, here it is. Do you want to take it home and put it in your scrapbook?" By this remark Dr. Ryan ridicules the degree of involvement in one's own medical condition which would induce a patient to save this kind of memento. Later in the same examination Dr. Ryan announces he will do a rectal examination and the (elderly) patient protests, "Oh, honey, don't bother." Dr. Ryan assures her jokingly, "It's no bother, really." The indirect message of all three jokes is that one should take gynecological procedures casually. Yet simultaneously an undercurrent of each joke acknowledges a perspective contrary to the medical definition.

While in most encounters the nurse remains quietly in the background, she comes forward to deal actively with the patient if the definition of reality is threatened. In fact, one of the main functions of her presence is to provide a team member for the doctor in those occasional instances where the patient threatens to get out of line. Team members can create a more convincing reality than one person alone. Doctor and nurse may collude against an uncooperative patient, as by giving each other significant looks. If things reach the point of staff collusion, however, it may mean that only by excluding the patient can the definition of reality be reaffirmed. A more drastic form of solidifying the definition by excluding recalcitrant participants is to cast the patient into the role of an "emotionally disturbed person." Whatever an "emotionally disturbed person" may think or do

does not count against the reality the rest of us acknowledge.

Perhaps the major safeguard of reality is that challenge is channeled outside the examination. Comments about the unpleasantness of the procedure and unaesthetic features of the patient's body occur mainly between women, two patients or a nurse and a patient. Such comments are most frequent while the patient gets ready for the examination and waits for the doctor or after the doctor leaves. The patient may establish a momentary "fellow-woman aura" as she quietly voices her distaste for the procedure to the nurse. "What we women have to go through" the patient may say. Or, "I wish all gynecologists were women." Why? "They understand because they've been through it themselves." The patient's confiding manner implies: "I have no right to say this, or even feel it, and yet I do." This phenomenon suggests that patients actually have strong negative reactions to gynecological examinations which belie their acquiescence in the actual situation. Yet patients' doubts are expressed in an innocuous way which does not undermine the definition of reality when it is most needed.

To construct the scene convincingly, participants constantly monitor their own behavior and that of others. The tremendous work of producing the scene is contained in subtle maneuvers in regard to details which may appear inconsequential to the layman. Since awareness may interfere with a convincing performance, the participants may have an investment in being as unselfconscious as possible. But the sociologist is free to recognize the significance of "inconsequential details" in constructing reality.

Conclusion

In a gynecological examination the reality sustained is not the medical definition alone, but a dissonance of themes and counterthemes. What is done to acknowledge one theme undermines the others. No theme can be taken for granted because its opposite is always in mind. That is why the reality of a gynecological examination can never be routinized, but always remains precarious.

The gynecological examination should not be dismissed as an anomaly. The phenomenon is revealed more clearly in this case because it is an extreme example. But the gynecological examination merely exaggerates the internally contradictory nature of definitions of reality found in most situations. Many situations where the dominant definition is occupational or technical have a secondary theme of sociality which must be implicitly acknowledged (as in buttering up the secretary, small talk with sales clerks, or the undertaker's show of concern for the bereaved family). In "business entertaining" and conventions of professional associations a composite definition of work and pleasure is sustained. Under many circumstances a composite definition of action as both deviant and unproblematic prevails. For example, while Donald Ball stresses the claim of respectability in his description of an abortion clinic, his material illustrates the interplay of the dominant theme of respectability and a countertheme wherein the illicitness of the situation is acknowledged.[19] Internally inconsistent definitions also are sustained in many settings on who persons are and what their relation is to each other.

Sustaining a sense of the solidity of a reality composed of multiple contradictory definitions takes unremitting effort. The required balance among the various definitions fluctuates from moment to moment. The appropriate balance depends on what the participants are trying to do at that moment. As soon as one matter is dealt with, something else comes into focus, calling for a different balance. Sometimes even before one issue is completed, another may impose itself as taking priority. Further, each balance contains the seeds of its own demise, in that a temporary emphasis on one theme may disturb the long-run balance unless subsequent emphasis on the countertheme negates it. Because the most effective balance depends on many unpredictable factors, it is difficult to routinize the balance into formulas that prescribe a specific balance for given conditions. Routinization is also impractical because the particular forms by which the themes are expressed are opportunistic. That is, persons seize opportunities for expression according to what would be a suitable move at each unique moment of an encounter. Therefore, a person constantly must attend to how to express the balance of themes via the currently available means.

Multiple contradictory realities are expressed on various levels of explicitness and implicitness. Sustaining a sense of solidness of reality depends on the right balance of explicit and implicit expressions of each theme through a series of points in time. The most effective gestures express a multitude of themes on different levels. The advantages of multiple themes in the same gesture are simultaneous qualification of one theme by another, hedging (the gesture lacks one definite meaning), and economy of gestures.

Rational choices of explicit and implicit levels would take the following into account. The explicit level carries the most weight, unless countered by deliberate effort. Things made explicit are hard to dismiss or discount compared to what is left implicit. In fact, if the solidification of explication is judged to be nonreversible, use of the explicit level may not be worth the risk. On the other hand, when participants sense that the implicit level is greatly in use, their whole edifice of belief may become shaken. "I sense that a lot is going on underneath" makes a person wonder about the reality he is accepting. There must be a lot he does not know, some of which might be evidence which would undermine what he currently accepts.

The invalidation of one theme by the concurrent expression of its countertheme must be avoided by various maneuvers. The guiding principle is that participants must prevent a definition that a contradiction exists between theme and counter-theme from emerging. Certain measures routinely contribute to this purpose. Persons must try to hedge on both theme and countertheme by expressing them tentatively rather than definitely and simultaneously alluding to and discounting each theme. Theme and countertheme should not be presented simultaneously or contiguously on the explicit level unless it is possible to discount their contradictory features. Finally, each actor must work to keep the implicit level out of awareness for the other participants.

The technique of constructing reality depends on good judgment about when to make things explicit and when to leave them implicit, how to use the implicit level to reinforce and qualify the explicit level, distributing themes among explicit and implicit levels at any one moment, and seizing opportunities to embody messages. To pursue further these tentative suggestions on how important explicit and implicit levels are for sustaining reality, implicit levels of communication must be explored more systematically.

Notes

1. P. Berger & T. Luckmann (1966), *The social construction of reality,* Garden City, NY: Doubleday.

2. The precarious nature of social interaction is discussed throughout the work of Erving Goffman.

3. The data in this article are based on observations of approximately 75 gynecological examinations conducted by male physicians on an obstetrics-gynecology ward and some observations from a medical ward for comparison. For a full account of this study, see J. P. Emerson (1963), "Social functions of humor in a hospital setting," unpublished doctoral dissertation, University of California at Berkeley. For a sociological discussion of a similar setting, see W. P. Rosengren & S. DeVault (1963), "The sociology of time and space in an obstetrical hospital," in E. Freidson (Ed.), *The hospital in modern society* (pp. 266–292), New York: Free Press of Glencoe.

4. "It takes severe biographical shocks to disintegrate the massive reality internalized in early childhood; much less to destroy the realities internalized later. Beyond this, it is relatively easy to set aside the reality of the secondary internalizations." Berger & Luckmann (1966), p. 142.

5. As stated by Lief and Fox: "The amounts and occasions of bodily contact are carefully regulated in all societies, and very much so in ours. Thus, the kind of access to the body of the patient that a physician in our society has is a uniquely privileged one. Even in the course of a so-called routine physical examination, the physician is permitted to handle the patient's body in ways otherwise permitted only to special intimates, and in the case of procedures such as rectal and vaginal examinations in ways normally not even permitted to a sexual partner." H. I. Lief & R. C. Fox (1963), "Training for 'detached concern' in medical students," in H. I. Lief et al. (Eds.), *The psychological basis of medical practice,* New York: Harper & Row, p. 32. As Edward Hall remarks, North Americans have an inarticulated convention that discourages touching except in moments of intimacy. E. T. Hall (1959), *The silent language,* Garden City, NY: Doubleday, p. 149.

6. For comments on embarrassment in the doctor-patient relation, see M. Balint (1957), *The doctor, his patient, and the illness,* New York: International Universities Press, p. 57.

7. Physicians are aware of the possibility that their routine technical behavior may be interpreted as sexual by the patient. The following quotation states a view held by some physicians: "It is not unusual for a suspicious hysterical woman with fantasies of being seduced to misinterpret an ordinary movement in the physical examination as an amorous advance." E. Weiss & O. S. English (1949), *Psychosomatic medicine,* Philadelphia: W. B. Saunders; quoted in M. Hollender (1958), *The psychology of medical practice,* Philadelphia: W. B. Saunders, p. 22. An extreme case suggests that pelvic examinations are not without their hazards for physicians, particularly during training: "A third-year student who had prided himself on his excellent adjustment to the stresses of medical school developed acute anxiety when about to perform, for the first time, a pelvic examination on a gynecological patient. Prominent in his fantasies were memories of a punishing father who would unquestionably forbid any such

explicitly sexual behavior." S. Bojar (1961), "Psychiatric problems of medical students," in G. B. Glaine, Jr., et al. (Eds.), *Emotional problems of the student,* Garden City, NY: Doubleday, p. 248.

8. Many other claims and assumptions are being negotiated or sustained in addition to this basic definition of the situation. Efforts in regard to some of these other claims and assumptions have important consequences for the fate of the basic definition. That is, in the actual situation any one gesture usually has relevance for a number of realities, so that the fates of the various realities are intertwined with each other. For example, each participant is putting forth a version of himself which he wants validated. A doctor's jockeying about claims about competence may reinforce the medical definition and so may a patient's interest in appearing poised. But a patient's ambition to "understand what is really happening" may lead to undermining of the medical definition. Understanding that sustaining the basic definition of the situation is intertwined with numerous other projects, however, we will proceed to focus on that reality alone.

9. Compare Donald Ball's account of how the medical definition is conveyed in an abortion clinic, where it serves to counter the definition of the situation as deviant. D. W. Ball (1967, Winter), "An abortion clinic ethnography," *Social Problems, 14,* 293–301.

10. Glaser and Strauss discuss the hospital prohibition against examinations and exposure of the body in the presence of intimates of the patient. B. Glaser & A. Strauss (1965), *Awareness of dying,* Chicago: Aldine, p. 162.

11. Sudnow reports that at the county hospital he studied, male physicians routinely did pelvic examinations without nurses being present, except in the emergency ward. D. Sudnow (1967), *Passing on: The social organization of dying,* Englewood Cliffs, NJ: Prentice-Hall, p. 78.

12. The following quotation suggests that euphemisms and understood references may be used because the staff often has the choice of using "lewd words" or not being understood. Our popular vocabulary for describing sexual behavior has been compounded of about equal parts of euphemism and obscenity, and popular attitude and sentiment have followed the same duality. Among both his male and female subjects, the interviewers found many who knew only the lewd words for features of their own anatomy and physiology. N. N. Foote (1955), "Sex as play," in J. Himelhock & S. F. Fava, *Sexual behavior in American society,* New York: Norton, p. 239.

13. The doctor's demeanor typically varies with his experience. In his early contacts with patients the young medical student may use an extreme degree of impersonality generated by his own discomfort in his role. By the time he has become accustomed to doctor-patient encounters, the fourth-year student and intern may use a newcomer's gentleness, treating the scene almost as an intimate situation by relying on elements of the "loving" demeanor previously learned in non-professional situations. By the time he is a resident and focusing primarily on the technical details of the medical task, the physician may be substituting a competent impersonality, although he never reverts to the extreme impersonality of the very beginning. The senior doctor, having mastered not only the technical details but an attitude of detached concern as well, reintroduces a mild gentleness, without the involved intimacy of the intern.

14. The management of closeness and detachment in professional-client relations is discussed in C. Kadushin (1962, March), "Social distance between client and professional," *American Journal of Sociology, 67,* 517–531. Wilensky and Lebeaux discuss how intimacy with strangers in the social worker-client relation is handled by accenting the technical aspects of the situation, limiting the relationship to the task at hand, and observing the norms of emotional neutrality, impartiality, and altruistic service. H. L. Wilensky & C. N. Lebeaux (1958), *Industrial society and social welfare,* New York: Russell Sage Foundation, pp. 299–303.

15. For a discussion of the socialization of medical students toward a generally detached attitude, see Lief & Fox (1963), pp. 12–35. See also M. J. Daniels (1960, November), "Affect and its control in the medical intern," *American Journal of Sociology, 66,* 259–267.

16. The following incident illustrates how a patient may exceed the limits. Mrs. Lane, a young married woman, was considered by the physicians a "seductive patient," although her technique was subtle and her behavior never improper. After examining Mrs. Lane, an intern privately called my attention to a point in the examination when he was pressing on the patient's ovaries and she remarked to the nurse: "I

have this pain in intercourse until my insides are about to come out." The intern told me that Mrs. Lane said that to the nurse, but she wanted him to hear. He didn't want to know that, he said; it wasn't necessary for her to say that. The intern evidently felt that Mrs. Lane's remark had exceeded the bounds of decorum. A specific medical necessity makes the imparting of private information acceptable, the doctor's reaction suggests, and not merely the definition of the situation as medical.

17. There is reason to think that those patients who would have most difficulty in maintaining their poise generally avoid the situation altogether. Evidence that some uncool women avoid pelvic examinations is found in respondents' remarks quoted by Rainwater: "I have thought of going to a clinic for a diaphragm, but I'm real backward about doing that. I don't even go to the doctor to be examined when I'm pregnant. I never go until about a month before I have the baby." "I tell you frankly, I'd like a diaphragm but I'm just too embarrassed to go get one." L. Rainwater (1960), *And the poor get children*, Chicago: Quadrangle, pp. 10, 31.

18. An example of such a struggle is analyzed in J. P. Emerson (1970), "Nothing unusual is happening," in T. Shibutani (Ed.), *Human nature and collective behavior. Papers in honor of Herbert Blumer*, Englewood Cliffs, NJ: Prentice-Hall.

19. Donald Ball (1967).

NEGOTIATING A WORKING CONSENSUS

19

"Precarious Situations" in a Strip Club

Exotic Dancers and the Problem of Reality Maintenance

Kari Lerum

(2001)

In her classic article, "Behavior in Private Places: Sustaining Definitions of Reality in Gynecological Examinations" (1970), Joan Emerson uses the example of a gynecological exam to demonstrate how social order can prevail even when a social situation is rife with contradictions. In this article, I use Emerson's work as a reference point for another contradictory social situation: a contemporary strip club. The point of this comparison is to examine some similarities and differences in how "reality" is created, threatened, and maintained in each setting, and to gain insight into how specific social conditions impact the process of reality maintenance.

DEFINING REALITY IN A PRECARIOUS SITUATION

Emerson explains that the process of undergoing a gynecological exam can bring about two diametrically opposed messages: (1) the gynecological exam is *sexual and/or intimate* because it involves the (female) patient's genitals being touched by a (male) physician, and (2) the gynecological exam is merely a *routine, scientific procedure;* therefore the exam is completely free of sexual or emotional meaning. Such contradictory messages create what Emerson calls "the problem of reality maintenance"; a problem that is particularly acute for the people most invested in maintaining a certain understanding of reality. In Emerson's case, those people are the gynecologists—since they (as well as most medical experts) base their professional legitimacy upon behaving in a scientific, professional manner, they have tremendous incentive to project an objective, detached image, while extinguishing any threats to this image.

For gynecologists, a contradictory image takes root when their client considers the following question: "Is this *truly* just a professional routine, or is it a sexual and/or intimate act?" Interestingly, in my research of the commercial sex industry, including field work as a waitress in a strip club,[1] I have seen the reverse question arise among clients of sex workers; that is, "Is this *truly* a sexual and/or intimate act, or is it just a professional routine?" In both cases these questions cast doubt on the definition of reality projected by the worker, thus jeopardizing their control over clients.

It is within these questioning moments, suspended between contradictory definitions of what is "really" going on, that Emerson sees a "precarious situation." The situation is precarious because the pendulum of meaning could easily swing either way; if it swings in favor of the worker's definition, the worker succeeds in performing her or his transaction with professional and personal integrity intact. If, however, the pendulum swings in favor of any contradictory definition, the routine is disrupted and the worker's grip on the situation is loosened.

To some extent, this problem is embedded everywhere; all social situations contain symbols or messages that people may interpret in numerous ways. However, this only becomes a problem when new perceptions of reality conflict with institutionalized ones. If people perceive an institution to have meaning contradictory to its "purpose," people are left with no established pattern, or guide, for behavior. Lacking any clear definition of what is "really" going on, the situation becomes one of confusion; people may get nervous and perplexed, and their behavior becomes unpredictable.

This is an unsettling possibility for anyone engaged in an activity requiring the full cooperation of others such as performing a gynecological exam or performing a private "lap dance"[2] at a strip club. While at first glance these two actions may seem to have little in common—the first being an unpleasant but necessary medical procedure performed on a woman for "her own good"; the second being an unnecessary act performed primarily on men simply because it "feels good"— workers in both situations face strikingly similar problems of reality maintenance.

In both cases, the medical worker and the sex worker perform actions that their clients may interpret in contradictory ways. Due to the precarious situation that this brings, a considerable amount of effort on the part of workers is needed to ensure client cooperation. Initially, the desired definitions of reality appear as opposites— medical workers want their actions understood as *standardized* and *non-intimate* while sex workers want their actions understood as *intimate* and *non-standardized*. However, in both cases workers also occasionally find it useful to intentionally project contradictory messages, or counterthemes. For example, the gynecologist occasionally includes a few personal (non-standardized) touches to keep the patient from feeling humiliated and dehumanized; the sex worker occasionally reminds the customer of his customer (standardized) role as a way to squelch any expectations that their relationship will carry on outside of work boundaries. As a result, skillful workers in both fields alternate between themes of standardized professionalism and personalized intimacy as it suits their immediate needs.

The point of these maneuvers is to get clients to succumb to the worker's definition of reality, thus allowing the worker to complete a successful transaction. However, since both transactions involve objects or behaviors with deeply symbolic meanings (for the gynecological exam, exposure to genitals = sexual intimacy; for the lap dance, sexual intimacy = a "real" relationship), convincing people to think otherwise is not an easy task. Reality maintenance in these circumstances requires considerable skill and collective effort; it is a process that works best when it is invisible to the client. As Emerson (1970) writes, successful reality maintenance creates the feeling that "reality seems to be out there before we arrive on the scene."

Due to the symbolic and contradictory meanings found in both gynecological exams and lap dancing, many of the ways that the medical worker's definition of reality is maintained in a gynecological exam also work toward maintaining the sex worker's definition of reality in a strip club. However, a number of structural and interactional factors make the process of reality maintenance in the strip club more precarious.

Factors That Exacerbate Precarious Situations

Perhaps the most important factor that impacts the management of a precarious situation is that of institutional legitimacy. Unlike the gynecological business, whose legitimacy is protected by massive institutions like the American Medical Association and the U.S. government, the social and legal legitimacy of exotic dancing is far shakier and subject to regional, state, and local variation.

This lack of institutional legitimacy in many strip club settings leads to a number of related problems, including the likelihood of intrusive troublemakers. Namely, a strip club's projection of reality is subject to constant and serious threat from troublemakers such as police officers, jealous lovers, and misguided customers (imagine a jealous husband or a police officer busting up a gynecological exam). All of these intrusions interfere with normal business, sometimes requiring workers to halt operations.

In addition to serious troublemakers, clients in strip clubs are generally less predictable and cooperative than clients in gynecological exams. In part, this lack of customer predictability is due to the nature of the business: One-on-one interactions with customers require the worker to individually tailor her approach. However, workers who provide other intimate, individually tailored services (such as hair styling, massage, counseling, or even gynecological exams) do not generally face uncooperative customers, so it is clear that the problem again stems from a lack of social legitimacy. In other words, customers might simply not see the worker as "legitimate"; thus an internalized sense of respect for the worker is lacking.

Additionally, the stigmatized work of selling and performing exotic dances may pose unique emotional requirements. As opposed to working within an arena built on emotional detachment (such as medicine), sex work requires the simultaneous *encouragement* of and *containment* of highly charged emotions. This, in addition to managing the stigma of sex work, may require more emotional labor for the sex practitioner in both managing her own and her customers' emotions. This in turn may make the process of reality maintenance more precarious.

Finally, the gendered, service-oriented nature of female erotic dancing might give customers the idea that control and power is in their hands rather than in the workers'. Since the broader culture still deems men more legitimately powerful than women, women in many occupations face problems of establishing interactional legitimacy. This combined with a culture of customer service (where the customer is allegedly "always right"), makes for a situation where worker control is not guaranteed.

In sum, with a lack of institutional, social, and interactional legitimacy, erotic dancers (and sex workers in general) cannot take their control for granted. Not only is their work itself often precarious legally, but on an interactional level, control over the definition of the situation must be continuously negotiated. Thus, in these settings, workers are more challenged in maintaining their definition of the situation.

MAINTAINING REALITY IN A STRIP CLUB

Despite differences in legitimacy, in both the gynecological examining room and the strip club, a successful reality maintenance campaign involves a practiced performance using several techniques. These techniques fall into two steps of reality maintenance: (1) *setting the mood* (setting and maintaining an overall message or atmosphere), and (2) *enforcing the rules* (enacting and enforcing that message with individual clients). When both levels of reality maintenance are employed, the likelihood of client cooperation increases.

Setting the Mood

The creation of an overall "mood" or atmosphere is accomplished through the use of several techniques, images, and props, all of which work in concert. In gynecological exams, an atmosphere of *objectivity, rationality,* and *standardization* is projected by normalizing and routinizing the exam, donning medical uniforms, and downplaying any emotional content. In the strip club where I worked (referred to here as "Club X"), an atmosphere of *excitement, intrigue,* and *exclusivity* was accomplished by heightening clients' emotions, making them believe that the experience was fun, sexy, exclusive, and slightly taboo, although also legitimate and professional. In both settings, workers intentionally influence the content and tone of clients' emotions. In one setting, the worker maintains control by making sure the client does not blush; in another setting, the worker maintains control by making sure the client *does.*

At Club X, the goal of making clients both emotionally "charged up" *and* compliant to workers' wishes was first accomplished by routinizing

and standardizing the club's "mood." This was achieved by manipulating the appearance, language, and behavior of staff members, the images projected, the music and lighting, and the DJ's announcements.

On a typical night at Club X, the DJ had the greatest immediate influence over the mood; thus this person's routine was key for reality maintenance. The DJ was responsible for controlling the television channel (linked to five TV monitors in the club), as well as the light level of the club and, of course, the music. Each DJ had their unique style (one favored loud music, another kept the light level low), but all DJs had to ultimately comply with the company CEO's standards—the club could not be "too" dark, "too" loud, and the music had to stay fairly upbeat.

The DJ was also the official "voice" of the club; his or her words and tone influenced the mood and acted as a vocal tour guide for customers, encouraging them to see the experience from the club's point of view. One such viewpoint was that the experience was exciting and fun, similar to a sporting event. This message was made most explicit once an hour, when the DJ announced that it was time for the "Texas Teaser." All the dancers (sometimes numbering over thirty) gathered on the front stage, smiling, posing, and flirting with the customers on the floor, while the DJ goaded the crowd:

> Just *look* at all those gorgeous ladies! Guys, what do you say?! Take your hands out of your pockets and show some appreciation! On the count of three I want you to all shout as loud as you can, and the guy who makes the most noise will get a *free pass* to the club!! One . . . Two . . . Threeeee!!!! [The crowd goes wild, some young men standing on their seats, yelling, and pumping their arms in the air.]

These exuberant displays of concentrated emotion might have resulted in a loss of control for the workers, but interestingly, it rarely did. Rather, customers seemed to clearly understand that this game was not serious and that the workers controlled the rules. This understanding was reinforced immediately after the contest—the dancers would descend from the stage, flood the floor, and choose a customer for a "free" dance (while the DJ explained that they must buy a second dance). Since not every customer could get chosen for this free dance, and since the choosing process was up to the dancer, in a matter of moments the customers' demeanor shifted from noisy swaggering to humble anticipation (or dread). If a customer was overlooked this would sometimes turn to embarrassment; as one young man said to me, laughing and pointing to his friend, "Look at him, he was sitting there waiting on the couch, but no one wanted to give him a dance!"

In addition to the vulnerability that comes with waiting to be chosen, customers were also put in their place by the DJ, who routinely teased them by questioning both their heterosexual virility ("What are ya, a bunch of wussies?! What's wrong with you, don't ya like naked chicks?!") and their manners ("Didn't your mother teach you any manners?! Show some appreciation and buy a dance. And buy that lady a drink while you're at it.").

During all this excitement and teasing, an implicit message of professionalism and customer service was also projected by workers. One way this was demonstrated was in the standardized dress of staff members. Just as medical professionals and staff wear specific and unique clothing to both distinguish themselves from their patients and to project a certain (detached) message, the dancers and staff of Club X also used clothing as a method of intentional reality maintenance. One obvious use of this method was found in the rule that all staff members—including waitresses, doormen, bartenders, DJs, floor managers, and the parking lot attendant—wear the same uniform: a white tuxedo shirt, black slacks, and black shoes. The one variation in this uniform was that male staff members (essentially, everyone except the waitresses) were additionally required to wear a

bow tie. As a fellow waitress explained to me, this dress code was established because "some of the waitresses were wearing really short skirts . . . but they [the management] wanted us to look classier."

This "professional" and sexually de-emphasized dress code for staff members also created a distinct contrast to the dancers—all of whom wore costumes meant to symbolize and create a sexually alluring image. None of the dancers wore identical outfits, and these outfits often changed by the night (and sometimes two or three times on the same night), but most of them fell within a narrow range of variability, ranging from short tight dresses to lingerie and g-string panties. These differences between the dancers' and staff members' costumes are not unlike the costume differences found within medical staff ranks where each variation symbolizes a difference in the person's status and role. However, in the strip club setting, costume variety between dancers and staff members also served to simultaneously portray a seemingly contradictory mixture of messages.

Another mood-shaping tool in Club X were the TV monitors. When I first began working at this club, every night brought a variety of soundless video images. Many of these images were of male sporting events, but sometimes the DJ would decide to watch the news, cartoons, or the Nature channel. Scrolling across these images were club advertisements such as "Welcome to Club X!," "$5 table dances; $12 couch dances, and $20 VIP dances!" and "If you've been overcharged, contact a manager." While these messages seemed congruent with images of football, race cars, and wrestling, the image of Dan Rather discussing Middle East politics made for a comically ironic fit. Eventually, these contradictory video messages stirred higher management to create new rules about acceptable video images. At one employee meeting, the general manager of Club X was particularly upset about the showing of cartoons, inspiring him to instigate a "no cartoon" rule.

Absolutely no cartoons! That drives me crazy! No more cartoons! You wanna know why? Cuz cartoons make you think of kids. When I see cartoons, I think of my kids. It makes me miss my kids, I wish I could see them more often. So if you've got some pervert in here, spending three, four hundred dollars, and he sees cartoons up on the TV, he's going to think of his kids, feel like shit, and he's going to leave. So no more cartoons!

In other words, the point of these televised images was to encourage a specific mood as well as to sustain customers' attention by keeping them entranced and undistracted by their external emotional ties.[3]

The language of the staff also shaped the club's mood. Just as the use of clinical terms in a gynecological office creates an atmosphere of emotional and sexual detachment, the language at Club X was used to create an atmosphere that was sexually exciting as well as professional and polite. The DJ would routinely describe a dancer as a "beautiful showgirl" or a "hottie," but the language in this club was generally not sexually explicit. Rather, body parts were euphemized or avoided altogether. As a result, the club could be distinguished as a "gentlemen's club" rather than as "pornographic" or "raunchy."

The language of waitresses and doormen also served to create an atmosphere of exclusivity and politeness to both customers and dancers. Club X advertised that it gave *every* customer "VIP" treatment, and staff members were instructed to treat dancers with old-fashioned respect (at least in front of customers). For instance, when a dancer was found sitting with a customer, waitresses were trained to formally ask the customer, "Would you like to buy the lady a drink?" As Emerson puts it, such scripted language serves to "embody intentional themes." In other words, by routinizing worker behavior, specific messages can be reliably portrayed to customers. Thus, by consistently referring to dancers as "ladies," the message was sent that—although this was a place where one

could get rowdy and receive good service—this was a place where one had to be polite to dancers.

In both the gynecological examining room and in the strip club, the work routine also includes similar specialized work areas—a table in the examining room; a couch in the strip club. Both also have "chaperones" (either a floor manager or a nurse) whose presence serves to discourage deviations from the intended reality.

Although the DJ was a heavyweight in creating the initial "mood," Club X's reality relied on the cooperation of all employees. Management was aware of this need for cooperation, judging by the messages staff members received such as a sign in the break-room which read: "T.E.A.M.—together everyone achieves more." Here the point of working together was to create a reality that was "respectable," service-oriented, and profitable. This emphasis on professional customer service is evident from the following quote from the general manager of Club X:

> Our competitors turned up the music, turned down the lights, and let the hand jobs fly . . . but that's not the kind of operation I'm running here . . . we need to stress service and entertainment. . . . When people go to a restaurant, they don't go there for the service, but it is what brings them back. So when customers come in, take care of them . . . be friendly, say, "Hey how's it going? If you see a girl you'd like, just let me know, and I'll get her for you." You know, take care of them.

From the worker's point of view, the ideal result of all these images, routines, and props is to prevent situations from becoming precarious—to barrage the client with consistent implicit (and sometimes explicit) messages, asserting that "this is how it's done here," and hoping for client cooperation.

Enforcing the Rules

Once the mood is set, a secondary process of enforcement is sometimes necessary. In both Emerson's observations of the gynecological exam and my own at Club X, rule enforcement was typically accomplished by simply instructing uninitiated clients (as well as co-workers) about their expected roles. In both settings, workers expect obedience and passivity from clients. And just as the physician guides the patient through the precarious scene by taking the initiative, controlling the encounter, and carefully monitoring the patient's reactions, so does the exotic dancer.

At Club X, once a dancer got a customer to agree to a dance, she was responsible for guiding the client into his or her proper role. While some role expectations were basic and mandatory (e.g., "no touching" and "keep your hands by your sides"), other role expectations were subtler—requiring the dancer to strategically combine her messages.

For instance, when an ambivalent customer conceded to a dance, dancers often found it useful to interact with the customer in a way that made him (or her) feel special and "really" cared for, yet also aware that the feeling came with a price. After getting paid, a dancer sometimes gave her customer a friendly hug and kiss on the cheek, reinforcing the message that she really did care about him. With younger male customers (who were notoriously "cheap" and who might have been embarrassed about paying for a temporary girlfriend), dancers would frequently walk with them hand-in-hand, leading them to the cash machine, but looking like high school kids going steady. With such shy, young, "cheap," emotionally sensitive, or uninitiated customers, subtle emotional management was often required.

For the hostile or uncooperative customer, rule enforcement relied upon the threat of physical force from male employee "chaperones." The primary chaperone at Club X was the floor manager, but all employees (especially male employees) were expected to jump in if trouble started. This club also had an informal enforcement team, composed of a few men who were allegedly not employees, but who were frequent visitors and known as "friends of the club." As one veteran

waitress explained to me, these "friends" "watch out for the girls and pitch in if they're needed."

Fortunately, the majority of customers accepted the reality of Club X and played along with the expected rules: that is, they applauded the dancers on stage, stood up and yelled when the DJ told them to do so, accepted all "free" dances, sat passively while a private dance was performed on them, and then graciously paid the previously negotiated price (mostly ranging from ten to forty dollars, with the average being twenty dollars a dance). However, some customers remained mystified or shy observers, some were arrogantly skeptical of the rules, and others became aggressive or hostile.

In one case, Nicki[4] had just finished two lap dances and had successfully collected her fee, but as she turned to leave the customer reached his hand up inside of her underwear and squeezed her buttock. Nicki became very upset and immediately told Aaron, who was working as the doorman. As Aaron later told me the story, he "told the guy to get the fuck out of here" before he "beat the shit out of him." The threat worked, and the deviant customer departed.

Other, perhaps even more troublesome intruders were jealous lovers of dancers, delusional customers who refused to accept that they could not have a "real" relationship with their favorite dancer, as well as customers who were simply belligerent and looking for a fight. Due to the highly explosive nature of these situations, staff members had to stay alert and immediately call for help if needed—even if this involved asking for help from another set of troublesome intruders, the police.

Despite their role as potential protectors, the most precarious situations often arose with the entrance of the police. Since this club was in a suburban area where strip clubs were a highly contentious political issue, police officers occasionally stopped by to make their presence known and to monitor the club's activities. When this happened, Club X's reality was severely interrupted. Word would quickly spread throughout the club that the police were there. If there was enough lead time, special red lights would flash behind the bar to warn workers that the police were coming. The manager would then put on a friendly face, greet the officers at the door, and give them a tour of the facility. While business appeared to continue, with waitresses serving drinks, the music continuing, and the DJ introducing each dancer as she appeared on stage, the money exchange would essentially halt; dancers would quit performing lap dances and sit quietly next to their customers or with each other. Sometimes, if a dancer was not notified quickly enough of the threat, she would get caught in the middle of an illegal lap dance[5] and be ticketed. The heart of the entire business (lap dances) would not resume until the departure of the police.

Although far less frequent, precarious situations also rose from the actions of dancers. Often coming from dancers who had previously worked in more sexually lenient clubs, their deviations came in the form of intimacy transgressions—in other words, they went "too far" with their customers. In my six months of work at Club X, there were several cases of dancers who were chastised and sanctioned by other dancers for such transgressions.

For example, Tasha, a dancer at Club X who routinely grabbed at men's genitals through their trousers, was overwhelmingly disliked by the other dancers and staff. As one waitress told me, "You know who I really don't like? Tasha. She's really not classy; that's when I hate working here, when it feels like a whorehouse." It probably was no coincidence that Tasha did not last long as a Club X dancer; without the respect of the other dancers and staff members, negotiation of precarious situations becomes far more difficult.

In some cases, the initiation of a new dancer or the sanctioning of an established dancer simply involved a cold shoulder. But many times the punishment of inappropriate behavior was more direct. In one case, Janessa—a dancer with experience at several other clubs around the United States—was surrounded by several dancers in the dressing room and scolded for putting her crotch in a customer's face. Janessa left her shift early, crying.

In another case, a veteran Club X dancer lashed out at a newer dancer who she felt had gone "too far." The verbal explosion (below) was witnessed by several other dancers and staff:

> I'm fucking old school! Remember how much shit you gave me when I started working here?! [directed at another veteran dancer, who nods her head.] That Regina girl's letting people grab her and shit and only charging twelve dollars! If she wants to do that she should put her ass on the street!! I'm fucking old school. She needs to be taught.

The newer dancer also took a verbal shot or two, but the veteran had publicly and definitively made her point. The manager then quickly intervened, taking both dancers into her office for a private "consultation."

If a manager directly witnessed an intimacy transgression, the dancer would risk harsher penalties. Officially, each dancer was allowed two warnings about such behavior, and on the third offense they would get "termed" (i.e., their independent business contract with the club would be terminated). In one case, a new dancer, Cyndi, performed stage shows that were more sexually graphic than the norm (which other dancers described as "gross"). She was also observed on a number of occasions physically groping the genitals of her customers (through their clothing)—which is against both the club's rules and the state's laws. In her short time at the club, Cyndi had already received two warnings. I observed Cyndi's third offense: She was on a female customer's lap, fondling her breast, and kissing her on the lips. It was the kissing more than anything that shocked the rest of the dancers and staff, since kissing in these circumstances was seen as outrageously intimate. The floor manager was notified and Cyndi was immediately termed.

In all of these examples, it is clear that when a dancer heightened her sexual intimacy with customers, the club's (as well as the dancers') definition of reality was threatened. These actions made the club more at risk of legal sanctions, increased customers' expectations (which subsequently created more competition between dancers), and threatened the "high class" aim of Club X. In an atmosphere where workers were greatly invested in distancing themselves from prostitutes, most dancers and staff members were personally offended by such behavior.

CONCLUSIONS

Comparing Emerson's observations on gynecological exams with my own observations of Club X leads to a number of insights about reality maintenance. One is simply that the process of creating and maintaining reality in both situations is strikingly similar. However, by examining the contrasting points of each case, one also finds that different settings create the need for different techniques. The most relevant contrasts are the *level of institutionalized legitimacy* and the *required amount of client management.* It seems that the higher the social legitimacy of an industry, and the lower the need to constantly monitor and manage one's customers, the lower the threat of a precarious situation. In such a situation, the worker's power is assured and automatic client compliance is likely. In contrast, lower social legitimacy combined with a "high maintenance" customer results in a more precarious situation that needs constant monitoring, manipulation, and rule enforcement.

While rule enforcement at Club X occasionally required the threat of physical force, the vast majority of this enforcement was enacted through the skillful manipulation of messages. Emerson claims that if one pays better attention to the interplay between implicit and explicit messages, then a richer understanding of reality maintenance will emerge. Unlike gynecological exams, contradictory *explicit* messages are the key to reality

maintenance at Club X. In other words, in order for the sex workers in this context to "pull it off," a simultaneous explicit expression of both professionalism and intimacy was not only possible, but necessary to maintain control.

In sum, strip clubs and gynecological exam rooms are both infused with contradictory messages, which can result in precarious definitions of the situation. In a sense, both are getting away with highly "intimate" acts in a commercial setting. However, Club X is doing so with a lack of social and legal legitimacy, making it more dependent on the efforts of individual workers to create a reality where business can be done.

NOTES

1. As part of my dissertation research, during 1998–1999 I spent six months working as a strip club waitress.

2. In contrast to a stage dance, where dancers perform for the entire audience and sometimes collect tips, lap dances are performed for the enjoyment of one customer and must be individually paid for. For most exotic dancers, the lap dance is the primary source of income.

3. Interestingly, pornography was rarely shown at Club X. During my six months of work, I only saw it shown twice. On both occasions, dancers complained loudly, calling these images lewd and disgusting.

4. All names have been changed.

5. Strip clubs within this police jurisdiction are subject to a "four-foot" rule; that is, erotic dances performed closer than four feet away from the patron are against the law. The problem is, it is virtually impossible for a dancer to make any money unless she dances closer than four feet.

REFERENCE

Emerson, J. P. (1970). "Behavior in Private Places: Sustaining Definitions of Reality in Gynecological Examinations." In P. Dreitsel (ed.), *Recent Sociology* (pp. 74–97). New York: Macmillan.

20

Encounters With the Hearing

Paul Higgins

(1980)

Outsiders are often characterized by the larger social world as odd, strange, or somehow other than normal. They are stigmatized. Consequently, encounters between outsiders and those who create and control the larger social world are often strained, inhibited, and awkward. . . . Unlike gays, ethnic Americans, and many other outsiders, the deaf are physically impaired. And like other outsiders who are physically disabled, their impairment and its accompanying limitations may disrupt encounters with those who are not disabled. These disruptions, however, are unrelated to whether the deaf are viewed as odd or not.

Encounters between the disabled and the nondisabled are often strained due to the impairments themselves and how they are managed. Certain features of a blind-sighted encounter can only be understood as the result of the strain that a visual impairment may create for the interaction. Blindness may interfere with establishing the interactants' identities and may create communication problems for both the blind and sighted (Scott, 1969a, 1969b). A wheelchair-bound individual may find that it is difficult to keep up with normally mobile companions on the sidewalk and into and through buildings. Similar problems occur for those with heart trouble or arthritis (Strauss and Glaser, 1975). Difficulty in muscle control and abnormality in appearance may interfere with face-to-face communication because facial and body gestures may convey unintended information (Richardson, 1969). . . .

Impairments, though, are not necessarily disruptive or limiting. Whether they are disruptive or not depends on the specific situation (Wright, 1960). Blindness does not interfere with telephone conversations, but it may disrupt face-to-face encounters, as mentioned above. Disabilities are disruptive in certain situations when they *cause the assumptions and related routine practices which usually successfully maintain interaction in those situations to become problematic*. A breach in the taken-for-granted interactional order has occurred. Coping strategies used by both the disabled and the nondisabled are attempts to compensate for those assumptions and practices which this time have failed. . . .

In this chapter, I analyze the often awkward and confusing interaction which occurs in short-term, usually mundane, and typically impersonal encounters between the deaf and the hearing. Interaction between a clerk and a customer is such an encounter. Interaction between the deaf and the hearing is often disrupted due to the impact of the impairment and of its accompanying limitations on social interaction. Once those disruptions have been identified, I examined how the deaf in particular, but also the hearing, cope with them. . . . Yet, in order to understand how deafness and its accompanying limitations disrupt interaction with the hearing, we need to examine the assumptions and routine practices of the hearing world.

CONVERSATION

. . . Much of human interaction is based on the assumption that people can hear and speak. We communicate through telephones, radios, television, intercom systems, and loudspeakers. Warning signals are often buzzers, sirens, or alarms. Time is structured by bells and whistles. And people talk. In conversation, which "assumes an easy exchange of speaker-hearer role," strain occurs between the deaf and the hearing (Goffman, 1974: 498).

An easy exchange of the speaker and hearer roles requires competence in the language used (Chomsky, 1965). It also requires competence in the norms and forms of interaction that the ethnographers and ethnomethodologists of communication have investigated—turn taking, whom to address, when to talk, what style of speech to use, and so on (Schegloff, 1968; Bauman and Sherzer, 1974; Hymes, 1974; Schiffrin, 1977). People typically must also be able to hear and speak, though not necessarily, as I explain later. Inadequate performances at each level of competence can inhibit conversation.

As I demonstrate throughout this chapter, interaction between foreigners and natives resembles in many ways encounters between the deaf and the hearing. Those who are foreigners in a country are typically outsiders in that country as well. Both the deaf and foreigners share a common problem, communication. And it is partly their communication problems which lead to their being outsiders. Therefore, the assumptions and routine practices which I examine for hearing and speaking seem to occur at other levels of competence involved in performing hearing and speaking *roles*—for example, linguistic competence.

Strain in encounters between the deaf and the hearing is due to the impact of deafness and of its accompanying limitations on conversation. The effects of deafness on conversation are fully realized within the assumptions and routine practices of hearing people. These assumptions and practices usually successfully maintain interaction. Yet they often lead to confusion when applied to encounters with the deaf.

NOTHING UNUSUAL IS HAPPENING

People typically initiate interaction with the assumption that "nothing unusual is happening" (Emerson, 1970). Even in problematic situations, we often act as if nothing is out of the ordinary. Only under certain circumstances are we likely to recognize that "something unusual is happening" (Emerson, 1970; 219–220). Such is the case in encounters between the deaf and the hearing. Hearing people typically assume that everyone can competently hear and speak. As an extension of that assumption, hearing people often infer that those who speak must be able to hear. Hearing and speaking are seen as naturally going together. Therefore, those who cannot hear may be viewed as unable to speak. These assumptions lead to awkward and confused encounters between the deaf and the hearing in two major ways.

First, the assumptions lead hearing people to overlook the very real limitations in the hearing abilities of deaf people. By literally assuming "more than meets the eye," hearing people make false attributions about whom they are interacting with. These mistaken attributions lead hearing people to act in inappropriate ways, given the limitations of the deaf.

Second, the stance that nothing unusual is happening is not always maintained. It sometimes crumbles when confronted by the disconfirming actions of the deaf. It sometimes is merely discarded when it is recognized as inappropriate. In either case, something unusual *is* happening which hearing people are rarely prepared for. As I will discuss later, participants may even have different ideas of what it is that is unusual. There should be little wonder, though, that the hearing are not prepared. Deafness is a relatively low-prevalence disability (Schein and Delk, 1974). Therefore, most hearing people have little experience with the deaf. Further, hearing people often assume that nothing unusual is happening, even when that is not the case (e.g., they have encountered a deaf person without realizing it). The stance that nothing unusual is happening, as well as the imputation that something unusual is happening, concerns both the hearing and speaking abilities of people and the interplay between the two.

Hearing

To point out the obvious, hearing people rarely initiate a conversation with the inquiry as to the other person's hearing ability. Though hearing people know that some people are deaf, they do not routinely act as if that were the case. Because deafness is an invisible impairment, interacting with a deaf person does not necessarily reveal the person's deafness. Deaf people can literally become victims of the assumption that everyone can hear. . . .

A . . . common instance may occur in a supermarket when a deaf person inadvertently blocks the aisle. The deaf shopper does not hear the approach of the hearing customer, the muted noises of impatience, or the request to move aside. . . . The deaf person is treated as an uncooperative hearing person.

Hearing people who know that the deaf person is impaired may nevertheless routinely act as if that were not the case. Deaf people may be conversing, however awkwardly, with a sales clerk when the clerk casually turns and involves other store personnel in the transaction. Such behavior is common and is not meant to nor does it exclude a *hearing* customer from what is happening. Yet, the store clerk's routine action for hearing customers effectively excludes deaf customers from being informed. Or a sales clerk may matter-of-factly ask for the telephone number of a deaf customer who is paying with a check. However, many deaf people do not own telephones. Again, though,

the ability to hear and/or the accounterments of it are routinely taken for granted.

Even hearing people who are acquainted with a deaf individual, friends, co-workers, or team members, may momentarily overlook that the individual is deaf. This seems to occur especially in gatherings of several hearing people. A deaf man recalled his involvement with a group of hearing individuals:

> The group was politically aware and very argumentative. Arguments, discussions become so heated that they'd just about forget me. I would be left out. All the time that I was left out, they didn't mean to leave me out. It was just circumstances. So that the social involvement with them was not very successful from my point of view.

Foreigners who do not know the native language well may find themselves in similar situations.

The stance that nothing unusual is happening is maintained due to several factors. Deafness is an invisible impairment. Except through self-disclosure, signing, display of a hearing aid, or inability to appropriately respond to auditory stimuli, hearing people may not realize that the person they have encountered is deaf. Even those potential cues are ambiguous and can be misinterpreted. Thus, deaf people look "normal." Routinely they unintentionally pass as hearing. This ambiguity makes it easier to assume that nothing is out of the ordinary (Emerson, 1970: 218). Further, to abandon that stance may require a more complex performance than to maintain it (Emerson, 1970: 219). For example, to overlook that one person in a group is deaf is much easier than continually to interrupt the conversation in order to make sure that the deaf person is completely informed. Finally, as I will discuss later, coping strategies that deaf people use may present the impression that little or nothing is out of the ordinary or may be interpreted by hearing people as such.

In other situations where the encounter between the deaf and the hearing is more direct and focused, the assumption that everyone can hear may crumble as hearing people repeatedly fail to make themselves understood and deaf people fail to understand them. As I will discuss later, the deaf cope with this potential problem through different strategies. . . .

Speaking

Hearing people start with the stance that everyone can talk. Some deaf people do have intelligible speech, but they still cannot hear. These deaf people find that if they talk to a hearing person they are spoken to as if they were hearing. The deaf individual may then disclose that they are deaf. Informing hearing people that one is deaf, though, may only elicit statements of "deaf and dumb" or visible indications that the hearing people are tense and do not know how to proceed.

However, because deafness is not immediately visible, hearing people may continue to act as if these deaf people who speak well are hearing, even though they declare their deafness.

> Everytime he [a deaf person] used his speech to place his request, the airline clerk would automatically answer orally, giving the necessary details which would most of the time contain numbers. The deaf man found that it was very easy to misread lips, and end up with reservations for wrong flights. Then he would have a very difficult time convincing the clerk that he could not hear and that it would be better for the clerk to jot down the needed information so that he could be 100 percent sure before confirming the reservation: the clerk could not understand that one who spoke so well could have a hard time understanding him in turn [Jacobs, 1974: 22].

Due to the ambiguity of the situation (i.e., the deaf person looks "normal" and speaks well), the stance that nothing unusual is happening may be maintained even in the face of disclaimers.

Other deaf people with usable, if not "perfect," speech have been mistaken for being German or English or African, if they were black, rather than recognized as being deaf. Not only were the deaf assumed to be hearing because of their serviceable speech, but an additional, mistaken characteristic was attributed to them. . . .

In other situations, though, the assumption that everyone can speak may not be maintained. Some deaf people cannot talk or their speech is unintelligible. Other deaf individuals' speech becomes intelligible only after hearing people have become familiar with it. Several respondents noted that, at schools for the deaf, their teachers judged their speech to be good, but once they left school they had difficulty being understood. For example, a deaf woman orders hot chocolate but receives a hot dog instead. After learning English, foreigners may encounter similar problems.

Deaf people who do speak, though, cannot auditorily monitor their speech. What was meant for only a few people may be broadcast throughout the entire room. Or, because their speech has become inaudible, deaf speakers may find their hearing listeners staring with incomprehension. The deaf may mispronounce words without realizing it because the mistakes are not heard. This inability of deaf people to obtain the auditory feedback of their speech also leads to what might be called "deafisms." During conversation or in reverie deaf people may emit strange vocal sounds, clicking noises, humming sounds, or grunts. Although they are unaware that they are producing such potentially distracting and disturbing noises, the result is to strain the interaction with the hearing.

COPING STRATEGIES

While encounters between the deaf and the hearing are often strained and confused, both parties usually attempt to complete the interaction successfully. The coping strategies used by both the deaf and the hearing are attempts to repair the breach in the taken-for-granted interactional order, to compensate for those assumptions and practices which have failed.

Deaf people are continually faced with these interactional problems, whereas any single hearing person may rarely encounter a deaf individual (Goffman, 1963). Consequently, the deaf are likely to have developed more effective strategies than have the hearing. Strategies used by the deaf may be practical, learned techniques developed over years of experience. The hearing, though, may base their strategies on "common sense." However, the strategies employed by the participants may be ineffective due to the same assumptions and practices which initially gave rise to the strain.

Here I want to focus primarily on the strategies used by the deaf. Strategies used by naive hearing people will be discussed to the extent that they interact with the strategies of the deaf. The deaf deal with potential conversational problems with the hearing in two major ways. One is to help maintain the hearing's orientation that nothing unusual is happening. The second way is openly to acknowledge that something is out of the ordinary and guide hearing people through the encounter. These two approaches relate both to hearing and speaking as well as to the interplay between the two. As I will mention throughout, similar strategies are used by other physically impaired people as well as by foreigners. In their own ways, of course, they too are outsiders.

Maintaining "Nothing Unusual Is Happening"

Though the deaf have very real limitations in hearing and often in speaking, they may still attempt to perform the hearer and speaker roles. The general approach is to act in what would be an appropriate way if one could hear and speak. This general strategy is carried out through four specific techniques: *pretense; being alive* to the situation; *substitution* of senses; and *collusion* with "wise" hearing people. These techniques apply to performing the hearer and speaker roles, though some are more likely to be used in performing one role rather than the other. Some of the techniques may be used even when the impairment has been disclosed. Their important feature is not to conceal the deafness, though they may do that. Rather, they allow the interaction to proceed as if the person were not deaf.

Pretense. Some deaf individuals pretend that they understand the speaker's talk. The deaf smile in agreement, and the speaker may proceed unthinkingly. As one deaf man remarked, if the conversation is not that important, then he lets it pass. Yet the conversation could become important without his knowing it. If the speaker asks a question or expects a comment, awkward silence may predominate for both. The deaf individual's smiles and nods no longer suffice as appropriate responses.

Similar techniques are used by foreigners as well as by those with other physical impairments. Foreigners too may smile or nod their heads even if they do not fully understand what is being said. Visually impaired people who agree with their sighted friends' comments concerning a painting may be pretending in order to pass as sighted. Yet, pretense need not be used only to manage stigmatization.

In general, those who do not understand what is being talked about, even though they hear what is being said, often pretend to understand. For example, children, inadequately prepared students, and patients may often use this technique. In these situations pretense may be used because the individuals know less than what they would like others to believe. They are managing their stigmata of ignorance. The deaf, too, pretend at times in order to conceal the fact that they do not understand what is being said. Yet, pretense may also be the easiest way to conclude an unimportant conversation. Thus, a technique which seems to be a way of managing stigma may be used merely to accomplish everyday activities.

Being Alive. A related technique to pretense is to be alive to ordinary, routine features of situations that others take for granted. Goffman (1963: 88) notes that those who pass must often be alive to aspects of the situation that others do not attend to. Again, such a technique can serve a purpose different than stigma management. The deaf may be alert to cues other than auditory ones in order to act appropriately. When in a restaurant deaf people may not hear the waitress's request for their order. However, by noticing the waitress's approach and the position of her pencil and order pad, the deaf may appropriately respond as if such a request has been heard. Deaf customers who cannot hear how much their purchases cost or may position themselves in order to see the total on the cash register. Others may hand the cashier "enough" money to cover whatever the amount might be. Foreigners who use the latter technique may do so at the risk of being short-changed. Color-blind drivers are alive to features of traffic and traffic control that normally sighted drivers take for granted. By noting the position of the light and movements of the surrounding traffic, color-blind drivers can successfully negotiate intersections. In this case, being alive means staying alive.

Substitution of Senses. Deaf people may substitute one sense or modality of action for another in order to perform the hearer and speaker roles. This technique is most widely used and misunderstood in connection with the hearing role.

Some of the deaf attempt to perform the hearer role through lipreading. Lipreading, though, is often inadequate. Many speech sounds are indistinguishable on the speaker's lips (e.g., /b/ and /p/). Hearing people often talk through pursed lips or enunciate poorly. Facial hair of male speakers can obscure the visibility of their speech. Strangers are more difficult to lipread than those who are familiar (Pintner, 1929). Foreign accents make lipreading even more difficult. Finally, a gathering of several people poses multiple problems: Sight lines

from the deaf person to the various potential speakers are not equally clear, and if they were, such an arrangement would inhibit the interaction; it is difficult to follow the talk as it moves from one speaker to another; and the talk itself may be composed of simultaneous emissions from several speakers.

Consequently, deaf people may silently sit in group situations or avoid them altogether if possible. Remember the deaf bowler in Chapter 2. Some tell their hearing workers to continue without them at the coffee break, while others may occasionally ask, "What's going on?" As one deaf man, who depended on a hearing aid, remarked:

> I don't go down for coffee with the others [hearing co-workers]. In a group I can't follow what's going on; plus the noise, cups and silverware clanking. Maybe in a one to one or one to two [situation] I might take a break. When Pete Kelly was here, he's a hearing person who can sign, I used to go down with him. He could fill me in. If there was any confusion, I'd ask him, "What gives?"

A few deaf people may even try to show hearing people how it feels to be left out.

> A deaf woman took a hearing co-worker to lunch with her and several deaf friends. The hearing worker felt left out, just as the deaf woman did when dining with the group of hearing workers. The deaf woman felt that the demonstration helped the hearing person to understand the situation from the deaf woman's viewpoint.

Thus, within a group of several learning people substitution of senses may not be very effective.

Those deaf who do lipread must contend with the coping strategies that many hearing people bring to the encounter when they learn that their interactional partner is deaf. Hearing people often exaggerate their mouth movements in the well-intentioned but mistaken belief that such movements make it easier for the deaf person to read their speech. Some, familiar only with the "hard of hearing" or using the "hard of hearing" as a model for the deaf, shout or move closer to the deaf person's ear. This action serves only to bring stares from passers-by and further inhibit the interaction. As described by a deaf lipreader, the approach of the speaker toward the deaf person's ear can also lead to the following:

> At all costs I must keep my line of vision to his face; so I step back. If this is a badly managed encounter we may begin to perform a kind of slow tango. Here is X advancing on my ear, myself retreating step for step, eyes fixed on my partner's face [Wright, 1969: 114].

What occurred is a distancing problem that Hall (1959, 1966) has discussed for cross-cultural encounters.

Americans who meet a non-English speaking foreigner, especially in the states, may cope with that situation in much the same way as hearing people do when they meet a deaf person. Americans may shout, exaggerate their English, or speak English with the "appropriate" accent, whereas hearing people, as noted above, shout, exaggerate their mouth movements, or move closer to the deaf person's ear.

The above incident illustrates another strain that may arise when deaf people attempt to play the hearing role through lipreading. In order to lipread, the deaf person must maintain relatively constant focus on the speaker's face. This constant attention can make hearing speakers uncomfortable because they are rarely used to continual eye contact from the listener (Argyle and Dean, 1965). It may also lead these speakers to shift the position of the face, thus causing the deaf lipreader to miss what was said.

Even if deaf people are successful in lipreading hearing people's spoken words, misunderstandings may still occur. The deaf may lose the information that speech conveys nonverbally—for example, through intonation or emphasis. Consequently, the emotion or intent of the speaker might be misinterpreted (Schiff and Thayer, 1974).

Although lipreading is often inadequate for successfully performing the hearer role, many hearing people commonsensically believe that it is very effective. This belief, which has been historically promoted by educators of the deaf, supports the technique of pretense. Even if the deaf do not understand what is being said, they can pretend to because many hearing people believe that all deaf people can lipread well.

To a lesser degree, deaf people may perform the speaker role through substitution of one modality for another. There is no equivalent to lipreading, but performing the speaker *role* requires only appropriate responses which need not always be verbal. As noted before, deaf people who smile and nod their heads in agreement are not only pretending to be hearers but are also giving appropriate responses as speakers. In situations of limited contact, pointing rather than speaking is often appropriate. Deaf people may point to the items on the menu which they wish to order. Who can fault someone for not being able to pronounce some foreign dishes? A few words may accompany the pointing. Though pointing may not be the ordinary response in a restaurant, it often suffices along with other techniques (e.g., collusion, to be discussed next) to maintain the stance that nothing is out of the ordinary.

Substitution is also employed by individuals with other impairments. Blind people who rely on their hearing to tell them when it is safe to cross the street are substituting one sense for another. Often those with impairments are explicitly trained to use their remaining senses and abilities as substitutes for those senses and abilities which are impaired.

In order effectively to substitute one sense or modality of action for another, physically impaired people must be alive to both features of and sensory cues in situations that others take for granted. Thus, the techniques of being alive and of substitution of senses are complementary. The success of each is based on there being *redundant* information in situations. Many different cues, often available through different sensory channels, can inform us of what is happening. The potential problem, of course, is that secondary cues and senses may not always give us as accurate or detailed information about what is occurring as the primary ones do.

Collusion. Other deaf people maintain the hearing's impression that nothing unusual is happening with a little help from their friends. Through collusion with "wise" hearing people, deaf people can often avoid potential communication problems with naive hearing people. The collusion may be intentional and well thought out in advance, or it may be a routine that has slowly, almost subconsciously, developed. Thus in a restaurant, one wise hearing person may order for the entire group of deaf and hearing people. The waitress may be none the wiser. A parallel situation exists when wise foreigners order dinner for their American friends in foreign restaurants. Again, a similar kind of collusion occurs in stigma management when, for example, the blind person's sighted companion guides the blind person through a room (Goffman, 1963).

Collusion is also used by the deaf to perform the speaker role. A hearing friend may do most of the speaking for a deaf person. More subtly, those who have difficulty moderating their speech due to a lack of auditory feedback may arrange for a hearing friend to accompany them and provide visual feedback (e.g., hand signals) in place of the auditory feedback. Backstage work may even take place in order to prepare deaf people for their performances—e.g., hearing friends may coach deaf people in pronunciation or volume. As is the case for training in the substitution of senses, educational programs for the deaf and for those with other impairments are expected to do such backstage work.

Through all four techniques—pretense, being alive, substitution of senses, and collusion—deaf people attempt to maintain the hearing's orientation that nothing unusual is happening and thereby successfully accomplish everyday activities. These four techniques often complement each other or are used in conjunction with one another. They are used by those with other physical impairments as well as by foreigners.

Managing "Something Unusual Is Happening"

In many situations, if not in most, deaf people cannot or choose not to maintain the impression that nothing is out of the ordinary. It may be more difficult and less effective to pretend to be hearing than to let others know of one's impairment. In these situations, the deaf often explicitly reveal their impairment and then try to indicate to the hearing how both can successfully manage the encounter. Three major strategies are used. Deaf people may implicitly or explicitly *disclose* that they have an impairment and then indicate what the hearing should do. Others use a *go-between,* a third party, to pass the messages back and forth. And some deaf people *manipulate* the hearing's impression of the type or extent of their impairment in order to facilitate interaction.

Disclosure. Most of the time, especially when the conversation with the hearing will entail more than a brief exchange, deaf people openly disclose their hearing and speech limitations to naive hearing people. Other physically disabled people often do the same. Something is out of the ordinary which deaf people attempt to guide hearing people through.

Deaf people often attempt to communicate with hearing people through writing or gestures. While they may be understood, the interaction is rarely smooth and uninhibited. Further, after reading a deaf person's written message and still relying on the assumption that everyone can hear, hearing people may speak to rather than write to the deaf person. When this happens, those deaf who do not lipread must explicitly state that they have a hearing impairment which requires the hearing to write rather than speak their message. Hearing people, though, are often uncomfortable with writing. They may even leave the deaf person standing with paper and pencil in hand.

Further, misunderstanding may occur because the writing or gesture of the deaf person is interpreted by the hearing individual within a different symbolic framework from that wherein it was produced (Stokoe and Battison, 1975).

A bank teller given a note asking for a coin bag mistook two deaf mutes for robbers.

"Please give me a zipper bag," read the note that a teenager dressed in white cut-off trousers passed to the teller at the First Federal Savings and Loan Association.

Thinking it was a holdup, the teller triggered an alarm, police said. The teller then stalled the youth, identified as Robert J. Pokorny, 19, of Painesville, Ohio.

An FBI spokesman said the teenager waited, but after a few moments scribbled another note: I will bring 2,500 coins.

The teller kept stalling, and the youth finally picked up his notes and left with his companion, Howard E. Shuping, 54, of Akron, Ohio.

Witnesses gave police officers and FBI agents a description of the car, which was traced to a residence in nearby Clearwater.

"The FBI followed Bobby to his grandmother's house," said his aunt, Elsie Pokorny of Clearwater.

"They pulled their guns and told them to stop as they got out of the car, but they couldn't hear it," she said. "I'm thankful they didn't shoot."

Pokorny and Shuping were taken to FBI offices in Tampa, 25 miles away, and detained for questioning. They were released after a Federal attorney said no charges would be filed [The Deaf American, 1973: 29].

While the meaning of the youth's notes seems clear, the bank teller misframed his actions because of the assumption that everyone can hear and speak. The deaf customer did not *explicitly* state that he was deaf, but only ambiguously implied it by writing his request. Therefore, if it is assumed that everyone can hear and speak, then the only reason that people would write a note in a bank is if they were attempting to rob it. Of course, not everyone can hear and speak. Thus, assumptions which are developed in a hearing world can lead to confusion when applied to outsiders in that world.

Go-between. Often deaf people rely on a "wise" hearing person to act as a *go-between* in encounters with naive hearing people. The wise hearing person, often a son or a daughter, will translate the remarks of the naive hearing person in sign language. If the deaf person does not speak intelligibly, the go-between will translate the sign language into spoken language. The parallel to encounters between foreigners is obvious. This technique often works reasonably well, but a few problems may arise.

If the go-between is unsophisticated in the matter being discussed, then satisfactorily conveying the information to both sides may be difficult. Such could be the case if the go-between for a deaf couple is their young hearing child. The same problem may occur when first-generation immigrant children interpret for their immigrant parents. These examples suggest a related problem. Personal matters (e.g., illnesses or financial dealings) are often embarrassing to discuss through a third party—particularly a third party who is a young, unsophisticated child.

The role of the go-between may also expand beyond what the impaired person intended. Normals may direct more of their attention to the go-between than either the impaired person or the go-between feels is necessary. Thus, waitresses may ask sighted companions of blind people what the latter wish to order (Gowman, 1956). On the other hand, the go-between may gradually monopolize the interaction. Rather than interpret what is said, the go-between makes decisions for the impaired person or the foreigner. As I noted in Chapters 2 and 3, deaf people often complain of not being fully informed when a go-between handles a telephone conversation for them. They become the third party.

Manipulation. Other deaf people may acknowledge that something unusual is happening, but manipulate the impression that hearing people have of what, exactly, is occurring. Goffman (1963: 94) argues that those pass may present signs of their failing as signs of another attribute which is less stigmatized. The deaf may use similar techniques, but not in order to manage their putatively spoiled identities. In fact, the deaf may present themselves as *more* impaired than they are in order to manage the encounter. The manipulations, though, fit the assumptions that the hearing bring to the encounters.

For example, those deaf individuals whose speech may lead hearing people mistakenly to identify them as hearing, sometimes use a simple strategy. In those situations where prolonged contact will not occur, the deaf may write their message rather than speak it. The deaf man who had problems at ticket counters does so now when requesting airline information (Jacobs, 1974). The deaf man not only avows his deviance of deafness (Turner, 1972), but implies a second discrediting trait of mutism which he does not possess. The strategy, though, allows the deaf person to complete the interaction successfully. The blind may use a similar strategy:

One totally blind boy who had a very normal appearance suffered so many unfortunate experiences from being taken for sighted that he began to carry a cane even though he made not the slightest use of it in getting about his environment [Lemert, 1951: 109–110].

Different strategies are used by those deaf whose speech becomes unintelligible to hearing people once hearing people know of the deafness. Some deaf people keep their impairment a secret from the hearing person. Others will reveal it as soon as they feel the hearing listener has become accustomed to their speech. Some use manipulation. They wear a hearing aid (Jacobs, 1974). Though the deaf person's speech does not improve, it remains intelligible to the hearing person because the deaf person is no longer viewed as a grossly defective hearer. The deaf person is only mildly defective (i.e., "hard of hearing") and still capable of speaking intelligibly. In passing as hard of hearing, these deaf people are not concerned with their spoiled identities. Rather, they are using a practical, learned strategy of manipulation which allows the interaction with the hearing person to proceed more smoothly.

As noted before, though, hearing people may treat deaf people as hard of hearing. The hearing shout or move closer to deaf people's ears (Webb et al., 1966: 150). Deaf people who wear a hearing aid so that their speech will remain intelligible to hearing people may find that it becomes even more difficult to lipread a hearing person as the latter shouts or advances toward their ears. A strategy to combat one strain may increase the likelihood of another.

Discussion

Unlike many other outsiders, the deaf are physically disabled. Their impairment and its accompanying limitations may profoundly disrupt interaction with the hearing. The same is true for other physically disabled outsiders. Consequently, stigmatization cannot fully explain the often awkward encounters between the deaf and the hearing.

Several factors seem to account for this overemphasis on stigmatization. Labeling theorists have often investigated or emphasized the visibly disabled (Davis, 1961; Barry 1973; Levitin, 1975). Therefore, the disabled's "differentness" was often apparent to both the nondisabled as well as to the sociologist. Further, much of the research has focused on the physically disabled who acquired their impairments later in life. Often they had not resolved issues of personal and social acceptance (Ladieu et al., 1948). While those born impaired or who have been impaired for a long time may continue to cope with stigmatization, that issue may not be paramount in their lives. . . . Members of the deaf community often deal with particular stigmatizing behaviors of the hearing by ignoring them. For example, members are so used to the stares that their signing attracts that they no longer pay attention to them. While members are ambivalent about their deafness, they derive a sense of belonging and wholeness from their fellow members of the deaf community. Consequently, the lack of social acceptance among members of the hearing world becomes less important, because acceptance is found within the deaf community. I suspect that much the same could be said for those who are members of other communities of outsiders. Finally, as in much previous thinking on outsiders in general (Goode, 1978), researchers have often assumed, even while denying it, that the physically disableds' lives are radically different from the nondisableds'. If that is so, then what problems they face and how they cope with them must be different too (Carroll, 1961).

Conclusion

An important task that the deaf face, as well as everyone else, whether they are outsiders or not, is to accomplish everyday activities competently. In trying to do so, the deaf often experience awkward, embarrassing, and unsatisfactory encounters with the hearing. Consequently, while the deaf cannot avoid the hearing world, they often seek out those with whom easy communication is possible—other deaf people. Awkward encounters with the hearing are part of the experiences which members of the deaf community share with one another. Those experiences reinforce the members' identification and participation with one another. Although the deaf community is not merely a response to the deaf's frustrating interaction with the hearing, it certainly does provide the social setting within which relaxed, uninhibited communication for the deaf typically takes place.

References

Argyle, Michael and Janet Dean (1965). 'Eye-contact, distance, and affiliation.' *Sociometry* 28: 289–304.

Barry, John R. (1973). 'The Physically Disabled.' Pp.99–115 in Don Spiegel and Particia Keith-Spiegel (eds.). *Outsiders USA: Original Essays on 24 Outgroups.* San Francisco: Rinehart Press.

Bauman, Richard and Joel Sherzer (eds.). (1974). *Explorations in the Ethnography of Speaking.* London: Cambridge University Press.

Becker, Howard S. (1974). "Labelling theory reconsidered." Pp. 41–66 in Paul Rock and Mary McIntosh (eds.). *Deviance and Social Control.* London: Tavistock.

Bender, Ruth E. (1970). *The Conquest of Deafeness.* Cleveland: The Press of Case Western Reserve University.

Carroll, Thomas J. (1961). *Blindness: What It Is What It Does, and How to Live With It.* Boston: Little, Brown.

Chicago Sun Times (1975). May 31: 5.

Chomsky, Noam (1965). *Aspects of the Theory of Syntax.* Cambridge: MIT Press.

Davis, Fred (1961). "Deviance disavowal: The management of strained interaction by the visibly handicapped" *Social Problems* 9: 120–132.

The Deaf American (1973). 25: 29.

Emerson, Joan P. (1970). "Nothing unusual is happening." Pp. 208–22 in Tamotsu Shibutani (ed.). *Human Nature and Collective Behavior.* Englewood Cliffs, New Jersey: Prentice-Hall.

Goffman, Erving (1963). *Stigma: Notes on the Management of Spoiled Identity.* Englewood Cliffs, New Jersey: Prentice-Hall.

Goffman, Erving (1974). *Frame Analysis.* Cambridge: Harvard University Press.

Goode, Erich (1978). *Deviant Behavior: An Interactionist Approach.* Englewood Cliffs, New Jersey: Prentice-Hall.

Gowman, Alan G. (1965). "*Blindness and the role of companion.*" Social Problems 4: 68–75.

Hall, Edward Twichell (1959). *The Silent Language.* Garden City, New York: Doubleday.

Hall, Edward Twichell (1966). *The Hidden Dimension.* Garden City, New York: Doubleday.

Hymes, Dell (1974). *Foundations in Sociolinguistics: An Ethnographic Approach.* Philadelphia: University of Pennsylvania Press.

Jacobs, Leo M. (1974). *A Deaf Adult Speaks Out.* Washington, DC: Gallaudet College Press.

Kramer, Ernest (1963). "Judgment of personal characteristics and emotions from nonverbal properties of speech." *Psychological Bulletin* 60: 408–420.

Lambert, W. E., R. C. Hodgson, R. C. Gardner, and S. Fillenbaum (1960). "Evaluational reactions to spoken languages." *Journal of Abnormal and Social Psychology* 60: 44–51.

Ladieu, Gloria, Dan L. Adler and Tamara Dembo (1948). "Studies in adjustment to visible injuries: Social acceptance of the injured." *Journal of Social Issues,* 4:55–61.

Lemert, Edwin M. (1951). *Social Pathology.* New York: McGraw-Hill.

Levitin, Teresa E. (1975). "Deviants as active participants in the labeling process: The visibly handicapped." *Social Problems* 22: 548–557.

Pintner, Rudolph (1929). "Speech and speech reading: Tests for the deaf." *Journal of Applied Psychology* 13:220–225.

Richardson, Stephen A. (1969). "The effect of physical disability in the socialization of a child." Pp. 1047–1064 in David A. Goslin (ed.). *Handbook of Socialization Theory and Research.* Skokie, Illinois: Rand McNally.

Safilios-Rothschild, Constantina (1970). *The Sociology and Social Psychology of Disability and Rehabilitation.* New York: Random House.

Schegloff, Emanuel A. (1968). "Sequencing in conversational openings." *American Anthropologist* 70: 1075–1095.

Schein, Jerome D. and Marcus T. Delk, Jr. (1974). *The Deaf Population of the United States.* Silver Springs, Maryland: National Association of the Deaf.

Schiff, William and Stephen Thayer (1974). "A eye for an ear? Social perception, Nonverbal communication, and deafness." *Rehabilitation Psychology* 21: 50–70.

Schiffrin, Deborah (1977). "Opening encounters." *American Sociological Review* 42: 679–691.

Scott, Robert A. (1969a). *The Making of Blind Men: A Study of Adult Socialization.* New York: Russell Sage.

Scott, Robert A. (1969b). "The socialization of blind children." Pp. 1025–1045 in David A.Goslin (ed.). *Handbook of Socialization Theory and Research.* Skokie, Illinois: Rand McNally.

Stokoe, William C. and Robbin M. Battison (1975*). Sign Language, Mental Health, and Satisfying Interaction.* Chicago: David T. Siegel Institute for Communicative Disorders, Michael Reese Hospital and Medical Center.

Strauss, Anselm and Barney G. Glaser (1975). *Chronic Illness and the Quality of Life.* St. Louis: Mosby.

Turner, Ralph (1972) "Deviance avowal as neutralization of commitment." *Social Problems* 19:308–321.

Webb, Eugene J., Donald T. Campbell, Richard D. Schwartz, and Lee Sechrest. (1966). *Unobtrusive Measures: Nonreactive Research in the Social Sciences.* Skokie, Illinois: Rand McNally.

Wright, Beatrice A. (1960). *Physical Disability-A Psychological Approach.* New York: Harper & Row.

Wright, David (1969). *Deafness; A Personal Account.* London: Allen Lane.

PART IV

PRODUCING SOCIAL SELVES

We come into this world as individuals, achieve character, and become persons.

—Robert Park (1952), *Human Communities*

We talk, therefore I am.

—Anna Quindlen (1989), *Living Out Loud*

Tell me who you love and I'll tell you who you are.

—Creole Proverb

FROM MASKS TO SELVES

Jodi O'Brien

What is the difference between the social performances (presentation of identities) that we engage in to establish a particular definition of the situation and expressions of the "true" self? One of my teachers and mentors, Phil Blumstein (1944–1991), used to tell the following story as an illustration of how identity presentation can eventually become an expression of self.

There once was a beautiful and intelligent princess who sought a husband. A decree was sent throughout the land that eligible men should present themselves at the castle for her consideration. The decree went on to announce that the qualities she desired in a husband were that he be kind, generous, loving, and respectful. Across the land lived a baron who was feared by all who knew him. He was ugly and misshapen and was so reclusive that people believed he was a wicked wizard of some sort. When the baron heard the decree, he knew he wanted nothing more than to marry the princess. But he despaired in the realization that he had nothing to offer her and none of the characteristics she desired. Then an idea struck him. He went immediately to a mask maker he knew and requested that the man make him a mask that displayed all the characteristics the princess desired. When the mask was completed, the baron put it on and rode throughout his village to see the effect. The people he encountered saw a man who appeared kind and thoughtful, and they responded to him with smiles and generosity. Pleased with the effect of the mask, the baron closed up his home and rode across the land to present himself to the princess. As soon as she saw him, the princess could see this was the man of her dreams. She sent out the announcement that her groom had been found, and they married shortly after in a grand ceremony that was celebrated far and wide.

In the days following their marriage, the baron was careful to always wear the mask and never let it slip even the slightest bit. He knew the princess was dearly loved by all, and he feared what would happen to him if anyone were to discover his underlying ugliness. The princess was delighted with her new husband. She took him on several journeys to visit her subjects throughout the kingdom. In each new village and hamlet, she would tell the people how kind and generous he was. Feeling the eyes upon him, the baron would do his best to appear respectful and loving. One day, after many months of travel, the couple and their entourage arrived in the town in which the baron had lived before marrying the princess. As she had done in each town, the princess held grand parties and invited the townspeople to attend. It was at one such party that a woman overheard the voice of a man she remembered as the one who had lived in isolation on the hill and was rumored to have put a spell on the town. Suspicious and curious, she turned to confront the man and encountered none other than the baron. "You imposter!" she screamed. "I know who you really are!" As she made this declaration, she ripped away his mask. Everyone gasped. The baron clutched his naked face and ran from the crowd. The princess ran after him and found him hiding in a darkened corner. "What's wrong, my love?" she inquired. "Certainly the woman is confused. She can't possibly be talking about you." At these words, the baron raised his head, prepared for the princess to see the truth: He was an ugly, selfish man. Imagine his surprise when the princess merely wiped his face with her handkerchief and said, "Come, let us rejoin the party so that they can see who you truly are." Startled and afraid, the baron protested, "You can't possibly want to be seen with someone as hideous as me," he said. The princess pulled a small mirror from inside her gown and held it up to his face. "I can't imagine why you are being so ridiculous," she laughed. "Look at yourself! You're beautiful—just the man I dreamed of." The baron looked into the mirror reluctantly and nearly fainted when he saw the image gazing back at him. There in the mirror, in the form of his own face, was the image of the mask.

Blumstein concocted this fairy tale to illustrate a process whereby "masks" become selves. Although note quite so simple a transformation as a toad being kissed by a princess and turning into a prince, the story illustrates that many of the characteristics we tend to associate with "personality" (for example, kindness, selfishness) actually emerge and become constant through social interaction. There are many masks that we wear frequently, but not all of these situated identities become stable aspects of our self-image. According to Blumstein, the factors that contribute to this transformation include repeated performance *and* role support from significant others. In other words, if we repeatedly perform a role that is significant to us and do so in the presence of people who find the role convincing and who are important to us and supportive of the performance, we are likely to eventually incorporate the performance into our own self-concept. This is the process whereby someone moves from engaging in a behavior, for instance, someone who studies, to being someone who *is* a scholar. Or someone who does the cooking to someone who *is* a chef. For Blumstein, performance is *behavior* that is manifest as *situated identities*. Identities are subject to considerable change and variation, depending on the situation and the audience. Selves are stable concepts—anchoring, organized ideas about our "true selves." This organized self-perception is the framework through which we view and judge our own actions and, eventually, make sense of who we are. In this essay, we will look at some of the differences between identity performances and the development of stable self-concepts. Sociologists consider the self to be an ongoing social process and not something that is inborn, fixed, and immutable. The stability that we appear to have as "personalities" is a product of interactional expectations and our desire for coherency and predictability.

SOCIALIZATION

Socialization is a process of learning the gestures, cues, and expectations that enable us to engage in successful impression management. When we become socialized into a role, we learn how to perform in ways that are consistent with the situation. For instance, whenever you begin a new job, you learn basic skills of the trade, but you also learn how to convey the attitude associated with the job. New teachers, for example, may be masters of their area of knowledge, but they have to practice giving the impression that they are in charge of the class and in control of the situation. A novice teacher may overdo the attempt to be seen as "in charge" and come across as "too authoritative." Likewise, a junior employee who is invited to drinks with the boss for the first time may worry later that she appeared "overeager" in her attempts to convey an impression of interest and respect. Like all new skills, the ability to project an identity that conveys the desired definition of the situation develops with practice. It's important to keep in mind that the source of our information about how to perform specific roles is interactional. We learn from others, including people we see represented in media, how we think a particular role is supposed to be played. Thus, in addition to practice, much of your performance is based on the type of imagery you hold in your minds (idealization) about how to behave in various situations. Someone may think of himself as a "nice guy" but have only one idea about how to approach women for potential dates. His friends may have convinced him that the only way to play this role is to perform with swagger and bravado. This approach is unlikely to be successful, but unless he becomes aware of alternative ways to convey his interest to potential dates, he is probably doomed to fail in his quests for romance.

One question that is of particular interest to students and scholars of social psychology is the question of the "self." The psychological theorist William James once remarked that our selves are as numerous as the number of people we interact with. This can be interpreted to mean that we are always putting on identities, or masks, in the presence of others. However, all of us know that some of these identities feel more consistent and real than others. It is these more enduring features of behavior that we associate with the core self or personality. What is the relationship between the identities that we put on to convey impressions to others and our inner sense of self—the core characteristics that we consider to be stable aspects of who we are across situations?

There are many ways to approach this question, and the comments in the remainder of this essay touch on the issue only briefly. The emphasis in the following discussion is on the *social self.* There are certainly aspects of who you are that do not fall into the pattern described below. However, if you concentrate on the implications of this theory of the social self, you may learn some useful things about how people come to see (name) themselves in particular ways.

ROUTINIZED IDENTITIES

One implication of interaction rituals is that they have the potential to become set or routinized. They may become so automatic that people fail to notice the extent to which they themselves engage in these performances. After spending some time at a job or in the company of old friends, people seldom recall the discomfort of the initial interactions—when the job was new or the people were strangers, when they were not sure whether their identity claims would be granted or how to define the situation.

How does an identity become a self? The answer, in part, is in the process of routinization. Identities that we perform repeatedly may become part of our general sense of who we are. On the other hand, some of us perform very routinized identities without ever considering them to be an aspect of our "true self." For example, many people who live and work in Los Angeles, when asked what they do, reply, "I work as a server/delivery person/janitor, but

I am really writing a screenplay," or "I am really an actor." The job, even if it is one that the person has performed for years, may not be an important aspect of the "real" self, whereas an identity that has yet to be realized may be the core of how the person sees herself or himself.

Before reading further, take out a piece of paper and write down twenty responses to the question "Who am I?" As you read through this section, ponder how each of these aspects of your "real" self came to be.

"I," "Me," and the Self as a Conversation

Even when interactions become routine, people still engage in impression management. Pause to consider for a moment how you observe and evaluate your own performances. In the Part II essay, I discussed the work of George Herbert Mead (see Reading 22), whose theory suggested that humans learn to treat themselves as objects that have meaning relative to other people and situations. The ability to treat the self as an object is what makes it possible for us to observe, reflect on, plan, and direct our own behavior. In other words, without the ability to perceive the self as an object, we would be unable to engage in impression management. As Mead explains it, we watch our own performances from the position of an overseer and attempt to bring our behavior into line with the expectations we have learned to associate with the situation. In this way, we are behaving as "socialized" beings.

An example I sometimes share with students, to their amusement, is my own behavior in the presence of a colleague who is completely bald. This colleague is much older than me, and in fact, for many years he was the chair of my department. For reasons I don't entirely understand, I often find myself wanting to rub his head when we sit together in meetings. In my mind, I can see myself reaching out to rub his head. At the same time, I can see how mortified everyone would be if I followed through on this action. Seeing all this in my head enables me to resist the temptation to rub his head. Mead would describe the impulse to head-rub as the potential action of the "I." The "me" is the overseer who observes the behavior and intentions of the "I" and brings them into line with cultural expectations. "You can't rub his head! That would be so embarrassing!"

The images and ideals you hold in your mind about proper behavior represent the attitudes and values of your culture. These expectations function as the *generalized other* (internalized social expectations) to give people an "ideal script" for acting the proper role in a situation. In understanding your "self," it is useful to think in terms of a conversation. When you guide, direct, and evaluate your own behavior, you are engaging in an internal conversation. This conversation might be with "generalized" expectations ("nice people don't pee on the sidewalk"), with your idea of the expectations of a particular group you associate yourself with ("I need a different haircut if I'm going to look as hip as the rest of the gang"), or with some specific person in your life ("my girlfriend is going to be so pissed if she catches me flirting this way"). According to Mead, these internal conversations are the basis of what we think of as our core self. Think for a moment about some of the audiences in your own head. Who are some of the significant people that you find yourself organizing your behavior in response to? What are some of the groups you reference in trying to make decisions about what do to and who to be?

Mead and other social psychologists emphasize the importance of "significant others" and significant "reference groups" in self-development. According to their theories, we are constantly engaged in internal self-evaluation based on our ideas about what we think significant others and groups we associate with expect of us.

THE SELF AS A PRODUCT OF INTERACTION

The process of identifying or naming behaviors that we come to see as an aspect of "self" involves this internal conversation. *In this way, the self is also a social construction that takes shape through interaction*—interaction outwardly with others and, especially, internal interactions or conversations we have with our images of significant others and reference groups.

In much the same way that we each learn to define the meaning of things in our environment, we learn about who we are through observing the responses of others to us as objects. Charles Horton Cooley, who wrote shortly before Mead, suggested the concept of the "looking-glass self" (see Reading 23). The looking-glass self consists of an internal image we generate about our self when we are trying to figure out what others think of us. We gain information about ourselves by casting ourselves in the role of an observer, *imagining* how our actions appear to that person, and then attaching some reaction (such as pride or mortification) to that perception. In short, we imagine what we think someone else thinks of us, and then we judge ourselves accordingly. Cooley refers to these self-assessments based on perceived reactions from others as "reflected appraisals." According to Cooley and most contemporary social psychologists, "significant others" and "primary groups" have a great deal of potential to shape our possible selves, because we use perceived assessments from them to shape our own self-assessment.

In other words, we name our own behavior (including how we feel about it) based on what *we think* others who are significant to us think about us. For example, a teacher whom you admire a great deal may appear to think very highly of your writing. This reflected appraisal may lead you to focus more intently on your writing; in time, your writing may become quite good, and you may begin to see yourself as a "writer." If you have a difficult decision to make regarding whether to take a high-paying job or attend a graduate writing program, you are likely to ask yourself what this teacher would think of your decision. In this process, you literally conjure up an image of yourself and hold it in front of your ideal of your teacher and develop a self-assessment accordingly. You may find yourself thinking, "This teacher will be so disappointed in me if I don't pursue my writing."

Some people don't like the idea of the self as being a product of social interaction. It can be very useful in your own understanding of your self to take some time to ponder your internal conversations; ask yourself who or what you're in conversation with, and then try to assess the accuracy of your ideas about how these people or groups think about you. The following exercise helps to illuminate the specific steps that occur in the process of moving from a series of identities to committed "selves" through interaction.

Begin a paper with the phrase: "I never thought I would become . . ." Then write about something that you could never see yourself doing (joining a religious cult, becoming a particular type of politician or other social role), and consider the ways in which persons who are significant in your life could actually change your ideals, beliefs, and sense of who you are.

Blumstein (1991) was particularly interested in the ways in which selves are produced in personal relationships. Blumstein's thesis is that significant others, particularly intimate partners, are important contributors to our sense of self because their reflected appraisals are so valued. For example, in the process of coordinating activities, a couple may name particular behaviors as identities, such as "provider" or "homemaker." The partners may become attached to, or grow into, these identities through routinization and the reflected appraisals of each other. This is especially likely to be the case when we perform situated identities that match highly idealized cultural expectations. For instance, a heterosexual couple who insist, early in their marriage, that they will not conform to gendered expectations about marital roles may find themselves surprised at the extent to which they have fallen into these roles anyway. If they trace it back, they may recognize many small, but cumulatively significant, moments when parents, friends, and others have focused on these behaviors and, in order to maintain the interaction, the married individuals may have played the expected situated identity. Friends and relatives who constantly comment on a man's "earning power" are singling out this behavior as an important characteristic of a "successful" married man. Each of these interactions reinforces a social expectation that "the man should be the breadwinner." In time, even though he may not think he subscribes to this expectation, the newly married man may find himself shifting his behavior more and more to fit the expectations of "the married man." Blumstein refers to this process as "ossification," meaning that identities have the potential to harden, like bone, into selves.

Under the right circumstances, we begin to think of everyday behaviors as "identities" and then, perhaps, to incorporate these identities into an organized sense of self. For instance, what's the difference between those of us who shop and those who consider themselves to *be* shoppers? The identity masks that we wear to convey information to others have the potential to become part of what we consider our "real" self. This is likely to occur when people whose opinions we value continually reinforce a specific behavior or identity ("I think you have a great sense of fashion"; "I think you are a remarkably kind person"; and so forth). The identity becomes solidified into an aspect of "self" as we incorporate it into our internal dialogue (internalization) and hold it up as a reflection of a personal, ideal sense of being. Consider the implications of this process as you reread your "Who am I?" list. Can you describe the social relations or social processes that occurred over time to give you a sense that you are these roles and possess these characteristics?

My own list includes the identity "teacher." How did I come to see myself this way? When I entered graduate school, like most graduate students, I was required to be a teaching assistant as part of my training. Most of us had been undergraduate students ourselves only a few years earlier, and we were quite nervous about trying to play the role of teacher. One exercise we engaged in was to try to remember a favorite teacher and consider what traits had made her or him a great teacher. With these images in mind, we would then perform the role of teacher in our own classes. All of us had to teach, but only a few of us began to eventually think of "teaching" as a central aspect of who we are. What made the difference? In my case, I received "role support" from several sources. My family thought that my teaching was a neat thing (otherwise, they had no idea what graduate school was and why I was there). When I talked with them about my studies, we talked mostly about my teaching. This they could understand. I was also invited by the chair of the department to participate in a pilot seminar that was part of a national project aimed at making scholars into better teachers (most graduate students receive little or no training to teach). This seminar functioned as a primary group. It became one of my primary reference points. Through this seminar, which included a lot of videotaping of our teaching, I began to think constantly about teaching: how to do it, what made it special, and so forth. My new seminar buddies and I talked together about these things as well. Within a few years, I was giving seminars to other graduate students on how to teach. I even wrote articles about teaching. I woke up one day and realized that over the course of several years and through engagement with a specific primary group I was not just a scholar who also taught classes, I was a *teacher*.

Role support from those who are significant is a central factor in the development of aspects of self that we consider to be core components of who we are. Significant others can sometimes be a source of conflicting information. In addition to the teaching support I received in graduate school, I also had faculty mentors who considered my teaching activities a waste of time. These professors wanted me to focus on scholarly writing and get a job at a top research school. They worried that I had become "too identified" with faculty at teaching schools and that I would "throw away" a good research career. These conflicts can be painful and difficult to reconcile. I will discuss this at length in the section of Part VI titled "Contradictions and Conflict in Self-Production." For now, it can be said that the conflicts are also a form of internal conversation that reveal our deepest values and commitments. I valued both primary groups—researchers and teachers—and I had significant relationships with mentors in both areas. The depth of my own conflict reflected these social relationships and commitments.

Ultimately, I was able to reconcile my conflict by engaging in an alternative conversation with myself. I didn't have to be one or the other—I could be both. I became aware of this *possible self* in a conversation with a retired faculty member who was very famous for his scholarly work on social research methods. This very famous scholar used to visit me in my graduate student cubicle and ask how my teaching was going. He was the one who told me I could do both. He introduced a new possibility into my existing definition of the situation. He reframed it. In so doing, he probably changed the course of my life. To the extent that I have a current vocation for teaching, I can trace it to the interactional effects of groups who provided me with a vocabulary for thinking about and performing the teaching role, and significant others who provided role support in the form of encouragement. Even those who were discouraging had an impact in making my commitment to teaching even stronger.

Possible Selves

Hazel Markus and Paula Nurius (1986) are known for their studies on how people develop ideas about who and what they think they can be. So far, this text has emphasized the idea that we learn cultural expectations from others. These expectations include scripts that provide details about appropriate behavior (identities) for various situations. Markus and Nurius are interested in the specific sources of information that individuals have for what roles they think they can play. They are also interested in how this information differs for different people in different walks of life. For instance, your economic class background, your racial or ethnic background, and your gender are some of the significant differences that shape ideas about who you think you can be. Markus and Nurius are particularly interested in studying the details of how we imagine ourselves in possible roles. According to their work, individuals who can "see" themselves in a particular social position are more likely to eventually achieve this position. However, it's not enough to have a general idea of the social role you would like to occupy; rather, you need to be able to imagine the actual *process* of getting into that role. They propose that people who have access to the information, or stories, that provide specific details of how to become a certain self will be more likely to be able to *imagine* themselves going through these steps and, in turn, will be better able to organize their lives so that they achieve their desired positions.

One example of their work focuses on the different expectations of fourth graders who are from either wealthy or low-income families. When asked what they want to be when they grow up, the children from higher-income families usually name a profession such as lawyer, doctor, software designer, and so on. What is noteworthy for Markus and Nurius is the children's ability to describe, in very specific detail, the paths to achieving these professional roles. The children have a well-mapped route, which includes an understanding that they will have to go to college (a good one), graduate school, and so forth. In contrast, children from low-income families often have highly unrealistic desires—for the most part, they want to be music stars or star athletes. When asked how this might come about for them, they have very little idea about what they might have to do to realize these desired selves. According to Markus and Nurius, the difference is in the type of information children receive about the actual processes of becoming specific social roles. If the information is specific and well charted, the children develop a highly articulated sense of a "possible self." They can hold this image in their minds and "rehearse" what it will be like to go through each stage of development toward the imagined end. Children who have no information about the path also have ideals, but they have no real sense of how to perform in each of the phases that leads to these ideals. Related research on athletic performance demonstrates that athletes who *imagine* themselves going through specific maneuvers actually perform better. These athletes take themselves through a mental workout that enables them to create a mental path through anticipated performance routines. Similarly, persons with specific information about expected performance routines can mentally rehearse by imagining themselves in, say, a job interview.

Markus and Nurius, along with many other educational researchers, observe that children in low-income schools receive very different information than those in high-income schools. Higher-income children are not only "tracked" for professional-level jobs, they are also exposed to considerable information about the specific steps required to progress toward these professions. For example, teachers and administrators in these schools routinely talk with parents and students about services that provide instruction and sample testing for college entrance exams. Not only do these conversations point students toward valuable services, they enable the students to imagine themselves in potential roles and to conceive the specific routes for getting there.

Significant Others and Reference Groups

Long before the term became a popular way of referring to an intimate partner, Cooley (1902) used the term *significant others* to refer to those people whose opinions and influence are particularly important in an individual's self-assessment. As we noted earlier, we pay more attention to the gestures and responses of those who are important to us. As we observe the reactions of those we are close to, we continuously evaluate and reevaluate our own behavior. For instance, consider a young man who identifies strongly with his grandfather as someone who is courageous and honest. While hanging out with a group of friends who decide to rob a store, this particular young man may find himself thinking about how his grandfather would react if he were to observe his grandson engaged in a robbery. Consequently, he might decide not to join his friends; he would rather appear noble in the imagined eye of his grandfather.

The beliefs, tastes, and habits of significant others are also an important source of cultural input that we use in trying on and discarding various social identities. Consider some of your own preferences for types of food, clothing, and music. Is there a type of food or music that you thought you didn't like, but you reconsidered because someone you were attracted to liked it? In such instances, you are putting yourself into the position of the other and willing yourself to simulate the other person's experiences. You are motivated to do so because you like the person, and in trying on new ideas and behaviors, you are stretching the boundaries of your own self.

In 1966, sociologist Norman Denzin conducted a study on the "significant others of a college population." Denzin tracked the shifts that college students went through during their college careers. He found that most traditionally aged freshmen remained strongly connected to their families and friends "back home." They talked with parents frequently, returned home for holidays and vacations, and were likely to discuss the material they were learning in terms of the beliefs and experiences of their parents and family. Denzin noted a distinct shift in students who were midway through their college careers. Advanced sophomores and juniors talked more about their friends at school and were more involved in school-related activities and less interested in what was going on "back home." Denzin was particularly interested in the observation that students in this group expressed much more conflict, frustration, and disenchantment with their parents than those in the freshman classes. The advanced students seemed to be experiencing a conflict between the ideals and expectations of new role models (especially faculty, who were sometimes more liberal than the parents) and those of their family. By the senior year, Denzin observed that most students were strongly identified with their college peers, the faculty, and peer groups in the local region. These students expressed beliefs and commitments very similar to those of the faculty and were somewhat disdainful of the ideas they had held just a few years earlier. According to Denzin, as the students became more identified with their college environment, their attachment to home shifted and, eventually, waned. This process of shifting identification was not always easy; students often experience tremendous guilt, conflict, and ambivalence. Denzin's interpretation is that these feelings reflect the shift away from significant others whose values and behaviors we have grown accustomed to sharing. Exposure to new groups, new peers, and new environments leads to shifts in alliances and commitments, which in turn lead to shifts in our sense of self. As Denzin notes, the process, while inevitable, is not without some pain, conflict, and grief.

Sometimes when observing our own behavior and imagining how it might appear to others, the "others" we have in mind are not specific significant others, but particular groups. Close association with specific groups (or our ideals of what those groups stand for) may lead us to adopt perspectives that are consistent with the behaviors, values, and beliefs of that group. Consequently, when we are making sense of a particular situation, or formulating assessments and making decisions, we use the perspective represented by this group as our reference point. When people use phrases such as "speaking as a Christian," ". . . as a Democrat," or ". . . as a sociologist," they are imaging themselves as members or representatives of a particular group and adopting the attitudes that they perceive to be consistent with this group. Reference groups can be specific groups that we associate with regularly; they can be dispersed groups whose values we have adopted; or they can be imaginary groups whose ideals we have derived from film, literature, and other cultural sources. Evaluating self-actions from the perspective of the "honorable hero" would be an example of an imagined reference group.

Our associations with reference groups have a powerful influence on our self-assessments and the decisions we make. A strong identification with particular reference groups is a central factor in the organization of our goals, values, and behaviors. For instance, newly married people have little or no experience actually being "wives" or "husbands," but the importance of their new social position leads them to identify strongly with these roles and, consequently, to make decisions in terms of what they think the ideal wife or husband might do. Major shifts in someone's behavior can usually be traced to the person's use of a particular reference group as a perspective for self-understanding and direction.

Reference group perspectives also help to explain why people who engage in very similar behaviors may adopt different self-images and, consequently, lead very different lives. Sexologists are interested in the gap between sexual behavior and sexual identification. Studies show repeatedly that a majority of people engage in sexual activity with someone of the same sex at some point in their lives. For example, many high school and college students report that they experiment with same-sex behavior. Yet, not all of these individuals go on to identify as gay or lesbian. Thus, the social psychologist might ask how it is that bisexual *behavior* results in different sexual *identities*. One immediate answer might be that those who don't like the behavior don't continue it. However, this is countered by evidence that indicates that many people who have had same-sex experiences continue to seek them (or would if they had the opportunity), they just don't *identify* as gay or lesbian (or even as bisexual).

Recall the article by Howard Becker, "Becoming a Marihuana User" (Reading 13)? According to Becker's model, people who use marijuana regularly for pleasure have *learned* to enjoy it through their association with others who have taught them how to smoke the drug and who provide an environment that enables them to think of this as an enjoyable activity. In a book called *Lesbian and Bisexual Identities*, sociologist Kristen Esterberg (1997) explores how women who have sex with other women *learn* to identify as either straight or lesbian.

Esterberg uses case studies to map the path that women who are behaviorally bisexual take toward a particular sexual identity. The primary factors along this route are significant others and reference groups. Esterberg's case studies suggest that bisexual women who are strongly identified with a boyfriend and with extended family and friends who are actively supportive of this relationship tend to settle into an identity as "straight." Similarly, women who become involved with other women who identify not only as lesbian, but with a gay and lesbian "community," tend to settle into "lesbian" identities. Repeated interaction with different groups, and the perspectives they represent, lead the women, eventually, to become more strongly identified with one or the other. This explanation suggests that sexual identities are fluid and shift over time depending on significant attachments and reference groups. Research in this area demonstrates that many people shift back and forth between sexual identities over the course of a lifetime. Reference group theories provide one framework for explaining these shifts, and they also provide a basis for understanding the potential conflict and stress related to certain behaviors: To the extent that we view certain behaviors from the perspective of conflicting reference groups (for example, "I'm a good Christian, how can I be gay?"), we are likely to be caught up in considerable personal turmoil. This kind of self-contradiction is explored more fully in Part VI.

CONCLUSIONS

One implication of these theories on the *social* self is that the company you keep and the ideas that you cultivate *do* matter. Before parents the world over start jumping for joy and saying, "See, I told you so, that person/group *will* be a bad influence," we should remember that these effects are (1) a process, and (2) the result of complex conversations we have with ourselves in which we reference multiple perspectives and consider many different significant others. We are not social robots; the attitudes of others are not simply poured into our heads, causing us to behave unthinkingly. Nor are we "Stepford" people who can be easily programmed to fulfill an ideal social role (such as husband or wife). As Mead has stated, the self is an *ongoing conversation*. Significant others are a part of our internal conversations, but just as we do not allow people to act as dictators over our external lives, neither are the "voices" of significant others an internal dictatorial process. We also adopt different reference group perspectives when we evaluate our behavior and make decisions. We conjure up these different perspectives as a way to enable us to see our possibilities from different points of view. Thus, the company you keep will certainly have an impact on your internal conversations and deliberations, but the form this influence takes will be (1) to allow new voices into your conversation—in the form of significant others, and (2) to cultivate new and alternative perspectives from which to make sense of and guide your own behavior.

Far from being robotic influences, a richly cultivated set of reference perspectives can actually make us freer. This will be the case to the extent that we understand the processes described in this essay and use this understanding as a guide to becoming *more observant* of the kind of conversation we are having with ourselves about who and what we can be. Other people and their ideas usually do not have a direct effect on our behavior, but they have an influence to the extent that the *expectations* of significant others make us feel more or less free to make certain choices and to behave in certain ways. One thing to keep in mind is that a broad range of possible selves and a carefully considered set of diverse reference groups will result in self-conversations that provide many different perspectives on how to see and direct your own behavior. This expansion of imagined possibilities provides you with a basis for bringing *more individuality* to various social roles. For instance, there are many different ways to be a minister or a teacher or a student or a spouse. The specific ways in which you grow into social identities, and eventually make them your own as part of your organized self-concept, will depend on the "models" you have for how you can play these roles. The broader your range of possibilities, the more variations you will be able to imagine, and the more individuality you will cultivate.

A final thing to keep in mind as we leave this topic is that significant others and reference groups can operate "oppositionally" as well as directionally. Most of us can recall occasions, at some time or another, when we have been focused primarily on *not* being something or on formulating a point of view that is in *opposition* to a significant other or reference group that feels problematic in our lives. Oppositional self-conversations can be very powerful in leading us to behave in emotionally charged ways. Thus, parents who are inclined to *protect* their children from *undesirable* external influences might consider whether their ways of doing so are teaching their children healthy ways of trying on various identities and reference perspectives so that they can judge for themselves, or rather, whether their methods are hindering their children from gathering the variety of perspectives that enable healthy self-engagement and development. In the case of the latter, one of the first strong oppositional perspectives the child might develop will be against the parent. In so doing, the child might be less selective about various identities he or she tries on and less inclined to assess the fit of these identities in terms of thoughtful self-process. Instead, in the eagerness to take on perspectives that challenge or oppose the parent, the child may actually eclipse or ignore other significant internal voices that are telling her or him that this identity is not a good fit. In short, trying on various identities under conditions of support and wisdom leads to the cultivation of a rich and healthy internal conversation whereby we learn the skill of mindful self-assessment and feel able to develop a variety of responses that we can feel good about in difficult situations. Conversely, external attempts to limit the opportunities for "identity play" may lead to less mindful rebellion aimed in opposition to single perspectives. The study of the self as a social process opens up the avenues to greater self-awareness and, consequently, to more nuanced ideas about who we think we can be and what we think we can do.

REFERENCES AND SUGGESTIONS FOR FURTHER READING

Blumstein, P. (1991). The production of selves in personal relationships. In J. Howard & P. Callero (Eds.), *The self-society dynamic* (pp. 305–322). Cambridge, UK: University of Cambridge Press.

Cooley, C. H. 1983. Looking-glass self. In *Human nature and the social order* (pp. 182–185). New York: Transaction Publishers.

Denzin, N. (1966, July). The significant others of a college. *The Sociological Quarterly, 7*(3), 298.

Esterberg, K. (1997). *Lesbian and bisexual identities: Constructing communities, constructing selves.* Philadelphia: Temple University Press.

Markus, H., & Nurius, P. (1986). Possible selves. *American Psychologist, 41,* 954–969.

Park, R. E. (1952). *Human communities.* Glencoe, IL: Free Press.

Quindlen, A. (1989). *Living out loud.* New York: Random House.

Sandstrom, K. L., Martin, D. D., & Fine, G. A. (2003). *Symbols, selves and social reality.* Los Angeles: Roxbury. [see especially Chapters 3–5]

Snyder, M. (1987). *Public appearances/private realities: The psychology of self-monitoring.* New York: W. H. Freeman.

————————))) ————————

THE SELF AS A PROCESS OF INTERACTION

Who am I really? This is a question we often ask ourselves. The psychologist William James once remarked that our selves are as numerous as the number of people with whom we interact. Most people believe that the self is a fixed and immutable set of "core personality traits"—something that we are born with. This section introduces the concept of the self as social process. Sociologists George Herbert Mead and Charles Horton Cooley were contemporaries of James, writing in the United States in the 1930s. They introduced the idea that people develop a sense of themselves in the same way that they develop an understanding of other social objects and events: We learn to "name" ourselves and our actions. This naming process occurs through interaction, especially with those who are significant to us. We learn how to think and feel about ourselves based on the impressions and "names" others have for us. For example, two young students with similar academic ability may learn to think very differently about their student "selves" if one has a teacher who treats the student as if her performance is "inspired" and the other has a teacher who considers his questions to be annoying and stupid. The first student, feeling encouraged and praised, may begin to see herself as having tremendous potential and therefore be inclined to study even harder. She may even begin to think of herself as "intellectual." The second student is likely to see himself as nonintellectual and be disinclined to study any more than he has to. The readings in this section provide the theoretical basis for understanding the social self.

"The Self, the I, and the Me" is based on the classic writings of George Herbert Mead. Mead discusses the process by which we come to see ourselves as objects and to describe our own actions. As this process develops, so does our ability to conceptualize our own actions as a separate, coherent self.

"Looking-Glass Self" is based on another classic article by Charles Horton Cooley. Cooley proposed that we learn what to think and feel about ourselves by watching how others react to us. Much like looking into a mirror, if we perceive someone as viewing our actions with admiration, then we feel pride. If we perceive them as viewing us with disdain, we feel mortification. Through these "reflected appraisals," we gain information from others about ourselves and our actions.

"Reference Groups as Perspectives" is written by sociologist Tamotsu Shibutani. Shibutani expands on the theories of Mead and Cooley by introducing the idea that we are particularly concerned about the "reflected appraisals" of groups that are significant to us. According to Shibutani, we use our images of these groups as a reference point, or measuring rod, for defining and evaluating our own actions, beliefs, and values. For example, if you think of yourself as a "leader," you probably have an idea of a general group of "leaders" whom you admire. When making decisions and judging your own actions, you probably reference this group in your mind. Or, if you are a devoted Christian, you may find yourself asking "What would Jesus do?" and using this reference as a perspective for making decisions. Reference groups can be close and tangible, they can be abstract and distant, they can even be fictitious. Shibutani's point is that they exert a strong influence on how we see the world and the choices that we make.

Questions for Discussion and Review

1. Make a list of twenty responses to the question, "Who am I?" How many of the characteristics on your list are "social roles"—that is, aspects of yourself that exist only in reference to others (for example, daughter)?

2. If you listed behavioral characteristics (for example, "friendly," "funny," etc.), try to recall how you came to think of yourself this way? Do you have significant others who notice, expect, and reinforce these self-images? How do you feel when you don't behave in ways that are consistent with these expected characteristics?

3. According to Cooley, we rely on the impressions of others in forming our own self-assessments. If we are watching others' perceptions of us, how do we know whether our read of their reaction to us is accurate or not? Does it matter?

4. For a few days, keep track of the "audience in your head" when you are making decisions or judging yourself. In these moments, stop and ask yourself who or what is in your mind as you go through the process of self-assessment and self-direction. This exercise can help you identify your significant others and reference groups.

5. Make a list of your most cherished beliefs and values and also some of the expectations and goals you have for yourself. Identify the groups reflected in this list of ideals. Now trace the origins of your identification with these groups.

6. Write a fantasy essay that begins with the sentence: "I never thought I would become . . ." Imagine the social circumstances that could lead, over time, to your becoming someone you just can't imagine (for example, a different political persuasion, a new religious affiliation). Be as specific as possible about the *process* that might lead to this change (for example, marriage to someone with very different views, a particular kind of job, etc.).

THE SELF AS A PROCESS OF INTERACTION

21

The Self, the I, and the Me

George Herbert Mead

(1934)

We can distinguish very definitely between the self and the body. The body can be there and can operate in a very intelligent fashion without there being a self involved in the experience. The self has the characteristic that it is an object to itself, and that characteristic distinguishes it from other objects and from the body. It is perfectly true that the eye can see the foot, but it does not see the body as a whole. We cannot see our backs; we can feel certain portions of them, if we are agile, but we cannot get an experience of our whole body. There are, of course, experiences which are somewhat vague and difficult of location, but the bodily experiences are for us organized about a self. The foot and hand belong to the self. We can see our feet, especially if we look at them from the wrong end of an opera glass, as strange things which we have difficulty in recognizing as our own. The parts of the body are quite distinguishable from the self. We can lose parts of the body without any serious invasion of the self. The mere ability to experience different parts of the body is not different from the experience of a table. The table presents a different feel from what the hand does when one hand feels another, but it is an experience of something with which we come definitely into contact. The body does not experience itself as a whole, in the sense in which the self in some way enters into the experience of the self.

It is the characteristic of the self as an object to itself that I want to bring out. This characteristic is represented in the word "self," which is a reflexive, and indicates that which can be both subject and object. This type of object is essentially different from other objects, and in the past it has been distinguished as conscious, a term which indicates an experience with, an experience of, one's self. It was assumed that consciousness in some way carried this capacity of being an object to itself. In giving a behavioristic statement of consciousness we have to look for some sort of experience in which the physical organism can become an object to itself.

When one is running to get away from someone who is chasing him, he is entirely occupied in this action, and his experience may be swallowed up in the objects about him, so that he has, at the time being, no consciousness of self at all. We must be, of course, very completely occupied to have that take place, but we can, I think, recognize that sort of a possible experience in which the self does not enter. We can, perhaps, get some light on that situation through those experiences in which in very intense action there appears in the experience of the individual, back of this intense action, memories, and anticipations. Tolstoi as an officer in the war gives an account of having pictures of his past experience in the midst of his most intense action. There are also the pictures that flash into a person's mind when he is drowning. In such instances there is a contrast between an experience that is absolutely wound up in outside activity in which the self as an object does not enter, and an activity of memory and imagination in which the self is the principal object. The self is then entirely distinguishable from an organism that is surrounded by things and acts with reference to things, including parts of its own body. These latter may be objects like other objects, but they are just objects out there in the field, and they do not involve a self that is an object to the organism. This is, I think, frequently overlooked. It is that fact which makes our anthropomorphic reconstructions of animal life so fallacious. How can an individual get outside himself (experientially) in such a way as to become an object to himself? This is the essential psychological problem of selfhood or of self-consciousness; and its solution is to be found by referring to the process of social conduct or activity in which the given person or individual is implicated. The apparatus of reason would not be complete unless it swept itself into its own analysis of the field of experience; or unless the individual brought himself into the same experiential field as that of the other individual selves in relation to whom he acts in any given social situation. Reason cannot become impersonal unless it takes an objective, non-affective attitude toward itself; otherwise we have just consciousness, not *self*-consciousness. And it is necessary to rational conduct that the individual should thus take an objective, impersonal attitude toward himself, that he should become an object to himself. For the individual organism is obviously an essential and important fact or constituent element of the empirical situation in which it acts; and without taking objective account of itself as such, it cannot act intelligently, or rationally.

The individual experiences himself as such, not directly, but only indirectly, from the particular standpoints of other individual members of the same social group, or from the generalized standpoint of the social group as a whole to which he belongs. For he enters his own experience as a self or individual, not directly or immediately, not by becoming a subject to himself, but only in so far as he first becomes an object to himself just as other individuals are objects to him or in his experience; and he becomes an object to himself only by taking the attitudes of other individuals toward himself within a social environment or context of experience and behavior in which both he and they are involved.

The importance of what we term "communication" lies in the fact that it provides a form of behavior in which the organism or the individual may become an object to himself. It is that sort of communication which we have been discussing—not communication in the sense of the cluck of the hen to the chickens, or the bark of a wolf to the pack, or the lowing of a cow, but communication in the sense of significant symbols, communication which is directed not only to others but also to the individual himself. So far as that type of communication is a part of behavior it at least introduces a self. Of course, one may hear without listening; one may see things that he does not realize; do things that he is not really aware of. But it is where one does respond to that which he addresses to another and where that response of his own becomes a part of his conduct, where he not only hears himself but responds to himself, talks and replies to himself as truly as the other person replies to him, that we have behavior in which the individuals become objects to themselves.

Such a self is not, I would say, primarily the physiological organism. The physiological organism is essential to it, but we are at least able to think of a self without it. Persons who believe in immortality, or believe in ghosts, or in the possibility of the self leaving the body, assume a self which is quite distinguishable from the body. How successfully they can hold these conceptions is an open question, but we do, as a fact, separate the self and the organism. It is fair to say that the beginning of the self as an object, so far as we can see, is to be found in the experiences of people that lead to the conception of a "double." Primitive people assume that there is a double, located presumably in the diaphragm, that leaves the body temporarily in sleep and completely in death. It can be enticed out of the body of one's enemy and perhaps killed. It is represented in infancy by the imaginary playmates which children set up, and through which they come to control their experiences in their play.

The self, as that which can be an object to itself, is essentially a social structure, and it arises in social experience. After a self has arisen, it in a certain sense provides for itself its social experiences, and so we can conceive of an absolutely solitary self. But it is impossible to conceive of a self arising outside of social experience. When it has arisen we can think of a person in solitary confinement for the rest of his life, but who still has himself as a companion, and is able to think and to converse with himself as he had communicated with others. That process to which I have just referred, of responding to one's self as another responds to it, taking part in one's own conversation with others, being aware of what one is saying and using that awareness of what one is saying to determine what one is going to say thereafter—that is a process with which we are all familiar. We are continually following up our own address to other persons by an understanding of what we are saying, and using that understanding in the direction of our continued speech. We are finding out what we are going to say, what we are going to do, by saying and doing, and in the process we are continually controlling the process itself. In the conversation of gestures what we say calls out a certain response in another and that in turn changes our own action, so that we shift from what we started to do because of the reply the other makes. The conversation of gestures is the beginning of communication. The individual comes to carry on a conversation of gestures with himself. He says something, and that calls out a certain reply in himself which makes

him change what he was going to say. One starts to say something, we will presume an unpleasant something, but when he starts to say it he realizes it is cruel. The effect on himself of what he is saying checks him; there is here a conversation of gestures between the individual and himself. We mean by significant speech that the action is one that affects the individual himself, and that the effect upon the individual himself is part of the intelligent carrying-out of the conversation with others. Now we, so to speak, amputate that social phase and dispense with it for the time being, so that one is talking to one's self as one would talk to another person.

This process of abstraction cannot be carried on indefinitely. One inevitably seeks an audience, has to pour himself out to somebody. In reflective intelligence one thinks to act, and to act solely so that this action remains a part of a social process. Thinking becomes preparatory to social action. The very process of thinking is, of course, simply an inner conversation that goes on, but it is a conversation of gestures which in its completion implies the expression of that which one thinks to an audience. One separates the significance of what he is saying to others from the actual speech and gets it ready before saying it. He thinks it out, and perhaps writes it in the form of a book; but it is still a part of social intercourse in which one is addressing other persons and at the same time addressing one's self, and in which one controls the address to other persons by the response made to one's own gesture. That the person should be responding to himself is necessary to the self, and it is this sort of social conduct which provides behavior within which that self appears. I know of no other form of behavior than the linguistic in which the individual is an object to himself, and, so far as I can see, the individual is not a self in the reflexive sense unless he is an object to himself. It is this fact that gives a critical importance to communication, since this is a type of behavior in which the individual does so respond to himself.

We realize in everyday conduct and experience that an individual does not mean a great deal of what he is doing and saying. We frequently say that such an individual is not himself. We come away from an interview with a realization that we have left out important things, that there are parts of the self that did not get into what was said. What determines the amount of the self that gets into communication is the social experience itself. Of course, a good deal of the self does not need to get expression. We carry on a whole series of different relationships to different people. We are one thing to one man and another thing to another. There are parts of the self which exist only for the self in relationship to itself. We divide ourselves up in all sorts of different selves with reference to our acquaintances. We discuss politics with one and religion with another. There are all sorts of different selves answering to all sorts of different social reactions. It is the social process itself that is responsible for the appearance of the self; it is not there as a self apart from this type of experience.

A multiple personality is in a certain sense normal, as I have just pointed out. There is usually an organization of the whole self with reference to the community to which we belong, and the situation in which we find ourselves. What the society is, whether we are living with people of the present, people of our own imaginations, people of the past, varies, of course, with different individuals. Normally, within the sort of community as a whole to which we belong, there is a unified self, but that may be broken up. To a person who is somewhat unstable nervously and in whom there is a line of cleavage, certain activities become impossible, and that set of activities may separate and evolve another self. Two separate "me's" and "I's," two different selves, result, and that is the condition under which there is a tendency to break up the personality. There is an account of a professor of education who disappeared, was lost to the community, and later turned up in a logging camp in the West. He freed himself of his occupation and turned to the woods where he felt, if you like, more at home. The pathological side of it was the forgetting, the leaving out of the rest of the self. This result involved getting rid of certain bodily memories which would identify the individual to himself. We often recognize the lines of cleavage that run through us. We would be glad to forget certain things, get rid of things the self is bound up with in past experiences. What we have here is a situation in which there can be different selves, and it is dependent upon the set of social reactions that is involved as to which self we are going to be. If we can forget everything involved in one set of activities, obviously we relinquish that part of the self. Take a person who is unstable, get him occupied by speech, and at the same time get his eye on something you are writing so that he is carrying on two separate lines of communication, and if you go about it in the right way you can get those two currents going so that they do not run into each other. You can get two entirely different sets of activities going on. You can bring about in that way the dissociation of a person's self. It is a process of setting up two sorts of communication which separate the behavior of the individual. For one individual it is this thing said and heard, and for the other individual there exists only that which he sees written. You must, of course, keep one experience out of the field of the other. Dissociations are apt to take place when an event leads to emotional upheavals. That which is separated goes on in its own way.

The unity and structure of the complete self reflects the unity and structure of the social process as a whole; and each of the elementary selves of which it is composed reflects the unity and structure of one of the various aspects of that process in which the individual is implicated. In other words, the various elementary selves which constitute, or are organized into, a complete self are the various aspects of the structure of that complete self answering to the various aspects of the structure of the social process as a whole; the structure of the complete self is thus a reflection of the complete social process. The organization and unification of a social group is identical with the organization and unification of any one of the selves arising within the social process in which that group is engaged, or which it is carrying on.

The phenomenon of dissociation of personality is caused by a breaking up of the complete, unitary self into the component selves of which it is composed, and which respectively correspond to different aspects of the social process in which the person is involved, and within which his complete or unitary self has arisen; these aspects being the different social groups to which he belongs within that process. . . .

Rational society, of course, is not limited to any specific set of individuals. Any person who is rational can become a part of it. The attitude of the community toward our own response is imported into ourselves in terms of the meaning of what we are doing. This occurs in its widest extent in universal discourse, in the reply which the rational world makes to our remark. The meaning is as universal as the community; it is necessarily involved in the rational character of that community; it is the response that the world made up out of rational beings inevitably makes to our own statement. We both get the object and ourselves into experience in terms of such a process; the other appears in our own experience insofar as we do take such an organized and generalized attitude.

If one meets a person on the street whom he fails to recognize, one's reaction toward him is that toward any other who is a member of the same community. He is the other, the organized, generalized other, if you like. One takes his attitude over against one's self. If he turns in one direction one is to go in another direction. One has his response as

an attitude within himself. It is having that attitude within himself that makes it possible for one to be a self. That involves something beyond the mere turning to the right, as we say, instinctively, without self-consciousness. To have self-consciousness one must have the attitude of the other in one's own organism as controlling the thing that he is going to do. What appears in the immediate experience of one's self in taking that attitude is what we term the "me." It is that self which is able to maintain itself in the community, that is recognized in the community insofar as it recognizes the others. Such is the phase of the self which I have referred to as that of the "me."

Over against the "me" is the "I." The individual not only has rights, but he has duties; he is not only a citizen, a member of the community, but he is one who reacts to this community and in his reaction to it, as we have seen in the conversation of gestures, changes it. The "I" is the response of the individual to the attitude of the community as this appears in his own experience. His response to that organized attitude in turn changes it. As we have pointed out, this is a change which is not present in his own experience until after it takes place. The "I" appears in our experience in memory. It is only after we have acted that we know what we have done; it is only after we have spoken that we know what we have said. The adjustment to that organized world which is present in our own nature is one that represents the "me" and is constantly there. But if the response to it is a response which is of the nature of the conversation of gestures, if it creates a situation which is in some sense novel, if one puts up his side of the case, asserts himself over against others and insists that they take a different attitude toward himself, then there is something important occurring that is not previously present in experience.

THE SELF AS A PROCESS OF INTERACTION

22

Looking-Glass Self

Charles Horton Cooley

(1983)

The social origin of [self] comes by the pathway of intercourse with other persons. There is no sense of "I" . . . without its correlative sense of you, or he, or they. . . . In a very large and interesting class of cases the social reference takes the form of a somewhat definite imagination of how one's self—that is any idea he appropriates—appears in a particular mind, and the kind of self-feeling one has is determined by the attitude . . . attributed to that other mind. A social self of this sort might be called the reflected or looking-glass self:

> Each to each a looking-glass
> Reflects the other that doth pass.

As we see our face, figure, and dress in the glass, and are interested in them because they are ours, and pleased or otherwise with them according as they do or do not answer to what we should like them to be; so in imagination we perceive in another's mind some thought of our appearance, manners, aims, deeds, character, friends, and so on, and are variously affected by it.

A self-idea of this sort seems to have three principal elements: the imagination of our appearance to the other person; the imagination of his judgment of that appearance, and some sort of self-feeling, such as pride or mortification. The comparison with a looking-glass hardly suggests the second element, the imagined judgment, which is quite essential. The thing that moves us to pride or shame is not the mere mechanical reflection of ourselves, but an imputed sentiment, the imagined effect of this reflection upon another's mind. This is evident from the fact that the character and weight of that other, in whose mind we see ourselves, makes all the difference with our feeling. We are ashamed to seem evasive in the presence of a straightforward man, cowardly in the presence of a brave one, gross in the eyes of a refined one, and so on. We always imagine, and in imagining share, the judgments of the other mind. A man will boast to one person of an action—say some sharp transaction in trade—which he would be ashamed to own to another.

The process by which self-feeling of the looking-glass sort develops in children may be followed without much difficulty. Studying the movements of others as closely as they do they soon see a connection between their own acts and changes in those movements; that is, they perceive their own influence or power over persons. The child appropriates the visible actions of his parent or nurse, over which he finds he has some control, in quite the same way as he appropriates one of his own members or a plaything, and he will try to do things with this new possession, just as he will with his hand or his rattle. A girl six months old will attempt in the most evident and deliberate manner to attract attention to herself, to set going by her actions some of those movements of other persons that she has appropriated. She has tasted the joy of being a cause, of exerting social power, and wishes more of it. She will tug at her mother's skirts, wriggle, gurgle, stretch out her arms, etc., all the time watching for the hoped-for effect. These performances often give the child, even at this age, an appearance of what is called affectation, that is, she seems to be unduly preoccupied with what other people think of her. Affectation, at any age, exists when the passion to influence others seems to overbalance the established character and give it an obvious twist or pose. It is instructive to find that even Darwin was, in his childhood, capable of departing from truth for the sake of making an impression. "For instance," he says in his autobiography, "I once gathered much valuable fruit from my father's trees and hid it in the shrubbery and then ran in breathless haste to spread the news that I had discovered a hoard of stolen fruit."[1]

The young performer soon learns to be different things to different people, showing that he begins to apprehend personality and to foresee its operation. If the mother or nurse is more tender than just, she will almost certainly be "worked" by systematic weeping. It is a matter of common observation that children often behave worse with their mother than with other and less sympathetic people. Of the new persons that a child sees, it is evident that some make a strong impression and awaken a desire to interest and please them, while others are indifferent or repugnant. Sometimes the reason can be perceived or guessed, sometimes not; but the fact of selective interest, admiration, prestige, is obvious before the end of the second year. By that time a child already cares much for the reflection of himself upon one personality and little for that upon another. Moreover he soon claims intimate and tractable persons as *mine,* classes them among his other possessions, and maintains his ownership against all comers. M., at three years of age, vigorously resented R.'s claim upon their mother. The latter was "*my* mamma," whenever the point was raised.

Strong joy and grief depend upon the treatment this rudimentary social self receives. In the case of M. I noticed as early as the fourth month a "hurt" way of crying which seemed to indicate a sense of personal slight. It was quite different from the cry of pain or that of anger, but seemed about the same as the cry of fright. The slightest tone of reproof would produce it. On the other hand, if people took notice and laughed and encouraged, she was hilarious. At about fifteen months old she had become "a perfect little actress," seeming to live largely in imaginations of her effect upon other people. She constantly and obviously laid traps for attention, and looked abashed or wept at any signs of disapproval or indifference. At times it would seem as if she could not get over these repulses, but would cry long in a grieved way, refusing to be comforted. If she hit upon any little trick that made people laugh she would be sure to repeat it, laughing loudly and affectedly in imitation. She had quite a repertory of these small performances, which she would display to a sympathetic audience, or even try upon strangers. I have seen her at sixteen months, when R. refused to give her the scissors, sit down and make-believe cry, putting up her under lip and snuffling, meanwhile looking up now and then to see what effect she was producing.

In such phenomena we have plainly enough, it seems to me, the germ of personal ambition of every sort. Imagination cooperating with instinctive self-feeling has already created a social "I," and this has become a principal object of interest and endeavor.

Progress from this point is chiefly in the way of a greater definiteness, fullness, and inwardness in the imagination of the other's state of mind. A little child thinks of and tries to elicit certain visible or audible phenomena, and does not go back of them; but what a grown-up person desires to produce in others is an internal, invisible condition which his own richer experience enables him to imagine, and of which expression is only the sign. Even adults, however, make no separation between what other people think and the visible expression of that thought. They imagine the whole thing at once, and their idea differs from that of a child chiefly in the comparative richness and complexity of the elements that accompany and interpret the visible or audible sign. There is also a progress from the naive to the subtle in socially self-assertive action. A child obviously and simply, at first, does things for effect. Later there is an endeavor to suppress the appearance of doing so;

affection, indifference, contempt, etc., are simulated to hide the real wish to affect the self-image. It is perceived that an obvious seeking after good opinion is weak and disagreeable.

NOTE

1. Darwin, F. (1959). *Life and letters of Charles Darwin.* New York: Basic Books, p. 27.

THE SELF AS A PROCESS OF INTERACTION

23

Reference Groups as Perspectives

Tamotsu Shibutani

(1961)

Each person acts on the basis of his definition of the situation. He categorizes the transaction in which he is involved, locates himself within it, and thereby decides upon his obligations. The consistency with which he defines a succession of situations arises from the fact that he generally uses the same perspective, one that he shares with his associates. Once he has adopted a particular point of view it becomes his working conception of the world, and he brings this frame of reference to bear upon each situation he encounters, whether or not anyone else from the group is actually on the scene. Since people with diverse orientations are selectively responsive to different aspects of their natural environment, identical events may be seen in divergent ways. A prostitute and a social worker walking down the same street in a slum area often have remarkably contrasting experiences. The leering men they pass,

the drunk sleeping on a doorstep, the drug addict purchasing a "fix"—all are seen differently. But their respective outlooks differ no more than those of a traffic officer and of a motorist stopped for excessive speeding. The offender is irked by the delay; much like a naughty child who has been caught misbehaving, he sulks. If the officer speaks curtly, the motorist is resentful of what he regards to be an unnecessary display of authority. It does not occur to him that only a half hour ago the same officer may have helped load the body of a dead child upon an ambulance, the victim of an accident involving two speeding automobiles. The diversity of interpretations often arises from the fact that key objects, though designated by the same symbols, assume different meanings for different people. It is not surprising, therefore, that immigrants and tourists almost invariably misinterpret much of what they see.

There have been a number of experimental studies demonstrating the manner in which the definition of identical situations varies with perspectives. Among them is one concerning the spectators of a crucial football game between Princeton and Dartmouth on November 23, 1951. It was a fiercely contested match in which a large number of penalties were called. In the second quarter a Princeton star who had been prominently mentioned for All-America honors had to leave the game with a broken nose and a concussion, and in the following period a Dartmouth player was carried off the field with a broken leg. Immediately after the contest there were charges in the press of "dirty" football. A week later undergraduate students in both universities were given a questionnaire concerning the game. All Princeton students described the game as "rough and dirty"; of the Dartmouth students a tenth thought it was "clean and fair," a third judged it as "rough and fair," and the remainder acknowledged that it was "rough and dirty." Of the Princeton spectators nine-tenths insisted that the Dartmouth players had started the foul tactics; but of the Dartmouth observers only a third held their own team guilty, and the rest blamed both sides. When the students were shown a motion picture of the game and asked to note and to evaluate infractions of the rules, the Princeton students detected twice as many violations and rated them as being more flagrant.[1] All of these students were either in the same stadium or were exposed to the same motion picture, but what they saw differed to a remarkable extent.

Divergent meanings can sometimes be reconciled by comparing assumptions, but misunderstandings become less amenable to clarification when differences exist over such fundamental categories as *time*. At first glance nothing appears as simple as the concept of time; it just passes on inexorably in increments like hours or days. But the passage of time is of different significance in different cultures. Precision in keeping time, for example, is relatively unimportant for a peasant, for he begins work soon after dawn and continues until sundown. He harvests his crops when they are ready and rests when weather conditions are such that he cannot work. In a peasant community that is becoming industrialized, however, keeping time takes on a new meaning, for men work by the clock. In some areas the owning of a wrist watch has become a status symbol among those desiring to be in line with the latest trends. At the other extreme are those who work for the railroads, among whom almost everything is measured in terms of accuracy in timing.[2] Such contrasts in the unstated premises about the passage of time sometimes lead people to conclude that others are indolent or unnecessarily aggressive.

Differences in the meaning of categories such as success can lead to serious misunderstandings, for the manner in which men organize their careers depends upon such conceptions. In the United States a high value is generally placed upon success. It is taken for granted that each individual will strive to improve his station in life, and those who do not succeed are often regarded as indigent. But there are many different conceptions of the kinds of goals that are regarded as worth pursuing. In some social worlds men in competitive situations are expected to exert themselves to the utmost to win; victory is all important, and considerations of decency and fair play are viewed as luxuries for "idealists." In intercollegiate athletics, for example, it has been reported that some athletes have been injected with amphetamine and similar stimulants by their coaches to make possible performances far beyond their normal capacity. Those who are familiar with the unreasonable pressures placed upon coaches and athletes view this practice with regret but with understanding. But many others are horrified, wondering what there could be about winning a contest that would justify risking the health of young men. Similarly, in some universities men doing research sacrifice themselves and their families, devoting themselves to their work 365 days a year; some of their colleagues wonder, however, whether anything such men may accomplish could really be worth the unbalanced lives they lead.[3] In some business circles the deception and exploitation of competitors and customers is regarded as perfectly natural; others wonder whether success built upon the misfortunes of other people can really be satisfying, and they condemn those who struggle so feverishly as being "power mad." Assumptions such as these provide the basis for deciding what goals are really worth seeking in life and the manner in which one is to go about pursuing his aspirations.

Many serious misunderstandings arise from differences in certain crucial values, especially in criteria of modesty, cleanliness, and sexual conduct. There are vast differences in standards of modesty. In some social worlds the exposure of the nude body, belching, and flatulence are simply accepted as a natural part of human life; in others such behavior is regarded as unforgivable and is concealed at all cost. The emphasis upon personal cleanliness ranges from high standards of sanitation to the retention of an outward appearance of neatness to a vague awareness of the problem. One person may be amused at those who are constantly washing themselves, while the latter wonder how their associate can possibly stand his own stench. There are norms in all groups concerning what constitutes proper sex conduct; this is true even in groups that are thought by outsiders to be without standards.[4] But there is remarkable variability in these norms, ranging from the open acceptance of sexual excitement as a part of human nature to the puritanical denial of sexuality. Practices that are condemned as sinful perversions in one circle are accepted as the normal part of life in another. Since each group takes it for granted that its own ways are right and natural, people are easily convinced that outsiders are either lewd or unduly inhibited. . . . Because understandings about sex are so deeply ingrained, people generally feel that there is something filthy or unnatural about the practices condemned in their group.

People with diverse cultural backgrounds often have different conceptions of human nature. In each universe of discourse explanations of the things men do are circumscribed by the available vocabulary of motives. There are a limited set of recognized intentions, approved and disapproved, which are thought to depict the natural inclinations of man. There are a limited number of words that are used to label these dispositions, and a motive that cannot be designated obviously cannot be imputed or avowed. Furthermore, in each social world there are shared assumptions as to the kinds of intentions that develop in each standardized context. In our society it does little good for a murderer to insist that his hand had been guided by the spirit of an ancestor for whom he had been named; he is more likely to receive a sympathetic hearing by claiming that he was the victim of a mysterious "inner urge" that he could not understand.

As one compares the perspectives that are shared in diverse social worlds, it becomes apparent that what differs are the premises underlying action. Identical situations are perceived differently because those starting out with unlike assumptions project contrasting hypotheses and are selectively responsive to different sensory cues. What makes the clarification of these divergences so difficult is that the differences are about matters that are taken for granted, matters on which alternatives are not considered. Beliefs concerning the importance of punctuality, cleanliness, or success, convictions about the proper contact between the sexes, as well as assumptions about the nature of love—all these meanings are intertwined with thousands of others into an organized scheme. A successful challenge to any basic assumption can lead to searching questions about all the others. To challenge such fundamental beliefs is to challenge a man's orientation toward life. If he takes it seriously, he may be left dazed and bewildered, not knowing what is true and what is false. . . .

The contention that men think, feel, and see things from the standpoint peculiar to the group in which they participate is an old one which has been repeatedly emphasized by anthropologists and students of the sociology of knowledge. But what makes this hypothesis so important for the study of modern mass societies is the fact that people may assume the perspectives of groups in which they are *not* recognized members, sometimes of groups in which they have never participated directly, and sometimes of groups that do not exist at all. For example, those seeking to raise their status are more responsive to the opinions of people in the social set to which they aspire than to the views shared in the circle to which they belong. Members of ethnic minorities who are becoming assimilated examine themselves from the standpoint of the dominant group; they often develop strong feelings of inferiority and condemn others in the minority for failing to live up to these outside norms. Servants and slaves sometimes accept the standards of their masters, and adolescent boys in slum areas sometimes adopt the code of the underworld, as they learn of it from motion pictures. There are many people, then, who try to live up to the standards of social worlds of which they learn from vicarious participation—through observation or through the various media of mass communication.

Furthermore, in societies characterized by cultural pluralism each person may acquire several perspectives, for he can participate simultaneously in a number of social worlds. Because cultures are products of communication a person develops a somewhat different perspective from each communication channel to which he is regularly exposed. Because of the ease with which one can gain access to a variety of channels, he leads a somewhat segmented life, engaging in turn in a succession of quite unrelated activities. Furthermore, the particular aggregate of social worlds of which one partakes differs from individual to individual; this is what led Simmel to declare that each person stands at that point at which the unique combination of social circles of which he is a part intersects.[5] This geometric analogy is a happy one, for it enables us to conceive of the almost endless permutations as well as the varying degrees of involvement in each circle. To understand any particular person, then, one must get a picture of his unique outlook. Since this is the product of his past experiences, real and vicarious, no two people are likely to have an identical outlook.

Since a given situation may be defined from so many different points of view, to understand what a man does an observer must get at the assumptions with which he begins. One of the most important things to know about a person is what he takes for granted. To take his role and to anticipate what he is likely to do it is necessary to identify the perspective he is using, the social world in which he is participating in a given act. The concept of *reference group* may be used to designate *that group, real or imaginary, whose standpoint is being used as the frame of reference by the actor.* This provides some notion of the meanings he is projecting upon the scene. Not only can different persons approach the same situation from diverse standpoints, but the same person in different transactions may utilize different perspectives. On a hockey field he has one orientation, and in a classroom he is participating in an entirely different social world. Each man acts, then, for some kind of *audience,* and it is important to know what this audience is and what kinds of expectations are imputed to it.

The reference group supports the values in terms of which a person estimates his own conduct; therefore, his line of activity depends upon the real or anticipated reactions of the other people for whom he is performing. There is a selective sensitivity to others; men are not equally responsive to the opinions of everyone present. Hardened criminals are well aware of the disapproval of most people but are not especially upset. Furthermore, the audience that counts need not consist of people whom one knows personally; frequently reference groups are quite large, and one can have direct contacts only with a few representatives. For example, those in ethnic minorities are usually highly responsive to the demands of others with whom they identify on the basis of common ancestry, but in most cases each knows on a personal basis only a small percentage of those who make up the category. In studying the behavior of human beings it is necessary to get "inside" the actor, to see the situation from his point of view, and the concept of reference group is useful for this purpose.

There are as many reference groups for each person as there are communication channels in which he participates, and individuals differ considerably in their range of participation. Each lives in an environment of which he is the center, and the dimensions of his effective surroundings are defined by the direction and distance from which news comes to him. Each time a man enters a new communication channel—subscribes to a new periodical, joins a new circle of friends, purchases a television set, or begins to listen regularly to some radio program—he is introduced into a new social world. People who communicate develop an appreciation of one another's tastes, interests, and outlook upon life; and as one acquires new standards of conduct, he adds more people to his audience. Each man's outlook is both shaped and limited by the communication networks in which he becomes involved.

A reference group, then, is any identifiable group whose supposed perspective is used by the actor as a frame of reference in the organization of his perceptual field. Men are usually most responsive to the views imputed to those with whom they are in direct and constant association, but reference groups may also be imaginary, as in the case of artists who are "born ahead of their time," scientists who work for "humanity," or philanthropists who give for "posterity." Such persons estimate their endeavors from a postulated standpoint imputed to people who have not yet been born. They sometimes undergo incredible sacrifices in anticipation of being appreciated by some future audience that presumably would be more sensible than the people who are now living. They are not concerned with immediate rewards and work slavishly for people who may actually never come into existence. There are others who live for a distant past, idealizing some period in history, longing for the "good old days" and constantly criticizing current events from a standpoint imputed to people long since dead—as in the case of the Southerner pining for the days of the Confederacy. There are some people who create a paradise in the next world—Valhalla, Heaven, or the "happy hunting grounds"—and forego pleasures in their present life on the assumption that they will be rewarded after death. An interesting problem is that of ascertaining how perspectives imputed to such imaginary audiences are constructed. One can learn about the typical ways in which people in the "Greek world" presumably lived, acted, and thought by reading history and studying archaeology, but what of the audiences that will not be born for another thousand years? The fact that there is no material basis for such reference groups does not make them any less important.

There are some categories of people with which men occasionally identify which are so amorphous that they may almost be regarded as imaginary groups. Two examples of vaguely defined audiences that play an important part in our society are public opinion and social class. Politicians, administrators, labor leaders, advertising men, and even dictators are constantly concerned with what they call "public opinion." Sometimes even the man of the street may refrain from doing something on the ground that "people won't like it." But who are these "people"? How does one go about ascertaining what it is that the "people" want? Although surveys and polls give some indications, there is no way of knowing for certain until after mass reactions are aroused. Public opinion is the source of so much concern precisely because a miscalculation of what people will tolerate can lead to disastrous consequences—embarrassing demonstrations, the loss of an election, demands for changes that threaten those in privileged positions, or a spectacular drop in the sales of some product. But most of the time those who are concerned with public opinion can only guess, and their conjectures are usually based upon very limited contacts. The same is true of social class. In a study of social stratification in England, where class lines are more clearly drawn than they are in the United States, Bott found that people are class-conscious and do act in terms of their understanding of their class position. But their conception of class structure is often vague and develops from the ways in which the various individuals personally experience prestige and power in their daily lives. Most people are conscious of class differences, but their conception of the system varies with their experiences. Bott concluded that a social class is a constructed reference group—an audience to which people project their own respective expectations and of which they do not in fact possess accurate knowledge.[6]

Actually, men become acutely aware of the existence of divergent standpoints primarily when they are caught in situations in which conflicting demands are made upon them. While they avoid making difficult decisions whenever possible, these contradictions sometimes force one to choose between two social worlds. Such inner conflicts are essentially struggles between alternative ways of defining a given situation, the options arising from each of two or more perspectives that might be brought to bear upon it. Examples of such dilemmas were provided by William James: "As a man I pity you, but as an official I must show you no mercy; as a politician I regard him as an ally, but as a moralist I loathe him." In playing roles in different social worlds, contrasting expectations are imputed to competing audiences, and sometimes these differences cannot be compromised.

The problem is that of selecting the standpoint from which the situation is to be defined. It is in contexts in which alternative definitions are demanded that problems of loyalty arise.

There are individual differences in the flexibility with which one shifts from one reference group to another. There are some people who have a dominant perspective and insist upon defining virtually all situations from this standpoint. Such persons are sometimes reluctant even to acknowledge the existence of other viewpoints and insist that everyone who disagrees with them is wrong. Most people have a limited number of perspectives and are aware of the existence of others, and though they may feel uncomfortable in the company of people whose views are too different, they can tolerate some diversity. Still others change with the wind so that even their close associates are not certain of where they stand. Some can compartmentalize their experiences into units; others apparently find it difficult to do so. . . .

Notes

1. Albert H. Hastorf and Hadley Cantril, "They Saw a Game: A Case Study," *Journal of Abnormal and Social Psychology*, XLIX (1954), 129–34.

2. Cf. W. Fred Cottrell, *The Railroader* (Stanford: Stanford University Press, 1940); and Hallowell, op. cit., pp. 216–35.

3. Cf. Alvin W. Gouldner, "Cosmopolitans and Locals: Toward an Analysis of Latent Social Roles," *Administrative Science Quarterly*, II (1957–58), 281–306, 444–80.

4. William F. Whyte, "Slum Sex Code," *American Journal of Sociology*, XLIX (1943), 24–31.

5. Georg Simmel, *Conflict and the Web of Group-Affiliations*, trans. Kurt H. Wolff and Reinhard Bendix (Glencoe: The Free Press, 1955), pp. 127–95.

6. Elizabeth Bott, "The Concept of Class as a Reference Group," *Human Relations*, VII (1954), 259–85. Cf. Kurt Riezler, "What is Public Opinion?" *Social Research*, XI (1944), 397–427.

———————— ⦚ ————————

SELF-DEVELOPMENT AND REFERENCE GROUPS

This section expands on the theoretical ideas presented in the previous section with three examples of the influence of reference groups on self-development and perspective.

"Girls, Media and the Negotiation of Sexuality: A Study of Race, Class and Gender in Adolescent Peer Groups" is an empirical study of the influence of contemporary media on girls' ideas about themselves. According to author Meenakshi Gigi Durham, the media is a powerful form of contemporary reference group—a common source whereby we get ideas about who we should be and how we should behave.

School environments provide significant sites for establishing peer reference groups. "Shades of White" is a selection from a book based on a study of two racially distinct high schools. Sociologist Pamela Perry was interested in the racial viewpoints that high school students develop based on the influence of their peers. Perry demonstrates that white students in predominantly white schools have very different racial perspectives than white students in a racially diverse school.

In his article "A Theory of Genius," sociologist Thomas Scheff uses reference group theory as a framework for explaining the development of genius. Scheff proposes that reference groups and significant others exert a powerful influence on self-development through the process of "shaming." According to his theory, "genius" is more likely to occur among those who are able to escape the interactional shaming processes that lead us to conform to the status quo.

Questions for Discussion and Review

1. Consider the magazines that you read and the television shows that you watch frequently. For a few days, pay close attention to the types of images you see. What information do you get about who is attractive and popular? What information do you get about who is successful? What information do you get about who is a social problem? How are your own gender, race, class, and sexuality most commonly portrayed?

2. Study the photos in your local newspaper for one week. Specifically, count the number of photos of men and women. Do you notice anything about where pictures of women are likely to be posted in comparison with pictures of men? Count the number of pictures of members of minority groups that appear, and make a note of the context in which they are portrayed. Do you think these images send particular messages about what kind of person is most likely to be a political leader? Fashion expert? Criminal?

3. Discuss the idea of "shame" as a process that preserves the status quo. How does this process work interactionally? How does it work internally? Consider experiences in which you have felt shame. Do you avoid certain behaviors or situations because you *imagine* you might experience shame? When you imagine this shame, who or what is the audience in your head?

SELF-DEVELOPMENT AND REFERENCE GROUPS

24

Girls, Media, and the Negotiation of Sexuality

A Study of Race, Class, and Gender in Adolescent Peer Groups

Meenakshi Gigi Durham

(1999)

Adolescence for girls in the United States has been characterized as "a troubled crossing,"[1] a period marked by severe psychological and emotional stresses. Recent research indicates that the passage out of childhood for many girls means that they experience a loss of self-esteem and self-determination as cultural norms of femininity and sexuality are imposed upon them.[2]

Much attention has been paid over the last decade or more to the role of the mass media in this cultural socialization of girls:[3] clearly, the media are crucial symbolic vehicles for the construction of meaning in girls' everyday lives. The existing data paint a disturbing portrait of adolescent girls as well as of the mass media: on the whole, girls appear to be vulnerable targets of detrimental media images of femininity. In general, the literature indicates that media representations of femininity are restrictive, unrealistic, focused on physical beauty of a type that is virtually unattainable as well as questionable in terms of its characteristics, and filled with internal contradictions. At the same time, the audience analysis that has been undertaken with adolescent girls

reveals that they struggle with these media representations but are ultimately ill-equipped to critically analyze or effectively resist them.

These studies are linked to the considerable body of research documenting adolescent girls' difficulties with respect to issues such as waning self-esteem,[4] academic troubles,[5] negative body image,[6] conflicts surrounding sexuality,[7] and other issues related to girls' development. Although the majority of these studies were conducted with upper-middle-class White girls, some of them take into account the impact of race, ethnicity, and class on girls' experiences of adolescence. These findings indicate that—contrary to popular belief—girls of color and girls from lower socioeconomic backgrounds are very hard hit by adolescence and have fewer available resources for help with problems like eating disorders, pregnancies, or depression.[8]

Bearing these issues and their implications for girls in mind, this study seeks to broaden and deepen our understanding of the role of the mass media in girls' socialization, with a particular emphasis on the context in which this socialization

AUTHOR'S NOTE: This study was supported in part by grants from the sociology department of the University of California at Berkeley and the Doreen B. Townsend Center for the Humanities. A grant from the Spencer Foundation supported the writing of this piece. I am solely responsible for all views and statements made. My deepest admiration and thanks go to all of the youth who participated in this project. I also thank Rob Benson, Robert Bulman, Katherine Rosier, Michael Wilson, Matt Wray, Ana Yolanda Ramos Zayas, and the anonymous readers for JCE for their helpful comments on this article.

takes place. New theories of child development contend that socialization is context-specific and that the peer groups of childhood and adolescence are responsible for the transmission of cultural norms as well as the modification of children's personality characteristics.[9] However, most of the research done to date on adolescence and mass media does not take into account the peer group dynamics involved in media use, nor the race and class factors that might influence these processes.

The key question in this study, then, is how peer group activity and social context affect adolescent girls' interactions with mass media, especially in terms of their dealings with issues of gender and sexuality. This study consisted of a long-term participant observation of middle-school girls combined with in-depth interviews with the girls and their teachers. A significant aspect of the study is that the girls were from sharply varying race and class backgrounds, and these factors were crucial components of the analysis.

METHOD

Background of the Study

In order to gain a deep understanding of the social processes at work in adolescent girls' peer groups, a participant observation was conducted over a five-month period at two middle schools in a midsize city in the southwestern United States. East Middle School was situated within the city limits, in an impoverished residential neighborhood that was very close to the interstate highway. Heavily trafficked streets bounded all sides of the schoolyard. The school building was a concrete block; inside, there was little natural light. East Middle School had a total student enrollment of 1,164, of which the majority were African-American (60 percent, or 704 students). The next largest student ethnic group comprised Latino students (26 percent, or 298 students). Thirteen percent (157) of the students were Anglo/White.

A majority of the students (76.5 percent) were categorized by the school district as "economically disadvantaged."

By contrast, West Middle School was located many miles outside of the city in a picturesque hilly area. It, too, was in a residential neighborhood, but the houses were half-million-dollar properties with landscaped yards. The school was on its own street. The surroundings were peaceful and quiet.

West Middle School had a total student enrollment of 804. Of these, 732 students (91 percent) were Anglo/White. The minority population was minuscule: 27 students (3 percent) were Latino; 6 students (.07 percent) were African-American; and 36 students (4 percent) were Asian/Pacific Islander. Only 2.5 percent of the West Middle School students were classified as "economically disadvantaged" by the school district.

ANALYSIS

While references to mass media abounded in the peer group conversations observed at both schools, it is important to note at the outset that none of the groups made any use of the *news* media in their day-to-day peer interactions. Discussions of politics and current events did not arise during the five months of observations; rather, popular culture was the common currency among the girls, and the media with the greatest communicatory utility were television, consumer magazines, and movies. These observations corroborate recent findings of declining use of the news media by young people.[10]

Media references cropped up much more frequently in the conversations of the students at West Middle School than at East. Students at East Middle School did use the mass media, but in their peer group discussions they were much more likely to talk about their community and church activities, their friends and relatives, and the incidents in their daily lives—for instance, the *quince-anera* celebrations which many of the Latina girls were planning. At West Middle School, by contrast, media references were almost constant: talk of movies, TV shows, and pop music featured in every conversation.

At both schools, mass media were in evidence. For example, most of the girls at both schools subscribed to *YM* and *Seventeen* magazines and carried them in their backpacks. Girls at both schools watched TV shows like *The X Files, Friends, Seinfeld, Daria, Sabrina the Teenage Witch,* and *Buffy the Vampire Slayer.* Girls at West Middle School were more likely to have seen current movies than the girls at East; they were also more involved with pop music.

The pervasiveness of popular culture at both schools was tied very closely to the single most important theme that emerged from the data: the dominance of the socio-cultural norm of heterosexuality in the girls' lives. While this was addressed and negotiated in different ways depending on various contextual factors, compulsory heterosexuality functioned as the core ideology underpinning the girls' interpersonal and intragroup transactions, although it was seldom explicitly acknowledged. What was striking was that this norm of heterosexuality was central to the social worlds of girls at both schools, and it guided the girls' behaviors and beliefs regardless of their racial, ethnic, and class differences, although it manifested itself in different ways based on these cultural variances.

The girls' efforts to understand and adapt to perceived social norms of heterosexuality played out principally through their ongoing constructions of femininity. The use of the mass media was woven into those constructions and served in various ways to cement the girls' identities within their peer groups as well as to secure their relationships to the broader social world. Themes of heterosexuality criss-crossed the girls' conversations and actions in multiple ways, but certain practices occurred frequently and repeatedly enough to constitute clearly discernible modalities

of mass mediated heterosexual expression. These are described and analyzed in detail, below, under the thematic headings of (1) the discipline of the body, (2) brides and mothers, (3) homophobia and sexual confusion, and (4) iconic femininity.

The Discipline of the Body: Cosmetics, Clothes, and Diets

Bartky points out that "femininity is an artifice" and that women engage in "disciplinary practices that produce a body which in gesture and appearance is recognizably feminine."[11] My observations of the school-girls at East and West Middle Schools indicate that these disciplinary practices are acquired fairly early in life and are essential to the maintenance of adolescent girls' peer group configurations. At both schools, peer relationships hinged on these techniques for molding the female body in group-sanctioned ways.

Cosmetics and Grooming. At East Middle School, the application of cosmetics was a common group occurrence and one that sometimes transpired with the aid of magazines like *YM, Seventeen,* and *Glamour.* This happened most often among the "gangsta" girls, and it usually occurred in the classroom when students were given unstructured work time. On several occasions I observed them braiding and styling each others' hair, painting each others' fingernails, and applying makeup. During the yearbook class one afternoon, for example, when some students were writing stories or working on layouts, a group of the "gangsta" girls drifted together; one pulled out a makeup bag and began to apply cosmetics to another, while several gathered around to watch and comment.

Mariana, the 14-year-old Latina girl who was doing the make-over, went about it with great concentration, first applying lip-liner, then lipstick, then powder foundation, then eyeshadows of various colors, and finally mascara to her friend

Mercedes' face. The girls were quiet and rapt while this was going on, watching the process in almost reverent silence, but after it was over they began to talk.

Laura: That looks good. That looks cute.

Mariana: I saw in *YM* that if you put white eyeshadow on like that, it makes your eyes look bigger.

Mercedes: (*opening her eyes wide*) Does it work?

Mariana: I don't know. Yeah. A little bit, maybe.

Nydia: Her hair is pretty. My hair is so ugly.

Laura: Your hair is pretty.

Nydia: Naw, it's all dry and damaged.

(*Much discussion about their hair . . .*)

Nydia: I like long hair. I want long hair. What shampoo do you use?

Mercedes: Pantene Pro-V.

Mariana: I use Wella conditioner.

Mercedes: My hair is all dry and I have split ends.

Nydia pulled a *Seventeen* magazine out of her backpack and flipped though it until she found an ad for Suave conditioner. "I need this," she said. "It's mois . . . tur . . . izing," she read from the ad, stumbling over the pronunciation. "'To replenish moisture in dry or damaged hair.' That's me."

This episode serves as an exemplar of the girls' preoccupation with the tools and techniques required to achieve physical beauty, and their use of mass media for guidance in the acquisition of those commodities. At East Middle School the girls who were more knowledgeable about beautification were also more "popular," which is to say that they were the central figures in their peer groups.

Clothes. Further, at East Middle School, peer groups were defined in part by their costuming. Conversations with the girls confirmed this: the main groups of girls were the "gangstas," students who were gang-identified; the "gangsta wannabes," who dressed and acted like gang affiliates, but who were not included in gang activities; the "preps," who were the honor students and the cheerleaders; and the "dorks," the social outcasts. The dorks, according to Ariana, a member of the prep group, "didn't know how to dress." The Latina girls in the "gangsta" group had thin plucked eyebrows, wore dark lipstick and heavy eye makeup, and had chemically lightened their hair color. The girls in the prep group wore minimal makeup, but they plucked their eyebrows and sometimes experimented with hairstyles within a very conservative range of options (ponytails or sometimes curled hair). Their clothes usually reflected current trends in shopping-mall fashions. The "dorks" wore blue jeans and t-shirts and tended not to draw attention to themselves via their costuming.

At West Middle School the groups, or "cliques" as they were called by the students, were also marked by their appearance, and costuming. As Judith, a 14-year-old Jewish girl, explained,

> Some of the cliques have um like certain styles. Like the most popular people are kind of like preps, and they wear like The Gap and J. Crew, and then the other groups that kind of get stuff like that are, the skater group who are like grunge influenced . . . and then um, like there's this one group of girls that are like really into Contempo clothes, and they wear that a lot.

Consumer fashion thus was the principal means by which group identity was demarcated, although pop music was also used in the same way. Fashion traits seemed to be derived from advertising; music was related to clothing, and these connections were made from MTV as well as peer references. The skaters listened to hard rock and heavy metal music; the preps made much of knowing which bands were currently "hot" on the charts.

Despite these identifiers, many students were emphatic about not conforming to group norms. In individual conversations, they were clear about the characterizing features of the different cliques, and they all identified themselves as iconoclasts and nonconformists even when they belonged to cliques:

Judith: My style is kind of different from everyone else's. I don't really think too much about what I wear as long as I like it.

Bobbi: If I feel comfortable, if I like what I'm wearing . . . I'm not out to please anybody else.

Lila: If I find something I like, then I wear it, but if everybody starts painting their nails silver or something then you'd have to stop.

Jenny: I try to be my own person. I just buy clothes that I like and that are comfortable.

Tara: I don't conform to fashion trends or whatever.

Jenny:
(to Tara): For fashion, you copy me.

In an interesting paradox, the West Middle School girls were quick to point out and criticize each others' compliance with mediated and peer standards for dress and appearance, but they denied their own participation in that system. Their peer group conversations, however, belied an intense interest in fashion and the fashion media.

Diet and Weight. At East Middle School the girls were extremely critical of those who showed no interest in conforming to media-driven standards of fashion and beauty, and they were also very open about their own interest in those standards.

This was particularly striking during a conversation about food and dieting that occurred at the lunch table among the "popular" girls at East. One of the girls, Ariana, had brought to the table a newspaper article about teenagers' eating habits, which the girls all looked at. The article described teenage girls' poor eating habits, stating that teen girls are "more likely to skip meals, avoid milk, eat away from home, and fret about their weight."

Brittany: It's true, this is how we eat. Milk has calcium, doesn't it? I don't drink milk.

Rachel: I only drink milk on cereal.

Brittany: I only drink water and tea.

Rosa: I drink everything except water and milk.

Brittany: I'm addicted to tea.

Marta: I'm addicted to Dr. Pepper.

Brittany: I used to starve myself.

Ariana: I did, too. It's easy after the first day. The first day is hard. But after that it's easy, you don't notice it.

Marta: We don't eat real food, we'd get food poisoning.

They were eager to reify the connections between themselves and the girls described in the article, and it was important to them to find points of similarity between themselves and the news article's mediated construction of "teenage girls," however negative that construction might be.

Despite this, these girls did not usually discuss their bodies or their weight to any significant degree in their peer group conversations; nor did the girls in the "gangsta" group. At West Middle School, however, there was more open talk about body norms and more criticism of girls whose bodies did not conform to the ideal.

Bobbi: There is a girl who will wear like really really tight pants and like stripes with flowers or something, things that don't go together at all.

Judith: Who?

Bobbi: Kathy Smith. [*author's note: name changed to protect privacy*]

Judith: That's a fashion faux pas right there. Not to say any names or anything, but she wears like tank tops with really thin straps but she doesn't really have the body for it . . .

The girls at West school were sensitized to issues of body image and eating disorders, and these topics cropped up frequently in their conversations. Eating disorders were a serious problem at this school; teachers informed me that a student had recently died of anorexia nervosa. Yet, interestingly, the girls' discussions hovered around *resistance* to dysfunctional images of body; they used discourse around these issues to find solidarity in critiquing problematic concepts of body.

Audrey: Like anorexia and all that stuff, I don't understand that. It's just so stupid, I don't get it. How can you not eat?

Jonquil: I couldn't ever be bulimic and keep throwing up.

Emma: And there are some people at school, these girls, they'll eat like a carrot, cause they're afraid the guys will see them eating. I hate that.

Audrey: At lunch, I eat like so much, I eat like three pieces of pizza every day. I don't care what guys think. People have to eat. That's just natural . . .

Jonquil: Biology.

Audrey: Yeah. And people, they're afraid they'll think they're pigs or something if they eat too much. So they'll like go to the bathroom and eat. Some people eat lunch in the bathroom.

Emma: It's so sad. You know Laurel. . . . She kind of copies things off magazines and TV and things. . . . she's into like being perfect and skinny and not eating.

Audrey: But you have to eat! I feel like saying, eat something!

Conversations with one of the teachers revealed that Jonquil in fact had had some problems with eating disorders; how many of the others had suffered from them was not ascertainable, but the issue was clearly on their minds. Here, the peer group served as a means of consolidating ideas about rejecting and resisting damaging ideals for female bodies. Individually, their engagement with their bodies may have been different, more self-critical and less defiant,[12] but the group context appeared to moderate those tendencies in more progressive directions. The conversation reflected the paradoxical nature of eating disorders and the culture of thinness in US society:[13] while the girls understood eating disorders as pathological and abnormal, they would not admit their own involvement with these problems even as they subscribed in their daily lives to mediated norms of slenderness and beauty. As Siebecker notes:

[Eating] disorders have been regarded as bizarre psychological phenomena that affect a minority of emotionally disturbed women. The problem has thus been isolated from the experiences of other women and marginalized into a psychological category. This has in effect thrown up a smokescreen between the clinically diagnosed eating disorder sufferer and the rest of women in society: If the smokescreen came down, what women would see is that, while we do not all actually have eating disorders, we are not so different from those sufferers.[14]

The girls' conversation kept the smokescreen up, distancing the girls with obvious eating problems from the sociocultural norms of thinness and beauty that pervaded the group members' everyday lives.

Brides and Mothers. Flipping through magazines in the classroom, Nydia and Maria pause at an advertisement featuring a bride in a formal white wedding dress. They examine the photograph for several minutes.

Nydia: Oh, that's a pretty dress.

Maria: She looks so beautiful.

Nydia: I want to have a long dress like that. I want a big veil and flowers.

At East Middle School mediated images of brides and motherhood were of vital interest to the girls. Again and again, they discussed TV and celebrity weddings with admiration and obsessive attention to detail.

Ariana: You know what I did? I saw this wedding on TV, and the guys all wore Wranglers and tuxedo shirts . . . and then the bridesmaids were late, and the bride got wet and her hair got all messed up . . .

Marta: What are you talking about?

Ariana: A wedding where these guys wore Wrangler jeans and tuxedo shirts and jackets . . .

Brittany: That's how you're gonna get married.

Marta: She's gonna have horses at the reception. (Giggles.)

Rosa: I want a formal wedding. Ariana, what color were the bridesmaids' dresses?

Ariana: Pink, a really gross pink, I'm having pastel colors for my wedding.

Brittany: Did any of you watch the Waltons reunion?

Rosa: I did!

Marta: I watched "The Brady Girls Get Married." Marcia and Jan were going to have a double wedding, but they kept fighting about what kind of wedding to have . . .

Brittany: What kind did they want?

Marta: I don't know, one wanted to go all formal, and the other one wanted something modern, I think. One ended up wearing a short gown, I think they call them tea-length? The other one was long.

Rosa: I want a long gown. And lots of bridesmaids. Big weddings are nice.

Ariana: Weddings should be special. It's your day, your special day.

On another occasion, when the girls were working in the computer lab on the Internet, a group of them found Madonna's home page and zeroed in instantly on photographs of her with her baby. They were especially delighted with one image of her when she was pregnant, exclaiming aloud about how "sweet" and "adorable" it was.

This valorization of marriage and maternity appeared to be in line with the trends in their lives. Teenage pregnancy is a significant problem at East Middle School—it is the main reason that girls drop out of that school. During the five months of this observation, on four different occasions, former seventh- and eighth-graders returned for campus visits with their babies in their arms. Their appearances were not greeted with any derision or gossip from their erstwhile classmates; rather, they were feted and embraced, the babies were cooed over, and the girls spoke with some longing of the day when they too would be mothers.

Culturally, teenage pregnancy was a norm among this student population. Many of the 14- and 15-year-old girls disclosed that their mothers were in their late twenties and early thirties. Some of the girls seemed to experience some conflict about the pressure toward maternity and their knowledge of other possibilities; they talked sometimes about the issue of abortion and whether it was sinful or not. The African-American girls tended to be more in favor of abortion as an option. The Latina girls were more opposed to it, for religious reasons.

Two of the "gangsta" girls had one extended conversation about their plans for the future; both intended to go to college and were clear and emphatic about not wanting to get pregnant before then.

Maria: I am not getting married until I'm older. Like, 60. And I'm not having no babies.

Nydia: I don't want a baby messin' up my life. I'm going to wait till after I go to college.

Maria became pregnant at the end of that academic year and dropped out of school.

By contrast, teenage pregnancy was invisible at West Middle School, and marriage and maternity were never mentioned in the girls' peer group conversations over the five months of this observation. The subjects did not seem to be relevant to the white, upper-middle-class girls' lives at all.

Homophobia and Sexual Confusion. On April 30, 1997, the TV show Ellen aired its notorious "coming-out" episode, in which the main character declared herself a lesbian. The show precipitated a discussion of homosexuality among the girls in the "prep" group at East Middle School; this conversation reiterated the refrain of homophobia that was a constant current in the students' lives at both East and West Middle Schools.

While overt discrimination based on race was rare at both schools, homophobia was an openly declared prejudice in the peer groups that were studied. Words like "fag" and "queer" were used casually as epithets; gossip about students' sexual orientations were a way of marking the social outcasts. At East Middle School the "coming-out" episode of *Ellen* served as a catalyst for a brief, impassioned exchange about the iniquity of homosexuality.

Rosa: I don't think she should have done that. It's just wrong to go on TV and put that in front of everybody.

Ariana: She should just keep it to herself.

Brittany: I think it's a sin and it shouldn't be on TV.

None of the girls in the peer group expressed opinions that differed from these, but later that day, Nona was looking through a *People* magazine in class and came across a photograph of Ellen DeGeneres. At that point she paused and said thoughtfully to her teacher, who was sitting nearby, "It's kind of good that they showed that on TV because it lets people who are gay know that people's lives are like that."

Her comment was unusual in a milieu where gay-bashing was considered high sport. At West Middle School homophobia was similarly open and aggressive. One student, Jenny—one of the most popular girls in the eighth grade—had a notebook covered with pictures cut out of magazines. The right side of the notebook displayed pictures of celebrity figures she disliked, and the left side was adorned with photos of people she admired. Prominent on the right side of the notebook was the band Luscious Jackson, and Jenny had written "Sucks! Dikes, too!" (*sic*) across their image.

The "regular girls" were very aware of the rhetoric of compulsory heterosexuality in teen magazines and talked about it with some anger. As Audrey put it, "They make it seem like if you don't have a boyfriend, you're just nothing, which really . . . I don't think it's true." Later, she added, "All of the articles are so superficial they make you think you have to be pretty to have friends or to have a boyfriend to be cool. . . . and that's kind of stupid . . ." Interestingly, in phrasing this resistance, she acknowledges her own susceptibility to the rhetoric. In other conversations these girls expressed aversion to the concept of homosexuality and distress at the idea of other students identifying themselves as gay or lesbian.

One of these girls, Lila, was very reflective about the homophobia that was rampant in the school. . . . Lila was clearly struggling with her sexuality and was conflicted about how to cope with her peer environment.

Lila: One of my friends and I, in order to help me dump my boyfriend, we pretended to be lesbians. . . . So that went on for about a week, and then we were like, oh it's just a joke, we were just trying to get rid of my boyfriend, you know, and people at school are still keeping it up. . . . There was this guy who like came up to me last week and said, "Why don't you leave our school so that we can get the scum out of here? Why don't you go to another school and stop polluting ours?" Some guy punched me six times and threw me on the ground.

Me: Hmm.

Lila: Although, I didn't really care, because you know, "Oh, no! He called me a dyke! I'm going to die!" and he's really mad at me because I didn't react. I mean, he calls me a lesbian and then walks away. I'm like, "Oh, no! I'm gonna die!"

Lila was derisive of the boy's bigotry, yet she was careful to couch her experience in terms of having "pretended" to be a lesbian. Students were open in their rejection of homosexuality and their need to position themselves in the heterosexual mainstream. In order to bolster this positioning, they chose role models whom they considered to epitomize femininity in terms of the heterosexual ideal.

Iconic Femininity. At both schools, the girls made frequent references to media figures who served as emblems or icons of ideal femininity.

All of the women who were chosen by the girls as role models or heroines exemplified media and sociocultural ideals of beauty; and they were admired by the girls specifically for their beauty, although other characteristics were sometimes mentioned as reasons for revering them. But none of the girls professed to admire women who had not been identified in the mass media as being physically beautiful according to dominant standards.

CONCLUSIONS

The girls' overall use of the mass media to reconstruct ideals of heterosexuality with regard to physical appearance, the goals of marriage and maternity, and active homophobia reveal a fairly direct appropriation of the dominant ideology of femininity. Race and class factors impacted the ways in which the parameters of ideal femininity were defined; but in general, the peer context was one in which emergent gender identity was consolidated via constant reference to acceptable sociocultural standards of femininity and sexuality.

This conformity was not seamless; pockets of resistance occurred in peer group discussions, but when they did, their functioning was paradoxical. In the West Middle School girls' dialogue about eating disorders, or the "gangsta" girls' rejection of the prospect of early motherhood, the privileged voices in the discussion shut out some of the participants in such a way that their personal struggles with these issues could not be recognized. Jonquil's history of eating disorders, Maria's sexual activity that culminated in pregnancy a few months later, Lila's sexual ambiguity could not be given full voice. Thus, the peer group served to achieve ideological closure in terms of how issues of gender and power could be addressed.

This functioning adds a new dimension to the studies that have looked at girls' individual responses to media texts. Duke and Kreshel found that girls "were not as uniformly vulnerable to media messages concerning the feminine ideal as was expected."[15] Frazer found girls to be aware of the distinctions between magazine portrayals and real life, although she did point out that the conventions and "registers" of discourse constrained what the girls said.[16] Numerous theorists have posited a fluid and mobile relationship between mass media and the receiver; especially in the cultural studies literature, it is supposed that readers are able to reappropriate the meanings of messages according to their various life circumstances.[17] It does appear that girls *on their own* may be somewhat more able to critically examine and deconstruct media messages than in the peer group context. Therefore, the role of the adolescent peer group is a complex one: the group dynamic serves to mask and neutralize individual experiences of social and cultural processes. The group is a microcosm for the creation of social structure via the renegotiation of dominant and oppositional ideological positions.

In the peer groups in this study, surface levels of resistance cloaked some of the participants' more private and interiorized struggles with dominant codes of femininity. The group discourse provided a text that could be analyzed, but the research cited earlier in this essay, as well as information gathered by this researcher from sources outside of the peer groups, point to the existence of subtexts that tended to be suppressed by the group process.

Some evidence of this kind of suppression was provided by the West Middle School girls' insistence that they were individuals when their outward behaviors indicated complete capitulation to the norms of the group. Another mark of such masking was the conspicuous absence of teen pregnancy in the peer discourse at West Middle School; it was a taboo topic in peer discussion, so if a girl at West had undergone a pregnancy, her experience would be completely invalidated by the group's tacit doctrine of denial.

Similarly, eating disorders were not openly discussed at East Middle School, yet the girls' casual references to starving themselves in one conversation indicated that body image issues were of more concern than was openly evidenced. Thompson points out that eating disorders among Latina and African-American women tend to be severe because they are not taken seriously or diagnosed quickly.[18] The girls at East Middle School were uncritical and unreflexive about the norm of thinness to which they subscribed.

Thus, this research indicates that while race and class were differentiators of girls' socialization and concomitant media use, the differences highlighted the ways in which their different cultures functioned to uphold different aspects of dominant ideologies of femininity.

Watkins suggests that minority youth in particular have generated cultural practices of resistance that have grown out of their social marginalization.[19] Such resistance was not obviously manifested among the girls at East and West Middle Schools, yet the potential for resistance was an ever-present subcurrent. At West Middle School, for example, the peer group discourse among the "regular girls" was more resistant than that of the "preps." Because peer acceptance is of paramount importance in girls' culture,[20] a real subversion of dominant norms *could* certainly happen in a peer group where that was part of the group identity. It is possible that the peer group's social standing with respect to other groups would influence the degree of resistance expressed in the group. A larger study in which more, and more diverse, peer groups were observed would be needed to further investigate these phenomena.

It could be argued that the girls' observed tendency to accept dominant norms of femininity was related to the fact that most of the subjects were honors students—academic achievers who conformed to social expectations in every aspect of their lives. Yet an adherence to codes of what might be called "hegemonic femininity" was also evident in the behaviors of the "gangsta" group from East Middle School, who were considered to be at risk of dropping out, delinquency, and other "antisocial" behaviors. In fact, they demonstrated even more interest in costuming, makeup, beautification, and maternity than did the more "prosocial" peer groupings. It can be tentatively concluded from these data, then, that the peer group generally serves to consolidate dominant constructions of gender and sexuality.

However, race and class factors appear to intercede in the process of meaning-making, within as well as around the peer group context. The predominantly white, upper-middle-class students at West Middle School were primary targets of advertising-driven media, and they concomitantly paid significantly more attention to the mass media than did students at East Middle School. Nonetheless, media were used to shore up systems of belief held by students at both schools.

Hermes has observed that "media use and interpretation exist by grace of unruly and unpredictable, but in retrospect understandable and interesting choices and activities of readers."[21] Among the girls in this study, a key strategy for blending into the peer group involved participating in activities that marked the limits of acceptable femininity; however, these were deployed within their racial, cultural, and class environments. Deviance from normative sexuality was a means of identifying the social outcast; conformity was a way of bonding with the group, and mass media were used as instruments in the bonding process.

These findings have multiple implications. First, they establish the centrality of mass media in adolescent society and underscore the links between socialization into dominant norms of sexuality and consumer culture. The teenagers in this study were hyperaware of the need to use the media to find their foothold in the group. Their uses of the media were more than discursive: consumption of the necessary products that openly established their acceptance and understanding of sexual norms was a necessary part of peer interaction. Thus socialization into femininity was linked to the multimillion dollar fashion, beauty and diet industries that thrive on women consumers.

Second, perhaps more important, it makes clear that the peer group must be taken into account in the contemplation of interventions or counteractions against the mediated norms that play into girls' gendered behaviors. Such interventions tend to be "top-down," devised and administered by adults; yet the significance of the peer group in girls' social lives indicates that the most effective resistant practices would germinate and take root within the peer group. In this study, the peer group was shown to be a training ground where girls learned to use the mass media to acquire the skills of ideal femininity, but it was also a place where rejection of these norms could sometimes be voiced.

While girls individually have some sense of the social environment that operates to regulate their expressions of gender and sexuality, and while they may try on an individual level to resist damaging normative constructions of femininity, the peer group dynamic tends to mitigate against such resistance. Effective interventions for girls must work within the peer context to try to encourage more nuanced and less univocal conceptualizations of normative femininity. Beyond this, the peer group's relationship to broader levels of society must be taken into account. Interventions such as media literacy efforts will not be effective unless they are sensitive to issues of race, class, and culture; a recognition of institutionalized networks of power that constrain and limit girls' autonomy is necessary before strategies for resistance and emancipation can be devised.

NOTES

1. Lyn Mikel Brown and Carol Gilligan, *Meeting at the Crossroads: Women's Psychology and Girls, Development* (New York: Ballantine Books, 1992).

2. Peggy Orenstein, *Schoolgirls: Young Women, Self-Esteem, and the Confidence Gap* (New York: Doubleday, 1994); Mary Pipher, *Reviving Ophelia: Saving the Selves of Adolescent Girls* (New York: Ballantine, 1994); Lori Stern, "Disavowing the Self in Female Adolescence," in *Women, Girls and Psychotherapy: Reframing Resistance,* ed. Carol Gilligan, Annie G. Rogers, and Deborah L. Tolman (New York: Haworth Press, 1991), 105–117.

3. Margaret Duffy and Michael Gotcher, "Crucial Advice on How to Get the Guy: The Rhetorical Vision of Power and Seduction in the Teen Magazine *YM,*" *Journal of Communication Inquiry* 21 (spring 1996): 32–48; Lisa Duke and Peggy J. Kreshel, "Negotiating Femininity: Girls in Early Adolescence Read Teen Magazines," *Journals of Communication Inquiry* 22 (January 1998): 48–71; Meenakshi Gigi Durham, "Dilemmas of Desire: Representations of Adolescent Sexuality in Two Teen Magazines," *Youth and Society* 29 (March 1998): 369–389; Ellen McCracken, *Decoding Women's Magazines: From Mademoiselle to Ms.* (New York: St. Martin's Press, 1993); Angela McRobbie, "Jackie: An Ideology of Adolescent Femininity," *in Mass Communication Review year book* vol. 4, ed. Ellen Wartella, D. Charles Whitney, and Sven Windahl (Beverly Hills, CA: Sage, 1983), 251–271; Angela McRobbie, "Shut Up and Dance: Youth Culture and Changing Modes of Femininity," in *Postmodernism and Popular Culture.* ed. Angela McRobbie (London: Routledge, 1994), 155–176; Kate Pierce, "A Feminist Theoretical Perspective on the Socialization of Teenage Girls through *Seventeen* Magazine," *Sex Roles* 23 (1990): 491–500; Kate Pierce, "Socialization of Teen age

Girls through Teen-Magazine Fiction: The Making of a New Woman or an Old Lady?" *Sex Roles* 29 (1993): 59–68.

4. Brown and Gilligan, *Meeting at the Crossroads;* Pipher, *Reviving Ophelia.*

5. Orenstein, *Schoolgirls:* American Association of University Women Educational Foundation, *How Schools Shortchange Girls* (Washington, DC: American Association of University Women, 1992).

6. Susan Bordo, *Unbearable Weight: Feminism, Western Culture, and the Body* (Berkeley; University of California Press, 1993); Naomi Wolf, *The Beauty Myth: How Images of Beauty Are Used Against Women* (New York: Anchor, 1991).

7. Sue Lees, *Sugar and Spice: Sexuality and Adolescent Girls* (Harmondsworth, England: Penguin, 1993); Naomi Wolf, *Promiscuities* (New York: Random House, 1997).

8. Jill McLean Taylor, Carol Gilligan, and Amy M. Sullivan, *Between Voice and Silence: Women and Girls, Race and Relationship* (Cambridge, MA: Harvard University Press, 1995); Becky W. Thompson, *A Hunger So Wide and Deep: American Women Speak on Eating Problems* (Minneapolis: University of Minnesota Press, 1994).

9. Judith Rich Harris, "Where Is the Child's Environment? A Group Socialization Theory of Development," *Psychological Review* 102 (1995): 458–489.

10. Kevin G. Barnhurst and Ellen Wartella, "Newspapers and Citizenship: Young Adults' Subjective Experience of Newspapers," *Critical Studies in Mass Communication* 8 (June 1991): 195–209; Kevin G. Barnhurst and Ellen Wartella, "Young Citizens, American TV Newscasts, and the Collective Memory," *Critical Studies in Mass Communication* 15 (September 1998): 279–305; Leo Bogart, *Commercial Culture: The Media System and the Public Interest* (New York: Oxford University Press, 1995).

11. Sandra Lee Bartky, "Foucault, Femininity, and the Modernization of Patriarchal Power," in *Feminism and Foucault: Reflections on Resistance,* ed. Irene Diamond and Lee Quinby (Boston: Northeastern University Press, 1988), 64.

12. See Duke and Kreshel, "Negotiating Femininity."

13. Bordo, *Unbearable Weight.*

14. July Siebecker, "Women's Oppression and the Obsession with Thinness," in *Women: Images and*

Realities, ed. Amy Kesselman, Lily D. McNair, and Nancy Schniedewind (Mountain View, CA: Mayfield, 1995), 107.

15. Duke and Kreshel, "Negotiating Femininity."

16. Frazer, "Teenage Girls Reading Jackie."

17. Ien Ang, *Watching "Dallas": Soap Opera and the Melodramatic Imagination* (London: Methuen, 1985); John Fiske, "British Cultural Studies and Television," in *Channels of Discourse, Reassembled,* ed. Robert C. Allen (Chapel Hill: University of North Carolina Press, 1992), 284–326; Stuart Hall, "Encoding/Decoding," in *Culture, Media, Language: Working Papers in Cultural Studies, 1972–1979,* ed. Stuart Hall, Dorothy Hobson, Andre Lowe, and Paul Willis (London: Hutchinson, 1980), 128–138; David Morley, *The Nationwide Audience: Structure and Decoding* (London: Hutchinson, 1980).

18. Thompson, *A Hunger So Wide and Deep.*

19. S. Craig Watkins, *Representing: Hip-Hop Culture and the Production of Black Cinema* (Chicago: University of Chicago Press, 1998).

20. Griffiths, *Adolescent Girls and Their Friends;* Brown and Gilligan, *Meeting at the Crossroads;* Evans and Eder, "No Exit."

21. Joke Hermes, *Reading Women's Magazines: An Analysis of Everyday Media Use* (Cambridge, England: Polity Press), 25.

SELF-DEVELOPMENT AND REFERENCE GROUPS

25

Shades of White

Pamela Perry

(2001)

"How would you describe white American culture?" I ask Laurie, a white, middle-class senior at Valley Groves High,* a predominantly white, suburban public school near the Pacific Coast of northern California. She pauses, her face looking visibly perplexed as if she did not understand the question or her mind was drawing a blank. Wondering if she heard me over the roar of the cappuccino machine in the background, I awkwardly reiterate, "Like, you know, what would you say white American culture is like?"

"I wouldn't be able to tell you. I don't know." She pauses again and laughs nervously. "When you think about it, it's like—[a longer pause]—*I don't know!*"

About twenty miles away from Valley Groves is the postindustrial city of Clavey. Clavey High School is composed of a brilliant mosaic of students from different ethnic and racial groups, about 12 percent of whom are white. In an interview with Murray, a white, Jewish, middle-class senior, he and I talked a great deal about the consequences of race in the United States and what privileges come with being a white person here. When I probed into his identification with being white or Jewish, he said,

[Cultural pride] doesn't make sense to me. To me it doesn't. I mean, what difference does it make what my great, great grandfather was or his whole

*All names of cities, schools, and individuals in this article are pseudonyms.

generation. That's not affecting my life. . . . I'm still here now. I've got to make what's best for me in the future. I can't harp on what the past has brought.

Laurie and Murray express what the racial category "white" means to each of them. Although their responses differ markedly, they share something fundamental; they perceive white raciality as cultureless. For Laurie, whiteness is not culturally defined. She lives within it but cannot name it. It is taken for granted. For Murray, to be cultural means having emotional attachment to tradition and history. He eschews culture, in this regard, and lives in the present, looking forward.

I chose these two excerpts from qualitative research I carried out in 1994–97 at Valley Groves, a predominantly white, suburban high school, and Clavey, a multiracial, urban high school. The focus of this research was on what differences, if any, the two demographically distinct contexts made on the ways white youth reflected on and constructed white identities. I found that it made a large difference: white students at Valley Groves did not reflect on or define white identity as a culture and social location to the extent that the white youth at Clavey did. Moreover, white identities at Clavey tended to be altogether more variable and contradictory than at Valley Groves. Elsewhere, I argue that these differences in white identities were conditioned by different experiences and structures of interracial association (Perry 1998).

I make a similar argument in this article but with a focus on the only similarity between the ways whites at both schools defined white identity. They defined white as cultureless. By that, I mean that white identity was understood to have no ties or allegiances to European ancestry and culture, no "traditions." To the white youth, only "ethnic" people had such ties to the past. The students would agree with George DeVos (1975) that a "feeling of continuity with the past" distinguishes an "ethnic" group from peoples with more "present-oriented" or "future-oriented" identities (p. 17)—such as whites.

However, although white students at Valley Groves and Clavey shared this perception of white identity, they did not arrive at it by the same processes. In what follows, I present and interpret ethnographic and interview data to argue that at Valley Groves, the tendency for youth to explicitly define themselves and other whites as people without culture came about through processes of *naturalization*—the embedding of historically constituted cultural practices in that which is taken for granted and seems "normal" and natural. At Clavey, culturelessness was achieved through processes of *rationalization*—the embedding of whiteness within a Western rational epistemology and value paradigm that marginalizes or subordinates all things "cultural."

Although there is some scholarly debate over whether there is such a thing as "white culture" (Ignatiev and Garvey 1996; Roediger 1994), my argument here is not so much about whether there is or is not a white culture but about the power whites exercise when *claiming* they have no culture. Culturelessness can serve, even if unintentionally, as a measure of white racial superiority. It suggests that one is either "normal" and "simply human" (therefore, the standard to which others should strive) or beyond culture or "postcultural" (therefore, developmentally advanced).

This work seeks to advance on theories and research in critical white studies, the sociology of education, and racial-ethnic identity formation by vividly illustrating the social construction of white identities and culture in schooling and the ways that different social-structural contexts differently influence constructions of whiteness, including the construction of white as cultureless or the norm. . . .

METHOD AND REFLECTIONS

The vast wealth of excellent scholarship on the social construction of identities in schooling fundamentally shaped my research focus and methodology (Bourdieu and Passeron 1977; Davidson 1996; Eckert 1989; Fordham 1996; Fordham and Ogbu 1986; Kinney 1993; MacLeod 1987; Thorne 1993; Valenzuela 1999). The main focus of my work was what role, if any, close interracial association in school had on the racial consciousness and identities of white youth. Therefore, in choosing my research sites, I looked for two schools: one predominantly white and located in a predominantly white town or city; the other multiracial, minority white and located in a minority white town or city. It also concerned me that the schools be in the same geographical region, of similar size and academic standing, and with student bodies of similar socioeconomic backgrounds to keep those factors as "constant" as possible. I studied census data and school statistics for different towns and cities across the United States before I decided on Valley Groves, which was 83 percent white, and Clavey, which was 12 percent white. Although Clavey was located in a city and Valley Groves a suburb, Clavey was very similar to Valley Groves in all respects besides racial composition, largely due to the fact that Clavey's catchment area encircled a largely middle- to upper-middle-class population. Particularly important for my research was that white students at Clavey were primarily middle class, which allowed me to focus on middle-class whites in both schools.

I spent two and a half years in the schools doing participant observation and in-depth interviewing. Daily practices included sitting in on classrooms with students, hanging out with them during breaks and lunch, attending school club meetings, and participating in student-administrator advisory committees, especially those concerned with race and cultural awareness on campus. I also observed or helped out with after-school programs and events, such as school plays, major rallies, games, and the junior and senior balls of each school. To familiarize myself with the music and leisure activities the students were involved in, after hours I listened to the local rap, R & B, punk, alternative, and classic rock radio stations; bought CD's of the most popular musical artists; went to live underground punk and alternative concerts; read fanzines and other youth magazines; watched MTV; studied music that students dubbed for me; and attended a large rave produced by some Clavey students.

Although I looked somewhat younger than my age (thirty-eight when the research began), I made concerted efforts to minimize the effects of age difference on how students related to me. I did not associate with other adults on campus. I dressed casually in attire that I was comfortable in, which happened to be similar to the attire students were comfortable in: blue jeans, sandals or athletic shoes, T-shirt or sweat-shirt, no jewelry except four tiny hoop earrings—one in one ear, three in the other. I had students call me by my first name, and I did not talk down to them, judge them, or otherwise present myself as an authority figure. To the contrary, I saw the students as the authorities, and they seemed to appreciate that regard. Those efforts, on top of having developed some popular-cultural frames of reference with the students; contributed to my developing some very close relationships with several of the students and fairly wide access to different peer groups and cliques on campus. Having stood in the middle of secret hideouts, food fights, fist fights, tongue lashings, and over-the-top fits of goofiness, I can say that in most cases, I seemed to have little impact on students' behaviors.

My other most apparent traits—race, gender, and middle-class/intellectual appearance—had both positive and negative effects. I connected most readily and easily with girls. The results were that I have more narrative data and in-depth material from girls than boys. At Clavey, however, I did make a few close relationships with boys that I believe helped balance my findings at that school. Similarly, my class background made crossing class differences awkward at times for me and for some participants, particularly working-class males. However, since I was focusing on middle-class white students, my own middle-class whiteness seemed to work mostly on my behalf. With respect to students of color, of which I interviewed quite a few, my race limited my ability to hang out with them in groups at school. Because my focus was on white students, I do not feel this limitation seriously compromises my argument, but deeper perspectives from students of color would certainly have improved it.

I formally interviewed more than sixty students at Valley Groves and Clavey. They included, at Valley Groves, fourteen white youth, one Filipino female, and a group of ten African-American students. At Clavey, I interviewed twenty-two white youth, ten African American youth, two Chinese American, one Filipino, and two Latino youth. A little more than half of my interviewees were female and the rest male. Most were middle class, but six were working class.

I did not randomly sample interview participants because I had very specific desires regarding to whom I wanted to speak: liberals and conservatives; whites, blacks, Asians, and Latinos; punks, hippies, homies, alternatives, rappers, and such; high achievers and low achievers; girls and boys; middle class and working class. So I sought out interviewees through multiple methods. Mostly, I directly approached students I observed in classrooms or in their cliques, but I also went to club meetings and asked for volunteers and, for the hard to find students, sought recommendations or introductions from youth.

Interviews took place on campus, in coffee shops, and in students' homes and generally lasted two hours. Students and their parents signed consent forms that explained that I was examining racial identities and race relations in the two demographically distinct contexts. In the interviews, I explored youth's experiences at school, their experiences of racial difference, how they thought of themselves racially, how they thought

of racial-ethnic others, their cultural interests and other significant identities, and what types of meanings they gave to their interests and identities. Interviews and informal discussions were also a time for me to discuss with youth my interpretations of school practices, youth cultures, and other events around campus. Students spoke candidly and openly; they seemed eager to talk to an adult who would listen to and treat them respectfully.

The interviews were tape-recorded and transcribed. They and my field notes were manually coded and analyzed along the way to illuminate processes, practices, terms, and conceptions calling for deeper investigation or changes in focus. Along the way, also, I read widely, looking for existing studies and theories that might shed analytical light on my observations. My final coding and analysis were carried out without the aid of software—only colored markers, a Xerox machine, and lots of post-its.

IDENTITY NATURALIZATION AT VALLEY GROVES HIGH: PASSIVE CONSTRUCTION OF WHITE AS CULTURELESS

Valley Groves is a suburban city of roughly 115,000 people. Its residents are solidly white and middle to upper-middle class. In 1990, 83 percent of the population of Valley Groves was white, and the median household income was $42,095. Inside Valley Groves High School's catchment area is Mapleton, a small suburb of about 7,500 people. Ninety percent of Mapleton residents are white, and their median household income in 1989 was $70,000.

The racial and class demographics of Valley Groves and Mapleton cities were reflected in the composition of the Valley Groves High student body and staff. In the 1995–96 school year, white youth made up 83 percent of the school population, followed by Hispanics (7 percent), Asians (5 percent), Filipinos (2 percent), and African

Americans (2 percent). The fifty-three teachers, five administrators, three campus supervisors, and fifty-odd service and administrative staff were 85 percent non-Hispanic white. There was only one African American among them.

Raymond Williams (1976) wrote,

Hegemony supposes the existence of something that is truly total . . . which is lived at such a depth, which saturates the society to such an extent, and which, as Gramsci put it, even constitutes the limit of commonsense for most people under its sway. (pp. 204–5)

At Valley Groves, whiteness "saturated" youth's lived experience. White youth and adults overwhelmed the demographic landscape. When I asked white students at Valley Groves how they would rate their experiences of people of color, most said "very little" or "none at all." In the school yard during lunch or break, students sauntered into the "quad," a large patio area in the center of the campus, to meet with friends and grab a bite to eat. At these times, the most open and public spaces were a sea of blonde- and brown-haired white girls and boys in blue jeans and T-shirts sporting logos of their favorite rock band or skateboard company. The popular and nondescript kids (usually called "normal") occupied the main quad, and the counterculture white students—druggies, skaters, hicks—claimed territory in outside areas adjoining the quad.

Some African American, Asian, or Latino students joined with white friends, and, when they did, they assumed the styles and demeanors of the crowd they were in, be it "popular," "skater," or merely "normal." Then, there were the students of color who clustered in groups of like-kind, racial ethnically. They wore their own styles; spoke in Tagalog, Spanish, or black English; and usually hung out in the cafeteria, classrooms, or distant corners of the campus, locations that kept them virtually invisible to the majority of students in and around the quad.

Similar spatial demographics, in which racial-ethnic difference was placed where it did not challenge the white norm, existed in the classroom structure (Fine 1989). The mainstream students—the popular kids, athletes, and college-bound youth—were in the honors and other high-tracked classes. The "regular" classes were made up of a hodge-podge of different types of youth—middle-class mainstream, working class, countercultural. With the exception of some of the high-tracked math classes, in which Asian American students were overrepresented, high and regular-tracked courses were disproportionately white, with small numbers of minority youth distributed equally among them. Just where the students of color were I am sorry to say I never learned the answer to, except that one day I saw a large (disproportionate) number of them in a remedial class.

Whiteness saturated Valley Groves school life not only demographically but culturally as well. The dominant culture at Valley Groves—that which oriented the social organization of students, common styles and practices, and expected behaviors—was homologous with the dominant culture outside of the campus, namely, a white European American culture. By "white European American culture," I refer to two features of American culture, broadly. First, although the dominant culture in the United States is syncretic, that is, composed of the different cultures of the peoples that populate the United States, several of its core characteristics are of European origin. These include, as I have already suggested, the values and practices derived from the European Enlightenment, Anglican Protestantism, and Western colonialism, such as rationalism, individualism, personal responsibility, a strong work ethnic, self-effacement, and mastery over nature. I include, also, carryover or "melted" material cultures of Western, Eastern, and Southern European peoples, such as hamburgers, spaghetti, cupcakes, parades, and line dancing. Second, by virtue of being numerically and politically dominant, whites tend to share certain dispositions, worldviews, and identities constituted by that, especially in predominantly white communities. Currently, a race-neutral or "colorblind" worldview and sense of oneself as normal are examples of that.

At Valley Groves, student cliques and social categories revolved around a norm-other dichotomy in which normal meant that one conformed to the dominant culture and expectations placed on them, and other meant one did not. For example, when I asked Billy how he would describe his group of friends he said,

> "Normal. We don't smoke or drink or anything and [we] wear clothes we would call normal."
>
> "And what is that?" I asked.
>
> "Not oversized, baggy clothes like the skaters wear, or, obviously, we don't wear cowboy hats or boots."

The normal clothes Billy referred to were the styles one might find at mainstream department stores like The Gap: loose, not overly baggy blue jeans; cotton T-shirts and blouses; sundresses; khaki shorts. The kids who did not dress or act normal served to define the boundaries of what was and was not normal. For instance, skaters wore excessively baggy pants and overall filthy clothes; "hicks" wore ten-gallon cowboy hats, tooled-leather boots, and tight jeans with big brassy pants buckles; and druggies flagrantly carried and consumed illicit drugs. (*Flagrant* is the key word here since, as a popular girl told me, "Popular kids do drugs. They just don't want anyone to know it.") Carli, a white girl who considered herself "hippie," referred to the nonmainstream kids as "rebels." She said, "I call them rebels 'cause they know the system sucks."

This norm-other dichotomy was race neutral. Maria, a popular senior of Mexican-American descent on her mother's side, told me that the "first cut of students starts with who is popular" and who fits in with the other cliques on campus. Anyone, regardless of racial-ethnic ascription,

could be popular, a skater, a druggie—even a "homie," which, as groups went at Valley Groves, was the most nonwhite. Price of admission was conformity to the styles and demeanor of the group. Hence, black kids who were skaters were not "black skaters," nor were white kids who were homies "white homies"; they were simply "skaters" and "homies," respectively. A white skater I spoke to pointed to an African American boy in his crowd and said, "That doesn't matter. We all love to skate together, hang out together." And when I asked black students if the white kids who were homies were considered "wanna-be black," they looked flatly at me and said, "No." Ron, who was a homie himself, said, "One of the guys who hangs out with us is white. He's not a racist and we've known each other for years."

Students' measuring sticks for gauging normal styles, behaviors, and expectations were the common, everyday practices and the system of rewards at school. On any given day at Valley Groves High, students attended classes and romped into the Quad at break and lunch to purchase anything from fresh cinnamon rolls, cupcakes, rice crispy bars, and fudge for snacks to pizza, hamburgers, meat loaf, and spaghetti for something more substantial. On occasion, leadership students played rock music over the loudspeakers while students talked among themselves in their friendship groups. Circulating through the youth were members of the administrative staff, who would greet students by their first names and engage them in casual conversation, and the team of grounds supervisors, all of whom were greying, middle-aged women. One was affectionately referred to as "Grandma."

"These are all good kids," is what administrators, teachers, and ground supervisors would say to me nearly every time I spoke with them. As Bourdieu (1977) argues, the embodiment of practices and ideas into that which feels normal, natural, and "common sense" requires collective reinforcement and approval. Adult approval rating of the students was high, and they let students know that with their smiles and friendly banter. It was demonstrated also, I believe, through the grounds supervisors, who, by virtue of their title (as opposed to "security") and appearance, demonstrated an implicit trust the adults had that students would, for the most part, comply with expected behaviors. (At least, adults trusted that the white students would comply. Students of color, especially black boys who wore hip-hop styles, told me that they experienced considerable racial profiling by school administrators and the grounds supervisors. This explicitly racial treatment of students of color was either not witnessed by whites or rubbed out of their minds, which I believe played a role in maintaining the pretense of race neutrality on campus.)

At schoolwide rallies and events, collective consensus, reinforcement, and approval of white American norms came from an even wider span of individuals: school adults, other students, and the outside community. Such events seemed to secure a broad consensus of what is true, right, and white but always through nondiscursive practice, never by saying and, thus, never sayable. For example, homecoming—a high school tradition that celebrates the school football team—was a time to raise school spirit and, thus, excite the interest and imagination of the most students possible. It was, for me, an excellent time to observe shared assumptions and normative expectations of students and observe the rewards and sanctions applied to different types of behaviors.

One day during homecoming week, students held rallies in the gym for the entire student body. To the thunder of heavy-metal music, rivers of white students flowed into the gym and took seats in different quadrants of the auditorium reserved for different grade levels. Just before the official ceremony began, two big, husky white males (appearing to be seniors) dragged into the center of the auditorium a small boy (appearing to be a freshman) whose feet and legs were bound

with silver duct tape. The crowd laughed and applauded. The two husky guys pumped their fists in the air to encourage the crowd then dragged the boy off center stage. After a brief greeting, members of the student leadership committee introduced the junior varsity and varsity football players. The players came out in succession and formed a line across the middle of the gym floor. The boys were all white except for three black players on the junior varsity team and, on the varsity team, two boys with Hispanic surnames. As his name was called, each player stepped forward to acknowledge the applause. Most did so with an air of shyness or humility, their heads bowed, cheeks blushing, shoulders pulled up to their ears. Two boldly strutted out, trying to play up the roar of the crowd, but their efforts fell flat.

Then, the varsity cheerleaders bolted to center stage, leaping energetically before getting into formation for their choreographed performance. The girls were all thin, some overly so, and wore uniforms with close-fitted bodices that made them look all the smaller. But their body size betrayed their strength. Their routine, driven by the firm beat of a heavy-metal tune, was rigorously gymnastic, with lots of cartwheels, flips, and pyramid constructions that were punctuated by the top girls falling trustingly into the arms of their comrades. Long, silky blonde hair parachuted out with each acrobatic stunt. Through the performance, the audience remained silent and attentive, with an occasional collective gasp at the girls' athleticism, until the show was over. At that time, the cheerleaders received roaring, vocal applause.

On the day after the rally was the homecoming parade. The parade took off from the basketball field and wound its way onto a residential side street. Four adult males, two of whom appeared to be Mexican American, led the parade mounted on prancing horses and wearing Mexican serapes and sombreros. The front two carried large replicas of the California and American flags. Following the horsemen were two convertibles, one of which was a white Corvette carrying the (white) city mayor, who waved ceremoniously to the onlookers on the sidewalks.

The music of the marching band, which followed closely behind the mayor, announced the arrival of the parade along its path. A group of eight white and one African American female dancers led the band, tossing and spinning colored flags in sync with the beat of the band's percussion section. The fifty musicians in the band, most of whom appeared white with five or six exceptions, marched militarily in tight formation and played their instruments with competence and finesse. Following the band was a procession of American-built pickup trucks carrying, first, the varsity and junior varsity football players, then the "royalty"—the senior "king" and "queen" and underclass "princes" and "princesses"—and finally, an open-bed truck loaded with seniors, hooting and cheering as if their graduation day had already arrived.

The parade made its way through several blocks of residences before returning to the main street and slowly making its way back to the school. Proud parents were perched on the sidewalks with their thirty-five-millimeter and video cameras in hand. Community residents stepped onto their front landings to wave and cheer as the parade passed their homes. Others peered out through large pane windows with cats in arms and dogs at heel.

The homecoming rally and parade were, in my view, packed with assumptions, values, behaviors, and origin stories that privileged white European American perspectives as well as gender, sexuality, and class-based norms (all of which tend to coproduce one another). At the rally, for example, the display of the hog-tied freshman reinforced that white (male) dominance is sustained not only through the subordination of nonwhite others but of "other" whites as well (Hartigan 1997, 1999; Thandeka 1999; Wray and Newitz 1997). Second, the virtues of personal mastery and self-effacement were

exemplified by the humble postures of the football players and reinforced by the slights the audience gave to those who presented themselves with more bravado. And, finally, the cheerleaders' thin, bounded physiques and gravity-defying athletic feats demonstrated that the girls had successfully learned to subjugate their bodies and overcome nature.

The homecoming parade, with its display of the national and state flags, American cars, marching band, and school royalty, was a stunning way to observe the coproduction of whiteness, Americanness, citizenship, and gendered codes of conduct. Included was even an origin story of white American colonial victory over Mexico. And, by virtue of who was there and who was not, the knitting together of the themes of mastery, domination, nationhood, and industry with whiteness was seamless. Other cultures in the school and community were not represented in the parade. There were no Filipino dancers, Asian martial artists, or African-American rappers. The event was performed by whites and for whites and, thus, little contradicted the cultural and political assumptions at play.

In sum, at Valley Groves High, white people and white European American culture saturated school life. White youth had little to no association with people or cultures that would place whiteness in relief in such a way that students might reflect on it and consciously define it.

No Ties

Given this sociocultural milieu, white youth could say nothing when I asked them to describe white culture; they had no words to describe that which comes naturally. Laurie, whom I quoted at the beginning of this article, struggled to describe white culture and finally succumbed to "I don't know!" Billy, a popular white senior, had a similar response. I asked him what he thought was culturally specific about white American culture. After a long pause in which he said only, "hmmm," he asked, "Like, what's American culture?"

"Uh-huh," I replied.

"Hmmm. [Another long pause]—I don't really know, 'cause it's like [pause]—just [pause]—I'm not sure! I don't know!"

However, Valley Groves white students were not always speechless about white identity. When my questions probed into the youth's social experiences and identities as whites and not their cultures, they could find something to say. Not too surprisingly, most told me that being white meant you had no cultural ties. Students I spoke to would explain that they had mixed European roots that held no significance to them; therefore they were "just white." For example, I asked Mara, a Valley Groves senior, what she would say if a census taker asked her, straight out without any prompting, "What are you?"

Mara: Like a race?

PGP: Could be a racial category.

Mara: I'd have to answer "Very white." I am, yeah. I am 100 percent white.

PGP: I noticed on your [consent form] you said you had a mix of European backgrounds, and you wrote, "Pretty much WHITE." Is that what "white" means to you, a European mix?

Mara: I just think that there's not much— I don't really think of myself as European. I think of myself as a white American girl. . . . I don't really go back to my roots, though I know I have family and where they come from but they're all white races.

PGP: You don't have any heartfelt devotion to your European past?

Mara: Not really. My family has lived here for generations, so I don't really draw on that.

Laurie had a similar response:

We're a bunch of everything. My great, great Grandmother is Cherokee. Whenever I fill out [questionnaires] about what's my ethnic background I write "white" because everything is so random. We have German, some family from Wales—but that means nothing to me. . . . I don't have ties to anything. I haven't heard about anything my parents have been through except for my grandparents in wars. It's all been about people, not culture.

Answers like Mara's and Laurie's, of which there were many, reflect that, although white youth at Valley Groves may not have thought about whiteness as a culture, they did think about it as a social category (Phoenix 1997), as a "group position" (Blumer 1958) with respect to other racial-ethnic groups. To Valley Groves students, whites were a group because they did not have culture, and "minorities" did. Through mixed-European and other cultural amalgamation, whites were a new breed, a hybrid, removed from a past that was meaningless to them and for the loss of which they held no remorse.

Valley Groves whites were speaking from the "postcultural" perspective that Rosaldo (1989) asserts is the perspective of all who are members of the dominant group of Western-style nation states. Naturalized whiteness complements and helps constitute this kind of postcultural identity because of the stability garnered from the fit between societal norms and the constructed identity of whites (powell 1997). The us-them construction revolves around "majority" (those who all look and act normal to one another) and the "minority" (those who do not look or act like the majority). Naturalized whiteness is securely grounded in and validated by the normal way of things in the present and therefore does not seek meaning in a cultural or past orientation.

CLAVEY HIGH SCHOOL:
WHEN WHITE IS NOT THE NORM

Once a port of entry for African American, Mexican, and Asian immigration into northern California, Clavey City today has one of the most racially/ethnically diverse populations for its size in the United States. Of its 372,000 residents, 33 percent are white, 44 percent are black, 19 percent are of Hispanic origin, and 15 percent are of Asian origin. Median household income in 1989 was $27,095. More than 16 percent of families in Clavey City live below poverty.

Clavey High School stands like a fortress overlooking a dense urban landscape. The schools magnet academies draw in youth from all over the city, bringing in a mosaic of students from different racial and ethnic groups. At the time of my research, whites comprised 12 percent of the two thousand students at Clavey. African Americans were the majority, making up 54 percent of the school. They were followed in numbers by Asian Americans (23 percent), then Hispanics (8 percent), Filipinos (2 percent), and a few Pacific Islanders and Native Americans. At any given moment during lunch break, one could tour the campus and hear students speaking in standard English, black English ("ebonics"), Eritrean, Cantonese, Mandarin, Korean, Spanish, Spanglish, Tagalog, Samoan, Russian, and Vietnamese, among others.

The racial composition of the administrative and teaching staff at Clavey was also quite diverse. The principal of Clavey was a white male, but the other top administrators, two assistant principals and the dean, were African American. Of all the administrators and their staff, 50 percent were African American, 25 percent were Asian, and 25 percent were white. Clavey teachers were 53 percent white, 30 percent African American, 8 percent Asian American, 6 percent Hispanic, and 3 percent Pacific Islander.

Life at Clavey High was very different from that at Valley Groves. White youth at Clavey were in daily, up-close association with marked racial and cultural difference to whiteness, and race was the primary means of sorting out who was who and where one belonged in the social organization of the school. Clavey's tracking structure, which I say more about later, was racially segregated, with whites and Asians disproportionally represented in the high-tracked classes and African Americans and Latinos overrepresented in the low-tracked classes. As well, certain areas on the campus were "where the white kids hang out"; others were "where the black (or Asian American or Latino) kids hang out." And student cliques and subcultures were racially marked such that "straights" (who were like "normal" kids at Valley Groves), alternatives, hippies, and punks were all "white people's groups"; rappers, athletes, gangsters, and "fashion hounds" were "black people's groups"; housers, natives, newly arrived, and martial artists were "Asian people's groups"; and so forth. This meant that the styles, slangs, vernaculars, and demeanors that marked identification with a certain clique or subculture simultaneously inferred racial identification. In a word, peer group activities *racialized* youth.

Speaking to this fact and the sanctions that came with crossing racialized boundaries in styles or leisure activities, Gloria, an immigrant from El Salvador, said to me,

> For my race, if you start wearing a lot of gold, you're trying to be black. If you're trying to braid your hair, you'll be accused of trying to be black. I'm scared to do things 'cause they might say, "that's black!" Or if you're Latino and you listen to that, you know, Green Day—that [alternative rock] kinda thing. If you listen to that, then you wanna be white.... "Oh my god, why you listening to that music?" they'd say, ... Aren't you proud of who you are?

Also different from Valley Groves was the dominant school culture. Overall at Clavey, African American youth claimed the majority of open, public spaces, and black popular cultural forms and practices shaped the normative culture of the school. By "black popular culture," I refer to the music, styles, and other meaningful practices that have risen out of black communities; are linked, if remotely, to diasporic traditions; and, most significantly, mark black identity and people-hood (Gilroy 1991, 1993; Rose 1994; Wallace 1992). Hall (1992) defines three things that are distinctive of black diasporic culture: (1) *style* as the "subject of what is going on," (2) *music* as the "deep structure of [black] cultural life," and (3) the *body* as "canvases of representation" (p. 27). Gilroy (1991) adds that the body in black culture carries "potent meanings" (p. 226) because it rests at the core of historical efforts of blacks to assert their humanity.

Unlike at Valley Groves, where the dress code did not diverge much from white adult main-stream style, at Clavey, basic elements of black hip-hop style were generalized into the normative styles for all youth. One informant called it the "leveler" style because it made all who wore it "the same." This basic style included clean, oversized, and sagging denim pants or sweatpants; large and long untucked T-shirts or hooded sweatshirts; large, bulky parkas; and sparkling-clean athletic shoes. The look was particularly common for boys, but girls' styles were also influenced by it. Only if and when students wanted to mark a distinctive style and/or racial identification did they embell-ish on this basic, baggy theme. Duncan, a middle-class, white male skater and "raver" (someone who frequents rave parties) told me,

> We all wear baggy pants, right? So parents think! But you find that ravers have cut-off bottoms to their [sagging] jeans, they wear bigger t-shirts they have hanging out of their pants, they carry packs that's full of crap that they take everywhere.

What Duncan specified as "raver" style, other students specified as "white," particularly the cut-off bottoms to large pants. Other markers of white kids' styles were Van shoes, instead of Nike or Fila brands (which marked black style), and macramé or silver-chain neck chokers.

Informal and formal activities on campus were also shaped by black popular culture. During breaks or at lunchtime, the ambient din of casual conversation was composed of the sounds, words, and inflections of black English and the most recent innovation in "street" slang. Lunchtime events, school rallies, and dances were enlivened with rap and R & B music, predominantly, with an occasional reggae tune or specially requested techno or alternative song. Often, students per-formed raps on the steps in front of the cafeteria or graced an audience with a spontaneous hip-hop dance performance.

Homecoming week at Clavey, like at Valley Groves, was a time to unite the school and raise the collective spirit. So, leadership students made attempts to appeal to the breadth of diverse interests and cultures of the school with "fashion shows" of traditional or native garments and a variety of games designed to mix students up. At lunch, they played a range of music, from R & B to techno and alternative rock, but songs by African-American and Afro-Carribean artists were predominant. The main events—the rally and game—were attended by and played predom-inantly to a majority-black audience.

The rally took place during lunch on the day of the "big game." Students, of which all but a few were black, crammed into the auditorium to the heartbeat pulse of a rap song. The rally opened with a greeting from the student body president and a soulful a cappella song performed by three African-American students. Then the cheerlead-ers, composed of one white and ten black girls, sprung out onto the gym floor. Their choreo-graphed routine was fluid, rhythmic, and dance-like, with movements drawn from traditional and contemporary African and African-American dance forms. To the infectious beat of an upbeat R & B song, the girls playfully flirted with their appreciative audience with beckoning hand and eye gestures. Several boys succumbed to the urge to dance in dialogue with the girls and leapt down to the floor to join them, but they were met by the arresting hands of campus security. Others, boys and girls alike, stood up and swayed or danced in place until the performance was over. Then, the varsity football players were called to line up in the center of the auditorium. The players were African American with the exception of two white boys and one Latino. When each name was announced, the football player leapt forward a few steps and embraced the cheers from the crowd. Each took his moment in the limelight proudly, with his fist in the air or maybe a little dance to augment the roar of his audience.

At Clavey, there was no homecoming parade that extended into the community, like at Valley Groves. At the game, a small procession of vehicles featuring the elected school "emperor" and "empress" circled the football field during half time. There was no marching band, either, but the award-winning school gospel choir sang several lively songs at halftime.

In short, school life at Clavey was heavily infused with styles, music, and activities that marked the identities and cultures of the majority black students. This had a few important implications for the experiences and identities of the white students. First, white was not the norm, either numerically or culturally. Barry, a middle-class, "straight" white male, told me, "School is like a foreign country to me. I come here to this foreign place, then go home where things are normal again." When I asked white students why they did not attend the rallies and dances, they said things like, "I don't enjoy the people," "They don't play my kind of music," and "I can't dance to that music." All in all, the message was that they could not relate to the dominant school culture.

Furthermore, whiteness was not entirely taken for granted. The racial organization of Clavey's social life, curricular structure, and schoolwide activities meant that white students were forced to grapple with their identities as whites and participate in active contestation over the meanings of white identity and culture. No white student I spoke to at Clavey was completely unable to describe something about white culture. All had reflected on it to some extent, even if only to ruminate on how difficult it was to define. And some youth could say a lot about white culture. One white, middle-class senior girl, Jessie, elaborated extensively on differences in attitudes toward food consumption that she noticed between her white, Filipino, and Chinese American friends, and she commented on how much more visible white culture is to her in places outside of California. She said, "Minnesota, Denver and . . . places like that. It seems like . . . you know, you've got the whole thing going on—beer bread, polka, parades, apple pie and things like that."

Most stunning to me about the white students at Clavey was not what they said explicitly about white culture but what they said implicitly. In our discussions about the types of music they liked and why, white students would tell me that they liked rock or punk or alternative music and not rap or R & B because "their" music spoke more to their "interests" or experiences as whites. For example, Kirsten and Cindi were good friends. They both were from middle-class homes, were juniors at the time, and liked alternative rock. Kirsten was white, European American, and Cindi was part white and part Chinese, although she admittedly "looked white" and hung out solely with other white youth. I asked them why they thought students tended to self-segregate on campus:

Cindi: I think there is . . . the factor that some people feel like they may not have very much in common with someone from a different race, which in some ways is true. Because you have, like, different music tastes, different styles of clothes. Also, like what your friends think.

Kirsten: Or like different things you do on weekends.

Cindi: Yeah, so I think that's something that separates the races.

Kirsten: It's kind of interesting because my musical interests have changed. . . . It seems like [in junior high school] everyone, regardless of if they were black or white or Asian, . . . listened to the [local rap and R & B station.] But then I think when you are little you don't really . . . have too much of an identity of yourself. As you get older and mature more you, like, discover what your "true being" is. So then people's musical tastes change. [Later in the conversation.] I think punk is more of a "I don't get along with my parents" kind of music and rap is more of "lets go kill someone" music.

Cindi: Punk . . . expresses a simpler anger. It's just kind of like "Oh, I broke up with my girlfriend" . . . something like that. Usually rap has more to do with killing and gangs—stuff that doesn't really relate to me.

In this discussion, Kirsten and Cindi defined white identity and culture in terms of interests and tastes in leisure culture. This "discourse of taste" (Dolby 2000) was the language of choice among all groups of students for articulating racial-ethnic differences. Behind it was the belief that different life experiences accounted for different tastes. Sometimes, white youth named fairly explicit experiences they believed were most common to or defining of whites. Class experience, expressed

by Kirsten and Cindi in terms of the type of neighborhood one lived in, was often evoked by youth. Other times, white youth spoke in terms of intangible but presumably race-based, emotional, aesthetic, and ethical sensibilities they felt when they listened to, say, punk or alternative music but not when they listened to rap.

ACTIVE CONSTRUCTION OF WHITE AS POSTCULTURAL

Ironically, even as Clavey whites demarcated white culture and identity boundaries through their popular-cultural tastes and leisure activities, they also imagined whiteness as cultureless, as postcultural. This was not as explicit as it was at Valley Groves. It would show its face when white students referred to people of color as people with "race" or "ethnicity," as though whites had neither. Tina, a working-class junior who had always been a racial minority in school and had many close black and Latino friends, told me that she "had a lot of ethnicity in [her] family . . . Hispanic, Korean. We all get along." By this she meant that white relatives had married "out" of whiteness and into culture, ethnicity.

Common also was the explicit and implicit definition of white as empty, meaningless, bland, and without tradition. This comment by Eric touches on all of those:

> I think it's more difficult [to define white culture] for Americans because the culture of America is more just consumption. In America, we buy stuff, and that's the basis of our culture. If you talk to people who want to come to America?—They want things. TV is a very American thing. We don't have lengthy traditions. . . . A lot has been lost because of the good ol' melting pot. I heard a cool one about a salad bowl—that's what America is, and along comes the dressing and turns everything into dressing flavor. Vegetables all got that white American spin on it.

Note, too, that Eric equates "white" with "American" until his last line, when he specifies "white American." That is a faux pas that whites often fall into because of the dominant construction of white as the "unhyphenated" American standard.

Finally, several Clavey white students told me that they did not like to think about themselves as "white" but as "human." These students also expressed a more explicitly rationalist construction of whiteness that denied the significance of a past orientation and exalted a more individualistic and present- or future-oriented construction of the self. White, middle-class boys expressed this most boldly, which might be expected given that they are triply constructed as the most rational by race, class, and gender.

Murray, whom I quoted at the beginning of this article, best exemplifies this latter perspective. In Murray's comments, we can read several tenets of Western rational thought and a postcultural identity: the irrationality of past-oriented values, the future orientation of the self, and individual responsibility. Daniel was a white, middle-class, "straight" male with some Portuguese ancestry. He made comments similar to Murray's:

> People have suggested I am a person of color or mixed. Then I decided, no, I'm European American. Ancestry doesn't matter. . . . People look back in the past and judge you for it, and I don't think that's right. Sure, people enslaved people. At one time every race had slaves. I think you need to move on and see what's going on now. History is important but you have to work on getting together now and don't use that as a divide.

A few scholars have observed a propensity among whites to deny the significance of the past, slavery particularly, in affecting the life chances of African Americans today. Some argue that this denial is a kind of defensive mechanism whites adopt to exonerate themselves from taking responsibility for the legacies of slavery and past

discrimination against African Americans and other minorities (Gallagher 1995). I take a slightly different position and suggest that white identity and culture is constructed in such a way that the values of individuality, personal responsibility, and a future-oriented self create a cognitive inability to see things any other way (see also Alba 1990; Blauner 1989). A past orientation simply does not make sense to many whites from their cultural perspective.

In sum, at Clavey, white culture was not entirely naturalized and taken for granted; it was reflected on and even defined somewhat, particularly through the language of tastes and popular culture. To an extent, however, white students also considered themselves unmarked American, nonethnic, unmarked human, and/or present oriented. In a word, they saw themselves as culture-less. I might add that several students of color I spoke to also were quick to define white culture in terms of styles and tastes but not in terms of tradition. Johnetta, an African American senior, said, "It's hard to generalize [about white culture] because there's no ready answer to what is white culture."

Whereas I have proposed that the naturalization of whiteness greatly facilitated the passive construction of postcultural whiteness at Valley Groves, I suggest that at Clavey, different and more active social processes were in play. Namely, Western rational ways of knowing and making sense of social relations permeated Clavey school and social practices. As I have argued, Western rationalism exiles tradition and culture from the realms of truth and relevance and replaces them with reason. That which is reasonable or rational is separated from and raised above that which is not, like the elevation of mind over body, intellectual over emotional, and order above chaos. Whiteness benefits from those hierarchical dualities by being linked with the higher value of each—with orderliness, self-control, individualism, and rationality, which, not coincidentally, are recognized as standard or normal behaviors. Otherness is defined in terms of that which is passionate, chaotic, violent, lazy, irrational, and—since marginal to the norm—cultural.

Two school practices in particular stood out for me in terms of the ways they seemed to structure the meanings all youth gave to their experience through a Western rational value paradigm. The first and most obvious of those was the tracking structure. Scholars have long argued that racial segregation in tracking reproduces racial inequalities in the wider society, largely by preparing high-tracked students, who tend to be middle-class white and Asian, better than low-tracked students, who tend to be black, Latino, and poor white and Asian (Gamoran et al. 1995; Oakes 1985, 1994; Oakes and Guiton 1995). Tracking also reproduces racial inequalities by reinforcing, if not constituting, racial stereotypes. Jeannie Oakes (1994) has argued that "all but the most extraordinary schools have their stereotypes and prejudices reinforced by racially-identifiable high- and low-tracked classes" (pp. 86–87). She asserts that tracking "institutionalizes racist conceptions of intellectual capacity" (ibid.). I would add to her argument that tracking also institutionalizes the values of mind over body and self-control over lack of restraint and racializes those who are superior and inferior in those respects.

At Clavey, the high-tracked classes, those designed to prepare students for high-ranking colleges and universities, were 80 percent white and Asian, according to a school survey. Conversely, "preparatory" classes, which filled graduation requirements, were overwhelmingly black and Latino. Remedial classes were 100 percent black and Latino. Although, officially, youth were tracked according to their intellectual or achievement levels, the discourses that surrounded tracking at Clavey suggested that *behavior* (including expected behavior) was just as relevant.

Students in the high-tracked classes were generally understood to be "well-behaved," "good" students. In those classrooms, students acted in the utmost orderly fashion: always listening attentively and taking notes, speaking only when called on. They considered themselves hard working and sophisticated in their abilities to defer gratification, such as to study during lunch instead of hang out and have fun with their friends. They justified their privilege to be in the accelerated classes on these grounds and blamed underachievement on the behaviors of the underachieved. Linda, a white Jewish girl in accelerated classes, represented this viewpoint in the following comment:

> It's so sad because these kids could be pushed so far beyond what they are [doing]. Like, it's unbelievable. When I see a twelfth grader holding a geometry book, I cringe inside me. Because, *you can learn*, you can do it! People are so lazy, they don't care. They have no goals, no ambitions. It's frustrating! I don't get it!

The "lazy" and unambitious kids Linda referred to were black and Latino students in the preparatory classes. Other commonly used terms to describe those classes and the students in them were "bonehead," "rowdy," and "out of control." And, indeed, some of those classes had students who were inattentive or disruptive and who could, on occasion, set the whole class off into a blaze of rowdiness. But those students were aware that they had been assigned to the least valued and negatively stereotyped classes in the school. If they did not hear it through common discourse, they deduced it from the classes themselves. They were overcrowded and short of chairs, books, and other course materials. Sometimes, they did not even have full-time teachers. It is not a stretch to suggest that preparatory students behaved in "bonehead" ways that they thought were expected of them (Eder 1981; Baron, Tom, and Cooper 1985; Lightfoot 1978; Ferguson 1998; Steele and Aronson 1998).

In sum, tracking at Clavey asserted more than, simply, intellectual superiority but also the values of mind over body and self-control over lack of restraint. Furthermore, it marked standard, acceptable forms of behavior—standards within which middle-class whites and Asians were squarely located practically and symbolically.

"Multicultural" programs and discourses were other school practices that positioned whites as the school's most rational and postcultural. At Clavey, there were two main, formal multicultural events: the "cultural assemblies" and "multicultural week." Once every other month or so, an ethnic club—the African-American Student Union, the Asian Student Union, Latino Student Union, or the Inter-Tribal Student Union—would put on a schoolwide assembly. A common assembly featured traditional ceremonial dances and rituals, music and song, poetry readings, historically informative slide shows, and clothing displays, all arranged and performed by the students.

Lunchtime activities during multicultural week were another opportunity for students to publicly display elements of their cultural heritage. Each day of the week was designed to feature a particular aspect of a culture—the music, dance, clothing, written texts, or narratives. For example, on a day featuring traditional or national clothing styles, youth held a fashion show in which African-American youth in dashikis, Chinese-American girls in brocade gowns, and Mexican-American youth in ceremonial dance costumes paraded before youth gathered outside the cafeteria.

These events had their merits. They gave voice and visibility to the cultures and perspectives of people historically silenced by white colonialism. African-American and Asian youth told me that they enjoyed having the opportunity to present their culture as well as learn about others. I propose, however, that multicultural events at Clavey coterminously reproduced white supremacist, rationalist tenets of white colonialism by making whiteness culturally invisible.

Rosaldo (1989) argues that, "as the Other becomes more culturally visible, the self becomes

correspondingly less so" (p. 202). I believe this was true for many Clavey whites. When white students spoke about the assemblies, they usually expressed enthusiastic appreciation for "the chance to learn about so many cultures." But learning about other cultures merely gave them more references by which to define what they were not. As well, when they spoke in this way, it was as if "cultures" were like books—objective things that existed outside of the self but could be consumed to pleasure the self (Farley 1997). In a conversation with four middle-class white girls at Clavey, I asked them how they thought their experience at Clavey would influence their adulthood.

Ann: I think it's going to be a very positive thing. [Melissa interjects: Yeah.] Because it teaches us how to deal with different kinds of people.

Sera: Yeah, you learn more about others. . . . It's a positive experience.

Melissa: Yeah, you gain street smarts. You gain stuff.

Greater knowledge of other cultures was something Ann, Sera, and Melissa appreciated because it gave them tools to enhance their sociability, but it did not make them reflect on their sociocultural location as whites. When other white students at Clavey spoke to me about the value of the multicultural events, they made very similar kinds of statements and inferences. Overall, multicultural events, as "add-on" school practices in which white students could pleasurably gaze on racial-ethnic others without putting themselves on the line, reinforced a sense of whiteness as center and standard (cultureless) and racial-ethnic others (by virtue of having culture to display) as different and marginal to that.

Furthermore, no white students I spoke to questioned why there was not a white-American cultural assembly. Granted, to most this was untenable, largely because it might be taken as a white-supremacist act. I talked to students about school clubs for whites only and they categorically dismissed the idea. One said, "There'd be a riot!" Another said, "It wouldn't be right. It would be taken all wrong." But it was also untenable because, as another student put it, "White is all around. It doesn't need special attention." The idea that white culture does not need special attention (read: white is the norm and standard) seemed to be another message multicultural events gave to white students. As if for the eyes of whites only, multiculturalism at Clavey gave white students new references to add to their mental cache of exotic others while further obscuring the invisible power of white culture.

CONCLUSION

For a while now, scholars of race and whiteness have understood that the construction of white culture as the invisible norm is one of the most, if not *the* most pernicious, constructions of whiteness in the post-civil rights era. However, very few have examined the everyday social processes by which white people come to think of themselves as normal and culturally empty (Frankenberg 1993; Kenny 2000a, 2000b; Twine 1997), and among those, no one has done a comparative study illuminating the ways that different social-structural institutional contexts influence different constructions of white identity as cultureless. My research suggests that, at Valley Groves, a predominantly white high school, white identity seemed cultureless because white cultural practices were taken for granted, naturalized, and, thus, not reflected on and defined. At Clavey, a multiracial school, white culture was not taken for granted— white youth thought about and defined it to an extent, particularly through their interests and tastes in popular culture. However, in part, whites also reflected on their sociocultural location

through the lens of European American rational authority, which school structures and practices helped construct and reinforce. That lens refracted whiteness into all that was good, controlled, rational, and cultureless and otherness into all that was bad, out of control, irrational, and cultural. It may be that when naturalization processes are not possible because of close interracial association, then rationalization processes must come into play to preserve white hegemony.

This argument has theoretical and practical implications for critical white studies, the sociology of education, and general theories and research in racial-ethnic identity formation. Within critical white studies, there are two prevalent sets of assumptions about white culture that this research advances. The first is that white people experience themselves as culturally empty because whiteness is hegemonic and, therefore, undefined. To disrupt the insidious power of white culture, then, we must expose and define it. My study suggests that this is true but not everywhere the truth. The multiracial experiences of white youth at Clavey suggest that making white culture visible is not sufficient for challenging the construction of white as norm. What is also necessary are efforts to expose, challenge, and transform the rule of reason that frames white culture as rational and, therefore, *beyond* culture, postcultural or even anticultural.

Another assumption among some scholars of critical white studies, particularly "New Abolitionists," is that white culture is experienced as empty because, simply, there is no white culture. I am less concerned with the question of whether there really is a white culture than with what is reproduced through *denying* there is a white culture. The argument I have presented here proposes that the concept of culture denotes more than, simply, a way of life organized around sets of symbolic practices. It connotes a relationship of power between those who "have" culture (and are, thus, irrational and inferior) and those who claim not to (and are, thus, rational and superior). More research and thought needs to go into examining the ways postcultural whiteness is inculcated in daily practice and into the profits whites gain by denying that they have a culture.

This research also contributes to the growing scholarship on social and cultural reproduction in education. Although considerable research has examined the reproduction and subversion of societal norms in schools, including racial norms (for example, Carter 1999; Conchas 2000; Davidson 1996; Fordham 1996; Fine et al. 1997; Kenny 2000a; McCarthy and Critchlow 1993; Valenzuela 1999), more is still needed that closely examines the symbolic impact of certain school practices on how white students make sense of their own identities and the identities of people of color. This research only touched the surface of that and came on some disturbing and unexpected findings, namely, the active construction of postcultural whiteness. Research and evaluations of multicultural and other programs designed to redress racial inequalities have focused primarily on students of color. Important insights might be gained from more attention to white students and the meanings they assign to their experiences of those same programs.

Finally, this research embellishes on theories of racial-ethnic identity formation by vividly illuminating the socially constructed and contingent nature of race. Racial identities are made, not born, and they are made through the interaction of the specific social, structural, political, and cultural composition of a given context (Blumer 1958; Pinderhughes 1997). This means that racial identities are not fixed or uniform but variable and multiple. They may even be contradictory. These observances are often lost among scholars of whiteness and white racism who tend to represent whites and white identities as everywhere and always the same and contradictions as a form of "contemporary race prejudice" (Williams et al. 1999). My research affirms that the hegemonic construction of white as cultureless is stubbornly persistent but that even *it* is not the same across all contexts. To more effectively dismantle white domination, we need to be aware of and ready to work with its different manifestations and internal contradictions. Future research and antiracist scholarship may benefit from deeper exploration of the variability of white racial identities and the processes by which white racial domination is reproduced and subverted in distinct contexts.

REFERENCES

Alba, Richard. 1990. *Ethnic identity: The transformation of white America.* New Haven, CT: Yale University Press.

Allen, Theodore. 1994. *The invention of the white race, vol. 1: Racial oppression and social control.* London: Verso.

Almaguer, Tomas. 1994. *Racial fault lines: The historical origins of white supremacy in California.* Berkeley: University of California Press.

Apple, Michael W. 1995. *Education and power.* New York: Routledge.

Baron, Reuben, David Y. H. Tom, and Harris M. Cooper. 1985. Social class, race and teacher expectations. In *Teacher expectancies,* edited by Jerome B. Dusek. Hillsdale, NJ: Lawrence Erlbaum.

Blauner, Bob. 1989. *Black lives, white lives: Three decades of race relations in America.* Berkeley: University of California Press.

Blumer, Herbert. 1958. Race prejudice as a sense of group position. *Pacific Sociological Review* 1 (1): 3–7.

Bourdieu, Pierre. 1977. *Outline of a theory of practice.* Cambridge, UK: Cambridge University Press.

Bourdieu, Pierre, and J. C. Passeron. 1977. *Reproduction in education, society and culture.* Beverly Hills, CA: Sage.

Carter, Prudence L. 1999. Balancing acts: Issues of identity and cultural resistance in the social and educational behaviors of minority youth. Ph.D. diss., Columbia University, New York.

Conchas, Gilberto Q. 2000. Structuring failure and success: Understanding the variability in Latino school engagement. Working paper, Harvard Graduate School of Education.

Davidson, Ann Locke. 1996. *Making and molding identity in schools: Student narratives on race, gender, and academic engagement.* Albany: State University of New York Press.

De Vos, George. 1975. Ethnic pluralism: Conflict and accommodation. In *Ethnic identity: Cultural continuities and change,* edited by George De Vos and Lola Romanucci-Ross. Chicago: University of Chicago Press.

Dolby, Nadine. 2000. The shifting ground of race: The role of taste in youth's production of identities. *Race, Ethnicity, and Education 3* (1):7–23.

Dyer, Richard. 1997. *White.* New York: Routledge.

Eckert, Penelope. 1989. *Jocks and burnouts: Social categories and identity in high school.* New York: Teachers College Press.

Eder, Donna. 1981. Ability grouping as a self-fulfilling prophecy: A micro-analysis of teacher-student interaction. *Sociology of Education 54* (3): 151–62.

Essed, Philomena. 1996. *Diversity: Gender, color and culture.* Amherst: University of Massachusetts Press.

Farley, Anthony Paul. 1997. The black body as fetish object. *Oregon Law Review 76* (3): 457–535.

Ferguson, Robert A. 1997. *The American Enlightenment, 1750–1820.* Cambridge, MA: Harvard University Press.

Ferguson, Ronald F. 1998. Teachers' perceptions and expectations and the black-white test score gap. In *The black-white test score gap,* edited by Christopher Jencks and Meredith Phillips, 318–74. Washington, DC: Brookings Institution.

Fine, Michelle. 1989. Silencing and nurturing voice in an improbable context: Urban adolescents in public school. In *Critical pedagogy, the state, and cultural struggle,* edited by Henry Giroux and Peter McLaren, 152–73. Albany: State University of New York Press.

Fine, Michelle, Lois Weis, Linda C. Powell, and L. Mun Wong, eds. 1997. *Off white: Readings on race, power and society.* New York: Routledge.

Fordham, Signithia. 1996. *Blacked out: Dilemmas of race, identity, and success at Capital High.* Chicago: University of Chicago Press.

Fordham, Signithia, and John Ogbu. 1986. Black students' school success: Coping with the "burden of 'acting white.'" *Urban Review 18* (3): 176–206.

Frankenberg, Ruth. 1993. *White women, race matters: The social construction of whiteness.* Minneapolis: University of Minnesota Press.

_____. 1997. *Displacing whiteness: Essays in social and cultural criticism.* Durham, NC: Duke University Press.

Gallagher, Charles A. 1995. White reconstruction in the university. *Socialist Review 24* (1&2): 165–87.

_____. 1997. White racial formation: Into the twenty-first century. In *Critical white studies: Looking behind the mirror,* edited by Richard Delgado and Jean Stefancic, 6–11. Philadelphia: Temple University Press.

Gamoran, Adam, Martin Nystrand, Mark Berends, and Paul C. LePore. 1995. An organizational analysis of the effects of ability grouping. *American Educational Research Journal 32* (4): 687–715.

Gilroy, Paul. 1991. *"There ain't no black in the Union Jack": The cultural politics of race and nation.* Chicago: University of Chicago Press.

_____. 1993. *The black Atlantic: Modernity and double consciousness.* Cambridge, MA: Harvard University Press.

Giroux, Henry. 1996. *Fugitive cultures: Race, violence, and youth.* New York: Routledge.

_____. 1997. Rewriting the discourse of racial identity: Towards a pedagogy and politics of whiteness. *Harvard Educational Review 67* (2): 285–320.

Goldberg, David Theo. 1993. *Racist culture: Philosophy and the politics of meaning.* Cambridge, UK: Blackwell.

Hall, Stuart. 1992. What is the "black" in black popular culture? In *Black popular culture,* edited by Gina Dent, 21–33. Seattle, WA: Bay.

_____. 1996. Introduction: Who needs identity? In *Questions of cultural identity,* edited by Stuart Hall and Paul du Gay, 1–17. London: Sage.

Haney Lopez, Ian F. 1996. *White by law: The legal construction of race.* New York: New York University Press.

Harris, Cheryl. 1993. Whiteness as property. *Harvard Law Review* 106:1707–91.

Hartigan, John, Jr. 1997. Locating white Detroit. In *Displacing whiteness: Essays in social and cultural criticism,* edited by Ruth Frankenberg, 180–213. Durham, NC: Duke University Press.

———. 1999. *Racial situations: Class predicaments of whiteness in Detroit.* Princeton, NJ: Princeton University Press.

Hill, Mike, ed. 1997. *Whiteness: A critical reader.* New York: New York University Press.

hooks, bell. 1992. *Black looks: Race and representation.* Boston: South End.

Ignatiev, Noel. 1995. *How the Irish became white.* New York: Routledge.

Ignatiev, Noel, and John Garvey, eds. 1996. *Race traitor.* New York: Routledge.

Jacobson, Matthew Frye. 1998. *Whiteness of a different color: European immigrants and the alchemy of race.* Cambridge, MA: Harvard University Press.

Kenny, Lorraine Delia. 2000a. Doing my homework: The autoethnography of a white teenage girl. In *Racing research, researching race: Methodological dilemmas in critical race studies,* edited by France Winddance Twine and Jonathan Warren. New York: New York University Press.

———. 2000b. *Daughters of suburbia: Growing up white, middle class, and female.* New Brunswick, NJ: Rutgers University Press.

Kinney, David A. 1993. From nerds to normals: The recovery of identity among adolescents from middle school to high school. *Sociology of Education* 66 (1):21–40.

Lightfoot, Sara Lawrence. 1978. *Worlds apart: Relationships between families and schools.* New York: Basic Books.

Lipsitz, George. 1995. The possessive investment in whiteness: Racialized social democracy and the "white" problem in American studies. *American Quarterly* 47 (3): 369–87.

Lott, Eric. 1993. *Love and theft: Blackface minstrelsy and the American working class.* New York: Oxford University Press.

MacLeod, Jay. 1987. *Ain't no makin' it.* Boulder, CO: Westview.

McCarthy, Cameron, and Warren Crichlow, eds. 1993. *Race, identity and representation in education.* New York: Routledge.

Morrison, Toni. 1993. *Playing in the dark: Whiteness in the literary imagination.* New York: Random House.

Oakes, Jeannie. 1985. *Keeping track: How schools structure inequality.* New Haven, CT: Yale University Press.

———. 1994. More than a misapplied technology: A normative and political response to Hallinan on tracking. *Sociology of Education* 76 (2): 84–89.

Oakes, Jeannie, and Gretchen Guiton. 1995. Matchmaking: The dynamics of high school tracking decisions. *American Educational Research Journal* 32:3–33.

Perry, Pamela. 1998. Beginning to see the white: A comparative ethnography in two high schools of the racial consciousness and identities of white youth. Ph.D. diss., University of California, Berkeley. Forthcoming publication by Duke University Press.

Pfeil, Fred. 1995. *White guys: Studies in postmodern domination and difference.* New York: Verso.

Phoenix, Ann. 1997. "I'm white! So what?" The construction of whiteness for young Londoners. In *Off white: Readings on race and power in society,* edited by Michelle Fine, Linda C. Powell, Lois Weis, and L. Mun Wong, 187–97. New York: Routledge.

Pinderhughes, Howard. 1997. *Race in the hood: Conflict and violence among urban youth.* Minneapolis: Minnesota University Press.

powell, john a. 1997. Reflections on the self: Exploring between and beyond modernity and postmodernity, *Minnesota Law Review* 81 (6): 1481–1520.

Roediger, David. 1991. *The wages of whiteness: Race and the making of the American working class.* New York: Verso.

———. 1994. *Towards the abolition of whiteness.* New York: Verso.

Rosaldo, Renato. 1989. *Culture and truth: The remaking of social analysis.* Boston: Beacon.

Rose, Tricia. 1994. *Black noise: Rap music and black culture in contemporary America.* Hanover, NH: Wesleyan University Press.

Saxton, Alexander. 1990. *The rise and fall of the white republic.* New York: Verso.

Segrest, Mab. 1994. *Memoirs of a race traitor.* Boston: South End.

Steele, Claude M., and Joshua Aronson. 1998. Stereotype threat and the test performance of academically successful African Americans. In *The black-white test score gap,* edited by Christopher Jencks and Meredith Phillips, 401–27. Washington, DC: Brookings Institution.

Thandeka. 1999. The cost of whiteness. *Tikkun 14* (3): 33–38.

Thorne, Barrie. 1993. *Gender play: Girls and boys in school.* New Brunswick, NJ: Rutgers University Press.

Twine, France Winddance. 1997. Brown-skinned white girls: Class, culture, and the construction of white identity in suburban communities. In *Displacing whiteness: Essays in social and cultural criticism,* edited by Ruth Frankenberg, 214–43. Durham, NC: Duke University Press.

Valenzuela, Angela. 1999. *Subtractive schooling: U.S.-Mexican youth and the politics of caring.* Albany: State University of New York Press.

Wallace, Michelle (a project of). 1992. *Black popular culture.* Edited by Gina Dent. Seattle, WA: Bay.

Ware, Vron. 1992. *Beyond the pale: White women, racism and history.* New York: Verso.

Wellman, David. 1977. *Portraits of white racism.* Cambridge, UK: Cambridge University Press.

Williams, David R., James S. Jackson, Tony N. Brown, Myriam Torres, Tyrone A. Forman, and Kendrick Brown. 1999. Traditional and contemporary prejudice and urban whites' support for affirmative action and government help. *Social Problems 46* (4):503–27.

Williams, Raymond. 1976. Base and superstructure in Marxist cultural theory. In *Schooling and capitalism: A sociological reader,* edited by R. Dale, 202–10. London: Routledge and Kegan Paul.

Wray, Matt, and Annalee Newitz, eds. 1997. *White trash: Race and class in America.* New York: Routledge.

SELF-DEVELOPMENT AND REFERENCE GROUPS

26

A Theory of Genius

Thomas Scheff

(1990)

The explanation of genius that is most common is that it is a product of inherited genes. Galton (1869) sought to demonstrate this point by studying the family lines of artists, scientists, and statesmen. Cox (1926) conducted a similar but more extensive study. Both show a strong relationship between genius in a certain field, for example, music, and a family background of talent in that field. Bach and Puccini, for example, were both descended from five generations of musicians. Although these two examples are extreme, the relationship is general; most of the great musicians came from families in which there was already musical talent.

This article is aimed not at dismissing the genetic argument but offers an alternative model of explanation which could either complement or replace it, depending on the findings of future research. As has been pointed out many times, family inheritance has both a biological and a social character. In the study of genius it is difficult to disentangle the two since we deal with a small number of cases. Since I propose only a necessary cause, not a sufficient one, there is no need to evaluate the validity of the genetic argument.

The theory proposed concerns two processes of development—one of *talent,* the other of *self-esteem.* I argue that both processes are necessary. The development of talent will be discussed first.

Modern linguistics has (unintentionally) contributed to the issue by the discovery that all humans have genius in language. Since this contention is not obvious, I first review the contribution that linguists have made: the competent use of language is an achievement of such staggering complexity that it seems a miracle.

There is a large literature on the complexity of even the simplest utterances. The attempt to program computers for automatic translation is one of the bases of the new appreciation of the immense intelligence required to use language. There is no way to program a computer to solve a relatively simple problem of competent language use: choosing from among fixed, multiple meanings of a word. This can be demonstrated by . . . the simple statement . . . , "The box is in the pen." Is pen to be construed as a writing instrument or an enclosure? To answer this question, the program would have to have access to an encyclopedia, not merely a dictionary, and would have to have the resources to know how to comb the encyclopedic reference for its relevance to the context in the sentence.

Compared with creating a metaphoric expression or even merely understanding one, words with two or more meanings are very simple problems indeed. There is the story of the computer program which translated the expression "The spirit is willing, but the flesh is weak" into Russian as "The whiskey is good, but the meat is bad," and "Out of sight, out of mind" as "First blind, then insane." These illustrations are apocryphal, but they make the point: using language correctly is a creative process beyond the power of even the most sophisticated computer program, or of living creatures other than humans, for that matter.

It will be helpful here to define what I mean by creative intelligence, the basis of genius. For my purposes, it is the ability to find a new solution to a new problem. In the living world outside humans, creatures that have even a modicum of this ability are very rare. The psychologist Köhler showed that a few of the most intelligent in the most intelligent of the primates, the chimpanzees, had a limited amount of creative intelligence. A representative problem was to reach fruit on a shed that was to too high to climb. The ingredients of the solution, jointed sticks and packing crates, were scattered around the yard. Only a few chimpanzees solved the problem: stacking the crates near the shed, carrying the jointed sticks to the top, joining them, using the pole created to get the fruit. This simple problem would confound almost all the non-human living world.

At the other end of the scale of complexity was the problem facing physicists at the turn of the century . . . when it was becoming apparent that classical physics was inadequate for dealing with the accumulating evidence on the nature of the physical universe. Hilbert (cited in Feuer 1982) raised the question of why it was that Einstein solved the problem rather than any one of a group of men, all of whom seemed to be so much better prepared than he: Lorentz, Hilbert himself, Poincaré, Mach, and Minkowski. His question can be used to illustrate my conception of creative intelligence. The others were all more erudite than Einstein, but their very erudition led them to keep applying the old solutions that were no longer appropriate. Only Einstein saw that it was the very successes of classical physics that were standing in the way of a solution. What was needed was not merely modifying the old solutions but discarding them entirely and starting over with new ones.

The physicist Boltzmann (1899) described the problem in general terms. He noted that when a new method yields "beautiful results," many become unconsciously wedded to it; they come "to believe that the development of science to the end of all time would consist in the systematic and unremitting application of it." . . .

Even among humans, many kinds of creative activity are rare: only a few solve an artistic or scientific problem in their lifetimes; that is, they do not create a new solution to a new problem. However, as already suggested, in one field, language, virtually every human by the age of five is a creative genius. Most five-year-olds can understand and even create a correct sentence that they have never heard before. Not infrequently, at a somewhat later age, a child can create a correct sentence that no one has ever heard before. In one field, language, almost everyone is creative, spontaneously creating new solutions to new problems as they arise in everyday life.

How do linguists account for the immense human creativity they have discovered? Chomsky (1957, 1965, 1969) offers what turns out to be a conventional genetic explanation. He suggests that linguistic competence is based on "deep structures," genetically programmed sequences, which would have been called instincts if that term had not been discredited. In his view, all humans are linguistically creative because that creativity has been genetically inherited.

I wish to broaden the linguists' question so that the issue includes all creative genius, not just language use. The question becomes: *Why is it that almost everyone is a genius at language, but only a few rare individuals are geniuses in all other spheres of activity?* As already suggested, Chomsky's answer to this question is genetic; he would assume that language creativity is genetically inherited by everyone and that genius in other areas belongs to only a few individuals with the right genetic inheritance, as Galton and Cox both tried to show.

My alternative explanation does not exclude genetics but opens several new areas of investigation. First, assume that the capacity for creative genius in all spheres of activity, not just in language, is genetically inherited by all human beings. Apparently the human brain is more complex and powerful than the largest and most sophisticated computer. Von Neumann estimated that it is capable of processing 140 million bits of information per second. The philosopher Emerson (whose conception of human nature will figure prominently in this essay) did not know this, of course, but he seemed to sense it: "We lie in the lap of immense intelligence" (1837).

If humans have the capacity for genius in all areas, not just in language, why does genius appear in everyone in language but almost never in other areas? Suppose we assume that the disparity is caused by differences not in genetics but in systems of instruction. That is, it is possible that the system of instruction which leads children to learn language is enormously effective, while the systems of instruction which lead children to learn other activities, such as musical composition or mathematics, are relatively ineffective. These two suppositions raise what seems to me to be a new question. *How is the system of instruction of children in language different from other systems of instruction?*

A careful answer to this question might require considerable investigation. In this paper I will attempt only a provisional answer in order to formulate a rudimentary theory of the origins of genius. I will describe only some of the most obvious characteristics which differentiate language instruction from all other types of instruction.[1]

1. Exposure to language begins at the moment of birth and goes on almost constantly throughout infancy and childhood, and indeed for the whole of the individual's life. In terms of sheer quantity, for most individuals, exposure to language is probably vastly greater than any other type of instruction.

2. Language instruction is supremely interactive. Only very early in infancy is the child merely passively exposed to language. Long before any speech is acquired, parents and others speak directly to the infant, usually seeking a response, any response, to their utterances. The immediate rewarding of the infant's responses, often with

boundless enthusiasm, is the beginning of a process of interaction between the infant and competent speakers which instructs the child in correct usage.

3. Virtually all an infant's prelanguage and language tutoring is with tutors who are, as has already been pointed out above, extraordinarily competent in the subject they are imparting. This characteristic of language instruction surely differentiates it from instruction in other subjects. With subjects other than language, the instructors are often only routinely competent, if that. As will be illustrated below for the case of musical creativity, most of the children who go on to become creative geniuses had been instructed by a teacher, usually a parent or other close relative, of much more than routine competence.

4. Language instruction is built upon the infant's own spontaneous gestures and utterances. Virtually all other systems of instruction require the learner to conform to the conventions of the subject to be learned. With a baby, however, one instructs by responding to its cooing, crying, or babbling with language, thereby gradually but relentlessly shaping native impulses. This characteristic may profoundly influence the results of instruction. It also serves to tie together the two parts of the present argument. Since language instruction appears to be so integral with the infant's spontaneous impulses and gestures, it would probably serve to affirm the infant's sense of self, resulting in small but cumulating additions to the level of self-esteem. By contrast, most other systems of instruction, which require the learner to adapt to an alien system of conventions, may cause small but cumulating deficits of self-esteem.

It is conceivable that a system of instruction for music or mathematics or other subjects could be constructed, as language is, out of the learner's spontaneous activities. In music, for example, the instructor could begin by responding to the infant's pitch and rhythms as if they were musical notes and shaping them as one does with language. Similarly a system of mathematical instruction could be built upon the learner's spontaneous counting activities.

The intention to build upon the learner's spontaneous actions appears to lie at the core of the Montessori method of teaching. Children are allowed to play with instructional toys which usually give rise to spontaneous mathematical, musical, and other types of activity. The teacher is trained to base his or her teaching on these spontaneous activities. Although this is an excellent idea, it is not able to capture many of the characteristics of language instruction in the family setting. It takes place only at certain hours of the day and only when the child has reached school age. The instructor may be at least routinely competent in the Montessori method but only routinely competent, if that, in the special area of music, mathematics, and so on. Finally, the teacher is a stranger, at least at the beginning of instruction, rather than being someone, like a parent or other relative, to whom the learner is already strongly attached.

The ideal teacher for a budding genius would be a close relative who is gifted in the area of instruction, always available because living in the same abode, who uses the learner's spontaneous acts as the basis for instruction. Also ideal would be the presence in the home of one or more back-up teachers, so that at least one teacher would be always available.

If we look at the families of the greatest composers, these conditions were usually met. Of course there is no way of knowing in detail their methods of instruction. Most of the greatest composers had at least one close relative who was a gifted musician: Bach, Beethoven, Bizet, Brahms, Chopin, Dvorak, Gounod, Grieg, Ives, Liszt, Mendelssohn, Mozart, Puccini, Rossini, Scarlatti, Schubert, Stravinsky, and Vivaldi. It would appear from their biographies that these composers had access to instruction from at least one gifted musician during infancy and early childhood. However, there are three composers who appear to be exceptions: Tchaikovsky, Verdi, and Wagner. I could find no obvious indication that there was a gifted musician available to them from the time of their births. Judging from these three exceptions, it would appear that although access to a gifted teacher from birth is strongly correlated with the appearance of genius, it is not a necessary condition. I will return to this issue after the discussion of self-esteem, below.

One last comment on musical instruction must be made with respect to Mozart, one of the most prodigiously gifted of the great composers. Like most of them, in his earliest years he had access to more than one competent musician. His father, Leopold, was a performer, composer, and teacher of music; and his older sister, Nannerl, a gifted performer. Of great interest for my argument, there is evidence that his father may have been extraordinarily gifted as a teacher of music. His manual of instruction for the violin, now almost two-hundred-years old, is still the standard text for that instrument. The vitality of his written teaching at least suggests that he may have also been a supremely competent teacher for his son.

The fifth characteristic which may differentiate instruction in language from instruction in other fields is the nature of the response to the learner's progress or lack of progress. In language acquisition in infancy, at least, the instructors seem to concentrate on rewarding correct speech rather than punishing error. Many parents seem to regard each new word as a miracle, often completely disregarding errors. One does not expect infants to know how to speak. We feel no contempt for their errors. (This is in contrast to our native reaction to the difficulties foreign adults have with our language.) At least in the earliest years of instruction, the young learner is not ridiculed for making errors. Perhaps this is one of the reasons for the remarkable effectiveness of learning in language

and the ineffectiveness of most other kinds of instruction: early language use may be almost completely free of shame.

In this section I have suggested that the methods that lead to language acquisition are vastly richer than other kinds of instruction. They begin at birth and are virtually continuous during the child's waking hours. They are carried on by a close relative who is extraordinarily gifted in the use of language. One or more back-up teachers are also usually available to ensure continuous training even in the absence of the primary teacher. Language instruction in infancy and early childhood is also intensely interactive, with the learner's getting virtually instant feedback on her or his fluency. I have also suggested that language instruction in the family is built upon the shaping of the learner's native impulses rather than the acquiring of new ones. This method may lead to high levels of self-esteem. A fifth characteristic may also build self-esteem: the overwhelming prevalence of positive, rather than negative, feedback in the early years of language acquisition. There seems to be a moratorium on criticism in the initial response of adults to children's early efforts at language.

THE REAL AND THE FALSE SELF

I introduce the topic of self-esteem and its relation to genius by referring again to Emerson's thought. He believed that self-reliance was the basic virtue because, he argued, at the core of every human is a self of unbelievable brilliance (1837, 18):

> What is the aboriginal Self, on which a universal reliance may be grounded? What is the nature and power of that science-baffling star, without parallax, without calculable elements, which shoots a ray of beauty even into trivial and impure actions, if the least mark of independence appear? The inquiry leads us to that source, at once the essence of genius,

of virtue, and of life, which we call Spontaneity or Instinct. We denote this primary wisdom as Intuition, whilst all later teachings are tuitions. This aboriginal self is the origin of intuition, and therefore of inspiration, of effortless genius.

Emerson points out that one aspect of genius, the completely accurate perception of reality, is totally involuntary:

Every man discriminates between the voluntary acts of his mind and his involuntary perceptions, and knows that to his involuntary perceptions a perfect faith is due. He may err in the expression of them, but he knows that these things are so, like day and night, not to be disputed. My willful actions and acquisitions are but roving; the idlest reverie, the faintest native emotion, command my curiosity and respect. Thoughtless people contradict as readily the statement of perceptions as of opinions, or rather much more readily; for they do not distinguish between perception and notion. They fancy that I choose to see this or that thing. But perception is not whimsical, but fatal. If I see a trait, my children will see it after me, and in the course of time all mankind—although it may chance that no one has seen it before me. For my perception of it is as much a fact as the sun.

If all humans have access to boundless intuition and perception, according to Emerson, why is not everyone a genius? The answer he gives is that with few exceptions, everyone is terrified by the specter of being deviants from the collective vision of reality that is held in the community. We conform out of shame.

A man must consider what a blindman's bluff is this game of conformity. . . . most men have bound their eyes with one or another handkerchief, and attached themselves to some one of these communities of opinion. This conformity makes them not false in a few particulars, authors of a few lies, but false in all particulars. Their every truth is not quite true. Their two is not the real two, their four not the real four; so that every word they say chagrins us and we know not where to begin to set them right.

Conformity to the popularly held version of what is real and what is possible blinds most individuals to their own inner visions. *Only that person whose self-esteem is so high that he can withstand social rejection will be able to propose new solutions to new problems.* Emerson's formulation of this issue is so lengthy that I have separated and enumerated the main components (emphasis added).

[1] To believe your own thought, to believe that what is true for you in your private heart is true for all men—that is genius. Speak your latent conviction, and it shall be the universal sense; for the inmost in due time becomes the outmost, and our *first thought* is rendered back to us by the trumpets of the Last Judgment.

[2] A man should learn to *detect and watch that gleam of light which flashes across his mind from within,* more than the lustre of the firmament of bards and sages.

[3] Yet he dismisses without notice his thought, because it is his. In every work of genius we recognize our own *rejected thoughts;* they come back to us with a certain alienated majesty.

[4] Great works of art have no more affecting lesson for us than this. They teach us to abide by our spontaneous impression with good-humored inflexibility then most when the whole cry of voices is on the other side. Else tomorrow a stranger will say with masterly good sense precisely what we have thought and felt all the time, and we shall be forced to take with *shame* our own opinion from another.

There are several important ideas in this passage, but they are not developed by Emerson, only mentioned casually in passing. Perhaps the most fundamental basis of his thought is found in

(2): "A man should learn to detect and watch that gleam of light which flashes across his mind from within, more than the lustre of the firmament of bards and sages." The key word is "flashes." In the context of the sentence, he seems to be suggesting that the flashes are extremely fast, so fast, perhaps, that unless one trains one's self, it is almost impossible even to become aware of them, much less try them out.

This sentence may serve to clarify what is otherwise a confusing issue in the advice that Emerson gives us. He tells us to trust ourselves but, aside from this sentence, does not give us any further guidance about what self it is that we are to trust. In the passage quoted earlier he calls it the "aboriginal self" and identifies it with intuition and spontaneity. But we have many different types of spontaneous impulses and thoughts, some of which are notoriously unreliable. We need a more specific description of the type of spontaneous intuitive thought.

In the sentence about the gleam of light, Emerson may have provided an important clue to what he meant. He seems to have anticipated Freud's discovery of the unconscious, the "aboriginal self" as Emerson calls it. In order to teach his patients "to learn to detect and watch" the gleam of light, Freud developed the method of free association. He devised a practical workaday technique for giving his patient's access to their "aboriginal" selves. Once the patient discovered this access, therapy usually advanced more rapidly.

In systematically applying the method of free association, Freud made a discovery that went beyond Emerson. He found that most of his patients actively resisted acquaintance with their aboriginal selves (the repressed parts of their experiences). . . .

The patient's resistance, Freud later found, was due to unresolved painful emotion that was often also a part of the aboriginal self. I will return to the issue of unresolved emotion below, in the section on shame and guilt. . . .

Emerson's idea and Freud's later work teach that intuitive thought is unsolicited and nonverbal, an "involuntary perception," to use Emerson's term; second, it appears and disappears so rapidly as to seem instantaneous; and finally, it is always the *first* thought, rather than the second, third, or later thought, that is unedited and uncensored and therefore uncompromised by bias. The unsolicited first thought appears always, "invariably" to use Freud's word, to be the most inclusive, complex, and original of our thoughts. (But this is not necessarily true; Emerson was careful to state that intuitive ideas always need to be tested in reality.)

Einstein, when he sought to explain the origins of his creative ideas, often hinted at these characteristics. He usually explained that ideas did not come to him in words but in "images." The greatest of the chess masters also explain their deliberation in a similar way, not in words or moves but in fluid images that come to them involuntarily. Like Einstein, they struggle in their descriptions because they are attempting to describe a nonverbal process in words. . . .

If we return to Emerson's passage, a second idea is suggested in (1), "To believe your own thought, to believe that what is true for you in your private heart is true for all men—that is genius." This statement makes a connection between self-esteem and genius. It evokes the idea, in the strongest possible terms, that what differentiates the genius most strongly from other, ordinary persons is not talent—no mention is made of that—but self-esteem. Emerson seems to suggest that for the genius, his or her unique vision does not lead to a feeling of alienation from others, of being "different," that is, a freak, as is usually the case, but of feeling connected with others in that what is true for you is also true of all others. In the discussion of the relationship between self-esteem and shame below, I suggest how such an extraordinary high level of self-esteem might come about.

One last thought in the original passage, (4), is in need of elaboration. I refer to the last part of this sentence, about the "whole cry of voices" being on the other side. The implication is that the person who expresses his or her unique vision will be persecuted for it. This sentence again implies a connection between genius and self-esteem. In this case it is implied that one will need a high level of self-esteem in order to withstand the cry of voices. The case of Galileo affords a familiar example. The tragic lives of the mathematician Georg Cantor and the physicist Boltzmann are less familiar. Relentless criticism of their work, which was far advanced over that of their contemporaries, drove Boltzmann to suicide and Cantor to the insane asylum. Emerson's paragraph appears to comprehend, in a single glance, the whole situation of the genius—his inner turmoil and his place in society. . . .

SELF-ESTEEM: COPING WITH SHAME AND GUILT

One last reference to Emerson evokes another aspect of genius—single-minded dedication to one's work: "I shun father and mother and wife and brother, when my genius calls me." Once again the image which Emerson evokes refers to a high level of self-esteem, in this case, the absence of guilt. I suggest that self-esteem rests upon a very specific process, the management of shame and guilt, and that this process, in conjunction with the development of talent, gives rise to genius.

I have been using the term "self-esteem" as if its meaning were self-explanatory. Actually, there is no agreed-upon definition of this idea. The nearest thing to be found in the literature is the idea that level of self-esteem concerns the degree to which one has positive feelings about oneself. Although this idea is a good place to start, since it concerns feelings rather than thoughts or images,

it is much too vague. It does not tell what kind of positive feeling: joy, love, pride, interest, thrill, and so on. In order to proceed further with the theory of genius, I discuss one particular feeling: shame. I define self-esteem as freedom from chronic shame.

Even a child who has no wish to express a unique vision, who wishes merely to be conventional in every possible way, must run a gauntlet of potentially shaming situations. The problem that the child faces is of almost inexpressible magnitude: in order to become an acceptable member of a community, she must learn a myriad of conventions and execute them in virtually perfect manner, as if each were second nature. There is a further characteristic of the job at hand. The child must learn to suppress her understanding that most of these conventions are completely arbitrary. The question "Why do we kiss on the lips rather than rub noses?" or a similar question is tolerated from a three-year-old, but in an older child it already is taken as intimating frivolousness or worse. These conventions "go without saying"; that is, they are sacred. Even to notice the arbitrariness of conventions, much less make an issue of them, invites ridicule and ostracism.

Rapid learning of a large mass of conventions makes errors inevitable. Mispronouncing a word is as much a part of learning as pronouncing it correctly, yet each error invites scorn or ridicule. (In a family I know, one of the members is still being teased about the time she thought that a friend of the parents named Dennis was a dentist.) A repeating error, such as lisping, stammering, or stuttering, creates a nightmare of ridicule. Language errors are particularly rife. There are millions of details of pronunciation, inflection, grammar, syntax, and nonverbal gesture that must be performed, letter perfect.

There is a further twist to language that must seem almost diabolical to the learner. On the one hand, the correct use of language requires creativity. As already indicated, one often needs to invent new linguistic solutions for new situations. A vexing problem faced by children, however, is that some of their inventions are accepted but others are ridiculed. . . .

THE SHAME CONSTRUCT

. . . A useful place to start is to compare shame with a much less complex and much more prestigious affect: guilt. In most cases, the feeling of guilt is evoked by a specific and quite delimited act or failure to act, for example, to forget one's spouse's birthday or to scream at one's helpless infant. The thread which seems to be common to the actions or inactions which produce guilt is that they all involve the possibility of injuring another. Whether one person steals another's purse or curses or berates him in public, the victim has been injured.

When a child misunderstands a word like "Dennis," however, or invents a motive for soccer players, no injury has occurred. Harmless errors of these kinds do not produce guilt in the perpetrator but a different emotion: shame. The possibility that one could injure another assumes a potent, powerful, *capable* self. Making a gross error raises a question about the *adequacy* of the self, its basic worth: If you could make an error like that, are you really a person like me, or are you some kind of freak that need not be taken into consideration?

When one feels guilt, one's self feels *intact*. In feeling shame, one experiences what must be the most vertiginous of all feelings, the *disintegration of the self,* or its potential for disintegration. It is for this reason that guilt is infinitely more prestigious than shame. Guilty persons may even feel pride (the reverse of shame) that they are feeling guilt: it shows that they are basically moral persons; that is, they have intact, capable selves.

A vast ocean of errors is built into the child's existence. These errors, for the most part, are

unavoidable, as is the normal shame that is the result of making errors. What may be avoidable, however, is to have innumerable experiences lead to *chronic* shame.

Shame is probably the most intensely painful of all feelings. Each person has spent what feels like an eternity of time and effort in constructing a competent, valuable self. The threat of losing that self may be more painful than the threat of losing one's life. In all cultures and historical eras, personal disgrace usually leads to extreme measures, even suicide.

There are two further premises about shame which need to be discussed before I return to self-esteem and genius. Many readers might agree that shame is a profoundly painful emotion but will assume that it seldom occurs and, when it does, one is fully aware of it. I am assuming, on the contrary, that shame is ubiquitous, not only in the lives of children but also in adult life, and virtually invisible. How can one be consumed with shame and still not be aware of it? To understand this issue, I will again review the concept of "unacknowledged shame" and the two forms this type of shame takes: "*bypassed* shame" and "*overt, undifferentiated shame*" (Lewis 1971).

According to Lewis, there are two opposite paths that one can take in order to avoid noticing the feeling of shame: one can bypass the feeling, swallow it, so to speak, so that one does not feel the pain at all (except for one extremely brief instant, when the shame is initially evoked). Although by following this path, one manages to decrease substantially the *intensity* of pain, at the same time the *duration* is increased. The shame is experienced as obsessive ideation or speech. During episodes of compulsive thinking or speaking, one experiences little feeling. On the contrary, one may be aware of an absence of feeling, of blankness or emptiness. Bypassed shame takes the form of too much ideation and too little feeling.

The other form, unacknowledged shame, the overt, undifferentiated type, leads to the opposite experience, too much feeling and too little ideation.

One is so flustered by the threat of incompetence (paralysis, disintegration) that one is unable to observe and analyze what is happening. "I feel like a perfect idiot" is one rendering. "Embarrassment," "humiliation," and "mortification" are examples of words used to describe overt shame; "bashfulness," "shyness," "modesty," and "discomfiture" are less-intense but longer-lasting variants.

Many of the commonly used references to undifferentiated painful feelings appear to be shame experiences, or mixtures of shame with another emotion, such as anger: awkward, uncomfortable, foolish, silly, strange, and "in a stew" are examples. In adolescent terminology, one is "bummed," "freaked," or "weirded out." These words appear to be substitutes or euphemisms for shame, just as there are many euphemisms for sexual and "toilet" terms. Shame, like these other functions, appears to be subject to taboo (Scheff 1984).

The discussion so far has focused on shame as a *response*, a stereotyped biopsychological response which is virtually omnipresent in human communities. To describe shame further, it is necessary to shift to the *stimulus* that is common to all situations in which shame arises. This stimulus seems to be social in character: shame appears to be the stereotyped emotional response to a threat of loss of connection to another person or persons. This element is fairly obvious in most cases of overt, undifferentiated shame. One becomes painfully embarrassed and flustered when one "loses face" in public: caught in a lie, a gross error, or caught unawares by an obvious trick (we feel humiliated that we "swallowed it hook, line, and sinker" without a trace of redeeming suspicion).

In bypassed shame, the social source is less obvious since this experience often arises when one is alone. Here is a characteristic moment described by a male college student:

> I am on campus, walking to class. On the way, I am remembering an earlier conversation with a great deal of pleasure. I believe I made a good impression on this woman that I am interested in. But then I remember a remark I made about her ex-boyfriend. At the time I felt witty saying it, but suddenly I saw it from her point of view. I felt like a turd. I kept replaying that scene, even when I was sitting in class, thinking what I might have said instead.

The obsessive replaying of the scene suggests that this experience involved bypassed shame. It occurred when the student shifted from his point of view to that of the woman. This shift exposes the social nature of the stimulus to bypassed shame. It occurred not in social interaction in the real world, as overt, undifferentiated shame usually does, but in imagined social interaction in the "internal theater," the interior dialogue that goes on in our minds.

The stricken feeling of shame indicated by the phrase "I just felt like an idiot" may occur in actual social interaction. Just as likely, it can occur in solitude, when one is reenacting a transaction from memory or inventing a meeting with another which has never taken place, and may never take place—imagining a conversation with "the man on the street" or with Shakespeare.

In interior dialogue, we are very often engaged with some other person, whose image we create for an inner enactment or reenactment: one's spouse, son, or daughter, boss or subordinate, or even one's self in some other guise, older or younger, in one or another of one's many hats or disguises. This internal theater often results in emotional responses. When we imagine the other as approving or accepting ourselves, we bask in the glow of self-generated pride. When we imagine the other as critical, contemptuous, or scornful, we roast in the hell of self-generated shame or guilt.

EMOTION AND CREATIVITY

The last step in describing the relationship of genius and self-esteem concerns feeling traps (Lewis 1971). Normal emotions—fear, anger, grief, and shame—are usually quite short-lived, a few seconds perhaps. They ordinarily are crisis responses. Referring to anxiety, Freud suggested that it has a "signal function"; it is an interior warning that something is wrong. If normal emotions are short-lived, how is it possible that one may be constantly angry, frightened, and, especially for our purposes here, ashamed? Chronic shame states are significant because they are probably the basis of what is called low self-esteem: one is usually not proud of one's self but ashamed.

The concept of the feeling trap may explain what otherwise might seem to be a paradox: emotional states which are virtually life long. Feeling traps occur when one has an emotional reaction to one's emotional reaction, and another reaction to that reaction, and another and another, and so on, ad infinitum. Panic seems to be one outcome of a fear spiral: of being frightened that one is so afraid. In fear panics, people may stampede like animals, inadvertently killing each other, or, as in the case of voodoo death, die of anoxia. Being ashamed of being ashamed is another spiral that has runaway possibilities: "What an idiot I am (how shameful it is) that I should get so upset (ashamed) over something so trivial." One outcome of this spiral, stage fright, can reach such proportions that the victim is paralyzed in mind and body.

In interpersonal relations, the lethal feeling trap seems to be the shame-rage spiral, of being ashamed that you are angry ("How could I be so angry at someone who loves me? What a monster I am.") and angry at self or at the other that you are shamed: "You asshole. Don't stand around moping over your ego. Get your ass in gear." The anger may be directed at the other rather than one's self: "It's all your fault. You made me feel bad." This particular spiral may be experienced as humiliated fury (e.g., the "wronged woman")—anger bound by shame. This state may not be represented in consciousness, however. Frequently it is not experienced at all since it has been going on so long as a virtually automatic response. Another possibility is that it is

experienced as the absence of any feeling at all, as blankness or emptiness.

Another of the isotopic representations of shame-rage is intermittent but lengthy bouts of resentment, jealousy, or guilt. These are all molecules of the same two atoms, but with the anger pointing in different directions. . . . In chronic jealousy, the anger may be pointed at the putative rival or at the love object or at both. In guilt, the anger seems to be pointed back at the self. One is enraged at the self for injuring another and, at the same time, ashamed both of one's actions and of being so enraged ("out of control").

Is there any possibility of escaping from a feeling trap, once caught up? The most common gambit used in daily life seems to be the attempt to talk one's self out of it, which seldom works. Telling one's self "You should be ashamed of being so upset at something so trivial" only sinks one deeper in the trap. In psychotherapy, a frequently used technique is to try to get the victim to express or discharge his anger. This seldom works either because it ignores the shame component of the trap. A common reaction is to become embarrassed (shamed) by the "artificiality" of showing anger when you are "not really mad," which is another variant of feeling that one's anger is not adequately justified, or feeling guilty about being loud or "selfish."

One method which almost always dispels shame is laughter, good-humored or affectionate laughter. This idea is very much in accord with popular belief that laughter relieves embarrassment. Lewis (1983) has shown that it is also supported by Freud's analysis of wit and laughter, although he does not make the idea explicit. Retzinger (1985, 1987) has shown that it is also implied by McDougall's analysis of laughter, although, like Freud, he does not make the sequence explicit.

If one laughs good-naturedly when shame is evoked, it will be quickly dispelled. If one does not laugh, one is often faced with unpleasant after effects. Usually the shamed person will blush or attempt to hide (cover face with hand, look away, try to leave the scene, or at least imagine he has left) or begin to talk or think obsessively. This is the setting for entry into a feeling trap. A common sequence is to become angry or hostile toward the other who is perceived as shaming one, then to feel guilty that one is angry, then to feel ashamed that one is so upset, and so on.

Good-natured laughter, if it occurs immediately when shame is evoked, avoids entry into the spiral. If it occurs when the spiral is in operation, it ends the cycle. Apparently when one laughs during a shame-rage spiral, the dispelling of the shame, which was binding the anger, allows the anger to discharge also. In her video studies of resentment, Retzinger (1985, 1987) has investigated the effects of laughter on anger. In the episodes where laughter occurred during the recalling of a resentment-laden memory, facial flushing and body heat, which are the markers of anger discharge (Scheff 1984), occurred simultaneously with the laughter. Retzinger showed that the frequency, intensity, and duration of verbal and facial anger expressions decreased dramatically after laughter.

The Laughing Genius

Having reviewed the concepts of unacknowledged shame and the shame-rage feeling trap. I return to genius and its relationship to self-esteem. I have argued that for genius to appear, the bearer must have extraordinarily high self-esteem, be able to catch his or her first thoughts in flight, and have the confidence to develop and express these thoughts. There are probably two paths which lead to this level of self-esteem. The first path concerns humane treatment: the budding genius may have undergone less humiliation than others and therefore spent less time in shame-rage spirals than the less gifted. . . .

It seems likely, however, that the development of ways of managing shame would be far more important in the development of self-esteem than the extent to which one was treated with respect or contempt. Shame seems to be an unavoidable aspect of the human condition, even for those who are fortunate enough to have been treated well in most of their relationships. The gamut of errors through which children must pass in learning their culture, and the shame which results, has already been mentioned. A second universal source of shame is that love is always ambivalent. Intimate relationships are invariably a source of frustration, and therefore of anger, as well as fulfillment, and a source of shame as well as pride. That is, intimacy inevitably leads to a situation in which one is rejected or feels rejected, a basic source of shame.

If, as has been argued here, shame is unavoidable, then self-esteem must rest on effective ways of dispelling shame. The most effective way of dispelling shame, I have suggested, is through laughter. If this is the case, the great geniuses should have been laughers. . . .

Although it is difficult to test the laughing-genius hypothesis with written biographies, it might be possible in interviews with living artists and scientists. I think that the laughing hypothesis probably is much more relevant to a certain type of creator, which I have termed the "easy" creator. These creators work very rapidly and with little revision. Goethe wrote *Werther* in 24 days; Nietzsche . . . wrote *Zarathustra* in 30 days. I suspect that creativity is extraordinarily rapid with this type because there is freedom from self-censure and therefore access to the aboriginal self. Schubert and Mozart were certainly composers of this type, and also the mathematician John von Neumann (the person most responsible for the invention of the computer). By investigating the nature of the emotional lives of these creators, and particularly the amount and quality of their laughter, it might be possible to clarify some of the issues that have been discussed here.

Conclusion

This paper has outlined a rudimentary theory of genius. Creative intelligence may arise out of two interrelated processes, the development of extra-ordinary talent and the growth of extremely high levels of self-esteem. Extraordinary talent, whether or not it also involves genetic inheritance of talent, also requires a system of highly effective instruction. The model for this system of instruction may be the kind of language instruction children receive for the first five or six years. The formulation of this model raises what may be an important question for investigation: In what ways is early language instruction different from all other types of instruction, and do these differences account for the creativity that occurs in the correct use of natural language?

The second process in the growth of creative intelligence may be the development of high levels of self-esteem. I argue that self-esteem is essentially freedom from chronic shame. This type of shame is usually unacknowledged. It is virtually invisible because it appears in multiform guises. The basic mechanism of chronic shame, it is argued, is the feeling trap, which may convert emotions, normally brief, into lifelong states. Finally it is suggested that chronic shame is most effectively dispelled by good-humored laughter. If this is the case, we should expect to find the genius, especially the easily creative genius, to be a laugher.

One final question: Is there any reason to believe that one or the other of these two processes, the one involving talent, the other, self-esteem, is in any way more important than the other in the appearance of genius? No doubt they are equally important in the lives of most geniuses. However, it seems possible, for theoretical reasons, that the development of self-esteem may be more important. It is possible that the early growth of high levels of self-esteem may allow the potential genius to find the effective instruction needed to develop extraordinary talent. This is one way of interpreting the three deviant cases—Tchaikovsky, Verdi, and Wagner—who do not appear to have had early access to a musically talented teacher. This possibility, like the others suggested here, awaits future research for clarification. . . .

NOTE

1. Howard Becker called to my attention a comparison of schooling and language acquisition which parallels mine, in Paul Goodman, "Education of the Young" (1969).

REFERENCES

Boltzmann, Ludwig. 1899. "The Recent Development of Method in Theoretical Physics." *Monist* 11:229–30.

Chomsky, Noam. 1957. *Systematic Structures.* The Hague: Mouton.

_____. 1965. *Aspects of a Theory of Syntax.* Cambridge, Mass.: MIT Press.

_____. 1969. *The Acquisition of Syntax in Children from 5 to 10.* Cambridge, Mass.: MIT Press.

Cox, Catherine M. 1926, *The Early Mental Traits of 300 Geniuses.* Stanford, Calif.: Stanford University Press.

Emmerson, R. W. 1837/1983. *Essays and Lectures.* New York: Library of America.

Feuer, Lewis S. 1982. *Einstein and the Generations of Science.* New Brunswick, N.J.: Transaction.

Galton, Francis. 1869. *Heredity Genius.* Cleveland: Meridian.

Goodman, Paul. 1969. *New Reformation.* New York: Vintage.

Lewis, H. B. 1971. *Shame and Guilt in Neurosis.* New York: International Universities Press.

_____. 1976. *Psychic War in Men and Women.* New York: New York University Press.

_____. 1983. *Freud and Modern Psychology.* 2 vols. New York: Plenum.

Retzinger, Suzanne. 1985. "The Resentment Process: Videotape Studies." *Psychoanalytic Psychology* 2: 129–51

_____. 1987. "Marital Conflict: Case Study of an Escalating Quarrel." Typescript.

_____. 1987a. "Resentment and Laughter: Video Studies of the Shame-Rage Spiral." In Helen B. Lewis, ed., *The Role of Shame in Symptom Formation.* Hillsdale, N.J.: Erlbaum.

Scheff, T. J. 1966. *Being Mentally Ill.* Chicago: Aldine (2d ed., 1984).

_____. 1984. "The Taboo on Coarse Emotions." *Review of Personality and Social Psychology* 5: 156–169.

SELF-PRESENTATION IN INTERACTION

This section builds on the ideas in Part III on the definition of the situation. Just as we have to project a definition of the situation to those with whom we're interacting, we also have to project definitions of ourselves. Other people can't read our minds or see at a glance how it is that we see ourselves. People put a lot of energy into presenting their sense of self to others. We wear clothing that reflects who we want to be and purchase cars and products that reflect our identification with particular reference groups. Some theorists have even proposed that we choose to date people based on the extent to which they complement our image of ourselves—we are attracted to people who reflect back the image we want to see of ourselves. The two articles in the section are examples of this process.

Why do people create personal websites? Charles Cheung addresses this question in "Identity Construction and Self-Presentation on Personal Homepages." Cheung analyzes homepages from a symbolic interactionist perspective in his quest to understand why people would want to display intimate personal details for anyone to see.

"Body Troubles: Women, Workplace and Negotiations of a Disabled Identity" is based on a study by Isabel Dyck. This study illustrates some of the ways in which women who have disabilities that are not easily noticeable negotiate their public image.

Questions for Discussion and Review

1. Think about the clothes you wear. What image of self are you conveying by your clothing choices? Who is the audience in your head when you get dressed and feel good about how you look? What clothes wouldn't you be caught dead wearing? Why?

2. Observe the various slogans on T-shirts, and consider the information they provide about the person's commitments and values. What T-shirt slogans would you not want to wear?

3. Hurt feelings and fights between close friends often occur when one or both persons feel that some aspect of their self is being mis-seen or unseen. Consider an experience in which you felt you were misunderstood by someone you're close to. What aspect of your self did you feel the other person was unable to see? Did you feel that the other person was reflecting an image of you that is different from how you see yourself?

4. Discuss situations in which you are keenly aware of trying to portray a particular image. Discuss situations in which you feel obligated to present a public image that is at odds with your private image of yourself.

SELF-PRESENTATION IN INTERACTION

27

Identity Construction and Self-Presentation on Personal Homepages

Charles Cheung

(2004)

How Many Personal Homepages Are There on the Web?

Although it is difficult to count the dispersed and ever-changing number of homepages on the Web, a look at the press relations sections of a handful of the sites offering free Web space shows that the numbers must add up quickly: large community sites like Yahoo! GeoCities and Angelfire claim over 4.5 million active homepage builders each, for example, and FortuneCity claims a further 2 million (July 2003). Millions more homepages reside in the numerous other free webspace services, and within commercial and educational sites. Personal homepage websites are also a popular Web destination. Nielsen/NetRatings' MarketView report shows that Yahoo! GeoCities had more than 27 million unique visitors within one month (October 2002). ComScore Media Metrix surveys also show that Tripod and Angelfire had around 16 and 12 million monthly unique visitors respectively (September 2002).

INTRODUCTION

If you are curious enough to browse through some personal homepages posted on the Web, you may quickly observe the following phenomena.

- Generally, personal homepages are websites produced by individuals, or sometimes a couple or family. On a personal homepage,

people can put up any information about themselves, including autobiography or diary material, personal photos and videos, creative works, political opinions, information about hobbies and interests, links to other websites, and so on.

- People from all walks of life have started to use the personal homepage to tell personal stories about themselves: cancer patients, retired scientists, kids with disabilities, vinyl collectors, kung fu movie fans, transsexuals, DIY enthusiasts, pornographic movie lovers, to name but a few.

- Certain personal homepages seem to be made to display the strong personality and identity of the homepage authors, as if declaring: 'It is me! I'm cool!' These pages usually have stylish design, and contain details of specific aspects of the author's life.
- Some personal homepages seem to be made more for self-exploration than for making a strong identity statement. These pages usually contain an online diary or journal, in which the homepage authors put down how they feel about what happens to them every day.
- Having said all this, many personal homepages tell you little information about the author. These pages are unbelievably dull—they only include things like vital statistics, one or two photos, some links to other websites, and nothing else.
- Even worse, many homepages are listed in Web directories but actually not available.

Personal homepages have their critics, of course. Some Internet commentators, for example, suggest that the contents of personal homepages reflect nothing but the narcissism and exhibitionism of many net users and the 'content trivialization' of the Internet superhighway. Some web designers are appalled by the amateur appearance of many personal homepages. But these responses are inappropriate. This chapter argues that, to make sense of the above phenomena, we need to take the personal homepage seriously as a significant social phenomenon. This article has two arguments.

1. The personal homepage is an emancipatory media genre. The distinctive medium characteristics of the personal homepage allow net users to become active cultural producers, expressing their suppressed identities or exploring the significant question of 'who I am,' often in ways which may not otherwise be possible in 'real' life.

2. Nevertheless, the fact that many personal homepages are poor in content, or have even been abandoned by their creators, suggests that the emancipatory potentials of the personal homepage are limited and often not fully exploited. In daily life, there can be a range of factors which preclude some people from producing 'content-rich' personal homepages.

People tell stories about themselves by making personal homepages, but not—to paraphrase Marx—in conditions of their own choosing, as this chapter will show.

"This is Me!": The Personal Homepage as a Stage for Strategic Self-Presentation

The first emancipatory use of the personal homepage is strategic and elaborate self-presentation. In everyday life, we usually try in vain to tell our partners, family, friends, employers, or at times even strangers who we 'really' are: Although we can one-sidedly complain that other people misunderstand us, sociologists suggest that self-presentational failure in everyday life actually involves other factors, such as social interactional contexts and our presentation skills.

According to Goffman, in everyday encounters, the social settings and audiences we face always define the kinds of 'acceptable' selves we should present—a teenager performs as a hard-working student in front of teachers in class, an office worker as a responsible employee in front of his or her boss and colleagues, a CEO as a responsible company leader who cares for shareholders in front of financial journalists at press conferences, and so on.

Nevertheless, sometimes we may wish to present certain identities but may not find the 'right' social settings and audiences, and if we present these identities in inappropriate social settings, we experience embarrassment, rejection or harassment. For example, a boy may entertain his friends with rap songs about his sexual conquests, but his grandparents might be a less receptive audience.

In face-to-face interaction, we present ourselves through the use of 'sign vehicles' such as clothing, posture, intonation, speech pattern, facial expression and bodily gesture. But Goffman also emphasizes that total control over these sign vehicles is difficult, since most face-to-face interactions proceed in a spontaneous manner and do not include an assigned block of time in which we can present ourselves in an orderly and systematic fashion. More often than not, our presentation of self in everyday life is a delicate enterprise, subject to moment-to-moment mishaps and unintentional misrepresentations. These mishaps typically lead us (again) to experience embarrassment, rejection or harassment and, consequently, the failure of self-presentation. To put it simply, the core problems of our self-presentation in everyday life are that we lack enough control over (1) what 'selves' we should display in a particular social setting and (2) how well we can present them. The personal homepage, however, can 'emancipate' us from these two problems.

First, the personal homepage allows much more strategic self-presentation than everyday interaction. The personal homepage is a self-defined 'stage,' upon which we can decide what aspects of our selves we would like to present. As previously mentioned, in everyday life we may wish to present certain identities but may not be able to find the 'right' audiences. On the personal homepage, however, this is not the case: once we put up our personal homepage on the Web, its global accessibility of the personal homepage means that we instantly have a potential audience of millions (with the emphasis on *potential*). In addition, even if some

people dislike our 'homepage selves' and send us negative responses by e-mail, these responses are not instantaneous, so we feel less pressure to respond to them—in fact, we can even ignore these comments. For example, if a kung fu movie lover really wants to tell others that he is an expert in kung fu movies, his simplest solution is not to force strangers in pubs to listen to him but to construct a personal homepage. By creating a website featuring his essays on kung fu movies, photo collection of kung fu stars, or even digital videos of him doing karate, he would have millions of net browsers who also love kung fu movies as his *potential* audience. Of course, not everyone stumbling across his homepage will admire his identity as a 'kung fu movie fan,' and sometimes people may even send him e-mails ridiculing his enthusiasm for these movies. But since these 'attackers' are not his targeted audience, he can always ignore their criticisms.

Second, the personal homepage is emancipatory for self-presentation since it allows the individual to give a much more polished and elaborate presentation, with more control over 'impression management,' compared with face-to-face interaction. Indeed, the 'sign vehicles' used in the homepage self-presentation are more subject to manipulation. As discussed in the preceding paragraph, since we are less likely to experience immediate rejection from those who read our homepages, before releasing our personal homepage to the net public, we can always manipulate all the elements until we are satisfied: we can experiment with the colour scheme, choose the most presentable head shot, censor the foul language accidentally written in the draft biography, and ponder as long as we like before deciding whether to tell the readers that our partner just dumped us. Mishaps that may affect one's self-presentation in everyday life can be avoided on the personal homepage. Of course, not all responses can be controlled—I cannot prevent a homepage visitor from thinking that I am a self-indulgent fool.

Research evidence shows that people from all walks of life have started to use the personal homepage for strategic and elaborate self-presentation.

One prominent use of the personal homepage is to promote one's professional achievement in ways which may not otherwise be possible in everyday life. People seeking jobs, for instance, use the personal homepage to highlight and embellish aspects of their professional achievements, so as to reach potential employers or to create more lasting impressions than brief phone or face-to-face job interviews (Rosenstein, 2000). Likewise, artists use their websites to promote their artistic persona, and young academics use faculty homepages to gain wider exposure. As one young academic confessed: 'For the person visiting the webpage of my department, I am more visible than the professors [who don't have pages]'.

Some homepages are more relationship-oriented. On these homepages, the authors often highlight particular personal qualities (personalities, hobbies or political opinions) so as to share opinions and experiences with like-minded individuals, or to attract potential romantic partners who admire those qualities (Rosenstein, 2000).

The personal homepage is also particularly valuable for those with difficulty presenting themselves in face-to-face interaction, such as introverts with weak self-presentational skills, and people with any kind of visible or invisible disability such as amputees, the visually impaired, or the hearing impaired. As one homepage author with traumatic brain injury said concisely: 'Our disability is *invisible* so people can't respond (original emphasis; Hevern, 2000: 16). These homepage authors may feel better able to express themselves through the use of biographies, online writing or their photos (Chandler, 1998). People with Down's syndrome, for example, have used the personal homepage to assert that in many ways they are no different from other people, because, like anyone else, they have distinctive cultural tastes and are

knowledgeable about certain things—such as making webpages.

The personal homepage may be most emancipatory for those whose identities are misunderstood or stigmatized in society—teenagers, gays and lesbians, fat people, the mentally ill, and so on—since they can reveal their identities without risking the rejection or harassment that may be experienced in everyday life. One gay respondent, for instance, explained how the personal homepage helped him to come out 'steadily':

> I was looking for some way of having a gay presence in the world and still feel protected from the adverse effects. [Making my personal homepage] was great because I didn't have to just 'come out' to somebody and risk rejection. I could do things a little at a time and build levels of trust along the way. (Hevern, 2000: 15)

Another gay author reports a similar experience. He would say to friends, 'Check out my website,' and let them see his positive expressions of gay identity, and 'think about it before reacting' (Chandler, 1998).

In fact, the emancipatory value of the personal homepage for self-presentation is even more evident if we look at how traditional mass media represent ordinary people. Generally, the mass media do not allow ordinary people to represent themselves on their own terms. Rather, ordinary people are represented by the creative personnel of the mass media, perhaps in stereotypical ways: the stupid teenager, the helpless disabled person, or the sexually available woman, for example. There may be radio phone-ins and TV audience talk-back programmes for the 'users' of these media to express their points of view, but the limited access to these shows, as well as the commercial nature of their topics, means that these media never allow people the degree of creative freedom offered by the personal homepage. Media scholars have longed for a medium which can help people who are often misrepresented in the mass media to move 'from silence to speech' (hooks, 1989: 9). The personal homepage can serve this very purpose.

"WHO AM I?": THE PERSONAL HOMEPAGE AS A SPACE FOR REFLEXIVE CONSTRUCTION OF IDENTITY

For some people, however, the personal homepage is emancipatory not because it is a stage for self-presentation, but because it can be a space for identity construction. My previous discussion on self-presentation more or less assumes that homepage authors have a stable sense of self-identity, and the only problem for these authors is to find some ways to present aspects of their identities. Some confident academics may use their webpage to advertise their academic persona, for example, and some lesbians who are very sure of their sexual identity may use their homepage to celebrate their lifestyle. However, for many people, their sense of 'who I am' is not that obvious, and may be highly uncertain. Their problem is not so much about presenting their identity, but concerns their exploration of 'who I am' and re-establishing a stable sense of self-identity. Much has been written on the sources of uncertain identity; here I have selected three examples for our discussion.

Multiple and contradictory identities. Unlike traditional society in which people only have a narrow range of ascribed identities, in late-modern society we are usually offered a bewildering range of choices over social and cultural identities, including those based on gender identity, nationality, religion, family relationships, sexuality, occupation, leisure interests, political concerns, and more. As Giddens (1991) suggests, these identity 'choices' are not marginal but substantial ones, since they allow us to define who we want to be. But Giddens (ibid.: 73) emphasizes that '[t]aking charge of one's life involves risk, because it means confronting a diversity of open possibility.' One 'unfortunate' consequence of this condition is identity confusion.

Take for example a Chinese-American lecturing in the USA, who feels passionate about gay fiction but also about heterosexual pornographic movies, who loves both academic books and PlayStation games, and who supports feminism yet likes Sylvester Stallone's movies a lot. Who is 'he' actually? Gay, straight or bisexual? Is he really an American? Is he an intellectual or just a lowbrow who loves video games but pretends to be an intellectual? Can someone who loves macho movie stars like Sylvester Stallone still be a feminist?

Disrupted lives. Late-modern society is always undergoing rapid and extensive change, and accordingly, our lives and sense of stable self-identity are prone to disruption more than ever: a CEO who loses his job and cannot find another post for years may have serious doubts about his identity as a member of the middle-class elite; an American girl who moves to Paris to be with her French fiancé may feel totally disoriented in a new country; a man who has been divorced five times may seriously question whether he can really be a 'good' husband in the future. Furthermore, victims of serious illness or injury may also feel uncertain about their identities and their ability to function as 'normal' people.

Stigmatized identities. We may be doubtful about certain identities of ours if these identity categories are controversial, stigmatized or unacceptable in society at large. For instance, a young woman who is attracted only to females may still feel uncertain about her sexuality, because she has been told for years in her traditional Catholic school that homosexuality is sinful.

So how do people with uncertain identities re-establish their stable sense of self-identity? Giddens (1991) argues that, in late-modern society, we construct our sense of self-identity by creating a 'coherent' self-narrative. In such a coherent self-narrative, we successfully make ourselves the protagonist of the story, and we know clearly who we are, how we became the way we are now, and what we would like to do in the future—all these elements help to give us a stable sense of self-identity. However, if our identities are being challenged by new events or experiences, the coherence of our self-narrative can be disrupted, and we may experience an unstable and confused sense of self. In order to re-establish a stable sense of identity, we have to reflexively reappraise and revise our 'disrupted' self-narrative until its sense of coherence is restored. Take, for example, how the aforementioned CEO may rework his self-narrative when his identity as a member of the middle-class elite becomes uncertain as a result of his long-term unemployment. He may insist on finding work as another CEO, and interpret his long-term unemployment as just one of the roadblocks that all successful people might face at some point. In this case, he makes minor modifications to his middle-class elite self-narrative, but the overall meaning of the narrative remains unchanged. Alternatively, he may choose to abandon his middle-class elite identity and adopt a new 'simple-life-is-good' identity, and interpret his previous middle-class life as a worthwhile experience, without which he would not have been able to discover the true value of his new 'simple life' philosophy. In this case, he almost completely rewrites the overall meaning of his self-narrative. Anyhow, our concern here is not which concrete self-narrative this CEO finally adopts. Our point is rather that, if our sense of self-identity becomes uncertain, it is only through reflexive reappraisal and revision of our self-narrative that we can re-establish a stable sense of self-identity. Giddens describes this process as 'the reflexive project of the self.'

The personal homepage is a form of media which facilitates the reflexive project of the self. I mentioned in the last section that people who use their homepages for self-presentation can lay out, arrange, retouch and manipulate their 'homepage selves' until the outcome reflects the self-identities they intend to present. But for people with uncertain identities, or with a more free and fluid sense of self, this flexible creative process has a totally different meaning—experimentation and

exploration of different identities. As Rosenstein (2000: 153) suggests, the 'hyper-media qualities of the home page can support linear, chronological narratives, but . . . they also lend themselves to a more episodic, situated and associational organization of materials that may be quite diffuse thematically and even spatially.' In other words, the hypertextuality of the personal homepage enables those authors who are in search of their self-identities—or who are happy to 'play' with their identities—to construct different self-narratives on their homepage and mull over which narrative (or narratives) makes most sense to them. This self-exploration process is akin to conducting internal dialogues within one's mind: 'I can be this or that, but who do I want to be?' However, the internal dialogue as a method of self-exploration has one major limitation. Since this dialogue is an internal mental process, it does not have any physical record. It is impossible to retrieve our internal dialogues conducted in the past without any loss and distortion of thoughts. In contrast, self-narratives on the personal homepage have a physical existence (at least as stored in webpage format) which can be completely retrieved for further self-contemplation whenever the author wants to. Undoubtedly, the self-narratives we compose in traditional written media such as a diary or biography also have a physical existence, but these forms often lack the revisability of the personal homepage, which allows or even invites the author to continually amend his or her homepage self-narratives. As Chandler (1998) suggests, completion of any personal homepages 'may be endlessly deferred' since every homepage is always 'under construction.'

In fact, recent research shows that people with uncertain identities have started to use the personal homepage to reflexively explore and reconstruct their identities. Personal homepages 'permit some authors to explore aspects of themselves in ways that they have never previously done,' claims Hevern (2000: 14). As one homepage author admitted: 'It helps to define who I am. Before I start to look at/write about something then I'm often not sure what my feelings are, but after having done so, I can at least have more of an idea' (Chandler, 1998). Another author commented: 'as a process for doing, for seeing yourself reflected on a screen, being able to draw connections where there weren't connections is really rich' (Rosenstein, 2000: 154).

By continually exploring and clarifying their thoughts and feelings, some people use the personal homepage to reclaim a sense of identity which is continuous with their previous one. As one homepage author who relocated from New York to California said: 'Moving to a place where I had to make so many changes, I needed a way to convince myself I was still okay and the things that were important to me are still important' (Rosenstein, 2000: 159). Some authors, however, may fashion new identities. For example, by building websites which provide health information, people whose lives have been disrupted by serious accidents or chronic illness may successfully re-establish a positive identity, as a health information producer (Hevern, 2000).

The personal homepage surpasses the internal dialogue and other traditional media in one more respect. The internal dialogue and traditional diary writing are 'private' identity construction activities, the audience of which is generally the author him/herself. But the global reachability of the personal homepage enables the homepage author to get validatory feedback from net browsers who empathize or share with the author's identity or narrative. I am not arguing that we cannot consider our self-identities in the absence of others, but getting recognition from other people is still important for establishing affirmative identities. After all, if no one ever tells you that you are smart, for how long can you convince yourself that you really are?

This identity validation function of the personal homepage is also identified in recent research. Undeniably, some homepage authors do not actively *seek* readers at all (Rosenstein, 2000: 96–9). As one author said: 'I was the intended audience, as strange as it sounds' (Chandler, 1998). Yet, many homepage authors use the personal homepage to re-establish their self-identities by getting positive comments from other net browsers. One disabled homepage author said: 'Do you have any idea how many people wallow in self-pity, spend the rest of their lives crying about what happened to them? Through the Internet I have been challenged to grow, to blossom, to meet others who understand me' (Hevern, 2000: 15). A gay author said: 'I think we all sometimes need to know that, no matter how alone we feel, there are witnesses' (ibid.: 14). A Spanish-speaking homepage author explained his motive for homepage publishing this way: 'I was looking for other people that were my color or listened to my kind of music or spoke my family's language . . . I was really looking for a part of me out there that I could make contact with' (Rosenstein, 2000: 168).

REALITY CONSTRAINTS ON THE MAKING OF PERSONAL HOMEPAGES

So far, our story of the personal homepage appears quite heartening. But some critics tell a more gloomy story, cautiously warning us not to uncritically celebrate the emancipatory potentials of the personal homepage and the creative autonomy of the homepage author. This more pessimistic story can be divided into two parts: (1) concern that social background may preclude certain people from making personal homepages; and (2) the view that commercial and ideological factors may work against the expressive creativity of homepage authors.

Who Can Build Personal Homepages?

One key factor that influences people's chances of reaping the emancipatory benefits of the personal homepage is their Internet access. The reason is simple: if a social group has less Internet access than others, members of this social group will have less opportunities to build personal homepages and, accordingly, they are less likely to benefit from the emancipatory potential of this media genre. One factor which influences one's opportunities to access the Internet is country of residence. Take some countries as examples: the Internet access rate of people living in China is 3.5 per cent; France, 28.4 per cent; Germany, 38.6 per cent; Greece, 13.2 per cent; Iceland, 79.9 per cent; Malaysia, 25.2 per cent; Russia, 12.4 per cent; Singapore, 51.9 per cent; Sweden, 67.6 per cent; Spain, 19.7 per cent; Thailand, 7.4 per cent; United Arab Emirates, 36.8 per cent; United Kingdom, 57.4 per cent; United States, 59.1 per cent (these are 2002 figures; see Nua.com, 2003). Indeed, Internet statistics show that, in many countries, additional factors such as ethnicity, gender, age, educational attainment and income level may also affect Internet access, although the significance of individual factors varies greatly from country to country.

Statistics show that demographic factors like gender, age, occupational status and educational level have noticeable effects on levels of Internet access. For example, a survey shows that, in 15 Western European countries, females, manual workers, the elderly and the less educated have less Internet access than males, professionals, the young and the well educated (European Commission, 2002). The USA shows similar Internet access patterns (except that females and males have virtually identical Internet access rate in the USA; see below). Nevertheless, the specific extent to which each demographic factor affects the Internet access rate of individual social groups varies from country to country. Take gender as an example. According to a recent survey of Internet users in 25 developed countries, the Internet access rate of females varies from country to country: in France, females make up 40.8 per cent of total Internet users; Germany, 38 per cent; Sweden, 46 per cent; the UK, 44.5 per cent; the USA, 51.9 per cent. (Nielsen//NetRatings, 2002). In some countries like Romania and Ukraine, females occupy less than one-third of the total population of Internet users (Taylor Nelson Sofres Interactive, 2002).

But will equal Internet access bring about equal opportunities in making personal homepages? Not necessarily. In a study of the homepages produced by students at four US universities and four German universities, Döring (2002) finds that females only make up 27 per cent and 13 per cent of the student homepage authors in the US and German universities respectively, despite the fact that at all of these universities there was an equal balance of male and female students. One possible explanation is that females tend to feel alienated from the male-dominated computer culture, making them less motivated to learn website-building skills. In other words, even if females and males have similar opportunities to 'log on' to the Internet (as is already the case in certain countries), females may not have the same degree of motivation and learned skills to create and maintain personal websites. In short, equal Internet access does not necessarily mean equal opportunities in making personal homepages.

Dominick's (1999) study illustrates how factors such as gender, age and occupation may influence people's chances of making homepages. From 317 English-language personal homepages randomly sampled from the Yahoo! homepage directory, Dominick found that 87 per cent of homepage authors were men, 79 per cent were under the age of 30; more than half of those who mentioned an 'occupation' were students, and around 90 per cent of the rest were white-collar workers. This data suggests that females, the unemployed and blue-collar workers may have less chances of building homepages than other people. (Note, however, that the gender balance, at least, is likely to have changed since the mid-to-late 1990s when this study was conducted; and note that the sample is based only on those homepage owners who submitted their site to the Yahoo! directory, and had that submission accepted by Yahoo! staff.)

The Poverty of Self-Expression and Creative Constraints

Undeniably, those who have no opportunity to make personal homepages are unable to enjoy the emancipatory benefits of the personal homepage. However, it is not necessarily the case that people who have already made personal homepages for themselves are able to fully realize the emancipatory potential of this media genre. From his sample of 500 English-language personal homepages, Dominick (1999) found that 30 per cent of the pages were either abandoned or no longer available, and most of the remaining 'analysable' homepages had been produced with little creative effort, offering predictable elements such as a brief biography, an e-mail address, some authors' photos, or links to other sites. Only 12 per cent of those analysable homepages included in-depth biographies, and only 23 per cent contained 'creative expressions' like original poems or stories. Dominick argues that most personal homepages show nothing but superficial self-expression. It is perhaps no wonder that some critics will say that many personal homepages lack creativity and thoughtfulness, since many homepage authors build their websites not for self-presentation or identity construction, but for instrumental reasons like passing time, learning HTML, distributing information to peers, and so on. This argument, however, cannot really explain why some personal homepages which are built for the purpose of self-presentation or identity construction still lack thoughtful and in-depth self-expression (Killoran, 2002). To answer this question, we need to examine how commercial homepage providers and ideological forces suppress the expressiveness of homepage authors.

Commercial Homepage Providers

Using Yahoo! GeoCities as an example, Harrison (2001) offers a number of compelling critiques of how major commercial homepage providers may undermine users' freedom of self-expression on the personal homepage. Two of these criticisms are as follows.

Standardizing homepages. Yahoo! GeoCities provides novice homepage authors with sets of pre-created homepage 'templates.' These 'templates' offer homepage authors standardized suggestions of where to place text, images and links, and encourage them to add Yahoo! services to their homepages. (Other major commercial homepage providers like Tripod, Angelfire and AOL Hometown also offer similar 'simple' homepage building tools.) Although these 'templates' enable novices to build homepages without the need to learn more advanced website-building tools like HTML, they indirectly lead homepage authors to produce 'cookie-cutter' personal homepages (ibid.: 55–62).

Homepage content control. All Yahoo! GeoCities homepage authors have to abide by the Yahoo! Terms of Service, which allow Yahoo! GeoCities to delete without prior warning those homepages with content the company and its advertisers deem inappropriate (ibid.: 62–4). Indeed, most commercial homepage providers such as Tripod, Angelfire and AOL Hometown, also have content regulation policies, which grant them the right to remove any homepages at any time, for any reason, with or without notice. According to some journalists and homepage makers, personal homepages deleted by commercial homepage providers often contain 'sensitive' content, including anti-abortion, death penalty and anti-Malaysian government opinion, nude photos of the author, and information that directly criticizes certain commercial homepage providers. Recently Yahoo! has signed a voluntary pledge with the Chinese government, promising that Yahoo! China will avoid 'producing, posting or disseminating pernicious information that may jeopardize state security and disrupt social stability'; it also pledged to monitor personal websites and will 'remove the harmful information promptly' ("Yahoo's China Concession," 2002).

Ideological Forces

Killoran's (1998, 2002) study shows that the poverty of self-expression on personal homepages is also caused by the ideologies of commercial and bureaucratic organizations as well as commercial homepage providers. He argues that since the personal homepage is a new media genre, it has no established generic conventions which homepage authors can follow when representing themselves in this medium. Under these conditions, the well-established, powerful and prevalent ideologies of commercial and bureaucratic organizations tend to 'colonize' the speaking spaces of the authors. Consequently, homepage authors abandon the opportunity to explore their distinctive self-identities, and represent themselves as 'domesticated, innocuous subjects and objects of a capitalist and bureaucratic order' (Killoran, 2002: 27). Killoran describes this process in which personal homepage authors adopt commercial and institutional ideologies to express themselves as 'synthetic institutionalization.' He argues that when individuals present themselves using visual styles borrowed from brands, organizations or corporations, or with devices designed to attract returning viewers (such as the promise of regular updates), they suppress their own creative identities in favour of institutionalized conformity. (Of course, it could be argued that the homepage authors are often wittily parodying corporate language, and that the promise of a regularly updated site does not necessarily represent some kind of tribute to capitalist 'customer loyalty' schemes, as Killoran seems to think.)

Gender ideologies may also affect personal homepage design. . . . Hess (2002) found that, generally, female academics were more hesitant and cautious than males about putting their personal photos on their faculty homepage. Many female academics explicitly admitted that they feared their photos may 'give off' sexist impressions and encourage people who read their homepage to focus on their appearance rather than their academic work. As one female lecturer said:

> Putting my own picture on my webpage . . . seems like something that would allow people to see me as vain (like, 'Oh, she thinks she's so good looking she put her picture on the Web') or at least read outside a professional context. (Hess, 2002: 181)

Instead of resisting these ideological pressures, some female academics opt for self-censorship—they choose not to put their pictures on their homepage and become 'faceless' authors (see also Cheung, 2000, for a discussion of self-censorship).

CONCLUSION

My analysis clearly demonstrates that, although the personal homepage is an emancipatory media genre for some people, its emancipatory potentials have not yet benefited everyone. Many people may still lack the resources and technological knowhow to build their own personal homepage. Even for those who are capable of making personal homepages, their individual expressiveness might still be suppressed by content censorship of commercial homepage providers or ideological pressures. Some statistics show that the Internet access gap between countries is narrowing (UNCTAD, 2002), and that in many countries the Internet access gap by gender is closing rapidly (Nielsen//NetRatings, 2002). These trends certainly imply that more people will be able to build personal homepages. But it remains the case that many constraints upon making personal homepages will not disappear in the near future: low-income groups in many countries still have great difficulty accessing the Internet; ideologies of various types will continue to exist and suppress individual expression; and control over homepage content may also be further heightened by some homepage providers. If more people are to enjoy the emancipatory benefits of a personal homepage, we must endeavour to remove these constraints. Homepage authors need to protest against any censorship of homepage content practised by commercial homepage providers; non-profit organizations may seek ways to provide free Internet access, censorship-free website hosting services, and even free training courses on website-building skills; academics and critics should also find ways to raise awareness among homepage authors about the commercial and ideological constraints which may suppress self-expression on the personal homepage. Only through such efforts can we hope that more people will be able to use the personal homepage to work through their identities, or present their suppressed selves to audiences around the world. Indeed, in a world where many people are plagued by identity problems, enabling more people to fully realize the emancipatory potential of the personal homepage is a timely and important task.

REFERENCES

Chandler, D. 1998. Personal home pages and the construction of identities on the Web. www.aber.ac.uk/media/Documents/short/webident/html

Dominick, J. R. 1999. Personal home pages and self presentation. *Journalism and Mass Communication Quarterly* 76:646–58.

Döring, N. (2002). Personal home pages on the Web: A review of research. *Journal of Computer-Mediated Communication* 7(3).

Giddens, A. 1991. *Modernity and self-identity.* Cambridge: Polity Press.

Harrison, A. Where are they now? Online identities on the commercial Web. Unpublished master's thesis, Georgetown University.

Hess, M. 2002. A nomad faculty. *Computers and Composition* 19, 171–89.

Hevern, V. W. 2000. Alterity and self-presentation via the Web. Paper presented at the First International Conference on the Dialogical Self. Katholieke Universiteit Nijmegen, The Netherlands.

Killoran, J. B. 2002. Under construction. *Computers and Composition,* 19, 19–37.

Rosenstein, A.W. 2000. Self-presentation and identity on the World Wide Web. Unpublished Ph.D. Thesis, U of Texas, Austin.

Yahoo's China concession. *Washington Post*, August 19, 2002, p. A12.

SELF-PRESENTATION IN INTERACTION

28

Body Troubles

Women, the Workplace and Negotiations of a Disabled Identity

Isabel Dyck

(1999)

INTRODUCTION

Throughout the social sciences the influence of cultural studies, feminisms and the challenges of post-modernism and post-structuralism have made space for sustained debate over the nature of human subjectivity, its constitution and its transformations. Difference, identity and the notion of the embodied self are being explored from various disciplinary perspectives, with geography focusing investigation on issues of space and place. The body, too, is attracting attention as the linkages between identity and the experience of specific spaces and places are theorised.

AUTHOR'S NOTE: The research was funded by grants from the British Columbia Health Research Foundation and the Social Sciences and Humanities Research Council of Canada. The co-investigator of the study was Dr. Lyn Jongbloed, School of Rehabilitation Sciences, University of British Columbia. Both investigators carried out some interviews but the majority were conducted by the research assistant to the study, Roberta Bagshaw. Our greatest debt is to the women who generously gave of their time and energy in participating in the research.

Centring the body in inquiry in geography has primarily been through work of feminist geographers interested in the connection between the body and situated knowledges, and geographers concerned with questions of sexuality, but recently the 'deviant' body of disability has also emerged as a focus of investigation (see, for example, Dorn and Laws 1994; Moss and Dyck 1996; Park *et al.* 1998; *Environment and Planning D: Society and Space* 1997). This work points to the discursive construction of ideas about the body and its abilities, and how dominant representations may be negotiated and contested in the context of particular spaces and places as 'disabled' women construct the meanings and materialities of their everyday geographies.

The purpose of this chapter is to investigate such contestation as this occurs in the workplace, as the subjectivity of women with chronic illness, specifically multiple sclerosis (MS), is transformed as they struggle with their 'body troubles.' The women were living with a sometimes failing, often unreliable body and one difficult to control. The severity of the women's impairments varied, but at some point most had experienced a period of 'invisible' disability. That is, although women experienced symptoms that caused feelings of illness and prevented, or made difficult, certain activities, the women appeared healthy. While workplace experiences varied, identity issues were a common and sometimes a profoundly disturbing concern. . . .

BODIES, IDENTITIES, SPACES: THE EMBODIED SUBJECT

In this chapter I am interested in how ideas about the body, identity and space nexus can inform the interpretation of the stories of women with multiple sclerosis and their experiences in the workplace. The body is receiving growing attention in discussions of social theory. Several different approaches have been used in theorising the body, ranging from essentialist understandings, through social constructionism,

to the 'body as text' of post-structuralism. . . . The body . . . is rejected, for it is understood as constantly in the making, embodying and contributing to social relations, and with its capacities constituted within cultural and historical specific moments (Grosz 1994; Shilling 1993). Shilling (1993: 4), for example, suggests that bodies are malleable and that the body is an ongoing project, never finished, but always 'in the process of becoming.'

Anti-essentialist feminist scholars have been interested in the ways dominant discourses, constructed within gendered power relations are part of this process of 'becoming,' mediating women's experiences of the body and providing ways of interpreting such experiences. . . .

Microscale studies, focusing on the materiality of everyday life, provide a useful entry point to the interweaving of the discursive and the material in investigating the formation of identities (Moss and Dyck 1996). They also permit exploration of 'competing' discourses as subjectivities are constituted and transformed. In this chapter, I am particularly interested in the tensions between the inscriptive processes of biomedicine as a powerful, cultural construction depicting the body as an 'object of science' (Fox 1993; Good 1994), other inscriptions of the body, and women's own experiences of living with chronic illness, as these interplay in reconstituting the body and subjectivity. Wendell (1996: 117) writes of the social and cognitive authority of Western scientific medicine in describing 'our bodies to ourselves and others' but its lack of ways of talking about and explaining the lived experience of illness or disability. As she wryly comments (1996: 122) of her own illness experience, 'my subjective descriptions of my bodily experience need the confirmation of medical descriptions to be accepted as accurate and truthful.' This comment picks up a central issue faced by the women in the study discussed here. Their bodies have been 'marked' through the language and practices of biomedicine, but this inscription interweaves with their bodily and social experiences following diagnosis in complex ways. While the analysis is grounded in the women's accounts, the following questions were posed: for women with chronic illness, how does bodily change threaten a continuity in self and social identification? how do such women live and renegotiate their subjectivity as corporeal changes are accompanied by the body's changing meanings and representation in the workplace? if the body is in a state of ongoing transformation and definition, how do events challenging its continuity (as an embodied self) enter and change the routinely experienced links between materiality, representations and subjectivity in the women's lives? As described in the remainder of the chapter, the women's bodies were in a 'process of becoming' threatening former physical capabilities and self and social identities, and including a potential categorisation of 'disabled.' Yet it would be mistaken to view biomedical authority as uncontestable. There are possibilities for resistance. As women resisted and negotiated the formation of a disabled identity and the meanings attached to this, there was a recursive interplay between the material body, its discursive constructions, and the workplace as a specific site of interweaving social relations and space.

THE STUDY[1]

Qualitative methods were used to investigate women's everyday experiences of domestic and wage labour following diagnosis with MS. In-depth interviewing was chosen due to the method's ability to reveal the women's relationship to the complex layering of environment, through their accounts of their illness experience. Interviews were semi-structured in that various topic areas were to be covered, but the interviewers were guided by the issues raised by the women. The women were recruited from two sources: a local branch of the Multiple Sclerosis Society and a

neurological clinic specialising in MS.[2] The analysis here concerns thirty-one women in either part-time (twelve) or full-time (nineteen) employment. They ranged in age from 25 to 49 years. Diagnosis of MS is predominantly associated with white people; this biological 'fact' was reflected in that the women recruited were white. Fourteen were married or lived in a stable heterosexual relationship, seven were divorced or separated, and ten were single. The women's employment ranged from service, sales and clerical work to professional occupational categories, although most of those still in employment worked in managerial, technical or professional occupations. All lived within Greater Vancouver, British Columbia, Canada. Interviewing produced many pages of detailed accounts of the women's day-to-day experiences in their home, neighbourhood and work environments following diagnosis. A thematic, interpretive analysis was employed, involving careful reading of all transcripts and a constant comparison across the women's accounts by the author and a coinvestigator interested in policy issues. In this chapter I focus on the issue of disclosure and on women's restructuring of the workplace as they struggled with their bodily changes.

Limited space precludes an extensive drawing on verbatim quotes from the interview transcripts; those I use are chosen as typical of women's concerns, although the particularities of the women's situations differed. As in any research concerned to link the particular with broader political economy relations, an attempt is made to balance the commonalities in women's experiences and the specificity of context in the analysis. However, in the interests of maintaining the women's anonymity details of context and demographic characteristics are not provided for each individual. Consistent with the aim of drawing on the women's voices in explicating my argument, however, I introduce the main issue addressed in the chapter with interview excerpts then contextualised in a brief summary of the two women's current situation:

Helen:	MS is very inconvenient. It's inconvenient because it doesn't show.
Interviewer:	Okay, what do you mean then?
Helen:	Well, I mean you can sit there, I mean I look perfectly healthy.
Interviewer:	Right.
Helen:	You don't know that my right leg's numb and maybe half my face is numb, that if I close my eyes I'll fall over. You don't know that I am tired, it doesn't show.
Elaine:	I don't have a problem with it right now . . . I only have a slight problem on my left side and nobody can notice it. And my speech is slurred occasionally but it's usually just when I'm tired.

Multiple sclerosis is a chronic and often progressive neurological disease which may be manifested in a variety of symptoms, but commonly involves profound fatigue and sensory and motor disturbances. Both 'Helen' and 'Elaine' were employed full time in positions in which career success and security were tied to high performance standards in the workplace. Helen was married with two teenagers, while Elaine was unmarried and living alone. The women talked about themselves as 'invisibles,' a category used by women in the study to distinguish between those with hidden disabilities and those who had clearly observable manifestations of the disease. Both recounted their struggles in maintaining their performance and position in the workplace. These struggles were not confined to physical difficulties in carrying out job-related tasks but extended to identity issues. While Helen's disability was in doubt, as her colleagues found it hard to understand she was sick when her body looked 'perfectly healthy,' Elaine in contrast was more concerned with appearing well and concealing disabling symptoms. She had not disclosed her illness in the workplace. Like other women in the study, their present concerns are subsequent to a process of biomedical inscription, starting with diagnosis, in which their body was defined as 'diseased' with a considerable, but uncertain, potential to become disabled.[3]

RESCRIPTING THE BODY: CHANGING POSSIBILITIES, CHANGING SUBJECTIVITIES

A recurrent theme in the women's accounts of their workplace experiences and decision-making was that of the medical uncertainty accompanying diagnosis. Diagnosis represented a point at which a biomedical script was drawn on in depicting and explaining a woman's changing experience of her body. For most of the women considerable medical uncertainty had accompanied such naming and explanation of their symptoms and ongoing illness experience. Diagnosis had often followed several months or even years of puzzling, sometimes transient, and debilitating symptoms. This period of illness was described by the women as a time when they felt a loss of control of their body. Eventual diagnosis brought relief to many women, in the sense of legitimising women's own illness experience and one that might have been doubted by others, whether physicians, family members, friends, or work colleagues, but the biomedical script also brought continuing uncertainty. Although it is known in biomedical science that MS is a progressive neurological disease with the potential for severe disability, there are various courses the disease may take. Women may have periods of remission with minimal or no symptoms or their bodily capacities may deteriorate steadily although with an unknown temporality. There is no known cure, although management strategies may relieve symptoms.

The women's 'reading' of the biomedical discourse describing their bodies and the material changes in them, however, varied and was interpreted within the context of their everyday relationships and day-to-day routines. Some talked explicitly about the tension between the text of MS and their own experience: while symptoms might match the information conveyed in the medical explanation, their meaning to women was not adequately covered by a medical focus and its terminology. The inadequate fit between the authoritative script of biomedicine and women's own bodily experiences was an issue that became a particular struggle in the workplace. The meaning of hidden disability varied for the women, but for all there was a destabilisation of identity that came into sharp definition in the workplace. The next sections focus on how women negotiated changes to the body's corporeality and the meanings conveyed by a biomedical scripting as their positioning in the labour force and its associated rewards were threatened.

THE WORKPLACE AS A PLACE OF RISK: FRAGMENTING IDENTITIES, DESTABILISED MEANINGS

Various strategies were employed by the women as they negotiated the changes in their material body and its associated meanings in the home, in large part away from the public gaze (Dyck 1998). In contrast, the workplace, reflecting the organisation of commodified labour within the social relations of capitalism, was for many women one where performative capacities were at a premium, and often visible to others. Abilities making up workplace performance were written into workplace social practices, whether informally or through policy. For instance, the lack of seating for retail store sales clerks or supermarket cashiers means that women having difficulty standing for long periods will lose such employment. In other work environments informal social practices that have become normative cues for behaviour, such as climbing stairs to the office instead of using the elevator, or

a high-paced work 'culture,' pose a threat to women's identity performance in the workplace. Struggles around the meaning of having MS in the workplace, as this related to work abilities, was a point of tension for many women, exemplified in one woman's comment:

> It's up to me to say whether I'm being affected to the point that I cannot do my job, not for them to say that. So, I just don't feel that I should be sick at this point in my life. Because I'm not ready, you know?

Although the demands of specific settings varied widely, for most women the workplace became a place of risk. Not being able to perform 'as usual' potentially threatened women's financial stability, and consequential access to a range of resources and opportunities, including housing. A woman's position as a social being in the world was also challenged. Threats to self-identity were commonly voiced. Women were concerned about being treated differently by others, and struggled with their own identity as an 'able self' as their performative acts no longer consistently matched their former interpretation of their 'place in the world.' Such an interweaving of concerns was expressed by one woman in the following way:

> I enjoyed me immensely and . . . you know, one of my big tasks since I've been diagnosed has been trying to . . . deal with changing that image. . . . I just don't want to identify with the disabled. But I think that that's only part of it . . . I think that there's discrimination out there that I don't know what to do with.

Other women drew a close association between their ability to work and both their self and social identity. One woman who had returned to employment stated:

> Working part time gives you this whole—not only a little bit more money, but it gives you this whole thing . . . because we have this culture that if you don't have a job . . . you're not a person. And then if you tell that you don't have a job because you're on

long-term disability—I mean you're even less of a person. . . . Even if you're working 15 hours . . . you have a place—you have an employer and you have a job and you have this thing that you do.

The intertwining of an able identity and work participation is implicated in the resources available to women. The material and financial rewards of a place of employment are jeopardised in part by physical limitations that circumscribe which job tasks women can or cannot continue to do. In addition, the representation in discourse of the body as diseased comes into play in the meanings attributed to women's performance in the workplace. The biomedical 'scripting' of the body provides an authoritative set of descriptions and meanings through which to interpret the women's struggles with their bodies. Women with hidden disabilities were often unsure of the implications of declaring their biomedical diagnosis, expressed in a common anxiety and dilemma surrounding the issue of disclosure.

Disclosure of diagnosis represented a pivotal and dynamic moment in which a 'marked' identity, that of disabled, had a potential to be 'fixed' with uncertain consequences for the women. While some women had greater control over their work environment than others, commonly cited fears associated with disclosure in employment situations included being unable to get work, losing a job, failing to gain promotion, or jeopardising eligibility for disability insurance or pensions. Yet women were also aware that a diagnosis may be drawn on in different ways as they negotiated their position in the labour force. It did not necessarily convey a single meaning. Its public knowledge may constitute a threat to continued employment, with consequent social marginalisation, but may also provide women with access to a social safety net of disability benefits and pensions, and sometimes access to help on the job allowing the completion of work tasks. In the next sections I explore women's management of meanings about their

destabilised identities and 'diseased' bodies. Central to the strategies of most was resistance to the dominant biomedical conceptions of their bodies as diseased and particular interpretations of this in the workplace.

NEGOTIATING THE WORKPLACE AND DEFERRING MEANINGS

Industrialisation, capitalism and the commodification of labour have been important in shaping the conditions under which dominant meanings of health, illness and disability and their categorisation are constructed (Barton 1996; Oliver 1990; Park *et al.* 1998; Zola 1991). Post-structuralist writing, however, suggests that meanings can be deferred and transformed, with a potential for their re-territorialisation as new meanings to be acted upon and bodies and spaces to be reinscribed (see, for example, Fox 1993, for the case of medicine). The women's accounts of their workplace experiences indicate slippage of meanings around the dichotomous categories of able/disabled, over which they struggled and in part managed through spatial strategies.

Helen, quoted at the beginning of this chapter, found her work colleagues underestimated or doubted the severity of her illness due to the invisibility of her symptoms, despite their legitimation through a medical diagnosis, but other women were concerned to remain invisible and hide their diagnosis. Non-disclosure and the concealment or management of symptoms were common strategies employed by women to manage this 'secret knowledge' and defer its meanings, as they negotiated both their ability to work and the threat to their able identity. Women may have disclosed their diagnosis in other contexts, for example to family members and friends, but disclosure in the workplace was resisted by women attempting to maintain the integrity of their existing social identity. This was particularly the case when there was a disjuncture between what women felt they were able to do and the meanings evoked by a diagnosis that suggested disability. Women whose symptoms were in remission might work for long periods with no or minimal symptoms, but exacerbations made concealment more problematic or impossible. Visibility of symptoms was situational too, occurring for some women only with tasks requiring mobility, or following the accumulation of physically demanding tasks over a day. The importance of appearing able was voiced by several women. One, for instance, talked of being upset when she had gone through periods of having to use a cane, 'I always look the same, but of course I have a cane and I'm limping and I don't look like I know what I'm doing, right?'

The ability of women to employ concealment strategies was linked not only to the severity of their symptoms, but also to the temporal-spatial organisation of work tasks. The management of space was integral to concealing deteriorating physical capacity. This included strategies such as avoiding walking and climbing stairs when possible, and the organisation of work tasks so that they were spread over more than one workspace, sometimes including the home. Each strategy involved the management of the body in the workplace in ways that reduced attention to its limitations. These are illustrated through examples from several women's descriptions of dealing with the issue of disclosure. Non-disclosure at work for one woman, for example, was facilitated by work assignments that took place in a variety of different spaces, as well as flexible work hours. Her work involved meeting clients in their workplaces, and her control over work scheduling allowed her to pace her travel and appointments in such a way that she was able to appear well and work competently. Her main problem of fatigue was accommodated by this scheduling and use of space. Another woman who had difficulty with handwriting took some of her work home, where she transcribed shakily written notes she would previously have given to a secretary.

Women in various forms of higher level sales involving work with professional clients used a variety of spatial strategies in avoiding the appearance of being disabled. One woman always allowed clients to leave the office ahead of her to cover the difficulty she had standing up from her chair and her limping. Another avoided lengthy tours of work sites when feeling fatigue by claiming time constraints and the need to get to another appointment.

Attempts by women to maintain the appearance of an able identity through substituting one way of moving through the physical environment of the workplace by another might be jeopardised, such as when the alternative was not consistent with workplace norms. For example, using an elevator instead of stairs was a common way of managing the physical environment for women with fatigue or mobility difficulties, but often women felt a need to provide a rationale. Similarly, being able to 'fake it' as one woman put it, sometimes involved a withdrawal from workplace social activities that were considered part of workplace collegiality. One strategy adopted in providing a rationale for lack of participation in an activity was claiming another illness or physical problem as the cause of difficulties in performance, which was perceived by women as less stigmatising than MS. A woman, for example, whose fatigue problems could be handled through a routine management of time and space, had difficulty when she was away from home at conferences. She explained her need to go to bed early or lie down and rest during the day as due to a back problem, a reason she saw as more socially acceptable than MS. Another, whose increasingly unsteady walking became a problem in a work environment that involved a good part of the day walking, standing and the use of stairs, avoided disclosure of her MS for several weeks as a broken ankle precluded these activities. Flu was the legitimising reason given by another woman for time taken off work due to an exacerbation of MS symptoms. Part of her job required walking outside from building to building to transfer information and a co-worker took over this task when she was first back to work, on the basis of her still recovering from flu. Another who had been asked what was wrong with her legs, replied 'I twisted my ankle.'[4]

The potential stigma of MS, together with uncertainty concerning access to long-term disability insurance for some women, were considerations for women struggling with the issue of disclosure. Yet, unless women enjoy a long remission of symptoms or symptoms are minimal, it is unlikely disclosure can be avoided in the longer term, particularly when women have little control of their work conditions. Furthermore, women in jobs requiring long periods of standing or other physically demanding activity had few options to use space in a way conducive to minimise symptoms or their visibility. By the time of the interviews most of the women had, in fact, disclosed and their diagnosis of MS was known in the workplace.

Negotiation and Contestation of Workplace Meanings

Following disclosure some women who appeared healthy found their claims of illness doubted by unsympathetic co-workers or supervisors, but more usually women remaining in employment had found supportive work colleagues and respect for their self-declared limitations. This is to be expected in the context of this study in that those able to retain their job were necessarily working under conditions where such support allowed this. Disclosure, however, was often selective with only an employer, supervisor or a few close colleagues being privy to this knowledge. This was particularly the case when women were in an environment with many co-workers or where they were able to carry out job tasks without major adjustments to tasks or the physical arrangement of the environment.

The demands of some jobs, particularly in sales and some service occupations, precluded continued employment for some women who had little option of occupational change without further training. For example, a hairdresser was forced to quit her job whereas a nurse with similar physical limitations was able to transfer to a job with lighter physical requirements. Being able to work part time or with flexible hours allowed some women to remain in the labour force. For others spatial strategies continued to be an important part of being able to retain employment in a variety of occupations, although now with the knowledge and cooperation of employers or colleagues. One woman, for example, who had difficulty walking omitted coffee breaks, taking instead a long lunch break and so decreasing the amount of walking required to reach the coffee room. Another working in a secretarial position had been able to continue to work through a rearrangement of the photocopying tasks required, accumulating these and doing them once a day and so reducing the amount of walking she had to do. Some workplaces had a room or a couch available for resting, but few made use of this provision. As one woman said, 'I have to give 110 per cent just to prove that I'm really with it and I can really do it: I wouldn't feel comfortable [lying down].' Her comment echoed other women's continuing desire to be seen as able to do their jobs well, although accommodations might have been made.

The sociopolitical organisation of the workplace also became important, with distinctions between unionised and non-unionised workplaces, public corporations and private sector companies, and with public service institutions concerned with health and education forming a further dimension in shaping women's experiences. Women most vulnerable to loss of employment were those in non-unionised, private sector jobs, of low seniority, and with little control in the scheduling or organisation of job tasks. One of the women, working in retail sales, for example, talked of the store management's gradual reduction in her hours and her feeling that she had been harassed out of her job. Other women with greater control of their work environment were more able to contest and negotiate normative meanings and practices of the workplace and, through this, their own position in the labour force. For example, an elementary school teacher discontinued supervising extra-curricular activities and resisted the scheduling of informal or formal meetings with staff, students or parents in lunch times or coffee breaks, which she needed to preserve as rest times. Those women most able to restructure their work environments in order to maintain their relationship to the labour force and its material and social rewards were those in employment situations willing and able to provide flexibility, whether in hours, pace or the organisation of workplace tasks. Seniority and 'track record' on the job were also important in some workplace settings in influencing responses to women's changing abilities. One woman, for example, who had worked in community health services with most of her work involving travel to different community settings had a job created for her which drew on her experience and skills, but was office based.

Workplace organisation, located within social relations shaped by political economy, the social practices of the workplace, and women's own work histories all circumscribe the range of options they have in responding to their illness experience. Furthermore, women are positioned differently in the relations and distributions of power that shape their future employment opportunities. Those with higher levels of education and jobs in professional and managerial occupations generally were more able to maintain their employment, at least for a period. Class positioning was therefore a dimension of women being able to control conditions in the workplace and being less vulnerable to surveillance practices. However, the situation is more complicated than one of class for some occupations with high performance expectations which require visible performance as an 'able' worker, just as in lower paid service work.

The workplace, too, may be open to reinterpretation, although again this is more possible for women with greater control over work conditions. For many of the women in this study, for example, negotiations of tasks, hours and space were ways of contesting dominant meanings of the workplace as a place for the 'healthy', able body as women redefined their relationship to their work environment. At this level women acted as individuals. One woman's situation, however, demonstrates the collective politicisation of her struggle in the workplace. While unusual among the women in the study, her situation helps to show the grounding of processes involved in the formation of a disabled identity and its embodiment in the contextual specificity of everyday material practices. It also demonstrates that dominant workplace meanings and practices can be contested, resulting in a redefinition of the workplace and the relationship of those with a 'disabled' identity within it. Her account includes, and brings together, components of other women's stories as it spans the time from her initial employment, her struggles with her body and identity, and her reinscription of herself and the workplace. As such, it acts as an empirical summary of the main issues of the paper. It speaks to commonalities among the women, while acknowledging the particular linkages of their personal histories with the work environment as a physical and social space located within wider political economy relations.

The woman, a teacher in a higher education institution, had been diagnosed with MS before she applied for her job. She did not disclose her diagnosis, although she felt uncomfortable not doing so at the time. She had weighed the pragmatism of getting a job, believing that knowledge of her disease might preclude this, against her personal scruples. She believed herself capable of doing the job and managed this through restricting her social life, cutting out extra-curricular college events and using concealment strategies in the workplace. Her symptoms worsened, however, and she could no longer work in what was a full-time position. She commented on her experience of working prior to this time:

> I'd been there three years with nobody knowing and that felt awful . . . withholding, walking around with that knowledge, and worry . . . I made up little stories about—why you don't take the stairs, why you don't go to the dance, why you don't do this and that . . . the answer to the questions always in my mind was MS, but that's not something I shared . . . so the whole thing felt quite foreign to me and to what I knew about myself, to what I'd done before.

Following a later improvement in health and a reorganisation of living space that reduced the demands of her household labour she felt able to work again, but part time. However, the only position to become available was defined as full time. With the encouragement of colleagues in the same unionised workforce she applied for the position but was not offered it. She said, 'I was the most senior person applying . . . [but] because I couldn't work full time they offered it to another person, so then we grieved it.' She and the union embarked on a grievance process, wanting to establish that the only reason for her not getting the job was that she could not work full time. After a long process involving the aid of a lawyer as several steps of the grievance process were gone through, eventually the grievance was resolved in her favour, and she received a contract for a permanent part-time position. She commented on the process, noting that she could not have won the case without the union but also saying:

> The only reason I didn't have a permanent job was not because of my ability or my experience or my recommendations, it was simply because I couldn't work full time . . . And that's what was so hard for me . . . because I had a career full of successes . . . and now here I was and I couldn't even get somebody to give me a permanent job . . . [I] felt so belittled by everything. At the same time the disease is ravaging my body, it's also ravaging my mind and my spirit, so I really needed to win that one. And I'm still feeling good about that . . . not marginalised, I'm legitimate.

This woman, like others in the study, had initially negotiated the work environment through her body in the form of concealment strategies, but once her ability to work full time became unrealistic for her, her body became a politicised site of struggle. The scripting of her body by bio-medicine and disclosure receded as issues of importance become irrelevant over time, to be replaced by a struggle over the tension between her bodily capacity and the normative, performance demands of the workplace. The struggle for employment was a struggle over both identity and body. This case of the redesignation of an employment opportunity to accommodate a woman's inability to work full time serves as apt example of the contestation of socially imposed meanings of the workplace and resistance to key players who order and interpret workplace practices. The workplace was an important site in the transformation of the woman's subjectivity and its embodiment, her winning of the case interrupting the formation of a disabled identity. Furthermore, just as her 'disabled' identity was reinscribed as 'able,' under the specific and negotiated conditions of employment, so too the meaning of the performative standards of the workplace were redefined.

DISCUSSION AND CONCLUDING REMARKS

It is likely the women of the study would agree, at least to some extent, with Wendell's (1996) comment about the need for subjective descriptions of bodily experience to be confirmed by medical descriptions in order to be accepted as valid and truthful. Certainly those that 'look perfectly well' need this legitimation to have their illness claims taken seriously, whether in negotiating workplace performance or gaining access to resources reserved for the disabled, such as long-term disability insurance or the Canada Pension Plan. For women with MS whose symptoms are in remission or transient, and who are able to work with the support of co-workers and various symptom management strategies, the potential or experienced stigmatising effects of their diagnosis is resisted by its concealment when possible. For them, disclosing their biomedical scripting may close off employment opportunities or open up possibilities for renegotiating their work tasks and conditions, depending on how employers 'read' and interpret such an inscription in relation to the work practices of a particular workplace. Disclosure of a diagnosis of MS was an important moment in the reconstitution of women's subjectivity. A disabled identity may become 'fixed' but with different consequences for women as they negotiate their position in the labour force.

Workplaces are recursively implicated in the reconstitution of subjectivity as women become defined as 'disabled.' As environments comprised of a layering of social relations and spatial organisation they provide the specificities of context for that cultural 'moment' of the discursive and material inscription of a disease category on women's bodies. However, the salience of a disabled identity may vary from setting to setting. Furthermore the concealment strategies women use to 'cover' potentially stigmatising symptoms and the case of the woman who worked with a union in resisting her social marginalisation indicate that the meanings and boundaries of what constitutes the workplace are potentially unstable. Hegemonic notions of the workplace and appropriate workers can be contested.

The women's accounts of their struggles with their body troubles support the argument that the corporeal body is continually in the process of 'becoming' as suggested by Shilling (1993), and always interpreted through available scripts, whether these be about ableness/disability, class, gender, 'race', sexuality, age, religion, caste or other axes of social differentiation accompanied by different insertions in distributions of power. These culturally produced scripts may be powerful, attaining a hegemony of understanding of the body, inclusive of ideas of ability or disability, but they may be resisted as women negotiate their identities and bodies in the materiality of their everyday lives. Yet there are limits to this resistance through individual body politics. Those inserted differently in distributions of power, such as supervisors, employers and disability insurance assessors, are in a position to use their interpretations, backed by a biomedical inscription, to contest or support women's attempts to renegotiate their position as participants in the labour force. Even when the body becomes a collectively politicised site of resistance, a woman will be constrained in the extent to which she can reinscribe herself in relation to a work environment. Relations of political economy forge the conditions of the workplace, although inclusive workplace policy and affirmative action may protect the position of workers in some settings. The divide between able to work or 'disabled' is one imposed through the machinations of social policy and private insurance schemes, rather than one that reflects the bodily experience of chronic illness as talked about by the women of this study.

To be able or disabled carries different connotations for the women. It is not a unitary experience, and how the biomedical script is drawn on varies, and conveys different meanings in different sites of interaction. As women struggle to defer meanings about their (dis)ability they do so within discursive and material practices, as played out in the particularities of time and space. The contingencies and local social and material practices of specific workplaces frame the fixing of the category of 'disabled,' and often place a woman in the oppositional category she sought to avoid. Such practices producing subjectivity, and its embodiment as microscale geographies and identity intertwine, are located within cultural and historical specificities (Walkerdine 1995). 'Coming out' as disabled is not just a personal moment but one embedded in processes of categorisation that rely on dualistic epistemologies that then maintain categories

(Pile 1994). As Natter and Jones (1997) comment, the category is a generalising and homogenising moment which serves to constitute both self and other. To be both able and disabled, or situationally or variably so, does not find a ready place within practices informed by biomedical representations of health, illness, disease, disability and body. As women make claims to the paid workplace through spatial practices, and experience exclusions from it, they are therefore also contesting claims of authenticity about the world. Their bodies have been marked through the language of biomedicine, but their performative abilities are reinterpreted as this inscription interweaves with their bodily and social experiences in complex ways in particular workplace contexts.

Notes

1. A second, separate, phase of the study consisted of a questionnaire survey, which derived its questions from this qualitative study. This is reported separately in Jongbloed (1996).

2. Reflections on the recruitment process in the context of feminist methodology can be found in Dyck (1996).

3. I use the terms sick and ill(ness) to indicate the experiential dimensions of symptoms associated with MS. Disease refers to the diagnosis of MS as represented in biomedicine. Disability is used to indicate limitations in performance in the context of the specificity of a workplace.

4. The women usually had neither the time or the energy to be involved in support groups. They were commonly isolated from other women with MS with whom such strategies might have been shared.

References

Barton, L. (ed.) (1996) *Disability and Society: Emerging Issues and Insights,* London: Longman.

Bell, D. (1995) 'Pleasure and danger: the paradoxical spaces of sexual citizenship,' *Political Geography* 14: 139–54.

Butler, J. (1990) *Gender Trouble: Feminism and the Subversion of Identity,* New York: Routledge.

Chouinard, V. (1997) 'Making space for disabling difference: challenging ableist geographies,' *Environment and Planning D: Society and Space* 15: 379–87.

Dorn, M. L. (1998) 'Beyond nomadism: the travel narratives of a "cripple"', in H. Nast and S. Pile (eds) *Places Through the Body,* New York: Routledge, 183–206.

Dorn, M. and Laws, G. (1994) 'Social theory, body politics, and medical geography: extending Kearns's invitation,' *The Professional Geographer* 46: 106–10.

Dyck, I. (1995) 'Hidden geographies: the changing life-worlds of women with disabilities,' *Social Science and Medicine* 40: 307–20.

_____. (1996) 'Whose body? Whose voice?', *Atlantis* 21: 54–62.

_____. (1998) 'Women with disabilities and everyday geographies: home space and the contested body,' in R. A. Kearns and W. M. Gesler (eds) *Putting Health into Place: Landscape, Identity and Wellbeing,* Syracuse: Syracuse University Press, 102–09.

Environment and Planning D: Society and Space (1997) 'Special issue: Geographies of Disability' 15: 379–480.

Featherstone, M., Hepworth, M. and Turner, B. (eds) (1991) *The Body: Social Process and Cultural Theory,* London: Sage.

Fox, N. J. (1993) *Postmodernism, Sociology and Health,* Buckingham: Open University Press.

Frank, A. W. (1989) 'Bringing bodies back in: a decade review,' *Theory, Culture and Society* 7: 131–62.

Freund, P. and McGuire, M. (1991) *Health, Illness and the Social Body,* Englewood Cliffs, NJ: Prentice-Hall.

Good, B. J. (1994) *Medicine, Rationality and Experience,* Cambridge: Cambridge University Press.

Grosz, E. (1994) *Volatile Bodies: Toward a Corporeal Feminism,* Bloomington: Indiana University Press.

Jongbloed, L. (1996) 'Factors influencing employment status of women with multiple sclerosis,' *Canadian Journal of Rehabilitation* 9: 213–22.

Katz, C. and Monk, J. (1993) *Full Circles: Geographies of Women over the Life Course,* New York: Routledge.

Longhurst, R. (1995) 'The body and geography,' *Gender, Place and Culture* 2: 97–105.

Moss, P. (1997) 'Negotiating spaces in home environments: older women living with arthritis,' *Social Science and Medicine* 45: 23–33.

Moss, P. and Dyck, I. (1996) 'Inquiry into environment and body: women, work and chronic illness,' *Environment and Planning D: Society and Space* 14: 631–783.

Natter, W. and Jones, J. P. (1997) 'Identity, space and other uncertainties,' in G. Benko and U. Strohmayer (eds) *Space and Social Theory: Interpreting Modernity and Postmodernity,* Oxford: Blackwell Publishers, 141–61.

Oliver, M. (1990) *The Politics of Disablement,* London: Macmillan Press.

Park, D. C., Radford, J. P. and Vickers, M. H. (1998) 'Disability studies in human geography,' *Progress in Human Geography* 22, 2: 208–33.

Philo, C. (1996) 'Staying in? Invited comments on "Coming out: exposing social theory in medical geography" ', *Health & Place* 2: 35–40.

Pile, S. (1994) 'Masculinism, the use of dualistic epistemologies, and third spaces,' *Antipode* 26: 255–77.

Pile, S. and Thrift, N. (eds) (1995) *Mapping the Subject,* London: Routledge.

Rose, G. (1993) *Feminism and Geography,* Minneapolis: University of Minnesota Press.

Shilling, C. (1993) *The Body and Social Theory,* London: Sage.

Valentine, G. (1993) '(Hetero)sexing space: lesbian perceptions and experiences of everyday spaces,' *Environment and Planning D: Society and Space* 11: 395–413.

Walkerdine, V. (1995) 'Subject to change without notice: psychology, postmodernity and the popular,' in S. Pile and N. Thrift (eds) *Mapping the Subject,* London: Routledge, 309–32.

Wendell, S. (1996) *The Rejected Body,* London: Routledge.

Zola, I. K. (1991) 'Bringing our bodies and ourselves back in: reflections on a past, present and future "medical sociology" ', *Journal of Health and Social Behaviour* 32: 1–16.

PART V

THE SOCIAL CONSTRUCTION OF REALITY

If [people] define situations as real, they are real in their consequences.

—W. I. Thomas and Dorothy Thomas (1928),
The Child in America

[People] make their own history, but they do not make it just as they please; they do not make it under circumstances chosen by themselves, but under circumstances directly encountered, given and transmitted from the past. The tradition of all the dead generations weighs like a nightmare on the brain of the living.

—Karl Marx (1963),
The 18th Brumaire of Louis Bonaparte

BUILDING AND BREACHING REALITY

Jodi O'Brien

STORIES WE LIVE BY

Writer and philosopher Antonin Artaud once remarked that humans are beasts with stories on their backs. Interactional routines and the coherent realities through which these routines take on meaning can be analyzed as stories. We use these stories to organize and give meaning to our lives. Stories have an organizational logic to them. They are contextual realities that provide the scripts for defining the situation and the identities appropriate to the situation. One question you might ask is what the connection is between the "performance scripts" described in Part III and "stories" or "realities." Think of scripts as possible lines of action that can take place within a particular type of story. Types of stories are referred to as "genres." For instance, you are probably familiar with the differences between the horror genre and the romance genre. There are many different scripts that can be written within the horror genre, but you recognize each of them as a manifestation of the particular genre, because it has familiar characters, plots, and story lines.

Similarly, social realities can be recognized in the ways in which people share expectations about the story line, the types of characters, and associated behaviors and feelings. These story lines, or realities, are often taken for granted until someone steps out of character or violates expected routines. These disruptions may cause us to stop and momentarily reflect on the expected story line. We then respond to the disruptions in ways that end up either changing the routine or reinforcing it. One of the most common (but also most taken-for-granted) realities or stories in contemporary U.S. culture comes in the form of a "romance genre." According to this story, our main life quest is to find our "true mate," form a union together, produce biological offspring, and live happily ever after. Even persons who have chosen not to pursue this quest are implicated in the story to the extent that they are constantly asked by others to justify or make sense of their nonparticipation. This story is so prevalent that we tend to think it is "natural" for all humans to want to do this, even though the emergence of (heterosexual) romantic love as a basis for family organization is a relatively recent historical development.

The prevalence of this "marriage" cultural reality, or story, is revealed in the fact that persons who are of marrying age, but who are not married, are expected to give "accounts." In other words, they are expected to provide an explanation for why they are not participating in the cultural story as expected. Some accounts are more acceptable than others. Explaining that you have chosen to devote your life to the Roman Catholic priesthood is acceptable. Announcing that you are gay may not be entirely culturally desirable, but it makes sense in this particular context and is acceptable as an explanation. It is less acceptable, especially for women, to simply say "that doesn't interest me." Such a response is likely to raise suspicion among friends and family. "What is wrong with that girl?" they might wonder. They may even begin to speculate that "she is hiding something." Simply not wanting to participate is a behavior that disrupts the taken-for-granted expectation that "everyone wants to get married." Being a priest or being gay is an individual deviation from the expectation that *makes sense* and also reinforces the general expectation: "If he weren't a priest, he would probably be married." Conversely, having no interest at all in the cultural practice of marriage is a "breach" or disruption that leads people to press for more of an explanation, an explanation that "makes sense" within the existing story line that dictates that everyone must be interested in marriage.

When people feel compelled either to go along with a cultural practice or to provide a "reasonable" explanation for their deviation, the practice can be said to be "compulsory." In contemporary U.S. culture, most socialized individuals feel compelled either to consider marriage or to provide themselves and others with an explanation for their nonparticipation. It's important to understand that *both* the act of marrying and the act of providing explanations are "performances" that highlight and reinforce the significance of marriage as a cultural practice.

Other "compulsory" practices include being employed. One of the most common ways that strangers begin conversations with one another about their own stories is through the question "What do you do?" Presumably, this is one of those questions that everyone understands. Even young children learn early how to respond to the question "What does your daddy or mommy do?" If you take the question literally, you could have a lot of fun with people by responding in ways that do not assume the question is connected to employment: "I do yoga, I do a lot of lunches, I do my daily prayers," and so on. If you did this, chances are people would look at you as if you were a bit crazy.

Think of other cultural expectations that are taken for granted and considered "just something everyone knows." Consider the underlying cultural stories that hold these expectations together, for instance, the idea that self-worth is reflected in type of employment. Recall the discussion of the *generalized other* in Part III. Cultural stories are reflected in the stories we tell ourselves about who and what we can and should be. Whenever you find yourself judging or assessing yourself in terms of a "should," you are in conversation with external expectations that you have internalized into your own self-story.

This section of the book explores the way in which people collectively participate in writing, rewriting, and performing various cultural routines or stories. If you view human behavior as a form of living through story, it may be easier to comprehend how and why people disregard or reinterpret contradictory evidence and behave in a way that results in self-fulfilling prophecies. Cognitively, we tend to pay attention to things that resonate with the situational story that is unfolding in any given moment. Behaviors and experiences that disrupt the story line tend to be ignored or "explained away." By acting as if nothing unusual is going on, we are able to maintain the impression that everything is going as expected.

In this way, realities become self-sealing. We either find some way to incorporate our experiences into mutually understood stories, or we disregard the experiences as much as possible. This amazing feat of collective reality making is described in detail in this essay.

MAKING SENSE

It has been suggested throughout this book that humans are meaning makers. We make sense of our experiences by naming them. The way in which we define experiences and situations carries with it cues for how we should feel and behave. An aspect of meaning making that is important to the process of constructing realities is the way in which humans create "theories." We don't just assign meaning to situations, the meaning holds an underlying logic and coherency, a working theory for what is going on. When things don't go as expected, we search our stockpile of working theories for the situation and make sense of things accordingly. For example, if you have a friend who is "always late," then you probably have a working theory to apply when he doesn't show up to meet you at the movies as planned. "That's typical," you say to yourself. And the situation is resolved. Your friend may call you later to apologize ("I'm so sorry, I got held up"). This apology reinforces the general working story (we did have a date, and that carries certain expectations) as well as making sense of the disruption of the general working story. Imagine instead that you believed you had made appointments with several different people for various things, but none of them showed up. And no one called to apologize or explain. Later, you encounter one of these people, and the person acts as if nothing occurred, saying nothing about having stood you up. At this point, you would probably be confused and begin to wonder what was going on. You would search back and try to apply a working theory to make sense of this "breach" in expectations. It would probably continue to nag at you until you were able to make sense of the situation in a way that was consistent with your general expectations—people make appointments and follow through. Eventually, someone might explain to you that in this particular subculture, people say things all the time such as "let's do lunch," but never actually mean it. "Ah," you might say to yourself, "now I get it. People here are just rude." By deciding that people are "rude," you have reinforced your original cultural expectations and also found a way to make sense of the breach.

All human interaction is grounded in story lines for what is going on and underlying theories for making sense of things when they don't go as expected. These working theories are a central aspect of social realities. Even something as simple as the "Hi, how's it going?" acknowledgment routine reflects very specific cultural expectations and underlying theories. The actual words spoken are completely incongruent with the expected response. If you speak the greeting to someone and they don't respond, you have a working theory for why. The theory might include the possibilities "she didn't see me," "she's distracted," perhaps even "she's annoyed with me." However, it's not likely that you would wonder if, perhaps today, you're invisible. This explanation is simply not part of your working theory.

An unquestioned assumption in the greeting ritual is that people can see one another. Recall the reading in Part III about encounters with people who are deaf. Similar to the assumption that people can see you if you're in their presence, there is an assumption that people can hear you. When someone doesn't respond immediately to a statement "obviously" directed at them, we file through several explanations, including "he's just being a jerk," before we hit on the possibility that "hey, maybe he can't hear me." Working theories, like other ways of making sense, are also a combination of individual experience and cultural information about how to make sense of those experiences. One of the features of socially constructed realities is that we have working theories that enable us to *generate* a vast number of explanations for situations that don't make sense, but even these theories are a product of social interaction.

Another feature of socially constructed realities is that they contain a great deal of information that "everyone just knows." However, taken literally, this knowledge may seem strange and contradictory when viewed out of context. In the acknowledgment routine described above, most people know that in response to this greeting, they are not supposed to actually go into detail about "how it's going." Someone who did so might be considered a little "off." In contrast, many people who are new to U.S. culture find this greeting routine perplexing: Why would you ask someone how they are and then not stop to hear the answer?

COMMON SENSE

This basic "what everyone knows" knowledge of "reality" is called *common sense*. Common sense is a set of shared cultural rules for making sense of the world. These rules are so well established and taken for granted that they often require no justification. To the question "How did you know that?" or "Why did you do that?" one can reply simply, "It's just common sense." These rules are the bedrock of cultural knowledge; they seem obviously true.

One of the most powerful ways of demonstrating that reality is a social construction is to show the limitations and arbitrariness of common sense, either by pointing out inconsistencies or by contrasting one culture's common sense to another's. One very popular counterculture book in the 1960s was written by two sociologists, Peter Berger and Thomas Luckmann (1966). In this book, *The Social Construction of Reality,* Berger and Luckmann describe the ways in which people create organizing systems with the intent of making their lives orderly and predictable. Eventually, they forget they were the creators of these systems, and, thus reified, the systems take on a life of their own. What were once useful recipes for living become calcified into "common sense" beliefs that "everyone knows."

There are several profound implications of "common sense" or socially constructed realities. Self-fulfilling prophecies and the (re)creation of the cultural status quo are two that are worth extensive discussion. Before turning to those implications, let's look in detail at some of the ways in which people actively work together, usually unknowingly, to create and recreate the stories and theories that we use for making sense.

A THEORY OF REALITY

Ethnomethodology is a research area in sociology that explores the folk methods ("ethno methods") that people use to construct systems of meaning and reality. Ethnomethodologists make visible the often invisible or unseen features of reality construction. Hugh Mehan and Houston Wood are two such ethnomethodologists. They have assembled a framework for analyzing collective reality construction. As part of this framework, they have identified five features that underlie all cultural realities (see Reading 30). These five key features of reality are reflexive, coherent, interactional, fragile, and permeable. You can read about each of the features in their article, but let's look at a few examples here.

Reflexive

Realities are *reflexive*. This means that all realities contain self-sealing beliefs—unquestioned beliefs that cannot be proven wrong. For example, if you place your pencil on your desk while you go for a snack and cannot find the pencil when you return, you will assume that you somehow misplaced it. If it reappears where you left it, you will assume that you just over-looked it the first time. In this culture, people hold an unquestioned belief regarding the immobility of "inanimate" objects, so it's unlikely that you would entertain the notion that your pencil left by itself and then returned. In other words, your working theory of reality does not include the possibility that inanimate objects move around on their own. This is just something everyone knows.

One of the interesting things about realities is that they often contain contradictions and inconsistencies. For instance, imagine a small child who fears monsters under her bed. Her parents might attempt to calm her by saying there are no such things as mon-sters, so they're not real. "But I can *see* them," she might insist. "I know they're real." Later, she may come down with the flu and ask what is making her so ill. "Germs," a parent might say. "Germs are little bugs that live inside you and make you sick, but you can't see them." How confusing is this information?! Tiny things that you can't see but that live in you and make you sick versus huge monsters you know you can see but apparently, you're told, are not real. All realities contain a series of working theories about how to deal with con-tradictory information. These working theories are called *secondary elaborations*. In response to information that may appear to contradict a taken-for-granted assumption, we explain away the contradiction with a secondary elaboration: "That girl actually answered the 'how's it going?' question because she's so weird. Everyone still knows that you don't really answer that question."

Consider this illustration: Do you watch the five-day weather forecast? A newcomer to this culture might assume that one needed to watch the forecast only once every five days: Presumably, a five-day forecast will give useful weather information for the next five days. Right? "No!" you exclaim. "You need to watch it every day." The newcomer looks at you, puz-zled. "Because the forecast changes," you continue. Now the newcomer is really confused. Why watch a "forecast" if you already know it will not be accurate? Think about this: You watch weather forecasts because you want to know what the weather will be, but you also recognize that the predictions are often inaccurate. So you watch the forecast again to see how it has changed. Does the frequent inaccuracy of the predictions make you doubt the "reality" that we can forecast the weather? No. Instead of questioning the validity of forecasting the weather, you probably explain away the inaccuracies as human error or the inadequacy of present meteorological technology. What you are not likely to do is question the taken-for-granted assumption that there is a pattern to nature, and that, with the right theories and technology, we can know this pattern and make predictions based on it. In other words, you are not likely to assume that the weather is actually random. An unquestioned belief of modern Western thought is that there is order in nature. The cultural enterprise of predicting weather is based on this assumption.

In one famous (and also controversial), study, a psychiatrist, David Rosenhan (1973), conducted a casual but effective experiment intended to determine whether the sane can be reliably distinguished from the insane. His hypothesis was that psychiatric practitioners were so entrenched in their own system of diagnosing patients that they would assume *anyone* who came for treatment was insane. Rosenhan sent several students to psychiatric admitting rooms and instructed them to say they were hearing voices but otherwise to show no symptoms of abnormality. All of the student posers were evaluated and judged to be in need of psychiatric hospitalization. Rosenhan concluded that psychiatric staff work in a context in which they *expect* patients to be insane, so they interpret the behavior of any person presumed to be a patient, even the behavior of "normal" researchers, as insane.

Unquestioned beliefs are often more easily noticed when examining a culture different from our own. In many cases, others' beliefs are described as superstitious or magical. However, Mehan and Wood demonstrate that any culture, including ours, is filled with unquestioned beliefs. When challenged with contradictions and inconsistencies, we reflexively "seal up" the contradiction with a secondary elaboration. This leads Mehan and Wood to conclude that "all people are equally superstitious." People continue to hold certain unquestioned beliefs in the face of contradictory evidence.

Coherent

A second feature of realities is that they have an order and structure to them; realities are *coherent*. Even realities that seem nonsensical and anarchical to outsiders reveal their own order and logic when carefully examined. Coherency is an outcome of the apparent human need to make order out of chaos. If things are orderly, then they are predictable. If you actually had to contemplate and question everything in your environment anew every day, you'd never make it out of the house. One interesting aspect of human life is that we create systems of order and theories for making sense and then tend to believe that these systems or theories reflect a general or real pattern.

Noncontingencies

Psychologists have conducted a series of intriguing experiments called "noncontingency" experiments. *Noncontingent* means that there is *no connection* between an outcome and something else in the environment. For instance, you may have a headache right now, but you know it is not contingent on (not connected to) having stubbed your toe earlier. Humans create working theories by formulating connections between what they perceive to be cause and effect. If I drink too much, I am likely to be hungover; feeling hungover is contingent on drinking too much. Or, my getting into graduate school is contingent on getting good grades.

Noncontingency experiments reveal some very interesting things about the construction of coherency. One is that we form "superstitious" or "neurotic" theories. A horse that receives a mild electric shock in its foot at the same time that a bell is rung will continue to raise its foot every time the bell rings even after the shocks have ceased. The horse associates the shock (and corresponding urge to lift its foot) with the bell, even though the shock is not connected to the bell. Similarly, humans who experience a strong emotion, such as shock or fear due to a particular event, may continue to experience that emotion in similar situations, even if the threat is no longer present. For example, someone who has been traumatized by a dog bite may panic in the presence of all dogs. This associative-emotive pattern is sometimes referred to as a *phobia*.

Even more interesting is an experiment in which a group of students was asked to develop a system for identifying "sick" versus "healthy" cells. It turns out that this is not a very difficult task if you already know the theory. However, if you don't have a working theory, you have to rely on trial and error. Students were shown slides and with each slide, they were asked to push a button indicating "sick" or "healthy." Lights on their panels then lit up indicating either a wrong choice or a right choice. Based on this information, the students studied the slide trying to come up with a working hypothesis (for example, "the nucleus looks broken"). When another slide was flashed, they could try out their hypothesis. The indicator lights letting them know their guesses were right or wrong provided the feedback they needed to revise and refine their working theories. Given correct feedback, cell identification turned out to be a simple task for most students. All of these students emerged from the task with a "theory," and their theories were very similar. They'd created a coherent way of cataloging the cells based on trial and error and feedback.

The interesting finding concerned another group who were participating in the same experiment, with one small difference. They were being given random feedback. In other words, their "right" and "wrong" buttons had no connection to their guesses. They too were trying to develop a theory of cell identification based on trial and error and feedback, but in this case, the feedback was not contingent on their guesses. Were they able to devise a theory? Yes! Not only did they develop theories, but the theories were very elaborate and complex. In an insightful conclusion, the researchers invited the student groups to talk with each other about their theories. The contingency group had very simple theories (based on the fact that they had received correct feedback), and when they questioned the noncontingency group about their more complicated theories, these students provided responses that were so compelling that the former group began to doubt their own theories and wonder if they were "missing something."

This experiment, and others like it, reveals several fascinating features of reality construction. Most significantly, we are able and inclined to create coherent theories out of even *random* information. It never occurred to the noncontingency group that there was no connection between their answers and the "feedback" they received. Further, when they were informed of this later, several of them insisted that, regardless of the randomness, their theories reflected "correct" assessments.

As you ponder this material, consider some of the ways in which you get the "feedback" that enables you to create coherent theories in your own life. It's a useful "reality check" to examine your sources of information, especially whether these are connected to outcomes in the ways that you believe them to be.

"It Makes Sense to Us!"

In discussing *coherency,* Mehan and Wood are particularly interested in the ways in which realities that may seem preposterous to outsiders are quite ordinary and plausible to insiders. Regardless of the ways in which a system of belief and expectations arose (that is, in spite of the noncontingencies and inconsistencies), it appears coherent to those who share the system of understanding. Persons of different religious or political persuasions often try to "poke holes" in one another's beliefs by pointing out what seem to be "obvious" contradictions. From an ethnomethodological perspective, this is a fruitless exercise and serves only to demonstrate the extent to which all belief systems have a coherency that includes secondary elaborations, or ways for explaining away inconsistencies. When the feature of *reflexivity* is added to *coherency,* we begin to see just how firmly entrenched belief systems can be. Challenges in the form of contradictions may actually serve to strengthen the original belief, especially as a person articulates the secondary elaborations that extend the coherency to cover all possible disruptions.

Interactional and Fragile

The process of creating and maintaining realities is *ongoing and interactional.* As noted in the example about greetings, we work together to create even the simplest realities such as the belief that we are seen by others as distinct and notable personages. Because realities are based on ongoing interactions, they are subject to performance breakdowns (recall the discussion in Part III). In this way, realities are *fragile.* We rely on one another to perform the expected roles and routines that make up significant cultural stories. One of the reasons that grand ceremonies, such as weddings, are a source of so much stress is because the participants are dependent on the actions of others in order for the event to go off well. This is why there are rehearsals for important events: We recognize that these are roles that are highly significant, but for which people don't have much firsthand experience.

Cultural realities actually break down much more than people acknowledge. In our day-to-day lives we encounter numerous disruptions that threaten to bring smooth interactions to an embarrassed halt. The reflexive and coherent features of reality are reflected in the ways in which people work together to repair these disruptions. "Tact" is one interactional strategy for repairing disrupted routines. Accounts are another. As was discussed in Part III, these strategies reflect a consensus about what the expected routine should be and a willingness to help restore it to a working definition. When disruptions in the expected routine occur, people often have no idea what to do next. They simply don't have a script for the situation. Such situations occur more frequently than we tend to realize. However, we're inclined to overlook the fragility of reality maintenance, in part because we have strategies for continuing on *as if* nothing unusual is happening.

Breaching

Imagine you attend a dinner party given by a friend, and you invite your girlfriend, who has never met the friend, to join you. Upon your arrival, your host takes your coats and says pleasantly, "Make yourself at home." The girlfriend replies, "Thank you, I will," and proceeds to take off her shoes and socks, turn on the television, and put her feet on the coffee table. Your friend is likely to look at you for an explanation of this seemingly bizarre behavior. You can only shrug and look on in dismay. Your shrug and look of dismay are cues to your friend that you share his view of reality: The girlfriend is behaving strangely and has violated the expected interaction rules for polite company behavior. Imagine further that you approach your girlfriend and ask what's going on. She replies, "He said I could make myself at home." In response to this, you try to explain that he didn't really mean for her to act like she was in her own home. She gives you a wilting look that suggests you're the crazy one and turns up the television.

In an article titled "A Conception of and Experiments With 'Trust' as a Condition of Concerted Stable Actions" (Reading 30), one of the founders of ethnomethodology, Harold Garfinkel, describes social "breaching experiments." Garfinkel achieved great fame and notoriety with the breaching experiments he and his students conducted at the University of California, Los Angeles (UCLA) in the 1960s. Breaching entails making the underlying structure of reality explicit by acting in a manner that is inconsistent with the taken-for-granted rules of interaction that maintain the reality. When reality is breached, interaction often comes to a confused halt. Garfinkel describes a variety of breaching experiments as well as people's reactions to these experiments. According to Garfinkel, we enter into interactional moments "trusting" that others share our expectations and definitions of reality. It is this trust that enables us to engage in stable, coherent, meaningful interactions.

The situation described above is a "breach." In this case, the woman has breached the expectation that certain phrases are intended as polite and are not meant to be taken literally. The host "trusts" his guests to know the appropriate "visitor" behavior. Otherwise, he would not have made a statement such as "make yourself at home." This example is based on an actual breach conducted by one of my students. Interestingly, she had put off doing the assignment until the last minute and didn't know what to do. As she explained later, when the host said "make yourself at home," she recalled reading in Garfinkel about taking statements literally and decided to give it a try. She actually went so far the evening of the party as to take a shower at her host's home.

Breaches reveal just how fragile and interactional (and meaningful) cultural realities are. Confronted with a breach, observers usually try first to ignore it (the "nothing unusual" bias). We do this whenever we walk away from people on the street who strike us as "off." If it is not possible to ignore, such as someone in an elevator asking you to examine the cut on her arm (another breach carried out by one of my students), people look to others to reaffirm that the breacher is "weird." This usually takes the form of strangers looking at one another, smiling knowingly, and perhaps rolling their eyes. This subtle communication is an effective interactional strategy for signaling that "normal people know the routine, and this person is not normal." Another strategy when confronted with a breach that cannot easily be ignored is to treat it as a joke. If the other person (the breacher) also laughs, then the expected reality is quickly restored, and all participants can sigh in the relief of knowing that they all share the same expectations of the situation.

In the breaching experiments designed by Garfinkel, students conducting breaches were instructed not to let the person repair the breach by treating it as a joke or something that could be ignored. When people do not find interactional support for repairing the situation, they tend to become agitated, in some cases even angry. They look for information that will help them make sense of the situation in ways that are consistent with their working definition of the situation. If they cannot do so, they become flustered and confused. The boyfriend of the woman who "made herself at home" was furious with her for days afterward. From his perspective, she had violated his "trust" by not behaving as expected and by making him look bad in front of his friends. This response, which is very understandable, illustrates just how much we depend on others to maintain basic definitions of reality, such as "this is just a nice friendly party." Her behavior resulted in a cascade of consequences that toppled several aspects of the taken-for-granted reality of the occasion and who these friends were to one another.

A couple more examples from my own classes include students volunteering to pay more than the posted price for an item. Another is shopping from others' carts in a grocery store. The taken-for-granted routine is that once you have placed an item in your cart, it belongs to you. The students who performed this "breach" matter-of-factly took items from the carts of others. When questioned, they responded simply that the item in the cart had been more convenient to reach than the one on the shelf. When assumptions are breached, people look for a "reasonable" explanation—something that reaffirms the underlying assumptions. "Oh, I'm sorry, I thought that was my cart" is an example of a reasonable explanation for taking something from someone else's cart. But to act as if there is nothing wrong with doing so confuses the other person and makes her or him question, just for a moment, the reality of the situation.

In another breaching experiment, a student cheerfully asked a McDonald's clerk for a Whopper, a menu item at rival Burger King. Rather than saying, "We don't carry that," the McDonald's clerk asked the student to repeat the order. When the request for a Whopper was repeated, the clerk looked around to see if fellow employees had heard this "bizarre" request. In other words, he searched for interactional corroboration of his reality that "everyone knows" the McDonald's menu, and anyone who doesn't is obviously weird. Something as simple as a sideways glance and raised eyebrows from a coworker can indicate that one's reality is intact and that the momentary experience is merely an aberration that can be ignored. In this case, however, the students were particularly tenacious in testing reactions to breaching. After the first person breached the fast-food order routine, another classmate stepped up and ordered a slice of pizza, which, of course, McDonald's restaurants don't serve.

Caveat Regarding Breaching Experiments

Occasionally, students using previous editions of this text have raised the concern that breaching experiments are a violation of social trust. This concern indicates an excellent insight regarding the theories of Goffman (1959; discussed in Part III) and Garfinkel—both are saying that social order (interaction routines) are based on trust. We *trust* one another to know the routines and to follow them through. In this way, we are able to carry on interactions with one another without the fear of being hurt or violated. I cannot speak directly for Goffman or Garfinkel, but the following is my own response to students and instructors who have concerns about breaching experiments.

Recall that one of the lessons in Part II is the extent to which we all participate in acts of categorization (stereotyping) that we may not be aware of. Much of our behavior is "mindless." Similarly, many of our interaction rituals are mindless and also taken for granted. I would never advocate the senseless disruption of another person's routine or status quo just for the sake of doing it. However, breaching experiments, handled with care and sensitivity, can be a way to raise consciousness and to invite others to think critically about their own participation in mindless routines. Keep in mind that there are many forms of breaching that do not have to involve someone else directly. Just thinking up the experiments can be a great exercise in consciousness raising. If you do decide to implicate others, consider situations in which the others are also likely to be able to learn something useful from the encounter. Breaching is not the equivalent of being mean or cruel. In my own experience with breaching, once people settle down and recover from the breach, they are often eager to discuss the experiment.

The important feature is that persons performing these experiments take the time to debrief their subjects and to engage with them in a discussion of what occurred. This can be a significant occasion in which to practice "interpersonal ethics"—that is, to use the situation to gain greater understanding among all parties involved. Remember, the point is to define and make explicit routines that reflect taken-for-granted assumptions about reality—not to hurt someone or make them needlessly uncomfortable. The best breaching experiments are those in which the person doing them is able to recognize her or his own participation in a taken-for-granted status quo.

Permeable

The fifth feature described by Mehan and Wood is that realities are *permeable*. We are constantly moving between different realities. In doing so, we alter our attitudes and behavior to bring them into line with the expectations of the reality of the moment. People who participate in nudist activities, for example, successfully maintain the reality while on their holidays that nudity is healthy and a source of family fun that is not associated with sexuality. They then return easily to work life, where it is commonly known that public nudity is not acceptable.

If the conditions are right, one can even move into a radically different reality. For example, soldiers move between a reality in which they are trained to kill other humans and another in which killing is defined as murder. The permeability of realities implies that we carry a variety of scripts for various routines, including routines that may seem contradictory, as well as rules and beliefs for bridging the gaps between the realities. In order to make a successful transition between the reality systems of war and civil society, soldiers have to learn and accept a cultural story that designates some people as "the enemy" and others as "those who need protection." One (among many) of the tragedies of war is the fragility of this particular system of belief. Hospitals and social service agencies are filled with men (and increasingly women) who find it difficult to maintain such distinct realities. Their psyches and spirits have broken down as a consequence. Soldiers who fought in Vietnam returned to a civil society that did not necessarily share the reality of the "enemy" these soldiers had been trained to fight and kill. One way to look at the post-Vietnam experience for veterans is to consider that they did not receive interactional support from the society they thought they had been protecting. This lack of support made it difficult for many of these veterans to maintain the belief that the killing they had done in one reality was indeed "honorable."

BELIEVING MAKES IT SO—SELF-FULFILLING PROPHECIES

Imagine an elementary school teacher who is told by school personnel that one group of children in his classroom are "gifted" and likely to be high achievers. Imagine another classroom where a teacher is told that some of her students have tested as "underachievers." An experiment similar to this scenario was conducted in the 1970s by Robert Rosenthal and Lenore Jacobson (1974). Rosenthal and Jacobson wanted to study the effects of preconceived beliefs about intelligence on the performance of schoolchildren. They told elementary school teachers that they had administered a test indicating that a number of the students in the teachers' classes were likely to show significant academic improvement over the course of the year. In fact, the researchers had simply picked a group of students randomly. However, by the end of the year, students who were expected by their teachers to improve had indeed improved (as measured by a standard IQ test). Rosenthal and Jacobson's study became famous and is known as the "Pygmalion in the Classroom" study. In recent years, their research has been criticized, especially for the use of standard IQ tests to measure student improvement. However, several aspects of the study are noteworthy and have been supported by related studies done by other researchers.

Rosenthal and Jacobson hypothesized that student performance was shaped, in part, by the way the teachers *treated* students. Subsequent studies of teacher behavior in the classroom indicate that teachers respond differently to students they perceive to be especially bright. They take more time with these students, encourage them to work on more complicated problems, and invite them to participate and share more with other students. In contrast, teachers are likely to "give up" quickly on students whom they perceive to be underachievers. Obviously, elementary school teachers are not the only factor in student performance, but the research highlights one important element: the power of beliefs to shape behavior.

A self-fulfilling prophecy is an event that comes true because we act in a way that brings about our initial expectations. In this case, if teachers perceive a child to be especially bright, the belief may set in motion a related set of actions that serves to make the expectation true. The teacher may treat the child differently, which may give the child more chances to develop academic skills. The child, upon recognizing that she is being treated as if she were very bright, may adjust her behavior to try to live up to that expectation. She may begin doing more homework, asking more questions, and generally behaving as if she were gifted. These actions are likely to result in increased performance over time.

Another set of studies that relates to this is work done by Paula Nurius and Hazel Markus (1986). (See also Part IV essay, pp. 235–248.) Nurius and Markus are interested in "possible selves": Who do you imagine you can be? What do you think you can do? Their research shows that children raised in homes where professional paths are discussed explicitly are likely to have a very articulated sense of who and what they are going to be. Fourth graders can describe in great detail where they intend to go to college, graduate school, and so forth en route to becoming a doctor, lawyer, engineer, and so forth. On the other hand, children who do not have such models available to them tend to think in terms of fantastic and generally unattainable goals (I'm going to be the next Britney Spears, a pro racer, an astronaut, and so forth). Nurius and Markus theorize that the ability to imagine a specific course of action—the path toward the result—enables us to make it so. They give several examples of professional athletes and musicians who "practice in their heads." This practice is, in a sense, a form of mental performance that provides people with some of the experience and insight necessary to actually bring about an intended course of action.

Conversely, people can become stuck in mental loops of despair in which they conjure up conversations and experiences that are likely to turn out badly. Psychologists such as Paul Watzlawick tell us that this kind of thinking can result in self-fulfilling outcomes (see Reading 31; Watzlawick, 1984). He uses the example of a couple in which the husband believes that his wife is a nag and the wife believes that her husband is withdrawn. These beliefs lead each to imagine that the other is going to behave as expected (nag/withdraw). When they encounter one another, each sees what he or she expects to see and is therefore poised to react in such a way that the expectations are made real. For instance, the husband, anticipating that his wife is going to nag him, comes home grumpy and withdrawn. This reinforces her perception ("He's withdrawn"), and she picks up with her nagging.

Self-fulfilling prophecies illustrate an important point made throughout this book: Often, what is important is not what is factually correct, but rather what is defined as real. People's actions are based on their *definitions* of what is real. That is, we respond not to the direct event but to our interpretation of it. An important message in Watzlawick's article is that, by becoming aware of self-fulfilling prophecies, we will be better able to recognize and resist potentially damaging outcomes.

Socially held beliefs about the characteristics of groups of people—in other words, stereotypes—often result in self-fulfilling outcomes. Another psychologist, Mark Snyder, studies the relationship between stereotypes and attraction (see Reading 32). Snyder has conducted experiments that demonstrate that the stereotypes about attractive versus unattractive people can be self-fulfilling. In one such study, participants speak on the phone with someone they perceive to be either "traditionally attractive" or "unattractive" based on pictures they've been shown. When speaking with a presumably attractive individual, participants tend to be more upbeat and friendly. This behavior induces similar responses in the person on the phone such that they are likely to be very friendly and outgoing. Participants usually conclude that the attractive people are also more friendly. Snyder points out that this stereotypical belief may be self-fulfilling, because we are likely to treat attractive people as if they are friendly and outgoing. In so doing, we elicit a friendly response.

Together, the features of reality yield a theory explaining why people pursue certain lines of action without noticing alternatives (reflexivity) and how these routines eventually take on the status of cultural stories or belief systems that are assumed to be natural and real. Through ongoing interaction, we reinforce these belief systems. Even disruptions and deviations serve to reinforce the original belief to the extent that we use secondary elaborations and behaviors to repair the breach and explain away inconsistencies. This theory is a powerful tool for understanding the maintenance of the status quo. It provides an explanation for the persistence of social patterns and the behaviors that sustain those patterns, even when people may think they are opposed to the status quo.

THE SOCIAL CONSTRUCTION OF THE STATUS QUO

Some cultural stories and routines are better established than others—that is, a large percentage of the population is likely to take them for granted and consider them as a source of authority for organizing social life. Well-established cultural practices that have widely recognized authority can be called *cultural institutions*. These institutions and practices constitute a cultural status quo. How are these institutional beliefs and practices enacted and maintained over time? This is the question we look at in this section. The theory of reality as a social construction can be used to address this question. As you read this material, another useful question to ask about these "dominant" cultural patterns is what alternatives might exist and how the situation might be defined and approached differently if others were in charge of the cultural definition of the situation.

One of the most well-established and least-questioned institutions in this country is the medical profession. Medicine is one of the relatively undisputed sources of authority regarding what constitutes "acceptable" behavior. Those who exhibit unusual or inappropriate behaviors are often referred for medical treatment. Both the cause and treatment of these behaviors are part of the body of organized knowledge that constitutes medicine. One feature of this form of knowledge is that certain types of actions and feelings are considered "natural." Deviations from the "natural" patterns are considered "pathological."

Medicalization

Sociologists Peter Conrad and Joseph Schneider (1944) have written extensively about the *medicalization* of behavior. They use the term *medicalization* to mean "defining behavior as a medical problem or illness and mandating or licensing the medical profession to provide some type of treatment for it." Our culture has a pervasive tendency to define everything from depression to alcoholism as a physiological disease. One behavior Conrad and Schneider examined closely is "hyperkinesis," or hyperactivity. In this study, they explore the emergence of a medical name (*hyperkinesis*) for hyperactivity in children—behavior that is considered distracting and "out of control" in everyday interactions. Hyperkinesis is particularly interesting because it exhibits none of the usual physiological correlates of disease (for example, fever, bacteria, viruses, changes in blood chemistry), and the symptomatic behaviors—rebelliousness, frustration, excitability—seem to have as much to do with social protest as with organic disease. Conrad and Schneider's thesis is that the increasingly high rates of diagnosed cases of hyperkinesis may indicate a social problem rather than individual behavioral disorders. This is a very controversial statement, but it's worth considering the point that parents and educators tend to look first at the child who appears to be disrupting the classroom status quo, rather than examining the underlying patterns of contemporary education. Such an examination might reveal factors such as extreme boredom, behavioral expectations that are not conducive to learning in small children, and so forth. Culturally, however, we tend to assume the infallibility of medicine and its ability to make the symptoms disappear, rather than examine underlying social patterns.

Conrad and Schneider (1994) also have written extensively on the medicalization of deviant behaviors. For example, all cultures have people who are "mad"—that is, people who violate behavioral boundaries that are maintained by the majority. Beliefs about what these people should be called, who should deal with them, and how they should be handled differ remarkably, however. Certain cultures see their "mad" as divinely inspired. In these cultures, madness is attributed to spiritual possession rather than natural pathology. For example, in ancient Hebrew, the term for "madness" is defined variously as "to rave," "to act beside oneself," and "to behave like a prophet." "Mad" people were considered to be so filled with spirits that they could not harness themselves to the chains of worldly conduct. Prophets and the "mad" were both "raving lunatics" who were thought to be "outside" society. An interesting question is what social definitions distinguished one from the other.

In our own culture, one social-psychological alternative to the medical model of madness and other forms of asocial conduct is based on the theory that those people who are unusually bright and creative experience an overload of contradictions when they try to meet standard expectations for behavior. These people are thought to be responding to a very complex and contradictory set of "generalized others," reacting rapidly to strong creative passions and urges. This complex creativity manifests as a resistance to socialization. And those who have the necessary interpersonal skills and material resources may avoid medical labeling and may become significant contributors in areas such as the arts. Because of their contributions, their "inappropriate" behavior is sometimes labeled "eccentric" rather than "mentally ill."

If you are interested in exploring this topic more, you might begin with some of the writings of one of the framers of this alternative perspective, Thomas Szasz. In a 1971 article, Szasz describes an extreme, even horrific, example of the medicalization of a "deviant" behavior. This historical case, reported in a prestigious medical journal in 1851, concerned a disease manifest among slaves. The primary symptom of the ominous-sounding disorder called "drapetomania" was running away from plantations!

Despite the increasing cultural awareness of the limitations and misapplications of the medical model of deviance, many medical practitioners continue to treat "conditions" such as transgendered behavior, homosexuality, and "female emotion" as symptoms of pathology. There are still respected scientists who use the medical model to claim that certain people may be more inclined to "social pathology" than others based on racial ethnicity. Medicine is a powerful and influential cultural institution that has done much to improve our quality of life, but it also warrants careful scrutiny. Be aware of its limitations and untold stories.

The Maintenance of Social Hierarchies

Science and medicine are prevailing cultural stories that are easy to recognize, even though we may take the authority of such institutions for granted. Much of the cultural status quo is less easy to see, but it is still profound in its influence. Economic class is a powerful influence in U.S. culture, but part of the routine connected to social class is the expectation that we should pretend it doesn't matter. Candace Perin (1988) is an anthropologist who did her dissertation field research in the suburbs of Minneapolis. Instead of going to a foreign country, she decided that the "suburbs" were rich with cultural practices worth studying from an anthropological perspective. Her book on the subject, *Belonging in America,* is an insightful examination of the day-to-day routines of suburbanites who attempt to maintain an image of middle-class wealth, prosperity, and the impression that "everything is always fine." One central suburban expectation is that it is "impolite" to directly confront neighbors about infractions and trespasses. As Perin points out, crabgrass does not respect property boundaries; if your neighbor does not maintain a crabgrass-free lawn, it's likely that some of the stuff will creep onto yours. Neighbors engage in all kinds of roundabout ways of trying to address these infractions without actually confronting the neighbor directly. Larger infractions—garbage cans left at the curb too long, rusty cars left sitting around for a period of time—are reported to the police. Perin noted that the majority of the calls received by police in the greater Minneapolis region during her months of fieldwork were from *anonymous* suburban callers "tattling" on their neighbors. Perin concludes that the interaction routines in the suburbs preserve the impression that all is rosy and well and conflict free. Meanwhile, suburbanites use many "backdoor" strategies to resolve conflict. This perpetuates an image of the suburbs as safe and problem free and may also explain some of the differences in urban versus suburban tolerance for conflict in group interaction.

One additional example illustrates the perpetuation of middle-class norms in mixed-class settings. Most people are aware of middle-class expectations, regardless of their own economic background. Students and faculty from working-class backgrounds can tell many stories about situations in which they have felt out of place with other students and faculty from middle-class backgrounds. Colleagues may suggest social gatherings that are beyond the price range of some of the members of the group, or they may engage in a lot of social conversation about the price of real estate in the area, their mortgages, and other class-related issues such as fancy vacation destinations and restaurants. What's interesting is that in such instances, people from working-class backgrounds rarely say anything that might indicate that they are unfamiliar or uncomfortable with the discussion. There is a tacit agreement to let the conversation continue on its own terms. Once in a while, someone may say, "I wouldn't know about that, I've never been able to afford to eat in such places." This usually brings the conversation to an awkward halt, leaving the speaker feeling as if he or she sticks out. Those whose taken-for-granted class reality has just been disrupted may, in theory, be aware of the class differences—some of us even teach this material—but in the interactional moment may just feel resentful about the awkwardness. The class norm "nice people don't talk about money" operates to maintain a cultural status quo in which profound class differences are never brought to the social stage.

Realities are constructed and maintained through interaction. Erving Goffman (1959) speaks of "dramatizing the ideal," of people employing the "ideals" suggested by their particular cultural reality in shaping their interactions with others. In acting out these ideals, people affirm and re-create them. Such behavior may help maintain realities that foster our dissatisfaction or oppression. Through our participation in various interaction routines, we reinforce the status quo. This is a particularly noteworthy process regarding the perpetuation of social hierarchies. Scholars who study social power emphasize the following points:

First, it is difficult or impossible to rule solely through raw force or oppression. In order for people "in charge" to rule over others, those "beneath" them must willingly comply to some extent. This compliance is accomplished through the performance of "legitimacy rituals" that establish and maintain the authority of those in power. Whether or not a person accepts the officials' authority in her or his private mind, participation in legitimacy rituals contributes to the construction of the status quo. The existing power structure is "realized" through the performance. There is an Ethiopian proverb that expresses this dual awareness: "When the great lord passes, the wise peasant bows deeply and silently farts." Cultural dominance is (re)affirmed in the gesture of the bow while the peasant's sense of self as outside this oppression is also affirmed by the private gesture of the fart. It is the public gesture that contributes to the production of the status quo, even as the private gesture helps to reconcile contradiction and conflict within the self.

Any social system, be it oppressive or humane, requires the cooperation of both the powerful and the weak. Both play a role in defining reality; both encounter limits. Some constraints arise from culture and tradition, which provide the precedents and the symbolic material that make some definitions so easy and others nearly impossible. Other constraints are the result of having or lacking tangible resources. Regardless of how you define a situation, if you are at the wrong end of a gun you can be hurt. But guns alone make for a very fragile social order.

Sociologist Cecilia Ridgeway describes a theory that she has developed to explain the perpetuation of gender inequality in employment (see Reading 33). Despite many formal legal changes in the past three decades that have made it unlawful to discriminate against women in employment, women still lag significantly behind men in promotions and raises. Ridgeway explains this lag as a manifestation of a particular status quo in which both men and women *perceive* women as being less competent than men in certain employment situations. According to prevailing cultural scripts and stereotypes, women just aren't as effective as men. This perception results in management decisions that may make the expectation self-fulfilling. This interactional explanation is an important contribution to understanding how gender inequality is perpetuated even when people intend to be fair.

CONCLUSION

The quotation from Karl Marx (1963) at the beginning of this essay suggests that people make their own history, but that they do so within the confines of the circumstances they encounter from others. When he spoke of "circumstances encountered from the past," Marx had in mind the economic conditions—the "mode of production"—that shaped the existence of a group of people. But the idea can be extended to the broader systems of belief that groups of people use to structure and make sense of their shared reality. The definitions that people use to organize and direct their own lives are generally based on, in Marx's terms, "the traditions of the dead generations."

As we discussed in Part II, language-based knowledge systems shape our perceptions. Hence, although several definitions of a situation may be possible, people actually work within a system of beliefs inherited from social ancestors. "Commonsense" stories and theories provide us with a means of making sense of our lives. These stories and theories are often useful and meaningful. However, "commonsense" theories can also limit certain lines of action and confirm arbitrary "truths" that hinder our capacity to make alternative or new sense of a situation. In this regard, it can be said that these traditions "weigh like a nightmare" on our existence. In acting out these traditions of thought uncritically, we both create and re-create the circumstances of the past.

The social construction of reality is perhaps the most central and profound topic treated in this book. The phrase deserves careful attention. Note first the claim that reality is a *construction*. This idea in itself can seem counterintuitive or even nonsensical. Surely reality is simply the objective world that exists "out there," the subject of study of our sciences. But the alternative claim is that reality is malleable. Different groups, different cultures, or different historical epochs may hold completely different (even diametrically opposed) beliefs about what is "real," what is "obviously true," what is "good," and what is "desired." The second noteworthy element in the title is that reality is a *social* construction. That is, the subjective realities that are created and maintained are the product not of isolated individuals, but of relationships, communities, groups, institutions, and entire cultures.

I have a colleague who had grown weary of a question constantly posed to her by other faculty: "Do you rent or own?" This seemingly innocent conversation starter is only innocent for those who are able to answer, "I own." The question itself implies a social hierarchy, and one has little choice in response but to affirm the hierarchy ("owning is a pinnacle of success in American life") and one's place in it ("I've arrived," or "I haven't"). Renters usually feel compelled to provide some account that indicates that they share the same class values but just haven't found the right place yet. In her private thoughts, my colleague was frustrated about her situation: She had worked hard most of her life but still couldn't afford to buy a home in her area. She also knew that most homeowners in her generation had been assisted by parents, spouses, or other sources of income. Mostly, she resented being put on the spot with an insensitive question. One day, she startled a group of people by responding to the question "do you rent or own?" with a raised eyebrow and glare at the person who asked. Then, in her best slow drawl she exclaimed, "Honey, I don't do mortgages. They are soooo bourgeois!" People actually gasped. With this single utterance, she had reframed the situation. Her answer turned the presumed status of the inquirer on its head and elevated her to a position of "interesting" and beyond the norm. My friend still wants to own a home, but she's found a provocative way to disrupt the taken-for-granted conversational routine that serves only to spotlight the status of the "haves" at the expense of the "have-nots."

Reality can be an amazingly malleable thing. But there are limits to how reality can be constructed. These limits include existing patterns of interaction and the taken-for-granted assumptions that underlie realities. Most of the time, expected definitions of the situation will prevail, because most of us know the routine and either follow it mindlessly or do not (or cannot) risk deviation. Power, in a symbolic interactionist sense, is the ability to define a situation in a particular way and to have others act in accordance with this definition. Reality may be a social construction, but we are not all equal participants in this construction.

Stories are a useful epistemology through which to understand how collective life comes to have recognizable patterns. Realities, like stories, do not exist unless people tell them to themselves and to others. Some realities, like some stories, are more comprehensible to the group than are others. Certain stories, and ways of telling them, are considered more or less acceptable. As you ponder the material in this part of the book, ask yourself what story line underlies each of the different realities described: What sort of meaning is attached to persons, situations, and events in each of these stories? Who has the power to write and rewrite stories? How conscious are you of the stories that constitute your realities? The concept of stories illustrates how realities continue and how they change.

References and Suggestions for Further Reading

Berger, P., & Luckmann, T. (1966). *The social construction of reality*. Garden City, NY: Doubleday.

Conrad, P., & Schneider, J. (1994). *Deviance and medicalization: From badness to sickness.* Philadelphia: Temple University Press.

Coupland, D. (1991). *Generation X.* New York: St. Martin's Press.

Goffman, E. (1959). *The presentation of self in everyday life.* Garden City, NY: Doubleday.

Marx, K. (1963). *The 18th Brumaire of Louis Bonaparte.* New York: International Publishing Company.

Nurius, P., & Markus, H. (1986). Possible selves. *American Psychologist, 41,* 954–969.

Perin, C. (1988). *Belonging in America.* Madison: University of Wisconsin Press.

Pollner, M., & Goode, D. (1990). Ethnomethodology and person-centering practices. *Person-Centered Review, 5,* 213–220.

Rosenhan, D. (1973). On being sane in insane places. *Science, 179,* 250–258.

Rosenthal, R., & Jacobson, L. (1974). Pygmalion in the classroom. In Z. Rubin (Ed.), *Doing unto others* (pp. 41–47). Englewood Cliffs, NJ: Prentice Hall.

Szasz, T. (1971). The sane slave: An historical note on medical diagnosis as justificatory rhetoric. *American Journal of Psychotherapy, 25,* 228–239.

Thomas, W. I., & Thomas, D. (1928). *The child in America.* New York: Knopf.

Watzlawick, P. (Ed.). (1984). *The invented reality.* New York: Norton.

A THEORY OF REALITY

This section focuses on the ways in which people create and maintain shared systems of belief. These belief systems or paradigms can be thought of as cultural stories that focus our perceptions, shape our perspectives, and provide guidelines about what is "real" and important. Culturally shared "realities" also provide the basis for making decisions and deciding what is true and right and good.

In "Five Features of Reality," Mehan and Wood describe five processes that combine to form socially shared systems of belief. As you read the remaining articles in Part V, consider how each of the five features is illustrated.

Harold Garfinkel's work is well known in sociology. The title of this selection, "A Conception of and Experiments With 'Trust' as a Condition of Concerted Stable Actions," sounds technical, but the idea is less complicated than it sounds. Garfinkel proposes that much of social action is based on shared and taken-for-granted expectations. We use a lot of social "shorthand" in our encounters with one another. We're able to do this because we share common beliefs about how the world works, and we "trust" others to do their part to maintain these beliefs. Garfinkel and his students at UCLA performed social experiments designed to demonstrate that realities actually require a great deal of interactional work and can be easily broken if one party "breaches" the expectations of the situation.

Questions for Discussion and Review

1. Find examples of each of the five features of reality in the essay that accompanies Part V. Make a list of your own examples of each of the five features.

2. Discuss the experiments described in Garfinkel's article and identify exactly what interactional expectation was breached in each one. Garfinkel states that people often respond to breaching with anger. Consider how this is connected to his use of "trust."

3. Think up other examples of breaching experiments that you could do. Do you find it easy or difficult to come up with ideas? How would you feel about doing a breaching experiment? What does this tell you about how the status quo is maintained?

4. Some students think that breaching experiments are unethical. Explain why they might think so. What does this indicate about social norms and how they are maintained?

5. Based on their theories, where would Goffman (see Part III) and Garfinkel say "society" is located?

A THEORY OF REALITY

29

Five Features of Reality

Hugh Mehan

Houston Wood

(1975)

REALITY AS A REFLEXIVE ACTIVITY

When the Azande of Africa are faced with important decisions, decisions about where to build their houses, or whom to marry, or whether the sick will live, for example, they consult an oracle. They prepare for these consultations by following a strictly prescribed ritual. First, a substance is gathered from the bark of a certain type of tree. Then this substance is prepared in a special way during a seancelike ceremony. The Azande then pose the question in a form that permits a simple yes or no answer, and feed the substance to a small chicken. The Azande decide beforehand whether the death of the chicken will signal an affirmative or negative response, and so they always receive an unequivocal answer to their questions.

For monumental decisions, the Azande add a second step. They feed the substance to a second chicken, asking the same question but reversing the import of the chicken's death. If in the first consultation sparing the chicken's life meant the oracle had said yes, in the second reading the oracle must now kill the chicken to once more reply in the affirmative and be consistent with its first response.

Our Western scientific knowledge tells us that the tree bark used by the Azande contains a poisonous substance that kills some chickens. The Azande have no knowledge of the tree's poisonous qualities. They do not believe the tree plays a part in the oracular ceremony. The ritual that comes between the gathering of the bark and the administration of the substance to a fowl transforms the tree into an oracle. The bark is but a vessel for the oracle to enter. As the ritual is completed the oracle takes possession of the substance. The fact that it was once a part of a tree is irrelevant. Chickens then live or die, not because of the properties of the tree, but because the oracle "hears like a person and settles cases like a king" (Evans-Pritchard, 1937, p. 321).

The Westerner sees insuperable difficulties in maintaining such beliefs when the oracle contradicts itself. Knowing the oracle's bark is "really" poison, we wonder what happens when, for example, the first and second administration of the oracle produces first a positive and then a negative answer. Or, suppose someone else consults the oracle about the same question, and contradictory answers occur? What if the oracle is contradicted by later events? The house site approved by the oracle, for example, may promptly be flooded; or the wife the oracle selected may die or be a shrew. How is it possible for the Azande to continue to believe in oracles in the face of so many evident contradictions to his faith?

What I have called contradictions are not contradictions for the Azande. They are only contradictions because these events are being viewed from the reality of Western science. Westerners look at oracular practices to determine if in fact there is an oracle. The Azande *know* that an oracle exists. That is their beginning premise. All that subsequently happens they experience from that beginning assumption.

The Azande belief in oracles is much like the mathematician's belief in certain axioms. Gasking (1955) has described such unquestioned and unquestionable axioms as *incorrigible propositions*:

> An incorrigible proposition is one which you would never admit to be false whatever happens: it therefore does not tell you what happens. . . . The truth of an incorrigible proposition . . . is compatible with any and every conceivable state of affairs. (For example: whatever is your experience on counting, it is still true that $7 + 5 = 12$.) (p. 432)

The incorrigible faith in the oracle is "compatible with any and every conceivable state of affairs." It is not so much a faith about a fact in the world as a faith in the facticity of the world itself. It is the same as the faith many of us have that $7 + 5$ always equals 12. (cf. Polanyi, 1958, pp. 190–193, 257–261).

Just as Gasking suggests we explain away empirical experiences that deny this mathematical truth, the Azande too have available to them what Evans-Pritchard (1937) calls "secondary elaborations of belief" (p. 330). They explain the failure of the oracle by retaining the unquestioned absolute reality of oracles. When events occurred that revealed the inadequacy of the mystical faith in oracles, Evans-Pritchard tried to make the Azande understand these failures as he did. They only laughed, or met his arguments:

> sometimes by point-blank assertions, sometimes by one of the evasive secondary elaborations of belief . . . sometimes by polite pity, but always by an entanglement of linguistic obstacles, for one cannot well express in its language objections not formulated by a culture. (p. 319)

Evans-Pritchard goes on to write:

> Let the reader consider any argument that would utterly demolish all Zande claims for the power of the oracle. If it were translated into Zande modes of thought it would serve to support their entire structure of belief. For their mystical notions are eminently coherent, being interrelated by a network of logical ties, and are so ordered that they never too crudely contradict sensory experience, but, instead, experience seems to justify them. *The Zande is immersed in a sea of mystical notions, and if he speaks about his poison oracle he must speak in a mystical idiom* [italics added]. (pp. 319–320)

Seeming contradictions are explained away by saying such things as a taboo must have been breached, or that sorcerers, witches, ghosts, or gods must have intervened. These "mystical" notions reaffirm the reality of a world in which oracles are a basic feature. Failures do not challenge the oracle. They are elaborated in such a way that they provide evidence for the constant success of oracles. Beginning with the incorrigible belief in oracles, all events *reflexively* become evidence for that belief.[1]

The mathematician, as Gasking suggests, uses a similar process:

> But it does lay it down, so to speak, that if on counting $7 + 5$ you do get 11, you are to describe what has happened in some such way as this: Either "I have made a mistake in my counting" or "Someone has played a practical joke and abstracted one of the objects when I was not looking" or "Two of the objects have coalesced" or "One of the objects has disappeared," etc. (Gasking, 1955; quoted in Pollner, 1973, pp. 15–16)

Consider the analogous case of a Western scientist using chloroform to asphyxiate butterflies. The incorrigible idiom called chemistry tells the scientist, among other things, that substances have certain constant properties. Chloroform of a certain volume and mix is capable of killing butterflies. One evening the scientist administers the chloroform as usual, and is dismayed to see the animal continue to flutter about.

Here is a contradiction of the scientist's reality, just as oracle use sometimes produces contradictions. Like the Azande, scientists have many secondary elaborations of belief they can bring to bear on such occurrences, short of rejecting the Western causal belief. Instead of rejecting chemistry they can explain the poison's failure by such things as "faulty manufacturing," "mislabeling," "sabotage," or "practical joke." Whatever the conclusion, it would continue to reaffirm the causal premise of science. This reaffirmation reflexively supports the reality that produced the poison's unexpected failure in the first place.

The use of contradictions to reaffirm incorrigible propositions can be observed in other branches of science. In the Ptolemaic system of astronomy, the sun was seen as a planet of the earth. When astronomers looked at the sun, they saw it as an orb circling the earth. When the Copernican system arose as an alternative to this view, it offered little new empirical data. Instead, it described the old "facts" in a different way. A shift of vision was required for people to see the sun as a star, not a planet of the earth.

Seeing the sun as a star and seeing it as a planet circling the earth are merely alternatives. There is no a priori warrant for believing that either empirical determination is necessarily superior to the other.

How is a choice between equally compelling empirical determinations made? The convert to the Copernican system could have said: "I used to see a planet, but now I see a star" (cf. Kuhn, 1970, p. 115). But to talk that way is to allow the belief that an object can be both a star and a planet at the same time. Such a belief is not allowed in Western science. So, instead, the Copernican concludes that the sun was a star all along. By so concluding, the astronomer exhibits an incorrigible proposition of Western thought, the *object constancy assumption.*[2] This is the belief that objects remain the same over

time, across viewings from different positions and people. When presented with seemingly contradictory empirical determinations, the convert to Copernicanism does not consider that the sun changes through time. Instead he says: "I once took the sun to be a planet, but I was mistaken." The "discovery" of the sun as a star does not challenge the object constancy belief any more than an oracular "failure" challenges the ultimate reality of Azande belief.

The reaffirmation of incorrigible propositions is not limited to mystical and scientific ways of knowing. This reflexive work operates in common-sense reasoning as well. Each time you search for an object you knew was "right there" the same reflexive process is operating. Say, for example, you find a missing pen in a place you know you searched before. Although the evidence indicates that the pen was first absent and then present, that conclusion is not reached. To do so would challenge the incorrigibility of the object constancy belief. Instead, secondary elaborations—"I must have overlooked it," "I must not have looked there"—are invoked to retain the integrity of the object constancy proposition.

Without an object constancy assumption, there would be no problems about alternative determinations. But, with this assumption as an incorrigible proposition, the person faced with alternative seeings must choose one and only one as real. In choosing one, the other is automatically revealed as false. The falsehood of the rejected alternative may be explained in various ways. It may be due to a defective sensory apparatus, or a cognitive bias, or idiosyncratic psychological dynamics. We explain the inconstancy of the experienced object by saying that inconstancy is a product of the experiencing, not a feature of the object itself.[3]

Once an alternative seeing is explained away, the accepted explanation provides evidence for the object constancy assumption that made the explanation necessary in the first place. By demanding that we dismiss one of two equally valid empirical determinations, the object constancy assumption leads to a body of work that validates that assumption. The work then justifies itself afterward, in the world it has created. This self-preservative reflexive process is common to oracular, scientific, and common-sense reasoning.

So far I have approached the reflexive feature of realities as if it were a form of reasoning. But reflexivity is not only a facet of reasoning. It is a recurrent fact of everyday social life. For example, *talk itself is reflexive* (cf. Garfinkel, 1967; Cicourel, 1973). An utterance not only delivers some particular information, it also creates a world in which information itself can appear.

Zimmerman (1973, p. 25) provides a means for understanding the reflexivity of talk at the level of a single word. He presents three identical shapes:

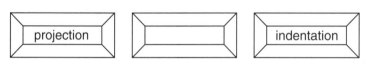

The first and third differ from the second: They each contain single words. These words interact with the box in which they appear so as to change the nature of that box. In so doing, they reflexively illumine themselves. For example, the word "projection," appearing in some other setting, would not mean what it does here. For me it means that I am to see the back panel and the word "projection" as illustrative of a projection. The word "projection" does not merely appear in the scene reporting on that scene. It creates the scene in which it appears as a reasonable object.

Similarly, the word "indentation" not only takes its meaning from the context in which it appears, it reflexively creates that very context. It creates a reality in which it may stand as a part of that reality.

These examples only hint at the reflexivity of talk. . . . Actual conversations are more complex than single words. The social context in which talk occurs, while analogous to one of these static boxes, is enormously ambiguous and potentially infinitely referential. Nonetheless, conversation operates like the printed "projection" and "indentation." An analysis of greetings can be used to show how talk partially constitutes the context and then comes to be seen as independent of it.[4]

To say "hello" both creates and sustains a world in which persons acknowledge . . . (1) [that] they sometimes can see one another; [and] (2) a world in which it is possible for persons to signal to each other, and (3) expect to be signaled back to, by (4) some others but not all of them. This is a partial and only illustrative list of some of the things a greeting accomplishes. Without the superstitious use of greetings, no world in which greetings are possible "objects" would arise. A greeting creates "room" for itself. But once such verbal behaviors are regularly done, a world is built up that can take their use for granted (cf. Sacks, Schegloff, & Jefferson, 1974).

When we say "hello" and the other replies with the expected counter greeting, the reflexive work of our initial utterance is masked. If the other scowls and walks on, then we are reminded that we were attempting to create a scene of greetings and that we failed. Rather than treat this as evidence that greetings are not "real," however, the rejected greeter ordinarily turns it into an occasion for affirming the reality of greetings. He formulates "secondary elaborations" of belief about greetings. He says, "He didn't hear me," "She is not feeling well," "It doesn't matter anyway."

Reflexivity provides grounds for absolute faith in the validity of knowledge. The Azande takes the truth of the oracle for granted, the scientist assumes the facticity of science, the layman accepts the tenets of common sense. The incorrigible propositions of a reality serve as criteria to judge other ways of knowing. Using his absolute faith in the oracle, the Azande dismisses Evans-Pritchard's Western science contradictions. Evans-Pritchard, steeped in the efficacy of science, dismissed the oracle as superstitious. An absolute faith in the incorrigibility of one's own knowledge enables believers to repel contrary evidence. This suggests that all people are equally superstitious.

REALITY AS A COHERENT BODY OF KNOWLEDGE

The phenomenon of reflexivity is a feature of every reality. It interacts with the coherence, inter-actional, fragility, and permeability features I describe in the rest of this chapter. These five features are incorrigible propositions of the reality of ethnomethodology. They appear as facts of the external world due to the ethnomethodologist's unquestioned assumption that they constitute the world. In other words, these features themselves exhibit reflexivity.

This reflexive loop constitutes the interior structure of ethnomethodology. This will become clearer as I describe the second feature of realities, their exhibition of a coherent body of knowledge. To illustrate this feature I will extrapolate from the work of Zimmerman and Wieder (n.d.), who investigated the life of a number of self-named "freaks," frequent drug users within America's counterculture. Both freaks and their academic ethnographers (e.g., Reich, 1970; Roszack, 1969) describe freaks as radical opponents of the straight culture from which they sprang. As Zimmerman and Wieder (n.d.) write:

> From the standpoint of the "straight" members of society, freaks are deliberately irrational. . . . They disavow an interest in efficiency, making long-range plans, and concerns about costs of property (etc.) which are valued by the straight members of American society and are understood by them as indicators of rationality. (p. 103)

On first appearance, here is a reality that seems anarchical. Nonetheless, Zimmerman and Wieder found that

> when it comes to those activities most highly valued by freaks, such as taking drugs, making love, and other "cheap thrills," there is an elabo-rately developed body of lore. Freaks and others use that knowledge of taking drugs, making love, etc., reasonably, deliberately, planfully, projecting various consequences, predicting outcomes, con-ceiving of the possibilities of action in more or less clear and distinct ways, and choosing between two or more means of reaching the same end. (pp. 102–103)

The most vivid illustration that freaks use a coherent body of knowledge comes from Zimmerman's and Wieder's discoveries about the place of drugs in the everyday freak life. At first glance such drug use appears irrational. Yet, among freaks, taking drugs "is something as ordinary and unremarkable as their parents regard taking or offering a cup of coffee" (p. 57). Freak behavior is not a function of the freaks' ignorance of chemical and medical "facts" about drugs. The freaks studied knew chemical and medical facts well. They organized these facts into a different, yet coherent corpus of knowledge.

One of the team's research assistants, Peter Suczek, was able to systematize the freaks' knowl-edge of drugs into a taxonomic schemata (see Table 1).

What the freak calls "dope," the chemist calls "psychotropic drugs." Within the family of dope, freaks distinguish "mind-expanding" and "body" dope. Freaks further subdivide each of these species. In addition, freaks share a common body of knowledge informing them of the practicalities surrounding the use of each type of dope. All knowledge of dope use is grounded in the incorri-gible proposition that dope is to be used. One must, of course, know how to use it.

Zimmerman and Wieder (n.d.) found the following knowledge about "psychedelic mind-expanding dope" to be common among freaks:

> The folk pharmacology of psychedelic drugs may be characterized as a method whereby drug users rationally assess choices among kinds of drugs, choices among instances of the same kind of drug, the choice to ingest or not, the time of the act of ingestion relative to the state of one's physiology and relative to the state of one's psyche, the timing relative to social and practical demands, the appropriateness of the setting for having a psychedelic experience, the size of the dose, and the effectiveness and risk of mixing drugs. (p. 118)

Freaks share similar knowledge for the rest of the taxonomy. Being a freak means living within the auspices of such knowledge and using it according to a plan, as the chemist uses his. Both the freaks' and the scientists' realities are concerned with "the facts." Though the facts differ, each reality reflexively proves its facts as absolute.

Consider how the freak assembles the knowledge he uses. He is not loath to borrow from the discoveries of science. But before accepting what the scientist says, he first tests scientific "facts" against the auspices of his own incorrigible propositions. He does not use the scientists' findings to determine the danger of the drug, but rather to indicate the particular dosage, setting, etc., under which a drug is to be taken.

Scientific drug researchers frequently attend to the experiences of freaks in a comparable way. They incorporate the facts that freaks report about dope into their coherent idiom. The two then are like independent teams of investigators working on the same phenomenon with different purposes. They are like artists and botanists who share a common interest in the vegetable kingdom, but who employ different incorrigibles.

The freak's knowledge, like all knowledge, is sustained through reflexive interactional work. For example, the knowledge contained in the drug

Table 1   The Folk Pharmacology for Dope

Types of Dope	Subcategories
Mind-expanding dope	(Untitled)
	"grass" (marijuana)
	"hash" (hashish)
	"LSD" or "acid" (lysergic acid)
	Psychedelics
	mescaline
	synthetic
	organic
	natural, peyote
	psilocybin
	synthetic
	organic
	natural, mushrooms
	"DMT"
	miscellaneous (e.g., Angel's Dust)
Body dope	"speed" (amphetamines)
	"downers" (barbiturates)
	"tranks" (tranquilizers)
	"coke" (cocaine)
	"shit" (heroin)

Source: Zimmerman and Wieder (n.d.), p. 107.

taxonomy (Table 1) sometimes "fails," that is, it produces not a "high" but a "bummer." The incorrigible propositions of freak pharmacology are not then questioned. Instead, these propositions are invoked to explain the bummer's occurrence. "For example," Zimmerman and Wieder (n.d.) write:

> A "bad trip" may be explained in such terms as the following: it was a bad time and place to drop; my head wasn't ready for it; or it was bad acid or mescaline, meaning that it was cut with something

impure or that it was some other drug altogether. (p. 118)

The reflexive use of the freak taxonomy recalls my previous discussion of the Azande. When the oracle seemed to contradict itself, the contradiction became but one more occasion for proving the oracular way of knowing. The reality of oracles is appealed to in explaining the failure of the oracle, just as the reality of freak pharmacology is used to explain a bad trip. It would be as futile for a chemist to explain the bad trip scientifically to a freak as it was for Evans-Pritchard to try to convince the Azande that failures of the oracle demonstrated their unreality.

The coherence of knowledge is a reflexive consequence of the researcher's attention. Zimmerman and Wieder, in the best social science tradition, employed many methods to construct the freak's taxonomy. Freaks were interviewed by sociology graduate students and by their peers. These interviewers provided accounts of their own drug experiences as well. Additional freaks not acquainted with the purposes of the research were paid to keep personal diaries of their day-to-day experiences. Zimmerman and Wieder used a portion of this massive data to construct the freak taxonomy, then tested its validity against further portions of the data.

Such systematizations are always the researcher's construction (Wallace, 1972). To claim that any reality, including the researcher's own, exhibits a coherent body of knowledge is but to claim that coherence can be found *upon analysis*. The coherence located in a reality is found there by the ethnomethodologist's interactional work. The coherence feature, like all features of realities, operates as an incorrigible proposition, reflexively sustained.

Consider the analogous work of linguists (e.g., Chomsky, 1965). Within language-using communities, linguists discover the "rules of grammar." Although the linguist empirically establishes

these grammatical rules, speaker-hearers of that language cannot list them. Rules can be located in their talk, upon analysis, but language users cannot describe them.

Similarly, freaks could not supply the taxonomy Zimmerman and Wieder claim they "really" know. It was found upon analysis. It is an imposition of the researcher's logic upon the freak's logic.

Castañeda's (1968, 1971) attempts to explain the reality of Yaqui sorcery further illustrates the reflexity of analysis. In his initial report, *The Teachings of Don Juan*, Castañeda (1968) begins with a detailed ethnography of his experiences of his encounter with a Yaqui sorcerer, Don Juan. In this reality it is common for time to stop, for men to turn into animals and animals into men, for animals and men to converse with one another, and for great distances to be covered while the body remains still.

In the final section of his report, Castañeda systematizes his experiences with the sorcerer. He presents a coherent body of knowledge undergirding Don Juan's teachings. Thus Castañeda, like Zimmerman and Wieder, organizes a "nonordinary" reality into a coherent system of knowledge.

In a second book Castañeda (1971) describes Don Juan's reaction to his systematization of a peyote session, a "mitote." Castañeda told Don Juan he had discovered that mitotes are a "result of a subtle and complex system of cueing." He writes:

It took me close to two hours to read and explain to Don Juan the scheme I had constructed. I ended by begging him to tell me in his own words what were the exact procedures for reaching agreement.

When I had finished he frowned. I thought he must have found my explanation challenging; he appeared to be involved in deep deliberation. After a reasonable silence I asked him what he thought about my idea.

My question made him suddenly turn his frown into a smile and then into roaring laughter. I tried to laugh too and asked nervously what was so funny.

"You're deranged!" he exclaimed. "Why should anyone be bothered with cueing at such an important time as a mitote? Do you think one ever fools around with Mescalito?"

I thought for a moment that he was being evasive; he was not really answering my question.

"Why should anyone cue?" Don Juan asked stubbornly. "You have been in mitotes. You should know that no one told you how to feel, or what to do; no one except Mescalito himself."

I insisted that such an explanation was not possible and begged him again to tell me how the agreement was reached.

"I know why you have come," Don Juan said in a mysterious tone. "I can't help you in your endeavor because there is no system of cueing."

"But how can all those persons agree about Mescalito's presence?"

"They agree because they *see*," Don Juan said dramatically, and then added casually, "Why don't you attend another mitote and see for yourself?" (pp. 37–38)

Don Juan finds Castañeda's account ridiculous. This rejection is not evidence that Castañeda's attempt at systematization is incorrect. It indicates that the investigator reflexively organizes the realities he investigates. All realities may *upon analysis* exhibit a coherent system of knowledge, but knowledge of this coherence is not necessarily part of the awareness of its members.

Features emerging "upon analysis" is a particular instance of reflexivity. These features exist only within the reflexive work of those researchers who make them exist. This does not deny their reality. There is no need to pursue the chimera of a presuppositionless inquiry. Because all realities are ultimately superstitious the reflexive location of reflexivity is not a problem within ethnomethodological studies. Rather, it provides them with their most intriguing phenomenon.

My discussion of these first two features of realities also shows that any one feature is separate from the other only upon analysis. In my description of reflexivity, I was forced to assume the existence of a coherent body of knowledge. Similarly, in the present discussion I could not speak about the existence of coherent systems of knowledge without introducing the caveat of "upon analysis," an implicit reference to reflexivity. This situation will continue as I discuss the remaining three features. Though I attempt to keep them separate from one another, I will only be partially successful, since the five are inextricably intertwined. Nevertheless, I will continue to talk of them as five separate features, not as one. I acknowledge that this talk is more heuristic than literal—it provides a ladder with five steps that may be climbed and then thrown away (cf. Wittgenstein, 1921/1961).

REALITY AS INTERACTIONAL ACTIVITY

Realities are also dependent upon ceaseless social interactional work. Wood's study of a mental hospital illustrates the reality of this reality work. He discovered that psychiatric attendants shared a body of knowledge. Wood's (1968) analysis of the attendants' interaction with the patients uncovered labels like: "baby," "child," "epileptic," "mean old man," "alcoholic," "lost soul," "good patient," "depressive," "sociopath," and "nigger" (p. 36). Though borrowed from psychiatry, these terms constitute a corpus of knowledge which reflects the attendants' own practical nursing concerns. These terms can be arranged in a systematic taxonomy (see Table 2). Each is shown to differ from the others according to four parameters of nursing problems.

Wood's study explored how the attendants used this taxonomy to construct meanings for the mental patients' behavior. One explanation of label use is called a "matching procedure." The matching model of labeling patient behavior is essentially a psychological theory. It treats behavior as a private, internal state, not influenced by social dimensions. The matching model assumes

Table 2   The Meaning of the Labels

Psychiatric Attendant Label	Nursing Trouble				Frequency × 60
	Work	Cleanliness	Supervisory	Miscellaneous	
Mean old man	yes	yes	yes	yes	2
Baby	yes	yes	yes	—	20
Child	yes	yes	—	yes	4
Nigger	yes	—	yes	yes	1
Epileptic	—	yes	—	yes	4
Sociopath	yes	—	—	yes	3
Depressive	—	—	—	yes	2
Alcoholic	—	—	yes	—	8
Lost soul	yes	—	—	—	12
Good patient	—	—	—	—	6

Source: Wood (1968), p. 45.

the patients' behavior has obvious features. Trained personnel monitor and automatically apply the appropriate label to patients' behavior.

Wood presents five case histories that show that labels are not applied by a simple matching process. They are molded in the day-to-day interaction of the attendants with one another and with the patients. The labeling of patients is a social activity, not a psychological one.

Wood (1968, pp. 51–91) describes the labeling history of patient Jimmy Lee Jackson. Over the course of his three-month hospitalization, Jackson held the same official psychiatric label, that of "psychoneurotic reaction, depressive type." However, the ward attendants saw Jackson within the web of their own practical circumstances. For them, at one time he was a "nigger," at another a "depressive," and at yet another a "sociopath." These seeings reflected a deep change in the meaning Jackson had for the attendants. When he was seen as a "nigger," for example, it meant that the attendants considered he was "lazy, and . . . without morals or scruples and . . . that the patient is cunning and will attempt to ingratiate himself with the attendants in order to get attention and 'use' them for his own ends" (p. 52). When

Jackson became a depressive type, all these negative attributes were withdrawn. The change in attribution, Wood shows, cannot be explained by a matching procedure. The attendants' social interactional work produced the change, independent of Jackson's behavior. This suggests that realities are fundamentally interactional activities.

One evening Jackson was suffering from a toothache. Unable to secure medical attention, he ran his arm through a window pane in one of the ward's locked doors. He suffered a severe laceration of his forearm which required stitches. When the attendants who were on duty during this episode returned to work the following afternoon, they discovered that the preceding morning shift had decided that Jackson had attempted suicide. Jackson was no longer presented to them as a nigger. The morning shift found that persons who had not even witnessed the event had given it a meaning they themselves had never considered. Nevertheless, the evening shift accepted the validity of this label change.

The label change indexed a far larger change. Jackson's past history on the ward was reinterpreted. He now was accorded different treatment by attendants on all shifts. He was listened to sympathetically, given whatever he requested, and no longer exhorted to do more ward work. All the attendants came to believe that he had always been a depressive and that they had always seen him as such.

A few weeks later Jackson became yet another person, a "sociopath." The attendants no longer accepted that he was capable of a suicide attempt. The new label was once again applied retrospectively. Not only was Jackson believed to be incapable of committing suicide now, he was thought to have always been incapable of it. The attendants agreed that the window-breaking incident had been a "fake" or "con,"—just the sort of thing a sociopath would do. Attendants who had praised Jackson as a hard worker when he was labeled a depressive now pointed to this same work as proof he was a "conniver." Requests for attention and medicine that had been promptly fulfilled for the depressive Jackson were now ignored for the sociopath Jackson, or used as occasions to attack him verbally.

Yet, as Wood describes Jackson, he remained constant despite these changes in attendant behavior. He did the same amount of work and sought the same amount of attention and medicine whether he was labeled a nigger or a depressive or a sociopath. What Jackson was at any time was determined by the reality work of the attendants.

In the final pages of his study, Wood (1968) further illustrates the power of interactional work to create an external world:

The evening that he [Jackson] cut his arm, I, like the PAs [psychiatric attendants], was overcome by the blood and did not reflect on its "larger" meaning concerning his proper label. The next day, when I heard all of the morning shift PAs refer to his action as a suicide attempt, I too labeled Jackson a "depressive" and the cut arm as a suicide attempt. When the label changed in future weeks I was working as a PA on the ward up to 12 hours a day. It was only two months later when I had left the ward, as I reviewed my notes and my memory, that I recognized the

"peculiar" label changes that had occurred. While I was on the ward, it had not seemed strange to think that cutting an arm in a window was a serious attempt to kill oneself. Only as an "outsider" did I come to think that Jackson had "really" stayed the same through his three label changes. (pp. 137–138)

As Wood says, Jackson could never have a meaning apart from *some* social context. Meanings unfold only within an unending sequence of practical actions.[5]

The *matching* theory of label use assumes a correspondence theory of signs (cf. Garfinkel, 1952, pp. 91ff.; Wieder, 1970). This theory of signs has three analytically separate elements: ideas that exist in the head, signs that appear in symbolic representations, and objects and events that appear in the world. Meaning is the relation among these elements. Signs can stand on behalf of the ideas in the head or refer to objects in the world. This theory of signs implies that signs stand in a point-by-point relation to thoughts in one's mind or objects in the world. Meanings are stable across time and space. They are not dependent upon the concrete participants or upon the specific scenes in which they appear.

Wood's study indicates that labels are not applied in accordance with correspondence principles. Instead, labels are *indexical expressions*. Meanings are situationally determined. They are dependent upon the concrete context in which they appear. The participants' interactional activity structured the indexical meaning of the labels used on the ward. The relationship of the participants to the object, the setting in which events occur, and the circumstances surrounding a definition determine the meaning of labels and of objects.

The interactional feature indicates that realities do not possess symbols, like so many tools in a box. A reality and its signs are "mutually determinative" (Wieder, 1973, p. 216). Alone, neither expresses sense. Intertwining through the course of indexical interaction, they form a life.

THE FRAGILITY OF REALITIES

Every reality depends upon (1) ceaseless reflexive use of (2) a body of knowledge in (3) interaction. Every reality is also fragile. Suppression of the activities that the first three features describe disrupts the reality. Every reality is equally capable of dissolution. The presence of this fragility feature of realities has been demonstrated by studies called "incongruity procedures" or "breaching experiments."

In one of the simplest of these, Garfinkel used 67 students as "experimenters." These students engaged a total of 253 "subjects" in a game of tick-tack-toe. When the figure necessary for the game was drawn, the experimenters requested the subject to make the first move. After the subject made his mark, the experimenter took his turn. Rather than simply marking another cell, the experimenter erased the subject's mark and moved it to another cell. Continuing as if this were expected behavior, the experimenter then placed his own mark in one of the now empty cells. The experimenters reported that their action produced extreme bewilderment and confusion in the subjects. The reality of the game, which before the experimenter's move seemed stable and external, suddenly fell apart. For a moment the subjects exhibited an "amnesia for social structure" (Garfinkel, 1963, p. 189).

This fragility feature is even more evident in everyday life, where the rules are not explicit. People interact without listing the rules of conduct. Continued reference is made to this knowledge nonetheless. This referencing is not ordinarily available as long as the reality work continues normally. When the reality is disrupted, the interactional activity structuring the reality becomes visible. This is what occurred in the tick-tack-toe game. A usually unnoticed feature of the game is a "rule" prohibiting erasing an opponent's mark. When this unspoken "rule" is broken, it makes its first public appearance. If we were aware of the fragility of our realities, they would not seem real.

Thus Garfinkel (1963) found that when the "incongruity-inducing procedures" developed in games

> were applied in "real life" situations, it was unnerving to find the seemingly endless variety of events that lent themselves to the production of really nasty surprises. These events ranged from . . . standing very, very close to a person while otherwise maintaining an innocuous conversation, to others . . . like saying "hello" at the termination of a conversation. . . . Both procedures elicited anxiety, indignation, strong feelings on the part of the experimenter and subject alike of humiliation and regret, demands by the subjects for explanations, and so on. (p. 198)

Another of the procedures Garfinkel developed was to send student experimenters into stores and restaurants where they were told to "mistake" customers for salespersons and waiters. . . . (see Reading 30, pp. 372–375, this volume, for details of one such experiment).

The breaching experiments were subsequently refined, such that:

> The person [subject] could not turn the situation into a play, a joke, an experiment, a deception, and the like . . . ; that he have insufficient time to work through a redefinition of his real circumstances; and that he be deprived of consensual support for an alternative definition of social reality. (Garfinkel, 1964; in 1967, p. 58)

This meant that subjects were not allowed to reflexively turn the disruption into a revalidation of their realities. The incorrigible propositions of their social knowledge were not adequate for the present circumstances. They were removed from the supporting interactional activity that they possessed before the breach occurred.

These refinements had the positive consequence of increasing the bewilderment of the subjects, who became more and more like desocialized schizophrenics, persons completely devoid of any social reality. These refinements produced a negative consequence. They were immoral. Once subjects had experienced the fragility, they could not continue taking the stability of realities for granted. No amount of "cooling out" could restore the subject's faith.

But what is too cruel to impose on others can be tried upon oneself. . . .

THE PERMEABILITY OF REALITIES

Because the reflexive use of social knowledge is fragile and interaction dependent, one reality may be altered, and another may be assumed. Cases where a person passes from one reality to another, dramatically different, reality vividly display this permeability feature.

Tobias Schneebaum, a painter who lives periodically in New York, provides an example of a radical shift in realities in his book, *Keep the River on Your Right* (1969). Schneebaum entered the jungles of Peru in 1955 in pursuit of his art. During the trip the book describes, he gradually lost interest in painterly studies. He found himself drawn deeper and deeper into the jungle. Unlike a professional anthropologist, he carried no plans to write about his travels. In fact, the slim volume from which I draw the following discussion was not written until 13 years after his return.

He happened upon the Akaramas, a stone age tribe that had never seen a white man. They accepted him quickly, gave him a new name, "Habe," meaning "ignorant one," and began teaching him to be as they were.

Schneebaum learned to sleep in "bundles" with the other men, piled on top of one another for warmth and comfort. He learned to hunt and fish with stone age tools. He learned the Akaramas'

language and their ritual of telling stories of their hunts and hikes, the telling taking longer than the doing. He learned to go without clothing, and to touch casually the genitals of his companions in play.

When one of the men in Schneebaum's compartment is dying of dysentery, crying out at his excretions of blood and pain, the "others laugh and he laughs too" (p. 109). As this man lies among them whimpering and crying in their sleeping pile at night, Schneebaum writes: "Not Michii or Baaldore or Ihuene or Reindude seemed to have him on their minds. It was as if he were not there among us or as if he had already gone to some other forest" (p. 129). When he dies, he is immediately forgotten. Such is the normal perception of death within the Akarama reality. As Schneebaum describes another incident: "There were two pregnant women whom I noticed one day with flatter bellies and no babies on their backs, but there was no sign of grief, no service . . ." (p. 109).

Gradually, Schneebaum absorbed even these ways and a new sense of time. At one point he left the Akaramas to visit the mission from which he had embarked. He was startled to find that seven months had passed, not the three or four he had supposed. As he was more and more permeated by the stone age reality, he began to feel that his "own world, whatever, wherever it was, no longer was anywhere in existence" (p. 69). As the sense of his old reality disappears, he says, "My fears were not so much for the future . . . but for my knowledge. I was removing my own reflection" (pp. 64–65).

One day, a day like many others, he rises to begin a hunting expedition with his sleeping companions. This day, however, they go much farther than ever before. They paint themselves in a new way and repeat new chants. Finally they reach a strange village. In they swoop, Schneebaum too, shouting their sacred words and killing all the men they can catch, disemboweling and beheading them on the spot. They burn all the huts, kidnap the women and children. They then hike to their own village, without pause, through an entire night. At home, a new dance is begun. The meat of the men they have murdered and brought back with them is cooked. As a new movement of the dance begins, this meat is gleefully eaten. Exhausted at last, they stumble together on the ground. Then the last of the meat is put to ceremonious use:

> We sat or lay around the fires, eating, moaning the tones of the chant, swaying forward and back, moving from the hip, forward and back. Calm and silence settled over us, all men. Four got up, one picked a heart from the embers, and they walked into the forest. Small groups of others arose, selected a piece of meat, and disappeared in other directions. We three were alone until Ihuene, Baaldore, and Reindude were in front of us, Reindude cupping in his hand the heart from the being we had carried from so far away, the heart of he who had lived in the hut we had entered to kill. We stretched out flat upon the ground, lined up, our shoulders touching. Michii looked up at the moon and showed it to the heart. He bit into it as if it were an apple, taking a large bite, almost half the heart, and chewed down several times, spit into a hand, separated the meat into six sections and placed some into the mouths of each of us. We chewed and swallowed. He did the same with the other half of the heart. He turned Darinimbiak onto his stomach, lifted his hips so that he crouched on all fours. Darinimbiak growled, Mayaarii-ha! Michii growled, Mayaari-ha!, bent down to lay himself upon Darinimbiak's back and entered him. (pp. 106–107)

Mass murder, destruction of an entire village, theft of all valuable goods, cannibalism, the ritual eating of the heart before publicly displayed homosexual acts—these are some of the acts Schneebaum participated in. He could not have done them his first day in the jungle. But after his gradual adoption of the Akarama reality, they had become natural. It would have been as immoral for him to refuse to join his brothers in the raid and its

victory celebration as it would be immoral for him to commit these same acts within a Western community. His reality had changed. The moral facts were different.

Schneebaum's experience suggests that even radically different realities can be penetrated.[6] We would not have this account, however, if the stone age reality had completely obliterated Schneebaum's Western reality. He would still be with the tribe. The more he permeated the Akaramas' reality, the more suspect his old reality became. The more he fell under the spell of the absolutism of his new reality, the more fragile his old reality became. Like the cannibals, Schneebaum says: "My days are days no longer. Time had no thoughts to trouble me, and everything is like nothing and nothing is like everything. For if a day passes, it registers nowhere, and it might be a week, it might be a month. There is no difference" (p. 174).

As the vision of his old reality receded, Schneebaum experienced its fragility. He knew he must leave soon, or there would be no reality to return to. He describes his departure:

> A time alone, only a few weeks ago, with the jungle alive and vibrant around me, and Michii and Baaldore gone with all the other men to hunt, I saw within myself too many seeds that would grow a fungus around my brain, encasing it with mold that could penetrate and smooth the convolutions and there I would remain, not he who had travelled and arrived, not the me who had crossed the mountains in a search, but another me living only in ease and pleasure, no longer able to scrawl out words on paper or think beyond a moment. And days later, I took myself up from our hut, and I walked on again alone without a word to any of my friends and family, but left when all again were gone and I walked through my jungle. . . . (p. 182)

The Akaramas would not miss him. They would not even notice his absence. For them, there were no separate beings. Schneebaum felt their reality obliterating "the me who had crossed the mountains in a search." Schneebaum was attached to this "me," and so he left.

In the previous section, I listed three conditions necessary for successful breaches: There can be no place to escape. There can be no time to escape. There can be no one to provide counter evidence. The same conditions are required to move between realities. That is, as Castañeda's (1968, 1971, 1972) work suggests, in order to permeate realities, one must first have the old reality breached. Castañeda has named this necessity the establishment "of a certainty of a minimal possibility," that another reality actually exists (personal communication). Successful breaches must establish that another reality is available for entry. Thus, as Don Juan attempted to make Castañeda a man of knowledge, he first spent years trying to crack Castañeda's absolute faith in the reality of Western rationalism.

Castañeda's work suggests many relations between the fragility and permeability features. It is not my purpose to explore the relations of the five features in this book. But I want to emphasize that such relations can be supposed to exist.

I relied on the "exotic" case of a person passing from a Western to a stone age reality to display the permeability feature of realities. However, any two subsequent interactional encounters could have been used for this purpose. All such passages are of equal theoretic import. Passages between a movie and freeway driving, between a person's reality before and after psychotherapy, between a "straight" acquiring membership in the reality of drug freaks, or before and after becoming a competent religious healer, are all the same. The differences are "merely" methodological, not theoretical. Studying each passage, I would concentrate on how the reflexive, knowledge, interactional, and fragility features affect the shift.

All realities are permeable. Ethnomethodology is a reality. This book is an attempt to breach the reader's present reality by introducing him to the "certainty of a minimal possibility" that another reality exists.

On the Concept of Reality

Many ethnomethodologists rely on Schutz's concept of reality (e.g., 1962, 1964, 1966). . . . My use of "reality" contrasts with Schutz's view. For Schutz (e.g., 1962, pp. 208ff.), the reality of everyday life is the *one* paramount reality. Schutz says that this paramount reality consists of a number of presuppositions or assumptions, which include the assumption of a tacit, taken for granted world; an assumed practical interest in that world; and an assumption that the world is intersubjective (e.g., 1962, p. 23). Schutz argues that other realities exist, but that they derive from the paramount reality. For example, he discusses the realities of "scientific theorizing" and of "fantasy." These realities appear when some of the basic assumptions of the paramount reality are temporarily suspended. The paramount reality of everyday life has an elastic quality for Schutz. After excursions into other realities, we snap back into the everyday.

My view of realities is different. I do not wish to call one or another reality paramount. It is my contention that every reality is equally real. No single reality contains more of the truth than any other. From the perspective of Western everyday life, Western everyday life will appear paramount, just as Schutz maintains. But from the perspective of scientific theorizing or dreaming, or meditating, each of these realities will appear just as paramount. Because every reality exhibits the absolutist tendency I mentioned earlier, there is no way to look from the window of one reality at others without seeing yourself. Schutz seems to be a victim of this absolutist prejudice. As a Western man living his life in the Western daily experience, he assumed that this life was the touchstone of all realities.

My concept of reality, then, has more in common with Wittgenstein (1953) than with Schutz. Wittgenstein (e.g., 1953, pp. 61, 179) recognizes that human life exhibits an empirical multitude of activities. He calls these activities language games. Language games are forever being invented and modified and discarded. The fluidity of language activities do not permit rigorous description. Analysts can discover that at any time a number of language games are associated with one another. This association, too, is not amenable to rigorous description. Instead, language games exhibit "family resemblances." One can recognize certain games going together. But one could no more articulate *the* criteria for this resemblance than one could predict the physical characteristics of some unseen member of a familiar extended family. Wittgenstein (1953, pp. 119, 123) calls a collection of language games bound together by a family resemblance, a *form of life*.[7] Forms of life resemble what I call "realities." Realities are far more aswarm than Schutz's terms "finite" and "province" suggest. Forms of life are always forms of life forming.[8] Realities are always realities becoming.

Notes

1. See Pollner's (1970, 1973) discussions of the reflexive reasoning of the Azande and Polanyi's (1958, pp. 287–294) examination of the same materials. In the Apostolic Church of John Marangue, illness is not bodily malfunction, it is sin. Sin is curable not by medicine, but by confessional healing. When evangelists' attempts to heal church members were not accompanied by recovery, Jules-Rosette (1973, p. 167) reports that church members did not lose their faith in the confessional process. They looked to other "causes" of the "failure." They said things like: Other persons must have been implicated in the sin, and untrue confession must have been given. Once again, contradictions that could potentially challenge a basic faith do not, as the basic faith itself is not questioned.

2. See Gurwitsch (1966) for a more technical discussion of the object constancy assumption. . . .

3. The . . . planet-star example [is] adapted from Pollner (1973). Much of this discussion of reflexivity derives from Pollner's thinking on these matters.

4. Riel (1972) illustrates how talk reflexively constitutes the context it then seems to independently reference. Trying to make a certain point, she reports turning away from an inadequate sentence she had written to explore notes and texts again. Forty-five minutes later she wrote the now-perfect sentence, only to discover it was exactly the same sentence she had rejected before.

5. Cicourel (1968) examines the interactional work that accomplishes external objects in greater detail. He shows that juvenile delinquents and crime rates are constituted by the social activities of law enforcement personnel.

6. For an account of a reality shift in the other direction, from the stone age to industrial Western society, see Kroeber's *Ishi in Two Worlds* (1961). Again the transition was never total, but this was a result of a political decision on the part of the author's husband. As Ishi's official keeper, he wished to keep him primitive for his own and anthropology's benefit.

7. Blum (1970) has previously explored the importance of Wittgenstein's notion of "form of life" for social science.

8. This phrase, like much of this chapter, has been adapted from the unpublished lectures of Pollner. For Pollner's published writings see Zimmerman and Pollner, 1970; and Pollner, 1970, 1973, 1974.

References

Blum, A. (1970). Theorizing. In J. D. Douglas (Ed.), *Understanding everyday life*. Chicago: Aldine.

Castañeda, C. (1968). *The teachings of Don Juan*. Berkeley: University of California Press.

Castañeda, C. (1971). *A separate reality*. New York: Simon & Schuster.

Castañeda, C. (1972). *A journey to Iztlan*. New York: Simon & Schuster.

Chomsky, N. (1965). *Aspects of the theory of syntax*. Cambridge, MA: MIT Press.

Cicourel, A. V. (1968). *The social organization of juvenile justice.* New York: John Wiley.

Cicourel, A. V. (1973). *Cognitive sociology.* London: Macmillan.

Evans-Pritchard, E. E. (1937). *Witchcraft, oracles and magic among the Azande.* London: Oxford University Press.

Garfinkel, H. (1952). *Perception of the other.* Unpublished Ph.D. dissertation, Harvard University.

Garfinkel, H. (1963). A conception of and experiments with "trust" as a condition of concerted stable actions. In O. J. Harvey (Ed.), *Motivation and social interaction.* New York: Ronald.

Garfinkel, H. (1964). Studies of the routine grounds of everyday activities. *Social Problems, 11,* 225–250 (Chapter 2 in Garfinkel, 1967).

Garfinkel, H. (1967). *Studies in ethnomethodology.* Englewood Cliffs, NJ: Prentice-Hall.

Gasking, D. (1955). Mathematics and the world. In A. Flew (Ed.), *Logic and language.* Garden City, NY: Doubleday.

Gurwitsch, A. (1966). *Studies in phenomenology and psychology.* Evanston, IL: Northwestern University Press.

Jules-Rosette, B. (1973). *Ritual context and social action.* Unpublished Ph.D. dissertation. Harvard University.

Kroeber, T. (1961). *Ishi in two worlds.* Berkeley: University of California Press.

Kuhn, T. S. (1970). *The structure of scientific revolutions.* Chicago: University of Chicago Press.

Polanyi, M. (1958). *Personal knowledge.* Chicago: University of Chicago Press.

Pollner, M. (1970). *On the foundations of mundane reason.* Unpublished Ph.D. dissertation. University of California, Santa Barbara.

Pollner, M. (1973). *The very coinage of your brain: The resolution of reality disjunctures.* Unpublished manuscript.

Pollner, M. (1974). Mundane reasoning. *Philosophy of social sciences, 4*(1), 35–54.

Reich, C. A. (1970). *The greening of America.* New York: Random House.

Riel, M. M. (1972). *The interpretive process.* Paper presented to a seminar led by Paul Filmer, University of California, San Diego.

Roszak, T. (1969). *The making of a counter culture.* Garden City, NY: Doubleday.

Sacks, H., Schegloff, E., & Jefferson, G. (1974). A simplest systematics for the analysis of turn taking in conversation. *Language, 50,* 696–735.

Schneebaum, T. (1969). *Keep the river on your right.* New York: Grove.

Schutz, A. (1962). *Collected papers I: The problem of social reality.* The Hague: Martinus Nijhoff.

Schutz, A. (1964). *Collected papers II: Studies in social theory.* The Hague: Martinus Nijhoff.

Schutz, A. (1966). *Collected papers III: Studies in phenomenological philosophy.* The Hague: Martinus Nijhoff.

Wallace, H. T. (1972). *Culture and social being.* Unpublished master's thesis, University of California, Santa Barbara.

Wieder, D. L. (1970). Meaning by rule. In J. D. Douglas (Ed.), *Understanding everyday life.* Chicago: Aldine.

Wieder, D. L. (1973). *Language and social reality.* The Hague: Mouton.

Wittgenstein, L. (1953). *Philosophical investigations.* London: Basil Blackwell & Mott.

Wittgenstein, L. (1961). *Tractatus logico-philosophicus.* London: Basil Blackwell & Mott. (Original work published in 1921)

Wood, H. (1968). *The labelling process on a mental hospital ward.* Unpublished master's thesis. University of California, Santa Barbara.

Zimmerman, D. H. (1973). Preface. In D. L. Wieder, *Language and social reality.* The Hague: Mouton.

Zimmerman, D. H., & Pollner, M. (1970). The everyday world as a phenomenon. In J. D. Douglas (Ed.), *Understanding everyday life.* Chicago: Aldine.

Zimmerman, D. H., & Wieder, D. L. (n.d.). *The social bases for illegal behavior in the student community: First year report.* San Francisco and Santa Barbara: Scientific Analysis Corporation.

A THEORY OF REALITY

30

A Conception of and Experiments with "Trust" as a Condition of Concerted Stable Actions

Harold Garfinkel

(1963)

SOME PRELIMINARY TRIALS AND FINDINGS

Since each of the presuppositions that make up the attitude of daily life assigns an expected feature to the actor's environment, it should be possible to induce experimentally a breach of these expectancies by deliberately modifying scenic events so as to disappoint these attributions. By definition, surprise is possible with respect to each of these expected features. The nastiness of surprise should vary directly with the extent to which the actor complies with the constitutive order of events of everyday life as a scheme for assigning witnessed appearances their status of events in a perceivedly normal environment.

Procedures were used to see if a breach of these presuppositions would produce anomic effects and increase disorganization. These procedures must be thought of as demonstrations rather than as experiments. "Experimenters" were upper division students in the author's courses. Their training consisted of little more than verbal instructions about how to proceed. The demonstrations were done as class assignments and were unsupervised. Students reported their results in anecdotal fashion with no controls beyond the fact that they were urged to avoid interpretation in favor of writing down what was actually said and done, staying as close as possible to a chronological account.

Because the procedures nevertheless produced massive effects, I feel they are worth reporting. Obviously, however, caution must be exercised in assessing the findings.

Demonstration 1: Breaching the Congruency of Relevances

This expectancy consists of the following. The person expects, expects that the other person does the same, and expects that as he expects it of the other the other expects the like of him that the differences in their perspectives that originate in their particular individual biographies are irrelevant for the purposes at hand of each and that both have selected and interpreted the actually and potentially common objects in an "empirically identical" manner that is sufficient for the purposes at hand. Thus, for example, in talking about "matters just known in common" persons will discuss them using a course of utterances that are governed by the expectation that the other person *will* understand. The speaker expects that the other person will assign to his remarks the sense intended by the speaker and expects that thereby the other person will permit the speaker the assumption that both know what he is talking about without any requirement of a check-out. Thus the sensible character of the matter that is being discussed is settled by a fiat assignment that each expects to make, and expects the other to make in reciprocal fashion, that as a condition of his right to decide without interference that he knows what he is talking about and that what he is talking about is so, each will have furnished whatever unstated understandings are required. Much therefore that is being talked about is not mentioned, although each expects that the adequate sense of the matter being talked about is settled. The more so is this the case, the more is the exchange one of commonplace remarks among persons who "know" each other.

Students were instructed to engage an acquaintance or friend in an ordinary conversation and, without indicating that what the experimenter was saying was in any way out of the ordinary, to insist that the person clarify the sense of his commonplace remarks. Twenty-three students reported twenty-five instances of such encounters. The following are typical excerpts from their accounts.

Case 1. The subject was telling the experimenter, a member of the subject's car pool, about having had a flat tire while going to work the previous day.

(S): "I had a flat tire."

(E): "What do you mean, you had a flat tire?"

She appeared momentarily stunned. Then she answered in a hostile way: "What do you mean? What do you mean? A flat tire is a flat tire. That is what I meant. Nothing special. What a crazy question!"

Case 2. (S): "Hi, Ray. How is your girl friend feeling?"

(E): "What do you mean, how is she feeling? Do you mean physical or mental?"

(S): "I mean how is she feeling? What's the matter with you?" (He looked peeved.)

(E): "Nothing. Just explain a little clearer, what do you mean?"

(S): "Skip it. How are your Med School applications coming?"

(E): "What do you mean, 'How are they?'"

(S): "You know what I mean."

(E): "I really don't."

(S): "What's the matter with you? Are you sick?"

Case 3. On Friday night my husband and I were watching television. My husband remarked that he was tired. I asked, "How are you tired? Physically, mentally, or just bored?"

(S): "I don't know, I guess physically, mainly."

(E): "You mean that your muscles ache, or your bones?"

(S): "I guess so. Don't be so technical."

(S): (After more watching) "All these old movies have the same kind of old iron bedstead in them."

(E): "What do you mean? Do you mean all old movies, or some of them, or just the ones you have seen?"

(S): "What's the matter with you? You know what I mean."

(E): "I wish you would be more specific."

(S): "You know what I mean! Drop dead!"

Case 4. During a conversation (with the male *E's* fiancee) the *E* questioned the meaning of various words used by the subject. For the first minute and a half the subject responded to the questions as if they were legitimate inquiries. Then she responded with "Why are you asking me these questions?" and repeated this two or three times after each question. She became nervous and jittery, her face and hand movements . . . uncontrolled. She appeared bewildered and complained that I was making her nervous and demanded that I "Stop it!" . . . The subject picked up a magazine and covered her face. She put down the magazine and pretended to be engrossed. When asked why she was looking at the magazine, she closed her mouth and refused any further remarks.

Case 5. My friend said to me, "Hurry or we will be late." I asked him what did he mean by late and from what point of view did it have reference. There was a look of perplexity and cynicism on his face. "Why are you asking me such silly questions? Surely I don't have to explain such a statement. What is wrong with you today? Why should I have to stop to analyze such a statement. Everyone understands my statements and you should be no exception."

Case 6. The victim waved his hand cheerily.

(S): "How are you?"

(E): "How am I in regard to what? My health, my finance, my school work, my peace of mind, my . . ."

(S): (Red in the face and suddenly out of control.) "Look! I was just trying to be polite. Frankly, I don't give a damn how you are."

Case 7. My friend and I were talking about a man whose overbearing attitude annoyed us. My friend expressed his feeling.

(S): "I'm sick of him."

(E): Would you explain what is wrong with you that you are sick?

(S): "Are you kidding me? You know what I mean."

(E): "Please explain your ailment."

(S): (He listened to me with a puzzled look.) "What came over you? We never talk this way, do we?" . . .

Case 8. Apparently as a casual afterthought, my husband mentioned Friday night, "Did you remember to drop off my shirts today?"

Taking nothing for granted, I replied, "I remember that you said something about it this morning. What shirts did you mean, and what did you mean by having them 'dropped' off?" He looked puzzled, as though I must have answered some other question than the one asked.

Instead of making the explanation he seemed to be waiting for, I persisted, "I thought your shirts were all in pretty good shape; why not keep them a little

longer?" I had the uncomfortable feeling I had overplayed the part.

He no longer looked puzzled, but indignant. He repeated, "A little longer! What do you mean, and what have you done with my shirts?"

I acted indignant too. I asked, "What shirts? You have sport shirts, plain shirts, wool shirts, regular shirts, and dirty shirts. I'm no mind reader. What exactly did you want?"

My husband again looked confused, as though he was trying to justify my behavior. He seemed simultaneously to be on the defensive and offensive. He assumed a very patient, tolerant air, and said, "Now, let's start all over again. Did you drop off my shirts today?"

I replied, "I heard you before. It's your meaning I wish was more clear. As far as I am concerned dropping off your shirts—whichever shirts you mean—could mean giving them to the Goodwill, leaving them at the cleaners, at the laundromat, or throwing them out. I never know what you mean with those vague statements."

He reflected on what I said, then changed the entire perspective by acting as though we were playing a game, that it was all a joke. He seemed to enjoy the joke. He ruined my approach by assuming the role I thought was mine. He then said, "Well, let's take this step by step with 'yes' or 'no' answers. Did you see the dirty shirts I left on the kitchenette, yes or no?"

I could see no way to complicate his question, so felt forced to answer "Yes." In the same fashion, he asked if I picked up the shirts; if I put them in the car; if I left them at the laundry; and if I did all these things that day, Friday. My answers were "Yes."

The experiment, it seemed to me, had been cut short by his reducing all the parts of his previous question to their simplest terms, which were given to me as if I were a child unable to handle any complex questions, problems, or situations.

Demonstration 2: Breaching the Interchangeability of Standpoints

In order to breach the presupposed interchangeability of standpoints, students were asked to enter a store, to select a customer, and to treat the customer as a clerk while giving no recognition that the subject was any other person than the experimenter took him to be and without giving any indication that the experimenter's treatment was anything other than perfectly reasonable and legitimate.

Case 1. One evening, while shopping at Sears with a friend, I (male) found myself next to a woman shopping at the copper-clad pan section. The store was busy . . . and clerks were hard to find. The woman was just a couple of feet away and my friend was behind me. Pointing to a tea kettle, I asked the woman if she did not think the price was rather high. I asked in a friendly tone. . . . She looked at me and then at the kettle and said "Yes." I then said I was going to take it anyway. She said, "Oh," and started to move sideways away from me. I quickly asked her if she was not going to wrap it for me and take my cash. Still moving slowly away and glancing first at me, then at the kettle, then at the other pans farther away from me, she said the clerk was "over there" pointing off somewhere. In a harsh tone, I asked if she was not going to wait on me. She said, "No, No, I'm not the saleslady. There she is." I said that I knew that the extra help was inexperienced, but there was no reason not to wait on a customer. "Just wait on me. I'll be patient." With that, she flushed with anger and walked rapidly away, looking back once as if to ask if it could really be true.

The following three protocols are the work of a forty-year-old female graduate student in clinical psychology.

Case 2. We went to V's book store, noted not so much for its fine merchandise and its wide range of stock as it is in certain circles for the fact that the clerks are male homosexuals. I approached a gentleman who was browsing at a table stacked neatly with books.

(E): "I'm in a hurry. Would you get a copy of *Sociopathic Behavior* by Lemert, please?"

(S): (Looked *E* up and down, drew himself very straight, slowly laid the book down, stepped back slightly, then leaned forward and in a low voice said) "I'm interested in sociopathic behavior, too. That's why I'm here. I study the fellows here by pretending to be . . ."

(E): (Interrupting) "I'm not particularly interested in whether you are or are only pretending to be. Please just get the book I asked for."

(S): (Looked shocked. More than surprised, believe me. Stepped around the display table, deliberately placed his hands on the books, leaned forward and shouted) "I don't have such a book. I'm not a clerk! I'm—Well!" (Stalked out of the store.)

Case 3. When we entered I. Magnin's there was one woman who was fingering a sweater, the only piece of merchandise to be seen in the shop. I surmised that the clerk must be in the stockroom.

(E): "That is a lovely shade, but I'm looking for one a little lighter. Do you have one in cashmere?"

(S): "I really don't know, you see I'm . . .

(E): (Interrupting) "Oh, you are new here? I don't mind waiting while you look for what I want."

(S): "Indeed I shall not!"

(E): "But aren't you here to *serve* customers?"

(S): "I'm not! I'm here to . . ."

(E): (Interrupts) "This is hardly the place for such an attitude. Now please show me a cashmere sweater a shade or two lighter than this one."

(The clerk entered.)

(S): (To clerk) "My dear, this—(pointed her face toward *E*)—*person* insists on being shown a sweater. Please take care of her while I compose myself. I want to be certain this (sweater) will do, and she (pointed her face again at *E*) is so *insistent.*" (*S* carried the sweater with her, walked haughtily to a large upholstered chair, sat in it, brushed her gloved hands free from imaginary dirt, jerked her shoulders, fluffed her suit jacket, and glared at *E*).

Case 4. While visiting with a friend in Pasadena, I told him about this being-taken-for-the-clerk experiment. The friend is a Professor Emeritus of Mathematics at the California Institute of Technology and the successful author of many books, some technical, some fictional, and he is most satirical in his contemplations of his fellow man. He begged to be allowed to accompany me and to aid me in the selection of scenes. . . . We went first to have luncheon at the Atheneum, which caters to the students, faculty, and guests of Cal Tech. While we were still in the lobby, my host pointed out a gentleman who was standing in the large drawing room near the entrance to the dining room and said, "Go to it. There's a good subject for you." He stepped aside to watch. I walked toward the man very deliberately and proceeded as follows. (I will use E to designate myself; S, the subject.)

(E): "I should like a table on the west side, a quiet spot, if you please. And what is on the menu?"

(S): (Turned toward E but looked past and in the direction of the foyer) said, "Eh, ah, madam, I'm sure." (looked past E again, looked at a pocket watch, replaced it, and looked toward the dining room).

(E): "Surely luncheon hours are not over. What do you recommend I order today?"

(S): "I don't know. You see, I'm waiting . . ."

(E): (Interrupted with) "Please don't keep me standing here while you wait. Kindly show me to a table."

(S): "But Madam,—" (started to edge away from door, and back into the lounge in a slightly curving direction around E)

(E): "My good man—" (At this S's face flushed, his eyes rounded and opened wide.)

(S): "But—you—I—oh dear!" (He seemed to wilt.)

(E): (Took S's arm in hand and propelled him toward the dining room door, slightly ahead of herself.)

(S): (Walked slowly but stopped just within the room, turned around and for the first time looked directly and very appraisingly at E, took out the watch, looked at it, held it to his ear, replaced it, and muttered) "Oh dear."

(E): "It will take only a minute for you to show me to a table and take my order. Then you can return to wait for your customers. After all, I am a guest and a customer, too."

(S): (Stiffened slightly, walked jerkily toward the nearest empty table, held a chair for E to be seated, bowed slightly, muttered "My pleasure," hurried toward the door, stopped, turned, looked back at E with a blank facial expression.)

At this point E's host walked up to S, greeted him, shook hands, and propelled him toward E's table. S stopped a few steps from the table, looked directly at, then through, E, and started to walk back toward the door. Host told him E was the young lady whom he had invited to join them at lunch (then introduced me to one of the big names in the physics world, a pillar of the institution!). S seated himself reluctantly and perched rigidly on his chair, obviously uncomfortable. E smiled, made light and polite inquiries about his work, mentioned various functions attended which had honored him, then complacently remarked that it was a shame E had not met him personally before now, so that she should not have mistaken him for the maître-d'. The host chattered about his long-time friendship with me, while S fidgeted and looked again at his pocket watch, wiped his forehead with a table napkin, looked at E but avoided meeting her eyes. When the host mentioned that E is studying sociology at UCLA, S suddenly burst into loud laughter, realized that everyone in the room was looking in the direction of our table, abruptly became quiet, then said to E "You mistook me for the maître-d', didn't you?"

(E): "Deliberately, sir."

(S): "Why deliberately?"

(E): "You have just been used as the unsuspecting subject in an experiment."

(S): "Diabolic. But clever, I must say (To our host) I haven't been so shaken since _____ denounced my theory _____ of _____ in 19 _____. And

the wild thoughts that ran through my mind! Call the receptionist from the lobby, go to the men's room, turn this woman to the first person that comes along. Damn these early diners, there's nobody coming in at this time. Time is standing still, or my watch has stopped. I will talk to _____ about this, make sure it doesn't happen to 'somebody.' Damn a persistent woman. I'm not her 'good man!' I'm Dr. _____, and not to be pushed around. This can't be happening. If I do take her to that damned table she wants, I can get away from her, and I'll just take it easy until I can. I remember _____ (hereditary psychopath, wife of one of the 'family' of the institution) maybe if I do what *this* one wants she will not make any more trouble than this. I wonder if she is 'off.' She certainly looks normal. Wonder how you can really tell?"

Demonstration 3: Breaching the Expectancy That a Knowledge of a Relationship of Interaction Is a Commonly Entertained Scheme of Communication

Schutz proposed that from the member's point of view, an event of conduct, like a move in a game, consists of an event-in-a-social-order. Thus, for the member, its recognizably real character is furnished by attending its occurrence with respect to a corpus of socially sanctioned knowledge of the social relationships that the member uses and assumes that others use as the same scheme of expression and interpretation.

It was decided to breach this expectancy by having students treat a situation as something that it "obviously" and "really" was not. Students were instructed to spend from fifteen minutes to an hour in their own homes acting as if they were boarders. They were instructed to conduct themselves in a circumspect and polite fashion: to avoid getting personal; to use formal address; to speak only when they were spoken to.

In nine of forty-nine cases students either refused to do the assignment (five cases) or the try was "unsuccessful" (four cases). Four of the "no try" students said they were afraid to do it; a fifth

said she preferred to avoid the risk of exciting her mother who had a heart condition. In two of the "unsuccessful" cases the family treated it as a joke from the beginning and refused, despite the continuing actions of the student experimenter, to change. A third family took the view that something of an undisclosed sort was the matter, but what it might be was of no concern to them. In the fourth family the father and mother remarked that the daughter was being "extra nice" and undoubtedly wanted something that she would shortly reveal.

In the remaining four-fifths of the cases family members were stupefied, vigorously sought to make the strange actions intelligible, and to restore the situation to normal appearances. Reports were filled with accounts of astonishment, bewilderment, shock, anxiety, embarrassment, and anger as well as with charges by various family members that the student was mean, inconsiderate, selfish, nasty, and impolite. Family members demanded explanations: "What's the matter?" "What's gotten into you?" "Did you get fired?" "Are you sick?" "What are you being so superior about?" "Why are you mad?" "Are you out of your mind or are you just stupid?" One student acutely embarrassed his mother in front of her friends by asking if she minded if he had a snack from the refrigerator. "Mind if you have a little snack? You've been eating little snacks around here for years without asking me. What's gotten into you?" One mother, infuriated when her daughter spoke to her only when she was spoken to, began to shriek in angry denunciation of the daughter for her disrespect and insubordination and refused to be calmed by the student's sister. A father berated his daughter for being insufficiently concerned for the welfare of others and for acting like a spoiled child.

Occasionally family members would first treat the student's action as a cue for a joint comedy routine which was soon replaced by irritation and exasperated anger at the student for not knowing "when enough was enough."

Family members mocked the "politeness" of the students—"Certainly Mr. Dinerberg!"—or charged the student with acting like a wise guy and generally reproved the "politeness" with sarcasm.

Explanations were sought in terms of understandable and previous motives of the student: the accusation that the student was covering up something important that the family should know; that the student was working too hard in school; that the student was ill; that there had been "another fight" with a fiancée.

Unacknowledged explanations were followed by withdrawal of the offended member, attempted isolation of the culprit, retaliation, and denunciation. "Don't bother with him, he's in one of his moods again." "Pay no attention but just wait until he asks me for something." "You're cutting me, okay. I'll cut you and then some." "Why must you always create friction in our family harmony?" A father followed his son into the bedroom. "Your mother is right. You don't look well and you're not talking sense. You had better get another job that doesn't require such late hours." To this the student replied that he appreciated his consideration, but that he felt fine and only wanted a little privacy. The father responded in high rage, "I don't want any more of *that* out of *you*. And if you can't treat your mother decently, you'd better move out!"

There were no cases in which the situation was not restorable upon the student's explanation. Nevertheless, for the most part, family members were not amused and only rarely did they find the experience instructive, as the student argued that it was supposed to have been. After hearing the explanation, a sister replied coldly on behalf of a family of four, "Please, no more of these experiments. We're not rats you know." Occasionally an explanation was accepted and still it added offense. In several cases students reported that the explanation left them, their families, or both wondering how much of what the student had said was "in character" and how much the student "really meant."

Students found the assignment difficult to complete because of not being treated as if they were in the role that they are attempting to play and of being confronted with situations to which they did not know how a boarder would respond.

There were several entirely unexpected results. (1) Although many students reported extensive rehearsals in imagination, very few of those that did it mentioned anticipatory fears or embarrassment. (2) Although unanticipated and nasty developments frequently occurred, in only one case did a student report serious regrets. (3) Very few students reported heartfelt relief when the hour was over. They were much more likely to report a partial relief. They frequently reported that in response to the anger of others they became angry in return and slipped easily into subjectively recognizable feelings and actions.

Demonstration 4: Breaching the Grasp of "What Anyone Knows" to Be Correct Grounds of Action of a Real Social World

Among the possibilities that a premedical student could treat as correct grounds for his further inferences and actions about such matters as how a medical school intake interview is conducted or how an applicant's conduct is related to his chances of admission, certain ones (e.g., that deferring to the interviewer's interests is a condition for making a favorable impression) he treats as matters that he is required to know and act upon as a condition of his competence as a premedical candidate. He expects others like him to know and act upon the same things; and he expects that as he expects others to know and act upon them, the others in turn expect the like of him.

A procedure was designed to breach the constitutive expectancies attached to "what-any-competent-premedical-candidate-knows" while satisfying the three conditions under which their breach would presumably produce confusion.

Twenty-eight premedical students of the University of California in Los Angeles were run individually through a three-hour experimental interview. As part of the solicitation of subjects, as well as the beginning of the interview, *E* identified himself as a representative of an Eastern medical school who was attempting to learn why the medical school intake interview was such a stressful situation. It was hoped that identifying *E* as a person with medical school ties would minimize the chance that students would "leave the field" once the accent breaching procedure began. How the other two conditions of (a) managing a redefinition in insufficient time and (b) not being able to count on consensual support for an alternative definition of social reality were met will be apparent in the following description.

During the first hour of the interview, the student furnished the facts-of-life about interviews for admission to medical school by answering for the "representative" such questions as "What sources of information about a candidate are available to medical schools?" "What can a medical school learn about a candidate from these sources?" "What kind of a man are the medical schools looking for?" "What should a good candidate do in the interview?" "What should he avoid?" With this much completed, the student was told that the "representative's" research interests had been satisfied. The student was asked if he would care to hear a recording of an actual interview. All students wanted very much to hear the recording.

The recording was a faked one between a "medical school interviewer" and an "applicant." The applicant was depicted as being a boor; his language was ungrammatical and filled with colloquialisms; he was evasive; he contradicted the interviewer; he bragged; he ran down other schools and professions; he insisted on knowing how he had done in the interview and so on.

Detailed assessments by the student of the recorded applicant were obtained immediately after the recording was finished. The following edited assessment is representative:

I didn't like it. I didn't like his attitude. I didn't like anything about him. Everything he said grated the wrong way. I didn't like his smoking. The way he kept saying "Yeah-h!" He didn't show that he realized that the interviewer had his future in his hands. I didn't like the vague way he answered questions. I didn't like the way he pressed at the end of the interview. He was disrespectful. His motives were too obvious. He made a mess of it. He finished with a bang to say the least. . . . His answers to questions were stupid. I felt that the interviewer was telling him that he wasn't going to get in. I didn't like the interview. I felt it was too informal. To a degree it's good if it's natural but . . . the interview is not something to breeze through. It's just not the place for chit-chat. He had fairly good grades but . . . he's not interested in things outside of school and didn't say what he did *in* school. Then he didn't *do* very much— outside of this lab. I didn't like the man at all. I never met an applicant like that! "My pal"—Just one of these little chats. I never met anybody *like* that. Wrong-way Corrigan.

The student was then given information from the applicant's "official record." This information was deliberately contrived to contradict the principal points in the student's assessment. For example, if the student said that the applicant must have come from a lower-class family, he was told that the applicant's father was vice president of a firm that manufactured pneumatic doors for trains and buses. If the applicant had been thought to be ignorant, he was described as having excelled in courses like The Poetry of Milton and Dramas of Shakespeare. If the student said the applicant did not know how to get along with people, then the applicant was pictured as having worked as a voluntary solicitor for Sydenham Hospital in New York City and had raised $32,000 from thirty "big givers." The belief that the applicant was stupid and would not do well in a scientific field was met by citing A grades in organic and physical chemistry and graduate level performance in an undergraduate research course.

The *S*s wanted very much to know what "the others" thought of the applicant, and had he been admitted? The "others" had been previously and casually identified by the "representative" as "Dr. Gardner, the medical school interviewer," "six psychiatrically trained members of the admissions committee who heard only the recorded interview," and "other students I talked to."

The *S* was told that the applicant had been admitted and was living up to the promise that the medical school interviewer and the "six psychiatrists" had found and expressed in the following recommendation of the applicant's characterological fitness.

> Dr. Gardner, the medical school interviewer, wrote, "A well-bred, polite young man, poised, affable, and self-confident. Capable of independent thinking. Interests of a rather specialized character. Marked intellectual curiosity. Alert and free of emotional disturbances. Marked maturity of manner and outlook. Meets others easily. Strongly motivated toward a medical career. Definite ideas of what he wants to achieve which are held in good perspective. Unquestioned sincerity and integrity. Expressed himself easily and well. Recommend favorable consideration." The six psychiatric members of the admissions committee agreed in all essentials.

Concerning the views of "other students," *S* was told that he was, for example, the thirtieth student I had seen; that twenty-eight before him were in entire agreement with the medical school interviewer's assessment; and that the remaining two had been slightly uncertain but at the first bit of information had seen him just as the others had.

Following this, *S*s were invited to listen to the record a second time, after which they were asked to assess the applicant again.

Results. Twenty-five of the twenty-eight subjects were taken in. The following does not apply to the three who were convinced there was a deception. Two of these are discussed at the conclusion of this section.

Incongruous materials, presented to *S* in the order indicated, were performance information, and characterological information. Performance information dealt with the applicant's activities, grades, family background, courses, charity work, and the like. Characterological information consisted of character assessments of him by the "medical school interviewers," the "six psychiatrically trained members of the admissions committee," and the "other students."

Subjects managed incongruities of performance data with vigorous attempts to make it factually compatible with their original assessments. For example, when they said that the applicant sounded like a lower-class person, they were told that his father was vice president of a national corporation that manufactured pneumatic doors for trains and buses. Here are some typical replies:

> "He should have made the point that he *could* count on money."
>
> "That explains why he said he had to work. Probably his father made him work. That would make a lot of his moans unjustified in the sense that things were really not so bad."
>
> "What does that have to do with values?!"
>
> "You could tell from his answers. You could tell that he was used to having his own way."
>
> "That's something the interviewer knew that *I* didn't know."
>
> "Then he's an out and out liar!"

When *S*s said that the applicant was selfish and could not get along with people, they were told that he had worked as a volunteer for Sydenham Hospital and had raised $32,000 from thirty "big givers."

> "He seems to be a good salesman. So possibly he's missing his profession. I'd say *definitely* he's missing his profession!"
>
> "They probably contributed because of the charity and not because they were solicited."
>
> "Pretty good. Swell. Did he know them personally?"

"It's very fashionable to work, for example, during the war for Bundles for Britain. So that doesn't—definitely!—show altruistic motives at all. He is a person who is subject to fashion and I'm very critical of that sort of thing.

"He's so forceful he might have shamed them into giving."

"People who are wealthy—his father would naturally see those people—big contributions—they could give a lot of money and not know what they're giving it for."

That he had a straight A average in physical science courses began to draw bewilderment.

"He took quite a variety of courses . . . I'm baffled.—Probably the interview wasn't a very good mirror of his character."

"He did seem to take some odd courses. They seem to be fairly normal. Not normal—but—it doesn't strike me one way or the other."

"Well! I think you can analyze it this way. In psychological terms. See—one possible way—now I may be all *wet* but this is the way I look at *that*. He probably suffered from an inferiority complex and that's an overcompensation for his inferiority complex. His *great* marks—his *good* marks are a compensation for his failure—in social dealings perhaps, I don't know."

"Woops! And only third alternate at Georgia. (Deep sigh) I can see why he'd feel resentment about not being admitted to Phi Bet."

"(Long silence) "Well! From what—that leads me to think he's a grind or something like that."

Attempts to resolve the incongruities produced by the character assessment of "Gardner" and "the other six judges" were much less frequent than normalizing attempts with performance information. Open expressions of bewilderment and anxiety interspersed with silent ruminations were characteristic.

(Laugh) "Golly!" (Silence) "I'd think it would be the other way around."—(Very subdued) "Maybe I'm all wro—My orientation is all off. I'm completely baffled."

"Not polite. Self-confident he certainly was. But not polite—I don't know. Either the interviewer was a little crazy or else I am." (Long pause) "That's rather shocking. It makes me have doubts about my own thinking. Perhaps my values in life are wrong. I don't know."

(Whistles) "I—I didn't think he sounded well bred at all. That whole tone of voice!!—I—Perhaps you noticed though, when he said 'You should have said in the first place' before he took it with a smile.—But even so! No, no I can't see that. 'You should have said that before.' Maybe he was being funny though. Exercising a—No! To me it sounded impertinent!"

"Ugh—Well, that certainly puts a different slant on my conception of interviews. Gee—that—confuses me all the more."

"Well—(laugh)—Hhh!—Ugh! Well, maybe he looked like a nice boy. He did—he did get his point across.—Perhaps—seeing the person would make a big difference.—Or perhaps I would never make a good interviewer." (Reflectively and almost inaudibly) "They didn't mention any of the things I mentioned." (HG: Eh?) (Louder) "They didn't mention any of the things I mentioned and so I feel like a complete failure."

Soon after the performance data produced its consternation, an occasional request would be made: "What did the other students make of him?" Only after Gardner's assessment, and the responses to it had been made were the opinions of the "other students" given. In some cases the subject was told "34 out of 35 before you," in others 43 out of 45, 19 out of 20, 51 out of 52. All the numbers were large. For 18 of the 25 students the delivery hardly varied from the following verbatim protocols:

[34 out of 35] I don't know.—I still stick to my original convictions. I—I—Can you tell *me* what—I saw wrong. Maybe—I—I had the wrong idea—the wrong attitude all along. (Can you tell me? I'm interested that there should be such a disparity.) Definitely.—I—think—it would be definitely the other way—I can't make sense of it. I'm completely baffled, believe me.—I—I don't understand how I could have been so wrong. Maybe my ideas—my evaluations of people are—just twisted. I mean maybe I had the wrong—maybe my sense of values—is—off—or—different—from the other 33. But I don't think that's the case—because usually—and in all modesty I say this—I—I can judge people. I mean in class, in organizations I belong to—I usually judge them right. So therefore I don't understand at *all* how I could have been so wrong. I don't think I was under any stress or strain—here—tonight but—I don't understand it.

[43 out of 45] [Laugh] I don't know what to say now.—I'm troubled by my inability to judge the guy better than that. [Subdued] I shall sleep tonight, certainly—[Very subdued] but it certainly bothers me.—Sorry that I didn't—*Well!* One question that arises—I may be wrong—(Can you see how they might have seen him?) No. No, I can't see it, no.— Sure with all that background material, yes, but I don't see how Gardner did it without it. Well, I guess that makes Gardner, Gardner, and me, me. (The other 45 students didn't have the background material.) Yeah, yeah, yeah. I mean I'm not denying it at all. I mean for myself, there's no sense saying—Of course! With their background they would be accepted, especially the second man, good God!—Okay, what else?

[23 out of 25] [Softly] Maybe I'm tired. (HG, "Eh?") [Burst of laughter.] Maybe I didn't get enough sleep last night.—Uhh!—Well—I might not have been looking for the things that the other men were looking for.—I wasn't—Huh!—It puts me at a loss, really.

[10 out of 10] So I'm alone in my judgment. I don't know, sir! I don't know, sir!!—I can't explain it. It's senseless.—I tried to be impartial at the beginning. I admit I was prejudiced immediately.

[51 out of 52] You mean that 51 others stuck to their guns, too? (Stuck to their guns in the sense that they saw him just as the judges saw him.) Uh huh. [Deep sigh] I still don't—Yeah! I see. But just listening I don't think he was a—very good chance. But in light of his other things I feel that the interview was not—showing—the real—him.—Hhh!

[36 out of 37] I would go back on my former opinion but I wouldn't go back too far. I just don't see it.—Why should I have these different standards?

Were my opinions more or less in agreement on the first man? (No.) That leads me to think.—That's funny. Unless you got 36 unusual people. I can't understand it. Maybe it's my personality. (Does it make any difference?) It *does* make a difference if I assume they're correct. What I consider is proper, they don't.—It's my attitude—Still in all a man of that sort would alienate me. A wise guy type to be avoided. Of course you can talk like that with other fellows—but in an interview? . . . Now I'm more confused than I was at the beginning of the entire interview. I think I ought to go home and look in the mirror and talk to myself. Do you have any ideas? (Why? Does it disturb you?) Yes it *does* disturb me! It makes me think my abilities to judge people and values are way off from normal. It's not a healthy situation. (What difference does it make?) If I act the way I act it seems to me that I'm just putting my head in the lion's mouth. I did have preconceptions but they're shattered all to hell. It makes me wonder about myself. Why should I have these different standards? It all points to me.

Of the twenty-five *Ss* who were taken in, seven were unable to resolve the incongruity of having been wrong about such an obvious matter and were unable to "see" the alternative. Their suffering was dramatic and unrelieved. Five more resolved it with the view that the medical school had accepted a good man; five others with the view that it had accepted a boor. Although they changed, they nevertheless did not abandon their former views. For them Gardner's view could be seen "in general," but the grasp lacked convincingness. When attention was drawn to particulars, the general picture would evaporate. These *Ss* were willing to entertain and use the "general" picture, but they suffered whenever indigestible particulars of the same portrait came into view. Subscription to the "general" picture was accompanied by a recitation of characteristics that were not only the opposite of those in the original view but were intensified by superlative adjectives like "supremely" poised, "very" natural, "most" confident, "very" calm. Further, they saw the new features through a new appreciation of the way the medical examiner had been listening. They saw, for example, that the examiner was smiling when the applicant had forgotten to offer him a cigarette.

Three more *Ss* were convinced that there was deception and acted on the conviction through the interview. They showed no disturbance. Two of these showed acute suffering as soon as it appeared that the interview was finished, and they were being dismissed with no acknowledgment of a deception. Three others inadvertently suffered in silence and confounded *E*. Without any indication to *E*, they regarded the interview as an experimental one in which they were being asked to solve some problems and therefore were being asked to do as well as possible and to make no changes in their opinions, for only then would they be contributing to the study. They were difficult for me to understand during the interview because they displayed marked anxiety, yet their remarks were bland and were not addressed to the matters that were provoking it. Finally three more *Ss* contrasted with the others. One of these insisted that the character assessments were semantically ambiguous and because there was insufficient information a "high correlation opinion" was not possible. A

second, and the only one in the entire series, found, according to his account, the second portrait as convincing as the original one. When the deception was revealed, he was disturbed that he could have been as convinced as he was. The third one, in the face of everything, showed only slight disturbance of very short duration. However, he alone among the subjects had already been interviewed for medical school, had excellent contacts, despite a grade point average of less than C he estimated his chances of admission as fair, and finally he expressed his preference for a career in the diplomatic service over a career in medicine.

As a final observation, twenty-two of the twenty-eight *Ss* expressed marked relief—ten of them with explosive expressions—when I disclosed the deception. Unanimously they said that the news of the deception permitted them to return to their former views. Seven *Ss* had to be convinced that there had been a deception. When the deception was revealed, they asked what they were to believe. Was I telling them that there had been a deception in order to make them feel better? No pains were spared, and whatever truth or lies that had to be told were told in order to establish the truth that there had been a deception.

SELF-FULFILLING PROPHECIES

Examples of self-fulfilling prophecies illustrate the features of reality that Mehan and Wood call "reflexive" and "interactional." *Self-fulfilling prophecies* are defined as beliefs that become true as a result of taking action based on the belief. For example, a husband who thinks his wife is "nagging" may withdraw from her to the extent that she actually begins to nag him in order to get his attention.

In "Self-Fulfilling Prophecies," Paul Watzlawick develops the definition of the process and gives several examples.

"When Belief Creates Reality" is a study based on the concept of self-fulfilling prophecies. Mark Snyder designed a study in which he observed the way people interacted with people perceived to be attractive and people perceived not to be attractive. He noticed that when people perceive someone to be attractive, they tend to act more friendly and engaged with the person, thus giving the other person more opportunity to be engaging in response. According to Snyder, this kind of behavior perpetuates the stereotype that attractive people are more friendly and engaging.

Questions for Discussion and Review

1. Watzlawick gives examples of self-fulfilling prophecies at both the individual and the collective levels. Discuss examples of contemporary world politics that can be explained in terms of self-fulfilling prophecies.

2. Make a list of behavioral stereotypes and consider how these stereotypes might become real and persistent as a result of self-fulfilling interactional expectations.

3. If someone has a preconceived notion and acts in a way that makes it real in the outcome, will the person ever know that it was his or her own behavior that caused the expected outcome? Does it matter? What feature of reality does this process describe?

SELF-FULFILLING PROPHECIES

31

Self-Fulfilling Prophecies

Paul Watzlawick

(1984)

A self-fulfilling prophecy is an assumption or prediction that, purely as a result of having been made, causes the expected or predicted event to occur and thus confirms its own "accuracy." For example, if someone assumes, for whatever reason, that he is not respected, he will, because of this assumption, act in such a hostile, overly sensitive, suspicious manner that he brings about that very contempt in others which "proves" again and again his firmly entrenched conviction. This

mechanism may be commonplace and well known, but it is based upon a number of facts that are by no means part of our everyday thinking and which have a profound significance for our view of reality.

In our traditional cause-and-effect thinking we usually see event B as the result of a preceding, causal event (A)—which in turn has, of course, its own causes, just as the occurrence of B produces its own sequel of events. In the sequence $A \rightarrow B$, A

is therefore the cause and *B* its effect. The causality is *linear* and *B* follows *A* in the course of time. Accordingly, in this causality model, *B* can have no effect on *A,* because this would mean a reversal of the flow of time: The present (*B*) would have to exert a backward effect on the past (*A*).

Matters stand differently in the following example: In March 1979, when the newspapers in California began to publish sensational pronouncements of an impending, severe gasoline shortage, California motorists stormed the gas stations to fill up their tanks and to keep them as full as possible. This filling up of 12 million gasoline tanks (which up to this time had on the average been 75% empty) depleted the enormous reserves and so brought about the predicted shortage practically overnight. The endeavor to keep the fuel containers as full as possible (instead of getting gas when the tank was almost empty, as had been done before) resulted in endless lines and hours of waiting time at the gas stations, and increased the panic. After the excitement died down, it turned out that the allotment of gasoline to the state of California had hardly been reduced at all.

Here the customary cause-and-effect thinking breaks down. The shortage would never have occurred if the media had not predicted it. In other words, an event that had not yet taken place (i.e., an event in the future) created an effect in the present (the storming of the gas stations), which in turn caused the predicted event to become reality. In this sense it was the future—not the past—that determined the present.

The objection could be raised that all of this is neither astonishing nor unheard of. Are not almost all human decisions and actions largely dependent on the evaluation of their probable effects, advantages, and dangers (or at least should they not be)? Does not the future therefore always play a part in the present? Significant as these questions may be, they do not seem to make much sense here. Whoever tries, usually on the basis of earlier experience, to evaluate the future effect of his decision

normally intends the best possible outcome. The specific action tries to take the future into consideration, and subsequently proves to be true or false, correct or incorrect; but it does not have to have any influence whatever on the course of events. However, an action that results from a self-fulfilling prophecy itself produces the requisite conditions for the occurrence of the expected event, and in this sense *creates* a reality which would not have arisen without it. The action that is at first neither true nor false produces a fact, and with it its own "truth."

Here are examples of both perspectives: If someone begins to suffer from headaches, sneezes, and shivers, he will, on the basis of past experience, assume that he is coming down with a cold; and if his diagnosis is correct, he can, with aspirin, hot drinks, and bedrest, favorably influence the (future) course of the illness by these means in the present. By doing so, he has correctly grasped a causal sequence that had at first been totally independent of him, and exerted a partial influence on it.

A fundamentally different sequence results from the practice of collecting taxes in certain countries. Since the revenue agency assumes a priori that no citizen will ever truthfully declare his income, the tax rate is dictated more or less arbitrarily. The revenue offices rely largely on the information of their assessment agents, who take into consideration such vague factors as a person's standard of living, his real estate property, the fur coats of his wife, the make of his car, and so forth. To the income, "ascertained" in this way, there is then added a certain percentage that is supposed to make up for any undeclared income, because—as we said—it is assumed a priori that the taxpayer cheats. This assumption, however, produces the situation in which a truthful declaration of income becomes unacceptable even for an honest taxpayer, and in which dishonesty is practically made a necessity if one wants to escape unfair taxes. Again an assumption believed to be true creates the assumed reality, and again it is irrelevant whether the assumption was originally true or false. And so we see that the difference lies in the fact that, in the example of the head cold, a development that is already taking place in the present is acted upon as best as is possible, and its course is influenced in this way in the present; whereas in the examples of the gasoline shortage and the income tax the course of events is induced by the very measures which are undertaken as a (supposed) reaction to the expected event in question. Therefore what is supposed to be a *reaction* (the effect) turns out to be an action (the cause); the "solution" produces the problem; the prophecy of the event causes the event of the prophecy.

This singular reversal of cause and effect is particularly obvious in interpersonal conflicts, where the phenomenon of the so-called *punctuation* of a sequence of events is invariably present. Making use of an example that has already been employed elsewhere (Watzlawick, Bavelas, & Jackson, 1967, pp. 56–58), we will imagine a married couple struggling with a conflict that they both assume to be basically the other's fault, while their own behavior is seen only as a *reaction* to that of their partner. The woman complains that her husband is withdrawing from her, which he admits, but because he sees his silence or his leaving the room as the only possible reaction to her constant nagging and criticizing. For her this reasoning is a total distortion of the facts: His behavior is the

cause of her criticism and her anger. Both partners are referring to the same interpersonal reality but assign to it a diametrically opposed causality. The diagram, Figure 1, may illustrate this discrepancy, although it postulates—unavoidably but wrongly— a starting point that does not really exist, because the behavior pattern between the two people has been repeating itself for a long time, and the question of who started it has long since become meaningless.

The arrows with the solid lines represent the behavior of the husband ("withdraws"), and the dotted lines that of the wife ("nags"). The husband dissects ("punctuates") the whole of the pattern into the triads 2–3–4, 4–5–6, 6–7–8, and so on, and so sees the interpersonal reality as one in which his wife nags (cause) and he *therefore* withdraws from her (effect). From her point of view, however, it is his cold passivity (cause) that causes her nagging (effect); she criticizes him *because* he withdraws from her, and therefore punctuates the pattern into the triads 1–2–3, 3–4–5, 5–6–7, and so on. With this opposed punctuation, both have literally brought about two contradictory realities and— what is perhaps even more important—two self-fulfilling prophecies. The two modes of behavior, which are seen subjectively as a reaction to the behavior of the partner, cause this very behavior in the other and "therefore" justify one's own behavior.

It goes without saying that self-fulfilling prophecies in an interpersonal context can also be

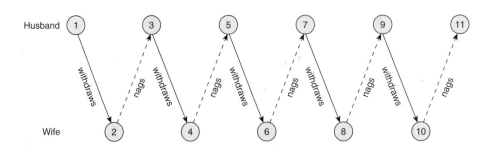

Figure 1

used deliberately and with a specific intent. The dangers of this practice will be discussed later on. As an example here let me only mention the well-known method of former matchmakers in patriarchal societies, who had the thankless task of awakening a mutual interest in two young people, who possibly cared nothing for each other, because their families had decided that for financial reasons, social standing, or other similarly impersonal motives, the two would make a good couple. The matchmaker's usual procedure was to talk with the young man alone and ask him whether he had not noticed how the girl was always secretly watching him. Similarly, he would tell the girl that the boy was constantly looking at her when her head was turned. This prophecy, disguised as a fact, was often quickly fulfilled. Skilled diplomats also know this procedure as a negotiating technique.[1]

Everyday experience teaches us that only few prophecies are self-fulfilling, and the above examples should explain why: Only when a prophecy is believed, that is, only when it is seen as a fact that has, so to speak, already happened in the future, can it have a tangible effect on the present and thereby fulfill itself. Where this element of belief or conviction is absent, this effect will be absent as well. To inquire how the construction or acceptance of such a prophecy comes to be would go far beyond the scope of this essay. (An extensive study of the social, psychological, and physiological effects of self-fulfilling prophecies was published in 1974 by Jones.) Too numerous and various are the factors involved—from the realities one fabricates for oneself during the course of the so-called noncontingent reward experiments (Watzlawick, 1976, pp. 45–54) . . . , to such oddities as the (perhaps unverified, but not improbable) assertion that since Bernadette had a vision of the Virgin Mary in February of 1858, only pilgrims, but not a single inhabitant of Lourdes, found a miraculous cure there.

Of this story one can say, *se non è vero, è ben trovato,*[2] since it helps to build a bridge from our previous, somewhat trivial reflections to manifestations of self-fulfilling prophecies that have a deeper human as well as scientific significance.

The oracle had prophesied that Oedipus would kill his father and marry his mother. Horrified by this prediction, which he undoubtedly believed to be true, Oedipus tries to protect himself from the impending doom, but the precautionary measures themselves lead to the seemingly inescapable fulfillment of the oracle's dictum. As is known, Freud used this myth as a metaphor for the incestuous attraction for the opposite sex inherent in every child, and the consequent fear of retaliation on the part of the parent of the same sex; and he saw in this key constellation, the Oedipus conflict, the fundamental cause of later neurotic developments. In his autobiography the philosopher Karl Popper (1974) refers back to a self-fulfilling prophecy that he had already described two decades earlier and which he called the Oedipus *effect:*

> One of the ideas I had discussed in *The Poverty* [*of Historicism*] was the influence of a prediction upon the event predicted. I had called this the "Oedipus effect," because the oracle played a most important role in the sequence of events which led to the fulfillment of its prophecy. (It was also an allusion to the psychoanalysts, who had been strangely blind to this interesting fact, even though Freud himself admitted that the very dreams dreamt by patients were often coloured by the theories of their analysts; Freud called them "obliging dreams.")

Again we have the reversal of cause and effect, past and future; but here it is all the more critical and decisive because psychoanalysis is a theory of human behavior that hinges on the assumption of a linear causality, in which the past determines the present. And Popper points to the significance of this reversal by explicating further:

For a time I thought that the existence of the Oedipus effect distinguished the social from the natural sciences. But in biology too—even in molecular biology—expectations often play a role in bringing about what has been expected.

Similar quotations, referring to the effect of such "unscientific" factors as simple expectations and assumptions in the sciences, could be collated in abundance—[*The Invented Reality*] is itself intended as such a contribution. In this connection one might recall, for instance, Einstein's remark in a talk with Heisenberg: "It is the theory that determines what we can observe." And in 1958 Heisenberg himself says, "We have to remember that what we observe is not nature in itself, but nature exposed to our method of questioning." And more radical still, the philosopher of science Feyerabend (1978): "Not conservative, but anticipatory suppositions guide research."

Some of the most carefully documented and elegant investigations of self-fulfilling prophecies in the area of human communication are associated with the name of the psychologist Robert Rosenthal of Harvard University. Of particular interest here is his (1968) book with the appropriate title *Pygmalion in the Classroom,* in which he describes the results of his so-called Oak School experiments. They concerned a primary school with 18 women teachers and over 650 students [see Reading 38]. The self-fulfilling prophecy was induced in the members of the faculty at the beginning of a certain school year by giving the students an intelligence test whereby the teachers were told that the test could not only determine intelligence quotients, but could also identify those 20% of the students who would make rapid and above-average intellectual progress in the coming school year. After the intelligence test had been administered, but before the teachers had met their new students for the first time, they received the names (indiscriminately picked from the student list) of those students who supposedly, on the basis of the test,

could be expected with certainty to perform unusually well. The difference between these children and the others thus existed solely in the heads of their particular teacher. The same intelligence test was repeated at the end of the school year for all students and showed *real* above-average increases in the intelligence quotients and achievements of these "special" students, and the reports of the faculty proved furthermore that these children distinguished themselves from their fellow students by their behavior, intellectual curiosity, friendliness, and so on.

Saint Augustine thanked God that he was not responsible for his dreams. Nowadays we do not have this comfort. Rosenthal's experiment is only one, although an especially clear example of how deeply and incisively our fellow human beings are affected by our expectations, prejudices, superstitions, and wishful thinking—all purely mental constructions, often without the slightest glimmer of actuality—and how these discoveries erode our comfortable conviction of the surpassing importance of heredity and innate characteristics. For it hardly needs to be expressly emphasized that these constructions can have negative as well as positive effects. We are not only responsible for our dreams, but also for the reality created by our hopes and thoughts.

It would, however, be a mistake to assume that self-fulfilling prophecies are restricted to human beings. Their effects reach deeper, into prehuman stages of development, and are in this sense even more alarming. Even before Rosenthal carried out his Oak School experiment, he reported in a book published in 1966 a similar experiment with rats that was repeated and confirmed by many scholars in the following years. Twelve participants in a laboratory course in experimental psychology were given a lecture on certain studies that purported to prove that good or bad test achievements of rats (for instance, in learning experiments in labyrinth cages) can become innate by selective breeding. Six of the students then received thirty rats whose genetic constitution allegedly made them especially good, intelligent laboratory subjects, while the other six students were assigned thirty rats of whom they were told the opposite, namely, that they were animals whose hereditary factors made them unsuitable for experiments. In fact and truth, the sixty rats were all of the same kind, the one that has always been used for such purposes. All sixty animals were then trained for exactly the same learning experiment. The rats whose trainers believed them to be especially intelligent did not just do better from the very outset, but raised their achievements far above that of the "unintelligent" animals. At the end of the five-day experiment the trainers were asked to evaluate their animals subjectively, in addition to the noted results of the experiments. The students who "knew" that they were working with unintelligent animals expressed themselves accordingly, that is, negatively, in their reports, whereas their colleagues, who had experimented with rats of supposedly above—average talents, rated their charges as friendly, intelligent, ingenious, and the like, and mentioned furthermore that they had often touched the animals, petted them, and even played with them. When we consider the surpassing role rat experiments play in experimental psychology and especially in the psychology of learning, and how often inferences are drawn from them to human behavior, these inferences now seem somewhat questionable.

Rats are known to be very intelligent animals, and the students' reports suggest that in the way they handled their animals, they literally "handed" them their assumptions and expectations. But the results of another research project, reported in 1963 by the research team Cordaro and Ison, suggest that it is not only a matter of such direct influence. In this project the laboratory subjects were earthworms (planaria), who are of great interest for the student of evolution and of behavior alike, in that they are the most primitive form of life possessing the rudiments of a brain. The supposition

therefore suggested itself that these worms were capable of training of the simplest kind, as, for instance, a change in direction (to the left or to the right) upon arriving at the crossbeam of a T-shaped groove arrangement. Experiments of this kind began in several American universities in the late fifties. As in the rat experiments, Cordaro and Ison caused the experimenters to believe that they were working with especially intelligent or especially incapable worms, and even here, at this primitive stage of development (which, moreover, left little room for emotional attachment), there grew from the conviction, once it was established, objectively discernible and statistically significant differences in the experimental behavior of the planaria.[3]

For the very reason that these experiments undermine our basic concepts, it is all too easy to shrug them off and return to the comfortable certainty of our accustomed routines. That, for instance, test psychologists ignore these extremely disturbing results and continue to test people and animals with unmitigated tenacity and scientific "objectivity" is only a small example of the determination with which we defend ourselves when our world view is being threatened. The fact that we are responsible to the world in its entirety and to a much higher degree than is dreamed of in our philosophy is for the present almost unthinkable; but it can penetrate our consciousness through a better understanding of the processes of human communication—a study that will encompass many disciplines that heretofore have been either considered as being quite independent of each other or not considered at all. Rosenhan's contribution [see Reading 39] illuminates the alarming possibility that at least some so-called mental illnesses are nothing but constructions, and that the psychiatric institutions actually contribute to the constructions of those realities that are supposed to be treated therein. The chronic problem that still plagues modern psychiatry is that we have only the vaguest and most general concepts for the definition of mental health, while for the diagnosis of abnormal behavior there exist catalogs perfected to the last detail. Freud, for instance, used the concept of the ability to love and work as a basic criterion for mature emotional normalcy (a definition that does not do justice to a Hitler, on the one hand, or to the proverbial eccentricities of men of genius, on the other). The other medical specialties work with definitions of pathology that refer to certain deviations from fairly well-known normal functions of the healthy organism. Quite irrationally, in psychiatry it is just the opposite. Here pathology is considered the known factor, whereas normalcy is seen as difficult to define, if it is definable at all. This opens the floodgates to self-fulfilling diagnoses. There is a great number of very definite patterns of behavior that in the terminology of psychiatry are so tightly associated with certain diagnostic categories (again I refer to Rosenhan) that they virtually function like Pavlovian buzzers, not only in the thinking of the psychiatrist but also in the family environment of the patient. An attempt to show how certain specific forms of behavior take on the meaning of pathological manifestations on the basis of their cultural and societal significance, and how these manifestations in turn become self-fulfilling prophecies, would go beyond the scope of this essay. Of the already quite extensive literature on this topic, *The Manufacture of Madness* by Thomas Szasz (1970) is particularly notable. Suffice it to say that an essential part of the self-fulfilling effect of psychiatric diagnoses is based on our unshakable conviction that everything that has a name must *therefore* actually exist. The materializations and actualizations of psychiatric diagnoses probably originate largely from this conviction.

"Magic" diagnoses, in the actual sense of the word, have of course been known for a very long time. In his classic paper "Voodoo Death," the American physiologist Walter Cannon (1942) described a number of mysterious, sudden, and scientifically difficult to explain deaths that followed curses, evil spells, or the breaking of moral taboos. A Brazilian Indian, cursed by a medicine man, is helpless against his own emotional response to this death sentence and dies within hours. A young African hunter unknowingly kills and eats an inviolably banned wild hen. When he discovers his crime, he is overcome with despair and dies within twenty-four hours. A medicine man in the Australian bush points a bone with magic properties at a man. Believing that nothing can save him, the man sinks into lethargy and prepares to die. He is saved only at the last moment, when other members of the tribe force the witch doctor to remove the spell.

Cannon became convinced that voodoo death exists as a phenomenon,

> characteristically noted among aborigines—among human beings so primitive, so superstitious, so ignorant, that they feel themselves bewildered strangers in a hostile world. Instead of knowledge, they have fertile and unrestricted imaginations which fill their environment with all manner of evil spirits capable of affecting their lives disastrously.

At the time when Cannon wrote these lines, hundreds of thousands of human beings who were neither superstitious nor ignorant had every reason to see themselves as bewildered victims of an unimaginably hostile world. From the haunted, shadowy world of the concentration camps Viktor Frankl (1959, pp. 74–75) reports a phenomenon that corresponds to voodoo death:

> The prisoner who had lost faith in the future—his future—was doomed. With his loss of belief in the future, he also lost his spiritual hold; he let himself decline and became subject to mental and physical decay. Usually this happened quite suddenly, in the form of a crisis, the symptoms of which were familiar to the experienced camp inmate. We all feared

this moment—not for ourselves, which would have been pointless, but for our friends. Usually it began with the prisoner refusing one morning to get dressed and wash or to go out on the parade grounds. No entreaties, no blows, no threats had any effect. He just lay there.

One of Frankl's fellow prisoners lost his will to live when his own prediction, seen in a dream, did not come true and thereby became a negative self-fulfillment. "I would like to tell you something, Doctor," he said to Frankl,

> I have had a strange dream. A voice told me that I could wish for something, that I should only say what I wanted to know, and all my questions would be answered. What do you think I asked? That I would like to know when the war would be over for me. You know what I mean, Doctor—for me! I wanted to know when we, when our camp, would be liberated and our sufferings come to an end. . . . Furtively he whispered to me, "March thirtieth."

But when the day of the prophesied liberation was near and the Allied forces were still far from the camp, things took a fateful turn for Frankl's fellow sufferer, the prisoner F.:

> On March twenty-ninth, F. suddenly became ill and ran a high temperature. On March thirtieth, the day his prophecy had told him that the war and suffering would be over for him, he became delirious and lost consciousness. On March thirty-first, he was dead. He had died of typhus.

As a physician, Frankl understood that his friend died because

> the expected liberation did not come and he was severely disappointed. This suddenly lowered his body's resistance against the latent typhus infection.

We admire human beings who face death calmly. Dying "decently," in a composed manner, without wrangling with the inevitable, was and is considered in most cultures an expression of wisdom and unusual maturity. All the more surprising and sobering therefore are the results of modern cancer research, which suggest that the mortality rate is higher in those patients who prepare themselves for death in a mature, serene way or who, like the concentration camp prisoner F., fall victim to a negative self-fulfilling prophecy. For those patients, however, who cling to life in a seemingly senseless, irrational, and immature way or who are convinced that they simply "cannot" or "must not" die because they have important work to do or family members to take care of, the prognosis is considerably more favorable. To the American oncologist Carl Simonton (1975), whose name is associated, above all, with the appreciation of the impact of emotional factors, now more and more recognized for their importance in the treatment of cancer, three things are of the utmost significance in this connection: the belief system of the patient, that of the patient's family, and, third, that of the attending physician. That each one of these belief systems can become a self-fulfilling prophecy seems credible in the light of what we have discussed so far. Furthermore, the studies and research reports about the susceptibility of the human immune system to mood swings, suggestions, and visual imagery (O. Simonton & S. Simonton, 1978; Solomon, 1969) are increasing.

How much can and should a physician tell his patients, not only about the gravity of their illnesses, but also about the dangers inherent in the treatment *itself?* At least in certain countries this question is becoming more and more rhetorical. The risk of getting hit with a malpractice suit because a patient has not been informed about his disease and its treatment down to the last technical detail causes many doctors in the United States, for example, to protect themselves in a way that can have serious consequences. The protection consists in asking the patient for a written consent to treatment in which the most catastrophic possible consequences of the illness and of the measures deemed necessary by the doctor are listed in every detail. It is not hard to imagine that this creates a kind of self-fulfilling prophecy that has a paralyzing effect on the confidence and will to recover of even the most sanguine patient. Who has not read the description of even a seemingly harmless medication and then had the feeling of swallowing poison? How does the layman (or, presumably, even the professional) know that he is not going to be the fourth of the three fatalities reported to date that were inexplicably caused by a medication so far used safely by millions? But *fiat justitia, pereat mundus*.[4]

Since in the patient's eye a doctor is a kind of mediator between life and death, his utterances can easily become self-fulfilling prophecies. The astonishing degree to which this is possible is portrayed in a case reported (but unfortunately not sufficiently documented) by the American psychologist Gordon Allport (1964). What is unusual here is that a misunderstanding shifted the prophecy from death to life:

In a provincial Austrian hospital, a man lay gravely ill—in fact, at death's door. The medical staff had told him frankly that they could not diagnose his disease, but that if they knew the diagnosis they could probably cure him. They told him further that a famous diagnostician was soon to visit the hospital and that perhaps he could spot the trouble.

Within a few days the diagnostician arrived and proceeded to make the rounds. Coming to this man's bed, he merely glanced at the patient, murmured, "Moribundus," and went on.

Some years later, the patient called on the diagnostician and said, "I've been wanting to thank you for your diagnosis. They told me that if you could diagnose me I'd get well, and so the minute you said 'moribundus' I knew I'd recover."

Knowledge of the healing effect of positive predictions is undoubtedly just as ancient as faith in the inescapable consequences of curses and evil spells. Modern use of positive suggestions and autosuggestions ranges from the "I will recover; I feel better every day" of Emile Coué, through numerous forms of hypnotherapeutic interventions (Haley, 1973), to influencing the course of an illness—and not only cancer—by positive imagery. The extent to which such imagery that a (future) event has already taken place can reach into the physical realm is suggested by several studies according to which it is possible to increase a woman's chest measurement by an average of four to five centimeters through the use of certain self-hypnotic techniques (Staib & Logan, 1977; Willard, 1977). I mention these "successes" with all due skepticism and simply as curiosities testifying to the towering importance of the female breast in the North American erotic ethos.

Brief mention should also be made of the modern physiological and endocrinological studies that indicate more and more the possibility of stimulating the functions of the immune system of the human organism by certain experiences and that these functions are by no means completely autonomous (that is, outside conscious control), as was assumed until quite recently. Medical research is likely to make astonishing discoveries in this field in the near future. For instance, it is now known that the organism itself produces a number of morphene-like substances—the so-called endorphins (Beers, 1979)—that are analgesic and whose production is stimulated by certain emotional processes. There is thus a wide-open, unexplored territory in which the phenomenon of self-fulfilling prophecies begins to achieve scientific respectability.

Just as decisive as a doctor's suggestive comments, expectations, and convictions are the measures he takes and the remedies he administers. Of special interest here are *placebos*[5] (Benson & Epstein, 1975), those chemically inert substances that resemble certain medicines in shape, taste, or color but which have no pharmaceutical effect. We must remember that until about 100 years ago nearly all medications were practically ineffective in the modern sense. They were only slightly more elegant tinctures and powders than the ground toads, the lizard blood, the "sacred oils," or the pulverized horn of the rhinoceros of even earlier times. During my childhood, people in the rural areas of Austria still believed that a necklace of garlic would protect them from the common cold, to say nothing about the well-known success of magic in the treatment of warts. Even in our time, old "tried and true" remedies or sensational new discoveries (as, for example, Laetrile) are always being unmasked as pharmaceutically ineffective. But that is not to say that they were or are *functionally* ineffective. "One should treat as many patients as possible with the new remedies, as long as these are still working," reads the maxim of a famous physician, attributed to Trousseau, Osler, or Sydenham. Scientific interest in placebos is rapidly increasing. In his contribution to the history of the placebo effect Shapiro (1960) points out that more articles on this topic were published in scientific journals between 1954 and 1957 alone than in the first fifty years of the twentieth century. Most of these reports discuss traditional pharmaceutical effectiveness studies, in which one group of patients receives the new medication while another takes a placebo. The purpose of this well-meaning procedure is to find out whether the course of the illness of the "actually" treated patients is different from that of the placebo group. Only people whose world view is based on classical linear causal thinking (for which there is only an "objective" relationship between cause and effect) react with consternation when they realize that the patients "treated" with placebos often show a quite "inexplicable" improvement in their condition. In other words, the claim of the doctor who administers the placebo that it is an effective, newly developed

medicine and the patient's willingness to believe in its effectiveness create a reality in which the assumption actually becomes a fact.

Enough examples. Self-fulfilling prophecies are phenomena that not only shake up our personal conception of reality, but which can also throw doubt on the world view of science. They all share the obviously reality-creating power of a firm belief in the "suchness" of things, a faith that can be a superstition as well as a seemingly strictly scientific theory derived from objective observation. Until recently it has been possible to categorically reject self-fulfilling prophecies as unscientific or to ascribe them to the inadequate reality adaptation of muddleheaded thinkers and romanticists, but we no longer have this convenient escape hatch open to us.

What all this means cannot yet be appraised with any certainty. The discovery that we create our own realities is comparable to the expulsion from the paradise of the presumed suchness of the world, a world in which we can certainly suffer, but for which we need only feel responsible in a very limited way (Watzlawick, 1976).

And here lies the danger. The insights of constructivism may have the highly desirable advantage of allowing for new and more effective forms of therapy (Watzlawick, 1978), but like all remedies, they can also be abused. Advertising and propaganda are two especially repugnant examples: Both try quite deliberately to bring about attitudes, assumptions, prejudices, and the like, whose realization then seems to follow naturally and logically. Thanks to this brainwashing, the world is then seen as "thus" and therefore is "thus." In the novel *1984* (Orwell, 1949) this reality-creating propaganda language is called *Newspeak,* and Orwell explains that it "makes all other modes of thinking impossible." In a recent review of a volume of essays published in London on censorship in the People's Republic of Poland (Strzyzewski, 1977–1978), Daniel Weiss (1980) writes about this magic language:

Compare for example the great number of adjectives, characteristic for Newspeak: Every development is nothing less than "dynamic," every plenary session of the party "historic," the masses always "proletarian workers." A sober communication scientist will find nothing but *redundance* in this inflation of mechanized epithets, drained of meaning. But after listening repeatedly, this automation is felt to have the equality of an incantation: The spoken word is no longer used to carry information, it has become the instrument of magic. (p. 66)

And finally the world simply *is thus*. How it was *made* to be this way was well known to Joseph Goebbels (1933/1976), when he lectured the managers of German radio stations on March 25, 1933:

This is the secret of propaganda: To totally saturate the person, whom the propaganda wants to lay hold of, with the ideas of the propaganda, without him even noticing that he is being saturated. Propaganda has of course a purpose, but this purpose must be disguised with such shrewdness and virtuosity that he who is supposed to be filled with this purpose never even knows what is happening. (p. 120)

In the necessity of disguising the purpose, however, lies the possibility of overcoming it. As we have seen, the invented reality will become "actual" reality only if the invention is believed. Where the element of faith, of blind conviction, is absent, there will be no effect. With the better understanding of self-fulfilling prophecies our ability to transcend them grows. A prophecy that we know to be only a prophecy can no longer fulfill itself. The possibility of choosing differently (of being a heretic) and of disobeying always exists; whether we see it and act on it is, of course, another question. An insight from the seemingly far-removed domain of the mathematical theory of games is of interest here. Wittgenstein (1956) already pointed out in his *Remarks on the Foundations of Mathematics* that certain games

can be won with a simple trick. As soon as someone calls our attention to the existence of this trick, we no longer have to continue playing naively (and continue losing). Building on these reflections, the mathematician Howard (1967) formulated his *existential axiom* which maintains that "if a person becomes 'aware' of a theory concerning his behavior, he is no longer bound by it but is free to disobey it" (p. 167). Elsewhere he also says that

a conscious decision maker can always choose to disobey any theory predicting his behavior. We may say that he can always "transcend" such a theory. This indeed seems realistic. We suggest that among socio-economic theories, Marxian theory, for example, failed at least partly because certain ruling class members, when they became aware of the theory, saw that it was in their interest to disobey it. (1971)

And almost a hundred years before Howard, Dostoevski's underground man writes in his *Letters from the Underworld* (1913),

As a matter of fact, if ever there shall be discovered a formula which shall exactly express our wills and whims; if ever there shall be discovered a formula which shall make it absolutely clear what those wills depend upon, and what laws they are governed by, and what means of diffusion they possess, and what tendencies they follow under given circumstances; if ever there shall be discovered a formula which shall be mathematical in its precision, well, gentlemen, whenever such a formula shall be found, man will have ceased to have a will of his own—he will have ceased even to exist. Who would care to exercise his willpower according to a table of logarithms? In such a case man would become, not a human being at all, but an organ-handle, or something of the kind. (p. 32)

But even if this kind of mathematical formulization of our lives could ever be achieved, it would in no way comprehend the complexity of our existence. The best theory is powerless in the face of an antitheory; the fulfillment of even the truest prophecy can be thwarted if we know about it beforehand. Dostoevski (1913) saw much more in the nature of man:

> Moreover, even if man *were* the keyboard of a piano, and could be convinced that the laws of nature and of mathematics had made him so, he would still decline to change. On the contrary, he would once more, out of sheer ingratitude, attempt the perpetration of something which would enable him to insist upon himself. . . . But if you were to tell me that all this could be set down in tables—I mean the chaos, and the confusion, and the curses, and all the rest of it—so that the possibility of computing everything might remain, and reason continue to rule the roost—well, in that case, I believe, man would *purposely* become a lunatic, in order to become devoid of reason, and therefore able to insist upon himself. I believe this, and I am ready to vouch for this, simply for the reason that every human act arises out of the circumstance that man is forever striving to prove to his own satisfaction that he is a man and not an organ-handle. (p. 37)

However, even the evidence of the underground man is likely to be a self-fulfilling prophecy.

NOTES

1. The following untrue story is a further illustration: In 1974, Secretary of State Kissinger, who is on one of his innumerable mediating missions in Jerusalem, is on his way back to the hotel after a private, late-evening stroll. A young Israeli stops him, introduces himself as an economist out of work, and asks Kissinger to help him find a job through his numerous connections. Kissinger is favorably impressed by the applicant and asks him whether he would like to be the vice-president of the Bank of Israel. The young man thinks of course that Kissinger is making fun of him, but the latter promises quite seriously that he will manage the matter for him. Next day Kissinger calls Baron Rothschild in Paris: "I have a charming young man here, a political

economist, talented, going to be the next vice-president of the Bank of Israel. You have to meet him; he would be a jewel of a husband for your daughter." Rothschild growls something that does not sound like total rejection, whereupon Kissinger immediately calls the president of the Bank of Israel: "I have a young financial expert here, brilliant fellow, exactly the stuff to make a vice-president for your bank, and most of all—imagine *that*—he is the future son-in-law of Baron Rothschild's."

2. *Editor's note:* Italian for "If it's not true, it is well written."

3. Here I will briefly mention an interesting sequel to these experiments: For reasons irrelevant to our topic, several researchers (McConnell, Jacobson, & Humphries, 1961) studied the fascinating theory that at the planaria's primitive stage of development information stored in a worm's ribonucleic acid (RNA) could possibly be directly transferred to other worms. For this purpose they fed untrained animals their already successfully trained fellow worms. Even we laymen can imagine the sensation among experts when the training of the worms provided with such food actually turned out to be much easier and faster. The euphoria lasted for a short while until the experiments, repeated under more rigorous controls, showed themselves to be inconclusive, and serious doubts arose concerning the transferability of intelligence through ground meat. The suspicion suggests itself, but was, as far as I know, never proven, that the original results were due to self-fulfilling prophecies, similar to those whose effects on the worms were already known. (The analogy, however, to the superstition of certain African tribes that eating a lion's heart will confer the lion's courage cannot be dismissed out of hand.)

4. *Editor's note:* Latin for "Let justice be done though the world perish."

5. Latin for "I shall please."

REFERENCES

Allport, G. W. (1964). Mental health: A generic attitude. *Journal of Religion and Health, 4,* 7–21.

Beers, R. F. (Ed.). (1979). *Mechanisms of pain and analgesic compounds.* New York: Raven.

Benson, H., & Epstein, M. D. (1975). The placebo effect: A neglected asset in the care of patients. *American Medical Association Journal, 232,* 1225–1227.

Cannon, W. B. (1942). Voodoo death. *American Anthropologist, 44,* 169–181.

Cordaro, L., & Ison, J. R. (1963). Observer bias in classical conditioning of the planaria. *Psychological Reports, 13,* 787–789.

Dostoevski, F. M. (1913). *Letters from the underworld.* New York: Dutton.

Feyerabend, P. K. (1978). *Science in a free society.* London: New Left.

Frankl, V. E. (1959). *From death camp to existentialism.* Boston: Beacon.

Goebbels, J. Quoted in Schneider, W. (1976). *Wörter machen leute. Magie und macht der sprache.* Munich: Piper.

Haley, J. (1973). *Uncommon therapy: The psychiatric techniques of Milton H. Erickson, M.D.* New York: Norton.

Heisenberg, W. (1958). *Physics and philosophy: The revolution in modern science.* New York: Harper & Row.

Howard, N. (1967). The theory of metagames. *General Systems, 2,* 167.

Howard, N. (1971). *Paradoxes of rationality, theory of metagames and political behavior.* Cambridge, MA: MIT Press.

Jones, R. A. (1974). *Self-fulfilling prophecies: Social, psychological and physiological effects of expectancies.* New York: Halsted.

McConnell, J. V., Jacobson, R., & Humphries, B. M. (1961). The effects of ingestion of conditioned planaria on the response level of naive planaria: A pilot study. *Worm Runner's Digest, 3,* 41–45.

Orwell, G. (1949). *1984.* New York: Harcourt, Brace.

Popper, K. R. (1974). *Unended quest.* La Salle, IL: Open Court.

Rosenthal, R. (1966). *Experimenter effects in behavioral research.* New York: Appleton-Century-Crofts.

Rosenthal, R., & Jacobson, L. (1968). *Pygmalion in the classroom: Teacher expectation and pupils' intellectual development.* New York: Holt, Rinehart & Winston.

Shapiro, A. K. (1960). A contribution to a history of the placebo effects. *Behavioral Science, 5,* 109–135.

Simonton, O. C., & Simonton, S. (1975). Belief systems and management of the emotional aspects of malignancy. *Journal of Transpersonal Psychology, 1,* 29–47.

Simonton, O. C., & Simonton, S. (1978). *Getting well again.* Los Angeles: J. P. Tarcher.

Solomon, G. F. (1969). Emotions, stress, the nervous system, and immunity. *Annals of the New York Academy of Sciences, 164,* 335–343.

Staib, A. R., & Logan, D. R. (1977). Hypnotic stimulation of breast growth. *American Journal of Clinical Hypnosis, 19,* 201–208.

Strzyzewski, T. (1977–1978). *Czarna ksiega cenzury PRL* (Black Book of Polish Censorship, 2 vols.). London: "Aneks."

Szasz, T. S. (1970). *The manufacture of madness: A comparative study of the Inquisition and the mental health movement.* New York: Harper & Row.

Watzlawick, P. (1976). *How real is real?* New York: Random House.

Watzlawick, P. (1978). *The language of change: Elements of therapeutic communication.* New York: Basic Books.

Watzlawick, P., Bavelas, J. B., & Jackson, D. D. (1967). *Pragmatics of human communication: A study of interactional patterns, pathologies and paradoxes.* New York: Norton.

Weiss, D. (1980). Sprache und propaganda—Der sonderfall Polen. *Neue Zürcher Zeitung, 39,* 66.

Willard, R. R. (1977). Breast enlargement through visual imagery and hypnosis. *American Journal of Clinical Hypnosis, 19,* 195–200.

Wittgenstein, L. (1956). *Remarks on the foundations of mathematics.* Oxford, UK: Blackwell.

32

When Belief Creates Reality

The Self-Fulfilling Impact of First Impressions on Social Interaction

Mark Snyder

(1977)

For the social psychologist, there may be no processes more complex and intriguing than those by which strangers become friends. How do we form first impressions of those we encounter in our lives? How do we become acquainted with each other? When does an acquaintance become a friend? Why do some relationships develop and withstand the test of time and other equally promising relationships flounder and fall by the wayside? It is to these and similar concerns that my colleagues and I have addressed ourselves in our attempts to chart the unfolding dynamics of social interaction and interpersonal relationships. In doing so, we chose—not surprisingly—to begin at the beginning. Specifically, we have been studying the ways in which first impressions channel and influence subsequent social interaction and acquaintance processes.

When we first meet others, we cannot help but notice certain highly visible and distinctive characteristics such as their sex, age, race, and bodily appearance. Try as we may to avoid it, our first impressions are often molded and influenced by these pieces of information. Consider the case of physical attractiveness. A widely held stereotype in this culture suggests that attractive people are assumed to possess more socially desirable personalities and are expected to lead better personal, social, and occupational lives than their unattractive counterparts. For example, Dion, Berscheid, and Walster (1972) had men and women judge photographs of either men or women who varied in physical attractiveness. Attractive stimulus persons of either sex were perceived to have virtually every character trait that pretesting had indicated was socially desirable to that participant population: "Physically attractive people, for example, were perceived to be more sexually warm and responsive, sensitive, kind, interesting, strong, poised, modest, sociable, and outgoing than persons of lesser physical attractiveness" (Berscheid & Walster, 1974, p. 169). This powerful stereotype was found for male and female judges and for male and female stimulus persons. In

AUTHOR'S NOTE: This research was supported in part by National Science Foundation Grant SOC 75–13872, "Cognition and Behavior: When Belief Creates Reality," to Mark Snyder. For a more detailed description of the background and rationale, procedures and results, implications and consequences of this investigation, see M. Snyder, E. D. Tanke, & E. Berscheid, Social perception and interpersonal behavior: On the self-fulfilling nature of social stereotypes. *Journal of Personality and Social Psychology,* 1977. For related research on behavioral confirmation in social interaction, see M. Snyder & W. B. Swann, Jr., Behavioral confirmation in social interaction: From social perception to social reality. *Journal of Experimental Social Psychology,* 1978.

addition, attractive people were predicted to have happier social, professional, and personal lives in store for them than were their less attractive counterparts. (For an excellent and comprehensive review, see Berscheid & Walster, 1974.)

What of the validity of the physical attractiveness stereotype? Are the physically attractive actually more likeable, friendly, sensitive, and confident than the unattractive? Are they more successful socially and professionally? Clearly, the physically attractive are more often and more eagerly sought out for social dates. And well they should be, for the stereotype implies that they should be perceived as more desirable social partners than the physically unattractive. Thus, it should come as little surprise that, among young adults, the physically attractive have more friends of the other sex, engage in more sexual activity, report themselves in love more often, and express less anxiety about dating than unattractive individuals do. But the effect is even more general than this. Even as early as nursery school age, physical attractiveness appears to channel social interaction: The physically attractive are chosen and the unattractive are rejected in sociometric choices.

A differential amount of interaction with the attractive and unattractive clearly helps the stereotype persevere because it limits the chances for learning whether the two types of individuals differ in the traits associated with the stereotype. But the point I wish to focus on here is that the stereotype may also channel interaction so as to confirm itself *behaviorally.* Individuals appear to have different patterns and styles of interaction for those whom they perceive to be physically attractive and for those whom they consider unattractive. These differences in self-presentation and interaction style may, in turn, elicit and nurture behaviors from the target person that are in accord with the stereotype. That is, the physically attractive may actually come to behave in a friendly, likeable, sociable manner, not because they necessarily possess these dispositions, but because the behavior

of others elicits and maintains behaviors taken to be manifestations of such traits.

In our empirical research, we have attempted to demonstrate that stereotypes may create their own social reality by channeling social interaction in ways that cause the stereotyped individual to behave in ways that confirm another person's stereotyped impressions of him or her. In our initial investigation, Elizabeth Decker Tanke, Ellen Berscheid, and I sought to demonstrate the self-fulfilling nature of the physical attractiveness stereotype in a social interaction context designed to mirror as faithfully as possible the spontaneous generation of first impressions in everyday social interaction and the subsequent channeling influences of these impressions on social interaction. In order to do so, pairs of previously unacquainted individuals (designated for our purposes as a *perceiver* and a *target*) interacted in a getting-acquainted situation constructed to allow us to control the information that one member of the dyad (the male perceiver) received about the physical attractiveness of the other individual (the female target). In this way, it was possible to evaluate separately the effects of actual and perceived physical attractiveness on the display of self-presentational and expressive behaviors associated with the stereotype that links beauty and goodness. In order to measure the extent to which the self-presentation of the target individual matched the perceiver's stereotype, naïve observer-judges who were unaware of the actual or perceived physical attractiveness of either participant listened to and evaluated tape recordings of the interaction.

Fifty-one male and fifty-one female undergraduates at the University of Minnesota participated, for extra course credit, in what had been described as a study of the "processes by which people become acquainted with each other." These individuals interacted in male-female dyads in a getting-acquainted situation in which they could hear but not see each other (a telephone conversation).

Before initiating the conversation, the male member of each dyad received a Polaroid snapshot of his female interaction partner. These photographs, which had been prepared in advance and assigned at random to dyads, identified the target as either physically attractive (attractive-target condition) or physically unattractive (unattractive-target condition). Each dyad engaged in a ten-minute unstructured telephone conversation that was tape-recorded. Each participant's voice was recorded on a separate channel of the tape.

In order to assess the extent to which the actions of the female targets provided behavioral confirmation of the male perceivers' stereotypes, twelve observer-judges listened to the tape recordings of the getting-acquainted conversations. The observer-judges were unaware of the experimental hypotheses and knew nothing of the actual or perceived physical attractiveness of the individual whom they heard on the tapes. They heard only those tape tracks containing the female participants' voices. Nine other observer-judges listened to and rated only the male perceivers' voices. (For further details of the experimental procedures, see Snyder, Tanke, & Berscheid, 1977.)

In order to chart the process of behavioral confirmation of stereotype-based attributions in these dyadic social interactions, we examined the effects of our manipulation of the target's apparent physical attractiveness on both the male perceivers' initial impressions of their female targets and the females' behavioral self-presentation during their interactions, as measured by the observer-judges' ratings of the tape recordings of their voices.

The male perceivers clearly formed their initial impressions of their female targets on the basis of general stereotypes that associate physical attractiveness with socially desirable personality characteristics. On the basis of measures of first impressions that were collected after the perceivers had been given access to their partners' photographs but before the initiation of the getting-acquainted conversations, it was clear that (as dictated by the physical attractiveness stereotype) males who anticipated physically attractive partners expected to interact with comparatively cordial, poised, humorous, and socially adept individuals. By contrast, males faced with the prospect of getting acquainted with relatively unattractive partners fashioned images of rather withdrawn, awkward, serious, and socially inept creatures.

Not only did our perceivers fashion their images of their discussion partners on the basis of their stereotyped intuitions about the links between beauty and goodness of character, but the stereotype-based attributions initiated a chain of events that resulted in the behavioral confirmation of these initially erroneous inferences. Analysis of the observer-judges' ratings of the tape recordings of the conversations indicated that female targets who (unbeknown to them) were perceived to be physically attractive (as a consequence of random assignment to the attractive-target experimental condition) actually came to behave in a friendly, likeable, and sociable manner. This behavioral confirmation was discernible even by outside observer-judges who knew nothing of the actual or perceived physical attractiveness of the target individuals. In this demonstration of behavioral confirmation in social interaction, the "beautiful" people became "good" people, not because they necessarily possessed the socially valued dispositions that had been attributed to them, but because the actions of the perceivers, which were based on their stereotyped beliefs, had erroneously confirmed and validated these attributions.

Confident in our demonstration of the self-fulfilling nature of this particular social stereotype, we then attempted to chart the process of behavioral confirmation. Specifically, we searched for evidence of the behavioral implications of the perceivers' stereotypes. Did the male perceivers present themselves differently to the target women whom they assumed to be physically attractive or unattractive? An examination of the observer-judges' ratings of the tapes of only the males' contributions to the conversations provided clear evidence that our perceivers did have different interactional styles with targets of different physical attractiveness.

Men who interacted with women whom they believed to be physically attractive appeared to be more cordial, sexually warm, interesting, independent, sexually permissive, bold, outgoing, humorous, obvious, and socially adept than their counterparts in the unattractive-target condition. Moreover, these same men were seen by the judges to be more attractive, more confident, and more animated in their conversation than their counterparts. They were also considered by the observer-judges to be more comfortable in conversation, to enjoy themselves more, to like their partners more, to take the initiative more often, to use their voices more effectively, to see their women partners as more attractive, and finally, to be seen as more attractive by their partners than men in the unattractive-target condition.

It appears, then, that differences in the expressive self-presentation of sociability by the male perceivers may have been a key factor in the process of bringing out those reciprocal patterns of expression in the target women that constitute behavioral confirmation of the attributions from which the perceivers' self-presentation had been generated. One reason that target women who had been labeled attractive may have reciprocated this sociable self-presentation is that they regarded their partners' images of them as more accurate and their style of interaction to be more typical of the way men generally treated them than women in the unattractive-target condition did. Perhaps, these latter individuals rejected their partners' treatment of them as unrepresentative and defensively adopted more cool and aloof postures to cope with their situations.

Our research points to the powerful but often unnoticed consequences of social stereotypes. In our demonstration, first impressions and expectations that were based on common cultural stereotypes about physical attractiveness channeled the unfolding dynamics of social interaction and acquaintance processes in ways that actually made those stereotyped first impressions come true. In our investigation, pairs of individuals got acquainted with each other in a situation that allowed us to control the information that one member of the dyad (the perceiver) received about the physical attractiveness of the other person (the target). Our perceivers . . . fashioned erroneous images of their specific partners that reflected their general stereotypes about physical attractiveness. Moreover, our perceivers had very different patterns and styles of interaction for those whom they perceived to be physically attractive and to be unattractive. These differences in self-presentation and interaction style, in turn, elicited and nurtured behaviors of the targets that were consistent with the perceived initial stereotypes. Targets who (unbeknown to them) were perceived to be physically attractive actually came to behave in a friendly, likeable, and sociable manner. The perceivers' attributions about their targets based on their stereotyped intuitions about the world had initiated a process that produced behavioral confirmation of those attributions. The initially erroneous impressions of the perceivers had become real. The stereotype had truly functioned as a self-fulfilling prophecy:

> The self-fulfilling prophecy is, in the beginning, a *false* definition of the situation evoking a new behavior which makes the originally false conception come *true*. The validity of the self-fulfilling prophecy perpetuates a reign of error. For the prophet will cite the actual course of events as proof that he was right from the very beginning. . . . Such are the perversities of social logic. (Merton 1948, p. 195)

True to Merton's script, our "prophets," in the beginning, created false definitions of their situations. That is, they erroneously labeled their targets as sociable or unsociable persons on the basis of their physical attractiveness. But these mistakes in first impressions quickly became self-erasing mistakes because the perceivers' false definitions evoked new behaviors that made their originally false conceptions come true: They treated their targets as sociable or unsociable persons, and, indeed, these targets came to behave in a sociable or unsociable fashion. Our prophets also cited the actual course of events as proof that they had been right all along. Might not other important and widespread social stereotypes—particularly those concerning sex, race, social class, and ethnicity—also channel social interaction in ways that create their own social reality?

Any self-fulfilling influences of social stereotypes may have compelling and pervasive societal consequences. Social observers have for decades commented on and demonstrated the ways in which stigmatized social groups and outsiders may fall victim to self-fulfilling cultural stereotypes. Consider Scott's (1969) observations about the blind:

> When, for example, sighted people continually insist that a blind man is helpless because he is blind, their

subsequent treatment of him may preclude his own exercising the kinds of skills that would enable him to be independent. It is in this sense that stereotypic beliefs are self-actualized. (p. 9)

All too often, it is the victims who are blamed for their own plight . . . rather than the social expectations that have constrained their behavioral options.

REFERENCES

Berscheid, E., & Walster, E. (1974). Physical attractiveness. In L. Berkowitz (Ed.), *Advances in experimental social psychology* (Vol. 7). New York: Academic Press.

Dion, K. K., Berscheid, E., & Walster, E. (1972). What is good is beautiful. *Journal of Personality and Social Psychology, 24,* 285–290.

Merton, R. K. (1948). The self-fulfilling prophecy. *Antioch Review, 8,* 193–210.

Scott, R. A. (1969). *The making of blind men.* New York: Russell Sage.

Snyder, M., Tanke, E. D., & Berscheid, E. (1977). Social perception and interpersonal behavior: On the self-fulfilling nature of social stereotypes. *Journal of Personality and Social Psychology, 35,* 656–666.

THE SOCIAL CONSTRUCTION OF THE CULTURAL STATUS QUO

When you combine everything that you have learned from this book up to this point, you will find that you now have a basis for explaining how major social patterns are created and maintained by small and seemingly insignificant everyday beliefs and actions. An important point to realize is that all of us may be contributing to the status quo, even when we sometimes believe we don't agree with it. The readings in this section provide examples of the maintenance of two kinds of *patterned* social discrimination. As you read, pay close attention to the everyday actions that perpetuate these social lines of division.

In "The Persistence of Gender Inequality in Employment Settings," sociologist Cecilia Ridgeway presents an explanation for the ongoing gender gap in upper-level management. Even laws such as affirmative action have not helped women to move into the highest ranks. Ridgeway finds the answer to this puzzle in an analysis of the preconceived *status expectations* that both men and women hold about management characteristics. All else being equal, when promotion decisions are discussed in groups, people often revert to stereotypical assessments that result in a default assumption that men are better suited for certain jobs. Through their conversations, the group upholds a gender status quo.

Scott Harris is another sociologist interested in the way in which interactions reflect and uphold preconceived status expectations. Harris explores how close friends handle social status differences between them. Does their behavior with one another break down status barriers or reinforce these barriers?

Questions for Discussion and Review

1. Review Ridgeway's discussion of "gender status beliefs" and make a list of other categories of "status beliefs" (for example, race, class, and so forth) Discuss how her theory might be used to explain persistent discrimination for these other statuses.

2. Make a list of social expectations that seem especially significant and taken for granted (for example, "everyone wants to get married," "everyone wants a good job," "everyone wants to own a home," "science provides true information"). Identify some of the social beliefs embedded in these expectations. Construct a detailed explanation for how these expectations are sustained through everyday interaction.

3. Some social situations may appear isolated and private but also reflect a strongly entrenched social hierarchy. Discuss the relationship between maids and their employers. Employers often engage in behaviors in the presence of their maids that they would never engage in around "polite company." This is a form of interactional "disappearance"—the maid is expected to act as if she does not exist. What consequences might this have for self-development?

4. Practice thinking about social institutions such as medicine, law, family, and religion from the perspective of an anthropologist from another culture. For instance, outsiders to modern Western cultures might consider Western medical practices, especially the reliance on pharmaceuticals, to be an intriguing form of magic. What kinds of public performances and interactional patterns maintain these cultural systems? What features of reality help to explain why the people of this culture tend to think that "their way is the only way"?

THE SOCIAL CONSTRUCTION OF THE CULTURAL STATUS QUO

33

The Persistence of Gender Inequality in Employment Settings

Cecilia Ridgeway

(2001)

Gender hierarchy is a system of social practices that advantages men over women in material resources, power, status, and authority. Oddly, gender hierarchy has persisted in Western societies despite profound changes in the economic arrangements on which it seems, at any given time, to be based. It has continued in one form or another despite major economic transformations such as industrialization, the movement of women into the paid labor force, and, most recently, women's entry into male-dominated occupations. What accounts for gender hierarchy's uncanny ability to reassert itself in new forms when its former economic foundations erode?

Although many factors are involved, one part of the answer lies in the way gender hierarchy in economic and other social arrangements is mediated by interactional processes that are largely taken for granted. Gender processes taking place as people interact during economic and other activities can operate as an "invisible hand" that rewrites gender inequality into new socioeconomic arrangements as they replace the earlier arrangements upon which gender hierarchy was based. To illustrate this point, I will describe some interactional processes that mediate gender inequality in paid employment and play a role in its persistence. First, however, we should consider how gender and interaction are related.

GENDER AND INTERACTION

Gender is an important part of the organization of interaction. It is striking that people are nearly incapable of interacting with each other if they cannot guess the other's sex. The television program *Saturday Night Live* illustrated this problem in its comedy sequence about "Pat," an androgynous person who wreaks confusion and havoc even in trivial, everyday encounters because the others present cannot place Pat as a man or a woman. The difficulty of dealing with a person whose gender is ambiguous suggests that gender categorization is a basic first step in the cultural rules we use for organizing interaction (West and Zimmerman 1987).

In order to interact with someone, you need some initial idea of "who" you are dealing with. You must classify the person in relation to yourself in socially meaningful ways so that you can draw on cultural knowledge about how "people like this" are likely to behave and how you should act in return. In other words, organizing interaction requires you to categorize the other as well as yourself in socially significant ways. Some of the social rules that you use for categorizing self and other must be so simplified and apparently obvious that they provide an easy means for initially defining "who" self and other are so interaction can begin at all. The cultural rules for classifying people as either male or female provide a quick initial category system—one that everyone takes for granted. Once interaction begins, definitions of self and other that are more complicated and specific to the situation can be introduced.

As research has shown, the cognitive processes by which we perceive others are hierarchically organized (Brewer 1988; Fiske and Neuberg 1990). They begin with an initial, automatic, and usually unconscious classification of the other according to a very small number of primary cultural categories and move on to more detailed typing depending on the circumstances. The evidence shows that gender is one of these primary categories in Western societies so that we automatically and unconsciously gender-categorize any specific other to whom we must relate.

In institutional settings, such as workplaces, there are often clear social scripts that define who self and other are and frame interaction (e.g., supervisor and worker). Yet gender categorization continues in these settings because the actual process of enacting a social script with a concrete other evokes habitual person perception and with it, the cultural rules that define gender as something that must be known to make sense of others. Research shows that when institutional roles become salient in the process of perceiving someone, those roles become nested within the prior understanding of that person as a man or woman and take on slightly different meanings as a result (Brewer 1988). We may be able to imagine an ungendered institutional script whereby "the student talks to the teacher" but we cannot interact with any actual students or teachers without first classifying them as male or female. The gender categorization of self and others, even in institutionally scripted settings, is a fundamental, unnoticed process that involves gender in the activities and institutional roles that people enact together.

Gender categorization in work-related encounters sets the stage for two interactional processes that contribute to and help preserve gender inequality in paid employment. Gender categorization cues gender status beliefs that can unconsciously shape people's assumptions about how competent women in the situation are compared to similar men. Gender categorization also unconsciously biases whom people compare themselves to. Comparisons, in turn, affect the rewards to which people feel entitled and the wages for which they will settle.

GENDER STATUS PROCESSES

Gender status beliefs are widely held cultural beliefs that posit one gender as generally superior and diffusely more competent than the other. Such beliefs are well established in Western societies. Gender categorization in interaction makes gender status beliefs implicitly accessible to shape actors' perceptions of one another.

In interaction, people are never just males or females without simultaneously being many other social identities (e.g., young or old, of a given ethnic group, a worker or a student). The impact of gender status beliefs (and other cultural assumptions about men and women) on people's perceptions and behaviors in a given situation depends on the relevance of gender to the situation compared to other identities that are also salient. In work settings, work-related identities are likely to be in the foreground of peoples' perceptions and shape behavior most powerfully. Gender often acts as a *background identity* that flavors the performance of those work identities. Research shows, however, that even when other identities are the strongest determinant of behavior, gender status beliefs are still sufficiently salient to measurably affect people's expectations and behavior under two conditions: in mixed gender settings and when gender is relevant to the purposes or context of the setting (e.g., a women's caucus group) (Berger et al., 1977; Deaux and Major 1987). This means that gender status beliefs are effectively salient in many but not all work-related interactions.

When gender status beliefs are effectively salient like this in a work setting, they have three types of effects on goal-oriented interaction that affect employment inequality. First, they cause both men and women to unconsciously expect slightly greater competence from qualified men than from similarly qualified women. These implicit expectations tend to become self-fulfilling, shaping men's and women's assertiveness and confidence in the situation, their judgments of each other's ability, their actual performances, and their influence in the setting (see Ridgeway 1993 for details).

Second, gender status beliefs, when salient, cause people to expect and feel entitled to rewards that are commensurate with their relative status and expected competence in the setting. Thus, if gender status beliefs cause people in a work setting to assume the men are more important and competent than women, both men and women in the situation will also presume that men are entitled to higher levels of rewards such as pay or "perks." Consequently, when gender status is salient, men may react negatively if they are placed on the same reward level as a similarly qualified woman. They may experience this situation as an implicit status threat.

Third, because gender status beliefs advantage men, men in interaction are less likely to notice, and more likely to discount if they do notice, information about self or other that might diminish or eliminate the effects of gender status beliefs on expectations for competence or rewards. This effect of gender status beliefs is due to the way people's interests in a situation unconsciously bias what they perceive. The effect makes it more difficult for women in the interaction to introduce information that would alter the lower expectations held for them. For example, there is a tendency in meetings for persons to attribute interesting or new ideas to a male speaker, even if a woman was the first to raise the point. Men who are "rewarded" for having expressed the good idea do not seem to notice that a woman may have mentioned the idea first. If the woman were to try to claim credit for the idea, and thereby lay claim to her competence, it is likely that she would be regarded as being pushy or out of line.

GENDER-BIASED COMPARISONS AND REWARDS

In addition to cueing gender status beliefs, gender categorization of self and other in workplace relations affects who people compare themselves to when they evaluate their own rewards or outcomes on the job. In general, people search out information about people whom they see as similar to them in order to evaluate whether they are receiving the rewards to which they are entitled. Automatic gender categorization causes people to unconsciously compare their own rewards more closely to those of the same gender than to those of opposite gender. If pay, perks, or other rewards are distributed unequally among men and women on the job, then the tendency to compare with same-gender others will cause men to form higher estimates of what the "going rate" is for people with their qualifications. Women, gathering more comparisons from other women, form lower estimates of the going rate for the same qualifications. Not recognizing that their estimates of what others earn on the job have been biased by their tendency to compare with same-gender others, women form lower expectations for the pay and rewards to which they are entitled than do similar men. Such reward expectations become self-fulfilling because they affect people's willingness to settle for a given level of pay or to press for more (see Major 1989 for research on this process).

GENDER INEQUALITY IN EMPLOYMENT

Gender inequality in employment is something of a puzzle. Theoretically, competitive market forces should wipe out gender discrimination because employers who prefer men and pay higher wages to get them will be driven out of business by smarter employers who hire cheaper but equally qualified women for the same jobs. Yet gender inequality in wages and gender segregation in occupations (i.e., the tendency for men and women to work in different occupations) have stubbornly persisted and improved only slowly over decades. England (1992) argues that gender inequality persists despite the flattening effect of market forces because it is continually being created anew, even if is worn down slightly over time. A consideration of how interaction drives gender categorization in work contexts and brings in gender status and comparison processes can help explain why the work world is so relentlessly gendered. It can also help explain why such gendering persists despite ongoing economic and organizational change.

Most work-related interaction takes place in organizational contexts with established job structures and institutional rules that heavily constrain what happens. Under business-as-usual conditions, gender status and comparison-reward processes occurring in these interactions are just part of the means by which existing gender-biased job structures and practices are enacted and sustained. Interactional gender processes, however, become important in themselves, rather than merely the agents of organizational structures and rules, at the interstices of organizations and under conditions that force change on an organization. In these transition zones where organizational structures are less clearly defined, gender categorization, status, and comparison processes play a part in shaping the interaction through which actors create new organizational rules and structural forms and map gender hierarchy into them as they do so.

Occupational arrangements and wage outcomes are mediated by interaction in many ways, whether it be face-to-face, computer-mediated (e.g., email), or indirect interaction through exchanges on paper. Workers learn about jobs and evaluate them through contact with others. Employers hire workers through direct (e.g., interviews) or indirect interaction (e.g., reviewing resumes and references). On the job, performance, evaluations, task assignments, and promotions involve interactions among people in complex ways. All these mediating interactions through which the world of work is conducted are potential sites where interactional mechanisms can map gender hierarchy into the occupational patterns and wages that result.

THE SEX LABELING OF WORKERS AND JOBS

Gender inequality in employment begins with the gender labeling of workers. This point seems so obvious and natural that we don't bother to explain it. Yet why should all workers be either male workers or female workers and not just workers? Why is gender a primary descriptor of workers at all? The answer lies in the way interaction evokes gender categorization, infusing gender in to the hiring processes as it mediates employers' recruitment and placement of workers. Because interaction triggers gender categorization, employers can never interview or read the resume of a gender-neutral worker. Similarly, workers cannot interact with a gender-unclassified co-worker, boss, subordinate, or client.

The taken-for-granted, unconscious gender labeling of workers begins a process that also leads to the labeling of jobs themselves as men's or women's jobs. As the economy changes and develops, jobs that have been traditionally labeled as men's or women's jobs may fade in importance and new jobs, such as computer programmer, are continually created. Theoretically, these new occupations could be gender neutral. Yet, in an example of the force of gender in the organization of work, most of these new occupations are themselves quickly labeled as either men's or women's occupations. The persistent gender labeling of new jobs continually renews the gender-segregated nature of our occupational structure.

Gender categorization in workplace interaction plays a role in the continual gender labeling of jobs by priming workers and employers alike to infuse stereotypic assumptions about gender into the institutional scripts by which a job is enacted and represented to others. Employers often begin the process by implicitly or explicitly seeking workers of a particular gender on the basis of assumptions about labor costs that are themselves suffused by the effect of gender status beliefs. Employees of one gender come to predominate in the job. Since gender categorization in interaction primes people's cultural beliefs about gender even in segregated contexts, workers and employees may use gender-stereotypic terms to justify the activities in a gender-segregated job even when those activities originally seemed gender irrelevant. Thus, electronic assembly comes to be represented as a woman's job requiring *women's* "attention to detail and manual dexterity." Selling securities becomes a *man's* job requiring masculine "aggressiveness."

As the stories and social scripts that represent a job in the media and elsewhere come to be gendered as masculine or feminine, the differential status attached to men and women spreads to the job as well. Research shows that a job or task, when labeled feminine, is viewed by both job evaluators and those in the job themselves as requiring less ability and effort and as worth less compensation than the identical job or task is when labeled masculine. Other research shows that the gender composition of a job alone has a significant impact on what it pays, as does the association of the job with stereotypically feminine tasks such as nurturance (see Ridgeway 1997 for more details). Continual

gender categorization in workplace interactions reinforces the tendency to apply gender labels to activities and perpetuates gender-based evaluations of jobs and activities.

MEN AND WOMEN AS INTERESTED ACTORS IN THE WORKPLACE

The interests of those in more powerful positions in employment organizations (e.g., bosses), who are more often men, are represented more forcefully than the interests of those who are in less powerful positions (e.g., secretaries). When gender status is salient in workplace interactions it creates a number of apparently gender-interested behaviors on the part of men, whether as employers, workers, or customers. The men themselves as well as observers of both genders will tend to see men in a situation as a bit more competent and deserving of rewards than similarly qualified women. They may miss or discount information in the situation that undermines these perceptions and perceive an implicit status threat when equivalent men and women are put on the same reward level.

All these effects usually occur as a modification or biasing of behavior during the enactment of an occupational or institutional identity that is more salient in the situation than the background identity of gender. A man acting in his role as an electrical engineer or union representative, for instance, may slightly bias his treatment of other men over women, usually in an implicit way that he himself does not recognize. Only occasionally will gender be so salient in the situation that men act self-consciously to preserve their interests as men. Yet the repeated background activation of gender status over many workplace interactions, biasing behavior in subtle or more substantial degrees, produces the effect of men acting in their gender interests, even when many men feel no special loyalty to their gender.

What about women in the workplace? Don't they pursue their interests as well? Yes, but the effect of gender status beliefs in interaction handicaps their efforts. It is in women's interests to introduce into a situation added information about their skills and accomplishments that undermines status-based assumptions about their competence compared to men and the rewards that they deserve. It is often difficult to introduce such information, however, precisely because gender is usually a background identity in workplace interactions. The participants do not explicitly think of gender as part of "what is going on here." The implicitness of gender in workplace interaction complicates the task of recognizing when bias is occurring and introducing countervailing information in the real time of actual interaction. The process is difficult as well because men's own status interests tend to make them more cognitively resistant to such information.

As a result, women on the job may periodically sense that something prejudicial is happening to them, but be frustrated in their efforts to act effectively against it. They will be vulnerable to "role encapsulation" whereby others define them in their work identities in implicitly gendered terms (e.g., "too nice" or "passive") that limit their effectiveness as actors in their own interests.

EMPLOYERS' PREFERENCES FOR MALE WORKERS

Reskin and Roos (1990) argue that employers show general preferences for hiring male workers, especially for "good," well-paying jobs. There are exceptions, of course, as when employers actually prefer female workers for jobs like nursery school teacher that involve tasks that are stereotypically associated with women. For other jobs, however, Reskin and Roos suggest that employers' preferences for male workers is a key factor that maintains gender inequality in wages and access to jobs with status and authority. While competitive market forces work against such preferences, they are nevertheless maintained by institutional rules and practices that embody them and by the implicit effects of gender status on workplace relations.

When an employer's automatic gender categorization of a potential employee cues gender status beliefs, these beliefs affect the employer's judgment of the worker's potential productivity. Expectations about competence based on gender status make the male worker appear "better" than an equally qualified woman. Also, an equally competent job or test performance by the two appears to the employer to be more indicative of ability and skill in the man than in the woman (see Ridgeway 1997 for a description of this research). On the surface merit is the basis of judgment. Yet the workers' gender is connected with merit by the way employers' evaluations of workers involve interactions that are unconsciously shaped by gender status beliefs. The result is what is called "error discrimination" where two workers who would perform equally are judged to be different and paid accordingly.

Gender status beliefs operating in the workplace can contribute to this process because they bias employers' expectations for workers' performances and these expectations tend to be self-fulfilling. This tendency often produces employer experiences with male and female workers that confirm the employers' initial judgments about them. A competent performance by a woman worker appears less competent coming from her than from her male co-worker. Also, and more insidious, the pressure of an employer's low expectations for them can actually interfere with some women workers' performances. Some male workers, on the other hand, may feel buoyed by their employer's confidence in them and perform even better than they otherwise might have. Thus, the effect of an employer's status-based expectations on some men and some women can create "real" differences in the average performance and productivity of groups of similar male and female workers. When interactional gender categorization makes gender salient in the hiring process, the employer's experience of these average differences also becomes salient. The employer may react by preferring male workers across the board (statistical discrimination). This form of discrimination is especially powerful in maintaining gender inequality in the workplace because it is more resistant to the equalizing effects of market forces than are other types of discrimination (England 1992).

WHY DO WOMEN WORKERS ACCEPT LOWER WAGES?

An employer's ability to attract and retain women workers for lower wages is also critical for maintaining gender inequality in employment. Why do women settle for less than similarly qualified men? Here, too, gender processes in interaction play a role by shaping different senses of entitlement on the part of similarly qualified men and women.

Although many women work in predominantly female jobs (e.g., nurses, secretaries, or elementary school teachers), their work performance is often evaluated through direct or indirect interaction with male supervisors, clients, or customers. Also, their work may have become typed a stereotypically female task. In any of these situations, gender categorization during interaction will activate status beliefs affecting women workers' own performance and expectations for rewards as well as their employer's and fellow workers' expectations for them. In fact, the evidence shows that women underestimate the quality of their performances in comparison with men. This makes them susceptible to arguments that they deserve less pay.

Gender categorization in work relations also unconsciously biases women's choices of whom to seek out in order to compare the pay they are receiving and evaluate whether it is fair. As we saw, women's tendency to compare their pay more closely with other women than similar men can cause them to underestimate the going rate for work by people with given qualifications. Such underestimates of possible pay rates is a second factor that causes women to peg the compensation they deserve at lower rates than do men.

If women workers inadvertently underestimate the rewards they are entitled to, employers can more easily force them to settle for lower wages (Major 1989). If corresponding gender status and biased comparison processes cause male workers to overestimate what they deserve, then employers find it harder to force lower wages on them. Out of such processes, women inadvertently accept lower wages than men. Women's unintentional acceptance of lower pay helps sustain gender hierarchy in employment over time by moderating women's resistance to pay differences.

WOMEN'S ENTRANCE INTO MALE OCCUPATIONS

In recent decades, women have entered male occupations in large numbers. Yet wage inequality and the gender segregation of jobs has not declined as much as one might expect. As Reskin and Roos point out (1990), the problem is that as women enter a male occupation in number, men often flee it so that it "turns over" to become a women's occupation. This has happened to the job of bank teller over the past couple of decades. Sometimes, when women enter a male occupation, instead of men leaving the occupation altogether, the occupation becomes reorganized so that some specialties within it are predominantly female while others are predominantly male. Thus, as women have entered medicine in recent years, pediatrics has become a women's specialty while neurosurgery has remained overwhelmingly male. Again, wage inequality and gender segregation of jobs are preserved despite women's entrance into the formerly male profession of medicine.

While many processes are behind these transformations of occupations, once again, gender processes during interaction are involved. Given employer preferences for male workers, women often gain access to men's occupations when the demand for workers in that occupation outstrips the pool of interested male workers available at an acceptable wage. As the shortage of male workers brings women into the job, gender-based status interests become increasingly salient in the workplace and may create tensions. Gender status beliefs activated by the mixed-sex context cause women's presence to subtly devalue the status and reward-worthiness of the job in the eyes of both workers and employers. Male workers may react to this perceived threat to their status and rewards by hostility towards women in the job. More men may begin to leave the job.

As women become more numerous in the job, supervisors' gender status beliefs and women workers' lower sense of entitlement exert self-fulfilling effects on women's pay and other rewards and these effects increasingly spread to the job itself. This situation makes it easier for employers to introduce organizational and technological changes to the job that further reduce the status and rewards that it offers. Although this scenario is not inevitable, when it occurs, it often results in the job becoming a women's job with lowered status and pay. Or the job may resegregate by specialty with lower pay and status for the female specialties.

Such transitions in occupations maintain gender hierarchy over a change in the technological and organizational structure of jobs. In the many interactions through which these transitions occur, activated gender status processes and biased reward comparisons create a complex mix of discrimination, status-based competitions of interests, differences in entitlement, and differential perceptions of alternatives. The result is a system of interdependent gender effects that are everywhere and nowhere because they develop through multiple workplace interactions, often in taken-for-granted ways. Their aggregate result is the preservation of wage inequality and the gender segregation of jobs.

CONCLUSION

Adding an interactional perspective to labor market and organizational explanations for inequality in employment helps explain why gender is such a major force in the organization of work. Hiring, job searches, placement, performance evaluation, task assignment, promotion, and dealing with customers, clients, bosses, co-workers, and subordinates all involve direct or indirect (e.g., via resumes) interaction. Interaction with a concrete other evokes primary cultural rules for making sense of self and of other, pushing actors to gender-categorize one another in each of these interactions. Gender categorization pumps gender into the interactions through which the world of work is enacted. It cues gender status beliefs and biases the choice of comparison others. The process is insidious because gender is usually an implicit background identity that acts in combination with more salient work identities and tinges their performance with gendered expectations.

In highly structured organizational work contexts, gender processes in interaction become part of the processes through which more formal structures that embody bias, such as job ladders and evaluation systems, are enacted. Gender processes in interaction contribute to the gender labeling of jobs, to the devaluation of women's jobs, to forms of gender discrimination by employers, to the construction of men as gender-interested actors, to the control of women's interest, to differences between men's and women's pay expectations, and to the processes by which women's entrance into male occupations sometimes leads to feminization of the job or resegregation by specialty.

In less bureaucratically organized work contexts, such as those at organizational interstices, in start-up companies, in newly forming professions, or in some types of works (e.g., screen writers), interpersonal processes come to the fore and are sufficient in themselves to create gender inequality in wages and gender typing of work. As they do so, interactional processes conserve gender inequality despite significant, ongoing changes in the organization of work and the economy, writing inequality into new work structures and practices as they develop.

If this inequality is to be reduced, it is vital to understand that gender inequality is maintained by structural processes and interactional processes acting together. Change will require intervention at both the structural and interactional level through policies such as affirmative action that change the interpersonal configuration of actors and, potentially, create stereotype disconfirming experiences for all.

While much has been learned about gender inequality in employment, the study of gender-based interactional processes may help to answer some of the stubborn questions that persist. These questions include the reasons why new jobs that develop as occupations change continue to acquire connotations as men's or women's jobs, how employer's apparent preferences for male workers persist even under competitive market pressures, why women's work is devalued, whether and how people act in their gender interests in employment matters, and why women accept lower wages than men for similar work.

REFERENCES

Berger, Joseph, M. Hamit Fisek, Robert Z. Norman, and Morris Zelditch, Jr. 1977. *Status Characteristics and Social Interaction.* New York: Elsevier.

Brewer, Marilynn. 1988. "A Dual Process Model of Impression Formation." Pp. 1–36 in *Advances in Social Cognition,* Vol. 1, edited by Thomas Srull and Robert Wyer. Hillsdale, NJ: Earlbaum.

Deaux, Kay, and Brenda Major. 1987. "Putting Gender Into Context: An Interactive Model of Gender-Related Behavior." *Psychological Review* 94: 369–389.

England, Paula. 1992. *Comparable Worth: Theories and Evidence.* New York: Aldine.

Fiske, Susan, and Steven Neuberg. 1990. "A Continuum of Impression Formation, From Category-Based to Individuating Processes: Influences of Information and Motivation on Attention and Interpretation." Pp. 1–73 in *Advances in Experimental Social Psychology,* edited by Mark Zanna. New York: Academic Press.

Major, Brenda. 1989. "Gender differences in Comparisons and Entitlement: Implications for Comparable Worth." *Journal of Social Issues* 45: 99–115.

Reskin, Barbara, and Patricia Roos. 1990. *Job Queues, Gender Queues: Explaining Women's Inroads into Male Occupations.* Philadelphia: Temple University Press.

Ridgeway, Cecilia L. 1993. "Gender, Status, and the Social Psychology of Expectations." Pp. 175–198 in *Theory on Gender/Feminism on Theory,* edited by Paula England. New York: Aldine.

———. 1997. "Interaction and the Conservation of Gender Inequality: Considering Employment." *American Sociological Review* 62: 218–235.

West, Candance and Don Zimmerman. 1987. "Doing Gender." *Gender and Society* 1: 125–151.

34

Status Inequality and Close Relationships

An Integrative Typology of Bond-Saving Strategies

Scott R. Harris

(1997)

Our close relationships are clearly a significant part of our happiness and quality of life. Who can deny the importance of our family and friends, our romantic partners, and our commiserating co-workers? Little in life would be worthwhile without companions such as these to share it with us. The fact that individuals seem to need meaningful connections with others has led some to believe that the maintenance of social bonds is "the most crucial human motive" (Scheff 1990, p. 4).

It is surprising, then, that little sociological research has investigated relationship maintenance and repair. Within the fields of communication and psychology, much (quantitative) research has been done in this area, focusing primarily on marital relationships in general states of decline (see Duck 1988 for a review). While the maintenance and repair of marital relationships is a significant topic, more attention should be given to the interactional practices that function to preserve all types of close social bonds: friendly, familial, *and* romantic. Additionally, more research could examine relationship repair within the contexts of specific types of problems, rather than assuming a general state of decay. In this paper I examine a distinctly sociological research question: *How do individuals in an intimate relationship remain close when they are confronted with a disruptive status inequality?*

EQUALITY AND CLOSE SOCIAL BONDS

Numerous sociologists have suggested that a state of equality is an integral component of close relations. Friendship is said to involve the "felt experience" of equality (Reohr 1991, p. 48), and it is thought to be difficult or impossible when significant status differences exist (Bell 1981, p. 85). Marriage is coming to be known as a partnership between equals (Leslie 1979, p. 51; Nock 1987, p. 125), and the level of happiness within the relationship is thought to depend on the degree of gender equality within it (Collins and Coltrane 1991, p. 13). Friendly sociability is regarded as the art of rendering status differences irrelevant and acting "as if" all were equal (Simmel 1950, pp. 45–6, 49); indeed, it is argued that even the friends of friends must treat each other as equals (Suttles 1970, p. 97).

Two rationales typically pervade such discussions of equality and close relationships. The first is based on the belief that cultural norms determine behavior; from this standpoint, individuals are socialized to behave as equals in close relationships. Thus, while it may be appropriate to act "bossy" with one's employees at work, to do so with one's friends would violate a norm of conduct. Other treatments stem from exchange theory, which views individuals as rational hedonists who weigh the costs and benefits of their actions. From this perspective, mutually satisfying interactions tend to occur between status equals because only they can evenly exchange rewards and escape the cost of admitting inferiority (Homans 1974, p. 302). Those who possess similar intelligence, wealth, or attractiveness are predicted to enjoy their associations more than those who are dissimilar.

A more recent approach centers on the emotions which underlie social interaction. Work by Scheff and Retzinger (1991) suggests that feelings of inferiority, unworthiness, and embarrassment (due to improper role enactment) are rooted in the emotion "shame." Their research demonstrates how unacknowledged shame is a frequent cause of anger, alienation, and aggression between individuals and groups, particularly married couples. From this third perspective, one might assume that feelings of equality must be maintained in close relationships in order to prevent shame from arising and damaging them.

Although much of the sociological literature assumes that equality is a prerequisite to successful close relations, little research has explored how individuals may try to save a social bond when it is disrupted by status inequality. Scheff and Retzinger (1991) argue that the destructive power of shame (which may result from status inequality) can be overcome if the participants acknowledge the emotion within a frank discussion of their relationship. Acknowledgment is in fact a reparative strategy discovered by this research; however, other types of remedial *and preventative* approaches should not be ignored. The literature on facework and embarrassment—a variant of shame (Scheff and Retzinger 1991)—suggests that strategies such as avoidance, offering "accounts" (excuses and justifications), and introducing humor can be used to cope with discrediting or embarrassing predicaments (Goffman 1967; Scott and Lyman 1968; Metts and Cupach 1989, 1994). My study examines how these and other strategies can be used to mitigate an alienating status difference. *The goal of my research is to construct a typology that integrates all types of interactional practices that may be used in an attempt to save a relationship threatened by status inequality. . . .*

A SYMBOLIC INTERACTIONIST VIEW OF EQUALITY

An investigation into the interpersonal management and social creation of relative status requires a theoretical framework that is sensitive to the nature of face-to-face interaction. Symbolic interactionism provides that kind of framework. . . . Human beings *think,* and their thinking is not merely the expression of psychological motives or drives. Self-interaction—in the form of interpreting, considering, and defining the situation—is a crucial determinant of action (Blumer 1969, pp. 64–5). A symbolic interactionist perspective assumes that, if we are to gain any insight into how relative status impacts close relationships, our focus must shift from preconceived causal directives to the substance and meaning of interaction within and among individuals.

Simple introspection and casual observation indicate that many types of relationships can be quite satisfying despite being characterized by status inequality. Parent-child, teacher-student, and mentor-protégé dyads are some obvious examples where intimacy might flourish untroubled by apparent status differences. Even among two close friends, there is probably one who tends to give more advice to the other or one who makes more decisions about what they should do together. Whether this tendency drives a wedge between them depends on how it is interpreted; its impact cannot be predetermined. . . .

THREE PROCESSES

We now have two sociological questions: when and how does an inequality actually become disruptive? It may be impossible to identify certain inequalities which will always disrupt a close relationship. It is possible, however, to outline three interpretive processes which must occur for an inequality to merit bond-saving attention: At least one participant in the dyad must (a) become aware of the inequality, (b) define it as problematic, and (c) decide that the relationship is worth the effort it would take to deal with the inequality.

To disrupt a close relationship, a status difference must first be noticed. As I argued earlier, individuals are complex, multifaceted creatures; how individuals isolate, identify, and evaluate their relative status is not a simple matter. William James' (1890, p. 402) discussion of the selectivity of human attention underscores the issue: "Millions of items of the outward order are present to my senses which never properly enter into my experience. Why? Because they have no *interest* for me. *My experience is what I agree to attend to.*" Our companions may be thinner, shorter, quicker, smarter, poorer, more humorous, or less popular; they may have great success in school and at work, or they may have serious troubles with their children and their marriages. Of all the attributes human beings possess, some quality or condition must first be identified before it can be judged unequal and problematic.

After the inequality is noticed, it must be experienced as distressing in order to threaten a relationship. Several factors seem to be involved in this process. First, the level of difference must be defined as significant. (*Does my spouse dance a little better than me or does she completely out-class me?*) Second, the inequality must be felt to occur in an important or "salient" area (Stryker 1981, pp. 23–4). One's ability to blow large bubbles with bubblegum is not likely to produce an emotionally charged status difference; however, wealth or success at one's career may spark envy. (*Does my spouse dance better than me even though* I *am the one pursuing a career as a professional dancer?*) Third, how generalizable the inequality is thought

to be affects its disruptive power. A status difference can be defined as a fluke or isolated occurrence, or it can be seen as an indicator of a larger, lasting condition. (*Do I usually dance better than I'm dancing tonight? Is my poor dancing being taken as a sign that I am always uncoordinated?*) Finally, an inequality will become problematic depending on whether it is defined in competitive terms. A companion's success can be an occasion for approval and applause or a time to engage in comparative evaluation. (*Am I proud of my spouse's dancing or am I envious and determined not to be bested?*)

Once a status inequality is noticed and experienced as problematic, an individual may either walk away from the relationship or attempt to deal with the uncomfortable feelings in some way. Here, the level of intimacy and one's investment in the relationship play a crucial role. While casual associations can merely be ended when an unwanted inequality arises, valued relationships cannot be so easily disregarded. Moreover, some relationships require recurrent interaction regardless of personal choice, such as those occurring within work or school settings. These situations may cause individuals to attempt to overcome a disruptive inequality, though they might prefer to simply disengage from the relationship.

In this paper, I focus on situations where an individual feels motivated to respond to a problematic inequality in some way, rather than merely ending the association.

DATA AND METHODS

The goal of this research is to identify the types of bond-saving strategies that individuals can use when a status inequality is perceived and felt to be disruptive by at least one participant in a close relationship. I hope to arrive at a general, universally relevant typology by analyzing numerous specific examples of such practices. Ideally, then, my data would have been collected by observing a large variety of subjects as they experienced and dealt with an alienating status inequality in naturally occurring, diverse relationships. Unfortunately, this would not be a very practical approach. First, it would be very difficult to position myself unobtrusively in many different social situations where I could expect to observe an inequality causing a problem in a relationship. Second, and more importantly, it could be impossible to remain with the participants long enough to observe them using one or more bond-saving strategies. It might take days or even months before my subjects attempted to resolve their problem—assuming they chose to do so.

Instead, I decided to obtain data by using open-ended, retrospective self-reports. During 1993, I collected 176 vignettes from students enrolled in undergraduate courses at a California State University. Respondents were asked to describe (in 500–750 words) an instance when a status inequality made a close relationship of theirs problematic in some way, the strategies one or both of the participants used to maintain the closeness of the bond, and how effective the strategies were. The self-reports were a required component of the students' course work, but contributing their papers to this study was voluntary.

Gathering data in this manner provided me with (a) numerous real-life examples of (b) individuals coping with various status inequalities (c) within different types of close social bonds (d) in diverse social settings (e) over time. My respondents did not restrict themselves to reporting classroom-oriented status differences (e.g., grades or intelligence); rather, they described a wide array of status inequalities occurring in many areas of social life, such as work, athletic, social, familial, and romantic settings. After reading and rereading their accounts, I felt that I had successfully immersed myself in my research topic. . . .

RESEARCH FINDINGS

My analysis of the respondents' vignettes yielded four basic types of bond-saving strategies that individuals can use to try to maintain or repair a close relationship threatened by a disruptive status inequality: They may (a) *accept* the status inequality; (b) *avoid* the situation which fosters feelings of inequality; (c) *alter* the status inequality by redefining or concretely mitigating it; or (d) *acknowledge* and discuss their problematic situation. Within the 176 vignettes, I found that each strategy appeared the following number of times: accept, 65; avoid, 48; alter, 107; acknowledge, 66. Moreover, each of these techniques can be undertaken by either the higher or lower status individual in the relationship. Examples from each perspective are included in my discussion.[1]

Accepting Status Inequality

The first type of bond-saving strategy makes no attempt to minimize the status difference or improve the relationship in any way. *Accepting status inequality* occurs when an individual experiences uncomfortable feelings of inequality in a close social bond, but does not vocalize or act upon those feelings. Rather than merely ending the relationship, the individual decides to "put up with" or "try to ignore" an unwanted element within the social bond.

Accept Higher Status

As might be expected, the vignettes offered little evidence of or support for the strategy of accepting higher status. It seems counter-intuitive that accepting one's own superiority could represent an effort to maintain an intimate bond. Nevertheless, certain vignettes did indicate that this is a possible bond-saving approach, as the following excerpts illustrate:

[My friend] would always complain of being "stupid," and would tell me how smart I was. This status difference made me very uncomfortable. [1][2]

Although I like [my friend], and it feels good to be admired, it is not what I consider a comfortable relationship. We have, consequently, drifted apart. [2]

Both of these individuals spurned attempts to place them in a superior status position in their relationships. But these examples do suggest that if individuals experience uncomfortable feelings of status superiority, and their partners insist on continuously reinforcing those feelings, then merely accepting higher status could be a plausible bond-saving strategy.

Accept Lower Status

Rather than end or try to repair a relationship disrupted by status inequality, individuals may also decide to accept a lower status position; that is, they may sacrifice their status to save the bond.

The following extract between two co-workers displays this technique. In this vignette, the respondent describes a problematic situation that arose because her friend received a promotion that both of them had wanted. After this event, the respondent was treated by her now higher-status friend with significantly less deference than before.

I tried playing the part of the insignificant member of the duo, but I knew this couldn't go on forever if I expected to maintain my sense of self-worth. I went along with [my friend] always making the decisions as to what we would do, whose opinion was correct, and whose lifestyle was more impressive. It seemed that the difference in status had occurred overnight; I kept hoping it would disappear the same way. [3]

For this person, accepting lower status was a temporary strategy, reflecting a hope that the relationship would return to its original state of approximate equality. Eventually, her patience wore thin. "I could not continue pretending that our relationship was perfectly acceptable," she says, and so she ended the friendship.

In contrast, another respondent permanently accepted being assigned lower status in a close relationship.

In [my friend's] mind, I will always be inferior. I can't be nearly as smart; I'm still in school and, at that, it is only a state school, not a university. Many view this friendship as nothing short of pathetic, but to me it has made me a stronger person, for I have learned tolerance, not to take myself too seriously, and if I can't like myself how are others supposed to? [4]

Here, an individual maintains a close relationship threatened by inequality by continuously accepting a lower "place" in the relationship.

Avoiding Status Inequality

A second way respondents coped with differential status in their close relationships was to avoid the situation that fostered feelings of inequality. Often it is a specific activity or conversational topic which accentuates the problematic status characteristic. In order to save the bond, then, individuals can attempt to edit out that portion of their relationship. Although avoidance has been described as a method of saving face and avoiding embarrassment (Goffman 1967), research has not yet examined it as a strategy for maintaining a sense of equality in a close relationship.

Avoidance by the Higher Status Individual

In the following extract, the respondent describes how he used avoidance to prevent his higher status from undermining a valued relationship. When this student and his best friend from high school started attending college, they both knew only a handful of people. However, this quickly changed for one of them when the respondent joined a fraternity and made many new friends. To his dismay, this student quickly discovered that his new status characteristic, popularity, would have a negative impact on his relationship with his friend from high school.

> [My friend] would make statements such as, "I don't have to pay for my friends." He felt awkward around me since he perceived I thought I was better than he was. At first, I had had no reservations about discussing my fraternity around my friend. As I gradually became aware of the fact that these discussions were a reinforcement of our status inequality (although they were never intended to be). I began diminishing talk about the fraternity until it eventually ceased altogether. [5]

Thus, the respondent purposefully used avoidance to prevent a sensitive topic from creating uncomfortable feelings of inequality between him and his friend.

Another respondent recalled using the same technique when she was admitted into an accelerated academic program while her friend was not.

> My best friend was very upset. I knew she was jealous that I had gotten into the "smart" class and she was still in the regular A-track. There were a few things we attempted to do in order to hold on to our friendship. [One was] I refrained from discussing what we did in [class]. [6]

Both of these examples illustrate the importance of role-taking (Mead 1934) in the maintenance and repair of close relationships. If these higher status individuals were not able to imagine the perspective of their partners, they could not have sensed the nature of their relationship problem, nor could they have determined what strategy might repair it. A person who does not take the role of the other in this manner risks stomping clumsily on his or her partner's feelings and losing the relationship.

Avoidance by the Lower Status Individual

Respondents also described situations where the lower status individual used avoidance to prevent status inequality from disrupting a close social bond. In the following vignette, a financial inequality threatened to disrupt a valued friendship. The respondent made only $22,000 a year, while her friend, upon marriage, had a combined income of over $100,000. To compensate, the less affluent woman avoided those occasions which accentuated the status difference between the two of them.

> I tried to plan activities that didn't involve money, such as inviting [my friend] and her husband over for dinner and cards, or to the park for a picnic. I would also decline the invitations that involved expenses beyond my means. Thus, I wouldn't get involved in an awkward situation. When she and her husband tried to pick up the tab when we went out, it made me feel inferior. [7]

This excerpt illustrates the significance of two other tenets of symbolic interactionism for the management of interpersonal relations—that individuals can (a) treat themselves as objects and (b) conceive and choose from different possible lines of action (Blumer 1969). This respondent made a conscious effort to anticipate future interactions and imagine how she might react to them. Because she could do this, she was able to plan events which would not produce unwanted feelings of inequality and yet would still help maintain the closeness of a valued social bond.

In another instance where status differentiating activities were avoided, a student's relationship with her fiancé became strained when they started taking classes together at the university. The respondent consistently received lower grades than her boyfriend even though she spent more time studying. Consequently, she began to feel "dumb," and "began inadvertently taking those feelings out on [her fiancé]." She tried to improve her grades by studying even harder, but to no avail.

There was only one solution and that was simply not take anymore classes together. There was a tremendous amount of unnecessary stress being put on us. Thus far, the solution has worked quite well. Although he still gets better grades than I do, it is different. We are not in the same class, and I do not feel as if I have to compete against him. [8]

As is evident in several of the vignettes above, the problem with avoidance is the way it detracts from the substance of the social bond (5, 6, & 8). To suddenly avoid a topic or activity reduces the repertoire of common interests within the relationship. This evidence substantiates Goffman's point that "Fear over possible loss of face often prevents the person from initiating contacts in which important information can be transmitted and important relationships re-established" (1967, p. 39). One respondent provided a partial solution to this dilemma, by avoiding *and replacing* inequality-producing situations with more congenial activities in order to preserve the closeness of the bond (7). Thus, avoidance may occur with or without an effort to replace the ties that have been edited out of the relationship.

Altering Relative Status: Redefining or Concretely Mitigating the Inequality

Rather than accept or avoid the problematic situation, individuals in a close relationship may attempt to neutralize disruptive feelings of inequality by directly manipulating their relative status. That is, they may try to redefine or take actions to mitigate the apparent inequality. There are four approaches to accomplishing this goal: Higher status individuals can attempt to (a) reduce their own status or (b) raise that of their partner; conversely, lower status individuals can attempt to (c) raise their own status or (d) reduce that of their partner. Like the strategies of acceptance and avoidance, status alterations can be undertaken without openly acknowledging that a problem exists.

Higher Status Individual Reduces Self-Status

One way to repair a relationship threatened by status inequality is for higher status individuals to reduce their own status. The following vignette describes how an educational inequality had the potential to disrupt a marriage. The respondent could tell that her husband felt less intelligent because she was attending college and he had stopped his education with a high school diploma. While the respondent did not perceive any important status difference, her husband did. His feelings of inferiority prompted her to reduce her own status in order to preserve their bond.

> While I knew that I was not smarter than he, my husband did not. So to counter his thinking, I exaggerated my own struggles I was having in class. I gave him the impression that my good grades were attributed to "easy classes" and "lucky guesses" on exams. By downplaying my grades, I subsequently proved I was not more intelligent. [9]

It is evident that the negotiation of relative status depends heavily upon the accounts individuals give for how they achieve their high (or low) status characteristics. "Accounts," as conceived by Scott and Lyman (1968), are used to excuse or justify unanticipated, untoward, or deviant behavior. My research shows that accounts also play an important role in mitigating the capacity of a negative *or positive* occurrence to differentiate one individual's status from another's (e.g., "I was just lucky" or "You were just unlucky"). Hence, I use the term "*discounts*" to refer to statements that attempt to defuse a potentially disruptive status difference.[3] The following vignette further illustrates this strategy:

> My friend was able to go to the college we both wanted to attend. I was unable to go due to financial reasons. When my friend comes home, she tries to tell me I'm not missing anything and that the school is really hard and she is struggling to get the grades. [10]

Here, a discount is used to undermine a status differentiating trait—choice of college—in an effort to prevent feelings of inequality and jealousy from disrupting a close social bond.

Rather than merely redefining a status inequality with a verbal discount, higher status individuals may take more active steps to lower their status. For example, one respondent found herself in a position of power over her teammates (and a particularly close friend) when she became the leader of her rifle team. In order to keep from alienating them, she purposefully tried behaving like an equal rather than a superior.

> I was suddenly elevated above [my friend] as well as the other team members. Simply bearing the title "Captain" immediately gave me a "one-up" position over them. My responsibility was to basically tell them what to do. Because [she] and I were such good friends, I found it difficult to use any authority over her. I did not want to "lord it over her." First, to somehow step down from my higher position, I made an effort to emphasize to her and the others that we were all a team. I did my best to incorporate their ideas into our routines instead of just being a drill sergeant forcing them to do what I always wanted. [11]

To maintain her social bonds with her teammates, this individual purposefully distanced herself from her superior role and portrayed herself as a friend and an equal. As Goffman notes, an individual who expresses role distance in this manner "does not draw into some psychological world that he creates himself but rather acts in the name of some other socially created identity" (1961, p. 120). By driving a wedge between her position and herself, "between doing and being" (1961, p. 108), the respondent attempted to undermine her own status and prevent it from disrupting her relationships.

Higher Status Individual Raises Partner's Status

When an apparent inequality disrupts a relationship, higher status individuals can also attempt to overcome it by elevating the status of their companions. In the following vignette, this strategy was used to mitigate a status difference between three co-workers. When three friends received temporary job appointments in the same office, they enjoyed working side-by-side. The problem arose, however, when one was "let go" while the respondent and the remaining friend were offered permanent positions.

> We told her that maybe the supervisor thought that, because she was older and more experienced, she could find a better job than what we had been offered. We tried to make our job look really pathetic and reassure her that she would find a different job that was ten times better. [12]

Thus, this student and her friend used discounts which focused on the cause of the differential status and the characteristic itself. First, they raised the third person's status by "excusing" why she was not hired (she was over-qualified). Second, they reduced their own status and raised that of their friend by "justifying" why it was not a status differentiating characteristic (she would find a better job).

In addition to applying simple discounts, higher status individuals can also make more concrete efforts to raise their partner's status, as shown in the next vignette. In this situation, the respondent went to work at the same airport as a friend, who had been there two months longer. An inequality became apparent when the respondent excelled at the work and was quickly promoted.

> Things became uneasy between us when I was asked to check all of [my friend's] work before she entered it into the computer. Sometimes I would let mistakes go by and later change them in the computer. I corrected her work and did not tell my employer about it; when he asked me how she was doing, I lied. I worked slower when we were together, and I even let her take credit for some of my work. [13]

This excerpt illustrates a myriad of strategies. First, by secretly correcting her friend's mistakes and giving her undue credit, the respondent attempted to raise her companion's status. Additionally, the respondent lowered her own status (by giving away credit) while successfully avoiding confrontations about her friend's performance (through her stealth). All of these strategies represent a coordinated effort to prevent a status difference from disrupting a close relationship.

This excerpt also illustrates how the management of "awareness contexts" (Glaser and Strauss 1964) goes hand in hand with the maintenance of close relationships. This respondent needed to create several closed awareness contexts in her work relationships in order to carry out her many strategies. First, she needed to prevent her boss from finding out about her friend's lackluster performance. Second, she had to keep her friend from observing her own mistakes. Third, she needed to hide her own perceptions (and actions) from *both* her boss and her friend.

Since our personal status depends on what others think of us, *who knows what* will obviously affect perceptions of equality and inequality. In this case, managing the awareness contexts was tantamount to the successful use of avoidance and alteration.

Lower Status Individual Reduces Partner's Status

When individuals in close relationships find themselves in lower status positions, they may feel compelled to undermine the status level of their companions in order to assuage their feelings of inferiority while remaining in the dyad. This strategy often comes in the form of a verbal "put down." When we "cut someone down to size," we are letting them know that they have become too "big" for the relationship; they have claimed a status much "higher" than our own.

This strategy was illustrated in an earlier vignette [5]. The statement, "I don't have to pay for my friends," was an attempt to mitigate a disruptive, status differentiating trait—popularity. A second example comes from a person whose friend felt threatened by their different educational backgrounds.

> [My friend] has told me that an education does not guarantee a job, especially in the field of my choice, thereby downplaying the importance of my schooling. [14]

A more subtle method of reducing someone's status is provided in the following vignette. Here a disruptive inequality arose when the respondent's friend began to succeed at track. At first, the respondent was proud of her friend, but, in time, she felt that her friend was taking herself too seriously.

> Slowly I began letting her know she wasn't the only one with talent. I no longer agreed or smiled when she bragged about herself. She began noticing that I paid less attention to her and that I didn't seem all that interested in track talk. [15]

By subtly withholding deference, the respondent attempted to undermine the alienating status claim being made by her friend.

Lower Status Individual Raises Self-Status

Individuals may decide to raise their own status if they perceive that they have lower status in a particular area. This strategy tends to be used by individuals who experience distressing feelings of inferiority or unworthiness. For example, one student reported being extremely nervous about meeting his girlfriend's family for the first time because all of her adult relatives had master's or doctoral degrees. To compensate, he writes [16], "I made my major sound more prestigious than it really is." Another felt inferior to her friend because of their financial inequality. She made a conscious effort to always "dress up" in order to "be in her league" [17]. Both stories indicate how impression management (Goffman 1959) is pervasive in the construction of relative status.

A more detailed example of raising self-status is found in the following vignette. Here, a close relationship was strained when the respondent's friend became a dancer in a prestigious ballet. The friend's new accomplishment made him the center of attention at social gatherings for some time. The respondent's feelings of inferiority increased as he became known as "[The dancer's] friend." To compensate, the respondent tried highlighting some of his own attributes for their companions.

> I started by introducing my experience in theater to impress the group. When the focus of the conversation was on [my friend] I would then introduce my involvement in a current local play. [18]

This respondent attempted to mitigate the inequality in his friendship by pointing out his own accomplishments, thereby sharing some of the spotlight with his friend.

A respondent who used the strategy of avoidance [8] also provides another example of the lower status individual attempting to raise her relative status. Recall that this woman felt inferior to her fiancé because he was getting better grades in a class without trying as hard.

> I tried studying harder and longer. Also, most of my study hours were now away from home so he wouldn't see me studying. I felt that if I could get a better grade than him on the next test without letting him see me study more, then he would see that I wasn't really dumb. [19]

It is important to note that this respondent put more time and effort into her studies *in secret.* Obviously, she felt that perceived intelligence, the relevant status characteristic, hinged upon how easily one can assimilate knowledge. Thus, her efforts at raising her status involved two processes: increasing her own level of learning so she could achieve better grades, and creating a closed awareness context by controlling what her fiancé knew about her actions.

Acknowledging Status Inequality

The previous bond saving strategies can all be used unilaterally and covertly; that is, individuals may attempt to accept, avoid, or alter status inequalities in close relationships without explicitly admitting to their partners that the relationships are strained. Therefore, acknowledging and discussing the problematic situation is the most openly interactive strategy in my typology.[4] This approach makes both participants aware that the relationship is at risk and allows them to cooperate in repairing it.

Higher Status Individual Acknowledges the Problematic Situation to Partner

The following description of a close friendship provides an example of the higher status individual acknowledging a disruptive status inequality. The relationship between these two women first began in high school; it continued despite the fact that the respondent went on to college while her friend dropped out and became a single mother. Nevertheless, a problem finally arose when various individuals outside of the relationship began treating the respondent with much more deference than her friend because of their respective life choices. One woman in particular complimented the respondent's choice of major and, in the next breath, criticized her friend's "irresponsible behavior." After this incident, the two began to see much less of each other.

> Finally, I asked her if she wanted to sit down and discuss what was going on. [My friend] was really angry that people felt that I was a better person because I was going to school. I was angry because people were always putting [her] down for the choice she made. We both realized we had unconsciously fallen into the categories in which people placed us. After talking for

a while, we decided we weren't going to let people's comments bother us. I was also going to quit talking about my work and school so much. [My friend] was going to become more actively involved in conversations and not assume people don't want to hear what she has to say. [20]

In this vignette, openly acknowledging the status inequality led to many possible solutions. First, the two women realized that *they* did not perceive an inequality between them; only certain others outside their relationship were doing so. This insight may have helped to reduce the animosity between the two. Second, the respondent agreed to avoid those topics which emphasized the status inequality—namely, her accomplishments at school and work. Third, her friend was going to make an effort to raise her own status by being more vocal in social settings. Their discussion made both participants in the relationship aware of the problem and allowed them to cooperate on various reparative strategies.

A second example where acknowledgment was initiated by the higher status individual is described in the next vignette. Throughout high school and junior college, this respondent maintained a very close friendship with a fellow athlete. Their relationship became strained, however, when the respondent's friend received an athletic scholarship to a university.

In my eyes, [my friend] was superior because he had a scholarship and I didn't. He could tell that something was wrong with me and sat me down for a talk. He told me that he wished he could be as tough a competitor as me and also a good student. When he got the scholarship, he didn't feel that our relationship had changed. He woke me up to the fact that there were tradeoffs in our friendship and that we were equals who excel in different things. Tom saved our relationship, and today we are still great friends.[21]

In this example, these two friends seem to have arrived at a rather effective solution to their status inequality. By agreeing that they are "equals who

excel in different things." they have paved the way for smooth relations in the future. If this sentiment can be maintained, then, when either of them acquires a new status characteristic (such as financial or marital success), they can be proud of each other rather than envious. This solution bears much resemblance to Simmel's notion of the pure form of sociation: "Sociability is the game in which one 'does as if' all were equal and, at the same time, as if one honored each of them in particular" (1950, p. 49). These two friends have honored each other by recognizing that they each excel in certain areas of their lives, yet they remain equal because they refrain from attempting to weigh one person's (overall) worth against the other's. They have simply "decided" to base their relationship on a vague sense of equality and mutual admiration.

Lower Status Individual Acknowledges the Problematic Situation to Partner

The student vignettes revealed that acknowledgment could be employed by either participant in a relationship threatened by inequality, but it was often difficult for the lower status individual to do so calmly. The following respondent reported using this strategy in an angry manner with her friend and co-worker. These two women enjoyed a "very close and strong" relationship until the respondent's friend received a promotion and began to treat her with less respect.

In order to deal with this situation, I went to her and laid out exactly how I felt, I told her that she was rude, and bossy, and uncooperative, and treats me poorly. When I began to tell her how I felt, she became very angry and defensive. [22]

Another respondent reported using "confrontation" in a similar work-related situation:

Confrontation usually occurs when I can no longer conceal my feelings of discontentment and frustration and must therefore voice them. This often brings few positive results and has the potential to create bad feelings. [23]

These extracts seem to suggest that the lower status individual resorts to an angry form of acknowledgment when a condition of status inequality becomes intolerable for her. Perhaps because we learn to be ashamed of being ashamed (Scheff and Retzinger 1991, p. 104; see also Lewis 1971), individuals may postpone acknowledging feelings of inferiority until they become unbearable. It may also be the case that admitting their feelings opens these individuals up to further humiliation; their partners may react insensitively, and their response may suggest that "You feel inferior because you are." These possibilities may account for those reported instances where the lower status individual acknowledged the problematic situation to her partner in a somewhat hostile manner.

One vignette provides an example where the lower status individual calmly acknowledged an inequality. In the following excerpt, the respondent reports a problematic situation that arose within a good relationship he shared with his supervisor. Although this student did not expect his supervisor to treat him like a complete equal, he felt he was being unfairly derogated by her behavior towards him. The respondent felt that he was an extremely proficient and experienced worker and expected to be treated as such.

> I felt that I was being treated with less respect and that she saw me at a lower status than I deserved, which I was unable to accept. I ventilated my concerns and asked if she was uncomfortable with me for any particular reason, to which she responded that she was relieved that I had brought this up. This opened up a wide range of dialogue and allowed her to ventilate that she did feel anxious at giving someone my age and with my range of experience and expertise assignments to do. She also expressed that she felt at times that I was trying to "one-up" her. The effects of the direct confrontation were very favorable. The awkwardness we had felt dissipated, and our attitudes toward each other improved greatly. [24]

The respondent was able to calmly raise the issue of the status inequality by taking the time to ask how his partner, the higher status individual, felt. By respectfully addressing her concerns at the outset, rather than merely conveying his own dissatisfaction, the respondent apparently avoided putting his supervisor on the defensive. Instead, they were able to calmly communicate and discover that, in fact, they both felt threatened by each other's status characteristics and that they both thought they were being treated with less deference than they deserved. Once they knew this, they were able to successfully change their relationship for the better.

SUMMARY AND CONCLUSION

I have attempted to construct a typology of strategies individuals can use to try to maintain or repair a close relationship when an inequality is perceived and felt to be problematic by at least one participant of the dyad. My analysis of 176 retrospective reports on this topic revealed that a disruptive inequality may be accepted, avoided, altered (that is, directly mitigated), or acknowledged by one or both participants in the relationship.

These four types are broad categories which encompass a wide array of behavior. Acceptance can take the form of a temporary [3] or permanent [4] tolerance of the uncomfortable element in the relationship. Status inequality can be avoided by editing its source out of the relationship [5, 6, & 8]; however, doing so may subtract from the substance of the social bond unless an effort is made to replace the missing activities or conversational topics [7]. A disruptive inequality can be mitigated by directly altering the participants' relative status through redefinition [9, 10, 12, & 14] or more concrete actions [13, 15, 18, & 19]. Acknowledging the existence of a problematic status inequality can resolve misunderstandings [20, 21, & 24] and allows for the cooperative use of avoidance and alteration [20].

While constructing this typology, I attempted to integrate previous research on related topics. Avoidance was originally conceived by Goffman (1967) as a way to avoid embarrassment and save face. This study shows that it can also be a strategy to minimize perceptions of inequality in a close relationship [5–8]. "Discounts," a variation on "accounts" (Scott and Lyman 1968), were described as strategies for directly altering relative status. These statements mitigate feelings of inequality by redefining a negative *or positive* status differentiating trait [9, 10, 12, & 14]. Role distance (Goffman 1961) was identified as another way of altering status by disregarding or undermining a status differentiating role [11]. In their research, Scheff and Retzinger (1991) present acknowledgment as the sole method of assuaging shame in close relationships. In my study, acknowledgment (here defined more broadly) was found to be one of many approaches for overcoming disruptive feelings of status inequality; in fact, acknowledgment facilitates the cooperative use of other types of strategies [20].

Individuals' skill at perceiving the nature of their relationship problems and applying the appropriate reparative strategies [5–6] depends on their ability to take the role of the other (Mead 1934). Those who are unwilling or unable to imagine their partners' perspectives will not adequately understand the source of their relationship troubles. Because individuals can mentally pre-construct different possible lines of action (Blumer 1969), they can guide the flow of interaction in directions that will not produce distressing feelings of inequality in themselves or their partners. This ability allows for the preventative use of avoidance [7]. Finally, managing "who knows what" is an integral part of the success of some strategies [13]. Individuals frequently keep their critical opinions of their partners to themselves; by doing so, they may hope to avoid feelings of superiority or inferiority that would otherwise arise in a

completely open awareness context (Glaser and Strauss 1964).

It is noteworthy that a symbolic interactionist perspective was purposefully adopted in the collection and analysis of these data. Consequently, relationship satisfaction was not presumed to be a simple function of equality, as some normative and rational choice theorists might conclude. Neither were certain inequalities considered inherently alienating; a status difference must first be identified and defined as problematic in order to disrupt a close relationship. However, my research design did assume that status inequality *can be* distressing, and that respondents could recall a time when such a predicament had occurred.

These findings validate the symbolic interactionist notion that status is a social object, the meaning of which is not intrinsic to any particular trait, but is, rather, the result of interpretation (Blumer 1969). By focusing on the process of interpretation, it is possible to see how status values are not merely handed down from the "macro" level or otherwise preordained. It is true that one's reference group may define attractiveness as being slender or wealth as a sign of prestige. However, such meanings may be renewed, renegotiated, or renounced by individuals in every relationship. As Blumer noted, "It is the social process in group life that creates and upholds the rules, not the rules that create and uphold group life" (1969, p. 19). The various forms of behavior reported in the vignettes clearly illustrate that relative status is a creature of interaction and interpretation.

Indeed, my findings reveal something important about the nature of social order. A typology of the creative strategies individuals use to maintain their close relationships begs the following questions: What would happen if people did not act this way? Would society be possible if close relationships flew apart at the slightest provocation? As Scott and Lyman (1970, p. 113) point out, "The threads of human association are constantly being rent. . . . If there were no way by which individuals might . . . repair their broken relationships, social relations would indeed be treacherous, perhaps coming to approximate Hobbes' state of nature." The stability of society rests, in part, upon the continuity of relations among its members. Since human agency, in at least the few ways discovered here, plays a role in the preservation of close relationships, it also contributes to the maintenance of social order. . . .

NOTES

1. I have tried to give the flavor of the strategies by examining instances of each type. However, the reader should not infer from my presentation that only one strategy was reported in a given vignette. Different types of strategies were often employed simultaneously or in succession. Additionally, the reader should not assume that a particular strategy was successful simply because I cite it. This is primarily a study of how individuals *attempt* to save relationships threatened by inequality.

2. I have assigned identification numbers to my excerpts for easier reference. The fact that I have numbered the excerpts sequentially does not mean that they were taken from the first vignettes in my data.

3. Status discounts should not be confused with "discounting" as explicated by Pestello (1991). Pestello's term refers to the statements and practices by which collectives make untoward or inconsistent actions non-problematic.

4. Note that I have defined acknowledgment as a verbal admission that a problem with status inequality is harming the relationship. Scheff and Retzinger (1991) have more stringent requirements for acknowledging shame.

REFERENCES

Bell, Robert. 1981. *Worlds of Friendship*. Beverly Hills: Sage.

Blumer, Herbert. 1969. *Symbolic Interactionism: Perspective and Method*. Englewood Cliffs, NJ: Prentice-Hall.

Collins, Randall, and Scott Coltrane. 1991. *Sociology of Marriage and the Family*, 3rd ed. Chicago: Nelson Hall.

Duck, Steve. 1988. *Relating to Others*. Pacific Grove, CA: Brooks/Cole.

Glaser, Barney G., and Anselm L. Strauss. 1964. "Awareness Contexts and Social Interaction," *American Sociological Review* 29:669–79.

Goffman, Erving. 1959. *The Presentation of Self in Everyday Life*. New York: Doubleday.

_____. 1961. *Encounters*. Indianapolis: Bobbs-Merrill.

_____. 1967. *Interaction Ritual*. New York: Doubleday.

Homans, George C. 1974. *Social Behavior: Its Elementary Forms*. New York: Harcourt Brace Jovanovich.

James, William. 1890. *The Principles of Psychology*, vol. I. New York: Henry Holt.

Katz, Jack. 1983. "A Theory of Qualitative Methodology: The Social System of Analytic Fieldwork." Pp. 127–148 in *Contemporary Field Research*, edited by Robert M. Emerson. Prospect Heights, IL: Waveland.

Leslie, Gerald R. 1979. *The Family in Social Context*, 4th ed. New York: Oxford University Press.

Lewis, Helen B. 1971. *Shame and Guilt in Neurosis*. New York: International Universities Press.

Lofland, John. 1976. *Doing Social Life: The Qualitative Study of Human Interaction in Natural Settings*. New York: Wiley.

Mead, George H. 1934. *Mind, Self, and Society*. Chicago: University of Chicago Press.

Metts, Sandra, and William R. Cupach. 1989. "Situational Influence on the Use of Remedial Strategies in Embarrassing Predicaments." *Communication Monographs* 56:151–162.

_____. 1994. *Facework*. Thousand Oaks, CA: Sage.

Nock, Steven L. 1987. *Sociology of the Family*. Englewood Cliffs, NJ: Prentice Hall.

Pestello, Fred P. 1991. "Discounting." *Journal of Contemporary Ethnography* 20:26–46.

Reohr, Janet. 1991. *Friendship: An Exploration of Structure and Process*. New York: Garland.

Scheff, Thomas J. 1990. *Microsociology: Discourse, Emotion, and Social Structure*. Chicago: University of Chicago Press.

Scheff, Thomas J., and Suzanne M. Retzinger. 1991. *Emotions and Violence: Shame and Rage in Destructive Conflicts*. Lexington, MA: Lexington Books.

Scott, Marvin B., and Stanford M. Lyman. 1968. "Accounts." *American Sociological Review* 33:46–62.

———. 1970. "Accounts, Deviance, and Social Order." Pp. 89–119 in *Deviance and Respectability,* edited by Jack D. Douglas. New York: Basic Books.

Simmel, Georg. 1950. *The Sociology of Georg Simmel.* Translated and edited by Kurt H. Wolff. New York; Free Press.

Stryker, Sheldon. 1981. "Symbolic Interactionism: Themes and Variations," Pp. 3–29 in *Social Psychology: Sociological Perspectives,* edited by Morris Rosenberg and Ralph Turner. New Brunswick: Transaction.

Suttles, Gerald D. 1970. "Friendship as a Social Institution." Pp. 95–135 in *Social Relationships,* by George J. McCall, Michal M. McCall, Norman K. Denzin, Gerald D. Suttles, and Suzanne B. Kurth. Chicago: Aldine.

Znaniecki, Florian. 1934. *The Method of Sociology.* New York: Farrar and Rinehart.

PART VI

AMBIGUITY, COMPLEXITY, AND CONFLICT IN SOCIAL INTERACTION

Advocating the mere tolerance of difference . . . is the grossest reformism. Difference must be not merely tolerated, but seen as a fund of necessary polarities between which our creativity can spark like a dialectic. Only then does the necessity for interdependence become unthreatening.

—Audre Lorde (1984),
"The Master's Tools Will Never Dismantle This House"

These conflicts which break forth are not between the ideal and reality, but between two different ideals, that of yesterday and that of today, that which has the authority of tradition and that which has the hope of the future.

—Émile Durkheim,
The Cultural Logic of Collective Representations

What I claim is to live to the full contradiction of my time.

—Roland Barthes (1957/2000), *Mythologies*

BOUNDARIES AND CONTRADICTIONS

Jodi O'Brien

I recall wondering as a child whether the people on television continued their activities when the set was turned off. What did they do when I was not around to operate the box they lived in? Why was it that whenever I wanted to invite one of the TV people to my birthday party, the adults in my life said the TV people couldn't come because they lived somewhere else? If they lived somewhere else, why were they always in my living room? And when some of the TV people frightened me, my parents always said not to worry because the TV people weren't real. How confusing it was to figure out what separated me and the adults I knew from the TV people!

Erving Goffman (1963), in one of his characteristically astute observations, notes that children must be taught not to call to people through walls. The reason for this, he suggests, is that children don't recognize the wall as a boundary between themselves and other people whom they know to be on the other side of the wall. Once people become aware of "walls," however, whether they are tangible or mental constructs, walls can have a profound influence on how reality is perceived.

BOUNDARIES

Two people huddled closely together in a public place, such as a coffeehouse, have an invisible wall around them. The wall is constructed from body language and gestures that we have learned to interpret as "intimacy." The action prescription that accompanies this knowledge is that it is impolite to "intrude" on someone's "walls" of intimacy. Goffman (1963) wrote an entire book, *Behavior in Public Places,* based on his observations of the manner in which persons who occupy the same physical space are able to construct unseen walls that delineate degrees of closeness and belonging. Walls also exist in the form of categorical boundaries about who we think we are or are not. Similarly, interactional routines consist of behavioral boundaries that denote what is within and without the realm of general acceptance in the situation, the group, or the culture.

Try this thought experiment: If you go to the bathroom in a public place in which there are two rooms, each with a single toilet, and the only difference is the signs that read "Men" and "Women," would you use the other bathroom if the one marked for your gender was occupied? I recently went to a public bathroom and found a couple of women waiting in line for the one marked "Women." The men's restroom was free. "Why don't we use that one?" one of the waiting women suggested. "We can keep a lookout for each other." Keep a lookout? For what? I wondered—the gender police? What would happen if the women suddenly climbed over the wall and used the men's toilet? In this case, the gender wall was invisible, but it was real to the extent that these women shared some mild anxiety about "getting caught" using the "wrong" bathroom.

The walls or boundaries that delineate experience and environment into "islands of meaning" are social accomplishments. When people define something, they trace boundaries around it; they wall it off and define what it is *not* in order to highlight and solidify what it *is*. Eviatar Zerubavel (1991), a sociologist, has written a compelling book on the topic, *The Fine Line: Making Distinctions in Everyday Life* (see also Reading 1). Zerubavel points out that the term *define* is derived from the Latin expression for boundary, *finis*. He tells this story:

> There is a joke about a man whose house stood right on the Russian-Polish border. When it was finally decided that it was actually in Poland, he cried out: "Hooray. Now I don't have to go through those terrible Russian winters anymore." (Zerubavel, 1991, p. 28)

Zerubavel continues:

> Such reification of the purely conventional is the result of our tendency to regard the merely social as natural. Despite the fact that they are virtually mental, most gaps—as well as the quantum leaps necessary for crossing them—are among the seemingly inevitable institutionalized "social facts" that constitute our social reality. (pp. 28–29)

The signs "Men" and "Women" signify more than the location of toilets. They reflect deeply etched mental lines representing gender, one of the most basic boundaries of difference in our culture. In contemplating whether or not to use the bathroom of the "other," we are contemplating crossing over into another territory entirely.

Another illustration of a social boundary that we tend to regard as natural is the Four Corners, a popular tourist destination for travelers in the southwestern United States. In this location, four states—Utah, Colorado, New Mexico, and Arizona—all meet at a common boundary. Thousands of tourists flock to the site and engage in the contortions necessary to claim that their bodies are in four states at once. They buy souvenirs and take pictures and home videos. Is there something special about this small patch of land? If you have visited the Four Corners site, you know that it is off the beaten path, and with the exception that it's the conjunction of the four states, it's relatively unremarkable terrain. However, the conception of being in one "state" or another is a powerful reference point for the visitors. Nothing about the physical land suggests that the states should be demarcated as they are currently, but our mental maps have a firmly etched knowledge of these social boundaries.

I lived in Switzerland in my youth. This small country is home to peoples representing at least four distinct ethnic cultures—French, German, Italian, and Romanian. The first three countries border Switzerland. In crossing from one region to another, a matter of only a few kilometers in some cases, I was always struck by the ethnic distinctness of the towns. By walking across a geopolitical line separating a German from an Italian village, I could travel between two completely different worlds. The Swiss are as obsessively tidy as the stereotypes emphasize. Cars are parked neatly within carefully painted lines, and people speak in hushed tones, queue up patiently, and always deposit their litter in one of the many handy trash cans—which are always sparkling clean. Just across the border, the Italians sing and chatter merrily as they jostle one another. Traffic rules are a fiction, and motorists park in any unoccupied space that is close to their destination and often simply stop to chat with passersby.

Near my home, in Zurich, was a complicated five-way intersection. In the middle stood an enclosed podium from which a single traffic cop directed traffic—except during lunchtime. At exactly noon every working day, the traffic cop would climb down from the podium and go home for lunch. No matter that this was the time many drivers were also driving home for the noon meal. For the traffic cop, it was time to go home. It didn't seem to make much of a difference whether the traffic cop was there, however. The Swiss took turns at the intersection with the same clocklike precision that prevailed when the traffic cop was present.

To this point, the theoretical perspective developed in this book suggests that the way humans make sense of and carve up our realities is a social process. We have looked at detailed information regarding the cognitive processes of "making meaning" and the interactional processes through which meaning is communicated, negotiated, and solidified. The processes have been elaborated at the personal, interpersonal, and cultural levels. By now, you know that realities are socially constructed and that organized systems of thought and rules for behavior differ from group to group. This picture is a useful representation of social reality, but it is too simple. Although it is accurate to say that boundaries are socially drawn and that different people and communities draw them differently, the impression left by much of the literature we have covered to this point is that these worlds exist as distinctly as do the worlds of the Swiss and the Italians. It may seem that negotiation proceeds, once it is routinized, as smoothly as the Swiss navigating the busy intersection at Kreuzplatz during lunchtime. However, social reality is often more complicated than this picture suggests.

CONTRADICTIONS

When different identities and cultural realities are mapped onto each other, it is evident that boundaries clash. Identities and cultures are not islands. They cannot be turned on and off like the people on TV. Different realms and territories overlap, and when they do, seemingly distinct selves and routines come crashing together. In the very process of trying to define who we are, as individuals and as groups, we encounter contradictions. We trespass across boundaries that we hold dear. We transgress against our own systems of meaning.

Boundaries depict differences in the beliefs, interests, and relative power *among* individuals and *among* groups. Trespasses and transgressions make evident the contradictions *within* ourselves and our groups. Émile Durkheim (1915/1965), one of the founders of sociology, wrote that in the act of defining deviance, a culture (or individual) defines and reinforces its own moral boundaries. George Herbert Mead's theory of the self (see Reading 22) is grounded in the notion of an ongoing internal conversation regarding struggle between the experiences and desires of the "I" and the moral boundaries drawn by the "me." The "self" is not one or the other; rather, it is a manifestation of the conversation between the socialized "me" and conflicting desires and ideals that occur through ongoing social encounters. Karl Marx represents society as an ongoing struggle between those who control the means of production and those who do not. Society is not the victor of one or another of these struggling groups, it is an expression of the continuous conflict between them. Social institutions and practices reflect the contradictions between the haves and the have-nots.

In this final part of the book, we develop the thesis that contradictions and transgressions make people continually aware of what the boundaries are. Wrestling with these contradictions is the dynamic force of self and society. The wrestling process reveals and shapes who and what we are.

CONTRADICTIONS AND CONFLICT IN SELF-PRODUCTION

The orderly precision of Swiss society belies the fact that foreigners, or even errant locals, often transgress codes of conduct. Many a hapless visitor has thoughtlessly dropped litter to the ground, only to have an observant Swiss pick it up and return it to its "owner" with the polite inquiry, "Did you lose this?" Parking the family car was always a traumatic event for my mother because, inevitably, just as she was about to exit the car, a vigilant local would tap on the window and describe to her the way in which she had misparked. This "helper" would then redirect her into the appropriate angle.

If you imagine this process of social correction as an internal conversation, you will have a picture of Mead's "generalized other" telling the "me" what to do. Both Mead and Sigmund Freud recognized that a person often engages in activities that conflict with or contradict expected routines of behavior. To the extent that the person has been socialized by the codes and expectations of the group, he or she will experience a voice, somewhat like the Swiss tapping the litterer on the shoulder, reminding the transgressor of what is expected. Thus, to a large extent, *intrapersonal* conflict as it is discussed by Mead and Freud emphasizes the conflict between the unsocialized will—individual passions, urges, and so forth—and the internalized voices of significant groups. This picture of cultural imprinting is a bit like that of a free-spirited animal that wants to belong to the herd but resists being fenced into a pasture.

In this discussion, we focus on yet another type of intrapersonal conflict. Certainly, much self-development occurs through channeling desires and urges into expected social forms, and learning to give these feelings and drives names and to harness them accordingly. However, socialized adults are likely to encounter many circumstances in which more than one set of "generalized other" voices compete for the reins. In those cases, the person is not struggling with the conflict between "unsocialized" drives and social expectations but rather with the clamorings and demands of distinct and contradictory voices representing different states of being, distinct commitments, and diverse "generalized others."

Consider this passage from *Living With Contradictions: A Married Feminist,* written by Angela Barron McBride in 1973:

I am a married feminist. What does that mean? Am I part of a new breed of women, or someone about to burst because of the contradictions in my person? There are weeks and months when I'm not sure which description best fits me, but such tensions are the essence of being a married feminist.

I am a woman who feels pulled in two directions—between traditional values and conventions on one hand, and a commitment to feminist ideology on the other. A woman who finds custom appealing and comforting, yet despises the patriarchal patterns that make women second-class citizens. I am a woman who wants a loving, long-term relationship with a man, but bitterly resents being considered only someone's other *half*. A woman who values family life, but deplores the sterile, functional view of man as the head of the family and woman as its heart. . . . A wife who wants to belong to one man, yet not be his private property.

The apparent contradictions felt by a married feminist are legion. I've listened to fashion plates sing the hedonistic pleasures of not being a mother, and felt like putting them over my knees and spanking them for their selfishness. I've heard gingham types say all they ever wanted out of life was to be a wife and a mother, and felt choked by their smugness. I bristle when people spit out the word "feminist" as if it were a communicable disease: I protest when others sneer at marriage as if it were an outdated misery. . . . Press the button and I can feel guilty about anything. I feel guilty that I never seem to have the time to make an assortment of Christmas cookies from scratch, *and* I feel guilty about feeling guilty about that. (pp. 1–3)

Note the teeter-totter between two roles, two selves—each is significant relative to specific groups, but both are defined in opposition to each other. McBride's conversation with herself is a veritable ricochet from one wall to another. In searching for her own sense of self, she wrestles with her generalized notions of what these possible selves represent. For middle-class white women in the 1960s and 1970s, the cacophony of voices about who and what they should be was loud and, in many ways, contentious.

Consider the content of these generalized voices today. Are people still inclined to represent the extremes in women's identities as "gingham types" and "radical feminists"? To some extent, these contradictions have been bridged, and the boundaries are now less sharply etched into the consciousness of young women (and men). This result stems from the attempts by the women of McBride's generation to establish some balance on the teeter-totter.

The search for new names for one's self is often prompted by the attempt to reconcile contradictions. The process can be much more complex than simply choosing one option or the other. Often the individual does not have a choice. Although contradiction and conflict may lead to change, the form of the change is always informed by the existing boundaries.

Terminology and Social Positions

In recent decades, many scholars have focused their attention on understanding the ways in which social position affects persons differently. It's obvious, for instance, that a wealthy person has a different perspective on her options when she is shopping than someone with a low-paying hourly job and a family to feed. But do these economic differences affect the self-image of each person, and if so, how? Certainly, both persons have the potential to have high self-esteem and a positive self-image, but it is also true that each is likely to have vastly different day-to-day experiences. These experiences combine to become the focus of the internal dialogue that make up a sense of self. In this way, social position can have profound effects on self-development. Regardless of what one thinks of oneself, certain features or characteristics denoting social status "mark" the interactional milieu in predictable ways. These "marked" interactions affect one's sense of self.

To continue the example, someone who is wealthy is likely to be treated with respect whenever she shops. Overall, a day of shopping is likely to be a positive experience for her, and the appraisals she receives from others will likely reflect her own sense of high self-worth. Conversely, there is a tendency among store clerks to treat persons who look poor as potential thieves. Thus, regardless of her own sense of personal integrity, a person "marked" as poor frequently encounters rude stares and attitudes of suspicion when she is shopping. Whereas the wealthy person takes her high self-worth for granted and has her self-impression reaffirmed through interaction, the poor person may have to continually remind herself that she really is a decent and valuable human being, despite interactions in which she is treated as if she may not be honest.

Many concepts have been developed to describe this process of differentiation in interaction. A few of these terms are reviewed here with the aim of providing a working vocabulary. Then we turn our focus to the ways in which these processes of interactional differentiation influence self-image.

Hegemonies

Some of the terms you may have encountered to refer to a person's social position are *hegemonic position, hierarchical status, center/margin, subject/object,* and *marked/unmarked.* Here is one way to make sense of this terminology: Although there are many different, often competing stories and perspectives that make up a culture, there are usually some stories or perspectives that are more acceptable and dominant than others. The dominant perspective is referred to as the *hegemonic* position. Whether they agree with it or not, most persons are aware of the hegemonic position, and its legitimacy is usually taken for granted. It is the position that is seen as "most normal" and "most desirable." In the contemporary United States, some of the hegemonic positions include "rational," "heterosexual," "middle-class," "Protestant," "male," and "white."

Some scholars refer to this hegemonic cluster as "the *center.*" Recall the discussion in Part II, and you will recognize the center as the default perspective. Those who do not have these centrist characteristics (for example, those who are not white) are considered "other" or "marginal." Some scholars study various hegemonies and look at the consequences for persons who are in marginal positions in the hegemony. Another way of saying this is that persons who are low in a particular social hierarchy are defined in terms relative to the hegemonic position. For instance, it can be said that economic status is a significant or hegemonic status marker in this society. There is a social hierarchy that exists according to economic status. "Middle-class" is the dominant or taken-for-granted position in this hierarchy (not necessarily the "best" position, but the one that is assumed to be "normal"). Persons who are poor are seen as low in the hierarchy and marginal.

Marked Positions and Subjectivity

For the purpose of understanding how these positions operate in interaction, we find the terms *marked/unmarked* and *subject/object* useful. When a person has characteristics that are consistent with the default position in a social hierarchy, then the status of the person is said to be "unmarked." The default position is *unmarked* because, cognitively, it is what people expect to see, all else being equal. A person's status is said to be "marked" if it is distinct from the expected norm. Thus, as was noted in Part II, when we refer to a "basketball player," we are inclined to think of a male basketball player. If we are talking about a basketball player who is female, we tend to mark this by saying, "the woman basketball player." Similarly, when white people mention someone who is not white, race is one of the first characteristics mentioned ("I was just talking to that black guy over there"). Alternately, when referencing a white person, mention is seldom made of race ("I was just talking to that guy over there"). The latter sentence is racially unmarked and thus reflects a cultural hegemony wherein white is considered "normal."

Subject refers to the person who is in an active role; *object* refers to the person upon whom the subject is acting. At least this is probably the definition you were taught in English grammar. In interaction routines, however, presumably all persons are subjects. They are all interacting. In any given moment, it can be said that a particular person who is projecting a definition of the situation is the subject and the persons to whom the subject is directing his or her actions are, in Goffman's (1963) terms, the audience (which is a more active position than "object"). In the vocabulary of symbolic interaction, persons are *subjects* to the extent that they are able to actively project their own contextual sense of self into the interactional dynamics. Someone is an *object* if he or she is seen by others only in terms of some marked social characteristic. If you came to talk with me about how much you want to go to law school and I responded by asking you how it was for you to be the only Chicana in your class, I would be responding to you as an *ethnic object* and denying you your self-presentation as a serious student interested in law. Or imagine I responded by stating that I'm sure you would do well because Asians are so smart. In this instance, I am treating you as an ethnic object and also imposing a particular ethnic stereotype on you. In both cases, I put you in a position in which (1) I am not granting you the specific subjective position that you are presenting, and (2) you have to adjust the interaction to respond to having been put into a categorical box that may or may not have anything to do with what you are trying to talk with me about.

The paradox of subject/object is that to some extent we are always objectifying others when we interact with them. As you have learned by now, we put others into categorical boxes (label them) in order to locate their role, and our own, in the interaction. A problem arises, however, when we interact with someone only in terms of stereotypical categories—when we do not give them the opportunity to project their own subjectivity. *Persons who can be identified by marginal, marked statuses are more likely to be treated as objects and less likely to be perceived as subjects.* A way to think about this is to ask yourself how free you are to write your own narrative in a given interaction. As we have seen, power determines who can do and say what in many interactions. To what extent does a highly marked status give you even less power in an interaction? Or, conversely, when do you find yourself treating someone else in terms of a social category (as an object) rather than as a subject?

We turn now to a discussion of some of the ways in which marked/unmarked statuses shape perception, interaction, and self-image. Keep in mind that the significant analytical point is the varying degrees to which persons in interaction have *control* over the roles and images they are able to present to others. We will look at just a few manifestations of this process: privilege and entitlement, marked positions and awareness, subjective freedom, stigmatized identities, interactional mirrors, and authenticity. Each of these processes reflects tensions and contradictions that occur as persons attempt to "realize" themselves in interaction with others.

Privilege and Entitlement

A noteworthy feature of hegemonic or unmarked positions is that those who occupy them are often unaware of their own relative subject freedom in interaction. They are more likely to pass through their everyday interactions without much friction. Their actions usually go unchallenged or don't need to be accounted for. They are generally given more space to express themselves, and their definition of the situation is likely to be accepted as the basis for the working consensus. For such people, the relationship between who they would like to be, who they think they are, and who they think they should be is likely to be isomorphic and noncontradictory. This unified and clearly delineated self-image is reflected back to them and reaffirmed in myriad small ways, especially through the ease with which they conduct their everyday interactions. This is not to say that such persons may not occupy contradictory roles—they simply have more control to make sure that these roles don't come clashing together.

Consider a small example: It is sometimes misassumed by middle-class people who live in suburbs that working-class people living in urban areas are more likely to engage in extramarital sex. In fact, the rates of extramarital sexual encounters may be the same across both classes, but middle-class people often have more resources for compartmentalizing their contradictory activities. Single-family homes ensure more privacy than do apartments with shared entries and thin walls. If you have money and credit cards, you can lead a duplicitous life farther away from prying eyes than if you do not have these resources. In short, it may be easier for a person with material wealth to move between one reality and another without experiencing too much social contradiction.

In *Carte Blanche,* a painting by Henri Magritte, a group of horseback riders is engaged in a fox hunt. In the foreground is a woman in fine riding clothes atop a handsome stallion. She sits astride her horse with ease and grace looking as if she hadn't a care in the world. In the background are several riders, less well clad, who are hunched low in the saddle, earnestly navigating their way around the trees of the forest through which they are riding. The woman, who represents privilege, is unaware of the trees because her horse is simply passing through them. The obstacles that exist for others don't exist for her. This is "carte blanche." The implication is that her life is like a blank check—relatively speaking, she can do as she pleases, because her social position eclipses obstacles that others must navigate.

One interactional consequence of this privilege is a sense of social entitlement. In a powerful essay about growing up as "poor white trash," author Dorothy Allison (1994) writes:

[My people] were the *they* everyone talks about . . . the ones who are destroyed or dismissed to make the "real" people, the important people, feel safer. Why are you so afraid? My lovers and friends have asked me the many times I suddenly seemed a stranger, someone who would not speak to them, would not do the things they believed I should do, simple things like applying for a job, or a grant, or some award they were sure I could acquire easily. Entitlement, I have told them, is a matter of feeling like we rather than they. You think you have a right to things, a place in the world, and it is so intrinsically a part of you that you cannot imagine people like me, people who seem to live in your world, who don't have it. I have explained what I know over and over, in every way that I can, but I have never been able to make clear the degree of my fear, the extent to which I feel myself denied: I was born poor in a world that despises the poor. (p. 14)

Entitlement in this sense can be defined as a taken-for-granted expectation that one has a *right* to pursue certain goals and to participate in various interactions. The person who feels entitled does not worry about being seen as an imposter or about being rejected or dismissed. Consider what sorts of internal conversations a person is likely to have if he or she feels entitled to participate in most realms of social life versus someone who would like to participate but is not sure if he or she has a right to do so. To what extent does this sense of entitlement provide someone with a script for pursuing such things as asking advice from professors, asking for letters of recommendation for graduate school, and so forth? A sense of entitlement is enhanced through repeated interactions in which a person is affirmed for her or his efforts. The more affirmed one feels, the more he or she will pursue new and risky opportunities that may lead to even greater social advantages. Relatedly, a person who feels entitled to certain things is more likely to get upset if things don't go as he or she planned. Relatively speaking, those with a strong sense of entitlement are more likely to hold greater expectations that situations will unfold according to their plans.

Marked Positions and Social Awareness

For those who occupy marginal, marked statuses, the simplest interaction may pose a contradiction between how they would like to see themselves and how others see them. A lack of role support combined with the necessity of pushing harder to project a definition of the situation can have profound effects on someone's sense of self. Social psychologists have studied the relationship between self-esteem and people's tendency to attribute successes and failures to external or internal factors. For instance, if you perform well on an exam and attribute this outcome to your own intelligence and the fact that you studied, you have made an internal attribution—the result is a consequence of something you did. If, on the other hand, you perform poorly and say that it was because the exam was too hard, you have made an external attribution—the outcome is due to factors beyond yourself.

A second attributional dimension is the extent to which you perceive the cause to be stable and within your control. For instance, if you perform poorly on an exam but attribute your performance to lack of study, you have made an internal attribution and concluded that the circumstances are potentially within your control: "I could pass that exam, I just need to study harder." If, however, you attribute your grade to the instructor's dislike of you, you have concluded that your evaluation is based on external factors beyond your control. Social psychologists are inclined to agree that external attributions lead to feelings of helplessness—the individual feels that nothing he or she can do will alter the outcome.

In a class exercise, I asked students to write a description of an occasion when they were uncertain about whether some outcome in their lives was due to personal (internal) factors or social (external) factors. Most of the students were middle class, but some interesting differences in their responses did appear. Without hesitation, the students of color and the women in the class bent their heads and wrote intensely for several minutes. What surprised me was the response of many of the white men. They chewed on their pencils, looked puzzled, and asked me to repeat the question.

When students read their responses, several of the women told of instances in which they had not gotten jobs or had not been allowed to participate in certain activities. They were unsure whether the outcome was because they were female or because they didn't have the right skills. Students of color had thought of similar instances. One Chinese American male told of winning an essay contest in his first year of college. Subsequently he was invited to a national forum to read the essay. When he arrived, he noted that all the other "winners" were also students of color. He was unable to decide whether he had won because he wrote a terrific essay or because of his ethnicity. Many of the Hispanic American and Asian American students related similar experiences. All of them were familiar with the day-to-day uncertainty about whether to attribute events in their lives to personal or social factors. For them, everyday self-awareness includes an ongoing internal conversation about whether their experiences result from ethnic, racial, or gendered processes or from personal skill and talent. One consequence of this ongoing deliberation is a feeling of walking along volatile boundary lines and never being certain if one is inside or outside.

The white men, meanwhile, looked increasingly ill at ease during this classroom activity. One by one, they read papers that began, "I'm not sure what the question is . . . " or "I'm not sure what you're getting at here. . . . " In subsequent reflective essays, however, many of these young men noted that they had gained a much greater recognition of how complicated self-awareness and self-evaluation are for people who cannot be certain whether or not an outcome in their lives is because of something within their control or because they are marked as particular objects. The white male students also began to take note of the many additional boundaries, such as social class and society's expectations for them (for instance, financial productivity, heterosexuality, and masculinity), that shape who and what they think they can be.

Whatever a person's status, greater self-awareness occurs as a result of recognizing the complex interplay among the positions that constitute social boundaries. Like other social routines that become ossified, and even naturalized over time, these positions are likely to be taken for granted by some and not by others. The less able a person is to take them for granted, the more likely he or she is to be aware of the boundaries—and the conflicts and contradictions—within all social systems. One outcome of dealing with contradiction is an ability to comprehend more social complexity.

Subjective Freedom

Subjective freedom can be described as how much freedom one has to successfully convey a definition of the situation. If others in the interactional setting see the person only in terms of a particular stereotypical status—as an object—then the person cannot expect to be seen on her or his own terms. For instance, in education research it has been demonstrated that students respond very differently to the same material depending on whether it is taught by a white man or a woman of color. The white man, who occupies the unmarked or expected position for the role of a college professor, is usually seen as "in control," "apolitical," "fair," and "informative" when he teaches material such as the ideas being discussed in this essay. A woman of color teaching exactly the same thing is often evaluated by students as being "too political," "too biased," "lacking authority," and "uninformed." Not only do perceptions differ dramatically, but in this case the man has more subjective freedom than the woman. A woman who is aware of these stereotypical reactions among students can develop strategies to counter this tendency, but in doing so, she has to shape the interaction in response to stereotypical perceptions. She is not as free to "be herself" in the same way that the man is. In presenting her subjective position (in this case as a teacher), she must navigate around the ways in which others mark her only as an object of her race and gender.

Persons who occupy highly marked positions are usually aware of the contradictions between how they see themselves and how others see them. The dilemma is complicated further by the fact that these marked positions are also a part of someone's subjectivity. A professor who is also a woman of color does not necessarily want to be treated *as if* she were white. This "color-blind" attitude reinforces the hegemony that white is the default and desired position. The challenge in developing *multicultural consciousness* is to overcome mindless stereotypes so that persons do not have to navigate their way out of boxes that objectify them in order to present their own subjectivity.

Ironically, dismantling stereotypes requires a *more* discriminating attitude. This does not mean discrimination in the sense of stereotyping, but discrimination as a form of discernment and awareness. We have to train ourselves to pay more attention to details that otherwise go unnoticed because they may not fit the stereotype. An employer who is mindfully discerning, for instance, will force herself to get over the fact that the job interviewee is in a wheelchair and focus instead on features such as the person's seemingly high intelligence and expert experience. At the same time, she will be aware that the person is in fact in a wheelchair and that this is obviously of some consequence for him. The ways in which it is of consequence should be the subject's own story to tell, however. The more he perceives that he is being treated genuinely as a subject within the situation—in this case, as a potential employee—rather than as a "handicapped" object, the freer he will be to present his own complex rendering of himself.

Stigmatized Identities

Some statuses are not only highly marked, but are marked in ways that are stigmatizing for the individual and for those associated with the individual. This stigmatization can have significant consequences for interaction and self-image. Consider a person who responds with the following profile to the "Who Am I?" question:

daughter	computer geek
granddaughter	cat lover
graduate student	girlfriend
white	feminist
middle-class	music lover

Are you formulating an image of this person? Can you tell something about the important things and people in her life from this list (for example, parents, grandparents, cats, school, and so forth)? This is her own subjective rendering of herself. All of these self-referential characteristics are features that she would probably be able to bring up in conversation with others and not expect conflict to occur (except maybe in terms of types of computers or favorite bands, but this would only reaffirm her commitment to these aspects of "self"). In other words, there doesn't appear to be a lot of role conflict in this initial list. Suppose, however, that she added "lesbian" to the list. Is this something that she can tell her grandmother about? Obviously that depends on the particular grandmother and the relationship between the two of them. Regardless, we can assume that this particular aspect of self may exist in conflict with some of the other relationships that she may value. Even if her parents are accepting of her lesbian status in their interactions with their daughter, they may find themselves in conflict when they encounter old friends who ask if their daughter is married yet. Do they "come out" as the parents of a lesbian or deflect the question in a way that will preserve their own unmarked (that is, heterosexual) status?

Add one more item to the list—"erotic dancer." Now what happens to your mental image of this person? Are you doing a bit of mental scrambling to make all the characteristics fit? For many people, once they are aware of this particular status, all other aspects of the person fade to the background. A stigmatized identity has a tendency to become a "master identity." Everything else about the person takes a backseat to, or is evaluated in terms of, the master identity. Stigmatized master identities also reflect archetypal social beliefs, such as the belief that someone can be a mother or an erotic dancer, but not both simultaneously. Someone might ask, for instance, "How can you be a feminist and also be a stripper? Or how can you be a graduate student and do that kind of work?" These sorts of questions reflect entrenched social expectations about which social roles go together and which do not. There is a tendency to assume that a person with a stigmatized role is nothing other than that particular role.

A person who engages in activities that are considered stigmatized has to do a great deal of interactional work to manage information. In this case, how free do you think the person is to share with classmates, teachers, family, and friends the fact that she dances nude for a living? Even when she does mention it, how likely is it that they will accept her definition of this particular subject position, rather than imposing their own?

This example illustrates a highly marked, problematic aspect of self (stigma) that has consequences in interaction with others. It also illustrates the fact that all of us have multiple, contradictory, shifting selves. We are many things both to ourselves and to one another. We enact various selves contextually. We may push out one aspect of self in one setting (erotic dancing) and another in another setting (participation in a seminar on the feminist implications of sex work). We may keep certain features hidden (lesbian) in order to preserve a valued relationship (with a grandmother). "Stigma" is an interactional feature. An aspect of self is stigmatized only to the extent that persons define it as beyond the boundaries of expected or acceptable practices. Yet stigma can have very real consequences in shaping how persons make sense of the contradictions they perceive in their own self-image and how they grapple with these contradictions in interaction with others.

Many stigmatized identities exist in the form of highly marked stereotypes (handicapped, homeless, ex-convict, hooker, drug addict, mental patient, welfare recipient, and so on). But any aspect of self about which someone feels extreme shame or embarrassment has the potential to operate as a stigmatized identity. If you are ashamed of being gay or lesbian, of being from a working-class background, of being a single parent, of your religious background, and so forth, then you may feel impelled to try to hide this aspect of yourself from others. Many social psychologists suggest that "shame" about an aspect of self-identity develops when a person internalizes social scripts that convey certain statuses as marked and undesirable. The person's own internal gaze or mirror is a reflection of social images whereby the identity is defined as loathsome. As a consequence of looking at this internal image, the person develops a sense of self-loathing. Persons who engage in behaviors that are stigmatized may or may not feel shame or embarrassment themselves. The extent to which they are able to deflect the shame directed at them by others depends on what sort of larger repertoire of self-understanding they have, their history of interactions with significant others, and their position in various social hierarchies.

For instance, when I am traveling in certain areas, I can expect to be called names or even spat at by persons who perceive me to be a lesbian. At times I feel unsafe in certain areas. However, for the most part I have the freedom to avoid these situations, and to the extent that I do have to deal with bigotry, I have a well-developed set of responses. My self-image as a lesbian (a nonstigmatized identity for me) is shaped by the fact that I am a tenured professor in a respectable university. I am aware that one part of who I am—my sexual identity—is socially stigmatized, but I view that part as normal and unremarkable. In interaction, I project a definition that invites others to treat me accordingly. And for the most part, they do. Students and colleagues may privately despise me for this part of who I am, but I don't provide any opportunity for them to project this definition onto my interaction. My ability to achieve this interactional destigmatization is based on much critical reflection about how I want to incorporate this aspect of myself into my everyday interactions; many positive experiences in which my own self-view has been affirmed by people who matter to me; and, perhaps most important, the fact that I have a great deal of power in the particular context in which I spend most of my time—a college campus.

All of us experience some degree of tension and contradiction (such as shame and guilt) in the various behaviors that we consider to be aspects of our core self. The way in which we work through these contradictions shapes our developing sense of self. Our resources for wrestling with these contradictions reflect personal interactional history and the repertoire of stories we have for ourselves, as well as our own relative power in situations.

Interactional Mirrors

One of the features of a hegemonic or central position is that persons who occupy these positions can be relatively certain of encountering others like them wherever they go. One outcome of this is that the person's reality is likely to be reflected back by others and thereby continually reaffirmed. In contrast, persons who occupy marginal positions and who interact primarily with persons who hold mainstream positions may often feel isolated and conflicted about how to interpret their own experiences. As the poet Adrienne Rich puts it, "It's like looking into a mirror and seeing nothing."

Being able to interact with others whose experiences and struggles match your own is not simply a privilege, it is an occasion to (re)affirm the reality of your own impressions and feelings. Many of us transgress boundaries every day because we are "outsiders." The vertigo of these experiences can be overcome, to some extent, if we are able to interact with others who share our conflicting circumstances and contradictory experiences. Conversations with those who share our experiences provide us with new names and meanings that help us bridge the contradictions. This opportunity to associate and redefine reality is one of the reasons why special interest groups and clubs are important for people who share marginalized, marked, or stigmatized statuses. These groups provide interactional mirrors that reflect the complexities of crossing through contradictory states of being. In encounters with others who experience similar contradictions and tensions, people broaden their repertoire, learn new scripts for acting, and have an opportunity to express more subjective freedom.

In this country, suicide is the leading cause of death among gay, lesbian, and transgendered youths aged fifteen to twenty-four (Herdt & Roxer, 1993). These young people often experience their sexual or gender feelings as being completely outside the boundaries of the self-images that have been inculcated by significant others, such as parents, family, friends, teachers, and church and community leaders. Without positive imagery and role models for how to incorporate their differences into the rest of their self-image, these young people may suffer the contradictions deeply. Irreconcilable feelings of helplessness can lead to extreme despair. The opportunity to encounter people whose self-image reconciles the identities of "homosexual" and "productive, accepted member of society" can turn these young people away from the brink of suicide.

Similarly, women and students of color benefit from programs designed specifically for them to interact with others who share similar points of view. For these alternative perspectives to be interactionally supported and to gain the stature of commonly understood realities, they must sometimes be enacted separately from mainstream culture. Renato Rosaldo (1993), an anthropologist who has participated actively in the development of such programs at Stanford University, calls the programs "safe houses":

> Why do institutions need safe houses? Safe houses can foster self-esteem and promote a sense of belonging in often alien institutions. Safe houses are places where diverse groups—under the banners of ethnic studies, feminist studies, or gay and lesbian studies—talk together and become more articulate about their intellectual projects. When they enter the mainstream seminars such students speak with clarity and force about their distinctive projects, concerns, and perspectives. The class is richer and more complex, if perhaps less comfortable, for its broadened range of perspectives. (p. xi)

Rosaldo is delineating the interactional steps whereby persons have an opportunity to express their subjectivity without having to navigate the imposition of stereotypes and prejudices. In the kind of interactional setting that he describes, persons develop a clearer and more articulate sense of who they are *in all their complexity.* When they bring this complexity into mainstream interactions, it can have the effect of altering the stereotypical routine.

It is important to note that status as an insider or an outsider is situational and may change with circumstance. In *Falling From Grace,* Katherine Newman (1988) describes the experiences of men in middle and upper managerial positions who have lost their jobs. For most of these men, selfhood pivots around their ability, as holders of privileged positions, to move with ease through a world in which they wield considerable control. When they lose their jobs, they lose access to a tremendous amount of interactional privilege (such as control over space and conversation) that was their basis for maintaining a positive self-image. Many of these men are unaccustomed to contradictory self-images and, as a result, are ill prepared for the quick downward spiral that they experience when they fall outside the lines of their primary reference group. Lacking alternative points of reference and feeling ashamed of having been "downsized," these men are at high risk for suicide. Support groups for these men do not simply provide a way to get through the hard times—they are interactional situations in which the men learn to project and juggle a new self-image, one that is quite different from the self they have been accustomed to being.

Authenticity

The preceding discussion reveals a picture of the social self as multiple, shifting, and contradictory. How we see ourselves and the selves we present to others shift from context to context and can be contradictory within a given situation. We are more committed to some aspects of self than others. We may be inclined to hide or deflect certain significant identities in some situations. These observations lead to the question, Who are you really? The question of "authenticity" is something that concerns many scholars as well as individuals. One answer to the question comes in the form of a paradox: We all live contradictory lives, but we tend to act *as if* our lives were not filled with ambiguity and contradiction. One cultural expectation that many of us share is the *norm of consistency.* Is consistency the same thing as authenticity? For many people, it is. We tend to believe someone is "authentic" when we observe him or her behaving consistently across different settings and circumstances ("She must be genuinely kind, because she is kind even when someone is mean to her"). It is possible that persons strive to make their behavior consistent because others expect us to behave consistently. Over the course of time, with repeated interactions and affirmation, we may develop self-routines that are so consistent that we believe them to be authentic expressions of self. Furthermore, to the extent that others strive to show us consistency and to hide the inconsistencies, we may come to believe that people are, indeed, consistent or authentic.

In a related way, we may strive to hide aspects of self that might strike others as contradictory according to preexisting social scripts about what sorts of behaviors go together ("He can't possibly be gay and also be a minister"). In doing so, we reaffirm these social scripts and fail to express the fact that selves are indeed multiple and contradictory.

From the perspective of symbolic interactionists who recognize the existence of multiple, shifting, contradicting self-expressions, one answer to the question "Who are you really?" is this: We are really the *way* in which we work through the contradictions that characterize our day-to-day interactions. We are the *process of wrestling contradiction.* This process is reflected in internal conversation and external expression. Two people can have a similar profile of self-referential identities and characteristics but very different self-images and interactional responses. Consider again the woman described in the "Who am I?" question above. She might keep her more stigmatized statuses (lesbian, erotic dancer) closeted from others whom she suspects will not be able to handle the "contradictions" these statuses imply, or she might reveal all and express an attitude of "I have a right to be *all* these various selves, even if it confuses you." How she views her own selves and how she chooses to portray them to others—in all their complexity and ambiguity—reveals the process of who she really is.

In this way, it can be concluded that selves are always in a state of becoming. This becoming is shaped through the processes of interaction and revealed through the internal dialogues in which we observe, comment on, feel, and try to make sense of our own complexity.

Recall some of the general principles that have been formulated throughout this book. All humans use language-based systems to create conceptual meaning. This process creates definitional boundaries. All people compartmentalize. Different individuals encounter these boundaries differently. The process of self-understanding is a continual interplay between personal experience and attempts to fit experience into existing conceptual categories and representations. All of us struggle to make sense of ourselves, to find ways of self-expression, and to be heard and understood. The self undergoes constant revision as it encounters friction, contradiction, and conflict among the various boundaries that give the self meaning.

CONFLICT AND CHANGE IN CULTURAL PRODUCTION

Cultural production, like self-production, is a dialectical process of definition. Within groups and societies, people struggle over what significant symbols mean and who has the authority to project public definitions. The struggle over frames of meaning organizes people's lives.

In this struggle to create definitions, cultural institutions are a resource—a source of privilege for some and an obstacle for others. Various institutions—family, government, religion, and the economy, for example—can wield great influence in the creation or maintenance of socially shared definitions. This influence may be unintended, or it may be consciously directed toward supporting a particular status quo. Again, however, power is an issue. Not everyone is equally able to participate in the construction of meaning. Some people's beliefs and interests are given more legitimacy than those of others.

Hegemonic practices of inequality persist because people play out the scripts expected of them—even when they may be privately opposed to these practices (see also the essay in Part V on the status quo). People participate in practices of domination and inequality for a variety of reasons: They may not realize the extent to which they contribute to the maintenance of particular definitions of the situation (hence the popular bumper sticker "Question authority"). Or, as is often the case, they may not have the resources necessary to break the chains of the existing reality. This complicity in oppression is what Marx refers to when he says that the "tradition of the dead generations weighs like a *nightmare* on the brain of the living" (italics added). Prevailing realities suggest certain lines of action and forestall others. The possibility for change is in the conception of alternative lines of interaction. Alexis de Tocqueville once observed: "A grievance can be endured so long as it seems beyond redress, but it becomes intolerable once the possibility of removing it crosses people's minds." To be realized, however, even the most eloquent theories must be acted out. Change must be performed on the social stage.

In a well-known essay called "Talking Back," the writer and activist bell hooks considers what happens when an oppressed person refuses to engage in expected forms of deference (see Reading 41). Oppression is a construction that requires the cooperation of many social actors—those doing the oppressing and those who are being oppressed. According to hooks, we choose to either join in the construction of oppression or to withdraw our support. She points out that we can all actively work to breach realities that work against our interests. Even if our resistance is only small, sometimes we find ways to talk back.

CONCLUSION

One of the paradoxes of human social life is that cultural practices both constrain us and make our lives meaningful. Another writer and activist, Gloria Anzaldua, who passed away recently, left a powerful legacy regarding cultural complexity. In one of her essays, "*La Conciencia de la Mestiza*/Toward a New Consciousness" (in Anzaldua, 1987), she describes the experiences of those who walk the boundaries and live the contradictions of being outsiders to various communities by virtue of class, gender, race, religion, sexuality, and so on. According to Anzaldua, such people develop a multiple, or *mestiza,* consciousness that makes them more aware of both the advantages and limitations of entrenched cultural practices. The *mestiza* is "a product of the transfer of the cultural and spiritual values of one group to another." This cultural transfer or border navigation can be tremendously difficult.

Anzaldua describes the clash this way:

> The clash of voices results in mental and emotional states of perplexity. Internal strife results in insecurity and indecisiveness. The mestiza's dual or multiple personality is plagued by psychic restlessness. . . . These numerous possibilities leave *la mestiza* floundering in uncharted seas. In perceiving conflicting information and points of view she is subjected to a swamping of her psychological borders. (p. 78)

How does *la mestiza* cope?

> The new *mestiza* copes by developing a tolerance for contradictions, a tolerance for ambiguity. She learns to be an Indian in Mexican culture, to be a Mexican from an Anglo point of view. She learns to juggle cultures. She has a plural personality, she operates in pluralistic mode. . . . Not only does she sustain contradictions, she turns the ambivalence into something else. (p. 79)

One of the implications of *la mestiza* or multiple consciousness is cultural awareness. Those who cannot take their social positions for granted, who cannot assume that their definition of the situation will be shared by others, are likely to have a more expansive awareness of the situation and its possibilities. This is what Anzaldua refers to as the "consciousness of the borderlands." Borderland consciousness, and the struggle it involves, is a central aspect of change.

Anzaldua concludes:

> The struggle is inner. The struggle has always been inner, and is played out in the outer terrains. Awareness of our situation must come before inner changes, which in turn come before changes in society. Nothing happens in the "real" world unless it happens first in the images in our heads. (p. 87)

Although Anzaldua is writing specifically about the borders that divide the consciousness of Chicana/os who are also Indians and also trying to live in Anglo worlds, her words resonate with many people who traverse multiple social borders. Contradiction is not necessarily a bad thing, especially when struggle leads to awareness. To the extent that each of us recognizes and learns to wrestle with the contradictions that are an inevitable part of social existence, we expand the definitions of who and what we imagine we can be. We increase our social muscle and enrich our repertoire of possibilities.

A similar process occurs at the societal level. As groups engage in boundary skirmishes regarding respective definitions of morality; entitlement; and the power to define cultural institutions such as politics, law, religion, and family, there is the possibility of increased awareness. This potential is shaped, in large part, by a group's power to participate in cultural definitions of what is "real" and "acceptable." If you live in the United States, consider what it means to live in a country that promotes the ideal of "freedom and justice" for all. Cultural pluralism is the bedrock of this freedom. For the ideal to become real, it is necessary to foster a national *mestiza* consciousness and all the struggle and debate that go along with it.

REFERENCES AND SUGGESTIONS FOR FURTHER READING

Allison, D. (1994). *Skin: Talking about sex, class and literature.* Ithaca, NY: Firebrand Books.

Anzaldua, G. (1987). *Borderlands/La Frontera: The new mestiza.* San Francisco: Aunt Lute Books.

Barthes, R. (2000). *Mythologies* (A. Lavers, Trans.). London: Vintage. (Original work published 1957)

Durkheim, É. (1965). *The elementary forms of the religious life* (J. W. Swain, Trans.). New York: Free Press of Glencoe. (Original work published 1915)

Goffman, E. (1963). *Behavior in public places.* New York: Free Press.

Herdt, G., & Roxer, A. (1993). *Children of horizons.* Boston: Beacon.

Lorde, A. (1984). *Sister/Outsider: Essays and speeches by Audre Lorde.* Berkeley, CA: Crossing Press.

McBride, A. B. (1973). *Living with contradictions: A married feminist.* New York: Harper Collins.

McIntosh, P. (1992). White privilege and male privilege. In M. L. Anderson & P. H. Collins (Eds.), *Race, class, and gender: An anthology* (pp. 70–81). Belmont, CA: Wadsworth.

Newman, K. (1988). *Falling from grace.* New York: Free Press.

Rilke, R. M. (1989). *The selected poetry of Rainer Maria Rilke* (S. Mitchell, Trans.). New York: Vintage.

Rosaldo, R. (1993). *Culture and truth: The remaking of social analysis.* Boston: Beacon Press.

Zerubavel, E. (1991). *The fine line: Making distinctions in everyday life.* Chicago: University of Chicago Press.

CONTRADICTIONS AND CONFLICT IN SELF-PRODUCTION

The previous sections have provided an explanation for the development of a social self through interaction. This section explores the more complicated process that occurs when our self-expectations and self-images are in conflict. People often identify with conflicting reference groups, for example. Similarly, we may receive ambiguous and confusing messages from various sources about who and what we should be. The articles in this section explore how people make sense of these contradictions. They also illustrate a powerful theme in the social psychology of the self: People have an amazing capacity to construct some kind of coherency out of the most extreme contradictions. This observation suggests that we are infinitely creative in constructing our own life stories.

"Double Consciousness and the Veil" is an excerpt from the writings of a famous sociologist, W. E. B. Du Bois. Du Bois was a highly influential thinker during the period known as the Harlem Renaissance in the 1920s. His ideas were instrumental in the advancement and politics of the "New Negro." Although his ideas were criticized by the next generation of black artists and intellectuals as being too bourgeois and too assimilationist in reference to a white middle class, Du Bois is widely regarded as one of the great intellectuals of his time. This selection is an early essay in which he considers the experience of being "other" and of cultivating a Negro self in a white world.

How do openly gay Christians make sense of the contradictions between Christian doctrine and being homosexual? Jodi O'Brien explores this question in "Wrestling the Angel of Contradiction: Queen Christian Identities." This study traces the ways in which openly gay and lesbian Christians define the contradictions they experience and the ways in which they reconcile these contradictions. This process of reconciling contradictions may have some surprising effects on mainstream Christian congregations.

In "We Are Graceful Swans Who Can Also Be Crows," Lubna Chaudhry describes the experiences of four Pakistani Muslim immigrant women's experiences in finding a sense of self. As this ethnographic study shows, persons from a similar background may have different ways of making sense of their experiences and contradictions.

Questions for Discussion and Review

1. Return to your list of responses to the question "Who am I?" (Part IV). Are there any items on this list that you would be embarrassed or ashamed to have someone close to you know about? If not, imagine what kinds of items might be on the lists of others that could be potentially conflicting.

2. Self-concept emerges from a person's unique intersection of social positions such as class, gender, race, religion, sexuality, age, and so forth. Review the concepts in the essay for this section and consider which aspects of your social position are more or less "central" and more or less "marginal." What impact might your specific position have had on your interactions and experiences?

3. Discuss the proposition that social power is the extent to which you can author your own position? What are some interactional factors that enable people to be more or less in control of how others define them?

35

Double Consciousness and the Veil

W. E. B. Du Bois

(1903)

O water, voice of my heart, crying in the
sand,
All night long crying with a mournful cry,
As I lie and listen, and cannot understand
The voice of my heart in my side or the
voice of the sea,
O water, crying for rest, is it I, is it I?
All night long the water is crying to me.

Unresting water, there shall never
be rest
Till the last moon droop and the last
tide fail,
And the fire of the end begin to burn
in the west;
And the heart shall be weary and wonder
and cry like the sea,
All life long crying without avail,
As the water all night long is crying
to me.

—Arthur Symons

Between me and the other world there is
ever an unasked question: unasked by
some through feelings of delicacy; by others
through the difficulty of rightly framing it. All,
nevertheless, flutter round it. They approach me
in a half-hesitant sort of way, eye me curiously or
compassionately, and then, instead of saying
directly, How does it feel to be a problem? they say,
I know an excellent colored man in my town;
or, I fought at Mechanicsville; or, Do not these
Southern outrages make your blood boil? At these
I smile, or am interested, or reduce the boiling to
a simmer, as the occasion may require. To the
real question, How does it feel to be a problem?
I answer seldom a word.

And yet, being a problem is a strange experience—peculiar even for one who has never been
anything else, save perhaps in babyhood and in
Europe. It is in the early days of rollicking boyhood
that the revelation first bursts upon one, all in a
day, as it were. I remember well when the shadow
swept across me. I was a little thing, away up in
the hills of New England, where the dark Housa-
tonic winds between Hoosac and Taghkanic to
the sea. In a wee wooden schoolhouse, something
put it into the boys' and girls' heads to buy gor-
geous visiting-cards—ten cents a package—and
exchange. The exchange was merry, till one girl,
a tall newcomer, refused my card—refused it
peremptorily, with a glance. Then it dawned upon
me with a certain suddenness that I was different
from the others; or like, mayhap, in heart and life
and longing, but shut out from their world by a
vast veil. I had thereafter no desire to tear down
that veil, to creep through; I held all beyond it in
common contempt, and lived above it in a region
of blue sky and great wandering shadows. That

sky was bluest when I could beat my mates at examination-time, or beat them at a foot-race, or even beat their stringy heads. Alas, with the years all this fine contempt began to fade, for the words I longed for, and all their dazzling opportunities, were theirs, not mine. But they should not keep these prizes, I said; some, all, I would wrest from them. Just how I would do it I could never decide: by reading law, by healing the sick, by telling the wonderful tales that swam in my head—some way. With other black boys the strife was not so fiercely sunny: their youth shrunk into tasteless sycophancy, or into silent hatred of the pale world about them and mocking distrust of everything white; or wasted itself in a bitter cry: Why did God make me an outcast and a stranger in mine own house? The shades of the prison-house closed round about us all: walls strait and stubborn to the whitest, but relentlessly narrow, tall, and unscalable to sons of night who must plod darkly on in resignation, or beat unavailing palms against the stone, or steadily, half hopelessly, watch the streak of blue above.

After the Egyptian and Indian, the Greek and Roman, the Teuton and Mongolian, the Negro is a sort of seventh son, born with a veil, and gifted with second-sight in this American world—a world which yields him no true self-consciousness, but only lets him see himself through the revelation of the other world. It is a peculiar sensation, this double-consciousness, this sense of always looking at one's self through the eyes of others, of measuring one's soul by the tape of a world that looks on in amused contempt and pity. One ever feels his twoness—an American, a Negro; two souls, two thoughts, two unreconciled strivings; two warring ideals in one dark body, whose dogged strength alone keeps it from being torn asunder.

The history of the American Negro is the history of this strife—this longing to attain self-conscious manhood, to merge his double self into a better and truer self. In this merging he wishes neither of the older selves to be lost. He would not Africanize America, for America has too much to teach the world and Africa. He would not bleach his Negro soul in a flood of white Americanism, for he knows that Negro blood has a message for the world. He simply wishes to make it possible for a man to be both a Negro and an American, without being cursed and spit upon by his fellows, without having the doors of Opportunity closed roughly in his face.

This, then, is the end of his striving: to be a co-worker in the kingdom of culture, to escape both death and isolation, to husband and use his best powers and his latent genius. These powers of body and mind have in the past been strangely wasted, dispersed, or forgotten. The shadow of a mighty Negro past flits through the tale of Ethiopia the Shadowy and of Egypt the Sphinx. Through history, the powers of single black men flash here and there like falling stars, and die sometimes before the world has rightly gauged their brightness. Here in America, in the few days since Emancipation, the black man's turning hither and thither in hesitant and doubtful striving has often made his very strength to lose effectiveness, to seem like absence of power, like weakness. And yet it is not weakness—it is the contradiction of double aims. The double-aimed struggle of the black artisan—on the one hand to escape white contempt for a nation of mere hewers of wood and drawers of water, and on the other hand to plough and nail and dig for a poverty-stricken horde—could only result in making him a poor craftsman, for he had but half a heart in either cause. By the poverty and ignorance of his people, the Negro minister or doctor was tempted toward quackery and demagogy; and by the criticism of the other world, toward ideals that made him ashamed of his lowly tasks. The would-be black *savant* was confronted by the paradox that the knowledge his people needed was a twice-told tale to his white neighbors, while the knowledge which would teach the white world was Greek to his own flesh and blood. The innate love of harmony and beauty that set the ruder souls of his people a-dancing and a-singing raised but confusion and doubt in the soul of the black artist; for the beauty revealed to him was the soul-beauty of a race which his larger audience despised, and he could not articulate the message of another people. This waste of double aims, this seeking to satisfy two unreconciled ideals, has wrought sad havoc with the courage and faith and deeds of ten thousand thousand people—has sent them often wooing false gods and invoking false means of salvation, and at times has even seemed about to make them ashamed of themselves.

Away back in the days of bondage they thought to see in one divine event the end of all doubt and disappointment; few men ever worshipped Freedom with half such unquestioning faith as did the American Negro for two centuries. To him, so far as he thought and dreamed, slavery was indeed the sum of all villainies, the cause of all sorrow, the root of all prejudice; Emancipation was the key to a promised land of sweeter beauty than ever stretched before the eyes of wearied Israelites. In song and exhortation swelled one refrain—Liberty; in his tears and curses the God he implored had Freedom in his right hand. At last it came—suddenly, fearfully, like a dream. With one wild carnival of blood and passion came the message in his own plaintive cadences—

Shout, O children!
Shout, you're free!
For God has bought your liberty!

Years have passed away since then—ten, twenty, forty; forty years of national life, forty years of renewal and development, and yet the swarthy spectre sits in its accustomed seat at the Nation's feast. In vain do we cry to this our vastest social problem—

Take any shape but that, and my firm nerves
Shall never tremble!

The Nation has not yet found peace from its sins; the freedman has not yet found in freedom his promised land. Whatever of good may have come in these years of change, the shadow of a deep disappointment rests upon the Negro people—a disappointment all the more bitter because the unattained ideal was unbounded save by the simple ignorance of a lowly people.

The first decade was merely a prolongation of the vain search for freedom, the boon that seemed ever barely to elude their grasp—like a tantalizing will-o'-the-wisp, maddening and misleading the headless host. The holocaust of war, the terrors of the Ku-Klux Klan, the lies of carpetbaggers, the disorganization of industry, and the contradictory advice of friends and foes, left the bewildered serf with no new watchword beyond the old cry for freedom. As the time flew, however, he began to grasp a new idea. The ideal of liberty demanded for its attainment powerful means, and these the Fifteenth Amendment gave him. The ballot, which before he had looked upon as a visible sign of freedom, he now regarded as the chief means of gaining and perfecting the liberty with which war had partially endowed him. And why not? Had not votes made war and emancipated millions? Had not votes enfranchised the freedmen? Was anything impossible to a power that had done all this? A million black men started with renewed zeal to vote themselves into the kingdom. So the decade flew away, the revolution of 1876 came, and left the half-free serf weary, wondering, but still inspired. Slowly but steadily, in the following years, a new vision began gradually to replace the dream of political power—a powerful movement, the rise of another ideal to guide the unguided, another pillar of fire by night after a clouded day. It was the ideal of "book-learning"; the curiosity, born of compulsory ignorance, to know and test the power of the cabalistic letters of the white man, the longing to know. Here at last seemed to have been discovered the mountain path to Canaan; longer than the highway of Emancipation and law, steep and rugged, but straight, leading to heights high enough to overlook life.

Up the new path the advance guard toiled, slowly, heavily, doggedly; only those who have watched and guided the faltering feet, the misty minds, the dull understandings, of the dark pupils of these schools know how faithfully, how piteously, this people strove to learn. It was weary work. The cold statistician wrote down the inches of progress here and there, noted also where here and there a foot had slipped or someone had fallen. To the tired climbers, the horizon was ever dark, the mists were often cold, the Canaan was always dim and far away. If, however, the vistas disclosed as yet no goal, no resting-place, little but flattery and criticism, the journey at least gave leisure for reflection and self-examination; it changed the child of Emancipation to the youth with dawning self-consciousness, self-realization, self-respect. In those sombre forests of his striving his own soul rose before him, and he saw himself—darkly as through a veil; and yet he saw in himself some faint revelation of his power, of his mission. He began to have a dim feeling that, to attain his place in the world, he must be himself, and not another. For the first time he sought to analyze the burden he bore upon his back, that dead-weight of social degradation partially masked behind a half-named Negro problem. He felt his poverty; without a cent, without a home, without land, tools, or savings, he had entered into competition with rich, landed, skilled neighbors. To be a poor man is hard, but to be a poor race in a land of

dollars is the very bottom of hardships. He felt the weight of his ignorance—not simply of letters, but of life, of business, of the humanities; the accumulated sloth and shirking and awkwardness of decades and centuries shackled his hands and feet. Nor was his burden all poverty and ignorance. The red stain of bastardy, which two centuries of systematic legal defilement of Negro women had stamped upon his race, meant not only the loss of ancient African chastity, but also the hereditary weight of a mass of corruption from white adulterers, threatening almost the obliteration of the Negro home.

A people thus handicapped ought not to be asked to race with the world, but rather allowed to give all its time and thought to its own social problems. But alas! while sociologists gleefully count his bastards and his prostitutes, the very soul of the toiling, sweating black man is darkened by the shadow of a vast despair. Men call the shadow prejudice, and learnedly explain it as the natural defence of culture against barbarism, learning against ignorance, purity against crime, the "higher" against the "lower" races. To which the Negro cries Amen! and swears that to so much of this strange prejudice as is founded on just homage to civilization, culture, righteousness, and progress, he humbly bows and meekly does obeisance. But before that nameless prejudice that leaps beyond all this he stands helpless, dismayed, and well-nigh speechless; before that personal disrespect and mockery, the ridicule and systematic humiliation, the distortion of fact and wanton license of fancy, the cynical ignoring of the better and the boisterous welcoming of the worse, the all-pervading desire to inculcate disdain for everything black, from Toussaint to the devil—before this there rises a sickening despair that would disarm and discourage any nation save that black host to whom "discouragement" is an unwritten word.

But the facing of so vast a prejudice could not but bring the inevitable self-questioning, self-disparagment, and lowering of ideals which ever accompany repression and breed in an atmosphere of contempt and hate. Whisperings and portents came borne upon the four winds: Lo! we are diseased and dying, cried the dark hosts; we cannot write, our voting is vain; what need of education, since we must always cook and serve? And the Nation echoed and enforced this self-criticism, saying: Be content to be servants, and nothing more; what need of higher culture for half-men? Away with the black man's ballot, by force or fraud—and behold the suicide of a race! Nevertheless, out of the evil came something of good—the more careful adjustment of education to real life, the clearer perception of the Negroes' social responsibilities, and the sobering realization of the meaning of progress.

So dawned the time of *Sturm und Drang:* storm and stress today rocks our little boat on the mad waters of the world-sea; there is within and without the sound of conflict, the burning of body and rending of soul; inspiration strives with doubt, and faith with vain questionings. The bright ideals of the past—physical freedom, political power, the training of brains and the training of hands— all these in turn have waxed and waned, until even the last grows dim and overcast. Are they all wrong—all false? No, not that, but each alone was oversimple and incomplete—the dreams of a credulous race-childhood, or the fond imaginings of the other world which does not know and does not want to know our power. To be really true, all these ideals must be melted and welded into one. The training of the schools we need today more than ever—the training of deft hands, quick eyes and ears, and above all the broader, deeper, higher culture of gifted minds and pure hearts. The power of the ballot we need in sheer self-defense—else what shall save us from a second

slavery? Freedom, too, the long-sought, we still seek—the freedom of life and limb, the freedom to work and think, the freedom to love and aspire. Work, culture, liberty—all these we need, not singly but together, not successively but together, each growing and aiding each, and all striving toward that vaster ideal that swims before the Negro people, the ideal of human brotherhood, gained through the unifying ideal of Race; the ideal of fostering and developing the traits and talents of the Negro, not in opposition to or contempt for other races, but rather in large conformity to the greater ideals of the American Republic, in order that some day on American soil two world-races may give each to each those characteristics both so sadly lack. We the darker ones come even now not altogether empty-handed: There are today no truer exponents of the pure human spirit of the Declaration of Independence than the American Negroes; there is no true American music but the wild sweet melodies of the Negro slave; the American fairy tales and folklore are Indian and African; and, all in all, we black men seem the sole oasis of simple faith and reverence in a dusty desert of dollars and smartness. Will America be poorer if she replace her brutal dyspeptic blundering with light-hearted but determined Negro humility? or her coarse and cruel wit with loving jovial good-humor? or her vulgar music with the soul of the Sorrow Songs?

Merely a concrete test of the underlying principles of the great republic is the Negro Problem, and the spiritual striving of the freedmen's sons is the travail of souls whose burden is almost beyond the measure of their strength, but who bear it in the name of an historic race, in the name of this the land of their fathers' fathers, and in the name of human opportunity.

CONTRADICTIONS AND CONFLICT IN SELF-PRODUCTION

36

Wrestling the Angel of Contradiction

Queer Christian Identities

Jodi O'Brien

(2004)

I wanted gays to be in the vanguard, battling against racial and economic injustice and religious and political oppression. I never thought I would see the day when gays would be begging to be let back into the Christian Church, which is clearly our enemy.

(Edmund White, author)

Seven reasons why you should absolutely, positively stay away from church . . .[reason number four]. The way some churches can get God to fit into those little boxes.

(Posted flyer, Spirit of the Sound: Gay and Lesbian Followers of Jesus)

I had to go to a non-Christian church for four years before I understood what it means to be a good Christian. A good Christian has a very big god.

(Larry, gay male and practicing Catholic)

INTRODUCTION

Several years ago I attended Gay Pride Parades in three different cities during the same month (San Francisco, Chicago, and Seattle). . . . Each parade felt distinct to me. The differences were not surprising. In many ways, they reflect the mosaic of responses to the proliferation of lesbian and gay presence and politics in recent decades. Perhaps this is why I was so surprised at one notable similarity that occurred at all three parades. Among the marchers in each parade were groups representing friends and supporters of lesbians and gays: PFLAG, AT&T Queer Allies, US Bank LGBT Employee Support, and so forth. In each case, the crowd responded enthusiastically to this display of support and acceptance. People clapped and cheered and whistled in appreciation. The marchers glowed in acknowledgement. This is not what surprised me. Rather, it was the contrast in the crowd's response to another group of marchers: lesbian and gay Christians and, specifically, Mormons (who march under the banner of Affirmation) and Catholics (who call their association Dignity). In these three very distinct US cities I wandered up and down the streets during each parade, watching as merry crowds fell silent at the appearance of these marchers. Everywhere the response was the same: silence, broken only by an occasional boo. I was stunned. These otherwise very "normal" looking but openly queer men and women (some of whom really did look like the stereotypical Mormon missionary) were being booed at their own Pride Parades. . . .

It is likely that many parade bystanders were genuinely confused at what must have seemed an obvious contradiction: openly queer, openly religious. For some parade-goers, the presence of these lesbian and gay Christians might even have been a form of betrayal given the active anti-homosexual preaching of both the Vatican and Mormon leaders. In any case, my curiosity was aroused. What compelled someone to want to parade both statuses? My initial impression was that lesbian and gay Christians must experience a form of "double stigma". . . . What seemed to confuse and unsettle the crowd was the open expression of such an apparent contradiction. Why would any self-respecting queer want also to embrace Christianity with its seemingly inevitable denouncement and exclusion? And why, especially, would they want to announce this involvement to fellow queers, knowing the disdain and rejection that this was likely to incur?

Compelled by these questions I began to research what I called "double stigma." Specifically, I was interested in lesbians and gays who are openly queer and openly Christian. How did they make sense of and manage this "double stigma" I wondered? The concept of "double stigma" was sociologically rigorous enough to garner me research support for the project. Armed with this idea, the financial blessing of the American Sociological Association, and a solid track record of ethnographic experience, I set off in search of answers. Five open-ended interviews into the project, I knew the concept of "double-stigma" was completely off the mark. I was missing the main point. When I raised the idea of "double-stigma"—How do you deal with it? Why do you deal with it?—the first round of interviewees all looked at me with similar confusion. Yes, they understood the question. Yes, they could

understand how others would see it that way. But it did not resonate for them. Each of these five people, none of whom knew one another, said the same thing. This was not about stigma. It was about "living a contradiction that defines who I am."

Forty-two interviews and many hours of congregational participation later I was still hearing the same thing: the contradiction of being Christian and being queer is who I am. When I gave talks describing the research project I noticed the vigorous head-nodding among self-described queer Christians at the mention of the phrase, "living the contradiction." My orienting perspective at the launch of this project reflected my penchant for sociological abstraction and personal experiences that disincline me toward participation in mainstream religions (I am a former Mormon with a typical "flight from religion" experience through the process of becoming a lesbian). Through sustained contact and participatory experience with self-described "queer Christians" and the congregations that welcome them, I developed an understanding of the deeply complex process of living the contradiction of being queer and Christian. In fact, over time, I have come to have considerable appreciation for this process.

RESEARCH SETTING AND METHODOLOGY

This article is based on a more comprehensive project in which I develop the thesis that the contradictions between Christianity and homosexuality are the driving tensions in the formulation of a historically specific expression of queer religiosity. These expressions are manifested in individual identities and practices, in community practices (i.e., Christian congregations), and in ideological discourses (i.e., theological and doctrinal discourses). The transformative processes occurring at each of these levels are mutually constitutive. In this article I focus specifically on the processes whereby lesbian and gay Christians[1] forge an integration of Christian doctrine, spirituality and sexuality.[2] My central interpretive claim in this paper is that this integrative struggle is experienced by lesbian and gay Christians as a raison d'être. Wrestling this contradiction has given rise to a particular expression of queer Christian identity. Among the many implications of these expressions of queer Christian identity is their impact on mainstream Christian congregations and Christian ideologies and practices. I describe these implications briefly in the conclusions.

As I have noted in the introduction, my original intent was to understand the motivations and experiences of lesbian and gay Catholics and Mormons who wished to be recognised explicitly for both their religiosity and sexuality. I began the project by talking with several such individuals, including my hairstylist, a self-described "flaming queen with a flair for building miniature houses" who is also active in his local Catholic parish. Larry's openly gay behavior was considered outrageous even by the standards of the gay-friendly hair salon that he worked in. Quite frankly, I could not imagine what his fellow parishioners made of his queerness. Yet Larry seemed to have found quite a home there. He spoke often and enthusiastically about his involvement with the parish. He invited me to attend services and, eventually, several meetings of the lay ministry, to experience for myself what his "contradictory" world was like. Another point of entry came through a colleague who had granted me a formal interview and then invited me to attend services at Seattle's First Baptist where he was an active participant. Later his congregation invited me to participate as a speaker in their ongoing "Adult Education" series—a version of Sunday School. They wanted to explore the theme of sexuality and asked if I would kick-off the topic. Jim, my colleague and interview subject, was instrumental in organising the series and in setting me up with subsequent interviews.

Through participation in these congregational activities I was introduced to more lesbian and gay

Christians who granted me interviews and put me in contact with other friends and colleagues throughout the western United States and British Columbia. I also learned first-hand of the tensions taking place within the congregations that were supportive of lesbian and gay members.[3] The late 1990s was a time of ferment within Christian congregations regarding the presence and affirmation of lesbian and gay members. In this respect, the timing of my research was serendipitous. In recognition of these community and organisational tensions, I expanded my interviews to include heterosexual congregants and clergy members. I also expanded my participation to several regional congregations representing Episcopalian, Methodist, Unitarian, and Presbyterian denominations, in addition to my initial participation with Baptist, Catholic and Mormon groups. My formal research process included 63 open-ended interviews and sustained contact with five congregations and two lesbian/gay Christian groups (Affirmation and Dignity) for a period of three years.

During this time I came to recognise what I term a "field of relations," which includes lesbian and gay Christians, the congregations in which they have found a "spiritual community," the general membership of these congregations, the congregational ministries, and the relationships between these congregations and their denominational organisations. There is awareness among these congregations that they are part of a historical moment that is fraught with considerable tension and debate regarding the very definition of Christianity. In this regard, I think it accurate to talk in terms of a social movement that is taking place within the pews (with a distinctly different genesis and process from LGBT political movements as they are typically presented in the social movements literature).

My research methods are consistent with ethnographic interpretive methodologies in which the intent is to articulate fields of relations and the intrapersonal and interpersonal relations that occur within these fields. My approach is especially informed by feminist methodologies, according to which my intent is to ascertain what persons within the field of inquiry have to say for themselves while remaining cognisant of my own relationship with these persons and my influence with the field of relations. At the same time, my work is strongly influenced by sociological theories that orient me toward ascertaining patterned discourses regarding how people make sense of themselves—what stories they tell themselves about who they are and what they can do—especially regarding conflict and contradiction (O'Brien 2001a; Plummer 1995). My observations and conclusions are interpretations that reflect my sociological orientation. Throughout the research process I presented myself as a sociologist with special interests in religion and sexuality. Early in the research process people became aware of my project and approached me about being interviewed and/or having me visit their congregations. This awareness and interest confirms my observation that a self-aware field of relations regarding queer Christian identities exists. My interpretations are limited to the specific context of this research project. However, my aim with this in-depth inquiry is to provide empirical insight and grounding for the conceptual frameworks through which scholars attempt to understand the integration of religion and sexuality generally.[4]

THE "GAY PREDICAMENT": AN IRRECONCILABLE CONTRADICTION

Homosexuality is intrinsically disordered.

(Catechism of the
Catholic Church 1994, 566)

The "question of homosexuality" has been a central focus of discussion in Catholic and Protestant denominations since the 1960s. Historically, homosexuality is forbidden in most Christian

doctrines. In these texts the homosexual has been variously defined as "disordered," "evil," and "sinful" (Conrad and Schneider 1980; O'Brien 2001b). In many texts homosexuality is rendered as absolutely irreconcilable with the basic tenets of Christianity. Recent revisions of a few doctrines offer a slightly more forgiving interpretation wherein homosexual behavior is separated from homosexual identity.[5] The new Catechism, for instance, defines homosexual inclinations (identity) as a "condition" that is not chosen and is experienced as a "trial" (Catechism of the Catholic Church 1994, 566). Grappling with this affliction can be a lifetime struggle and those who are "successful" in taming the beast of homosexuality can expect the same joys and blessings as other good Catholics.[6] In this rendering the act is the sin, while desire is an affliction. In an accompanying passage, the text admonishes all Catholics to treat persons who suffer the condition of homosexuality with "respect, compassion and sensitivity" (1994, 566). Progressive Catholics see this doctrine as at least an acknowledgement that homosexuality exists. The separation of act and identity is considered by some to be a statement of acceptance. Still, even in this supposedly progressive statement, the "homosexual" is rendered as someone (something) lacking, someone whose desires are a potential source of shame and exile.

Doctrines that condemn homosexuality constitute the ideological backdrop against which Christians initially experience their homosexuality. At worst, they are irredeemable sinners: at best, they suffer from problems or afflictions. Given this discourse of rejection, non-Christians might assume that the simplest path would be the renunciation of religion. For many Christians struggling with feelings of homosexuality the path is not so simple.

Psychologists of religion offer a holistic explanation for sustained Christian participation, even when the participation involves conflict. According to this thesis, Christianity is a well-established and deeply meaningful cosmology that weaves together spirit, intellect, body and community (Fortunato 1982). Christianity offers answers to big questions such as the meaning of life and death. Religious participation is also a means of transcending the oppressions and banalities of everyday living. For many Christians, the traditional ceremonies of religious expression are both evocative and comforting. Thus, motivation for participation is not so much the puzzle. In fact, to frame the question this way, as many studies of religion and homosexuality (including my own initial research proposal) do, is arguably to impose a secular perspective on a religious question.[7] Rather, the puzzle becomes: How does the homosexual make sense of the fact that, by definition, he/she is considered an exile who is beyond the promised redemption of Christian theology? Christian therapist John Fortunato refers to this as the "gay predicament." The "gay predicament," simply put, is that one cannot be a good Christian and also be queer.

The intensity of this contradiction can only be fully understood within a framework of Christian experience. Within a heteronormative culture, lesbians and gays are (often painfully) aware that they are social cast-offs. Within Christianity, active homosexuals are also aware that, in addition to their being social cast-offs, their souls have been cast off as well. This predicament poses a tremendous existential crisis. To experience homosexual desires, and certainly to pursue fulfillment of these desires, will result in being cast out from the cosmology through which one makes sense of one's life. One obvious solution is to cast off Christian theology in favor of the homosexual identity. This is easier said than done, however. Bending the rules is one thing, but shedding an entire structure of meaning may leave one cast adrift in a sea of meaninglessness—which may be even less tolerable than the knowledge that one is potentially damned. This is a defining predicament for lesbian and gay Christians. It is also a profound set of contradictions. Abandoning Christianity may mean

losing a sense of meaning and purpose, yet keeping this particular religion means facing the prospect of damnation.

Queer Secularism

In addition to the predicament of exile, lesbian and gay Christians who are open about their religiosity face rejection from other queers. Lesbian and gay political activists, scholars and writers tend to be critical and dismissive of Christianity. The following remark from gay author John Preston (known especially for his anthologies of gay male short stories) is indicative of the discourse of disdain prevalent among lesbian and gay activists and artists. Preston was invited by Brian Bouldrey to write a chapter for his anthology, *Wrestling with the Angel: Religion in the Lives of Gay Men*. This is his response:

> I'd have nothing to say in your anthology. As an atheist I have no angels with which to wrestle, and, to be honest, I think adults who worry about such a decrepit institution as organized religion should drink plenty of fluids, pop an aspirin, and take a nap, in hopes that the malady will pass. (Quoted in Bouldrey 1995, xi).

Thus, lesbian or gay Christians who seek comfort and insight among fellow queers may be setting themselves up for further disdain and rejection because of their religious affiliation. The queer Christian is doubly damned: according to Christian doctrine, homosexuality is an affliction; among fellow (non-Christian) lesbians and gays, religious affiliation may be the affliction. Not only can one not be a good Christian and be queer, apparently one cannot be a good queer and be religious. Or, as Elizabeth Stuart, author of a guide for LGBT Christians, so aptly phrases it, "queer Christians find themselves caught as it were between the devil and the rainbow, aliens in both lands" (1997, 13).[8]

Persons who have been "spun off from their galaxy of meaning" (Fortunato 1982)—in this case, heteronormative acceptance and Christian systems of meaning and purpose—seek reintegration into new systems of meaning. For instance, heterosexual persons who are inclined, for whatever reasons, to denounce their religious roots usually construct new systems of meaning within secular frameworks. Persons who find themselves spun off from heterosexual culture often find meaning in queer groups that have articulated anti-straight philosophies and practices. . . .

Responses to the Gay Predicament[9]

Anecdotal and experiential information suggests three general sorts of responses to the gay predicament: denunciation and flight, acceptance of the doctrine of shame, and articulation of an alternative (queer) religiosity. The first, denunciation and flight, is a well-known story among many lesbians and gay men. Many "coming out" stories involve a process of renouncing religious roots. These stories can be interpreted as a statement of renunciation and opposition against a system of meaning in which lesbians and gays find no place for themselves. These expressions involve a process of reshaping one's sense of self and identity in opposition to religious teachings and practices. For many individuals, this is a painful and alienating process that involves not only casting off an entire system of meaning and belonging, but forging a new (non-Christian) ideology. As one former Mormon missionary-turned-lesbian put it:

> Non-Mormons don't get that Mormonism answers your questions about everything. Now I have to wonder about every little thing. Do I still believe in monogamy? Or is that something I should throw out along with Mormonism? Do I still believe in life-after-death? Marriage? Commitment? What do I believe in? It's all a big gaping hole for me now. (Lori)[10]

For many the struggle is about how to (re)integrate with society more generally. This is often done through alignment with other queer groups and the articulation of a discourse whereby the religious community, not the individual, is seen as the problem. In this instance, throwing off the cloak of religious shame is seen as an act of liberation:

> Healthy living means finding ways to throw off the guilt. It's not just the guilt of feeling like you've betrayed your family and friends and their expectations for you. It's the guilt that comes from messages all around you that you don't belong. That you're an aberration. Until one day you start to get it and say, hey, I'm here. I'm doing okay. I must belong. When you figure that out you have the courage to walk away from the [church] and realize the problem is them. They're not big enough to let you belong. (Brian)

This group of "recovering Christians" may be the least tolerant of lesbians and gays who attempt to find a place for themselves within Christianity.

Another familiar, and similarly complex, response is to learn to accept Christian teachings that render homosexuality an affliction. In such instances, the struggle to be a good Christian (and a good person generally as defined through adherence to Christian principles) revolves around the struggle to sustain celibacy. Homosexual reintegration into Christianity involves accepting the definition of an afflicted self, donning a cloak of shame regarding one's homosexuality (or, minimally, a cloak of sickness), and embarking upon the struggle indicated by this affliction. The literature on ex-gay therapies and ministries, most of which consists of personal narratives and "undercover" participant observation, indicates that those who seek out these "therapies" are likely to come from strong Christian backgrounds. Often they are referred to the therapies by a Church leader in whom they have confided (see, for instance, Harryman 1991). In these cases, the homosexual Christian who is not "cured" is encouraged to remain "closeted" if he/she wishes to maintain a position in the religious community.

My focus is on those individuals who endeavor to maintain both a strong Christian identity and an open and "proud" lesbian or gay identity. These people recognise their distinct position with respect to those who renounce Christianity and those who accept Christian definitions of affliction. A defining feature of this group is the desire to (re)integrate within a Christian system of meaning while maintaining a queer identity and, ideally, to integrate both identities within a common community. Given this, especially viewed within the framework of the other paths of response, it is possible to assert that lesbian and gay Christians are a distinct group who have at least some awareness that they are forging a unique response to their predicament. It must be noted, however, that, at least initially the responses to this predicament are local and individual. In this regard, the convergence of responses into similar themes is sociologically noteworthy.

In this paper, I am particularly interested in the content of themes that lesbian and gay Christians have articulated. As I note in the concluding section, it is the expression of these themes and the performance of a queer Christianity within congregations that creates a critical mass, or groundswell, that can be interpreted as a particular form of queer Christian religious movement. In other words, none of the individuals in this project started out with an inclination to reform religion or to make a socio-political statement. Rather, each was primarily interested in the question of (re)integrating within a Christian community. Given this context, meaningful research questions include: how do lesbian and gay Christians make sense of and manage their predicament? What motivates their involvement in a system of meaning from which they have been spun off, socially and spiritually? What (if any) source of (re)integration do they articulate for themselves?

Raison d'être

Despite the threats of damnation and rejection among other queers, lesbian and gay Christians remain undaunted in their commitment to both a queer identity and Christian religiosity. Each of the 42 lesbian and gay Christians that I interviewed described having a sense of deep spirituality. Many of them offered details of what they felt to be an "early sense of vocation." As one interviewee phrased it, "religion has always been a natural and necessary part of existence for me."

At the same time, lesbian and gay Christians recognise that these proclamations of Christian spirituality put them at odds with other queers. Detailed statements about religious conviction are usually accompanied by accounts of having to defend this spirituality as a "thoughtful, meaningful enterprise and not some sort of brain-numbing self-denial" (Sean). He continues, "When I see it through the eyes of other gays, I often wonder if my religiosity is a character flaw."

Each of the interviewees articulated an awareness of a secular hegemony in this culture ("educated professional people in general are often embarrassed about their spiritual leanings"). To be religious in a secular society is a struggle. To be religious and queer is to expect ongoing struggle. The theme of struggle is constant throughout my own interviews, in my ethnographic participation in various congregations and in related writings.

The theme of struggle is also familiar and persistent throughout Christian doctrine and teachings. For example, in the Catechism, persons are instructed that appropriate sexual behavior (chastity) is an "apprenticeship in self-mastery which is a training in human freedom" (Catechism of the Catholic Church 1994: 562). This mastery (which culminates in sexual expression contained within a marriage blessed by the Church) will bring happiness and fulfillment. Failure to achieve it will lead to enslavement by the passions. "Struggle" may be a definitive trope of Christianity itself. Certainly one of the religion's most enduring themes is that persons will confront challenges and afflictions. The implied lesson is that the way they handle these struggles shapes their character. In this regard, lesbian and gay Christians can be seen as playing out a variation on an old theme: the contradiction of spirituality and sexuality is their particular struggle; the manner in which they engage the struggle defines their character. Struggle is paramount in each of the three responses to the "gay predicament"—struggle to reinterpret or renounce a dominant system of meaning; struggle to suppress and hide homosexual desire. A common distinction among the lesbian and gay Christians in this study is the extent to which struggle with a contradiction is a definitive aspect of self-understanding and identification (cf. White and White 2004). Two themes in particular emerged from my interviews and observations. First, wrestling the contradiction of spirituality and sexuality defines that self-proclaimed lesbian or gay Christian. Second is the sense among them that they are better Christians—indeed, better persons—as a consequence of this struggle. In other words, the struggle is the crucible in which their character is forged.

Articulating the Self as a Process of Contradiction

There is a version of social psychology that suggests the "articulated self" develops through the process of managing tensions and contradictions in aspects of life that the person considers most meaningful. In my own work I make the claim that the "self" can be usefully defined in terms of this process. In other words, the ways in which we make sense of and manage these contradictions are the definitive features of the social self (O'Brien 2001a). One common experience among the persons I interviewed was an early awakening of both spirituality and homosexuality.[11] Several participants indicated that their awareness of both their spirituality and their homosexuality was simultaneous. For each of them this was a profound realisation, and one that was followed almost immediately by a sense of dread and panic:

I was about 14 or so. I had this heightened sense that I was very special. Very spiritual. God has something special in mind for me. At the same time I had this sense of myself as sexual and that felt so good and so right. And then it occurred to me that these two feelings didn't fit and were going to get me into big trouble. That's when I started trying to figure out what God wanted with me. What was this struggle supposed to teach me? I was really a mess about it for a long time. I think I have some answers now. But I still struggle with it every day. (Jim)

Fortunato remarks that it is "no surprise that gay people ask an inordinate number of spiritual questions." For those who fit comfortably within an accepted system of meaning such as Christianity, the extent to which they think about their spirituality is probably in terms of some benign Sunday school lesson, or perhaps something that is mildly comforting in times of need.[12] Christians who have acknowledged their homosexuality do not have the luxury of semi-conscious spirituality. The discovery that one's sexuality is so deeply contradictory "requires awakening levels of consciousness far beyond those necessary for straight people" (Fortunato 1982, 39). Thus, lesbian and gay Christians may have a more articulated sense of what it means to be a Christian precisely because the have to make ongoing sense of deeply felt contradictions.

For the most part this struggle for articulation is seen as positive and definitive. Every interviewee remarked in some way or another that her/his core sense of being was shaped significantly by the struggle to reconcile homosexuality and religiosity. Comments such as "I wouldn't be me if I didn't have this struggle" were typical.

This is what has forged me, my defining battle. I'd probably be a very conservative evangelical Christian if I wasn't gay—everything is different as a result, especially my spirituality. Wrestling this marginality has become the thing that shapes me more than anything else. (Jim)

For these individuals, self-understanding comes through the process of engaging with persistent contradiction. The experience of contradiction is ongoing, both in conversations with oneself and in interactions with others. Lesbian and gay Christians constantly find themselves in situations in which they must explain (and often defend) their seemingly contradictory statuses to others. This experience is seen both as an occasion that can be tiresome and also as an occasion for growth and self-articulation. As one lesbian Baptist put it:

> You can never take yourself for granted. If I go to an event with lesbians and somehow it comes up that I'm an assistant pastor, I have to listen to this barrage of criticism about the history of Christianity and what it's done to us. I get soooo tired of that. What's amazing is that it never seems to occur to them that maybe I've thought about this. Maybe I have complicated reasons for being who I am. But they don't ask. As tiresome as it can be, it's still a good experience for me. I tend to go home and ask myself, why are you doing this? And I find that I understand my own answers better and better. Does that make any sense? (Carol)

Or this comment from a gay Methodist:

> It's like coming out over and over again. Every time someone new joins [the congregation] we're going to go through the same ol' dance about how the Sunday School coordinator is this gay guy. Thankfully, I'm so well-known now that the other members warn the newcomers. But there's always someone who wants to bait you, y'know, corner you at a social or something and quiz you on doctrine. Like they know doctrine!. . .I wanted to be able to scoff at their ignorance. The funny thing is, now that I know what I do, it turns out I want to educate them instead of show them up. I guess this whole thing has made me much more conscious of being a good Christian. (Mark)

This comment is from a student of Theology and Ministry:

> It seems like everyday, everywhere I go I'm a problem for somebody. It's a problem for white America that I'm black. It's a problem for gay America that I'm in the ministry. It's a problem for the ministry—a big, big problem—that I'm gay. Always a problem. Weird thing is, and you might think this is funny, but being a problem has made me really strong. I mean, as a person. I'm always having to think about who I am and not let it get to me. That makes you strong in yourself. You really know who you are. (Everett)

Another common feature in these narratives is the prevalence of contradiction.

These experiences are similar in tone and expression to some of the narrative reflections on multiple consciousness (for example, Anzaldua 1987). Persons who occupy contradictory social positions find themselves traversing the boundaries, or borders of multiple worlds. In so doing they develop a consciousness that reflects their marginal position. Persons in such positions usually have a heightened awareness of their own marginality; they are also more likely to be critically aware of expressions and practices that less marginalised persons take for granted. Most individuals perceive this heightened awareness as an advantage. At the very least, as noted in the illustrative quotes, contradictory positions are an occasion for reflection and articulation.

A significant outcome of these reflections among lesbian and gay Christians is the articulation of contradiction itself as useful and worthwhile in the shaping of a Christian identity. Not only is contradiction a catalyst for self-reflection, but ultimately it is a source of challenge for Christian congregations. Lesbians and gays who denounce Christianity and leave often make sense of their departure by recognising that their religion is "too small" to accept "the likes of me." This (re)conception of the church and/or God as being too small to accommodate difference is a common basis for renouncing religious affiliation among lesbians and gays. Among those who remain (or become) active participants in their religious communities, there is a slightly different and highly significant twist to this discourse. The strands of this twist include the articulation of the theme that "my gay presence in this too small church is an opportunity for members to stretch their own limits of love and acceptance" and the even more radical notion, "homosexuality is a gift from God." The articulation and convergence of this uniquely queer response to Christianity is the subject of the next section.

ARTICULATING A QUEER CHRISTIAN IDENTITY

Biography and faith traditions intersect to produce discursive strategies toward religion.

(Wade Clark Roof)

Homosexuality is a gift from God.

(John McNeill,
formerly of the Society of Jesus)

In the foregoing comments I have suggested that lesbian and gay Christians are aware that they occupy a unique, marginal and contradictory position with regard to fellow (heterosexual or closeted) Christians and to (former-Christian or non-Christian) lesbians and gays. This contradiction is experienced as a source of insight and as an occasion for articulating a self that these individuals perceive as stronger, more purposeful and, in many cases, indicative of the true meaning of Christianity. In other words, I suggest that rather than attempt to resolve the apparent contradiction of being queer and Christian, these individuals see "living the contradiction" as a purpose in itself, a raison d'être.

One additional theme that emerged from my conversations with lesbian and gay Christians is this: "my contradictory presence is good for the Church." This revision of the discourse on homosexuality

(from problem to useful challenge) serves to reintegrate the homosexual into Christianity (at least in terms of her/his personal articulation of the religion). Further, it renders the homosexual a sort of modern-day crucible with which Christianity must grapple. In doing so, mainline Christian denominations must revisit and redefine the message of love and redemption. In this regard, lesbian and gay Christians redefine "affliction" as an ability; the ability to embrace contradiction and ambiguity is articulated as a manifestation of Christian goodness and character.

This articulation can be interpreted in terms of Roof's thesis of religious individualism (Roof 1999). Individuals enter into a "creative dialogue with tradition" and articulate discursive strategies that enable them to retain significant (often contradictory) aspects of self while maintaining religious commitments.[13] In this instance, the homosexual biography intersects with familiar aspects of Christianity—faith in God's divine wisdom, acceptance of challenge, struggle, oppression, awakening and rebirth—to produce a particularly queer discursive response toward religion. The lesbian and gay Christians who took part in my research, as well as those interviewed by Wilcox (2000), are a unique group in that they have not rejected religion altogether, nor have they accepted the terms of a "divinely ordered closet" (i.e., donning the cloak of shame and silence in order to maintain Christian commitments and status). Instead, they have articulated a position that can be interpreted as a unique queer Christian identity. This identity merges elements of essentialist reasoning, Christian doctrines of love and acceptance, Christian histories of oppression, and collective struggle to attain godly virtues. The emergence of a common discourse among individuals who are, for the most part, engaged in solitary struggle, is noteworthy. I attribute this emergent queer Christian discourse, in its initial phases, to the common threads in Christianity generally. In articulating a queer Christianity, lesbians and gays take up similar threads regarding the formation of identity and their position within their congregations.

The most common theme I heard among both the lesbian and gay Christians I came to know and the congregants who fully accepted them was that we are "all God's children." A point of reconciliation with one's homosexuality and Christianity seems to be the acknowledgement that "God created me; He must have created me this way for a reason." This "realization" is marked by many lesbian and gay Christians as a turning point: "All of a sudden it hit me, I believe in God, I believe He is perfect and has created a perfect world. Why would I have these desires if they weren't part of a perfect plan?" Or as one lesbian pastor phrased it, "Yes I've been reborn through my faith in God's love. Turns out I was born queer."[14]

Coupled with the theme of struggle, this discourse becomes a narrative whereby homosexuality is "both a gift and my cross to bear." In this regard, homosexuality becomes a personal crucible for forging character. This discourse is buttressed by the Christian belief that God creates everything for a purpose. The good Christian's task is to nurture faith in God and to live out the purpose evident in her/his own creation—in this case, the creation of homosexuality. Queer Christians find doctrinal support for their homosexuality in the principle, "God is love." A loving God loves and accepts all Her/His creations; a Church founded on these principles must make room for all that God has created and loves. From this thread comes the idea that a Church is only as big as its god, and its god is only as big as the extent of her/his love. Thus, a truly Christian church is a church that is big enough to love and accept homosexual members.

The third and most critical thread in this discourse combines with the others to weave the theme whereby the homosexual is a necessary and useful challenge for contemporary Christianity. In the words of former Jesuit and self-declared gay liberation theologian John McNeill, "God is calling us to play an historical role" (1996, p. 192). This role is to extend to Christian congregations and denominations the challenge of stretching to accept all who enter and wish to belong—in short, to become as big as God's love, which is infinite. This discourse reclaims the proverbial phrase, "love the sinner but hate the sin," but it reframes sin as failure to love and accept all God's creations. In this conceptualization, God and Christianity *per se* are not the problem; rather, the problem is the institution through which God's intent is interpreted. In the words of a gay Methodist minister, "I never had any doubts about my relationship with God. It's the church that's been a problem for me." Thus, the institution of Christianity becomes the problem and lesbian and gay Christians become the chosen few whose special calling it is to redeem institutional Christianity by liberating its narrowly defined god.

Articulating a queer Christian identity involves transforming a discourse of shame and silence (with the promise of exile) into a narrative of pride and expression. For lesbian and gay Christians, pride is based on a belief that homosexuality has a place in God's plan. The particular place at this particular moment in history is to foment Christian renewal and reformation. In this way, lesbian and gay Christians manage their original predicament by renaming themselves and their positions within their congregations in terms of a gay Christian activism. This discursive strategy is consistent with both lesbian and gay social movements and a Christian tradition of faith-based struggle and martyrdom. It elevates the homosexual from a position of "irredeemable problem" to one of "path to redemption." In this particular instance, it is institutional Christianity that is in need of redemption. Just as the individual must struggle in order to grow and to achieve character and, ultimately, exaltation, so too must the institution of Christianity struggle. The "latter-day homosexual" is the occasion for this institutional metamorphosis. Within this discourse, lesbian and gay Christians become both modern-day Christian soldiers and sacrificial lambs. . . .

Implications: Theology

What are the ideological consequences of a gay and lesbian presence in mainstream Christianity? I have suggested that lesbian and gay Christians are authoring a historically specific queer religiosity to make sense of their predicament of exclusion. This queer Christianity is likely to have transformative effects at the individual, community and organizational levels—all of which are mutually constitutive. Similarly, there are implications for Christian ideologies as well. I offer the following as preliminary observations. Whether one is in agreement with it or not, the articulation of a queer Christian theology, especially as it has emerged within the ranks of individuals trying to make sense of their own contradiction, has implications.

Queer Christian theologies resituate and redefine the parameters for discussions of sexuality and morality. Regardless of one's views, the conversation is different as a consequence of acknowledging homosexuality. Another significant implication is the authoring of a "gay liberation theology" whereby homosexuality is identified as a gift from God. Again, regardless of whether one agrees, this particular discourse is already leading to a re-examination in many denominations of what it means to say that theology should be a "living guide" that reflects its times.

In my own assessment, one of the most noteworthy ideological considerations is the implication of focusing on "unconditional love" as a discursive strategy for accepting and affirming a homosexual presence. Concerning the case of homosexuality, the belief that "god is love" sits in tension with the notion of a patriarchal god who, like the unchallenged parent, sets down rules

that are not to be questioned. An ideology of unconditional love implies a love that is growing and stretching; a love that is manifest among members of a community who interpret for themselves the extent and expression of this love. This is a longstanding tension in Christian theology. Deliberations regarding homosexuality that are framed in terms of "god's unconditional love" tip the equation one degree further toward a rendering of a Christian god who is not an anthropomorphic figure handing down his particular rules. Rather, this god is an expression of agreement and affirmation among a collective body united in spirit and intent. In short, "god" becomes the extent of the community's expression of love. The larger the reach of the group's love, the bigger their god.

A Final Note Regarding "Oppositional Consciousness"

In an attempt to explain lesbian and gay involvement in Christian organizations, some lesbian and gay political activists have suggested that religion is one of the "last citadels" of gay oppression (see Hartman 1996 for a review). These observers see the struggle for inclusion in mainstream religions as a final step toward attaining cultural and political acceptance. In this literature, lesbian and gay Christian involvement is interpreted as a form of political expression whereby queers are taking on traditional homophobia by acting from within. This thesis presumes an "oppositional consciousness" (Mansbridge 2001) that conflates outcomes (religious reform) with motivation and presumes a motivation (desire to reform religion) that is not necessarily reflective of the actual experiences of lesbian and gay Christians. My research suggests that there are several stages in self-awareness and articulation that occur before any form of "oppositional consciousness" develops among lesbian and gay Christians. To the extent that such a consciousness is developing, I suggest that it is historically unique and should be understood within the context in which it is developing. Specifically, the motivation should be understood in terms of the homosexual Christian's desire for self-understanding in Christian terms and reintegration into a system of meaning from which he/she has been cast off.

Sociological theses such as Mansbridge's "oppositional consciousness" or Roof's "creative dialogue" are useful in providing a general framework of analysis, but they miss the mark in interpreting motivations and commitments. Roof's thesis is intended to explain what he views as a "shopping" mentality regarding contemporary religion, in which the individual shops around in search of a congregation or denomination that fits personal needs. Queer Christian identities appear to be motivated more by the desire for (re)integration within Christian traditions, at which point the individual may begin to "shop" for a welcoming congregation. Similarly, while it is certainly possible to view the growing lesbian and gay visibility within Christian organizations as a manifestation of "oppositional consciousness," I think it would be inaccurate and misleading to assume a political motivation for this involvement. An intended contribution of this study is to make clear that lesbian and gay Christian participation (and related activism) must be understood on its own terms, in its own context and in terms of the particular historical moment.

NOTES

1. In this paper I use the phrase "lesbian and gay" because it is the most accurate description of the group about which I am writing. The term "lesbian/gay/bisexual/transgender" (LGBT) is politically strategic and meaningful, but often not descriptively accurate in specific case studies.

2. Several colleagues and interviewees have indicated that the experiences of Jewish lesbians and gays

are similar. In this project, I have maintained a focus on mainstream Christian denominations because of my familiarity with Christian theology. For studies in Jewish queer experience, see Schneer and Aviv (2002) and Balka and Rose (1991).

3. During the course of my formal research, Seattle First Baptist was one of a handful of recent Baptist denominations in the United States that were threatened with revocation of their charter for affirming lesbian and gay membership. Other congregations that were the spiritual homes to several of my interviewees struggled with similar tensions within their denominational organizations, especially congregations attempting to appoint lesbian and gay ministers and those that supported standing ministers who had recently "come out" to the congregation.

4. This ethnography is limited, especially in what it suggests regarding variations of gender, race, and geography on the articulation of and circumstances surrounding a queer Christian identity. I expect that there are significant variations in terms of the dimensions of gender and race, and I suspect these interact differently in different geographical regions. This study highlights one variation on the theme of individual reconciliation of homosexuality and Christianity. It should be read in terms of what it can suggest for further research regarding different variations on this theme.

5. There is a notable historical correlation between gay political movements, Christian denominations' heightened discussion of the "homosexual question"—including the revision of the Catechism—and the removal of "homosexuality" as a category of pathology in the 1974 *Diagnostic and Statistical Manual* used by the American Psychiatric Association to identify and diagnose psychological disorders.

6. Article Six, section 2359: "Homosexual persons are called to chastity. By the virtues of self-mastery that teach them inner freedom, at times by the support of disinterested friendship, by prayer and sacramental grace, they can and should gradually and resolutely approach Christian perfection" (Catechism of the Catholic Church 1994, 566).

7. This explanation is consistent with a social psychological literature demonstrating that dominant belief systems are usually not rejected in the face of contradiction. Rather, individuals attempt to make

sense of the contradictions through "secondary elaborations" (Mehan and Wood 1975, 197). The motivation for continued engagement in the belief system is the desire to maintain a coherent system of meaning regarding the meaning and purpose of one's life. Even problematic positions within the system of meaning can be less threatening than having no sense of meaning or basis for self-understanding. This literature can be used to explain seemingly incomprehensible behavior such as attendance at one's own "degradation ceremony" (e.g., the Mormon who participates in her/his own excommunication process).

8. Stuart also points out the similarities with other Christians, such as Christian feminists or Christian ecologists, who must also explain and justify their religious commitments.

9. I am not implying that these responses are mutually exclusive or fixed. Rather, it is probable that during the course of a queer Christian career individuals try on aspects of each these responses. It is beyond the scope of this paper to develop an explanation for primary self-expression through one response or another—a settling in to a particular expression of identity. I assume that various reference groups play a part in this process and that, over time, the proliferation of an articulated queer Christianity will in itself serve as one such point of reference for a new generation of queer youth. I offer some suggestions toward such an explanation in the conclusions.

10. All quotes from subjects used in this article are intended to be illustrative (rather than analytically definitive). For this reason I do not give detailed subject descriptions. These descriptions are available on request. All of the interviewees in this study elected to use their real names. For reasons of "voice" this is my preferred ethnographical practice.

11. Although nothing conclusive can be ascertained from my few interviews, this phenomenon of simultaneous awakening of homosexuality and spiritual vocation may be more prevalent among young men. Nineteen of the 25 men I interviewed spoke of this experience. Only two of the women mentioned a similar feeling. In fact, the women tended to develop a strong sense of spirituality and desire for religious involvement sometime after coming to terms with their homosexuality. Two of the men offered an explanation of their early sense of vocation as being a means of making them feel better about their homosexuality. As one put it, "God wouldn't have made me this way if he didn't have something special in mind for my life." Another noted that he considered his experience somewhat normal "for someone who was meant to be a priest. . .after all, aren't all priests supposed to be gay? I figured that my attraction to men, including one of the teachers at my [Catholic] school, was just God's way of making it clear that I was meant to be a priest."

12. Evangelicalism is another domain of Christianity whose members experience struggle and are likely to view this struggle as a definitive aspect of themselves and their religious commitment. Smith, C. 1998. American Evangelicalism: Embattled and Thriving. Chicago: University of Chicago Press.

13. For another interesting example, see Gloria Gonzalez-Lopez's (2004) study of Catholic Mexican immigrant women and their sex lives.

14. In the past two decades, many lesbian and gay Christians embraced the hypothesis that homosexuality is genetic rather than socially determined. This essentialist position was consistent with the idea that if homosexuality exists, God must have intended it. Catholicism has accepted the essentialist proposition of biological determinism explicitly without accepting the corollary that homosexuality is a positive characteristic. The latter is the queer twist on the essentialist proposition. But belonging to a denomination that accepted the initial proposition made it easier to make the case for the possible goodness and purpose of homosexuality. Other denominations, notably Mormonism, state explicitly that homosexuality is a "lifestyle choice" that a person should resist by every possible means, no matter how strong the inclination. For a discussion of the intersection of essentialist and constructionist reasoning within Christian considerations of sexuality, see Boswell (1997).

REFERENCES

Anzaldua, G. 1987. *Borderlands/La Frontera: The new Mestiza*. San Francisco: Aunt Lute Books.

Balka, C., and Rose, A., ed. 1991. *Twice blessed: On being lesbian, gay and Jewish*. Boston, MA: Beacon.

Boswell, J. 1997. Concepts, experience, and sexuality. In *Que(e)rying religion: A critical anthology*, ed. G. D. Comstock and S. E. Henking. New York: Continuum.

Bouldrey, B., ed. 1995. *Wrestling with the angel: Faith and religion in the lives of gay men*. New York: Riverhead Books.

Catechism of the Catholic Church. 1994. United States Catholic Conference, *Libreria Editrice Vaticana*. Mahwah, NJ: Paulist Press.

Comstock, G. D. 1997. *Que(e)rying Religion: A Critical Anthology*. New York: Continuum.

Conrad, P., and Schneider, J. 1980. Homosexuality: From sin to sickness to lifestyle. In *Deviance and medicalization: From badness to sickness*, ed. P. Conrad and J. Schneider. Philadelphia: Temple University Press.

Cornell-Drury, P. 2000. Seattle First Christian Church unanimously becomes "open & affirming Letter to the congregation, 6 November, Seattle, WA.

Fortunato, J. 1982. *Embracing the exile: Healing journeys of gay Christians*. San Francisco: Harper Collins.

Gill, S., ed. 1998. *The lesbian and gay christian movement: Campaigning for justice, truth, and love*. London: Cassell.

Gluckman, A., and Reed, B., ed. 1997. *Homo Economics*. New York: Routledge.

Gonzalez-Lopez, G. 2004. *Beyond the bed sheets, beyond the borders: Mexican immigrant women and their sex lives*. Berkeley: University of California Press.

Harryman, Don D. 1991. With all thy getting, get understanding. In *Peculiar people: Mormons and same-sex orientation*, ed. R. Schow, W. Schow and M. Raynes, Salt Lake City: Signature Books.

Hartman, K. 1996. *Congregations in conflict: The battle over homosexuality*. New Brunswick, NJ: Rutgers University Press.

Mansbridge, J. 2001. The making of oppositional consciousness. In *Oppositional consciousness: The subjective roots of social protest*, ed. J. Mansbridge and A. Morris, Chicago: University of Chicago Press.

McNeill, J. 1996. *Taking a chance on god: Liberating theology for gays, lesbians, and their lovers, families, and friends*, Boston, MA: Beacon.

Mehan, H., and Wood, H. 1975. Five features of reality. In *Reality of ethnomethodology*, ed. H. Mehan and H. Wood. New York: Wiley.

Nestle, J. 2002. How a "liberationist" fem understands being a Jew. In *Queer Jews*, ed. D. Schneer and C. Aviv. New York: Routledge.

O'Brien, J. 2001a. Boundaries and contradictions in self articulation. In *The production of reality*, ed. J. O'Brien and P. Kollock. Newbury Park, CA: Pine Forge Press.

O'Brien, J. 2001b. Homophobia and heterosexism. In *International encyclopedia of the social and behavioral sciences*. London: Elsevier Science.

Plummer, K. 1995. *Telling sexual stories: Power, change, and social worlds*. London: Routledge.

Roof, W. C. 1999. *Spiritual marketplace: Baby boomers and the remaking of American Religion*. Princeton, NJ: Rutgers University Press.

Schneer, P. and Aviv, C. 2002. *Queer Jews*. New York: Routledge.

Smith, R. L. 1994. *AIDS, gays and the American Catholic church*. Cleveland, OH: Pilgrim Press.

Stuart, E. 1997. *Religion is a queer thing: A guide to the Christian faith for lesbian, gay, bisexual and transgendered people*. Cleveland, OH: Pilgrim Press.

Tigert, L. M. 1997. *Coming out while staying in: Struggles and celebrations of lesbians and gays in the church*. United Church Press, Cleveland, Ohio.

White, D. and White, O. K. 2004. Queer Christian confessions: Spiritual autobiographies of gay Christians. *Culture and Religion* 5 (2).

Wilcox, Melissa. 2000. Two roads converged: Religion and identity among lesbian, gay, bisexual and transgender Christians. Doctoral Dissertation, University of California, Santa Barbara.

37

"We Are Graceful Swans Who Can Also Be Crows"

Hybrid Identities of Pakistani Muslim Women

Lubna Chaudhry

(1998)

This is the story of four young women: Nida, Aisha, Fariha, and Sabeen.[1] All four identified themselves as Pakistani, Muslim, and immigrant. When I met them in the spring of 1992 after I moved to Northern California, they had all been living in the United States for six, ten, or more years. With the exception of Aisha, they were born in Pakistan and immigrated to the United States directly from there.

In April 1992, Nida was in her mid-twenties and finishing up her premedical requirements. She lived in the Bay Area with her mother, daughter, and husband. She entered a private medical school in the fall of that year. When we started to interact, Aisha was almost nineteen and in her first year of college. She had moved from Southern California, where her parents were at that time, to live in the same university town as I did in April 1992. At that time, Fariha was around sixteen, attending high school, and living with her mother and siblings in a town in the Central Valley. Sabeen was fifteen and also lived in the Central Valley with her parents and brother. She had been out of school for four years. She had managed to elude school authorities because her family moved around a lot. At one point, she was sent to Pakistan to attend school, but her mother became ill, so she came back to the United States to take care of her.

When I first began to interview and observe the four women, I had some notion of figuring out how they were oppressed as women, as Pakistanis,

and as Muslims. The more I got to know them, the more I realized how complex their lives were. There was no neat and simple way I could reduce their multifaceted everyday realities to tidy categories. Their experiences in different family, community, and institutional contexts, and their perceptions of these experiences, were interconnected in some ways and yet very distinctive in others.

Ultimately, I became more interested in analyzing how these young women forged new cultural identities, hybrid identities, in their bids to empower themselves in the community and in school. I was struck by how consistently these women were confronting power structures through everyday practices that could be seen as acts of creative resistance.[2] I wanted to understand more fully how their identities were socially reconstituted by their individual responses to cultural symbols, power relations, and material conditions that limited and shaped opportunities in particular social contexts.[3] I wanted to focus particularly on how, in reconstructing their ethnic identities, these women were bringing together very different traditions of thought.[4]

I grounded my analysis of the identity formation processes in women-of-color feminist theories. I was especially influenced by theories of differential oppositional consciousness.[5] These theories refer to the guerrilla strategies developed by women of color in response to oppressive conditions. Flexibility becomes a key to survival, as women of color self-consciously take up and discard various identities for various lengths of time and in different contexts as an oppositional tactic to power structures.

Here, I will describe the manner in which hybrid identities were deployed by Pakistani Muslim immigrant women to resist power relations in some contexts. The stories of Nida, Aisha, Fariha, and Sabeen enabled me to grasp more clearly the relationship between a multiplicity of identities and resistance to power relations. First, I will present an overview of the relationship between hybridity and resistance that emerged from these stories. Next, for each of the four young women, I will provide specific instances of how resistance was articulated through the maneuvering of hybridity.

THE NATURE OF HYBRIDITY: MULTIPLE IDENTITIES AND WORLDVIEWS

The concept of hybridity encompasses the fluid state of having multiple, shifting identities which are constructed and differentially privileged in response to contextual demands for alienation and allegiance. It also subsumes the protean condition of possessing multiple systems of meaning. Such multiple worldviews synthesize modes of cognition drawn from traditions of thought or cultural systems generally perceived as distinct or disparate.

The four women saw being Pakistani and Muslim as their primary identities. Their conceptions of what these identities symbolized were, however, contingent upon experiences and encounters in the United States. Fresh interactions opened up the possibilities for different kinds of identification and distancing processes. Their identities and their conceptions of these identities shifted depending on the context and the power relations. In a given context, one identity became more salient than others. Thus, their identities in different times and places could be contradictory or inconsistent.

The four young women were born and raised in families who adhered to cultural values and traditions which supposedly have their origins in different parts of Pakistan. Yet given the history of conquest, multiple colonizations, and immigration through the centuries in that part of the world, the idea that there ever was a pure culture in any region of Pakistan is a myth. Pakistan itself is a legacy of colonialism, as India was partitioned by the British before they left. The identities and value systems of those who live in the country continue to be ruptured and hybridized by neocolonial processes. The four young women and their families already had hybrid cultural systems when they came to the United States. In order to survive and function in the United States, they had to extend and modify their systems of meaning in accordance with previously unknown power relations. Furthermore, at times they had to learn and enact behaviors that sometimes contradicted each other. The hybridization of cultural systems for Aisha, Nida, Sabeen, Fariha, and their families was not additive, in that their worldview, at a certain point in time, could not be neatly segmented into its Pakistani or American parts or traced back to its antecedents.

The hybridity of the four women, then, was dynamic—simultaneously an attribute and a phenomenon, always transforming to suit the needs of changing contextual realities. Identification processes, systems of meaning, memories of past experiences, and power relations intersected in complex ways to produce their particular situations. In numerous contexts specific types of hybridization processes were deemed mandatory by the workings of power structures. The women, for instance, had little choice in refusing their identities as immigrants when seeking health services or renewing their green cards. Still, in some contexts, the women had more choice about the deployment of their hybridity. In such instances, the young women could either conform to the demands of the power relations or resist them through adhering to a certain identity or a particular discourse. It is this exercise of agency in resisting power relations that interested me.

Although the four women identified themselves as Pakistani Muslim women, and were exposed to cultural influences in Pakistani families and U.S. society, each young woman's hybridity was distinctive, rooted in her life circumstances and experiences. Each of the four women was marginalized, silenced, and oppressed in different contexts as a woman, as a Muslim, as a Pakistani, as a perceived minority in the United States, or as a conglomerate of these identities, yet they varied in how they interpreted the same identity labels. Their interpretation of their identification as Pakistani, Muslim, and female, and their hybrid worldviews, were shaped by such factors as family income and status in U.S. society, their links with Pakistan, immigration history, regional and ethnic affiliation, religious sect, age, relationships with family members, peer-group influences, and community, as well as neighborhood affiliations. It followed that their use of their hybridity to enact resistance would also be circumscribed by their particular realities. The potential for resistance, then, emerged from the effects of the same power centers structuring the marginal existence of these women and forcing them to hybridize their worldviews and identities. Nida's hybridity and resistance, for instance, were delimited by her family's higher socioeconomic status, just as Sabeen's were defined by her working-class background. Although they both shared a marginality born of their Pakistani and Muslim origins, this marginality manifested itself differentially because of their different circumstances.

Through the manipulation of their hybridity, the four women, in different ways and in different contexts, articulated resistant practices. The resistance was sometimes a reaction to perceived threats to identities or values. When it was felt, for instance, that Muslims, either individually or as a group, were being attacked, verbally or otherwise, the women performed behaviors which they saw as being true to their Muslim heritage. At other times, the resistance was a strategy to satisfy needs or desires arising from hybrid realities which certain power centers might be attempting to suppress. Although different identities were sometimes privileged in

different contexts, it was also very important to the women to be recognized as Pakistani Muslim young women in America, and not just Pakistani Muslim or American. They asserted their "Americanness" in contexts where it was overlooked and stressed their Muslim and Pakistani origins when these were negated. To varying degrees, they were very aware that their being Muslim and Pakistani was influenced by being in the United States. Many times the resistance was an attempt to carve out circumstances where threats were dispelled and needs were fulfilled. Hybridity was then deployed to validate hybridity itself.

Resistance took on a variety of forms. For example, the women, depending on their intent, engaged in acts of cultural translation.[6] They executed behaviors in contexts where they appeared anomalous as a challenge to power relations. These behaviors were drawn from their hybrid repertoire of diverse cultural practices. The cultural practices had a specific meaning within the context of either their personal histories or the history of a group with whom they identified. Another form of resistance was the skillful conformity to the demands of various contexts in order to serve a cause of objective which otherwise would be jeopardized.

SABEEN: DEFYING RELATIONAL BOUNDARIES

Sabeen did not go to school in the United States after fourth grade, and her contact with the outside world was minimal. When I knew her, she spent most of her time in the one-bedroom apartment she shared with her parents and two brothers. In addition to instructing children about the Koran and teaching Urdu at the local Islamic center, she would occasionally go grocery shopping, visit me, or sneak out to see her friend Anna and Anna's mother, Mimi. Despite her limited exposure to U.S. society, she was the only one of the four young women who had an intense, close friendship with someone who identified herself as "just American." Sabeen's friendship with

Anna, a white teenager, was an act of resistance on many different levels.

In fact, Sabeen was going against the patriarchal norms her father upheld, values which he claimed were integral to his honor as a member of the Pushtun clan, an ethnic group from the northwestern mountains of the Indian subcontinent. As the daughter of an upstanding Pushtun family, she could violate the family honor by befriending a woman who would be considered immoral by their clan. Women born and raised in the United States were suspect in general, especially non-Muslim women, and Anna did not hide her intimate connections with men. Sabeen incurred her father's wrath several times by allowing Anna to visit her (Sabeen's father's sense of hospitality as a Pushtun prevented him from being outright rude to Anna) or by arranging to meet her in the grocery store. She also faced the possibility of very serious repercussions by secretly accompanying Anna to parties and other outdoor expeditions on a few occasions.

Sabeen's friendship with Anna crossed racial, ethnic, and cultural borders. Sabeen had never had a Caucasian friend before, and all of Anna's other friends were white. On the surface the two teenagers had very little in common. The power balance in the friendship could easily have tilted in Anna's favor. Not only was she white and an American by birth, but she was also the one in school. Sabeen, however, asserted her own terms, and despite occasional friction, their friendship survived because of a mutual empathy deriving to a large extent from shared class and gender affiliations. The fondness they both exhibited for slapstick comedy also helped.

Through the building and maintenance of an alliance along class and gender lines, the two teenagers went beyond the racial barriers enacted by power centers to support the status quo in capitalistic societies. These divisions operate by drawing attention away from the common issues of those who are at the bottom of the totem pole. Sabeen and Anna, however, while acknowledging their own limitations, displayed an overall willingness to explore each other's worldviews and learn about each other's realities. Their friendship, thus, challenged power structures that sanctioned "othering" processes which have historically been used to rationalize colonization and slavery of "other" races in different parts of the world.

Sabeen's approach to friendship and the manner in which she expressed that friendship, verbally and otherwise, could be perceived as cultural translation. She exhibited strong feelings toward Anna. Her involvement with Anna and the life of Anna's mother was intense. She displayed and expected a level of commitment from the friendship which was not typically associated with nonsexual relationships between teenage girls in Anna's circle of friends. The politics of emotions which characterized her friendship, according to mainstream patriarchal ideas in U.S. society, were reserved for the domain of romantic love between males and females.

Since she did not go to school for long and she did not work a lot outside the home, Sabeen had not been socialized into establishing the transient, working kind of relationships which are intrinsically bound up with the functioning of capitalist societies. Throughout her life Sabeen had been exposed to very strongly positive views about the value of friendships between people of the same sex. The better-known stories in her clan, which her father related to Sabeen and her brothers, were about men and boys dying for each other. Her mother, and during her childhood her relatives in Pakistan, had narrated to her tales about powerful connections between women or girls and the sacrifices these females for each other. Sabeen found the script for friendship handed to her through these stories infinitely more appealing than her reading of the dynamics of female friendships in U.S. society. She felt that relationships with boys were given priority. She told me how she had spent years imagining a very close friendship with another girl. Her relationship with Anna gave her the chance to prove her mettle as someone who could love her friend.

In her friendship with Anna, Sabeen deployed modes of relationality that she had learned at home in the United States and in Pakistan through her interactions and experiences with her immediate, as well as extended, family. As a member of an ethnic culture which was segregated on the basis of gender, Sabeen had been socialized into a strong sense of solidarity with the other females in her life. Her refusal to continue her formal schooling reflected, at one level, her determination to ally herself with her mother's sphere. She was close to her father and loved her brothers, but her first loyalty was to her mother and other kinswomen. It was this loyalty, underpinned by the realization that as females they all needed to support one another in a world where men made most of the rules, which she extended to Anna and her mother.

Sabeen was very conscious of her friendship as being transgressive on these different counts. She admitted that at times she was herself surprised at her closeness with Anna. She had never thought she could be friends with a white girl, because all the white girls seemed arrogant, superficial, and uncaring, especially toward other females. Her impressions, based on television representations and observations in stores, were validated by her memories of the bitter experiences she had as a child in school. Both white boys and girls had mistreated her, but she had been more disappointed and hurt by the girls' behavior. Evidently, she had not expected anything better from the boys. Sabeen's responsiveness toward Anna's bid for friendship was, therefore, in itself a hybridization process. She was revising her worldview vis-à-vis white females even as she tentatively reciprocated Anna's friendliness. The hybridization of her system of meaning continued as her friendship with Anna evolved.

Sabeen's friendship with Anna created new identities for her. In keeping with the context, she was, by turns, a friend, a teenaged female, and a lower-class person. She learned she could sometimes identify with a white girl, with someone who did not share her primary identities as Pakistani, Muslim, and Pushtun.

In addition to providing the terrain for complex identification processes, the friendship proved to be instrumental in offering Sabeen the opportunity to reaffirm and reevaluate her identities as Pakistani, Muslim, and Pushtun. Interactions with Anna, Anna's family, and Anna's other friends were at times characterized by a different kind of hybridizing process—alienation or distancing processes which entailed sharp, and often poignant, realizations of her differences in worldview, experiences, and allegiances from her friend. Sabeen extended her repertoire of acceptable behaviors and experiences to be around Anna or to take care of her. She found, however, that certain values were integral to her sense of self, especially when she felt someone expected her to give them up.

In cultivating the friendship with Anna and then honoring the commitment to the friendship, Sabeen was satisfying her need for companionship with someone of her age, as well as her desire to have a meaningful relationship on her terms. The satisfaction of the desire entailed resisting multilayered power regimes. The friendship became an assertion of agency on Sabeen's part. This agency in its turn derived its impetus from Sabeen's interpretation of multiple systems of meaning and the resulting conception of what it meant for her to have a fulfilling life.

FARIHA: ROMANCING RESISTANCE

For Fariha, a romantic liaison, which led to an elopement, became the means to resist her mother's authority. It also became a recourse to demonstrate to her peers at school that she did not have to compromise on the values she held sacred in order to have a man in her life. Fariha's idea of romance stemmed from her viewing of films from the Indian subcontinent. Her ideas were further nurtured by her attempts to read translations of the love stories written by famous Punjabi Sufi poets. In many East Indian and Pakistani films and in most of the Sufi renditions of heterosexual love, passion between men and women is a subversive force capable of undermining the dominant order, for which the segregation of sexes served as a mechanism of control. Such love was untainted by earthly considerations, and its consummation involved a union at the spiritual level. The physical realm was secondary or completely insignificant.

Fariha's mother had high expectations of her. Fariha was her oldest child and daughter, and she saw Fariha as responsible for her younger siblings. She was the one who was supposed to set an example of good performance at school, as well as proper behavior in line with Islamic principles and Punjabi cultural traditions. She desperately wanted Fariha to excel at school and pave the way for the advancement of the family. She also believed she had to be strict with Fariha and protect her from the negative influences of U.S. society. Her husband had not been able to withstand the temptations and the pressures of living in a comparatively less morally structured culture. He had taken to alcohol and womanizing, eventually abandoning his wife and the children. Fariha's mother felt Fariha was even more vulnerable to external societal forces. She was, after all, at an impressionable age.

Fariha, on the other hand, felt pressured by her mother's expectations and frustrated because her mother did not seem to understand the dilemmas and demands of having to cope with more than one culture. She respected her mother's faith in education and agreed, to a large extent, with her attitudes about morality and codes of behavior. Yet even as she judged her peers for being immodest or too invested in the physical side of love, she envied them their freedom to spend more time with people of their own age and to experiment with flirtation and sexually charged situations. Moreover, she craved acceptance by the very same peers she sometimes viewed as immoral. Fariha thought she could obtain that acceptance if young men were interested in her or if she led a less restricted existence. On several occasions, her sheltered existence was the butt of unkind jokes and cutting comments.

Despite he pressures of her situation, Fariha could not bring herself to be involved with someone who did not share, or at least understand, her upbringing and value systems. When boys at her school, at different points in time, exhibited behaviors which she perceived as attempts at flirtation, even seduction, Fariha backed off in trepidation. It was not until she met Razzaq, a young man who had just arrived from Pakistan, that she felt comfortable enough to explore the possibility of a romantic relationship. Razzaq might not have shared Fariha's idealized notion of romantic love, but he was definitely familiar with the conceptions structuring her reality. Besides realizing her romantic fantasies, Fariha's relationship with Razzaq gave her an opportunity to be really close to someone. This closeness was probably only approximated by her connection to one of her aunts before she got married and went to live with her husband. Razzaq was her best friend, as well as someone who could take her away from the miseries she encountered at school and the restrictions she lived with at home.

Fariha's elopement with Razzaq was a bold gesture of defiance. When her mother found out about the romance, her outrage at her daughter's behavior seemed to push Fariha further towards rebellion. She later told me she had insisted on getting married right away because she had not wanted to besmirch her family's honor in any way. Any kind of love that violated honor was not pure and sincere. Her subsequent return to her mother and insistence on an annulment of her marriage were never really clarified. From hints and certain details she revealed during our conversations, my inference was that she had been insulted by Razzaq's attempts to have sexual intercourse even before they had spent time to get to know each other better. She also started to suspect that Razzaq might have married her because she had an American passport.

Within the context of Fariha's life and circumstances, romance became a way of simultaneously resisting and satisfying the demands of various power relations structuring her reality. As a teenager in American society, she felt compelled to assert her sexuality. However, Fariha shared her family's general negative attitude toward the open expression of physical desires. She also shared their mistrust of those who were perceived as too "American" and unable to relate to people at a deep spiritual and emotional level. Despite her internal conflicts, the belief system she had internalized in home and community contexts with respect to love and sexuality prevented her from following the example of her peers.

Fariha constructed her script for romance, to a certain degree, from alternatives offered to her by sources from her region of origin. However, this script was mediated by the immediacy of her American existence. Her take on love and passion reflected her hybrid positioning. Her meeting with Razzaq resulted in further hybridization processes. She initially identified with Razzaq as a Pakistani and as someone who shared her view on love. Such a view privileged emotional closeness. Her romance with Razzaq, therefore, allowed her to assert her agency in the face of the narratives of romance imposed on her by U.S. society and by family traditions. She could have the kind of love in her life that she wanted and remain true to her cultural traditions. Her peers might not believe in the existence of love which was founded on bonds other than the physical, and her mother might not have faith in marital arrangements which departed from traditional norms in that they were based on love before marriage. But she could show them, through here experiences, that she could bring these different worlds together!

Fariha's romance did not unfold in the manner that she had expected. Her resistance to power structures continued when she did not give in to Razzaq's demands. She opted for an annulment because he had disappointed her in certain ways. Again it was important to her that she live up to her own expectations, and she manipulated prescribed scripts to suit her situation. Her family ended up helping her get the annulment. Patriarchal notions which represented daughters as the receptacles of family honor were harnessed to override the obligations decreed by other kinds of patriarchal norms pertaining to the institution of marriage.

AISHA: TRANSPLANTING THE *HIJAB*

The *hijab*, in the initial stages of the spread of Islam, was a strategy adopted by women to protect themselves from unwanted advances.[7] Aisha's adoption of the *hijab* while attending a university in the United States was a strategic, creative response to what she perceived as the undue stress on sexuality in her present environment. It was also a proclamation of her affiliation with Muslims. She especially wanted to represent her identification with young Muslims at college in the United States who believed in the inevitability of an Islamic state where people would live peacefully according to Koranic injunctions. Such a belief was very much a by-product of the anti-Muslim sensibility evident in the Euro-American media and the global political scene.

Aisha's use of the *hijab* constituted an act of cultural translation. Aisha articulated a cultural practice in an incongruous context in such a manner that the practice retained its historicity and the articulation expressed an awareness of and challenge to dominant relations of power. By covering her hair she resisted prescribed norms of beauty in U.S. society, which objectified women. Aisha deeply resented not being appreciated for her intellect and qualities other than her physical attributes. She decided to don the *hijab* in order to discourage attention from the "wrong kind of men." In reality, the *hijab* proved to be an effective screening mechanism, and Aisha was not very happy about the number of suitors and admirers she lost! Although her rationale was anchored in her realization of the historic significance of the *hijab* for Muslim women, Aisha's reasoning was motivated by her own experiences in U.S. society. The subversive potential of the *hijab* for Aisha stemmed from her interpretation of her surroundings. She found parallels between Medina in a state of civil war and the aggressive emphasis on sexuality around her.[8] The *hijab* took on a new meaning in the context of her life and the power relations structuring it.

Aisha's choice to wear the *hijab* reflected an attempt to exhibit a specific kind of Muslim identity. Her family identified themselves as Muslim, but neither her mother nor her sister wore the *hijab*. In fact, her mother strongly discouraged her from covering her hair because she was worried that "educated and modern Muslim men" would not want to marry Aisha. She would be seen as "backward." For Aisha, the *hijab* as an option emerged from her participation in Muslim students' organizations on the various campuses she attended. Within the context of the on-campus activities of these organizations, the *hijab* was a symbol of the Muslim woman's allegiance to the collective empowerment of Muslims in general, and Muslim students on U.S. campuses in particular. Aisha's decision to don the *hijab* was not just a declaration of loyalty to the causes of these organizations. Still, her interactions with other Muslim students she met in college and university did generate complex identification processes which were instrumental in her consideration of the *hijab* as an option. The donning of the *hijab* did seem to signify a crystallization of her Muslim identity as a form of politics. It was, therefore, not coincidental that she decided to incorporate an expression of her experiences and perspectives as a Muslim woman in her art and writing soon afterward.

Aisha's covering of her hair by the *hijab* could also be perceived as a subscription to patriarchal values generated by power centers within Muslim students' organizations in particular, and larger Muslim institutions in general. Aisha, however, did not regard the *hijab* as oppressive. She argued that pious Muslim men as well as pious Muslim women were supposed to cover their sexualized parts. Moreover, she felt the *hijab* liberated her from certain constraints that characterized interactions between Muslim men and women. She felt men were more comfortable with her, since she did not present herself as a sexual object. The one major concern she had with the *hijab* was that too many practicing, strict, Muslim young men decided she would be a suitable partner for them after just a few cursory meetings.

Aisha did seem to use her *hijab* strategically to gain respect from Muslim men. To a certain degree, the *hijab* ensured her more voice in Muslim organizations. Nonetheless, the *hijab* was politically useful to Aisha only because of her specific commitment to the causes of Muslim women, her oppositional consciousness, and her interest in negotiating with those who shared her religious and cultural affiliations.

However, Aisha did not wholly subscribe to the notion of purdah.[9] She wore the *hijab* but continued to interact with men, Muslim and non-Muslim. She occasionally went through fits of remorse because she felt she engaged in an inordinate amount of verbal flirtation. She admitted that she enjoyed flirtation a lot. She could not understand why men sent her marriage proposals without getting to know her better even when it was pointed out to her that it was customary to do so in Pakistan. The *hijab* guaranteed her a certain kind of safety, as well as a sense of belonging to a collectivity, but she invested it with a hybrid meaning which echoed her own hybridity.

In certain contexts as an act of cultural translation, in other contexts as an act of strategic conformity, the *hijab* represented Aisha's attempts to negotiate her multiple realities. The negotiation involved resisting dominant ideas of sexuality so as to develop and assert alternative conceptions. The negotiation also meant conforming to patriarchal prescriptions for proper behavior based on Islamic teachings in order to perform a Muslim identity. This performance, given the anti-Muslim sensibilities in U.S. society, assumed a political significance.

NIDA: NEGOTIATING FORMAL EDUCATION

In order to realize her dream of going to medical school, Nida had a baby at eighteen to appease her in-laws. Her marriage had taken place at seventeen. As soon as she graduated from high school, her parents became anxious about her going to college in a coeducational setting. They did not want her to follow American customs of dating. The Syed clan to which she belonged was generally endogamous. Their tradition dictated that marriages happen as soon as possible after the onset of puberty. Moreover, her father's health was bad, and he wanted to perform his duty as a parent in an expedient manner.

Nida's husband was himself a graduate student. He initially supported her educational aspirations wholeheartedly even in the face of opposition from some of his family members. Nida and her parents had made sure he would be supportive when he was chosen as a suitable partner for her. After Nida's marriage and the birth of her daughter, her mother ensured that Nida pursue her goals by helping out with domestic responsibilities and child care herself. She also provided resources in the form of appropriate babysitters brought to the United States from Pakistan.

Nida's position as the daughter of an upper-class, landed family in Pakistan, which strictly adhered to the traditions of its clan, was responsible, to a large degree, for her early marriage and her obligation to have a child just after the marriage. Nida's socioeconomic class in Pakistan, as well as in the United States, and her status as the daughter of landed gentry in Pakistan also paved the way for the continuation of her education after her marriage. She, however, did have to struggle against customs in the family which frowned upon a married woman's perceived neglect of her husband and child. Her access to higher education and her husband's at-times grudging acceptance of her endeavors had a lot to do with her being financially independent. The business her father had set up continued to generate an income for her even after his death. Her mother also had the time to help take care of Zaini, Nida's daughter, because she did not have to work outside the house.

During high school in the United States, Nida was encouraged by her teachers to aim for an advanced degree because of her diligence and intelligence as a student. After she had transferred to U.S. schools from her colonial-style institution in Pakistan, she did not encounter any academic difficulties. However, college was harder because she had to juggle her marriage and her education. She did not enjoy her overextended schedule, but took it in her stride by thinking of it as the American way of life. In her opinion, it was her determination to learn to function effectively in U.S. society by getting to know the rules for different settings that led to her success at different levels.

Although the privileges of her class positioning facilitated her success in the educational sphere, it was Nida who decided that a degree in medicine would provide her the means of self-actualization. She learned to adapt herself strategically to what was required of her in different contexts in U.S. society and her home. She, thus, resisted patriarchal norms within her clan which restricted her roles to that of wife and mother. She also resisted institutionalized sexism within U.S. society which forces women to make a choice between being a mother and having a career. Her worldview juxtaposed devotion to her family and commitment to her educational career, and therefore reflected her hybridity. This hybridity manifested itself externally in her ability to take on multiple identities in keeping with the demands of the multiple contexts.

CONCLUSION: THE POINT OF RESISTANCE

During the summer of 1994, I was visiting Fariha and her mother when Fariha said what ultimately became the title of this essay. Fariha and I were getting ready to see an art exhibition at a local Chicana/o center. Before we left, we dutifully went to the kitchen to take leave of her mother. After surveying our all-black "hip" and "cool" denim outfits, Fariha's mother shrugged her shoulders and uttered a well-known Urdu proverb: "When the crow imitates the walking style of a swan, it forgets even its own walk." Fariha laughed and said, "No, it is the other way around. We are graceful swans who can also be crows. We remember all the ways of walking."

Underlying the resistance exhibited by the four women here was a consciousness of the effects of power relations. This consciousness was born out of their hybridity, their capacity to slip in and out of cultural systems. Of course, with the exception of Aisha, they did not couch their consciousness in terms of the theoretical language about "centers of power" and "marginality" that I am employing in this chapter. Neither was their consciousness constant in all contexts, nor was it complete in that they were always aware of the influences of power regimes in their entirety.

Nevertheless, fragmentary or otherwise, the consciousness of oppressive power structures and their effects led them to articulate practices of resistance. The practices were assertions of their agency, their ability at least to attempt to construct their own realities and control their lives. The conceptions of what constituted resistance and agency were shaped by the array of discourses available to them in different contexts which still surrounded them or which they had internalized during the course of their lifetime. The articulation of resistance and assertion of agency were tied up with their hybrid identities and hybrid worldviews. These complex relationships could only be adequately understood if scrutinized from within the context of their lives.

Although Aisha deployed the *hijab* (an icon transplanted from the Middle East) in her enactment of resistance, the mode she employed was the one that most obviously could be recognized by Euro-American standards. Her resistance, in its utilization of a piece of clothing to perform identity and express a viewpoint, was reminiscent of the methods employed by youth subcultures in Western contexts. Moreover, she was an active participant in Muslim organizations that followed Western-derived norms of resistance.

The resistance exhibited by Nida, Fariha, and Sabeen did not fall under the rubric of organized politics in the sense in which it is understood in common parlance in the United States. Yet in their everyday lives they continued to conform to or defy power relations in accordance with their perceived needs and desires. In doing so, they highlighted the multiplicity in the effects of the

centers of power, as well as the potential for everyday practices to challenge these centers. Although they were not engaged in supporting political agendas in the style accepted as bona fide resistance, they were hardly passive victims of the power structures around them.

The resistance displayed by the four young women, organized or otherwise, points to the existence of spaces on the margins where the effects of power structures are attenuated. The four young women, through engagement with collectivities, acts of cultural translation, as well as strategic conformity and defiance in different contexts, effectively executed resistance to oppressive power structures. Their stories clearly illustrate that through a strategic use of hybridity, multiple systems of thought can be deployed to subvert power relations.

NOTES

1. All names have been changed to preserve anonymity.

2. My conception of everyday practices as creative resistance was developed through a reading of M. de Certeau's *Practice of Everyday Life* (Berkeley: University of California Press, 1984).

3. M. P. Smith and B. Tarallo, "The Postmodern City and the Social Construction of Ethnicity in California," in M. Cross and M. Keith (eds.), *Racism, the City, and the State* (London: Routledge, 1993), 61–76, write about how cultural identities of new immigrants are socially reconstituted when they construct themselves as "social actors" who "respond to the material conditions, semiotic codes, and power relations shaping the opportunities and constraints of a historically specific time and place" (61).

4. S. Hall, "New Ethnicities," in J. Donald and A. Rattansi (eds.), *Race, Culture, and Difference* (New York: Sage, 1992), 252–59, refers to this reconstruction of diasporic identities as "new ethnicities." H. Bhabha, "The Third Space: Interview with Homi Bhabha," in J. Rutherford (ed.), *Identity* (London: Wishart, 1990), 206–21, writes of this cultural reconstitution as cultural hybridization, a process which involves the "yoking together of unlikely traditions of thought" (212). Those engaged in hybridization processes are hybrids.

5. According to C. Sandoval, "U.S. Third World Feminism: The Theory and Method of Oppositional Consciousness in the Postmodern World," *Genders* 10 (1991): 1–24, theories of "differential oppositional consciousness" refer to the "grace, flexibility, and strength" developed by women of color as a response to oppressive conditions, which enable them "to confidently commit to a well-defined structure of identity for one hour, day, week, month, year," and "to self-consciously transform that identity according to the requisites of another oppositional ideological tactic if readings of power formations require it" (15).

6. Bhabha sees hybridity and cultural translation as inextricably linked. Hybridity is the "third space which enables other positions to emerge, . . . sets up new structures of authority, new political initiatives, [and] a new area of negotiation of meaning and representation" (207). Hybrids, those in a state of hybridity, engage in acts of cultural translation whereby certain behaviors

are executed in temporal and spatial realms which have been hitherto atypical contexts for those actions.

7. The Arabic word *hijab* refers to what is commonly called the Muslim veil in Western contexts. It is a scarf worn by some Muslim women to cover their hair.

8. F. Mernissi, *The Veil and the Male Elite: A Feminist Interpretation of Women's Rights in Islam* (New York: Addison-Wesley, 1991), traces the institutionalized adoption of the *hijab* by Muslim women to the early years in Islamic history, when there was a civil war in Medina, a city in Saudi Arabia. She argues that women had to don the *hijab* as a protective strategy because unsafe conditions were created by masculinist warring agendas. During the civil war, the street became a space where the raping of women was permitted, and one way women could avoid being persecuted was to cover themselves.

9. Purdah in a broad sense encompasses traditions in Islam which decree segregation of the sexes and the covering of sexualized body parts.

————————))))) ————————

CONTRADICTIONS AND CHANGE IN CULTURAL PRODUCTION

The examples in the last section of Part V, "The Social Construction of the Cultural Status Quo," explored some of the ways in which interaction results in the persistence of the status quo. This section looks at examples of conflict and change in cultural production.

The idea of a Native American tribe using computer technology to sustain cultural traditions may seem contradictory at first glance. Ellen Arnold and Darcy C. Plymire present the case of a group of Cherokee Indians who are using the Internet as a means of cultural production. As they explain in "Continuity Within Change," the Cherokee find many similarities between Internet technology and the oral traditions used historically to pass on cultural beliefs and practices.

In "Patients, 'Potheads,' and Dying to Get High," Wendy Chapkis analyzes the battle to legalize medical marijuana. Based on an ethnographic study of providers and users of medical marijuana, she notes that the struggle revolves around attempts to redefine traditional beliefs about "patients" and "pharmacies." The process is complicated further by reactions to the experience of "getting high" and the varying interpretations of this experience.

"Adventures in Desocialization" is an excerpt from a book by two creative sociologists, Inge Bell and Bernard McGrane. Writing within the Buddhist tradition of "mindfulness," these authors invite us to step outside our taken-for-granted realities and see the world anew.

"Talking Back" is a short essay from renowned contemporary author and scholar bell hooks. In this brief autobiographical sketch, hooks recalls an event in which it became impossible to maintain the social routine.

Questions for Discussion and Review

1. Describe other examples of contemporary social conflicts that seem similar to the medical marijuana conflict (for example, decriminalization of sex work, abortion, the "war on terror," and so forth). What kind of language does each side in these conflicts use to describe the situation and those involved? Discuss some of the conflicting values and beliefs reflected in the different terms. How does language serve to help establish a particular perspective?

2. In the examples from the previous exercise, describe how conflicting groups attempt to establish themselves as the "authority." What social-psychological processes would explain why people are persuaded by one side or another?

3. Do some of the exercises suggested by Bell and McGrane and discuss your experiences.

4. Discuss one taken-for-granted belief or practice you have reconsidered as a result of studying the material in this book.

CONTRADICTIONS AND CHANGE IN CULTURAL PRODUCTION

38

Continuity Within Change

The Cherokee Indians and the Internet

Ellen L. Arnold and Darcy C. Plymire

(2004)

Current use of the Internet by the Cherokee Indians reflects many aspects of the historical situation of the Cherokees since the early 1800s. The Cherokee people, who called themselves *Ani '-Yun 'wiya,* or the 'Principal People,' at the time of first European contact occupied approximately 135,000 square miles in parts of what are now eight southeastern states. By the early 1800s, their territory had been drastically reduced through treaties and other actions by the US government. One of the so-called Five Civilized Tribes of the Southeast, the Cherokees were quick to adopt many of the ways of the Europeans. In 1821, Sequoyah created the Cherokee Syllabary, which enabled their language to be written, and the Cherokee people quickly gained a greater degree of literacy than their EuroAmerican contemporaries. They drafted their own constitution, published the first Indian newspaper (the *Cherokee Phoenix,* still being published today), and established the town of New Echota in Georgia, which served as both a seat of government and an economic centre for a thriving independent nation.

Under pressure from EuroAmerican settlers seeking gold and land, the US Congress made plans to remove the Cherokee people from their land. Progressive Cherokees, proponents of Americanization, fought in the American courts to force the US government to honour its treaties with the Cherokee Nation, arguing its sovereign status. Many traditionals opposed assimilation into American society; yet the Cherokee Memorials, eloquent documents arguing against removal, demonstrated that even the progressive leaders who drafted them wished to preserve a distinct cultural identity as well as their newly acquired status as 'civilized.' When the Cherokees lost their battle in the courts, 16,000 Cherokees were forced by the US Army to relocate 1000 miles to the west to Indian Territory. On this infamous Trail of Tears, called *Nunadautsun't,* 'the trail where we cried,' in the Cherokee language, more than 4000 Cherokees died.

Several hundred Cherokee people, mostly traditionals, remained in the East, hiding from settlers and soldiers. Eventually they re-established themselves as a nation and, in 1848, were formally recognized by the US government as the Eastern Band of Cherokee Indians. The Eastern Band now numbers about 12,500 enrolled members, a majority of whom live on the Qualla Boundary in western North Carolina, a 56,000-square-acre portion of their original homeland which has its seat in the town of Cherokee. This land, purchased by Will Thomas, the adopted white son of a Cherokee leader, and transferred to the Cherokees in the late 1800s, is now held in trust for the Cherokee people

by the US government and is administered as a reservation. Like other reservations, Qualla Boundary has a complex status as a semi-sovereign nation, exempt from the jurisdiction of state governments in most matters, yet subject to a great deal of control by the federal government. The Western Band of Cherokees, known officially as the Cherokee Nation of Oklahoma, now occupies a jurisdictional service area of 4,480,000 square acres with a capital at Tahlequah, and has approximately 281,000 enrolled members. The United Keetowah Band, a third federally recognized band of Cherokees also located in Oklahoma, numbers more than 7,950. The Cherokees, including numerous bands not recognized by the government, form the largest tribal group in the USA.

The question of assimilation remains relevant to contemporary Cherokee Indians. The construction and use of the official websites of the Eastern Band (www.Cherokee-nc.com) and the Cherokee Nation of Oklahoma (www.Cherokee.org) reflect many elements of the historical relationship of the Cherokee Nation to the nation and government of the USA. (The website of the United Keetowah Band (www.uark.edu/depts/comminfo/UKB) was created in 1997–98 on an academic server, and does not appear to be currently maintained; therefore, we do not include it in our study.) The Oklahoma site primarily serves its community by providing links to human services, political news and organizations, and cultural and historical information. The Eastern Band site provides access to cultural and historical information as well, but because of its proximity to the popular Smoky Mountains National Park and the Blue Ridge Parkway, the Eastern Band has also been able to use its website to help build a thriving tourist economy. Observing the websites as outsiders, we suggest that they are skilfully designed aspects of increasingly successful political and economic efforts to use the dominant paradigm and its technologies to protect and preserve the unique cultural heritage and identity of the Cherokee people and, at the same time, to expand their control over their own affairs and influence on American culture.

THE DEBATES

Cherokee use of the Internet must be considered in light of wider debates about whether computer technology and the Internet medium help to preserve or tend to destroy indigenous cultures and traditions. Mark Trahant (1996), a member of the Shoshone-Bannock tribe of Idaho, speculates that the Internet might be a medium particularly well suited to teaching in Indian communities, because it is more like traditional oral and pictographic forms of communication than are the typical written forms of the dominant culture. The imagery and fluidity of the web, like pictographs, allow the user to enter where he or she will and continue in whatever direction he or she chooses; like the storytelling tradition, in which both teller and audience participate in the exchange of stories and their meaning, the Web undermines both the power of the individual author and the presumed linearity of history. The stories told on the Web, like the stories told in pictographs or oral narration, change according to the teller, listener or user.

According to Trahant, in 1996, the growing numbers of Native Americans using the Internet were onto something. He speculated that growing use of the Internet by tribal groups would have several beneficial consequences. Since the medium requires less capital outlay than print media, Native groups might get their perspectives on political and social issues into circulation more easily. Second, tribes might use the sites to teach language and history, as do the Navajos and the Cherokees. Third, Trahant states that 'one of the oldest battles in the Native American press is over who controls information' (ibid.: 19). Print media may give tribal governments of federal agencies the power of censorship, while the Internet grants individuals a greater voice. Finally, individuals might use the net to communicate with one another, through newsgroups and listservs, to build the bonds of community across time and space.

Trahant's high hopes for the new medium mirrored the utopian tenor of much mainstream scholarship on the Internet. Because of the comparative affordability and accessibility of the Internet, many came to view the medium as a virtual democratic utopia (Levinson, 1997). If Michel Foucault (1980) is correct that the producers of knowledge have power over those who are the subjects of knowledge, then the established media will typically produce relationships of power that privilege those who already hold positions of social power in capitalist societies. The Internet, which opens the publishing field to groups who lack capital and power, can in theory allow marginalized individuals and groups to produce their own knowledge, put it in circulation, and, as a result, gain a greater measure of social power. Kurt Mills (2005) believes the Kurds, oppressed 'inhabitants of a transnational territory' (2002: 81), are living examples of the Internet's potential. They use the medium to create a 'cybernation' (ibid.: 81) of Kurdistan to spread political information and to offer a place where Kurds around the world can express their aspirations for self-determination. In an earlier case, the 1994 Zapatista uprising in Chiapas, Mexico, used the Internet to generate international support in their struggle against the Mexican government for indigenous self-determination and economic survival.

In addition, scholars such as Sherry Turkle claim that 'on the Internet . . . people [may] recast their identity in terms of multiple windows and parallel lives' (1997: 72). Theoretically, one may produce an online identity that does not correspond to one's real-life race, class or gender, or one may produce multiple identities, all of which may be in circulation concurrently. This may make the Internet a particularly effective medium for negotiating the complex and often conflicting demands of both American and tribal cultural identities. According to the cybertopian world-view, 'The Internet deemphasizes hierarchical political associations, degrading gender roles and ethnic designations, and rigid categories of class relationships found in traditional, visually based and geographically bound communities' (Ebo, 1998: 3). Communities online, therefore, have the potential to create meaningful social groups that do not merely reproduce inequalities among real life social groups. If that is the case, then the medium might be a force for building more egalitarian communities by breaking down race, gender and class barriers.

Many question the cultural implications of virtual community for Native Americans, however. *New York Times* writer Elizabeth Cohen summarized concerns of Native spokespersons she interviewed that 'Web sites may not always represent the people and tribes they say they do, and that certain sacred and guarded cultural knowledge could be misunderstood or misused if it ends up on the Web' (1997: 2); she especially decried '"cyber-shamans" [who] feign tribal affiliation to sell various so-called native goods and services' (ibid.: 3). Lakota scholar Craig Howe argued that, because land and geographic location are fundamental to specific tribal identities, 'the pervasive universalism and individualism of the World Wide Web is antithetical to the particular localities, societies, moralities, and experiences that constitute tribalism' (1999: 7). Or, as Dakota/Salish writer Philip Red Eagle put it in an online discussion of the subject in 1999 (NativeLit-L@raven.cc.ukans.edu), 'Community is about responsibility to a specific group of people who practice culture with one another.' Although writing before the invention of the Web, Jerry Mander (1991), a non-Native writer, insisted that the computer destroys ways of thinking and acting fundamental to oral cultures and inculcates values inimical to Indian traditions. Because computers rely on an information exchange model of communication, he argued, they contribute to a world-view that reduces the natural world to resources to be managed and controlled, at the expense of embodied interrelationship with the world that is characteristic of traditional indigenous

lifeways. Bowers, Vasquez and Roaf conclude that the problems identified by critics are unavoidable. The computer is not a neutral technology but a teacher of the sort of 'rootless individualism' (2000: 186) endemic to postmodern consumer culture, in which personal tastes and choice take precedence over belongingness and group identity.

The Internet also may reproduce rather than challenge social inequalities. Though users cannot see each other, they may not have abandoned all judgements on the basis of race, class, gender and ethnicity. While individuals and minority groups may more easily 'publish' on the Internet, readership may be more limited, so knowledge and ideas that challenge the status quo may remain marginalized. Similarly, access to the Internet is not equally distributed along lines of race, class, gender and ethnicity. It could be argued that the democratic potential of the Internet has not yet been fully realized.

As in many other disciplines, research and critical attention to Indian use of the Internet is ghettoized, limited primarily to studies specifically about Native Americans. Such a practice reproduces what many have called 'the vanishing Indian syndrome' by implying that Indians no longer exist as a vital and influential part of the American population. A 1999 report by the National Telecommunications and Information Administration (NTIA) failed to include statistics on Native Internet use. The Digital Divide Network (Twist, 2002) reports that the exclusion of Indians from the NTIA study hampers the efforts of individuals and groups lobbying lawmakers for continued funding of federal programmes such as the Technological Opportunity Program (TOP) and Community Technology Centers (CTC) programme, which provide opportunities for Natives to narrow the technology gap. These programmes are important, since Native communities are some of the poorest in the USA, with rates of access to telephone service, computers and the Internet currently about two-thirds of the national average (Yawakie, 1997; National Telecommunications and Information

Administration, 1999). As a result, Native Americans often rely on community centres for Internet access (NTIA, 1999).

Despite this, the *New York Times* reports a 70 per cent increase in Native American use of the Internet in the first six months of 1998 alone, and Internet sites for and about Indians abound. In 1994, the Oneida Indian Nation was the first Indian nation to 'claim territory in cyberspace' (Polly, 1998: 37). The Indian Circle Web Ring (www.indiancircle.com) now lists 111 active tribal webpages (out of the more than 550 federally recognized Indian tribes of the continental US and Alaska).

THE WEBSITES

The sheer number of sites pertaining to Cherokee Indians makes a general survey impractical; in addition, there are many 'unofficial' sites for and about the Cherokees, many of which are interesting and informative, and some of which are appropriative and/or unreliable. We chose to limit our study to the official home pages of the Eastern and Western Bands. Since our first comparative analysis three years ago, in the first edition of *Web.Studies,* the primary focus of each site remains the same, but there have also been significant changes to the design and content of both sites.

Both homepages are produced by outside organizations under the direction of tribal members, but the two sites still offer striking contrasts. The Oklahoma homepage is designed primarily for Cherokee users. Undergoing revision at the time of writing, it has been retitled from *The Official Site of the Cherokee Nation* to *The Cherokee Nation,* with the words 'Official Site' displayed in smaller font on the line below and an image of the official Seal of the Cherokee Nation displayed to the left. The homepage features changing photographs of community members involved in contemporary activities, and foregrounds news items relevant to local and national Indian politics and services. The

site includes links to: the *Cherokee Advocate* and *Cherokee Phoenix,* and their archives; information about tribal government and services; cultural, historical and language instruction sites; employment opportunities; community calendars; and genealogy and enrolment information. A category labelled 'Associations' includes links to Sequoyah High School, Talking Leaves Job Corps, Cherokee Heritage Center, Cherokee Nation Housing Authority, Cherokee Nation Industries, and the Cherokee Gift Shop. Significantly, the only potentially tourist-oriented links on the Western Band homepage, the Gift Shop and the Casinos, are relatively hidden in the 'Associations' category. Furthermore, the gift shop features items that do not seem to be geared toward the tourist trade, such as Cherokee Holiday T-shirts with lettering in the Cherokee syllabary. With the exception of a few of the 'Association' links, the Cherokee Nation now maintains all of the links on the site. Notably, links to Federal Government agencies that appeared on the 1999 page have been removed and replaced with links to services provided by the Cherokee Nation itself, and there are no hints of the internal corruption within the tribal government reported in news releases on the site three years ago. These changes suggest, and have perhaps contributed to, a new sense of self-definition, self-containment and sovereignty on the part of the Western Band of the Cherokee Nation.

Changes in the Western Band page also reflect improved relationships with the Eastern Band. Three years ago, the only link to the Eastern Band homepage was an indirect one via an *Indian Circle Web Ring* link, and the only references to the Eastern Band were historical. The new page offers a direct link to *Cherokee-nc.com* on the Genealogy page, and news stories featured on the site frequently cover recent events in North Carolina. An archived news release reports a historic Joint Council meeting in August 2002, to discuss issues and share ideas of mutual interest, and a September 2002 story covers the opening of a new Cherokee

Visitor Center at the Chief Vann House Historic Site in Spring Place, Georgia, attended by both Western Band Chief Chad Smith and Chief Leon Jones of the Eastern Band. Both Chiefs emphasized the need for historical information to combat stereotypes, and 'reiterated the need not to portray the Cherokee as helpless victims of hopeless circumstances' but to remember 'the proud legacy of a strong people who survive and prosper' (www.cherokee.org/NewsArchive/News2002).

In contrast to the Western Band page, the Eastern Band homepage reflects few changes since 1999. The description 'The official homepage of the Cherokee Nation,' which appeared at the bottom of the page in 1999, has been incorporated into the body of the text as 'the official home page of the Eastern Band of Cherokee Indians.' The homepage now bears an image of the official Seal of the Eastern Band, similar to that displayed on the Western Band site. The combined effect of changes on the two homepages has been to identify each Band more specifically as a member of a larger Cherokee Nation. Importantly, the link to the Western Band homepage (under 'Related Links'), which was present in 1999 but not working, is now activated. However, many of the links to historical and cultural information have disappeared, and the page of language links which was in an early stage in 1999, has not been developed; as a result, the Eastern Band site at present seems even more directed toward tourism than it did three years ago. Still titled simply *Cherokee,* the homepage features changing images of local attractions, including a potter with her craft, and museum scenes. Links take the user directly to information on tourism and gaming on the Cherokee Reservation and in the Great Smoky Mountains National Park. Attractions on the reservation mirror those in the surrounding park—fishing, hiking and camping—but *Cherokee* also offers visitors cultural attractions, such as Oconoluftee Indian Village, 'Unto These Hills' Outdoor Drama, and Qualla Arts and Crafts Mutual, as well as museums,

shopping and an invitation to gamble at Harrah's Cherokee Casino.

In her analysis of 96 official tribal websites comprising the Indian Circle Web ring, Rhonda Fair notes that sites designed for Native American users typically emphasize a 'specific tribal identity' (2000: 204), while those produced for tourists and other outsiders tend to reproduce stereotypical images of the 'White Man's Indian' (Berkhofer, 1978). Fair offers the website of the Eastern Band of Cherokee as an example of the latter trend, but she acknowledges that Cherokee adoption of 'Hollywood' images of Indians reflects a 'dialectical process of identity formation' (2000: 208), in which the Cherokee have the agency to create images for their own purposes. Examination of the current Eastern Band homepage and interviews with its producers reflect that this dialectic process continues. However, at the present time, the Eastern Band Cherokees seem to be recreating their image in ways that will both appeal to non-Native visitors *and* reclaim their specific tribal heritage.

Tribal member Dave Redman (personal communication, 1999), who originated the North Carolina website in 1997, confirmed that the homepage was intended primarily to expand tourism and economic growth on the reservation. 'Gaming'—incorporating casino gambling, video gaming, bingo parlours, stick and bone games, and many other pursuits—is the linchpin of the Cherokees' development strategy, as it has been on other reservations. Like other tribes, many Cherokees view gaming as 'simply a profitable business, upon which economically dormant Indian nations can regain long lost territory, cultural prerogatives, and community structures built on respect'. Capital acquisition, however, is not an end in itself for the Cherokee Nation in North Carolina. Gaming proceeds are reinvested in the community. Projects funded by gaming revenues include a new youth centre, which provides access to computers and the Internet, and a community computer centre. Other beneficiaries include a new Cultural Resources Division, the newly redesigned museum, a language preservation programme (which records native speakers of Cherokee language on CD-ROM), and the Cherokee school system.

Robert Jumper, who took over management of the website from Redman, reaffirms the Cherokees' interest in building tourism (personal communication, 2002). However, he notes that the nature of tourism has changed. Tourists, especially those from the USA and Japan, have become impatient and lose interest in sites that do not change rapidly and are not technologically exciting. In addition, contemporary tourists want more education and more cultural information. Though there is still a market for the generic Indian items sold by Cherokee Publications (such as beaded belts, medicine wheels and '"Totemscents" Ceremonial Packs'), a growing number of tourists prefer interactive media that teach Cherokee culture, language and history. The site's content already reflects some of the changes Jumper describes. For example, links to the outdoor drama 'Unto These Hills' and the recreated Oconoluftee village contain video clips as well as text and still pictures. To match the 1998 renovation of the Museum of the Cherokee Indian, which combines 'high-tech wizardry and an extensive artifact collection' (www.cherokee-nc.com), the Museum website has been redesigned to feature colour graphics of traditional artefacts, and an online demo of a virtual tour of the Museum available on CD, as well as opportunities to buy historically and culturally specific books, and video and audio tapes.

At the time of writing, Jumper is taking bids for the design of a new website, to be launched early in 2003. Planned to meet both the changing desires of tourists and needs of the Cherokee community, the new website will feature more cultural information and education in the Cherokee language, which Jumper expects to be used by local people engaged in language reacquisition. An exciting element missing from the present webpage is a link to the Cherokee Elementary School and the homepages of Cherokee fifth graders. In 1999, users could access each child's page, with a photograph, his or her name in Cherokee, and an autobiographical statement. The site also invited visitors to click on a 'culture' option to hear a native storyteller recite Cherokee legends in English with Cherokee translations. Unfortunately, while computer use continues among Cherokee students, links to the Elementary School's pages have been discontinued in the interest of the security of the students. Jumper hopes that security issues can be worked out so that the link can be restored, and with it, an additional involvement of the Cherokee community with the website.

Conclusion

In our examination of the two websites, we attempted to address the question: does use of this potent Western technology necessarily lead to the degeneration of Native communities, or can Indians use the medium to further the goal of 'reindigenization'—the process of strengthening tribal ties while asserting sovereign rights and fostering self-determination? We conclude from our study of the Cherokees that tribal websites can be powerful agents for community development and cultural continuity within change. The Cherokee Nation of Oklahoma site offers the possibility of developing community by linking people to services, organizations, news, language instruction and free e-mail accounts; both Bands' sites literally enlarge community by providing information about genealogy and enrolment that will assist people with Cherokee ancestry to become members of the tribe, while screening out non-Native 'wannabes' or those merely interested in gaming profits.

The Eastern Band website and its links continue to both reflect and contribute to increasingly successful efforts by Cherokees to recover and retain participation in the capitalist economy of the larger nation. Profits are not only channelled into community services and cultural preservation, but have also expanded the actual land base of the community by funding the purchase of an ancient burial site, and supported business ventures such as the Nation's new bottled water industry and small business loans. Thus the Eastern Band website actively alters the way Qualla interfaces with surrounding cultures, drawing non-Natives from around the world to contribute to cultural preservation and economic recovery (a large percentage of site visitors are German, French, Japanese and other nationalities). At the same time, the Internet helps to control access by the dominant culture to Eastern Band Cherokee culture and its representations, and appears to be a significant part of a recovery of their success in the early 1800s as a thriving community in the inter-sections of EuroAmerican and tribal cultures. While the Internet may not yet have become the 'great equalizer' that many had hoped, these two websites suggest that some communities are now beginning to realize the Internet's potential for democratic and material equality.

REFERENCES

Berkhofer, R. 1978. *The white man's Indian: Images of the American Indian from Columbus to the Present.* New York: Vintage-Random House.

Bower, C. A, Vasquez, M. and Roaf, M. 2000. Native people and the challenge of computers: reservation schools, individualism, and consumerism. *American Indian Quarterly,* 24 (2), 182–199.

Cohen, E. 1997: For Native Americans, the net offers both promise and threat. *The New York Times on the Web.* http://www.nytimes.com/library/cyber/week/041697natives.html.

Ebo, B. 1998: Internet or outernet? In Ebo, B. (ed.), *Cyberghetto or Cybertopia?: Race, Class, and Gender on the Internet.* Westport, CT: Praeger, 1–12.

Fair, R. S. 2000. Becoming the white man's Indian: An examination of Native American tribal web sites. *Plains Anthropologist,* 45 (172), 203–213.

Foster, D. 1997: Community and identity in the electronic village. In Porter, D. (ed.), *Internet Culture.* New York: Routledge, 23–37.

Gurak, L. 1997: *Persuasion and Privacy in Cyberspace: The Online Protests over Lotus Marketplace and the Clipper Chip.* New Haven, CT: Yale University Press.

Hill, J. 2000. Virtual trade routes. *American Indian NMAI,* 1 (2), 10–11.

Howe, C. 1999: Cyberspace is no place for tribalism. Rptd.from *Wicazo-Sa Review* 13.2. http://www.ualberta.ca/~pimohte/howe.html.

Johnson, T. 1995: The dealer's edge: Gaming in the path of Native America. *Native Americas* 12, 16–24.

Levinson, P. 1997: *The Soft Edge: A Natural History and Future of the Information Revolution .* New York: Routledge.

Mander, J. 1991: *In the Absence of the Sacred: The Failure of Technology and the Survival of the Indian Nations.* San Francisco: Sierra Club Books.

Mills, K. 2002. Cybernations: Identity, self-determination, democracy and the "internet effect" in the emerging information order. *Global Society,* 16 (1), 69–87.

National Telecommunications and Information Administration. 1999. Fact sheet: Native Americans lacking information resources. www.ntia.doc.gov/ntiahome/digitaldivide.

Polly, J. A. 1998. Standing stones in cyberspace: The Oneida Indian Nation's territory on the internet. *Cultural Survival Quarterly* 21 (4), 37–41.(available online through ProQuest)

Trahant, M. N. 1996: The power of stories: Native words and images on the Internet. *Native Americas,* 13 (1), 15–21.

Turkle, S. 1997: Multiple subjectivity and virtual community at the end of the Freudian century. *Sociological Inquiry* 67, 72–84.

Twist, K. 2002. A nation online, but where are the Indians? *Digital Divide Network.* www.digitaldividenetwork.org/contents/stories/index.

Wilbur, S. P. 1997: An archaeology of cyberspaces: Virtuality, community, identity. In Porter, D. (ed.), *Internet Culture.* New York: Routledge, 5–22.

Wolf, A. 1998: Exposing the great equalizer: Demythologizing internet equity. In Ebo, B. (ed.), *Cyberghetto or Cybertopia?: Race, Class, and Gender on the Internet.* Westport, CN: Praeger, 15–32.

Yawakie, M. P. 1997: Building telecommunication capacity in Indian country. *Winds of Change,* 12, 44–46.

RADICTIONS AND CONFLICT IN CULTURAL PRODUCTION

39

Patients, "Potheads," and Dying to Get High

Wendy Chapkis

(2005)

The Wo/Men's Alliance for Medical Marijuana (WAMM) is an organization that is not easily classified. WAMM is not, as the federal Drug Enforcement Administration (DEA) might suggest, a cover for illicit drug dealing to recreational users, but neither is it properly characterized as a pharmacy dispensing physician-recommended medicine. In this article, I describe briefly the origins of WAMM and then discuss the problem of trying to divide medical marijuana users into "real patients" and "potheads." Such classification is complicated further by the relationship between medicinal cannabis use and the experience of getting "high."

WHAT IS WAMM?

WAMM was founded in California in 1993 by medical marijuana patient Valerie Corral and her husband, Michael Corral, a master gardener. In April 2004, WAMM drew national and international attention when it successfully won a temporary injunction against the U.S. Justice Department; as a result, the alliance now operates the only non-governmental legal medical marijuana garden in the country. The organization is unique in other respects as well. It is organized as a *cooperative*. Marijuana is grown and distributed collectively and *without charge* to the 250 patient participants.

Instead of paying for their marijuana, members are expected, as their health permits, to contribute volunteer hours to the organization by working in the garden; assisting with fund-raising; making cannabis tinctures, milk, capsules, and muffins; or volunteering in the office.

Over a five-year period (from 1999 to 2004), I conducted more than three dozen interviews with WAMM members about their involvement with the organization and their therapeutic use of marijuana. The WAMM members interviewed for this article reported use of marijuana with a physician's recommendation for a range of conditions including nausea related to chemotherapy (for cancer and AIDS), spasticity (multiple sclerosis), seizures (epilepsy), and chronic and acute pain. In order to become members of WAMM, each of the patient participants had to discuss with his or her doctor the possible therapeutic value of marijuana and to have been told explicitly (and in writing) that cannabis might prove useful in managing the specific symptoms associated with his or her illness, disability, or course of treatment. The number of members the program can accommodate is limited by the amount of marijuana the organization is able to grow. There is an extensive waiting list to join the organization; with more than 80% of its members living with a life-threatening illness, the standing joke is that "people are literally dying to get into WAMM."

Financial support for the organization comes largely from external donations. In 1998, however, the federal government revoked WAMM's non-profit status on the grounds that it was involved in supplying a federally prohibited substance. WAMM's struggle for survival further intensified in the fall of 2002 when the federal DEA raided the WAMM garden and arrested the two cofounders (to date, no charges have been filed against them). Despite these challenges, WAMM has continued to operate with the full support of California's elected officials and in close cooperation with local law enforcement. In April 2004, Judge Jeremy Fogel of the federal district court in San Jose (citing a recent Ninth Circuit Court of Appeals decision, *Raich v. Ashcroft,* soon to be reviewed by the U.S. Supreme Court) barred the Justice Department from interfering with the Corrals, WAMM patients, or the collective's garden. The federal injunction has provided at least temporary respite in the ongoing battle with the federal government.

WHO ARE THE WAMM MEMBERS? "WORTHY PATIENTS" OR "UNWORTHY POTHEADS"

Dorothy Gibbs is the sort of patient voters are encouraged to imagine when the question of medical marijuana is before them. At ninety-four and confined to a bed in a Santa Cruz nursing home, this WAMM member is hardly the stereotypical "pothead" many critics believe to be hiding behind the medical marijuana movement. Cannabis, for Dorothy Gibbs, has never been anything but a medicine, a particularly effective analgesic that relieves severe pain associated with her post-polio syndrome:

> I never smoked marijuana before; I had no reason to. But the relief I got was wonderful and long lasting and pretty immediate, too. I didn't really have any misgivings about using marijuana; I figured it had to be better than what I'd got. They had me on lots of

other medications, but I couldn't stand them; they made me so sick.

Most Americans (80% according to a recent CNN/Time poll; Stein, 2002) support the right of seriously ill patients like Dorothy Gibbs to access and use medical marijuana. This broad support is coupled, however, with lingering concerns that medical marijuana may be, as described in *Time* magazine, largely "a kind of ruse" (Stein). From this perspective, medical marijuana campaigns are seen as a cover for drug legalization and most, if not all, "medicinal use" as nothing more than a recreational habit dressed up in a doctor's recommendation.

Tensions between medical and social uses of marijuana are unavoidable in a political context in which nonmedicinal use is at once widespread, formally prohibited, and often severely punished. Because of the social and legal penalties associated with recreational use, it is reasonable that some consumers would attempt to acquire a measure of legitimacy and protection by identifying a medical need for marijuana. Medical marijuana users, then, become divided in the public arena between patients, like Dorothy Gibbs, who have never used marijuana except as a medicine, and "pretenders" who have a social relationship to the drug. As with other discreditable identities (like the prostitute, the poor person, or the single mother), a line is then drawn between a small class of deserving "victims" and a much larger group of the willfully bad who are unworthy of protection or support.

Such divisions are both illusory and dangerous. In the case of marijuana use, the identities of medical and social users are not neatly dichotomous. Some medical users have had prior experience with marijuana as a means of enhancing pleasure before they had occasion to become familiar with its potential in relieving pain. Other patients discovered the reasons for the plant's popularity as a recreational drug only after being introduced to it for a more narrowly therapeutic purpose.

With the majority of WAMM members living with life-threatening conditions and many of the chronically ill confined to wheelchairs, this is an organization that presents the legitimate face of medical marijuana, the sick and dying who are widely seen as deserving of the drug. Yet even within this population, neat divisions between medical and social users are unworkable. "Di," for example, a WAMM member in her midforties living with AIDS, acknowledges,

I'm just going to be totally honest—it wasn't AIDS that introduced me to pot. I had smoked marijuana as a kid and I liked it even then. When I tested positive in 1991, I felt that it was kind of a benefit that I got to use the term "medical marijuana," but I didn't quite own it as medicine because it had just been my lifestyle. But then, a few years ago, I traveled out of state [without access to marijuana]. I spent a week traveling and then went to Florida with my mom. By the time we got there, I was in so much pain from the neuropathy, I couldn't get up. We went to Urgent Care and they gave me morphine. The pain just wouldn't go away. I took the morphine for a week until I got back to California. When I got home, I started smoking pot again as normal and it took about three or four days and I stopped taking the morphine. I realized I had probably kept myself from having this really severe nerve pain for a long time by smoking every day. It was like this big validation that I really was using good medicine.

"Maria," a fifty-two-year-old single mother living with metastatic ovarian cancer, had no current relationship to marijuana when she fell ill, but she did associate the drug with the recreational use of her youth. This past association made it difficult for her to accept that cannabis might have therapeutic value:

I don't even know if I would have believed [that marijuana was medicine] if I hadn't tried it for medical purposes myself. I hadn't smoked for many years since I had my daughter. But a good friend said that they had heard it was really good for the nausea

[related to chemotherapy] and turned me on to WAMM. . . . What an incredible difference; the pharmaceuticals don't hold a candle [to marijuana] in terms of immediate relief . . . I don't think I would have believed it because it had always been recreational to me.

A COVER FOR DRUG DEALING OR AN ALTERNATIVE PHARMACY?

Because of confusions about the legitimacy of marijuana as medicine and of users as patients, provider organizations such as WAMM are often misunderstood as well. Even within communities largely tolerant of marijuana use, such as Santa Cruz, suspicions remain about the role of a provider organization. "Betty," now a WAMM volunteer, initially assumed WAMM was little more than a cover for recreational users to obtain their drug of choice:

A friend of the family developed stomach cancer, and when he got the prescription for marijuana he said to me, "I got into this organization; it's called WAMM." I had heard of WAMM but had never been involved with it or anything. Anyway, he says, "Everybody wants to be my caregiver but they all smoke and they're going to steal my pot. I know you don't do marijuana, so would you do this for me?" At first I said, "No, I don't think so." A couple of weeks later, he came back and asked again. So I said, "I'll tell you what—I'll go and check this out, but I'm not going to be sitting around with a bunch of potheads. I'm really not into that, I might as well be honest. But I'll go with you and check it out." So I went and I was really surprised at what I found. These people aren't potheads. These people aren't drug addicts. They're not derelicts. It's nothing like I had envisioned in my mind. I was very surprised . . . these people are really sick. And it's not like they all sit around and get stoned. I was amazed.

Similarly, "Hal," a seventy-year-old with severe neurological pain from failed back surgery, remembers that when a friend suggested he consider marijuana to manage the pain and WAMM as a way to access that marijuana, he was suspicious:

> Right, "medical" marijuana, sure. But [after trying it] I couldn't deny I felt better. I didn't know anything about WAMM; I'd never even heard of a cannabis buying club. I just wasn't in that world. I immediately jumped to the wrong conclusion. I thought "you're a bunch of potheads who are scamming the system." Right? So I'll be a pothead and scam the system. I don't care because I need it. I need it.

Hal's suspicion that WAMM was largely a cover for drug dealing to recreational users was shattered only when he attended his first weekly membership meeting:

> The first time I went to WAMM, with all these misconceptions in my mind, I looked around the room and thought, "My god, these people are really not well." I went home and said to my wife, "I'm going to have to rethink this whole thing. I'm going to have to stop jumping to conclusions here because this was an incredible experience.

Attending a WAMM meeting is indeed consciousness altering; new patients and guests enter expecting a room thick with marijuana smoke and instead find a room filled with human suffering and a collectively organized attempt to alleviate it. In fact, no marijuana is smoked at WAMM membership meetings. Rather, the hour-and-a-half gathering is spent building community: sharing news about the needs of the organization and the needs of the membership. Announcements are made not only about volunteer "opportunities" to work in the garden or the office, but also about members needing hospital visits, meals, or informal hospice support. Memorials are planned for those who have recently died, and holiday parties are organized for those with a desire to socialize and to celebrate. Information is exchanged about the practical dimensions of living with chronic or terminal illness and about coping with the often cascading challenges of pain, poverty, and social

isolation. The meetings conclude with members picking up a week's supply of medical marijuana.

NEITHER DRUG DEALING NOR A PHARMACY: A NEW MODEL OF COMMUNITY HEALTH CARE

Although WAMM is not, then, a cover for recreational drug dealing, neither is it simply a pharmacy dispensing physician-recommended medicine. Indeed, by its very design, the organization does not "dispense" marijuana at all. Rather, members collectively grow, harvest, clean, and store the plants; transform them into tinctures, baked goods, and other products; and draw their share throughout the year according to medical need. This is made all the more remarkable by the fact that WAMM never charges for that medicine. The paradigm-breaking phenomenon of patients collectively producing their own medicines not only challenges the "pharmaceuticalization" of healing, it also creates a therapeutic setting that effectively disrupts the atomized experience of illness and treatment characteristic of conventional medical practice. And, because WAMM members are on the front lines of legal and political battles around medical marijuana, the organization also necessarily facilitates civic engagement.

In short, WAMM approaches "health care" in the most expansive terms, addressing "afflictions" of the body, mind, and spirit, as well as those of the body politic. In this way, the organization more closely resembles women's health care cooperatives (originating in the feminist health care movement of the 1970s) and AIDS self-help and community support organizations (organized through the gay community in the 1980s and 1990s) than it does a pharmacy.

Like these earlier manifestations of community-based health initiatives, WAMM, too, deliberately challenges the monopoly of medical professionals, the pharmaceutical industry, and the state to determine the conditions of treatment, access to drugs, and even the terms of life and death. The objective of WAMM activists is not simply to add another drug to a patient's medicine cabinet but rather to create community. WAMM cofounder Valerie Corral observes:

> We came together around the marijuana, but it's not just the marijuana, it's the community. If the government has its way, and we have to go to a pharmacy to get our prescriptions filled, then we do it all alone. We would lack that coming together, and that is as important as anything else. Totally important. There is magic in joining together with other beings in suffering. That's the "joyful participation in the sorrows of the world" that the Buddhists talk about. It's how you recognize something is bigger than you and it's a paradigm breaker.

Patient participants initially may join WAMM for no other reason than to access doctor-recommended medication. But it is difficult for members to relate to the organization as nothing more than a dispensary. Weekly attendance at a ninety-minute participants' meeting is required for pickup of marijuana. At a minimum, this means that members must become familiar with each other's faces, witness each other's suffering, and confront repeated requests for assistance by both the organization and by individual participants. In other words, just because the marijuana in WAMM is free and organic doesn't make it without cost, at least in terms of emotional investment. For some, like thirty-seven-year-old "John," living with HIV, the price feels very high indeed.

> I've had a strange relationship to WAMM because a dispensary is really what I would have rather had it be. I'm a matter-of-fact kind of person, and if I have to have this condition, and I have to use a substance, I want to be able to get it and go and not be a part of anything. I don't want to know who my pharmacist is. That's exactly how I feel about WAMM. I go to the meetings because it is a requirement, but it's not necessarily what I would opt to do. I bet everybody who goes just wants to pick up their medicine and

leave. Basically, what we want is our medicine and to get on with our lives.

Indeed, those "with a life" and, perhaps more important, an income may prefer a dispensary or buyers' club over a demandingly intimate self-help collective. But for many who remain members, marijuana becomes only one of a number of threads tying them to the organization. "Joe," a forty-year-old man with a severe seizure disorder, explains:

> The medicine is actually turning into a secondary or tertiary part of what WAMM is all about for me now. It's more about the group itself, the fellowship that goes on, the ways we help each other. Actually that's the biggest thing I want to rave about: that deisolation that takes place. Isolation that accompanies illness gets to everybody eventually. Suddenly you are removed from any kind of social matrix, like being in school or at work so you don't have the day-to-day contacts with people that make all the difference in your life. WAMM takes you out of that isolation by putting you in contact with other people, like it or not. That's what I really like about the requirement that you come every week to get what you need. You have to be there. That's the only rule actually, and that's what makes it work. People get there whether they'd rather stay at home and then they start finding things in themselves that relate to other people. It's a way for patients to get a hold of their own lives and feel whole, feel human.

One of the most distinctive features of belonging to the WAMM community is, in the words of one participant, the possibility of "dying in the embrace of friends." Because the majority of members are living with life-threatening illness, death is a close companion. For the most active members, this is both the source of great social cohesion and, simultaneously, an almost unbearably painful aspect of collective life. "Kurt," a forty-two-year-old living with AIDS, explains:

> At first I came because I heard that this Mother Teresa was giving out the best medicinal marijuana in the

fucking world. And I wanted to know what this was about. What I found was a collective. WAMM has become the most unique group I've belonged to in my whole life. Sometimes it's hard for me, though, because it's a place for the sick and dying. And I'm sick but I'm not dying. I've pulled away from WAMM these past years because every time I become close to someone, they've died. And I was like "fuck this. I'm not going to go through this every time." But what WAMM has done for me—and for everybody they've supplied—is what nobody could do. Whether it's the marijuana or the tincture, or Valerie just coming and sitting by your side. So many people have died, but at least they had somebody sitting by their side.

DYING TO GET HIGH

Given decades of condemnation in this country of "reefer madness" and the supposedly dangerously intoxicating high produced by marijuana, it is not surprising that medical marijuana advocates have steered away from any discussion of the consciousness-altering properties of the substance. In an effort to distinguish medical from recreational use, the medical marijuana movement has focused almost entirely on the utility of medical marijuana in physical symptom management (that is, on its effects on nausea, pain, appetite, muscle spasms, ocular pressure, and seizure disorders). It is as if the "high" that inspires recreational use either disappears with medicinal use or, at best, is an unintended and unfortunate side effect. The medical marijuana movement, in other words, seems to have decided that talking about the psychoactive properties of cannabis will serve only to further discredit the drug, working against efforts to transform it into a "medicine."

WAMM cofounder Valerie Corral has resisted this impulse. In addition to gathering data on how marijuana affects members' physical symptom management, Valerie has been encouraging members to reflect on how marijuana might be affecting their psychospiritual well-being. Valerie observes:

I've gotten criticism for even talking about "consciousness"—I think people are afraid it will be used against us. But I really think it's interesting that the government is so determined to take the "high" out of marijuana before they legalize it as a prescription medicine. You never hear them talking about taking the "low" out of opiates; we allow medicine that relieves pain and is addictive but puts a veil over consciousness. So why is it so important to remove access to a drug that relieves pain and allows for an opening of consciousness?

My interviews suggest that living with severe and chronic pain and with an enhanced awareness of death is, in itself, profoundly consciousness altering. Medical interventions that ignore this dimension are increasingly recognized as inadequate by those involved in palliative care. "Healing," in such situations, is necessarily distinct from "curing" and involves interventions in body, mind, and spirit. Dr. Bal Mount, the founder and director of the Palliative Care Unit at the Royal Victorian Hospital in Montreal argues, "Healing doesn't necessarily have to do with just the physical body. If one has a broader idea of what healing and wellness are, all kinds of people die as well people," (quoted in Webb, 1999, p. 317).

"Bill," a fifty-three-year-old gay man who has been a caregiver to several WAMM members living with and dying of AIDS, was a cofounder of the local AIDS project in the 1980s and has extensive experience with the medical use of marijuana. He reports:

The gay community was well aware of marijuana, and early on in the AIDS epidemic we realized that it solved several major things: it solved problems of appetite when somebody wouldn't eat anymore; and it solved nausea, which I didn't think it would, but it did. And it seemed to really help somebody get past the stuck spot they were in of being sick and not being able to be helped, being in that all-alone space. Get them stoned and they got past that.

Deborah Silverknight, a fifty-one-year-old African American/Native American woman with chronic pain from a broken back, notes that this association between marijuana and a sense of enhanced well-being is an old one:

> My great-grandmother referred to marijuana as the "mother plant"—the one you smoke that helps you medicinally and spiritually. Marijuana is a meditative thing for me. It's not only about the physical pain, but relief of pain of the spirit. If I'm having a terrible back spasm, then it's mostly about the need for physical pain relief. But even then, it has that other dimension as well.

The psychospiritual effects of marijuana were frequently remarked upon by WAMM members who reported that the consciousness-altering properties of marijuana were a necessary component of its therapeutic value. Altered consciousness enhances physical symptom relief by helping them to deal with situational depression associated with chronic pain and illness.

"Barb," a forty-five-year-old white woman with post-polio syndrome, observes:

> When I get a pain flair, I smoke and it helps to relieve the pain and relieve the spasms but it also means I don't get as depressed. My attitude is more like, "oh, okay, I'm going to be in pain today, but I'm going to enjoy what I can enjoy and get through the day." Marijuana never fails to lift my mood. I smoke and think "okay, I'm just going to have to go with the pain today. It's beautiful outside and I'm going to go tool around the garden in my chair." It takes you to another level mentally of acceptance about being in this kind of pain. So when I'm in that "I can't handle this another minute stage," it produces a positive shift and I can go on to something else. The other drugs I'm prescribed have such major side effects, but if I smoke a joint, the biggest side effect is a mental lift. And that's a side effect I can live with.

"Hal," the seventy-year-old living with severe neuropathy, notes:

> When you are in constant pain, your focus is 100% on yourself: I can't move this way, I can't twist this

way, I can't put my foot down that way. That kind of thing. It's terrible.
>
> I'd never been one who was self-absorbed to the extent that I would forget about other things. I became that way [because of the pain]. I don't know how my wife could stand it. But, I find at this point [with the marijuana], I am in a sense witnessing my pain; what's happened as a result is that I am no longer so absorbed in my pain. I can rise above it, and then I'm able to do whatever I have to do.

One common objection in antidrug literature to the "high" associated with psychoactive drug use is that it offers only a "distortion" or "escape" from reality. The implication is that escape is somehow unworthy or undesirable, and the "alternative reality" accessed through drugs is illegitimate. But, in the context of chronic pain or terminal illness, one might question whether, in the words of Lily Tomlin, reality isn't "greatly overrated."

Pamela Cutler, a thirty-eight-year-old white woman in the final stages of living with metastatic breast cancer, observes:

> Marijuana kind of helps dull the reality of this situation. And anyone who says it's not a tough reality . . . I mean your mind will barely even take it in. It does dull it, and I don't think there is anything wrong with that if I want to dull it. That's fine. . . . I was diagnosed with breast cancer and had a radical mastectomy . . . the whole thing was a big shock. I mean I was thirty-six. I was like, "What?" And ever since then it's been like a roller coaster: okay, it's spread to your bones, and then it's spread to my lungs, and then my liver. . . . [Marijuana] makes it easier to take for me. It doesn't really take it away. It just dulls the sharpness of it—like "Oh my god, I'm going to be dead." I just think that's just incredible.

Although most of the individuals I interviewed commented on the therapeutic value of the psychoactive properties of marijuana, a number were careful to make a distinction between the psychoactive effect of marijuana when used medicinally and the effects when used recreationally. For many of them, the contrast between "getting loaded for fun" and medicinal use was described as profound. In part, this difference may be a question of, as Norman Zinberg (1984) has phrased it, the effects of "set" (the user's mindset) and "setting" (the context in which the drug is taken). A substance taken in expectation of pleasurable intoxication by a healthy individual may produce a substantially different effect from that experienced by an individual living with a life-threatening illness or in chronic pain.

"Kurt," the forty-two-year-old white man living with AIDS, notes:

> I used to smoke recreationally, but it became a whole different thing when I became HIV positive and needed it as a medicinal thing. I had never had a life-threatening disease, and now I was watching everyone die in front of me. It wasn't just getting high anymore; it let me think about why I am still here after they are all gone.

Some individuals suggested that the different experience of marijuana when used medicinally was less about changed context and more about simple drug habituation. "Cher," a fifty-two-year-old white woman with chronic pain and seizure disorder, reports:

> I have to use marijuana every day to deal with pain . . . I feel like I'm so habituated that it really doesn't do that much to my mood anymore. Or at least it's hard to tell. . . . It was more fun being a big pothead than it is being a medical user, for me. You get higher when you are a recreational user. Anytime you use something every day, your system almost naturalizes it. And frankly, I do not really feel stoned anymore unless I smoke because I am so habituated to eating it. . . . And when I smoke, I remember how wonderful it was when marijuana actually got you high. It's like any drug; your body gets habituated.

Hal too reports a diminishing "high" as he became more accustomed to the drug:

> After a couple of months, I found that I wasn't getting high as much as I was getting calm. It took a couple of months though. At first, I'd smoke and get really high and have a wonderful afternoon or evening or whatever. But then it started to change and I just got calm.

Hal's shift from "high" to "calm" may be the result not only of biochemical tolerance but also the effect of increased familiarity with the altered state so that it becomes the quotidian reality rather than the "alter."

Interview subjects who had a history of drug abuse and recovery were especially insistent on making a clear distinction between a recreational "high" and the effects of medicinal marijuana use. By drawing a clear line between "getting loaded" and "taking medicine," these individuals were able to maintain their sense of sobriety while using cannabis therapeutically. Inocencio Manjon-McFaline, a fifty-four-year-old African American/Latino man with cancer and a former cocaine addict who got sober in 1998, described the difference like this:

> What's strange now is that I don't feel the effects [from marijuana] that I remember from when I would smoke it before, smoking to get loaded. It's a different time for me. I'm not smoking it looking for a high. Maybe it's just psychologically different knowing I'm smoking it for medicinal use. But I haven't felt loaded. I smoke only for the pain. It gets me out of there, out of that frame of mind. I'll smoke and I'll tend to focus on what I want to focus on. Generally, that's my breathing and my heartbeat. And I'll get really into plants. I just really get into that and forget about pain. . . . Every breath I take is a blessing. I don't fear death, but I don't look forward to it. I really treasure life.

Inocencio's comments raise an important question about what it means to get "high." Clearly he is no longer looking to "get loaded" and argues that he no longer gets "high." Yet, his description of his medicinal use suggests that the marijuana assists him not only in dealing with pain and nausea but also in "focusing" on his breath, on his heartbeat, on the blessings of being alive. This state may seem more "altered" when there are more conventional demands on one's time than when one is in a state of dying. The present-tense focus, which is an aspect of getting "high" that is often commented on, matches the needs of the end-of-life process and therefore may not feel "altering" but rather "confirming" or "enhancing."

Qualities associated with the psychoactive effects of cannabis—such as present-tense focus, mood elevation, and a deepened appreciation of the "minor miracles" of life—may be especially usefully enhanced in the face of anxiety over death or chronic pain. Given antidrug rhetoric in our culture, it is not surprising that some medical marijuana patients may downplay the psychoactive effects of cannabis use. And certainly some medical marijuana users may become habituated to the effects of the THC and to the altered or enhanced state to which it provides access. But "habituation," "tolerance," or "familiarity" are not synonymous with "no effect." For those living with chronic pain,

terminal illness, or both, the psychotherapeutic and metaphysical effects of marijuana may complement the mindset and setting in which the substance is used. As these accounts suggest, although medical marijuana use is most certainly not just about getting "loaded" in any conventional recreational sense, its therapeutic value may be strongly tied to the psychoactive properties of *the plant* (rather than "of cannabis"). This suggestion has significant implications for both the practice of medicine and the transformation of public policy.

REFERENCES

Stein, J. (2002, November 4). The new politics of pot. *Time.* Retrieved March 4, 2005, from http://www.time .com/time/archive/preview/0,10987,1101021104-384830,00.html

Webb, M. (1999). *The good death.* New York: Bantam.

Zinberg, N. (1984). *Drug, set, and setting.* New Haven, CT: Yale University Press.

CONTRADICTIONS AND CONFLICT IN CULTURAL PRODUCTION

40

Adventures in Desocialization

Inge Bell

Bernard McGrane

(1999)

When I was teaching, I tried to find a way of using sociology to make students aware of the ways in which society has trained them to look at the world and at themselves. The object was to free people from the influence of society—specifically, to begin to undo the indoctrination that each of us has undergone growing up in this particular society. I believed that as we became conscious of the many specific ways in which our inner experience of reality had been conditioned, we might throw off this conditioning and create greater inner freedom for ourselves. In line with this, I developed a course called "Ventures in Desocialization."

Socialization is the name sociologists give to the process by which a child is inculcated with the beliefs of its culture. Sociologists study this process in great detail, demonstrating how we are, completely, creatures of our culture. However, they never seem to step beyond this stage and actually try to free us from social conditioning, nor do they point out that this freedom is even possible.[1] Yet their studies of resocialization during adulthood—when someone goes into prison or into the army, for example—demonstrate that we are capable of changing enormously if our environment changes. We know that it is possible to resocialize people, but is it possible to desocialize without taking on any new set of beliefs and pressures? The Buddhists say yes, that this, in fact, is the path to enlightenment.

In this section I will offer you a series of exercises that were successful in helping students to begin to free themselves from conditioning. Of course, the exercises are only a first step, but they can introduce you to new ways of observing the world and yourself. They are the initial wedge entering between you and your internalized beliefs and habits. I suggest that you do each exercise before reading about the way my students responded, so that you will have your own experience first, before you see what you have in common with or how you differ from others.

THE SELF: REALITY OR ILLUSION?

We have said that wisdom consists of self-knowledge. We have to look at this in greater detail. None of us is very fond of a person who is constantly thinking about himself, analyzing himself, and talking about himself. All of us like somebody whose "self" doesn't intrude very much, in the sense that such a person has plenty of attention and energy available for people and things outside. They probably engage in relatively little self-criticism and self-laceration. We sense that, somehow or other, their self is not a problem. So, perhaps what we wish to eliminate is something we might call the "problematic self," the one that gives us problems.

It may help us to look at the way "self" has been conceptualized in more than one culture. We can compare our view of self with that of a radically different cultural system, that of Zen Buddhism. The New Testament strongly advised people not to take the self seriously. Are you worried about how you are dressed? The New Testament tells us to be like the lilies who never worry about how they look but are nevertheless beautiful. It warns us not to inflate the self through the possession of wealth, power, or fame. It even advises us to "lose ourselves" to attain salvation: not in the hereafter, but in the sense that we may find refuge from all worry right here in this life. These messages accord closely with Zen Buddhism, which goes so far as to call the self an illusion that has been implanted in us by society: a sort of bogeyman who scares us but, when we look, is not there at all. Unfortunately, over the centuries, European Christianity perverted the meaning of the scriptures. "Selflessness" came to mean self-condemnation. We were supposed to despise the flesh as sinful and to engage in all sorts of self-laceration to drive the devil out of ourselves. Thus, subtly perverted, the message became one of paying constant and fearful attention to ourselves, lest we fall from grace through a wrongful feeling or thought. The self, far from being dropped as an illusion, became the center stage on which the drama of salvation and damnation was played out. On top of our troublesome earthly self, we now had an eternal self to worry about, and because the afterlife was fraught with terrible hells, our anxieties have increased accordingly.

A reaction to a bad system is all too frequently another bad system that really is the mirror image of the first. During the 19th century, American mainstream culture began to throw off the idea of sin and hell, salvation and damnation. Yet we were not to become lighthearted, as the scriptures suggested; "self" remained the central concern, only now salvation meant the worldly success of the self, and damnation meant poverty and failure. These changes in the culture paralleled the dissolution of family and communal bonds that actually left the individual very much alone. For the first time in history, most of us human beings must now reckon with the fact that no group will accompany us from birth through death. We will move through many groups, even several nuclear families. Essentially, we will be alone on our journey. This socially isolated self became psychologically isolated because, as the old bonds dissolved, competition came to take their place.

Today we even have a magazine called *Self.* We are constantly bombarded with images of celebrities whose lives consist of nothing but self-adornment, self-glorification, and self-seeking competition. Such folk are our heroes and role models. As in the perverted version of Christianity, the self remains at the center of the stage, and we all have stage fright.

Now let us return to the Buddhist idea of the self as illusion. Actually, this idea accords rather closely with sociologist's view of self, as both regard the self as a socially learned construct, even though sociology does not go as far as Buddhism in asserting that we might get rid of the illusion. At first this may seem preposterous. Our own self seems to be the one most solid, unavoidable thing with which we are in direct touch. In what sense can it be illusion? To approach this question, I would like you to do a little exercise that I do with my students. Take a piece of paper and list on it all of the aspects of the self you can think of, beginning with such obvious items as "my reputation," "my clothes," "my grades," and so on. When you

have finished your list, come back to the book and see how it corresponds with one I have compiled from various student lists (see Table 1).

As you look over this list, you will notice that it is very long. No wonder the self is problematic. It is a huge, overblown contraption. You will also notice that the items on the list are, indeed, items we have learned from our culture. Even "my body," which would seem to be a given, existing prior to culture, is socially learned in the sense that how we regard it (too fat, beautiful, clumsy, etc.) is learned from our culture. Even the way we relate to our body—for example, whether or not we are sensitive to its aches—depends on cultural conditioning.

But surely some of the items on this list are worth collecting. "Knowledge" and "opinions," for instance, are in very high repute in the academy. You are here to gather these, and your professors are paid for having lots and lots of them. Buddhism speaks to us very clearly on this point. The scholar's type of knowledge is considered one of the greatest hindrances to enlightenment. The great spiritual teacher Krishnamurti has defined the expert as "somebody who knows so much that he can't learn anything more." Buddhism tells us that, if we wish to attain wisdom, we must come with "beginner's mind," we must come with an empty cup, otherwise nothing new can be poured into it.

Even the habit of intellectual speculation gets in the way. Krishnamurti tells a delightful story about a drive he took in the country with two scholars who had come to learn from him. Unfortunately, the driver of the car wasn't looking and ran over a goat. The two scholars in the back seat didn't notice it because they were so busy discussing awareness.

In studying people's ideologies, it is easy to see how our assumptions blind us utterly to the reality we are living through. Two men can go into combat in war, and one will come out a convinced pacifist while the man next to him comes out a confirmed and aggressive patriot who believes we must be

Table 1   Exercise: Components of the Self

MY:	MY:	MY:
reputation	hobbies	physical space
clothes	future	youth
grades	past	writing
body	life story	hates
sex appeal	family	dislikes
friends	ethnicity	spiritual development
lovers	status	
acquaintances	prestige	peak experiences
opinions	neuroses	security
tastes	career	religion
image	style	competitive position
ideal self	sense of humor	grudges
real self	dreams	regrets
talents	daydreams	self-accusations
virtues	role models	desires
vices	ideals	credentials
habits	knowledge	personality
accomplishments	skills	titles
fears	beliefs	privileges
wishes	credit	uniqueness
ambition	ancestors	honor
goals	looks	name
IQ	life	sins
memory	moods	bank balance

constantly ready for war. They lived through the same experience, but it was only the same outwardly. Just so, you can take a group of students to see a terribly poor inner city neighborhood. The left-wingers will see pure evidence of economic oppression, while the right-wingers will see confirmation of their belief that poor people are just lazy, dirty, and vicious.

To keep reality from intruding and upsetting our ideas, our brains keep up a constant babble. Above all, this babble is designed to keep the illusion of self alive. We are constantly rehearsing something we need to do next week or going over an argument we had yesterday, trying to improve on the line we took. We daydream about improving ourselves or adding luster to our name. This stream of ideas not only keeps the illusion of self ever alive, it also comes between us and our bodies, so that people can strain themselves until their heart or their stomach lining gives way without ever having heard the warning signals of impending disaster. They are too busy thinking to listen to their bodies or to see the world around them. They are self-absorbed in the sense that they are constantly working on the illusory self.

Surely we cannot just throw all knowledge out the window. How could we live? Krishnamurti again comes to our aid in differentiating "psychological thinking" from "technical thinking." The latter is the knowledge we need to lead our lives, from knowing our address to knowing how to cook. The knowledge you need to carry out your job also falls into this category, although this can become complex when your job seems to require opinions. It is clear, however, that most of the daily thinking we do, the thinking that makes us uncomfortable, is just the sort of rehearsing and rehashing we described above. Thinking about the self is psychological thinking, and it is this that takes up most of our time and emotional energy.

Exercises: The Self/No Self

Now, let us do two exercises on the self/no-self. First, we will do a meditation on the self. Allow about fifteen minutes. Sit up straight in a comfortable position and close your eyes. Now, review as many of the aspects of the self as come to your mind, concentrating on those that are especially troublesome to you. As you bring up each item, imagine it turning into a heavy weight that you must hold and carry. Each time, tense the muscles holding the items. You may pile these up in your arms, pile some on your head, lay some on your lap, your feet, and so on. Gradually increase the tensions in every part of your body that must bear the weights. Then, when you have built up maximum tension, imagine all of the weights lifting away from you and simply floating off. Relax all muscular tension and stay in the sitting position, eyes closed, for several more minutes, enjoying the feeling of lightness and relaxation that comes from letting go of the self.

For the second exercise, find a friend who will join you. Both of you write down four items that you regard as important aspects of your "ideal self" and four that you believe describe your "real self." Make these lists separately. Now, compare notes. Do you think your friend's version of her "real self" is correct? Does she think your list is

realistic? After discussing this, go over the list for the real self and see if you can remember how each item was inculcated into you by the adults around you when you were growing up.

If no friend is handy, at least jot down four items for your real and ideal selves before reading on.

Ideal Self, Real Self: Both Illusions

Most people show a disastrous gap between their real and ideal selves. The ideal is usually something like: confident, successful, energetic, friendly; the real is often: fat, lazy, shy, incompetent. Right away we see why such a self is highly troublesome. Most students assume that their ideal self is a kind of daydream, but their "real self" is just a straight report of the facts. Actually, both versions are pure fantasy without the slightest substance. If you had a tough parent, for example, you may think that your real self is pretty awful. The same biological you, having had loving, self-confident parents, would feel much more self-approval, even though this second person had the same looks, brains, or energy level. It all depends on who held up the mirror to us as we were growing up.

Buddhism tells us that, to get rid of the problematic self, we need not change any aspect of it. We only need to accept what is there. Of course, to truly accept, we need to know what is there. A person who cannot admit to herself that she is afraid cannot accept her fear; hence, she will be constantly wrestling with it and will remain tense and anxious. The suppression of laziness is a good example of this. Our culture demands much difficult effort from us from early childhood. It disapproves most strongly of laziness. In school, "lazy" and "stupid" are about the worst things you can be. "Vicious" and "cruel" would be mild condemnations by comparison. This means that, to get approval, we had to deny all our urges to rest.

As we deny them, they collect and grow bigger. It takes constant effort to keep this huge pile of laziness under cover. Simply everybody suspects themselves of laziness. Had we grown up in a different culture, the accusation might never have entered our minds.

A note of caution: Don't interpret letting go of the self to mean that you should ignore your feelings. On the contrary, as we sweep away concern with the problematic self, it leaves the mind more available to stay in touch with our body, its physical sensations and feeling-states or emotions. Mind should look after body and feelings the way a good parent looks after a child. There is a saying in Buddhism, "When you are tired, lie down." I often think this should be engraved over the entrance of all college dormitories.

EXERCISE: THE CRITICAL VOICE

Here is an exercise designed to make you more aware of how your insides function. Take paper and pencil and begin by giving your particular inner critical voice a name. Students come up with a wonderful variety of such names: the clobberer (a mean one), the nag (slightly less mean), the cold-eyed commentator, the nudge, the judge, the accuser, the perfectionist, mother, father, the quibbler, and many others. Freud called it the superego, some call it conscience. Most people have to cope with some form of critic; only a small number of lucky ones don't.

Now write out a list of the most frequent criticisms you hear from this voice. It is important to get your inner workings out on paper where you can get a different perspective on them than if you only go over them in your head. One tricky aspect of this task is that, in many people, the criticisms are not consciously heard. All that is conscious is the self-justification and self-defense about something: "I do spend my money wisely. I saved by not buying that dress last week," or "I do well in many of my classes—the ones that are important. I never mess those up!" and so on. The unheard or subconscious part is "You are a spendthrift," or "You mess up in all your classes." Whenever you defend yourself like this, you know there is a silent accusation afoot. For your list, you may infer these accusations from the self-justifications and self-defenses.

Now, go over your list and rate the correctness of each criticism. Then give an overall assessment to the critical voice: right 50% of the time, 90%, 10%, and so on. If you have a friend who will join you in this exercise, put your heads together over each list and see what your friend thinks about the accuracy of your critical voice. In the next step of the exercise, let the critical voice (always address yours by the name you've given it) justify itself: Make a list of justifications. Let the voice claim various benefits it brings you—perhaps it will claim that you couldn't function without it, and so on. Now assess the believability of the defense: very believable, somewhat believable, not too believable, or utterly wrong.

Although there is a wide variety of forms taken by the voice in different individuals, the accusations are usually rather similar: too lazy, too fat, not nice enough to parents, procrastinating on schoolwork, and so on. You can easily see that the content of the accusation is learned from the attitudes of the people around you as you grew up. Had you been born a Trobriand Islander, for example, you might have criticized yourself severely for any playful or slightly intimate interaction with your brother or sister.

The severity or even the presence of such an element of personality depends on culture, specifically on the severity with which children are treated during their upbringing. In a [1985] study of Polynesian culture, Bronislaw Malinowski tells us that, when he asked people whether there was anything the individual wanted to change about himself, he usually found that the respondent couldn't think of anything at all.

How people rate their critical voice on believ-ability seems to vary greatly, but the rating appears to have no correlation to the individual's talents or personality. Some really wonderful people believe the worst accusations about themselves. This, again, is related to childhood experiences.

You have to see the critical voice as a saboteur who constantly undermines and rattles you while claiming to be your friend. The voice makes you dread failure, and fear of failure is one of the most common causes for failure. In many years of teach-ing, I learned that very, very few low-scoring students were failing because of lack of intelli-gence. Rather, self-confidence was the major ingre-dient in success. When you are confident you procrastinate less. We all hate to spend time at something that makes us feel bad. The confident student talks more in class and learns more by ask-ing questions. She is likely to be more adventurous and creative. In short, whatever destroys your faith in yourself undercuts your performance. Learn to see the critical voice for the enemy that it is.

This doesn't mean that you are unable to see and correct errors in your work. You have to be able to see, matter-of-factly, where you are wrong—that is a necessary part of the process of learning. But that is quite different from the Voice. You can see your error in a flash—your understanding is that quick. The nagging and inner backbiting of the Voice comes on top of this quick knowing. It drags the whole affair out and makes you a culprit for having been wrong. If you knew everything already, why should you get an education?

Next time you have a severe attack of self-criticism (it may also feel like depression), take it as a perfect occasion for catching the critic. Sit right down and make a list of the accusations—get them out into the daylight. Read them to your-self out loud. Share them with a friend.

When working on the critical voice, notice that this part of your brain is very agile. When it sees you coming after it, it may quickly switch sides and join in the new game by criticizing you for being self-critical. It is perfectly capable of such treach-ery. What you have to learn to recognize is not so much what it says, but the tone of the criticism and the way that tone makes you feel.

The critical voice is tremendously subjective. It is, in fact, incapable of objective, fair judgment. For example, it will blame you for things it would never criticize in another person. In fact, if you criticized your friends so severely, you probably wouldn't have any friends. To strengthen your capacity for cool, unbiased self-judgment, try the following exercise: At various moments during the day, whenever you think to do it, just observe what you are doing—not what you are thinking or feeling—briefly and quite unemotionally and without judg-ment: "I am walking to my math class," "I am watching a movie," "I am reading an assignment," "I am having coffee and a chat with a friend." This exercise should be done over a period of at least three weeks—catching yourself about once or twice a day—don't overdo. If you forget easily, wear something unusual to remind yourself occa-sionally of the exercise. Everyone will obtain his own result from this exercise, and I won't spell out what your result might be. Try it and see. After three weeks, go back and look at your list of accusations and your assessment of their correctness. See if your feelings toward the critical voice have changed.

The following short essay by an undergraduate student illustrates a major change in relating to our socialization and to our life:

ZEN AND THE ART OF RIDING THE SCHOOL BUS

When I was in second grade, I started taking the bus to school. To occupy myself on the hour-long bus ride, I would draw pictures. When I first started rid-ing, I was awed by the power of the bus. I wouldn't even try to draw by myself. I just placed my pencil in the center of a sheet of paper and I let the bus draw with its bumps and turns. What I got was scribble, but to me it was beautiful because I had made the bus come alive. I had made it draw.

After a while, though, I tired of the bus's random scribbles and I tried to guide the scribbles into simple pictures like stars and hearts. Soon, though, I tired of this as well. The bus's pictures were dry and boring. I decided to forget the bus and draw by myself so I could make intricate designs, much better that those the bus made. With this, though, I quickly grew frustrated. The bus's jiggling and bouncing made my lines wiggly and uneven. I was angry at the bus for invading my beautiful pictures with its ugly squiggles. I hated riding the bus.

Over time I had lost respect for the bus. I had forgotten its power and forgotten that every morning when I stepped onto it, I became a part of the bus, accepting its twists and turns as if they were my own. I wanted to escape the bus in hopes that without it my pictures would be perfect. I blamed the bus for my imperfections. My ego took over.

Now I find myself coming around in a circle . . . only now the bus is the world, and I don't have a choice whether I want to get on it in the morning. I'm stuck here for good, 'til death do us part. I want to let the bus draw again, but I keep getting frustrated with it. It's difficult to accept that my problems are not the fault of the world but of myself. I don't want to be imperfect.

I don't yet understand my feelings, or where I stand in relation to the bus or the rest of the world. I won't pretend to understand either. Everyday I learn more and I see more, and with each experiment my world becomes more whole. But in this realm of massive change I am lost. I don't know who I am anymore. I am very much like Carlos Casteneda in his book *Journey to Ixtlan:* The doors of opportunity have been opened, I just don't know which one to choose. It's like some sort of demonic version of "Let's Make a Deal." I want the microwave, but I'm hoping for a Porsche. Where's a strange man in a chicken suit to give advice when I really need it?

On my first day of this "Ventures in Desocialization" class I believed that self was an independent individual, free from restraints, limitations, and expectations placed on it by others. I felt that I was the most important self, that I was independent of all others, and that life was a survival of the fittest. I had a superiority complex and I wanted to be told that it was OK. (Boy, did I get a reality check!)

What I learned has nothing to do with independence or individuality. What I learned is that we are all the same, not just all people, but all things. I'm no different than a mountain or a piece of grass, and I'm no more significant.

The search for self is not about finding out who you are to gain independence; it's about finding yourself in an effort to be rid of it. Self-identity is ego, and with ego comes deceit.

Long ago Shakespeare said that all the world is a stage, and he was right. Very few people are actually who they want to be. We're all bitter extras who didn't get the lead, and we're all fighting over who gets the most lines. Our actions and behaviors are all acts. We do what we think we're supposed to do without ever putting thought into it. Our personalities are all facades that we put on to gain the approval of other people with equally fake personalities. Our lives are based on deceit, and our neverending quest for acceptance is based on the false hope that acceptance will bring us happiness.

Equally, we hope that material goods will bring us satisfaction. By wanting more, we constantly reaffirm how inferior we are. We create a self-perpetuating cycle of want leading to our own demise. We are constantly striving for more of what we already decided didn't work. We'll never achieve happiness if we enforce such socially prescribed standards.

Eliminating standards and preconceptions was a major theme in this course. By trying to adhere to society's rules, we eliminate freedom of the soul, of self. All of the reading stressed this point in one way or another. One author wanted people to enjoy life, not feel restrained by grades and rules and appropriate behavior; another said that we can't define love, or fall into the misconception of romantic love, because real love just is; another said that we need to see the world from other perspectives, that "I" gives only a limited view. They all agreed that we need to distinguish our own beliefs from those of society.

The largest social misconception we need to eliminate is the conviction that humans are a superior species (beyond, of course, admitting that we as individuals are not the most important). All living things are equal because, regardless of how much money we make or what technology we have, we will all die. Death is an equal opportunity abductor. (This is not to say that living things are superior to the inanimate, for I believe that life is an abstract and that all things hold some life despite their vital statistics.)

Once we learn that all things are equal and interconnected, and after we've eliminated our preconceptions, we need to learn to experience life. We need to experience not as we have in the past, but in a new way, with full consciousness at every moment. We need to open our eyes and see things as we've never before seen them. We need to be able to question why we do things. Do we do them out of habit, because it is what society dictates, or because we truly want to do things that way? We spend so much time trying to figure out how to make our lives great and overcome obstacles that we forget to appreciate the experiences that we actually do have. For most people, life has become a nuisance, an obstruction of happiness. They have not realized that it is the act of living life that breeds genuine happiness.

What I realize now is that I shouldn't have been drawing pictures on the bus, I should have been experiencing the bus ride. I have no happy memories of the bus, I don't remember my friends or the excitement, or the long drive, because I didn't pay attention. I drew pictures to make the time pass quickly, and now all I remember is the sadness because my pictures weren't perfect. Part of my life passed me by and I don't even remember it. That's much more important than a few messy pictures. (Kristin Rydberg)

EXERCISE: ROOTS

Before you can let go of this troublesome self of yours, you will have to explore it and study it and understand it. (Don't use what I am saying to think about yourself incessantly. Watch instead. The "understanding" I am talking about comes as a flash of insight, not as the result of endless rumination.)

To a much larger extent than our culture lets on, we are still the products of quite distinct subcultures. In my course, I had every student research his or her ancestry as far back as they could go. They interviewed relatives and wrote letters to all the older members of their families they could find. Then we had a come-as-you-were party: come as your grandfather or great-grandfather or one of your parents. As we exchanged family histories, we began to get a strange sensation of how much of a melting pot this society really is.

Here is a third-generation German Jewish immigrant whose grandparents fled from Hitler in the 1930s. Here is a Chicano student whose family has lived in a Chicano neighborhood near the Mexican border for generations. They were former landowners, pushed out when the Anglos grabbed California and reduced the family to the poverty of farm laborers. Here is a black student whose grandparents made it out to California from Arkansas to work in the shipyards during World War II and whose parents made it up to the level of skilled blue-collar workers. Here is an individual whose family of Presbyterian New England farmers has been in America for many, many generations. Here is a young woman who was, herself, born in Taiwan and whose own parents had an arranged marriage. She tells us that it seemed to work about as well as most marriages she sees around her in the United States. Here is a young man whose ancestors were queens of Hawaii. Had we gone back two generations we would have spoken in a babble of tongues; we would have come from rags and riches. We would have exchanged passionate enmities; in no sense would we have been members of a common enough culture so that we could easily understand one another.

We tend to be fooled by externals. All of these disparate people now look pretty much alike. Not only do we dress the same, we organize our faces similarly. We wear the same expressions; our body language signals the same reserved friendliness, the same underlying disapproval of our bodies. On the surface we are indeed alike, but it is amazing how the old ethnicity hangs on. If we look at any trait, from a person's politics to the way he disciplines his children, we will always find that differences in ethnic and social class origins still show up.

I put ethnicity and class position into the same bag because they come combined in patterns that reflect the historical circumstances under which each group came to be part of the United States. Black people came in chains, and black ethnicity is still correlated with lower-than-average class position. The Italian immigrants came without money or urban skills, primarily during the years 1880 to 1920. They began at the bottom but were only partially blocked by racism and hence managed to get into better-paid working-class positions and into the lower middle class. The wave of Jewish immigrants who came in the 1930s were mostly middle class and came into our economy at that level, and thus it goes. The patterns vary from family to family. Some families moved up fast; others remained in the same economic position for generations.

There are so many subtle aspects to this heritage of ours. I was the first-generation child of Austrian Jewish parents who fled from Hitler. By a fluke, my family moved to Southern California, away from the other immigrants who stayed on the East Coast. Luckily, there wasn't much anti-Semitism among my young schoolmates in Claremont, California, and I grew up feeling myself to be totally "American." Yet, one day I found myself majoring in sociology in graduate school at the University of California at Berkeley. I looked around me in seminar and realized that 80% of my classmates and professors were Jewish. "Isn't it strange that I ended up in this group?" I thought, and then I began to put it together. My father had been a socialist and had raised me as one. Many of the sociologists at Berkeley at that time were socialists or ex-socialists of some stripe or persuasion. They had gravitated naturally to sociology because it was the newest and most militant social science, and it counted Karl Marx as one of its most influential intellectual parents. Jews have historically often been political radicals because they lived for so many centuries as outcasts within the Christian nation-states of Europe.

I married twice, both men with backgrounds completely different from my own. Neither marriage lasted. And then I found Ted and a kind of immediate understanding, as though for the first forty years of our lives we had thought roughly the same thoughts and found the same comedians funny. There was something even more subtle afoot. The way he played with me and teased me reminded me very much of my father. Ted's mother was thoroughly American, but he is a throwback to two Russian-Jewish grandfathers with whom he lived during his childhood and who teased him and played with him in the same way my Austrian Jewish father had played with me. One of them was a labor organizer and a radical.

Another thing we discovered at our come-as-you-were party was that some people had large, cohesive, happy families with lots of positive ties and common sociability, but other people came from tiny fragments of once-extended families in which bad feelings had eaten like acid into the old kinship ties. Happiness seems to run through generations and so does unhappiness. Don't take this as an edict from fate; every human being can remake his family situation during his lifetime, at least up to a point. You cannot will a warm, extended family into being, but you can create a small happy family on the strength of your own wisdom. In fact, it is quite possible to learn as much from bad examples as from good ones, so long as you are clear about which is bad and which is good.

Many of the interviews and letters from relatives turned out to be wonderful. Perhaps it was just a chance for young folks to talk with old folks and find out about old times. That used to happen naturally because people lived near each other and weren't segregated so sharply by generations. I once read a study in which it was found that children who have close ties with grandparents feel more optimistic about life and about getting old than children who are cut off from those ties. "Roots" was a way to bring a little of this contact about.

Do your own roots. Perhaps you could do it as a half-credit independent study or in connection with a course. In that case, there are many interesting books, fiction and nonfiction, which you could read on just about any ethnic group. A sociologist should be able to help you here. Or, organize a come-as-you-were party among a group of friends who are willing to put a little time into it. You will find clues to your own identity and broaden your sympathies toward others from different origins.

EXERCISE: SLOWING DOWN

Time is our modern nemesis. We are slaves of our wristwatches in a social system in which five minutes is considered a significant interval—the difference between being "on time" or "late" to class. Imagine living in a society whose smallest unit of discussible time is "the time it takes to boil rice"—and not instant rice, either. It is ironic that, although previous cultures had far fewer labor-saving mechanisms, they possessed a feeling of plenty of time; whereas we, with all our labor-saving devices, feel chronically time poor.

Evans-Pritchard (1940) describes an African herding people, the Nuer:

> [T]he Nuer have no expression equivalent to "time" in our language, and they cannot, therefore, as we can, speak of time as though it were something actual, that passes, can be wasted, can be saved, and so forth. I do not think that they ever experience the same feeling of fighting against time or of having to coordinate activities with an abstract passage of time, because their points of reference are mainly the activities themselves, which are generally of a leisurely character. Events follow a logical order, but they are not controlled by an abstract system, there being no autonomous points of reference to which activities have to conform with precision. Nuer are fortunate. (p. 47)[2]

One of the reasons we have to time everything so carefully is that we must coordinate our actions with a highly complex system of activities, and we must do this alone. You don't move from class to class to luncheon date with any single group. You are generally entirely on your own, and the structure sets up unyielding demands. Another reason our machines don't make life leisurely is that our society is so competitive. Having your own jet doesn't put you safely ahead of other executives who also have private airplanes. Having a calculator in math class doesn't put you ahead of other students similarly equipped. As soon as everybody has a labor-saving device, nobody is benefited by it. Twenty years ago, social scientists were predicting that the coming of the computer would shorten everybody's work week. We got unemployment instead, and there hasn't been a decrease in the work week since World War II.

The sense of urgency that fills our days has been turned into a virtue by the folks who lead our institutions. A number of years ago, I decided to try enlightening my faculty colleagues at Pitzer College by sending out a brief questionnaire that simply asked whether the individual felt he had "plenty of time," "just enough time," or was "short of time" in connection with his work at the college. As I had expected, most people checked "short of time." I had planned to make this situation known to the faculty to see what we might do about it. I was stopped short by the marginal comments that graced at least half of the questionnaires. Next to the box "short of time" people had penciled, "I am glad about this, it keeps me going," "Short of time—of course, what professional is not?" and so on. In other words, they celebrated the shortage. This is not really surprising in a society where the answer to "how are you?" is frequently "keeping busy," which means the same as "well, thank you."

Yet there is probably no single cause of tension greater than this chronic feeling of time nipping at our heels. As one surveys this scene, there is a feeling that we are caught in a social structure much larger than ourselves—a structure whose wheels just revolve too fast for our comfort. But we can change these feelings for ourselves as individuals and do so without becoming incompetent. You may begin to see this for yourself by trying the following day-long exercise.

Get up twenty minutes early tomorrow and do twenty minutes of the "slow walk"[3] before starting your day: That is, for twenty minutes, walk around your room as slowly as you possibly can without losing your balance. It may take you ten minutes to cross the room. Just concentrate on the body-feelings of walking slowly. Don't do anything special with your mind—let it relax and go along for the ride.

Now, for the rest of the day, do all your accustomed tasks at about 50% of your normal speed— even less when it seems possible. Walk to class slowly, take notes slowly, eat your lunch slowly, do your assignments slowly, go out on your date slowly, and so on. Another way of getting into the feel of this exercise is to think of each separate activity as a "time frame." Our usual habit is to "lean forward" into the next time frame (e.g., as we walk to class we are already thinking about class; as we shower, we are already dreaming about seeing our date). This time, try "leaning back" into your present time frame. Say to yourself, "How nice, I have a five-minute walk now. I hope it lasts a long time, so I can settle into it comfortably." With practice, you can learn to "lean back" even into quite short time frames.

At the end of the day, for your own records, jot down your impressions. Try to see what you have learned about yourself, other people, institutions, and so on. Do this before reading on.

Students generally come back from this exercise astounded about something. Perhaps they sense for the first time how much they habitually rush. "I don't usually taste my food, I eat so fast," says one student; "I never realized how fast everybody dashes around," says another. But the greatest surprise is, "I got everything done just about as well as usual," or "I actually got more done than usual because I felt so sane"; also, "I wish I could do that every day. . . ." Well, why not? It is possible to change one's inner experience of time. Nobody need be the wiser. You won't look that different from the outside. Experiment has shown that runners actually make better time when instructed to run at just 80% of their normal speed. When tension decreases, we actually become more efficient.

Of course, this exercise, like all consciousness-changing exercises, requires much practice. You spent twenty years learning to feel hurried. It will take time and practice to undo that. A problem with such practice is that you forget to do it once the novelty wears off. One way to help yourself is to wear or carry something unusual that will remind you to do the practice. You may wear an unaccustomed bracelet, or change the arm on which you wear your watch, or carry a bright notebook cover, and so on. The slow walk, by the way, is a very nice meditation that you can use any time to calm down. I would recommend you look at Thich Nhat Hanh's (1985) *A Guide to Walking Meditation.* The activity of the mind is tied to the physical body. When you slow the body down, the mind also slows down.

Desocializing doesn't have to be as severe as it sounds. Although escaping reality can be a form of removing yourself from socialization (and society in the process), desocialization may be much softer. Desocialization is more like drifting to the edge of the fish bowl we're all in rather than jumping out. Once you are at the edge, it is possible to view everyone in the middle with less biased lenses. Try this: at some point during the day when you have a break between classes that's more than ten minutes, go to a quiet spot in the campus. It may be the park in the center of the school or just a quiet block along the main street. Put your stuff down and sit quietly or walk slowly. Allow your mind to wander away from the stresses of school. Do this until a feeling of calmness comes over you. If you can achieve this peacefulness, you will be able to, at least temporarily, remove yourself from the routine pressures of school. Do this every so often and you should start to see these pressures in a different light.

MAXIMIZING AND MINIMIZING

One of the basic, underlying styles of our culture is the tendency to maximize and minimize everything: to push everything as far as possible in a given direction—to always expand to the limits of endurance. We have seen how we do this with time. We are always "making the best use of our time"; we can never allow ourselves to "waste time." If we get an extra piece of time thrown our way we immediately find something to fill it—something that had not been pressing before suddenly becomes pressing. Thus, we seldom allow ourselves a leisurely sense of time.

We see this tendency at work most dramatically in our attitudes toward spending money. The average American spends to the limit of his or her capacity. When we get a raise, we immediately increase our purchases accordingly. Thus, we are always financially uncomfortable, no matter how much we make. We could feel rich if we simply stayed at our present spending level when we get a raise, but we just cannot do this because we are so surrounded by appeals to spend.

Just as surely as we maximize our spending of time and money or our attainment of sexual satisfaction, we minimize in other directions. Many of us are constantly on a diet, minimizing our food intake; at home, we minimize our housework; at school, we must minimize our errors. Not for us the golden mean of the ancient Greeks or the middle way of the Buddhists. The inevitable accompaniment of this style is strain. Ask anybody on campus whether they feel strained by time, by finances, by sexual needs and you will usually find a strainer. At the same time, the culture demands that we maximize "happiness." To be less than happy is to be somehow in disgrace. Yet happiness just cannot be found in this basic mode. The demand is a cruel contradiction in terms.

I know of no way to break through this pervasive pattern except by pulling yourself up short when you are about to maximize or minimize some situation and asking yourself, "Would it not be better to find the golden mean, the middle way? Suppose I don't try to write the longest paper for glory or the shortest paper to minimize the discomfort of research? Suppose I write a paper of middle length? Suppose I hit for the medium price range in my purchases? Suppose I settle for being slightly overweight? Suppose I don't change my spending patterns when I get the raise? Suppose I don't rush through every country in Europe so I won't miss anything?" It will perhaps seem inglorious to you, but it is certainly more comfortable. You may still choose to maximize some area of activity, but don't let the culture rush you into doing so every time. Be aware of this tendency and use your awareness to increase your freedom.

DAYDREAMS AND GREAT EXPECTATIONS

Zen Buddhism has a very simple recipe for enlightenment: attention to the present moment. At first it may seem to us that, of course, we pay attention to the moment. We don't, after all, fall downstairs or run into trees very often. We couldn't survive if we paid no attention. As we begin to observe the workings of our mind, we find that the attention we pay is usually minimal. Most of the time we are relying on habit and an occasional glance to get us through the environment. As we dress, brush our teeth, walk to class, or drive into town, our heads are usually filled with thoughts about ourselves. We see ourselves as heroes and heroines of many a dramatic fantasy. In short, we daydream.

If you want to see for yourself what happens to your attention during habitual tasks, try this simple experiment. Next time you are washing and getting dressed, try keeping your mind firmly glued to the present moment by describing each little action to yourself: "I am walking into the bathroom," "I am washing my face," "I am drying my face," "I am putting the towel back," and so on. You may be surprised by what you find.

Over the years I have been impressed by the stubbornness with which students defend their right to daydream. "But I don't want to stop daydreaming" is a frequent response to the stricture of Buddhism to remain in the present moment. Daydreaming is enjoyable; it seems to fulfill some great inner need, and, anyway, the ordinary world seems repetitive and boring much of the time. In view of this resistance by my students I had to ask myself: **"What is wrong with daydreaming? What is the price we pay for daydreaming?"**

One clear price that we pay is that daydreaming stirs up our emotions when we could be perfectly calm. Even though we are only walking down a quiet street, our body chemistry is responding to our thoughts of adventure, danger, revenge, triumph, and so on. Hence, we are seldom as serene and inwardly quiet as we could be if we were only responding to our environment. Thus we tend to be either "up" or "down." We do not find our inner center and so cannot respond to the happenings of the day from this center. Rather, the day's problems flow into the daydreaming and we really cannot separate and deal with the real problems realistically.

There is a kind of clean simplicity and innocence in our experience during those rare times when we are "just" in the physical environment.

Our daydreams are very frequently dreams of fulfilling our every wish. Our thoughts run so far ahead of our real acquisitions that we feel forever in need of more and more goodies about which we have fantasized. The daydreams make us dissatisfied with what we really have.

Daydreams can also deprive the real happenings in our life of the luster they would have if we came upon them innocent of expectation. Indeed, expectation is the great enemy of satisfaction. When we begin a flirtation with someone, our mind immediately rushes ahead to what it could be like to make love to this person—to travel with them—to be wonderfully flattered and complimented by them. By the time a real relationship develops, we are primed for disappointment. It will

never be anything like our daydream. Perhaps we will never see the potentialities for new experience with this other person because we are looking through the old stuff of our daydreams.

In reality, it is our daydreams that are old and repetitive and hackneyed. It is reality that is ever new and continually amazing and challenging, but we live so little in this reality that it doesn't penetrate to us. We blunt its impact. One day in class I remarked on the beautiful and fragrant citrus tree by our classroom door. I discovered that most students just had not seen or smelled it. Daydreamers are like people who spend nearly all their time watching movies. Perhaps they are really in a splendid natural scene and surrounded by interesting people, but they only take out a few minutes between movies. During those few minutes, the last movie is still so much in their mind that nothing in the real scene penetrates their emotions. Immersion in the media is a good analogy to immersion in daydreams. The media are the stuff that feeds our dreams, and our constant exposure to them helps to make daydreamers of us.

In *Great Expectations,* Dickens relates the story of a woman who was jilted on her wedding day. Refusing utterly to face the reality of this, she spends the rest of her life dressed in her wedding gown and sitting at the banquet table that was to have been her wedding feast. When she is very old, she upsets a candelabra and sets her finery, herself, and the whole house on fire. Her great expectation consumed her entire life.

Ted and I had some interesting experiences with expectations as we began to plan for our early retirement. Ted's dream since childhood had always been to go to the South Seas. He thought that perhaps he might even want to live there. So, we set out on a six-month tour of the South Sea Islands. Having always centered my travel interests on Europe, I had never even thought about going to the South Pacific.

During our tour we had our good and bad times, as one always does when traveling. The worst thing was that it rained much more than usual and spoiled a lot of our planned outdoor activities. An unexpected delight, on the other hand, was the marvelous diversity and beauty of the art, music, and dance of the peoples of Melanesia and Polynesia.

Our responses to the trip were very different. I experienced the journey as a great pleasure. Every new, unexpected facet of the area surprised and delighted me. At the same time, I took the bad weather rather philosophically. Ted, on the other hand, found the trip unexpectedly depressing. It did not come up to his life-long expectations and, whenever it fell short, he suffered a real sense of loss.

Some years later, when we had decided to settle in Northern California, we bought three acres that had been a once-beautiful but long-neglected garden. Gardening had always been my passion. I had always been "land-hungry" on my little city lots. During all the years in which lack of space constrained me, I avidly read garden books and magazines and seed catalogues. **The media are specialists in promoting unrealistic daydreams.** Just as the houses shown in home magazines are generally only affordable by millionaires, so the garden magazines contained doctored photographs of perennial borders made beautiful by the last-minute addition of hidden pots of flowers grown in greenhouses. How many such perennial borders had I planted in my mind (while skipping the chapters called "Pests and Diseases")? Ted, on the other hand, had no expectations of the garden. He didn't even know whether he would enjoy gardening. He just sort of went along with me in picking this particular acreage.

Of course, the results were predictable. As I began to face the real difficulties of getting three acres under control, I suffered a good deal. Although I had pictured myself working six or seven hours a day in my dream garden, I discovered that, at fifty-three, working even four hours is very likely to land you a tennis elbow. All in all, the

garden quickly became my nemesis. In the meanwhile, Ted innocently began to prune the trees and found that he hugely enjoyed the activity. He was able to take pleasure in the garden just as it was at any given moment, but I always saw "weeds" and other errors crying out for correction. We both learned about the influence of expectations the hard way. Luckily, reality is always there to wake us up. As I bow to the realities of my garden, I find that the garden is reshaping me quite as much as the other way around.

Often, our daydreams seem to function as rehearsals, and we have convinced ourselves that rehearsals are as useful in real-life interaction as they are in staged presentations. Without them, we might not be prepared to meet various situations. That this is an error you can substantiate for yourself. Observe whether or not an encounter for which you have rehearsed ever comes off the way you expected. In my experience, real encounters are always grossly different from rehearsals. In fact, if we didn't quickly drop the rehearsed material, we would be incapable of dealing with the real situation. The very best way to meet any difficult encounter—whether an oral examination or a painful dialogue with a friend—is to go into it with a calm, quiet mind, primed to be totally alert and open to the situation as it develops.

If you want to get a handle on your own daydreaming, carry paper and pencil around with you for one day and make a tally for every time you catch yourself daydreaming. You can also make a quick note of the subject of each daydream. At the end of the day you can take a look at what goes on in your mind.

That is exercise number one. For number two, wait until some event is coming up from which you expect either pleasure or pain. When such an event appears on your horizon, make it your practice to forego absolutely any kind of daydreaming about that particular occasion. Of course, you may do some necessary preparation for the occasion. But this is different from daydreaming. Pick just one event at a time, as this is difficult and will take energy to carry out. Be absolutely ruthless about this one event. Whenever you catch your mind wandering even near it, strike at the roots swiftly, as if you were wielding a very sharp sword. If you discover that you are in the middle of such thoughts, drop them immediately. (Don't prolong it by berating yourself.) Then, when the real event happens, see if there is any difference in your experience of it.

Books I Used for the Desocialization Course[4]

Cohen, Stanley, and Laurie Taylor. *Escape Attempts.*
Fromm, Erich, D. T. Suzuki, and Richard DeMarino. *Zen Buddhism and Psychoanalysis.*
Fischer, Louis. *The Essential Gandhi.*
Herrigel, Eugen. *Zen in the Art of Archery.*
Krishnamurti, J. *Freedom From the Known.*
Maslow, Abraham H. *Toward a Psychology of Being.*
Matthiesen, Peter. *The Snow Leopard.*
Powell, Robert. *Zen and Reality.*

Putney, Snell, and Gail J. Putney. *The Adjusted American.*
Stevens, Barry. *Don't Push the River.*
Suzuki, Shunryu. *Zen Mind, Beginner's Mind.*
Trungpa, Chogyam. *Meditation in Action.*
Watts, Alan. *Psychotherapy East and West.*

Notes

1. For an exception, see Dennis Wrong's classic article "The Oversocialized Conception of Man in Modern Sociology" in the *American Sociological Review* (April 1961, pp. 183–193).

2. From *The Nuer* by E. E. Evans-Pritchard. Copyright © 1940. Used by permission of Oxford University Press.

3. I learned the "slow walk" at the Nyingma Institute in Berkeley, California. This is a Tibetan Buddhist Institute founded by Tarthan Tulku, Rinpoche. Although the founder is in retreat, the teachers he trained are running the institute, which offers many workshops, classes, and an academically accredited program in certain subject areas.

4. All these books are available through http://www.amazon.com.

CONTRADICTIONS AND CONFLICT IN CULTURAL PRODUCTION

41

Talking Back

bell hooks

(1989)

In the world of the southern black community I grew up in, "back talk" and "talking back" meant speaking as an equal to an authority figure. It meant daring to disagree and sometimes it just meant having an opinion. In the "old school," children were meant to be seen and not heard. My great-grandparents, grandparents, and parents were all from the old school. To make yourself heard if you were a child was to invite punishment, the back-hand lick, the slap across the face that would catch you unaware, or the feel of switches stinging your arms and legs.

To speak then when one was not spoken to was a courageous act—an act of risking and daring. And yet it was hard not to speak in warm rooms where heated discussions began at the crack of dawn, women's voices filling the air, giving orders, making threats, fussing. Black men may have excelled in the art of poetic preaching in the male-dominated church, but in the church of the home where the everyday rules of how to live and how to act were established it was black women who preached. There, black women spoke in a language so rich, so poetic, that it felt to me like being shut off from life, smothered to death if one was not allowed to participate.

It was in that world of woman talk (the men were often silent, often absent) that was born in me the craving to speak, to have a voice, and not just any voice but one that could be identified as belonging to me. To make my voice, I had to speak, to hear myself talk—and talk I did—darting in and out of grown folk's conversations and dialogues, answering questions that were not directed at me, endlessly asking questions, making speeches. Needless to say, the punishments for these acts of speech seemed endless. They were intended to silence me—the child—and more particularly the girl child. Had I been a boy they might have encouraged me to speak believing that I might someday be called to preach. There was no "calling" for talking girls, no legitimized rewarded speech. The punishments I received for "talking back" were intended to suppress all possibility that I would create my own speech. That speech was to be suppressed so the "right speech of woman-hood" would emerge.

Within feminist circles, silence is often seen as the sexist "right speech of womanhood"—the sign of woman's submission to patriarchal authority. This emphasis on woman's silence may be an accurate remembering of what has taken place in the households of women from WASP backgrounds in the United States, but in black communities (and diverse ethnic communities) women have not been silent. Their voices can be heard. Certainly for black women, our struggle has not been to emerge from silence into speech but to change the nature and direction of our speech, to make a speech that compels listeners, one that is heard.

Our speech, "the right speech of womanhood," was often the soliloquy, the talking into thin air, the talking to ears that do not hear you—the talk that is simply not listened to. Unlike the black male preacher whose speech was to be heard, who was to be listened to, whose words were to be remembered, the voices of black women—giving orders, making threats, fussing—could be tuned out, could become a kind of background music, audible but not acknowledged as significant speech. Dialogue—the sharing of speech and recognition—took place not between mother and child or mother and male authority figure but among black women. I can remember watching fascinated as our mother talked with her mother, sisters, and women friends. The intimacy and intensity of their speech—the satisfaction they received from talking to one another, the pleasure, the joy. It was in this world of woman speech, loud talk, angry words, women with tongues quick and sharp, tender sweet tongues, touching our world with their words, that I made speech my birthright—and the right to voice, to authorship, a privilege I would not be denied. It was in that world and because of it that I came to dream of writing, to write.

Writing was a way to capture speech, to hold onto it, keep it close. And so I wrote down bits and pieces of conversations, confessing in cheap diaries that soon fell apart from too much handling, expressing the intensity of my sorrow, the anguish of speech—for I was always saying the wrong thing, asking the wrong questions. I could not confine my speech to the necessary corners and concerns of life. I hid these writings under my bed, in pillow stuffings, among faded underwear. When my sisters found and read them, they ridiculed and mocked me—poking fun. I felt violated, ashamed, as if the secret parts of my self had been exposed, brought into the open, and hung like newly clean laundry, out in the air for everyone to see. The fear of exposure, the fear that one's deepest emotions and innermost thoughts would be dismissed as mere nonsense, felt by so many young girls keeping diaries, holding and hiding speech, seems to me now one of the barriers that women have needed and still need to destroy so that we are no longer pushed into secrecy or silence.

Despite my feelings of violation, of exposure, I continued to speak and write, choosing my hiding places well, learning to destroy work when no safe place could be found. I was never taught absolute silence, I was taught that it was important to speak but to talk a talk that was in itself a silence. Taught to speak and yet beware of the betrayal of too much heard speech, I experienced intense confusion and deep anxiety in my efforts to speak and write. Reciting poems at Sunday afternoon church service might be rewarded. Writing a poem (when one's time could be "better" spent sweeping, ironing, learning to cook) was luxurious activity, indulged in at the expense of others. Questioning authority, raising issues that were not deemed appropriate subjects brought pain, punishments—like telling mama I wanted to die before her because I could not live without her—that was crazy talk, crazy speech, the kind that would lead you to end up in a mental institution. "Little girl," I would be told, "if you don't stop all this crazy talk and crazy acting you are going to end up right out there at Western State."

Madness, not just physical abuse, was the punishment for too much talk if you were female. Yet even as this fear of madness haunted me, hanging over my writing like a monstrous shadow, I could not stop the words, making thought, writing speech. For this terrible madness which I feared, which I was sure was the destiny of daring women born to intense speech (after all, the authorities emphasized this point daily), was not as threatening as imposed silence, as suppressed speech.

Safety and sanity were to be sacrificed if I was to experience defiant speech. Though I risked them both, deep-seated fears and anxieties characterized my childhood days. I would speak but I would not ride a bike, play hardball, or hold the gray kitten. Writing about the ways we are hurt by negative traumas in our growing-up years, psychoanalyst Alice Miller makes the point in *For Your Own Good* that it is not clear why childhood wounds become for some folk an opportunity to grow, to move forward rather than backward in the process of self-realization. Certainly, when I reflect on the trials of my growing-up years, the many punishments, I can see now that in resistance I learned to be vigilant in the nourishment of my spirit, to be tough, to courageously protect that spirit from forces that would break it.

While punishing me, my parents often spoke about the necessity of breaking my spirit. Now when I ponder the silences, the voices that are not heard, the voices of those wounded and/or oppressed individuals who do not speak or write, I contemplate the acts of persecution, torture—the terrorism that breaks spirits, that makes creativity impossible. I write these words to bear witness to the primacy of resistance struggle in any situation of domination (even within family life); to the strength and power that emerges from sustained resistance and the profound conviction that these forces can be healing, can protect us from dehumanization and despair.

These early trials, wherein I learned to stand my ground, to keep my spirit intact, came vividly to mind after I published *Ain't I a Woman* and the book was sharply and harshly criticized. While I had expected a climate of critical dialogue, I was not expecting a critical avalanche that had the power in its intensity to crush spirit, to push one into silence. Since that time I have heard stories about black women, about women of color, who write and publish (even when the work is quite successful), having nervous breakdowns, being made mad because they cannot bear the harsh responses of family, friends, and unknown critics, or becoming silent, unproductive. Surely, the absence of a humane critical response has tremendous impact on the writer from any oppressed, colonized group who endeavors to speak. For us, true speaking is not solely an expression of creative power; it is an act of resistance, a political gesture that challenges the politics of domination that would render us nameless and voiceless. As such it is a courageous act—as such, it represents a threat. To those who wield oppressive power, that which is threatening must necessarily be wiped out, annihilated, silenced.

Recently, efforts by black women writers to call attention to our work serve to highlight both our presence and absence. Whenever I peruse women's bookstores I am struck not by the rapidly growing body of feminist writing by black women but by the paucity of available published material. Those of us who write and are published remain few in number. The context of silence is varied and multidimensional. Most obvious are the ways racism, sexism, and class exploitation act as agents to suppress and silence. Less obvious are the inner struggles, the efforts made to gain the necessary confidence to write, to rewrite, to fully develop craft and skill—and the extent to which such efforts fail.

Although I have wanted writing to be my life-work since childhood, it has been difficult for me to claim "writer" as part of that which identifies and shapes my everyday reality. Even after publishing books, I would often speak of wanting to be a writer as though these works did not exist. And though I would be told, "you are a writer," I was not yet ready to fully affirm this truth. Part of myself was still held captive by domineering forces of history, of familial life that had charted a map of silence, of right speech. I had not completely let go of the fear of saying the wrong thing, of being punished. Somewhere in the deep recesses of my mind, I believed I could avoid both responsibility and punishment if I did not declare myself a writer.

One of the many reasons I chose to write using the pseudonym bell hooks, a family name (mother to Sarah Oldham, grandmother to Rosa Bell Oldham, great-grandmother to me), was to construct a writer-identity that would challenge and subdue all impulses leading me away from speech into silence. I was a young girl buying bubble gum at the corner store when I first really heard the full name bell hooks: I had just "talked back" to a grown person. Even now I can recall the surprised look, the mocking tones that informed me I must be kin to bell hooks—a sharp-tongued woman, a woman who spoke her mind, a woman who was not afraid to talk back. I claimed this legacy of defiance, of will, of courage, affirming my link to female ancestors who were bold and daring in their speech. Unlike my bold and daring mother and grandmother, who were not supportive of talking back, even though they were assertive and powerful in their speech, bell hooks as I discovered, claimed, and invented her, was my ally, my support.

The initial act of talking back outside the home was empowering. It was the first of many acts of defiant speech that would make it possible for me to emerge as an independent thinker and writer. In retrospect, "talking back" became for me a rite of initiation, testing my courage, strengthening my commitment, preparing me for the days ahead— the days when writing, rejection notices, periods of silence, publication, ongoing development seem impossible but necessary.

Moving from silence into speech is for the oppressed, the colonized, the exploited, and those who stand and struggle side by side a gesture of defiance that heals, that makes new life and new growth possible. It is that act of speech, of "talking back," that is no mere gesture of empty words, that is the expression of moving from object to subject—the liberated voice.

EPILOGUE

The mind that has conceived a plan of living must never lose sight of the chaos against which that pattern was conceived.

—Ralph Ellison, *Invisible Man*

God can be shaped. God is Change.

—Octavia Butler, *Parable of the Sower*

In the book *The Sword and the Stone,* by T. H. White, a wise old badger tells his young apprentice, Wart, how all the creatures of the earth came to be as they are. According to the badger, God assembled a multitude of fledgling embryos before him on the sixth day of creation and explained that He was going to hand out gifts. The embryos could each choose two or three gifts. These gifts would serve as a set of tools that would mark the creature's unique existence on earth. The embryos chattered excitedly among themselves about the possible combinations of tools each might ask for. When the time came, each embryo stepped forward and requested its gifts from God. Some asked for arms that were diggers or garden forks, some chose to use their arms as flying machines, and others asked for bodies like boats and arms that were oars. One of the lizards decided to swap its entire body for blotting paper. Still others asked to be able to use their mouths as drills or offensive weapons. Finally, it was the turn of the embryo called "human." This small, naked creature approached God and stammered shyly, "I have considered your generous offer, and I thank you for it, but I choose to stay as I am."

"Well chosen," thundered God. "In deciding to retain your embryonic form you will have use of all the gifts that mark the being of each of the other creatures. You will exist always as potential: the potential to take up and put down the tools of the other creatures, the potential to create uniforms and tools of your own design and to wear and discard them as you see fit. You have chosen wisely, human. We wish you well in your earthly journey."

An important lesson of symbolic interactionism is that humans exist as embryonic potential. We are capable of creating, taking on, and casting off various identities and cultural institutions. Our potential is limited only by our imagination and our ability to assemble the materials necessary to realize our visions.

As social beings, the ability to create shared meaning is the distinctive mark of our species. However, the history of Western consciousness suggests a somewhat paradoxical acceptance of this ability. We are eager to embrace our creative potential but at the same time reluctant to recognize our own authority as social creators and the responsibility that this implies. As conclusion to this text, we offer a few thoughts on this conundrum, which has come to be known more commonly as the "postmodern crisis of meaning."

SYMBOLIC INTERACTION AND THE "POSTMODERN CRISIS OF MEANING"

How do you determine what is true and right and good? This is the question with which we opened this book. The intellectual tradition known as *postmodernism* arose as a critique of the "modernist" ideals that there is a single universal truth, or reality, and that this truth is revealed in the patterns of nature and can be discovered using the methods of science. Modernist reasoning applied to questions of justice suggests that, within this "natural order," some ways of being are better than others according to "natural law" (for example, heterosexuality is "more natural" than homosexuality; poor people are poor because they are intellectually inferior). Postmodernist scholars dismantled this line of reasoning by demonstrating that, in human societies, there is no single truth; no simple, noncontradictory reality; and no single version of justice and authority. In contrast to modernist notions of a *universal, univocal* truth, postmodern theories set out to demonstrate that social reality is *contextual, multivocal,* and *complex.*

The postmodernist approach, called *critical theory,* employs a method known as *deconstructionism.* Postmodern scholars use critical theory to demonstrate that dominant (hegemonic) forms of social order are not "natural," but actually represent the perspective and values of a privileged few. They demonstrate this by "deconstructing" the taken-for-granted assumptions underlying modern Western thought. The goal of deconstructionism is to demonstrate that the ideas of the dominant group are in fact self-fulfilling realities and not instances of a natural order that inevitably controls all of us. Exponents of critical theory have demonstrated that many social institutions reflect the interests and values of groups who control the means of cultural and economic production. Critical inquiry also led to the conclusion that many of the aims and "findings" of science have reflected the interests of upper-middle-class Anglo European men. Critical theorists have tried to show that the science practiced by this class is not, in fact, based on natural law, as its proponents have claimed, but rather on a socially constructed reality that serves to maintain the privileged position of this small group.

A critique that some scholars have made against postmodern theories is that the perspective results in a "crisis of meaning." Any and all cultural institutions can be disassembled to point out the prejudices and taken-for-granted assumptions embedded in a group's beliefs and values. In general, the practice of deconstructionism is a sound one. It instructs us to dig beyond the obvious to uncover the philosophies and interests that perpetuate our social institutions. These nonobvious special interests often lead to unintended and undesirable personal and social consequences. Thus, it is useful to be *critically* aware of the assumptions underlying our own ideals. Many observers have noted, however, that this line of reasoning leads to cynicism and cultural disaffection. Deconstructionism becomes a sort of cultural wrecking ball for tearing down all that a group holds meaningful and leaving nothing in its place except the rubble of dismantled values. To the extent that this is so, some critics have gone so far as to call postmodern or critical theory an immoral practice.

Symbolic interactionism as a form of intellectual inquiry predates postmodernism. The two traditions do share the premise that realities are multiple, shifting, contradictory, and situationally specific. However, whereas critical theorists have focused on deconstructing cultural beliefs and practices, symbolic interactionists have focused on studying *how* people learn and sustain certain culturally specific practices and beliefs through everyday patterns of interaction. Similar to postmodernism, symbolic interactionism also has been criticized as perpetuating cynicism and social dissolution. If you really follow the logic of the symbolic interactionist perspective, you will note that it implies (1) interactions are always fraught with misunderstandings, miscues, misinformation, and possibly even attempts to mislead and manipulate; and (2) meaning is *always negotiated*: It is always in flux and always reflects the interactional context and the relationship between persons in the interaction. In concert with the postmodern dictum, symbolic interactionism states that there is no universal meaning or "truth."

Therefore, students of these perspectives sometimes conclude that it is not worthwhile to participate in social life because, ultimately, there is no *real* meaning. The conclusion they draw is that nothing really matters. The dilemma, as they represent it to themselves, is whether to participate in social relations that are, theoretically, always in flux.

This is especially a dilemma for people who are newly aware of the complex, contradictory, and shifting aspects of social relations. However, the crisis is not so much a crisis of meaning that has been brought about by symbolic interactionist studies and critical inquiries, but a crisis that arises because people who learn these perspectives remain stuck in a modernist mindset—the lingering premise in modernist thought that there *should be* a stable and transcendent truth. *The real postmodern dilemma is not that there is no universal meaning, but that persons fail to comprehend the significance of their own expressive and creative potential.*

Meaning, Stability, Authority, and Authenticity

Some of the vestiges of the modernist mindset include the belief that something is meaningful only if it is stable and if its authority transcends the persons who "created" it. Thus, if the implications of symbolic interactionism listed earlier are correct, meaning is unstable (always negotiated and in flux), and there is no ultimate authority. Given this (taking the logic of deconstruction to its extreme), why even bother to produce this text? If I actually believe what I'm saying, then the underlying premise is that nothing, not even the tenets of the theory that we have tried to lay out here, are "real." What seems to bother people about the implications of this perspective is that meaning is not stable, and there is no ultimate authority outside of situational human relations. Furthermore, if people's selves are always shifting, where is the authenticity?

Stability and "Outcomes"

Imagine using a similar logic if you intended to build a sand castle on the beach. It will only be washed away by the tides or eroded by the wind. It's fragile and temporary, so why bother? *Why* do people build sand castles? Certainly not so that they will endure, but rather for the sheer pleasure of doing so. The experience lingers long after the sand form has crumbled away. Why do people form friendships, get married, or invest time and energy in pursuing a vocation (such as graduate school or the ministry), even though they may have doubts about its "permanence"? Presumably, these activities are more stable than the sand castle, but is this so because they are "naturally" more stable, or because we care enough to remain continually engaged in their ongoing creation?

Modernist assessments of meaning and value are rooted in notions of "outcomes." What is the likely *outcome* of your education? Will you be able to get a good job? Make more money? Is the outcome worth the effort and the cost involved? Presumably, education is a stable, predictable course of action toward a desired end. The meaning and worth of the education are assessed in terms of this end. If someone were to demonstrate for you that the link between education, occupation, and income was a social construction, would that make it any less real in the consequences? And what about other aspects of your education, such as the *process* of learning? Does this have any meaning and value in itself? A cynic who explored the connections between education and business in a capitalist world might conclude that higher education was nothing more than a means to train workers for docile servitude. This critical theory may have some truth to it, but it doesn't necessarily have to lead *you* to conclude that *your* education has to turn out that way *for you*. Through critical awareness and mindful engagement, you have the potential to turn the *process* of your experience in higher education into a meaningful activity.

Another lesson of the symbolic interactionist perspective is that *there are stable, predictable patterns of behavior and systems of belief.* A central focus of this perspective is to demonstrate the existence of these patterns and to show the ways in which ordinary people create and re-create them. Just because these patterns are the result of human activity does not make them any less meaningful. The pertinent question is whether people are *mindfully engaged* in these practices or *mindlessly* rattling around in old routines and beliefs that may have lost their meaning.

Authority and Authenticity

Another vestige of modernism is the notion that there is a real truth in the authority of nature or God. Postmodern thought has deconstructed the idea that God and nature are sources of authority that exist independently of human relations. The resulting "crisis of authority" seems to be the crux of the problem. A central implication of social constructionism is that humans are the sole authors of the shared cultural meaning that makes their existence worthwhile. Somehow this notion disappoints many people. They would rather trade in their creative, observable embryonic potential for an unseen, elusive form of natural order. The latter presumably offers more security. It also frees people from assuming responsibility for the existence and perpetuation of embarrassing or undesirable social institutions. If these institutions can be attributed to forces beyond our control, then we do not have to participate in changing them. But to embrace this logic is to allow the ghost of a philosophy of natural order to haunt the possibilities of purposefully constructed realities. This logic also implies that, because cultural forms are human creations, they are somehow less worthwhile than if they were the result of an extrahuman force. This is a rather odd and hasty dismissal of human potential as a creative entity. It implies that our own constructions are not worth anything simply because we have the ability to deconstruct them as well.

Consider the Great Wall of China, a remarkable feat of human coordination and labor. Are you any less amazed by its existence when you pause to ponder the reasons for its construction or the fact that it could also be disassembled, stone by stone, by the same human hands that initially constructed it? Why are we so reluctant to experience a similar awe and wonderment when we contemplate human culture, which is also the product of a highly complex and intricate set of coordinated human actions?

A new way to think of this is to consider the idea that *we are the gods*. We create and re-create our own systems of meaning and ideals. The fact that we are the creators doesn't make these beliefs and practices any less real. In fact, our ability to analyze, critique, and *change* our practices for the common good is a mark of our creative potential. Again, the pertinent point is the extent to which persons are mindfully engaged in the process of social relations. When you are engaged and critically aware of the role you play in various systems of meaning, then you are also able to take responsibility for your actions and to participate in ongoing discussions about what is "right" and "good." Authority, morality, and authenticity are *embedded* in these social relations. The actual process of involvement can be seen as an enactment of morality and authenticity.

We like to think that most people who were given a choice between (1) living a life in mindless ignorance of the social processes that shape who and what we are, and (2) becoming mindfully and critically aware of these processes, would choose mindful awareness. This process of becoming aware can itself be an act of meaningful engagement. At the same time, it can also be painful. Kahlil Gibran once wrote that pain is the experience of breaking the shell that encapsulates understanding. The implication is that, in the process of stretching one's intelligence and understanding, there will always be the pain of breaking old habits and relinquishing old ways of knowing. Meaningful living is mindful living, and this can be a risky enterprise.

MINDFUL (RE)CONSTRUCTION

If, as we have suggested, social realities are fragile and require maintenance, then it is reasonable to conclude that our active participation is required to keep personal and social routines meaningful. Of course, it is possible to maintain many cultural institutions through mindless, unexamined participation in taken-for-granted routines. To the extent that we each do so, we perpetuate realities that have little meaning for us and that fail to consider ways we might actively and meaningfully produce alternative realities. But learning about alternative realities teaches ways to grapple with complexity and provides an awareness of other possible scripts. Through critical reflection and analysis, we learn to discern taken-for-granted beliefs and practices; through engaged, mindful participation, we contribute to the ongoing creation of a mindful existence. Let's identify two pitfalls that should be avoided in the pursuit of a mindful, meaningful existence: ossification and entropy.

Ossification

We have discussed the tendency for human routines and ideas to harden, or "ossify," into habits and entrenched systems of belief (see the introductory essay in Part IV). We have also discussed some of the reasons why this occurs in human relations (desire for predictability, cognitive efficiency, mindlessness). Ossified social practices (aka "social institutions") are not necessarily bad. The problems arise when we forget the purpose of the initial routine or practice or fail to remain mindful about the fact that these are socially created routines. What may have served as a useful basis for achieving some particular end becomes an ideology and an end in itself. We may persist in maintaining these ossified constructions simply because they have become permanent, hardened features of our social landscape. But at the same time, we may be contributing to the maintenance of our own prisons.

People usually know when to tear down a building that has ceased to serve any useful function and may even be a source of danger. However, we sometimes rattle around in social institutions that are cracked and crumbling simply because we fail to realize that it is within our power to step beyond the confines of these structures and build others. The point is not that all old social institutions should be torn down; it is that we should be mindful of the purposes of the social institutions that our actions (or inactions) help to perpetuate. Unfortunately, such purposes become increasingly difficult to recognize—and change becomes more difficult—the more hardened, or ossified, the institution becomes.

Consider the social routine prevalent in U.S. universities of giving exams. In a seminar for graduate students on how to teach, I ask prospective college teachers to provide a rationale for giving exams. At first, this seems like a simple task, but the seminar participants usually end up struggling once they begin to think about it. The practice of giving exams has become such an ossified element of the educational landscape that many instructors engage in the practice mindlessly. They really don't know why they do it. If exams are written and administered with a particular purpose, such as providing feedback for the student and the instructor or as an incentive to organize chunks of information, then teachers are participating in the mindful maintenance of this social institution. But to give exams simply because "that's what's always been done" is to perpetuate a potentially meaningless social routine.

Once the purpose for a particular social routine is isolated, it is possible to devise potentially more useful routes to achieve it. For example, one unfortunate outcome of the exam procedure may be the unnecessary rank ordering of students. If the purpose of exams is to motivate students to organize and articulate their knowledge, then it may be possible to create an alternative exercise that more directly serves the intended purpose and avoids the pitfalls. It is possible, however, that the purpose of exams is indeed to rank-order persons—perhaps to facilitate their entrance into a stratified institution, such as the labor market. In that case, instructors should be mindfully aware that their examination procedures serve to perpetuate social stratification, and that they are performing a gate-keeping role for other social institutions.

The point is to understand how one's participation in particular cultural routines perpetuates the existence of social institutions. Here, in the exploration of ossified structures, is where the tools of deconstruction serve a useful end. Such explorations need not lead to the conclusion that the entire structure should be dismantled, however. Mindful construction instructs us to ask what purpose the social routine serves and whether we want to participate in that purpose.

Two points are worth underscoring here. First, social institutions are created and maintained through the active participation of individuals. To the extent that we are aware of our reasons for participating in various cultural productions, we can be said to be mindfully engaged in the construction of reality. If, however, we are simply participating in patterns that "have always been," then we risk being social robots living in the brittle houses constructed by previous generations for their own purposes. Second, change does not occur simply by tearing down these structures. A meaningful existence requires that we construct other institutions in place of those that have been torn down.

Entropy

If any pattern in nature seems to play itself out in human relations, it is entropy—the natural process that results in decay. According to the laws of thermodynamics, coherent molecular systems require constant input of energy to maintain their structure. If this energy is diverted, the system (whether molecule, leaf, or earlobe) will erode or fall apart into increasingly random elements. This tendency toward randomness is entropy. Similarly, the meaning and purpose of many of our social routines are constantly threatened with erosion unless participants infuse these routines with mindful energy.

As we have pointed out, a great deal of mindful intellectual energy has been devoted to deconstructing ossified social realities. But often this activity produces isolated individuals cut adrift from any meaningful social activity—in other words, cynics. The path toward cynicism is exacerbated by the process of entropy. If we do not invest energy in those social productions that matter, they will cease to exist as meaningful systems.

What are some of the meaningful activities or relationships in your life that you take for granted? Do you have a spouse or family member whom you love but "don't have enough time for"? Consider the trap that people set when they depend on ossified routines to provide a sense of meaning and purpose while neglecting to contribute adequate energy to the maintenance of the routine. Imagine an attorney who decides to commit her services to assisting those who cannot afford legal counsel. After mindful consideration, she has decided to devote her time and talent to fighting what she perceives to be an injustice. In effect, she has chosen to actively chip away at one social system that she perceives to be culturally unfair, economic inequality in the legal system. Now imagine this same woman explaining to her spouse and children that she does not have time to celebrate birthdays and anniversaries because she is busy fighting for an important social cause. She is often absent from family meals and other everyday rituals as well. One day she awakens to the discovery that she is no longer meaningfully engaged with her family—they seem to be living their lives without her.

This example illustrates the simple but profound point that if we do not actively participate in the production of those realities that we wish to maintain as the foundation of our lives, they will be eroded by the forces of entropy. Love and family involvement require ongoing, active participation in the ritual interactions that maintain these institutions. We can't take for granted even seemingly well-established social institutions such as "the family." These social institutions do not endure without active maintenance.

Mindful Engagement

Together ossification and entropy suggest that, left to themselves, our social institutions will harden into brittle and unserviceable cultural forms that bind us even while they cease to hold much meaning for us. This is not a pleasant outcome. Yet it has been predicted by many of the classical sociological thinkers. Max Weber, for example, referred to the stultifying process of the "Iron Cage." Karl Marx warned that individuals who were denied meaningful forms of social activity would suffer alienation and cynicism. Émile Durkheim proposed that groups would not be able to regulate the behavior of members if the groups failed to produce meaningful social rituals; members would suffer from a sense of purposelessness and lack of regulation known as *anomie*. The challenge for students of sociology is to understand these processes so they can be guided more purposefully.

The messages are the following: (1) be choosy about the realities that you intend to produce or reproduce, and (2) recognize that the production of any reality requires your participation. To the extent that you participate mindfully, your life will take on increased meaning and purpose.

Trudy the bag lady, introduced in Reading 2 by Jane Wagner, is a true hero from the perspective of the mindful construction of reality. She has scrutinized the social institutions in which she dwells and found them to be unacceptable. Rather than turn away in despair, she has created a rich, lively alternative reality for herself. Now, as she describes it, her days are "jam-packed and fun-filled." Trudy is both a product of the general social realities that form this society and a commentator on them. Her commentary is compelling because it is both informed and hopeful. She is neither a social robot nor a cynic. She has taken responsible control of the construction of her own reality, and she invests in this production with enthusiasm and vigor. She is an intriguing character in that, although she is a street person, I do not feel pity for her. In fact, I feel a bit envious of her insightful, energetic reality, mad though it may appear by conventional standards. Trudy is bursting with potential.

Our own realities can be similarly produced, whether by doing something as simple as participating wholeheartedly in small daily rituals with those you love or as revolutionary as "talking back to outrage" in the form of large-scale collective protest. The message is that it takes insight, courage, and responsibility to engage in the mindful production of reality. This is the basis of a meaningful existence.

CREDITS

Chapter 1

"Islands of Meaning" reprinted and edited with the permission of The Free Press, a Division of Simon & Schuster Adult Publishing Group from *The Fine Line: Making Distinctions in Everyday Life* (pp. 1–4, 5–20) by Evitar Zerubavel. Copyright © 1991 by Evitar Zerubavel. All rights reserved.

Chapter 2

Excerpts from *The Search for Signs of Intelligent Life in the Universe* (pp. 13, 15–21, 23, 26, 29, 212–213) by Jane Wagner. Copyright © 1986 by Jane Wagner, Inc. Reprinted by permission of HarperCollins Publishers, Inc.

Chapter 3

"Truth, Objectivity and Agreement" reprinted by permission of Waveland Press, Inc. from Earl Babbie, *Observing Ourselves* (pp. 19–28). Long Grove, IL: Waveland Press, Inc. Copyright © 1986 (reissue 1998). All rights reserved.

Chapter 4

"Constructivist, Interpretivist Approaches to Human Inquiry" by Thomas A. Schwandt. From *Handbook of Qualitative Research*, 2nd edition (pp. 118–125) edited by Norman K. Denzin and Yvonna S. Lincoln. Copyright © 1994. Reprinted by permission of Sage Publications, Inc.

Chapter 5

"That Powerful Drop" from *The Langston Hughes Reader* (p. 201) by Langston Hughes. Copyright © 1953 by Langston Hughes. Copyright renewed 1981 by George Houston Bass. Reprinted by permission of Harold Ober Associates Incorporated.

Chapter 6

"A Clue to the Nature of Man: The Symbol" from *An Essay on Man* (pp. 42–44) by Ernst Cassirer. Copyright © 1944 by Yale University Press. Reprinted by permission of Yale University Press.

Chapter 15

"Acknowledgment Rituals" by Carl Edward Pate from *Everyday Inequalities: Critical Inquiries* (pp. 97–129) edited by Jodi O'Brien and Judith A. Howard. Copyright © 1998 Blackwell Publishers Ltd. Used by permission of Blackwell Publishing Ltd.

Chapter 16

"Embarrassment and the Analysis of Role Requirements" by Edward Gross and Gregory P. Stone from *The American Journal of Sociology, 70:* pp. 1–15. Copyright © 1964 by The University of Chicago Press. Reprinted by permission of The University of Chicago Press.

Chapter 17

Excerpts from *The Managed Heart: Commercialization of Human Feeling, 20th Anniversary ed.* (pp. ix-x, 24–25, 95–96, 98–101, 104–105, 110–111, 126–128, 131) by Arlie Russell Hochschild. Copyright © 1983 by The Regents of the University of California. Used by permission of the Regents of the University of California and the University of California Press.

Chapter 18

"Behavior in Private Places" by Joan P. Emerson from *Recent Sociology* (pp. 74–97) edited by Han Pieter Dreitzel. New York: Macmillan. Copyright © 1970. Reprinted by permission of the author.

Chapter 19

This paper, " 'Precarious Situations' in a Strip Club: Exotic Dancers and the Problem of Reality Maintenance" by Kari Lerum, is based on research for the author's dissertation, titled *Doing the Dirty Work: Emotion Work, Professionalism, and Sexuality in a Customer Service Context.* University of Washington, 2000.

Chapter 20

"Encounters with the Hearing" from *Outsiders in a Hearing World: A Sociology of Deafness* (pp. 145–167) by Paul C. Higgins. Copyright © 1981. Reprinted by permission of Sage Publications, Inc.

Chapter 21

"The Self, the I, and the Me" by George Herbert Mead from *Mind, Self, and Society: From the Standpoint of a Social Behaviorist* (pp. 136–144, 195–196) edited by Charles W. Morris. Copyright © 1962 by The University of Chicago Press. Reprinted by permission of The University of Chicago Press.

Chapter 22

"Looking Glass Self" from *Human Nature and the Social Order* (pp. 182–185) by Charles Horton Cooley. Copyright © 1983 by Transaction Publishers. Reproduced with permission of Transaction Publishers via the Copyright Clearance Center.

Chapter 23

"Reference Groups as Perspectives" from *Society and Personality* (pp. 251–260) by Tamotsu Shibutani. Copyright © 1961. Reprinted by permission of Pearson Education, Inc., Upper Saddle River, NJ.

Chapter 24

"Girls, Media, and the Negotiation of Sexuality" by Meenakshi Gigi Durham from *Journalism and Mass Communication Quarterly, 76.* Copyright © 1999 by the Association for Education in Journalism and Mass Communication. Used by permission.

Chapter 25

"White Means Never Having to Say You're Ethnic" by Pamela Perry from the *Journal of Contemporary Ethnology, 30:* pp. 56–91. Copyright © 2001 by Pamela Perry. Reprinted by permission of Sage Publications, Inc.

Chapter 26

"Language Acquisition versus Formal Education" from *Microsociology: Discourse, Emotion, and Social Structure* (pp. 156–175) by Thomas J. Scheff. Copyright © 1990 The University of Chicago Press. Reprinted by permission of the University of Chicago Press.

Chapter 27

"Identity Construction and Self-Presentation on Personal Homepages" by Charles Cheung from *Web.Studies: Rewiring media studies for the digital age,* 2nd ed. (pp. 53–67) edited by David Gauntlett. Copyright © 2000, 2004 Edward Arnold (Publishers) Ltd. Reproduced by permission of Edward Arnold, a member of the Hodder Headline Group.

Chapter 28

"Body Troubles" by Isabel Dyck from *Mind and Body Spaces* (pp. 119–137) edited by Ruth Butler and Hester Parr. Copyright © 1999. Used by permission of Taylor & Francis.

Chapter 29

"Five Features of Reality" from *Reality of Ethnomethodology* (pp. 8–33) by Hugh Mehan and Houston Wood. Copyright © 1975 by John Wiley & Sons. Reprinted with permission of John Wiley & Sons, Inc.

NAME INDEX

SUBJECT INDEX

ABOUT THE AUTHOR

Jodi O'Brien is Professor of Sociology at Seattle University. She teaches courses in social psychology, social inequalities, sexualities, and classical and contemporary theory. She writes and lectures on the cultural politics of transgressive identities and communities. Her other books include *Everyday Inequalities* (Basil Blackwell) and *Social Prisms: Reflections on Everyday Myths and Paradoxes* (Pine Forge Press).